W9-BZA-739

LET'S GO

■ THE RESOURCE FOR THE INDEPENDENT TRAVELER

"The guides are aimed not only at young budget travelers but at the independent traveler; a sort of streetwise cookbook for traveling alone."

—*The New York Times*

"Unbeatable; good sight-seeing advice; up-to-date info on restaurants, hotels, and inns; a commitment to money-saving travel; and a wry style that brightens nearly every page."

—*The Washington Post*

"Lighthearted and sophisticated, informative and fun to read. [Let's Go] helps the novice traveler navigate like a knowledgeable old hand."

—*Atlanta Journal-Constitution*

"A world-wise traveling companion—always ready with friendly advice and helpful hints, all sprinkled with a bit of wit."

—*The Philadelphia Inquirer*

■ THE BEST TRAVEL BARGAINS IN YOUR PRICE RANGE

"All the dirt, dirt cheap."

—*People*

"Anything you need to know about budget traveling is detailed in this book."

—*The Chicago Sun-Times*

"Let's Go follows the creed that you don't have to toss your life's savings to the wind to travel—unless you want to."

—*The Salt Lake Tribune*

■ REAL ADVICE FOR REAL EXPERIENCES

"The writers seem to have experienced every rooster-packed bus and lunar-surfaced mattress about which they write."

—*The New York Times*

"A guide should tell you what to expect from a destination. Here Let's Go shines."

—*The Chicago Tribune*

LET'S GO PUBLICATIONS

TRAVEL GUIDES

Alaska & the Pacific Northwest 2003
Australia 2003
Austria & Switzerland 2003
Britain & Ireland 2003
California 2003
Central America 8th edition
Chile 1st edition **NEW TITLE**
China 4th edition
Costa Rica 1st edition **NEW TITLE**
Eastern Europe 2003
Egypt 2nd edition
Europe 2003
France 2003
Germany 2003
Greece 2003
Hawaii 2003 **NEW TITLE**
India & Nepal 7th edition
Ireland 2003
Israel 4th edition
Italy 2003
Mexico 19th edition
Middle East 4th edition
New Zealand 6th edition
Peru, Ecuador & Bolivia 3rd edition
South Africa 5th edition
Southeast Asia 8th edition
Southwest USA 2003
Spain & Portugal 2003
Thailand 1st edition **NEW TITLE**
Turkey 5th edition
USA 2003
Western Europe 2003

CITY GUIDES

Amsterdam 2003
Barcelona 2003
Boston 2003
London 2003
New York City 2003
Paris 2003
Rome 2003
San Francisco 2003
Washington, D.C. 2003

MAP GUIDES

Amsterdam
Berlin
Boston
Chicago
Dublin
Florence
Hong Kong
London
Los Angeles
Madrid
New Orleans
New York City
Paris
Prague
Rome
San Francisco
Seattle
Sydney
Venice
Washington, D.C.

CHILE

STEFAN JACOB EDITOR
HUMA YUSUF ASSOCIATE EDITOR
LAURA GORNOWSKI ASSOCIATE EDITOR

RESEARCHER-WRITERS
VICTOR TAN CHEN
ALEX LEARY
JONGSOO JAMES LEE
JANE A. LINDHOLM
TOM MERCER
KISHAN KUMAR PUTTA

ERIC BROWN MAP EDITOR
MARLA KAPLAN MANAGING EDITOR
EDUARDO L. MONTOYA TYPESETTER

ST. MARTIN'S PRESS ⋈ NEW YORK

HELPING LET'S GO If you want to share your discoveries, suggestions, or corrections, please drop us a line. We read every piece of correspondence, whether a postcard, a 10-page email, or a coconut. Please note that mail received after May 2003 may be too late for the 2004 book, but will be kept for future editions. **Address mail to:**

> Let's Go: Chile
> 67 Mount Auburn Street
> Cambridge, MA 02138
> USA

Visit Let's Go at **http://www.letsgo.com,** or send email to:

> feedback@letsgo.com
> Subject: "Let's Go: Chile"

In addition to the invaluable travel advice our readers share with us, many are kind enough to offer their services as researchers or editors. Unfortunately, our charter enables us to employ only currently enrolled Harvard students.

Maps by David Lindroth copyright © 2003 by St. Martin's Press.

Distributed outside the USA and Canada by Macmillan.

Let's Go: Chile Copyright © 2003 by Let's Go, Inc. All rights reserved. Printed in the United States of America. No part of this book may be used or reproduced in any manner whatsoever without written permission except in the case of brief quotations embodied in critical articles or reviews. Let's Go is available for purchase in bulk by institutions and authorized resellers. For information, address St. Martin's Press, 175 Fifth Avenue, New York, NY 10010, USA.

ISBN: 0-312-30560-5

First edition
10 9 8 7 6 5 4 3 2 1

Let's Go: Chile is written by Let's Go Publications, 67 Mount Auburn Street, Cambridge, MA 02138, USA.

Let's Go® and the LG logo are trademarks of Let's Go, Inc.
Printed in the USA on recycled paper with soy ink.

HOW TO USE THIS BOOK

ORGANIZATION. Our coverage begins in Santiago, the dynamic capital of Chile. The Middle Chile chapter continues in a clockwise spiral beginning in Valparaíso. Coverage then extends northwards through Norte Chico and Norte Grande to the Bolivian and Peruvian borders. We then skip back and continue south from Santiago through the Lakes District to Aisén, with a short digression to the island of Chiloé. Tierra del Fuego and the Far South frigidly conclude our coverage of Chile. The black tabs on the side of the book should help you navigate your way through.

PRICE RANGES AND RANKINGS. Our researchers list establishments in order of value from best to worst. Our absolute favorites are denoted by the Let's Go thumbs-up (☒). Since the best value does not always mean the cheapest price, we have also incorporated a system of price ranges in the guide. The table below lists how prices fall within each bracket.

CHILE	❶	❷	❸	❹	❺
ACCOMMODATIONS	Less than CH$3500	CH$3500-7000	CH$7000-14,000	CH$14,000-24,500	CH$24,500 plus
FOOD	Less than CH$2100	CH$2100-3500	CH$3500-7000	CH$7000-10,500	CH$10,500 plus

PHONE CODES AND TELEPHONE NUMBERS. Area codes for each region appear opposite the name of the region and are denoted by the ☎ icon. Phone numbers in text are also preceded by the ☎ icon.

WHEN TO USE IT

TWO MONTHS BEFORE. The first chapter, **Discover Chile,** contains highlights of the region, including Suggested Itineraries (see p. 9) that can help you plan your trip. The **Essentials** (see p. 36) section contains practical information on planning a budget, making reservations, renewing a passport, and has other useful tips about traveling in Chile.

ONE MONTH BEFORE. Take care of insurance, and write down a list of emergency numbers and hotlines. Make a list of packing essentials (see **Packing,** p. 49) and shop for anything you are missing. Read through the coverage and make sure you understand the logistics of your itinerary (catching buses, ferries, etc.). Make any reservations if necessary.

2 WEEKS BEFORE. Leave an itinerary and a photocopy of important documents with someone at home. Take some time to peruse the **Life and Times** (p. 13), which has info on history, culture, flora and fauna, recent political events, and more.

ON THE ROAD. The **Appendix** (p. 497) includes a guide to Chilean Spanish, including notes on pronunciation, a Spanish phrasebook (check the Menu Reader to ensure you don't order eel diced in *pebre* without knowing it), and a Spanish glossary.

A NOTE TO OUR READERS The information for this book was gathered by *Let's Go* researchers from February through August of 2002. Each listing is based on one researcher's opinion, formed during his or her visit at a particular time. Those traveling at other times may have different experiences since prices, dates, hours, and conditions are always subject to change. You are urged to check the facts presented in this book beforehand to avoid inconvenience and surprises.

CONTENTS

Chile: Regions

RESEARCHER-WRITERS

Victor Tan Chen *Southern Middle Chile and Northern Lakes District*

Taking skills perfected through editorial work for the online journal *Inthefray.com*, and expertise that only a know-it-all ne'er-do-well first-year Sociology and Social Policy grad student could have, Victor set off to Chile to practice his Spanish and get in some hard-core snowboarding. What he did instead was wrangle space heaters, discover that the Mapuche never switched over to Spanish, and produce fine copy enriched with fascinating historical and cultural detail.

Alex Leary *Aisén and the Far South*

Alex just couldn't get enough of South America; he skipped school to traipse around Brazil, Peru, and Bolivia, pausing to catch his breath for three months while studying in Buenos Aires. This escapade didn't cure his Latin-fever; consequently, he edited *Let's Go: Central America 2002*. It was flying to Chile that finally stilled the wandering beast—after traversing treacherous rapids and scouring the wilds of the Patagonia he decided to settle down and look for a job.

Jongsoo James Lee *Norte Grande and northern Norte Chico*

You saw him in *Let's Go: South Africa 2001* and *Let's Go: New Zealand 2002*, but this here is his real blockbuster. Hailing from Seoul and having traveled to over 65 countries, Chile was the latest feather in James's cosmopolitan cap. Having just submitted his dissertation on international 20th-century history, James embarked on this adventure with renewed gusto, prancing through national parks, splashing about in thermal baths, and dancing the night away in Arica.

Jane A. Lindholm *Norte Chico and central Middle Chile*

For Jane, arriving in Valparaíso felt just like coming home. Having spent time studying Andean languages and culture in Santiago as an anthropology undergraduate, traipsing through vineyards in Middle Chile and cooking spaghetti with would-be aliens in La Serena was second nature to Jane. Can't get enough of her keen wit, charming prose, and amusing anecdotes? Catch her stellar work on the Weekend Edition Saturday on NPR.

Tom Mercer *Santiago, Chiloé, and southern Lakes District*

No *Let's Go* virgin, Tom's time in Chile was his third researching stint (New Zealand and Alaska were also graced with his presence). The lively, perfectly formatted, and timely copy he churned out (complete with scandalous marginalia) is proof of his experience as editor of the *Let's Go: Southwest USA 2002*. It remains a miracle that he got any work done between downing *pisco sours* in Barrio Bellavista and getting amorous on aphrodisiacal oysters in Ancud.

Kishan Kumar Putta   *Central Lakes District*

Kishan's work appears in the *Los Angeles Times, The Providence Journal,* the *Times of India, The Straits Times* in Singapore, and *Let's Go: India and Nepal 1999*—this however is his real tour de force. Kishan skipped around the southern lakes and literally had a blast visiting active volcanoes and gushing hot springs. What he did most often, however, was remind the unforgettable Chileans he met every day that his last name has two T's in it.

CONTRIBUTING WRITERS

Derek Glanz was the editor of *Let's Go: Spain, Portugal, and Morocco 1998.* He is now a freelance journalist who recently began pursuing post-graduate studies in international relations. He has been published in *The Associate Press* and *The Miami Herald,* and served as a guest TV analyst on Colombia's *TeleCartagena.*

Sarah Kenney was the editor of *Let's Go: Barcelona 2002.* She is now working in publishing.

Brian Milder was a Researcher-Writer for *Let's Go: New Zealand 2000.* He has spent the past year in Chile as a Rockefeller Fellow living in Santiago and volunteering at the Nonprofit Enterprise and Self-sustainability Team (NESsT).

Amity Wilczek is a graduate student in evolutionary biology at Harvard University.

Megan Brumagin   *Editor: Peru, Ecuador & Bolivia*

Genithia Hogges   *Associate Editor: Peru, Ecuador & Bolivia*

David Huyssen   *Associate Editor: Peru, Ecuador & Bolivia*

Amy Cooper   *Researcher-writer: Southern Peru*

Brian King   *Researcher-writer: Southern Bolivia*

Jacob Rubin   *Researcher-writer: La Paz, Bolivia*

ACKNOWLEDGMENTS

LET'S GO

Team Chile thanks: Our amazing RWs for keeping us on our toes; PEB for comic relief; Eric for the long hours; Prod for the endless lovin'; Megan and Joanna for being there; Marla, Matt and Brian for making our bookteam a whole family again; Alex for her help and snacks; sugar-daddy Noah; our relentless typists and anal proofers; and Tom Malone.

Stefan thanks: Huma for the long, crazy nights; Laura for her incredible strength, commitment & sense of humor; Marla for helping with everything always; Ben for "quick" breaks, long talks, and the fever; Megan for her crazy bookteam & lots of Snoop; Eric & the Prod boys for endless answers; Adam & Matt for a chill room; John for late-night runs; the Dinner Posse; the Block for crazy roadtrips & international adventures; Genevieve for *arroz con leche* and late mornings; And my parents for the car, laundry and love.

Laura thanks: Stefan, for making this book terrific, against all odds; Princess Huma, for your endless wit—you are "grand;" Marla, for taking care of us all; Aly and Age, for being the sisters I should have had; Sarah and Erin, for the endless laughs and unfaltering support; Alex, for believing in the best version of me and for the butterflies; Mom, for showing me the meaning of strength and unconditional love; And Dad, for always being my biggest fan and proving that believing can make anything possible. I love you.

Huma thanks: Stefan, for keeping the faith and licking my neck; Laura for letting me write in a British accent; Marla for whining enough for all of us; DJ David-sen for supplying the soundtrack; Maria, for cleaning out Dave's trash; Brenna for being a Bhen...Matt for all the lovin'; Eric for being fantastic; Chris, Caleb, Meuhlke for being the bestest; Proust, for inspiring our RWs; *huasos* for being cool; and the Imperial House of Yusuf for holding down the fort.

Eric thanks: Stefan, Huma, and Laura. Indebted to Mom, Dad, and Kate. For Anna on her birthday.

Editor
Stefan Jacob
Associate Editors
Laura Gornowski, Huma Yusuf
Managing Editor
Marla Kaplan
Map Editor
Eric Brown

Publishing Director
Matthew Gibson
Editor-in-Chief
Brian R. Walsh
Production Manager
C. Winslow Clayton
Cartography Manager
Julie Stephens
Design Manager
Amy Cain
Editorial Managers
Christopher Blazejewski,
Abigail Burger, D. Cody Dydek,
Harriett Green, Angela Mi Young Hur,
Marla Kaplan, Celeste Ng
Financial Manager
Noah Askin
Marketing & Publicity Managers
Michelle Bowman, Adam M. Grant
New Media Managers
Jesse Tov, Kevin Yip
Online Manager
Amélie Cherlin
Personnel Managers
Alex Leichtman, Owen Robinson
Production Associates
Caleb Epps, David Muehlke
Network Administrators
Steven Aponte, Eduardo Montoya
Design Associate
Juice Fong
Financial Assistant
Suzanne Siu
Office Coordinators
Alex Ewing, Adam Kline,
Efrat Kussell

Director of Advertising Sales
Erik Patton
Senior Advertising Associates
Patrick Donovan, Barbara Eghan,
Fernanda Winthrop
Advertising Artwork Editor
Leif Holtzman
Cover Photo Research
Laura Wyss
President
Bradley J. Olson
General Manager
Robert B. Rombauer
Assistant General Manager
Anne E. Chisholm

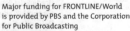

DISCOVER CHILE

Chile is Latin America's best kept secret. While Peru is known for its Incas, Brazil for its beaches, and Central America for its rainforests, Chile is remembered by many only for being narrow. It's that extra-hard-to-color-in strip of land smashed on one side of South America's jumble of countries. The thin country is truly a cartographer's nightmare, impossible to present in any handy and detailed form from tip to toe. And yet therein lies its temptation for travelers. Spanning more than half the length of South America, Chile is home to a remarkable diversity of climates, terrain, and wildlife. In the far north, at the base of the highest volcanoes in the world, flamingo-filled lakes surround the driest place on earth. In the south, enormous glaciers flow down into national parks, which protect trees born thousands of years ago. And in between all that, world-renowned vineyards share Chile's rolling valleys with rheas, guanacos, and pudús.

Chile offers even more than incredible natural attractions. Its culture and history are a fusion of Spanish and English influences. Additionally, this unmistakably European feel is augmented by its indigenous roots, which add a unique flavor to the cultural mix. The diversity of terrain and climate are echoed in a diversity of culture. The eerie, desert landscape of the north is inhabited by a laid-back, almost spiritual people, while the rolling, fertile hills of the Central Valley play host to a frantic, high-energy urban lifestyle. And farther south, the rugged, untamed forests and mountains are home to a cultural heritage that mixes the fierce independence of the Mapuche and the resilience of rural farmers. Wherever you go, however, a distinctly Chilean way of life is perceptible— characterized by a rapid, rhythmic incarnation of Spanish, hearty cuisine typically doused in a hot chili pepper sauce or mashed avocado, and a strong sense of national identity.

Even from its isolated perch behind the Andes mountains, Chile has managed to distinguish itself among its sibling nations. It is a country with a long democratic tradition, still struggling to deal with a brutal interlude of authoritarian rule. Yet it has managed to return to steady democracy despite the serious political and social challenges it faces. Chile also excels in the arts, boasting two celebrated Nobel Laureate poets, Pablo Neruda and Gabriela Mistral, the latter the only Latin woman to date to be distinguished with the honor. Finally, over the last few decades, Chile has gained a level of economic stability and development that well surpasses its Latin neighbors.

Currently on the verge of taking its place among the leading countries of the world with modern social programs and stronger economic and political ties to both Europe and Asia, Chile offers many of the conveniences and reliability of a developed nation while maintaining the amazing sights and fascinating culture that make Latin America a popular tourist destination.

DISCOVER

▨ LET'S GO PICKS

BEST PLACE TO SEE PLUTO: Mamalluca, an observatory outside of **La Serena,** was built especially for nonscientists, since the four other massive observatories in northern Chile are tightly controlled by multinational alliances.

BEST GATHERING OF FUZZY LITTLE CREATURES: Parque Nacional Chinchilla protects the last remaining wild colonies of the furry creatures that are its namesake. Picture short, fat, ultra-furry mice with big ears.

BEST NAME FOR A TREE: Chile's national tree, the **Monkey Puzzle Tree,** is native to the southern Andes region. According to legend, an Englishman thought its snaking branches with rows of stiff, sharp leaves would be quite a "puzzle" for a monkey to climb. Good thing monkeys don't actually live in Chile.

BEST FLOWERING DESERT: Although it is the driest desert in the world, the **Atacama** can surprise you. Once every 5 years or so a surge of rain brings out its hidden floral beauty, especially around **Vallenar.**

BEST PLACE TO PASS OUT FROM LACK OF OXYGEN: Rising over 22,400 feet above sea level, **Ojos del Salado** is the highest mountain in Chile and the highest active volcano in the world.

BEST PLACE TO FREEZE TO DEATH: Just a few hundred miles from Antarctica, **Puerto Williams** on **Isla Navarino** is the most southerly human settlement in the world. Bring warm clothes...

BEST SAND PICTURE: Just outside **Iquique** is the **Gigante de Atacama** (Giant of Atacama), an enormous 400 foot drawing of a man that is said to be created in the same style as the mysterious pictures in Nasca, Peru.

BEST PLACE TO MEET DIONYSUS: The valley of the Río Maule is one of Chile's largest **wine** producing areas. Over 23 vineyards cover the land around the city of **San Javier.** Most will allow tours—just make sure you have a designated driver.

BEST PLACE TO BE GENE KELLY: You'll be "Singing in the Rain" for sure in **Valdivia.** Gathering over 100 inches of rain a year, it is Chile's wettest city.

BEST RENDITION OF THE APOCALYPSE: In 1960, the area between Temuco and Valdivia was hit by the worst **earthquake** in Chile's history, which caused four volcanoes to erupt, dropped the coastline by more than six feet, provoked landslides, and sent out a tsunami that flattened fishing villages up and down the coast and was felt in New Zealand and Japan.

WHEN TO GO

Anytime, all the time, whenever your heart desires. Chile's different climatic zones ensure that a variety of weather conditions prevail year-round, making a wide array of activities available at all times. Chile is divided into three significant climatic areas: the arid north; the cool and damp south; and the temperate, almost Mediterranean, central Chile which experiences heavy rainfall between May and August and bright sunshine the rest of the year. The spring and summer seasons in Chile (between October and March, as in all countries of the Southern Hemisphere), tend to see the most tourist traffic, as foreigners and Chileans from far and wide flock to the white-sand beaches of the glamorous Viña del Mar and other coastal resorts. Santiago is warm and sunny this time of year (25°C Dec.-Mar.), trekking is pleasant in the Lakes District (13°C Oct.-Apr.), and the erratic weather of Patagonia simmers down to warmer days (daytime highs 15°C Oct.-Mar.). The peak tourist season that ushers in fully-booked hotels, packed *discotecas*, and exorbitant prices is between the end of December and the beginning of February, when locals are on summer vacation.

However, the Chilean winter is not an altogether unpleasant time to travel—ski slopes among the Andes are at their best, the Atacama desert in northern Chile offers warm and sunny days on beautiful beaches, and almost all prices are discounted by 5-30%. The downside? Many smaller towns in Middle Chile and the Lakes District are practically deserted, temperatures in the Far South are frigid, and heating is not always provided in budget accommodations, leaving you shivering under slight sheets. Consider heading to Chile during "shoulder season" travel periods, in Oct.-Nov. and Mar.-Apr., when extremes of weather are less frequent, prices are moderate, and neither ghost towns nor much-too-crowded hostels get you down.

TO DO	IN THE NORTH	MIDDLE CHILE	LAKES DISTRICT	CHILOÉ	PATAG- ONIA
Biking	Year-round		Nov.-Apr.		Nov.-Mar.
Volcano tours	Year-round		Nov.-Mar.		Nov.-Apr.
History tours	Year-round	Year-round	Year-round	Nov.-Mar.	Year-round
Archaeology	Year-round				
Lake tours			Nov.-Apr.	Nov.-Apr.	Nov.-Mar.
Mountaineer	Year-round	Nov.-Apr.	Oct.-Apr.		Nov.-Mar.
Skiing		June-Oct.	June-Oct.		
Trekking	Year-round	Nov.-Apr.	Oct.-Apr.	Dec.-Mar.	
Hot springs	Year-round	Year-round	Year-round		Nov.-Apr.
Festivities	Year-round	Year-round	Year-round	Oct.-Apr.	

THINGS TO DO

Being horizontally-challenged has never been a stumbling block for Chile, and with regards to the tourism industry, the country's natural and geographical idiosyncrasies are a palpable godsend. The diversity of climate and terrain that Chile enjoys creates a wide array of exciting and gratifying adventures for the budget traveler to embark upon. And although the healing *termas* in Chillán will invite you to relax, the deep still waters of Lago Llanquihué will cause you to take a moment to catch your breath, and the laid-back fishermen's way of life in Chiloé will move you to abandon your own frenzied, touristy pace; Chile's offerings are so unique and abundant that even the most sluggish visitor will want to keep moving. See the **Highlights of the Region** section at the beginning of each chapter for specific regional attractions.

EAT

Eat cheap seafood at the renown open-air fresh fish market, **La Recova** in La Serena (p. 228). Or head south to **Dalcahue** (p. 426) for dirt cheap, decadently delicious oysters. Lobsters cost next to nothing and taste even better among the hustle and bustle of Coquimbo's chaotic **Caleta** (p. 221). Cheap mackerel and even cheaper mussels at every restaurant in **Mejillones** (p. 264) are spiced up with dreamy sauces. Gorging on a hearty *paila marina* for a pittance in **Antofagasta** (p. 257) is a real treat too. You get the idea...when in Chile, eat cheap!

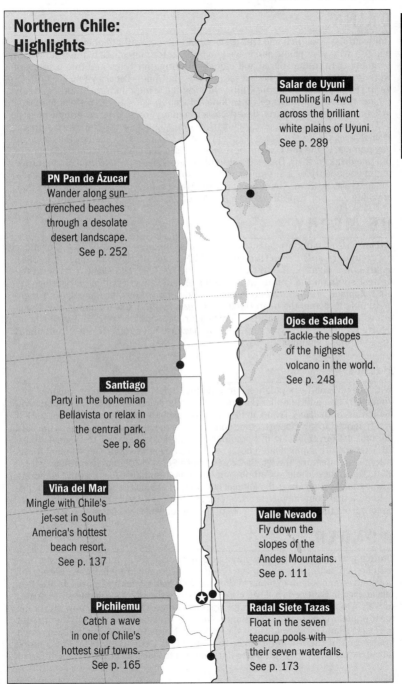

Northern Chile: Highlights

Salar de Uyuni
Rumbling in 4wd across the brilliant white plains of Uyuni.
See p. 289

PN Pan de Ázucar
Wander along sun-drenched beaches through a desolate desert landscape.
See p. 252

Ojos de Salado
Tackle the slopes of the highest volcano in the world.
See p. 248

Santiago
Party in the bohemian Bellavista or relax in the central park.
See p. 86

Viña del Mar
Mingle with Chile's jet-set in South America's hottest beach resort.
See p. 137

Valle Nevado
Fly down the slopes of the Andes Mountains.
See p. 111

Pichilemu
Catch a wave in one of Chile's hottest surf towns.
See p. 165

Radal Siete Tazas
Float in the seven teacup pools with their seven waterfalls.
See p. 173

DRINK

Bold and flavorful, rich and fruity, sweet and subtle; world-famous Chilean wines will flirt with your palate and leave you begging for more. Satiate the wino within by going right to the source and enjoying informative tours and free tastings of wine from the cellars of the largest producer in Chile—**Concha y Toro** (p. 119). Or venture deeper into Middle Chile, the original wine country, to enjoy a truly tongue-titillating experience on **La Ruta del Vino** (p. 172). Sip in style at **Matilla,** a luscious too-good-to-be-true desert oasis legendary for its overpowering wines (p. 303). However, if you prefer guzzling to savoring, knock back a few *pisco sours* at **Planta Capel,** the largest *pisco* plant in Chile (p. 234). And if you enjoy that, you can pay homage to the rife Chilean beverage at **Pisco Elqui,** a town named in honor of the fine drink (p. 236). Decided not to ply yourself with poison? Be content drinking in the beauty of a sublime sunrise at the ethereal **El Tatio Geysers** (p. 283). Chances are, however, that if you go white-water rafting on the **Futalefú,** more than anything else, you'll swallow down gallons of pristine river water (p. 446).

BE MERRY

Salsa, salsa, and more *salsa* is the name of the game at *discotecas,* or more appropriately, *salsatecas* throughout Chile. **Dance** till dawn in Iquique (p. 293), **splurge** on a night on the town in Valparaíso (p. 123), and **shake** it down in the hottest spots on the continent in Barrios Bellavista and Ñuñoa in Santiago (p. 103). **Applaud** *muy machista huasos,* Chilean cowboys, at Rancagua's rough-'n'-tumble Rodeo in the heart of *tierra huasa* (p. 160). **Cheer** on the Talca Rangers with other *fútbol* fanatics in Talca's largest stadium (p. 175). **Laugh** wholeheartedly at the embarrassing bray of "jackass" penguins in the Monumento Nacional Los Pengüinos (p. 467).

PRAY

With over 90% of the population perpetuating Chile's Catholic fervor, you may find yourself acting a little holier-than-thou. Stir your spirituality by gazing upon vivid depictions of the Holy Trinity in the grand **Iglesia Catedral de Concepción** (p. 194). If you're moved to get closer to your god, just ride the elevator to the top of the 93ft. tall **Cruz del Tercer Milenio** in Coquimbo—Catholicism's answer to Disneyland (p. 222). On a more sophisticated note, consider La Serena's churches—famed for its colonial architecture, the **Iglesia Catedral de La Serena** is definitely worth a visit (p. 229). Meanwhile, Chilean Catholicism takes on a Buddhist flavor at the elaborate shrine to the Virgin Mary, the **Mirador la Virgen,** in Vicuña (p. 235). If you need more help than that, join the pilgrims from far and wide who still crawl to Andacollo to benefit from the miraculous powers of the sacred **Virgen del Carmen** (p. 218).

WONDER

Chile's assortment of quaint museums harboring odd, miscellaneously mismatched collections, is one of the country's most endearing features. Forget the polished cosmopolitan exhibits at the **Museo de Bellas Artes** and **Museo de Arte Contemporaneo** in Santiago (p. 110); consider instead the irony of the life-sized poster of Walt Whitman in Pablo Neruda's Valparaíso home, **La Sebastiana,** now one of the most popular museums in the country (p. 129). You can save yourself the trip out to Easter Island by stopping in at the excellent **Museo Fonck** in Viña del Mar, which boasts one of the few *moai* ever to have left the island (p. 141). For a more unusual exhibit, stop by the **Museo Bomberil Benito Riquelme** in Talca for a different

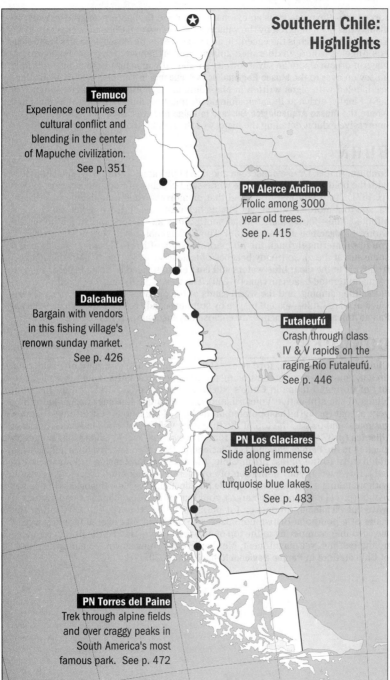

Southern Chile: Highlights

Temuco
Experience centuries of cultural conflict and blending in the center of Mapuche civilization. See p. 351

PN Alerce Andino
Frolic among 3000 year old trees. See p. 415

Dalcahue
Bargain with vendors in this fishing village's renown sunday market. See p. 426

Futaleufú
Crash through class IV & V rapids on the raging Río Futaleufú. See p. 446

PN Los Glaciares
Slide along immense glaciers next to turquoise blue lakes. See p. 483

PN Torres del Paine
Trek through alpine fields and over craggy peaks in South America's most famous park. See p. 472

sort of art—the museum is an extensive tribute to firefighters and the artwork on display has been inspired by the valiant efforts of several Chilean firemen (p. 178). Taking it up a notch is the eccentric and largely eclectic **Museo de la Alta Frontera** in Los Angeles, where taxidermied animals are presented alongside exquisite displays of ornate Mapuche silver jewelry (p. 196). If you're bit by the indigenous bug, mosey on over to the **Museo Regional de la Araucanía** in Temuco, where all displays are labeled with signs written in Mapudungun, the original Mapuche tongue (p. 358). Finally, arrive at the archaeological capital of Chile, San Pedro de Atacama, where the **Museo Arqueológico Gustavo le Paige** features ancient mummies and an impressive exhibit detailing the history of the region (p. 281).

BURN

Sunburn, that is. Or use sunscreen and don't burn at all. Either way, rub shoulders with the bold and beautiful on the white-sand beaches of ritzy, resorty **Viña del Mar** (p. 137). But if you just don't feel that glamorous when languishing in the sun, escape to a more secluded, yet just as beautiful, beach town along the coast of Middle Chile—**Cartagena.** Or head south a few kilometers and sunbathe on the shores of **Algarobbo** instead (p. 133). The Chilean coast is never-ending, so even if you're sauntering through the *altiplano* deserts of Norte Grande, you can catch some sun at the oh-so-trendy beaches of **Iquique** (p. 293). And if all of this endless frolicking in the clear blue waters still isn't enough, head to **Bahía Inglesa,** a haven of unadulterated beach nirvana (p. 250). The views, the fishing, the strolls, the kayaking, the camping, and the warm sands of the picturesque beach resort are unrivaled in all of Chile—except maybe by stunning sandy coves in the **Parque Nacional Pan de Azúcar,** where beaches are enclosed by luscious patches of forest (p. 252).

CONQUER

Climb every mountain, ford every stream—and while you may not find your dream, you will encounter stunning natural expanses and a mind-blowing diversity of flora and fauna in Chile's world-famous national parks. Ignore the rumblings of the still-active Volcán Llaima in the **Parque Nacional Conguillío** during your ascent (p. 358). Disappointed in the lack of poisonous sulfur fumes? Grab a gas mask and trek to the top of the turbulent Volcán Villarrica in **Parque Nacional Villarrica** (p. 372). If you're looking for a more serene ascent, slide along gorgeous glaciers in the **Parque Nacional Los Glaciers** (p. 483). If you need a little help getting uphill, turn to the oldest lift in Chile, the **Ascensor Concepción** in Valparaíso (p. 131). However, if your definition of conquering a peak entails coming downhill without taking a bad fall, head to **Valle Nevado,** famed to have the best skiing in the region (p. 111). If mountains aren't your cup of tea, conquer the temperamental waves at **Pichilemu,** the mecca for persistent *surfistas* (p. 165). Or refute the claim of a pompous British colonizer who declared that even a monkey would have trouble scampering to the top of an *araucaria*, and be the first to scamper up the baffling, yet magnificent, Monkey Puzzle Trees as you conquer the quirks of Chilean flora in **Parque Nacional Nahuelbuta** (p. 207).

SUGGESTED ITINERARIES

MOUNTAIN, BEACH, AND DESERT:
THE NORTH

MOUNTAIN, BEACH, AND DESERT—THE NORTH (4 WEEKS)

Before exposing yourself to the most extreme environs of Chile, you might as well soak up some sun in the relaxed beach town of **Arica** (p. 308). As the major international gateway from Peru and Bolivia, it's an easy place to start. From there, head west to **Parque Nacional Lauca** (p. 324) to enjoy its vast alpine fields, snow-capped mountains, and diverse wildlife. Be sure to plan a trek through neighboring **Reserva Nacional Las Vicuñas** (p. 327) to see the brilliant white salt plains of the Salar de Surire. After walking in the clouds with the vicuñas and guanacos, find another slice of heaven in **Iquique** (p. 293). Often called the Miami Beach of South America, this coastal city is an interesting contrast of 19th-century colonial port and 21st-century luxury beach resort. Heading south, you'll enter the vast **Atacama Desert,** the driest place on earth, via an otherworldly forest of strange trees—the **Reserva Nacional Pampa de Tamarugal** (p. 302) protects the last of the tenacious *tamarugo* trees, which manage to survive and even thrive in the dry, saline soils at the edge of the desert. You can skip over the majority of this wasteland to its very heart, **San Pedro de Atacama** (p. 275), an oasis village that is the jumping-off point for some of the best sights of the region. From here you can watch the volcanic water spouts of **El Tatio Geysers,** catch sunrise over the eerie landscape of **El Valle de la Luna,** and frolic with flamingos in **Reserva Nacional Los Flamencos** (yes, there are flamingos in the desert). When you are ready to get back to civilization, swing through **Calama** (p. 269), Chile's highest-altitude city. Take some deep breaths before catching a bus to **Antofagasta** (p. 257), the largest city in the northern region, where you'll find plenty of urban excitement. After a short break to recoup, head south again to **Copiapó** (p. 242). From this commercial mining town, you can easily attack **Parque Nacional Nevado Tres Cruces,** home to some of the best hiking and climbing the Andes have to offer, including **Ojos del Salado,** the highest volcano in the world. But don't get yourself sacrificed to the gods because you will want to be on the road again to reach **Vallenar** (p. 239) before finally arriving in **La Serena** (p. 222). This thriving port city with its colonial facade claims to be the premier beach resort in Chile (much to the chagrin of residents of Viña del Mar), and has enough sun-drenched coast to keep an avid beach bum busy for weeks. Despite this temptation, make sure to take the time to jump around with the penguins in the **Reserva Nacional Pingüino de Humboldt** (p. 230) and sample the Chilean national liquor in **Pisco Elqui** (p. 236).

CHILLIN' AND MILLIN'—MIDDLE CHILE (2 WEEKS)

If you're strapped for time, the incredible number of sights and activities packed into Middle Chile make it a must-see area. There's no better place to start than the thriving metropolis of **Santiago** (p. 86). Enjoy the wide boulevards and bustling crowds of *el centro* or groove into the early morning hours in the bohemian Barrio Bellavista. Escape the urban insanity to indulge in the internationally recognized

DISCOVER

CHILLIN' AND MILLIN': MIDDLE CHILE

wines of Concha y Toro or ski the slopes of Valle Nevado. Then get moving to the coast, starting with the sprawling **Valparaíso** (p. 123). Spend time wandering through picturesque neighborhoods that surround the downtown and check out one of Pablo Neruda's houses. Then head south to **Isla Negra** (p. 134) to see more of his eclectic collection of artifacts and curios. After getting your fill of culture, it's time to see the other side in **Viña del Mar** (p. 137). One of the hottest resort towns in South America, Valpo's little sister will have you relaxing on white-sand beaches and jumping in the clubs 'til dawn. When the high-life gets too much, head north again to **Quintero** (p. 144), where you can walk along the coast in the shade of cypress trees while watching the sea lions sun themselves in the many secluded bays. Before winding up your whirl-wind tour of Middle Chile, make sure to head over to **Parque Nacional La Campana** (p. 145).

OVER THE RIVER AND THROUGH THE WOODS—THE LAKES (3 WEEKS) Get ready to roll through one of the most beautiful regions of Chile. Your starting point is **Temuco** (p. 351). A vital commercial city and the heart of the remaining Mapuche indigenous population, this gateway to the Lakes District has a definite mix of cultures. Head south from here to **Villarrica** (p. 360), a good place to spend the night while daytripping to the more expensive **Pucón** (p. 366). This popular lakeside town is great not only for relaxing on black-sand beaches, but also for organizing trips into **Parque Nacional Villarrica** (p. 372) to climb the majestic Volcán Villarrica. When you are finished playing on the snow-capped peak, it's time to move on to the Seven Lakes. **Pan-**

guipulli (p. 379) lies on the shores of its namesake lake and is the perfect spot to begin exploring this incredible region. Seven major lakes are surrounded by lush forests, sandy beaches, popular camping grounds, and quaint little towns, making it well worth a few days' venturing. Before completely losing yourself, though, find your way back to the Pacific coast. Set among rolling farmlands, **Valdivia** (p. 380) is the capital of this region and is the rainiest place in Chile. Its Germanic heritage gives the city a little extra *sabor*, although much of the original construction has been lost to earthquakes over the years. On the road again, make sure to stop in **Osorno** (p. 387), an agricultural city that shares the Germanic roots of its northern neighbor. The city lies at the center of the Lakes District and is a short hop from many major destinations in the area. The most popular of these is **Lago Llanquihué,** with its sparkling blue waters and the imposing backdrop of the Volcanes Osorno, Calbuco, and Puntiagudo. One of the most picturesque towns on the lake is **Frutillar** (p. 396). Relax along the shore and take in the incredible landscape or set off hiking. When you're ready to get back to civilization, continue on to **Puerto Varas** (p. 397), just around the

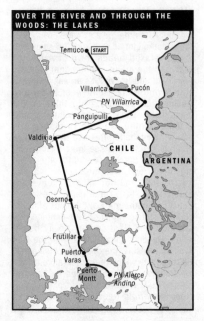

OVER THE RIVER AND THROUGH THE WOODS: THE LAKES

lake. Much more of a commercial and tourist center than the surrounding towns, Varas is a fun place to kill a day or two and still be by the water. Then move on from the residential suburb to the larger **Puerto Montt** (p. 409). The only major city for miles, Puerto Montt is the meeting point of the Panamerican Highway out of the Lakes District, the Camino Austral out of the Aisén, and the ferry from the Island of Chiloé. Before finishing up your tour, don't forget to see **Parque Nacional Alerce Andino** (p. 415), which protects *alerce* trees, some of which are over 4000 years old.

ICE, ICE BABY—THE FAR SOUTH (3 WEEKS)

Looking for some rugged adventure and don't mind a little cold and wind? The Far South is the place for you. Start off in the southernmost city in the world, **Punta Arenas** (p. 461), a sheepherding town that has managed to survive and grow while keeping its quiet origins. From here you can head over to **Monumento Nacional Los Pingüinos** (p. 467) and waddle with some of these well-dressed birds. When you're ready to get down to business, go north to **Puerto Natales** (p. 468), a quiet city that serves as a jumping-off point for some of the most incredible parks in South America. At the top of that list is **Parque Nacional Torres del Paine** (p. 472). Vast forests, alpine fields, rocky ravines, and blue-green lakes surround the impossibly steep and smooth *torres* (towers) that give the park its name. You could easily spend weeks wandering in this incredible park—but keep pushing on to reach **El Calafate, ARG** (p. 475). This tiny town in the Argentine Patagonia sits at the base of some of the largest glaciers in the world. Walk within a few feet of the towering Glacier Perito Moreno or take a boat up to an *estancia* perched over the vast Upsala Glacier. If you're looking for terrain more suited to hiking, continue north to **El Chaltén, ARG** (p. 480), where you can climb the well-known Fitz Roy. Don't be in too much of a rush to leave Chile's more flamboyant neighbor. First trek on down to the touristy **Ushuaia** (p. 488), in the Argentine Tierra del Fuego. The "Land of Fire" isn't quite the burning place you thought it would be—**Parque Nacional Tierra del Fuego** (p. 493) is actually the best place from which to arrange trips to Antarctica. Before wrapping up this short jaunt, be sure to visit **Puerto Williams** (p. 495) on Isla Navarino so you can say you visited the southernmost human settlement in the world!

THE BEST OF CHILE (1 MONTH)

So you want big cities, rugged wilderness, burning deserts, towering glaciers, and gorgeous beaches, and black-sand beaches? Sounds like you want all of Chile! Although seeing all of Chile would take months or even years, if you move quickly and are willing to spend a little on airfare, you can do a super-speedy greatest-hits-of-Chile tour. Your first stop (and likely entry point) is the bustling metropolis of **Santiago** (p. 86). Gape at the soaring skyscrapers of *el centro* and get your groove on in the hip Barrio Bellavista. Then jump to the far north and land in **Arica** (p. 308), gateway to Peru and Bolivia. From there, head over to **Parque Nacional Lauca** (p. 324) and run with the llamas, alpacas, vicuñas, and guanacos, or move south to see the blindingly white salt plains of the Salar de Surire. From alpine plains and snow-capped mountains to the barren desert, **San Pedro de Atacama** (p. 275) is your next stop. Try catching the sunset at El Valle de la Luna and the sunrise over El Tatio Geysers. When you're ready to head back to civilization, continue to **Antofagasta** (p. 257), the region's largest city. This is a great place to rest up before attacking the highest volcano in the world, Ojos del Salado, in **Parque Nacional Nevado Tres Cruces** (p. 247). Back on the Pacific coast, **Val-**

THE BEST OF CHILE

paraíso (p. 123) is a great place to take in a little culture and see Pablo Neruda's old haunts. Or swing over to Valpo's sister city **Viña del Mar** (p. 137), one of the hottest, wildest beach resorts in South America. If sand isn't your favorite thing, continue on to **Chillán** (p. 180), famous for the longest ski slopes in South America and the most relaxing hot baths. Don't stay too long, because it's off to **Puerto Montt** (p. 409) and nearby **Puerto Varas** (p. 397). With a laid-back atmosphere and incredible views of the Andes, they are two of the most popular cities in the Lakes District. From there it's an easy ride to **Castro** (p. 427) on the Island of Chiloé. Be sure to spend time wandering through some of the quaint fishing villages that dot the coast and drop by the picturesque Parque Nacional Chiloé. After that, head down to **Punta Arenas** (p. 461), where you can spend time with penguins and prep yourself for a trek through **Parque Nacional Torres del Paine** (p. 472), one of the most well-known parks in South America. When you've had enough of alpine fields, blue-green lakes, and craggy peaks, move on to **Ushuaia, ARG** (p. 488). Although it claims to be *"el fin del mundo"* (the end of the world), no trip would be complete without a trip to the actual southernmost human settlement in the world, **Puerto Williams** (p. 495), on Isla Navarino. Now take a deep breath and tell yourself you'll never be crazy enough to do something like that again.

LIFE AND TIMES

LAND

Bounded by the Andes to the east and the Pacific Ocean to the west, Chile is one of the most isolated, yet environmentally diverse countries in South America. Spanning over 4300km (2700mi.) from north to south (nearly half the length of South America), Chile averages only 177km (100mi.) in width. Nevertheless, the range of geographic formations packed into this narrow country gives rise to an incredible mix of environments from the arid desert regions of the north to the lush rolling farmland of the Central Valley and the rocky glacial fields of the south.

GEOGRAPHY AND CLIMATE

THE ANDES. Stretching along the entire eastern border, the **Andes** are an omnipresent feature of the Chilean landscape. Highest in the far north, they contain peaks reaching well over 6000 meters (20,000 feet). **Ojos del Salado** (6893m) is the highest peak in the country and the highest active volcano in the world. Aconcagua (6959m), the highest peak in the world outside the Himalayas, lies just across the border in Argentina. Towards the south, the mountains gradually decrease in elevation, while mountain passes occur more frequently and are easier to negotiate.

The creation of the Andes due to the collision of two teutonic plates also makes this region a hotbed of seismic activity. Some 2000 volcanoes are scattered throughout the mountain range, almost 50 of which are still active. **Earthquakes** have also had a major impact on the country—in 1960, one of the biggest quakes in Chile's history (8.75 on the Richter Scale) decimated cities throughout the Central Valley and sunk some parts of the coast nearly two meters into the ocean.

NORTE GRANDE AND NORTE CHICO. The far north of Chile is arid and rugged, dominated by the **Atacama Desert,** one of the driest deserts in the world. To the west, cold air brought up by the Humboldt current meets the steep cliffs of the Cordillera Domeyko that line the coast and forms banks of fog that roll down into the desert valley. This cold air current significantly moderates the climate in the region, with the average temperature ranging between 14°C (58°F) and 21°C (70°F). Despite the relative coolness, the Atacama region still receives little rain and, in some parts of the desert, there has never been any recorded precipitation.

Despite the desert conditions, Norte Grande boasts some of Chile's most fantastic landscapes. Sublime sunsets highlight an incredible range of earthy colors derived from the rich mineral deposits that cover the area. These mineral deposits, especially the vast salt plains, also make Norte Grande one of Chile's most valuable regions. The **copper exports** that have formed the foundation of the Chilean economy for decades all come from this region.

CENTRAL VALLEY AND THE LAKES DISTRICT. The region stretching from Santiago south to the Island of Chiloé is the most fertile and populated part of Chile. Just north of the capital city, the scrublands of Norte Chico break into the beginnings of the Central Valley. This region of rolling farmland is home to Chile's lucrative wine industry. The vast tracts of grapes that make their white wine famous grow well in the seasonal rain and mild, almost Mediterranean climate. The region is also home to some of Chile's largest cities, including Santiago, Valparaíso, and Concepción.

The farther south you go, the rainier it becomes. The city of Valdivia in the heart of the Lakes District, for example, receives over 2535mm (115in.) of rain a year. Dozens of beautiful lakes dot this damp region and the everpresent background of snow-capped mountains makes this one of the most picturesque parts of Chile. Industry has also capitalized on its grassy pasture lands and vast forests, turning it into the center of lumber production and cattle ranching.

AISÉN, CHILOÉ, AND THE FAR SOUTH. Beyond the port city of Puerto Montt, the Central Valley drops below sea level, creating a perplexing maze of islands, inlets, and fjords. The sheer cliffs of the Andes move closer and closer to the water's edge until they too disappear into the ocean. The landscape is dominated by alpine forests and grasslands that break into tundra plains in the far south. The frigid Humboldt Current flowing north from Antarctica brings with it cold temperatures and bitter winds; in many places enormous **glaciers** cover the mountains and plains below.

The rugged nature of this part of the country has made it difficult to develop. Nevertheless, the region is extremely important in Chile's overall economy, as lumber and livestock are in abundant supply, and petroleum is also an important product in the area surrounding the **Strait of Magellan.** The Strait is an important connection between the Atlantic and Pacific Oceans that allows both passengers and cargo ships to avoid the dangerous trip around Cape Horn.

FLORA AND FAUNA

Due to its relative physical isolation and its diversity of geographic regions, Chile boasts an incredible variety of plants and animals, many of which are endemic to the country (they do not live anywhere else). Many of these species such as the vicuñas and guanacos of the northern *altiplano* or the Alerce and Monkey Puzzle trees of the Lakes District are characteristic of Chile's varied and unique wildlife. Unfortunately, most of these are also in serious danger of extinction. Unchecked hunting, trapping, logging, and clearing have pushed dozens of once-widespread plants and animals onto the endangered species list. Weak or non-existent environmental laws have facilitated serious environmental damage from industrial pollution and over-population. Despite these problems (and partially in response to them), the government has built one of the largest and most successful national park systems in the world.

PLANTS

The diversity and uniqueness of Chile's plant life can be seen in every part of the country. Some of the most interesting and rare species are found in the most sparsely populated regions, a phenomenon seen most vividly in the case of the northern desert region. Although what little life there is in the desert and *altiplano* is, expectedly, dominated by various types of cacti, the area is also home to the **tamarugo,** a spiny acacia tree, and the **queñoa,** which lives at slightly higher altitudes. Shrubs cover most of the land to the south, although the Santiago area has vestiges of the previously extensive **Southern Beech** forests (also called the Chilean palm). The climate becomes more tolerable for wildlife in the Central Valley and Lakes District. The increase in rain and milder temperatures support a wide variety of trees, flowers, and grasses. Most notable among these are the national flower, the **Chilean Bell Flower,** and the national tree, the **Monkey Puzzle.** One of the other well-known species in this region is the **Alerce,** a relative of the sequoia tree that can survive for over 4000 years. Heavy logging of these enormous trees, however, has brought critical attention from international conservation groups.

ANIMALS

Although Chile's severe climate zones and relative isolation has limited the breadth of animal species that populate the country, it has allowed for the development of a number of rare and interesting species. In the highlands surrounding the northern deserts live a large number of the **llamas** and **alpacas** so well-known in Peru and Bolivia. However, Chile also is home to two other members of the llama family, **guanacos** and the endangered **vicuñas.** The soft fine coat of the vicuña made it the fabric of choice for the ancient Incan royalty and nearly drove it to extinction when it became widely popular at the turn of the century. The rodent-like **chinchilla** has a very similar story—it was hunted so thoroughly that almost none exist today except as household pets. Its close cousin, the mountain **vizcacha,** has survived, although only in the southern highlands.

The **Rhea,** or ñandú, is Chile's version of the ostrich, and makes its home in the southern highlands, along with the **Andean Condor.** With a wing span of over three meters, the condor is often spotted floating lazily on the updrafts that blow through the mountain peaks. The endemic **huemul,** an endangered Chilean deer, lives within the rocky Patagonia. In the more hospitable temperate regions, Chile boasts a richer diversity of wildlife: look for **pumas** and other wild cats; the **pudú,** a small deer-like mammal; and a wide range of birds.

Although Chile's terrestrial wildlife is somewhat limited, its assorted and abundant marine life more than compensates. The shores of the country are teeming with the incredible variety the Pacific offers. **Penguins, sea lions, seals,** and **otters** can be found along Chile's extensive coastline. The coastal waters are home to a wide range of **whales** and **dolphins** and produce the enormous selection of fish and shellfish that are such an important part of the Chilean cuisine.

HISTORY

PRECOLONIAL TIMES AND SPANISH COLONIZATION (1492-1550). Think twice before arguing with a Chilean—considering their history of unrelenting resistance, they're bound to put up quite a fight. When the Incas attempted to conquer Chile in 1460 and 1491, they encountered fierce resistance from the indigenous **Araucanians,** specifically, members of the **Mapuche** tribe, and were only able to establish some forts in the Central Valley.

The Araucanians, a fragmented tribal society consisting primarily of hunters and farmers, constituted the largest Amerindian group in Chile. The Araucanians' almost mythical ability to withstand foreign attempts at colonization of their land served them well when the Spanish conquest of Chile began in 1536-37. **Francisco Pizarro** invaded Chile in search of an 'Otro Peru' (Another Peru). Disappointed at not finding gold, Pizarro returned to Peru immediately, but in 1540-41 agreed to **Pedro de Valdivia's** request to conquer and colonize the region.

Santiago was founded on February 12, 1541, but Valdivia did not undertake the conquest of the southern regions until 1550, and the conquest of Chile was consolidated in the late 1550s under **Governor Don García Hurtado de Mendoza.** To resist colonization, the Araucanians added horses and European weaponry to their arsenal, and were able to hinder the Spaniards until the late 19th century. The chieftain, **Lautaro,** who staged a revolt that led to the capture and death of Valdivia, is still revered by Chilean nationalists. Unfortunately, however, a century of European conquest and disease decimated about half of the original Araucanian population of a million.

50,000-9000 BC
Adventurous Chileans-to-be cross the Bering Strait

12,000 BC
Araucanian natives set up shop in the foothills of the Andes

1460
Incas invade Chile and are driven out

1491
Incas attack again and still can't subdue the mighty Araucanians

1536
After defeating the Incas, the Spanish try their hand at conquering Chile... and fail.

February 1541
Pedro de Valdivia leads Spaniards back to Chile and founds Santiago

1578
Sir Francis Drake loots and pillages Valparaíso

1544-1759
Chile develops as a farming colony

COLONIAL PERIOD (1550-1759). Despite the corruption of the political system and the mediocrity of Spanish officials posted in Chile, Chileans exhibited loyalty to crown authority for three centuries of colonial rule. Ironically, the colonizers themselves often circumvented royal laws—in the countryside, local landowners and military officials often established their own rules.

Settlers had accepted Chile as a primarily agricultural colony due to the scant amounts of precious metals available. The Chilean colony depended on coerced labor, and the labor force was comprised mainly of *mestizos* who worked on *haciendas*. Chile was regarded as a "deficit area" in the Spanish empire, and maintaining officials and an army in Chile proved to be a cumbersome expense. Meanwhile, Chileans resented their reliance on Peru for governance and trade. Although the economy expanded under Spanish rule, Chileans found taxation, and particularly, the restrictions on trade and production, stifling.

In addition, the stratification of colonial Chilean society on the basis of race, ethnicity, and class irked many. *Peninsulares* (recently arrived Spaniards) and *criollos* (Chilean-born children of Spanish immigrants) dominated the upper class. The increasing population of *mestizos* (mixed European and Indian blood) were next, followed by indigenous populations, and the few African slaves. The Spaniards were in favor of the subjugation and extermination of *indígenas;* the Roman Catholic Church, the primary instrument of social control whose influence on social affairs was often decisive, served as the main defender of the indigenous population from Spanish atrocities.

Chile hosted one of the largest standing armies in the Americas and so became a garrison to protect against potential Araucanian encroachment and Spain's European enemies (**Sir Francis Drake** invaded Valparaíso in 1578). Lacking a printing press until the Wars of Independence (1810-18), Chile remained isolated from the outside world.

THE ROAD TO INDEPENDENCE (1759-1818). The **French Bourbon** monarchs came to power after the **Habsburg** dynasty's rule over Spain ended in 1700. The attempt to restructure the empire to improve its productivity caused a period of reform in Chile that lasted from the coronation of **Charles III** in Spain to the end of **Governor Ambrosio O'Higgins y Ballenary's** tenure in Chile.

The **Bourbon Reforms** of 1759-96 allowed for increased independence in Chile from the Viceroyalty of Peru. Irish-born Governor O'Higgins's promotion of self-sufficiency in both economic production and public administration initiated the independence movement. Free trade with other colonies and independent states was encouraged, and this exposure through trade brought knowledge of foreign politics to Chile.

News of European liberalism, the independence of 13 American colonies, and descriptions of the French Revolution made the notion of independence enticing to a Chilean elite.

The real possibility of independence materialized after the authority of the crown was undermined by Napoleon's invasion of Spain in 1807. Spanish loyalists formed cliques that decided to govern both Spain and her colonies until the rightful king was restored. Chileans found themselves wondering who the rightful regional authority was now—the French monarch, the Spanish rebels, or local leaders? On **September 18, 1810** (a date now celebrated as Chile's independence day), *criollo* leaders of Santiago declared that they would govern the colony until order was restored in Spain, and immediately opened the ports to all traders.

This initial experiment in self-government was led by the new president, **José Miguel Carrera Verdugo** (1812-13). Carrera's militaristic tendencies provoked **Bernardo O'Higgins Riquelme** (an advocate for complete independence), who opposed Carrera's ideas by launching a rival faction. This caused civil war to break out among the *criollos* because for many, temporary self-rule escalated into the possibility of permanent independence. However, troops in Peru seized their opportunity and reasserted control in Chile in 1814 after winning the **Battle of Rancagua.**

The harsh rule of Spanish loyalists after *La Reconquista* (the Reconquest) of 1814-17 convinced Chileans of the need for independence. However, the *criollos* who sought independence and equality for Chilean society were more interested in assuming leadership positions previously held by *peninsulares* than liberating the Chilean masses. In a sense, the Chilean independence war played out as a class struggle.

O'Higgins, who was in exile in Argentina, joined forces with José de San Martín. Their army launched a daring attack on the Spaniards over the Andes in 1817, ultimately defeating the colonizers at the **Battle of Chacabuco** on February 12. Chilean independence was formally granted after San Martín crushed the last Spanish force on Chilean soil at the **Battle of Maipú** on April 5, 1818.

BUILDING THE REPUBLIC (1818-1879). Although when he came out of the War of Independence, Bernardo O'Higgins seemed to have a tight hold over Chile, his position as a dictator was soon being challenged. Internal divisions that had been forced below the surface during the war were now returning as resentment over his heavy-handed rule increased. By 1823, his attempts to draw more of the oligarchy into his administration had been thwarted and he was ousted from power.

For Chile, the fall of O'Higgins set the stage for seven years of bad luck. From 1823 to 1830, 30 different governments tried to establish themselves. However, divisions including conservatives, liberals, authoritarians, and federalists made it nearly impossible to hold together a coherent coalition. As government after government failed to gain control, lawlessness and economic troubles increased, and the elites became increasingly frustrated with broad-based attempts at forming a stable regime. In 1830, **Diego Portales** changed all that.

1759-1796
Bourbon reforms cause food for thought

1807
Napoleon invades Spain, but is not cured of his complex

September 1810
Loyalists declare independence until "real" Spanish government restored

1814
Divisions in leadership allow the Spanish to reconquer Chile

January 1817
After kicking butt in Buenos Aires, José de San Martín crosses the Andes and overruns Santiago

February 1818
Chilean independence declared

April 1818
Argentine-Chilean army finally drives out the last of the Spanish and heads North to Peru

1823
Bernardo O'Higgins, supreme dictator, no longer reigns supreme, but gets plazas named after him nonetheless

1823-1830
Chile suffers from political schizophrenia

1830
Diego Portales establishes a stable government

1833
Chile gets its first Constitution; too bad no one but the elite get a say in it

1836-39
Chile breaks up a Peru-Bolivia Confederation

1840s and 50s
Economic booms create a new elite and more social stratification

1851
Liberal forces lead an attempted coup

1879
Needy Chile finds a good way to get greenbacks—take them from your neighbors

1881
Peruvian resistance forces Chile to sack Lima

By hammering out a compromise amongst the most powerful elites, Portales was able to catapult **José Tomás de Ovalle** into the presidency and establish an incredibly strong, conservative government. This new government was further strengthened by the adoption of a new constitution, pushed by Portales, in 1833 that called for a powerful central presidency and a parliament controlled by the oligarchy.

The new regime earned its legitimacy militarily and economically. In 1836, Peru and Bolivia formed a confederacy that Chile believed threatened its security. A series of skirmishes over the next three years reasserted Chilean dominance and broke up the two rivals. A subsequent boom in exports due to higher world demands for grains and metals filled state coffers, smoothed over internal divisions, and created a whole new class of wealthy businessmen.

This economic growth also brought many changes. With the help of British investment, the government embarked on a massive modernization project. This included building railroads, expanding education, and encouraging more entrepreneurs. However, the new members of the elite, who had made their money through business, trade, and industry rather than exploitation of the land, were less tied to traditional values and were more in tune with changes sweeping across Europe. As their numbers and power increased, so did the push for secularization and the diminishment of the role of the Roman Catholic Church in government, as well as liberalization and the inclusion of more Chileans in the politcal process. After decades of stability and unity, the late 1850s and early 1860s brought a hint of new divisions and impending upheaval. But first, Chile would have to beat on its neighbors one more time.

WAR OF THE PACIFIC AND THE NEW PARLIAMENT (1879-1920). The massive influx of investment and industrial goods from Europe caught up to Chile in the 1870s. Faced with a serious balance-of-payments crisis, the government began looking toward the region north of Antofagasta for revenue. Although the incredible mineral wealth of the area was extracted by Chilean-European conglomerates, the territory was still claimed by Bolivia and Peru. In 1879, Chile found just the excuse it was looking for to change all that.

In 1878, Bolivia tried to impose a series of new taxes on the mining companies. When they refused to pay, the Bolivian government seized the firms, infuriating the Chilean elites. When Chile declared war in 1879, Peru announced its intention to honor a secret alliance and support Bolivia. So began the war of three totally unprepared states with almost no armies. In fact, the war became more of a naval contest between Chile and Peru (since Bolivia had no navy). Each nation had two ironclad ships and when Chile managed to sink one of Peru's and capture the other, it was declared the inevitable victor. Unfortunately, Peru did not see it that way. In 1881, the Chilean army was forced to land troops in central Peru and capture the capital city of Lima. Even then, the

Peruvians refused to give up and fought a bloody land war for two more years.

The result of the War of the Pacific was extraordinarily beneficial for Chile. It gained an enormous amount of new territory (a third more), most of which was mineral-rich. However, as is always the case, more money equaled more greed. In 1886, **José Balmaceda** was elected president in what seemed like a continuation of the trend over the last two decades towards more liberal governments. Nevertheless, Balmaceda was a liberal in his ideology but not in his rule. Instead, he tried to reestablish the power of the president and gain control over the distribution of the new mineral wealth. The brewing conflict came to a head in 1890 when a budget crisis broke down into civil war. Enraged by his heavy-handed rule, the congress actually raised an army to overthrow Balmaceda. After several brutal battles outside of Valparaíso, the President was defeated and a new government was created.

Under the new government, the presidency was eliminated entirely and the parliament became the ruling body. However, this new parliamentary government had a variety of new issues to tackle. As the Chilean economy had changed, so had the social structure. Business, trade, and industrialization facilitated the growth of the middle class and the working class. Both classes became increasingly aware that their urban orientation and social concerns were not in any way linked with the landed oligarchy and that they had to get politically involved. The first widespread strikes occurred around the turn of the century, and the old conservative elite were suddenly contending not only with the traditional liberal party but also a new wave of Radicals, including Democratic Socialists and even Communists. As the country headed into the 20th century, the elite-dominated parliament was becoming progressively more isolated and out-of-touch.

A NEW CONSTITUTION AND THE RISE OF THE LEFT. In 1920, widespread discontent among the middle class catapulted the reformist **Arturo Alessandri Palma** into the presidency. However, the powerful, elite-controlled parliament blocked most of his initiatives. Four years later, frustrated by the deadlock, middle-class military officers led a military coup. Alessandri was kept as president and the parliament was forced to pass the reform measures. However, conflicts within the new government forced the president to flee to Argentina and set the stage for another more sweeping set of changes.

Soon after Alessandri's flight, another group of military officials led by **Carlos Ibañez del Campo** staged a second coup and invited the ex-president to return. With their support, Alessandri drafted a new constitution that strengthened the presidency and instituted a number of welfare guarantees and reforms never present in the original document. Following his own ambitions, however, Ibañez soon forced the president to resign, setting himself up to be elected in 1927. The next five years were chaotic for the country due partially to

1883
Peru finally admits defeat, Chile landlocks Bolivia and winds up rich, rich, rich!

1886
José Balmaceda goes from prince to pauper

1890
The Chilean congress raises an army to fight the President's army—talk about political deadlock

1891
The Congress wins, the Presidency is abolished, and Parliamentarism is established

1920
President Alessandri issues in middle-class reform era

1924
Military intervenes to push through reforms

1925
Chile's second constitution established

1925-32
Chile relapses into political schizophrenia

LIFE AND TIMES

LIFE AND TIMES

1927-1931
Carlos Ibañez brings momentary stability through military rule

1930
World depression wreaks havoc on the Chilean economy, increasing tensions

1932
Alessandri returns again to reestablish order

1938-52
Middle-class Radicals rain on the old elite's parade and gain power

1952
Mounting frustrations result in the return of Ibañez, this time as elected President

1958
Socialist, Communist, and other leftist parties make major showings in the elections

1964
Eduardo Frei elected; begins major liberal reforms

the interesting contradiction between Ibañez's brutal autocratic style of rule and his leftist reform policies. Nevertheless, most of the ensuing troubles arose from the economic disaster of the Great Depression. Unable to halt the nation's downward spiral, Ibañez was ousted in favor of a traditional elite, **Juan Montero Rodríguez,** who was then ousted by a civilian-military coalition that founded the Socialist Republic. Order was finally restored after the elections of 1932 and the return of Alessandri. This time, however, he faced a very different political landscape.

In less than 10 years, several decades of social change finally emerged on the political scene. The government was no longer dominated by the parties of the old elite, the Conservatives and Liberals. Now, the middle-class based Radicals held the center and a multitude of groups had formed on the left, including the Socialist and Communist Parties. After Alessandri's term ended, the Radicals gained power and remained there until 1952 (helped somewhat by the economic boom during World War II). However, frustration with the slow pace of reform allowed for the reelection of Carlos Ibañez as an "apolitical" candidate. But by 1958, the political discontent and divisions were growing. The candidate of the old oligarchy, **Jorge Alessandria Rodríguez** (the son of Arturo), just barely obtained a plurality above the leftist **Salvador Allende** and **Eduardo Frei,** representing the newly formed, centrist Christian Democrat party. The power of Allende's leftist coalition, *Frente de Acción Popular* (Popular Front Action), frightened the elites. The working-class had been gaining rights and benefits slowly but continuously over the last few decades and each new addition only made them more demanding. This well-organized coalition posed a serious threat to the elite's dominance.

In an effort to ensure the defeat of Allende in the 1964 election, the Liberal and Conservative parties, now united as the National Party, along with many foreign interests (especially the United States), threw their support behind the Christian Democrat Eduardo Frei Montalva. They got far more than they bargained for. Hoping to solidify support both with the middle-class and the lower-class, Frei instituted a serious of major reforms that attacked the power of the elites. Furthermore, to return the profits of the copper industry to the state and use it to finance other initiatives, the government began the process of "Chileanization" whereby they gained control of 51 percent of all of the US-owned industry. Frei then instituted a massive agrarian reform allowing the government to expropriate uncultivated farmland and to redistribute it to peasants. This attacked the heart of the landed oligarchy's support. For decades they had had complete control over the lives of the peasants that worked their vast *haciendas* and therefore had control over their votes. By the time the next elections rolled around in 1970, the National Party was significantly weaker and the peasants and working-class were suddenly highly active and involved.

THE FALL AND SLOW RETURN OF DEMOCRACY. In response to the independent efforts of both the National Party and the Christian Democrats to recapture the presidency, the Socialists, Communists, and Liberals in both the Radical and Christian Democrat parties formed a coalition party called *La Unidad Popular* (Popular Unity). Allende, as their candidate, managed to just beat the other two candidates, but it was not enough to win outright. Instead, the decision had to be ratified by congress. In exchange for his promise to respect the democratic institutions of the country and continue with elections, the Christian Democrats gave him the support he needed to become president. For the first time in its history, Chile had a socialist president.

The goals of Allende's government were not all that more radical than Frei's. He wanted to nationalize major industries, speed up agrarian reform, and institute a massive redistribution of wealth, efforts for which the foundations were already in place. However, the speed with which these changes were implemented shocked supporters and critics alike. Within a year, dozens of major industries had been nationalized and all of the large *haciendas* were disbanded—Allende had ended an economic system that had dominated Chile for centuries.

As the initial steps of the reforms were completed, the government began to run into problems. The immense financial burden of the nationalizations and a ballooning public sector threatened to evolve into an unpayable debt. This combined with a fall in world copper prices and the incredible complexity introduced by state-management industry to form the beginnings of a serious economic crisis.

At the same time, support for the government began to waver. The seizures and nationalizations had produced a powerful opposition alliance between the landed elites and foreign investors (especially the United States). On the reverse side, radical leftists frustrated by the continued moderation of reforms became increasingly violent. The formation of the *Movimiento Izquierda Revolucionario* (MIR), a radical guerilla group, marked the beginning of a dangerous time for Chile. Meanwhile, within the UP itself internal disagreements about the pace and direction of reforms were dividing the party. Middle-class backing eroded as the economic and social situation deteriorated and when an elite- and US-supported truckers' strike paralyzed the country, popular support evaporated. Lower, middle, and upper class alike felt that the country was headed towards a chaotic collapse and for only the third time in its independent history, the Chilean military stepped in to rule.

In 1973, the army launched a major coup, ending decades of stable democracy. At first, the military regime was supposed to be a temporary solution. It enjoyed widespread support from citizens who believed that its main goals were to regain economic and social stability while rebuilding the political institutions that had been severely weakened. However, it soon became evident that **General Augusto Pinochet,** who had emerged as the head figure of the coup, had no such intentions.

1967
Frei institutes massive land reforms, expropriating millions of acres

1969
Socialists, Communists, and some Christian Democrats and Radicals form Popular Unity

1970
Popular Unity candidate and Marxist Salvador Allende elected President

1971
Nationalization of the copper industry

March 1973
UP actually gains seats in mid-term elections despite ensuing turmoil

September 1973
Pinochet launches a bloody coup against government; Allende commits suicide

1973-75
Period of "social stabilization" lead by DINA, Pinochet's secret police

LIFE AND TIMES

1975
Initiation of "economic stabilization" with austerity plan

1976-1981
Chilean Miracle — rapid economic growth and reduction in inflation

1977
Pinochet disbands political parties permanently, crushing hope for democracy

1980
New constitution passed giving Pinochet 8 more years in the driver's seat

1982
Debt crisis sweeps through Latin America; Pinochet forced to implement austerity

1983
Opposition to Pinochet becomes obvious in first major labor protests

Within the first few weeks of the military overthrow, thousands of political activists, journalists, professionals, union leaders, and anyone else considered a subversive individual were arrested and executed. Tens of thousands more were imprisoned and tortured or forced to flee the country. Newspapers and other media were shut down or taken over, trade unions were disbanded, all political parties were suspended, and the Communist and Socialist parties were banned from the country. Soon after, the national congress was dissolved and Pinochet appointed himself dictator. To consolidate his rule, the general created the *Directoria de Inteligencia Nacional* (DINA), which was in charge of "homeland security" and became one of the most atrocious state-sponsored terrorist groups in the world.

Along with this "social stabilization" (a pretty name for brutal oppression) came an entirely new economic orientation. With the help of the so-called Chicago Boys (economists trained at the University of Chicago in the US), Pinochet introduced a series of radical market-oriented reforms. All of the state-owned industries were privatized, public spending and employment were slashed, and trade and investment were liberalized. This "shock treatment" was designed to halt inflation and eliminate state-created inefficiency—its effects were brutal and immediate. Unemployment jumped to well over 20 percent and salaries plummeted, hitting the middle and lower classes the hardest. Although the policies were successful in controlling inflation and sparking economic growth, the costs were enormous. Public services deteriorated, unemployment remained high, and the radical shift in income distribution impoverished huge portions of the population.

By 1980, international experts began talking about the "Chilean miracle," a Latin American country that had managed to escape the chaos and poverty of a radical government and build a stable, growing economy. Pinochet felt confident enough in his standing that he decided it was time to create a new constitution to silence some of the rising criticism of his dictatorship and to secure his position as the leader of Chile. That year he called for a plebiscite to approve a new constitution that would guarantee his position for at least eight more years and allow for another eight-year extension in the future. Strictly controlling the plebiscite, Pinochet managed to obtain the two-thirds vote he needed and Chile had a new constitution.

Soon after the installation of the new constitution, Chile's national situation suddenly deteriorated. In 1982, international credit vanished as the US spiraled into a major recession, plunging countries all across Latin America into serious debt crises. Although Chile's public debt had never been high, many of its private firms and banks were in major trouble. Faced with a serious economic setback, Pinochet once again instituted austerity policies. This second wave of salary cuts and unemployment seriously undermined support for the regime.

By 1983, serious signs of the regime's weakness were visibly manifesting themselves. For the first time in nearly a decade, leftist groups were successfully staging massive demonstrations. Even more worrisome for the military government was that militant opposition groups were beginning to form in the urban shantytowns created by high rates of unemployment and poverty. The stable, peaceful environment which had been one of Pinochet's few sources of legitimacy was fading rapidly. Political activists did not take long to capitalize on this uncertainty—the Christian Democratic Party, Chile's largest political party, was resurrected along with many others, and a center-left coalition, the Democratic Alliance, was formed to put pressure on the crumbling regime. By the middle of 1984, even the Catholic Church had swung behind the democratization movement and, in August, a church-mediated accord was signed by parties in the center and right to move for immediate elections.

Despite this growing protest movement, Pinochet refused to yield and intensified his ban on political activity instead. There was to be no discussion of elections until after the constitutionally-prescribed plebiscite in 1988 decided whether or not Pinochet would be granted another eight years as the nation's leader. Nevertheless, the opposition he faced was more than just a leftist uprising. Conservative business leaders and foreign investors were becoming more and more nervous about the increasing instability in Chile. International pressure, especially from the normally reticent United States, increased as a trend towards democracy swept through Latin America. Confronted by such broad-based opposition, the General was not able to control the plebiscite and, in October of 1988, 55% voted "No" to extending his rule. In December of 1989, Patricio Aylwin lead the Concertación, a coalition of the major centrist parties, to electoral victory, defeating the military-backed candidate Hernán Büchi Buc. For the first time in 16 years, Chile had a democratic government.

THE DEMOCRATIC 90S. The return to democracy has not been a simple or quick process for Chile. In many ways, the peacefulness of the transition has made it even harder. Unlike many other South American countries, such as Argentina, whose military was thrown out of power in bitter disgrace, Chile ended its dictatorial regime during a period of economic growth and recovery when the government still had a significant amount of support. The compromises that were reached in order to guarantee military support of democracy have thus made the task of dealing with the Pinochet legacy complicated.

One of the most significant compromises was that all of the top military officials were granted immunity from prosecution and were given the option to become "bionic" senators, or senators for life. General Pinochet remained the commander of the armed-forces and the civilian government was prohibited from replacing him until he choose to retire. Another major concession was that military officials would be granted a major presence in the new cabinet and play a role in executive decision-making.

1984
11 resurrected political parties sign accord to push for elections

1988
Plebiscite votes on extension of Pinochet's reign... and says "No!"

1989
Patricio Aylwin elected as first democratic president in 16 years

1993
Eduardo Frei isn't elected again, but his son is

1998
Asian financial bug crosses the Pacific and bites Chile

March 1998
Pinochet retires to a life as Senator, and is promptly arrested in London

January 2000
Socialist Ricardo Lagos ekes out a presidential win

March 2000
General Pinochet returns home to more charges and furious controversy

LIFE AND TIMES

LIFE AND TIMES

The effects of these agreements go beyond simply protecting those responsible for the decade and a half of oppression. It has allowed conservative groups to remain a force to be reckoned with. Aylwin's four years in office were fairly uneventful as a result. Without the two-thirds majority needed for constitutional changes, he could not push through major reforms and was forced to continue with most of Pinochet's economic policies. Fortunately for the Concertación, the world economy had stabilized and export prices were on the rise. The resulting economic boom, combined with a few successful social programs, helped Eduardo Frei (son of the Ex-President Eduardo Frei) win the 1993 election.

During his six-year term, Frei was able to make even more progress on many fronts. Economically, many of the liberal reforms were developed, allowing for a diversification in Chile's export profile. This reduction in copper dependence helped bring more stability to the country. Frei was also able to push through several more major social reforms aiming to reduce the extreme levels of poverty and lower the unemployment resulting from the Pinochet regime. On the human rights side, a Chilean judge finally sent General Manuel Contreras to jail for his role in several assassinations. Activists still debate whether this verdict had any significant impact; its symbolic import remains unquestioned, however.

1998 proved to be Chile's most volatile year since the democratic transition. The nation had developed strong ties with its neighbors across the Pacific and the Asian financial crisis hit them hard. After 10 years of sustained growth averaging over 6 percent annually, the Chilean economy slipped into recession. On top of that, General Pinochet finally retired and took up his position as life senator, only to be indicted by a Spanish judge and arrested in London for the torture and murder of Spanish citizens during his rule. The resulting controversy became a major issue in Chile. Still unable to incur the wrath of the military and other conservative groups, the Frei government lodged a formal protest, saying that Pinochet should be tried in Chile if he was to be tried anywhere. With this issue still unresolved and the economy still struggling to recover, the Concertación faced a serious challenge from conservative candidate Joaquín Lavín. Ultimately, however, their candidate Ricardo Lagos managed to sneak by in a run-off election.

TODAY

The last few years for Chile have been years of new challenges and old issues. The presidency of Ricardo Lagos, the first socialist president since Salvador Allende, has marked a serious political shift. Already following a decade of liberal leaders, Lagos has shaken things up by appointing women and liberal activists to important positions, enacting constitutional reforms, and increasing funding for social reforms and protection programs. Nevertheless, divisions in the Concertación have allowed the conservative Right to gain ground. This has been clearly shown through the continued inability of the government to rid the Senate of the nine Pinochet-appointed senators.

Martial-civil relations are somewhat volatile, but have been improving in recent years. The retirement of Pinochet and the appointment of General Izurieta has led to a growing trust in the military's commitment to democracy. The subsequent prosecution of the officers responsible for Pinochet's "Caravan of Death" and the first sentencing of an active-duty officer has gone a long way to eliminate military impunity and reduce social tension over the issue. However, contention over the Pinochet question continues. After being declared unfit to stand trial in Spain, he returned to Chile only to be indicted by a Chilean judge and kept under house arrest. Although he was again declared unfit to stand trial, documents released by the Chilean government and the US CIA have prompted a series of new accusations against Pinochet and his officers in Chile, Argentina, and France.

Economically, the country is still trying to get back on its feet. Although the economy has returned to positive growth, improvement has been slow due to the troubled economies of Argentina and the US. Lagos and his government have worked to counter this by solidifying and diversifying the nation's economic ties. The President was part of the Asian free trade talks and recently signed a free trade agreement with the European Union. Nevertheless, unemployment has continued to remain high and the combination of volatile financial markets and slumping export prices may mean Chile is in for a rough ride.

Throughout all of these controversies and issues, social reform has remained one of most pressing national issues. At the end of Pinochet's regime, over 40 percent of the population was living in poverty, with 13 percent in absolute destitution. Through increased investment in education, health services, and social protection, those numbers have been reduced to 17 and 4 percent respectively, an incredible feat for any country; unfortunately, problems still remain. Unemployment is still high and is especially prevalent among young adults. Inequality levels are also very high. Despite the economic growth of the last decade, the gap between rich and poor has expanded significantly, raising serious concerns about the effectiveness of current social programs.

Chile has come a long way over the last decade, politically, economically, and socially. Nevertheless, some of the country's most difficult issues remain unresolved. Combined with a turbulent international scene, these will make the next couple of years vitally important to the future direction and success of the nation.

PEOPLE

DEMOGRAPHICS

Mestizaje, the blending of races resulting from centuries of migration, explains why over 70% of Chile's 15 million residents are *mestizos*, a racial mixture of Europeans and *indígenas*. Unfortunately, Chileans maintain an ambivalent attitude towards their native heritage—while indigenous culture is celebrated, Chileans tend to consider indigenous people inferior and instances of neglect, disrespect, and mistreatment are not rare. Indigenous communities still constitute about 3% of the population: 40,000 **Aymara** inhabit the northern areas bordering Bolivia; **Araucanians** reside in the south of the country, especially around Temuco; and several thousand **Mapuche** populate the Central Valley. In recent years, the Mapuche have been organizing to preserve their language and traditions—prepare to be engulfed in traditional ceremonial rituals like the *ñgillatun* celebration, the great festival of crops and fertility. If passing through Osorno and Temuco, look out for the most visible members of Chile's society—her cowboys. Intent on maintaining a separate identity from Argentina's mythical *gauchos*, Chilean cowboys, *huasos*, still work on ranches and sport impressive attire.

Descendants of 19th-century European migrants—most notably **German** settlers—continue to make up a significant portion of the residents of the Lakes District. Valdivia, with its own German newspaper, resembles a German city, while Osorno manifests distinct German influences. Other Europeans who factor significantly in Chilean society are arrivals from the former **Yugoslavia**; Chile's **Croatian** population is the fifth largest in the world, consisting of both a native and first-generation population. **Middle Eastern** migrants are now respected members of the Chilean business community, and dominate financial circles and manufacturing operations. Christian communities from Lebanon, Syria, and Palestine escaped to

Chile at the time of the devolution of the Ottoman Empire. Consequently, since their ports of embarkation were under Turkish control, migrants with a Middle Eastern heritage are commonly, although incorrectly, referred to as *turcos* (Turks). Since a tropical plantation economy never developed, there is no significant black culture in Chile.

Despite these multi-faceted demographics, there is a strong sense of a unified Chilean identity, provided by the homogenizing influence of the prevalent Spanish language, the Roman Catholic religion, a pride in the Chilean literary tradition, and Chile's relative isolation from bordering South American countries.

LANGUAGE

Spanish is the official language of Chile. However, peppered with terms from Indian languages, English, German, Italian, and even Serbo-Croatian, Chilean Spanish is a vital cultural expression reflecting the varied ancestry of the people that call Chile home. That Chileans remain implicitly aware of the singularity of their spoken Spanish is evident, as people prefer to say **castellano** rather than *español*. In Chile, the question *"¿Habla español?"* seems to ask "Do you speak Spanish (like a Spaniard)?", so say *"¿Habla castellano?"* and curry Chilean favor. Besides contending with the speed of spoken Chilean Spanish, the uninitiated tourist will not find the language incomprehensible, but stay attuned to quirky regionalisms and peculiar pronunciation, or refer to the Appendix (p. 497) for common words and phrases unique to Chilean Spanish. Other languages you may encounter while in Chile include **Aymara,** spoken in the mountains of the extreme north, around Arica and Iquique; **Huilliche,** spoken by several thousand Chileans between Valdivia and Chiloé; **Rapa Nui,** spoken mainly on Easter Island; and **Mapudungun,** the language of the Mapuche. English speakers don't abound (even among tourist office staff, hostel owners, waiters, and bus and taxi drivers), so brush up on basic Spanish and don't feel self-conscious trying it out on amiable Chileans.

RELIGION

Eighty-five percent of Chileans identify as **Roman Catholic,** and rather than remain allied with conservative elements, the Roman Catholic Church exists as a religious body that is representative of Chilean society as a whole. Chilean Catholics, whether practicing or not, tend to respect the tenets of their Church (although some reject the more rigidly conservative views of the Vatican on several issues including artificial birth control, marriage of the clergy, and abortion). Chileans maintain ties to the Church through sacraments such as baptism, marriage, and last rites, while attendance at Sunday Mass varies across the country. The movement to support social change with religious backing, known as Liberation Theology, remains appealing to Chileans primarily concerned with social issues.

Protestant sects, such as the **Anglican** and **Lutheran** churches, mainly serve members of the small English and German communities that remain in Chile. Chileans dissatisfied with the Roman Catholic Church prefer to embrace Evangelical denominations that were introduced to Chile through missionaries from the United States during the 20th century. Other Christian groups that are now established include **Baptists, Evangelicals, Methodists, Mormons, Presbyterians,** and **Seventh-Day Adventists.**

CULTURE

FOOD AND DRINK

MEALS AND MEALTIMES. The Chileans seem to have figured out the whole 'eat-drink-be-merry' thing, as evidenced by the fact that they usually eat four leisurely meals a day. **Desayuno** (breakfast) has a southern-European flair, and standard breakfast fare usually consists of *café con leche* (strong coffee and hot milk) and toast with butter and jam.

Almuerzo (lunch), the main meal of the day, is taken between 1 and 3 pm. A generation ago, Chilean employees were given up to 2½ hours off to return home, partake of an unhurried *almuerzo*, and even sneak in a quick *siesta* before returning to work. While rampant capitalism and longer commutes have made this traditional midday break implausible, lunch remains an elaborate and comparatively elongated affair, and it is not unusual for offices to close their doors during this time. However, for motivated Chileans and tourists on the go, quick meal options are available at the innumerable food stalls, delis, and convenience stores embedded in nooks and crannies across cities.

Even the most copious lunch will, however, be followed by 'tea time' in the illustrious manner of the British. This light meal referred to as **el té** (tea time) or **las onces** (elevens) is taken at anytime between 4 and 6 p.m. *Café con leche, café helado* (iced coffee), or hot tea (Brit-style with milk) are normally served along with either toast, *marraqueta* (a traditional bread loaf), or fancier cakes and pastries. Restaurants cater to this cultural habit and remain open for tea, while some establishments identify specifically as 'tea rooms'.

La comida (dinner, or literally, the meal) is typically eaten at 9pm, and is served even later at social events. The meal resembles lunch but is generally less opulent. Try not to use the Spanish word *la cena* (supper) to refer to this meal, for although it's universally understood, it immediately identifies you as a non-Chilean.

CHILEAN CUISINE. Chilean cuisine is a wonderful melange of fare from native Indian, Spanish, French, German, English, Italian, Mexican, and Asian origins. Chileans also fully relish their natural resources through the generous use of fruits and vegetables in their recipes and innovative preparation of the varied supply of fresh seafood. As in the rest of the region, **corn** (*maíz* in Spanish, but *choclo* in Chile) is the basic ingredient of most Chilean foods.

Traditional national foods commonly enjoyed for *almuerzo* include **humitas** (akin to Mexican *tamales*), **pastel de choclo** (a corn casserole containing beef, chicken, raisins, onions, olives, and spices, and reflecting both Indian and European origins), and **cazuela** (a clear broth with rice, potato, corn, and chicken or beef). Particularly voracious eaters have *cazuela* as an appetizer and continue with **empanadas** (fried flour tortillas filled with cheese, meat, or seafood).

Other well-known Chilean dishes include **porotos granados** (cranberry beans with squash and corn), **pan amasado** (a common heavy bread), and **pernil de chanco a la chilena** (braised fresh ham with chili sauce). Although dishes with less meat and more vegetables are typical of rural Chilean cuisine, **parrillas** (a popular type of restaurant that serves a variety of meat cuts and sausages) abound. **Lomo a la pobre** (poor man's steak) is filling and widespread.

With its 4300km coastline, an abundance of **seafood** is available in Chile, and is commonly incorporated into local cuisine. Popular dishes to look out for are: **budín de centolla** (a pudding of crab, butter, onions, flour, cream, egg yolks, and cheese); **chupe de marisco** or **chupe de locos** (sea scallops or abalone with white wine, butter, cream, cheese, and spices); **paila marina** (a soup made from various shellfish); **caldillo de congrio** (an eel and vegetable soup); and the ever popular **curanto** (a hearty stew of fish, shellfish, chicken, pork, lamb, beef, and potato). Unusual seafood dishes to try are **picoroco** (a dish using a barnacle with white crab-like meat) and the overwhelmingly flavorful **piure.** Many recommend that fish should be had **al vapor** (steamed) or **a la plancha** (grilled), rather than **frito** (fried). While enjoying marine munchables, keep in mind that *marea roja* (red tide), a deadly seaborne toxin, has been detected off the southern coast of Chile. Since the Chilean government is carefully supervising the sale of shellfish so as to screen for the toxin, the threat of infection remains minimal; however, be cautious and only consume seafood purchased from reliable sources.

One can circumvent these plentiful offerings by opting to have increasingly popular **lunchtime snacks** instead. Prevalent sandwiches are the **churrasco** (steak) and **jamón y queso** (ham and cheese). Sandwich combos to try are the **Barros Luco** (beef and cheese), named for the Chilean president Ramón Barros Luco (1910-1915), and the **Barros Jarpa** (containing ham, and consequently named after the 19th-century Chilean writer-lawyer-diplomat-politician, Ernesto Barros Jarpa). The **chacarero,** named after Chilean farm workers, contains beef, tomato, chili, and green beans, and comes highly recommended. An **ave-palta** (chicken and avocado) sandwich is largely considered a staple of the corporate luncheon crowd.

You'll definitely come across **pebre,** a varyingly mild or spicy sauce, that can accompany any or all of the listed victuals. Traditionally an accompaniment to red meat and rice, Chileans generally like their *pebre* with most of their food.

If you have any room left, partake of the notorious **Chilean sweets.** Diverse fresh fruit options from the Central Valley aside, try out Chile's most distinctive desserts that originated with German immigrants. **Kuchen** is a delicious pastry loaded with fruits like raspberries and apricots. **Macedonia** is another offering dripping fruit syrup. **Alfajor,** a common Chilean pastry, consists of an excess of *dulce de leche* (caramelized milk, also known as *manjar*) sandwiched between thin pastries and powdered sugar. Or try **arroz con leche** (chilled rice with milk, sugar, and cinnamon), and *semola con leche* (a *flan* with sweet corn flour and caramel). Simpler *tortas* and *queques* (cakes) abound in pastry shops across the country.

While the cosmopolitan Santiago offers food to suit even the most finicky palate (the German culinary influence is evident, vegetarian options are not lacking, and Chinese restaurants abound), other regions are not as well endowed, culinarily speaking. The best restaurants are restricted to resort towns such as Viña del Mar, La Serena, and Puerto Varas, while Arica and Iquique boast good **chifas** (Chinese restaurants). Nevertheless, good Chilean food is available throughout the country, and most establishments oblige **vegetarians** on request. Make sure that you articulate your desire for vegetarian entrees, many so-called vegetarian dishes in rural Chile include ham.

DRINKY-DRINKS. Neither occupation, nor age, economic background, nor locality, can prevent Chileans from having **vino** (wine) with their meals. It is not surprising that this essential element of the Eucharist is universally enjoyed throughout Chilean society. The abundance of **vineyards** (Chile's wine country stretches for 875km from just north of Santiago to Concepción) producing excellent **reds** and **whites** for both domestic and foreign markets ensures that fine, inexpensive varieties remain readily available. Notable vineyards include Undurraga, Santa Carolina, Cousiño Macul, and particularly, Concha y Toro, Chile's largest wine maker with 1845 hectares of land just south of Santiago. Concha y Toro's reds, especially the **Cabarnet Sauvignon** and **Merlot,** have won international critical acclaim, while their **'Cassillero del Diablo'** (the devil's workshop) is considered among Chile's finest wines. Consider daytrips to vineyards around Santiago (see **Concha y Toro,** p. 119) for tours and tastings.

When in the mood for something that packs more of a punch, Chileans drink **pisco,** a powerful grape-based distilled spirit produced in northern vineyards in the Limari and Elqui valleys. **Pisco sour,** Chile's answer to the Mexican margarita, is notorious for its ability to intoxicate and inflict severe hangovers on uninitiated tourists. *Pisco* can also be added to Coca-Cola to produce the popular *piscola.* If your tolerance level is flailing, try **chicha** instead. A punch made from grapes beginning to ferment, this beverage is common during Independence Day celebrations on September 18.

If passing through Chile around Christmastime, check out the Chilean equivalent of eggnog. **Cola de mono** is an enjoyable mixture of milk, coffee, sugar, and *aguardiente*, a clear Chilean brandy. While **beers** are commonly available on tap, Chile is not exactly known for its ales or lagers. A full bodied beer to try is Escudo; otherwise, stick to popular draft beers (know in Chile as *schop*) such as Cristal.

If you're hoping to stay hydrated, **non-alcoholic** options abound as well. Delectable juices of in-season fruits are available at most restaurants year-round, but remember that Chileans have a penchant for added sugar, and specify that you'd prefer *"puro jugo sin azucar"* (pure juice without sugar) if that is indeed the case. American soft-drinks, both of the regular and diet variety, are readily available, as is water. Tap water in Chile is usually potable, but err on the side of caution, and drink bottled water whenever possible. Chileans enjoy both still (*sin gas*) and carbonated (*con gas*) water, both of which are available throughout the country.

CUSTOMS AND ETIQUETTE

GREETINGS AND PUBLIC BEHAVIOR. South Americans are generally warm, tactile people who converse in close proximity—get used to being cozy with your Chilean companions, because backing away is considered offensive. When greeting a group of Chileans, it is important to smile, make eye contact, and shake hands firmly with everyone present, as a group greeting can seem standoffish. Closer male friends may hug and pat each other's backs affectionately; women often greet each other by touching check to cheek and quickly kissing in the air.

Smoking at social functions is pretty standard, but if you are going to light up, offer a cigarette to your companions first. Always arrive fashionably late for social functions—15 to 30 minutes after the invitation time is customary. If you get there on time or early, you may catch your host or hostess off-guard. (Promptness is essential, however, for business functions—see **Business Etiquette,** below.)

HOUSEGUEST CUSTOMS. Bringing a **gift** to a home you are visiting is an appropriate gesture, as long as you don't choose anything too expensive that might seem flashy. Gifts from your home country that aren't available in Chile, such as your country's native handicrafts, candy, or liquor, are a good bet. You'll also score points if you bring small tokens, such as candy or games, to any children in the household that you are visiting.

Flowers are acceptable gifts, but you should send them before your arrival or bring them with you so that they don't seem an afterthought. Avoid yellow roses, a sign of contempt, and black or purple flowers, which symbolize death. If you receive a gift, open it immediately in front of your host and express enthusiastic thanks.

TABLE MANNERS. Chilean manners can be a bit more formal than those of other South American countries, but keeping a few things in mind will help you make a good impression on your Chilean acquaintances. Be sure that you know the correct utensils to use for each course—eating anything with your hands is a definite faux pas. Placing your hands in you lap while at the table is a sign of deception, so take care to keep both hands above the table at all times. It is polite to sample everything that is served and to compliment the host or hostess on all of the eats.

Meals in Chile are often more about conversation and visiting than the food itself. Enjoy leisurely meals with your Chilean friends—stay for conversation rather than taking off when your plate is clean.

If you go out to eat, the person who makes the invitation often pays. Don't expect to share in the bill, but plan to reciprocate with a similar invitation at a later date. Arrange ahead of time to pay the bill in a restaurant if you made the invitation. You will have to ask for the bill at the end of the meal—the waiter won't rush you out by bringing it automatically.

BUSINESS ETIQUETTE. Chilean businesspeople are big on exchanging business cards, so it's a good idea to have yours translated into Spanish on the back of your standard card; the swap of cards usually occurs after the ritual handshake.

Meetings and business gatherings begin with chit-chat. Arrive on time, but don't be surprised if others, especially the seniors of the meeting, arrive half-an-hour late. Status at meetings is important, and an age hierarchy is assumed. You should expect to defer to the eldest person present—if you are unsure who is the eldest, keep an eye on the behavior of others at the meeting.

Be aware that feelings are often the driving force in business interactions. A respectful and humble approach to discussion is your best bet—attempting forceful negotiations, cracking excessive jokes, or putting people down will lead only to embarrassment among your Chilean colleagues.

TABOOS. If you make some gestures common in other areas of the world, you may unintentionally offend your new Chilean friends. Be careful not to slap your right fist into a left open palm—this is a strong insult in Chile. Displaying an open palm with fingers splayed is taken to mean "stupid." Make sure to point and beckon with your entire hand instead of your index finger. Also, do not raise your right fist near your head—this is a communist taboo in Chile.

THE ARTS

HISTORY AND THE CURRENT SCENE

ARCHITECTURE. Due to the frequent earthquakes in Chile, many **architectural monuments** from the colonial period are no longer standing. Founded in 1536, **Valparaíso** is the oldest Chilean city, but none of its colonial buildings remain because of a massive earthquake that leveled all of its structures in 1730. The city, however, was rebuilt immediately and has continued to develop architecturally since, with a mix of imposing professional buildings and older residential structures in the north of the city. Southern cities, including Valdivia and Osorno, reflect the impact of their German heritage in the few buildings that have survived earthquakes.

In **Santiago**, the architecture is a merging of remains from ancient monuments, some colonial buildings, and modern skyscrapers of 30 or more stories. The perfectly calibrated city blocks of old Santiago are centered around the **Plaza de**

Armas, which is flanked with several significant historical buildings in the **colonial** style. In the early 20th century, the plaza was embellished with several new buildings in the **Art Nouveau** style, including the **Cousiño Palace,** the **Church of the Sacramentinos,** the **Palace of Fine Arts,** and the **Tribunal.** The city expands out from the original center to include additional buildings and homes in the **Neo-Gothic, modern,** and **"California"** styles.

FINE ARTS. Colonial art from the 17th and 18th centuries in Chile is composed almost entirely of religious images. Early colonial sculptures, paintings, and murals depict dramatic images of Christ, the Virgin Mary, and the Catholic saints. Toward the end of Spanish domination in Chile, colonial artists became increasingly interested in depicting the most wealthy and influential citizens, especially those of Santiago, in their work.

Romanticism, which ruled the Chilean art scene at the beginning of the 19th century, was created primarily by European artists who came to Chile after it gained its independence. The classic landscapes and portraits of Romanticism replaced the predominantly sacred images of the previous colonial period.

Chile's premier 20th-century painter, **Roberto Matta,** is a pioneer in the style of **abstract realism.** Matta is noted for his abstract style that "has one foot in architecture and the other in dreams."

LITERATURE. Latin America's first **epic poem,** *La Araucana,* was penned by the Chilean soldier-poet **Don Alonso de Ercilla** in the late 16th century. *La Araucana,* which captures the beauty of the Chilean countryside, paved the way for all Latin American poets to come, and is ranked among the epics of Homer, Virgil and Lucano.

Alonso de Ovalle is considered the finest poet of 17th-century Chile. The friar composed his best-known work, *Histórica relación del reino de Chile,* while he was abroad in Rome—distance allowed him to capture the country with nostalgia and insight. His poems map the cities, valleys, rivers, lakes and mountains of Chile to perfection. Much of 18th-century Chilean poetry is narrow in focus because it was composed mainly by men in the Catholic Church. In the later 18th and 19th centuries, Chilean **romanticism** flourished in the wake of the Spanish romantics.

Chile's greatest literary pride lies in the two 20th-century **Nobel Laureates** who secured the country's reputation as "the land of poets". **Gabriela Mistral,** a Vicuña native, worked as a schoolteacher until her early poems of mourning, *Sonetos de la muerte (Death Sonnets),* made her famous throughout Latin America. Mistral won the Nobel Prize for Literature in 1945 and continued to publish poetry while serving in the League of Nations, helping to reform the Chilean and Mexican school systems, and teaching Spanish Literature at several reputed North American Universities. **Pablo Neruda,** who was influenced by Mistral during his youth in Temuco, published poetry on a wide range of political, social and sentimental subjects and experimented with many literary styles, including the "esoteric surrealism" of his 1933 breakthrough *Residencia en la tierra (Residence on Earth).* After returning to Chile from political exile due to his alliance with the communist party, Neruda was awarded the Nobel Prize for literature in 1971.

Perhaps Chile's best-known 20th-century novelist is **Isabel Allende,** whose works of **magical realism** are best-sellers in both Latin America and in translation in the United States. Her classic novel, *La casa de los espíritus (The House of the Spirits),* follows in the path of the Colombian Nobel Laureate, Gabriel García Márquez's novel *Cien años de soledad (One Hundred Years of Solitude),* adopting its cyclic storytelling and magical possibilities while introducing new ideas about gender and social movements. Allende's work is also said to be influenced by 20th-century novelist **José Donoso,** known for his epic novel of family, *Casa del campo*. Allende continues to pen novels today; her latest work, published in 2000, is entitled *Retrato en sepia (Portrait in Sepia)*.

MUSIC. Chile's **folkloric music** is rich and diverse, influenced by Spanish, Argentine, Peruvian, and Mexican traditions. Music for the **cueca,** the national dance of Chile, is one of the country's classic styles, featuring exact, quick rhythms sung with accompaniment from guitar, piano, and accordion. Other styles such as the **Tonada,** a more improvisational folkloric style, and the **Chilean Waltz**, a melding of Peruvian and Argentine waltzes, are traditional throughout the country.

Popular music tends to be more prevalent on the radio and in *discotecas*. Prepare to be regaled with Latin pop from celebrities such as Ricky Martin and Shakira. Successful Chilean acts to look out for include rapper DJ Mendez, Los Javias, Los Prisioneros (a pop group), La Ley (a Latin-rock group), and Miriam Hernandez (a popular singer of moving ballads).

DANCE. The national dance of Chile, **la cueca,** is widely considered the best expression of the Chilean spirit, despite the fact that there is some controversy as to whether the dance originated in Chile or in Lima, Peru. Regardless, the dance has been appropriated by Chileans since colonial times and is a time-honored component of Chilean culture. The tranquil and hesitant movements that define *la cueca* are meant to evoke the behavior of the rooster and chicken during an amorous conquest. Partners brandishing handkerchiefs and accompanied by musicians on guitar, piano, accordion, or harp, dance separately, never touching, yet remaining connected through fluid movements, eye contact, and facial expressions. The flirtatiousness of the dance is gradually intensified through complex footwork that steadily brings the male dancer closer to his female partner. *La cueca* is still an integral part of any celebration or festival in the Chilean countryside and is performed year-round by *huasos* around Temuco and Osorno. But don't expect to practice your rooster imitation in a hip urban nightclub. Known as *discotecas* in Chile (the term "nightclub" refers to strip clubs or other shadier operations), dance clubs blast popular Top 40 American hits and Latin-pop numbers while youngsters groove and gyrate on crowded dance floors.

FILM AND TELEVISION. Pinochet's military regime was not kind to the **Chilean film industry,** but the current dearth of a national cinema has not always been the case in Chile. Cinema originated in Chile before World War I, and although film production was initially spasmodic, and the introduction of talkies dealt an early blow to the industry, in 1958 a new Chilean cinema emerged.

Developed by the *cineclub* at the University of Chile and the Film Institute at the Catholic University in Santiago, cinema became an integral mode of popular cultural expression that vigorously supported the socialist cause. Rather than be harmed by the introduction of television to Chile in 1962, the film industry benefited from increased distribution through made-for-TV films. Thematically, Chilean cinema of the 1960s echoes the history of the Popular Unity government, and becomes particularly influenced by politics during the cultural upheaval of the Allende years. Director Miguel Littin's famous film *El chacal de Nahueltoro (The Jackal of Nahueltoro)* is regarded as a prophetic, national allegory, while his 1972 film *La tierra prometida (The Promised Land)* eerily anticipates the *coup d'état* of September 11, 1973.

Although Chilean films developed specifically as aesthetic as well as ideological products, they were not embraced by the public until positively reviewed in European journals such as *Cahiers du Cinéma*. However, the popular socialist bent of the new Chilean cinema made it one of the main targets for the military's repression, and strict film censorship policies were implemented after Pinochet established military rule.

After the destruction of the national film institute of the Popular Unity government, the Chilean film industry basically disappeared. The distribution of films in Chile came under the control of the monopoly formed by companies such as Warner Brothers, Paramount, Columbia Pictures, and 20th Century Fox. Similarly, if you turn on the TV for an authentic Chilean visual experience, you're in for a disappointment. Today, Chile's 350 theaters exhibit European and especially American Hollywood films with Spanish subtitles. Even the lift of film censorship in 1997 did not reinvigorate the Chilean film industry. Meanwhile, increasingly popular cable TV packages bring CNN, MTV, Discovery Channel, and American shows such as *Friends* and *Seinfeld* into millions of homes. Chilean soap operas, however, are the one exception—*telenovelas* (several-month-long soap operas) consistently get good ratings and are watched by men and women alike.

SPORTS AND RECREATION

SOCCER. Soccer, known in South America as **fútbol,** is undoubtedly the most important sport in Chile—almost all Chilean men and many women take pride in their *fútbol* skills. Don't be surprised to see young children playing in blocked off parking lots and entire families playing in their yards during their free time.

Although the national team tends to fall in the shadows of star South American teams such as Argentina, Brazil, and Uruguay, Chile is proud of having hosted the World Cup in 1962, when its national team made it to the semi-finals for the first (and only) time. Many Chileans enthusiastically follow the ongoing competition between the rival professional teams from the **Universidad de Chile** (University of Chile), **Colo Colo,** and the **Universidad Católica** (Catholic University). It is definitely worthwhile to see a professional game at the **Estadio Nacional** if you are visiting Santiago.

TENNIS. Although Chile's enthusiasm for **tenis** (tennis) never quite matches its love of soccer, the country is proud of its world-renowned tennis players. The current Chilean tennis stars are **Marcelo Ríos,** who has won numerous championships and was ranked #1 in the world in 1999, and **Nicolás Massú,** considered Chile's second-strongest player.

SKIING. Chile's **ski season** lasts from June to October, so skiing and snowboarding fanatics from the Northern Hemisphere flock to the country each winter to join the many South Americans who hit Chile's famous slopes. **Portillo Ski Resort** is the oldest and perhaps most widely known ski establishment in South America, but its steep prices and exclusivity make it inaccessible for many budget travelers. **Valle Nevado, La Parva,** and **Farellones-El Colorado,** all within 60km of Santiago, are perhaps the best choices for extended stays or daytrips from the capital.

SURFING. During the summer months, Chileans trade their skis for surfboards, hitting the numerous **surf spots** along the coast in northern and central Chile. The type of surfing available varies by location—in the **northern region,** between Arica and Iquique, the waves are small, but the water is warm and there are many unexplored beaches for the adventurous surfer to navigate. The **central region** of the country boasts larger waves, but the waters are colder and the surf season is consequentially slightly more limited.

HOLIDAYS AND FESTIVALS

Most of Chile's **nationally observed holidays** are religious, despite the official separation of Church and State that occurred in 1925. Traditional Catholic holidays are generally solemn, including a celebration of Mass, processions in the street, elaborate costuming, and reenactments of Bible stories. Secular holidays, such as Independence Day, often involve dancing and preparation of traditional foods.

CHILEAN FESTIVALS

DATE	NAME & LOCATION	DESCRIPTION
January 1	Año Nuevo (New Years Day)	Family and social celebrations, often held outdoors.
March 1	Día del Trabajo (Labor Day)	Schools and businesses closed; parades and worker demonstrations throughout the country.
April 13-20 (varies)	Semana Santa (Holy Week)	Week leading up to Easter; schools and businesses closed in many places. Precessions and masses.
April 20 (varies)	Día de Pascua (Easter Sunday)	Masses held and time spent with family.
April 27 (varies)	Domingo de Cuasimodo (Middle Chile only)	Sunday after Easter; houses are decorated and costumes worn; parade in the streets—priests, accompanied by huasos, or cowboys, give communion to the poor and elderly.
May 21	Glorias Navales	Commemoration of the naval battle at Iquique, in 1879; celebrations, military parades, and speeches.
June 23	Corpus Christi	Streets are lined with decoration; costumed performances in or near churches.
June 29	Día de San Pedro y San Pablo (St. Peter and St. Paul)	Masses held; schools and businesses closed—homage paid to St. Peter and St. Paul.
August 15	Asunción de la Vírgen (Assumption of the Virgin Mary)	National Holiday; masses held.
September 3	National day of Reconciliation/ National Unity Day	Celebration of national unity after Pinochet's regime.
September 18	Día de Independencia (Independence Day)	Eating, drinking, and dancing the national dance "cueca" are customary; unofficial beginning of summer.
September 19	Army Day	Military celebration of independence, parade in Santiago draws crowds and is watched on TV throughout Chile.
October 12	Día de la Raza (or Día de la Hispanidad)	Originally established by Franco's regime in Spain to celebrate Spain's former colonies, now commemorated with school and office closings.
November 1	Todos los Santos (All Saints Day)	Religious holiday observed by churches; the following day flowers are placed on loved ones' graves.
December 8	Inmaculada Concepción (Immaculate Conception)	People attend church and gather to honor the Virgin Mary.
December 24	Christmas Eve	Many attend Miso de Gallo—midnight mass—and await Viejo Pascueo (old man Christmas).
December 25	Navidad (Christmas Day)	Time spent with family, preparation of traditional foods.

ADDITIONAL RESOURCES

GENERAL HISTORY

Culture and Customs of Chile, by Guillermo I. Castillo-Feliú.

The Breakdown of Democratic Regimes, ed. Juan Linz, et.al. A great compilation of Latin American political thinkers on the fall of Chilean democracy in the 1970s.

Chilean Democracy, by Arturo Vanezuela. Written by one of Chile's foremost political theorists, it looks at the country's political history.

Chile Since Independence, Leslie Bethell. General history of Chile.

FICTION AND NON-FICTION

A Gabriela Mistral Reader, by Gabriela Mistral. A good compilation of Mistral's works, translated into English.

The House of the Spirits, by Isabel Allende. Allende's best-known magical realism novel.

La Araucana, by Alonso de Ercilla y Zâuäniga. The classic epic poem of the Chilean literary canon.

Portrait in Sepia, by Isabel Allende. The author's latest novel, in its English translation.

Residence on Earth, by Pablo Neruda. The poet's breakthrough work of surrealism.

Twenty Love Poems and a Song of Despair, by Pablo Neruda. One of Neruda's most famous collections.

ESSENTIALS

FACTS FOR THE TRAVELER

ENTRANCE REQUIREMENTS
Passport (p. 37). Required for all visitors.
Visa (p. 37). Required for stays of over 90 days; required anytime for citizens of New Zealand, Poland, Russia, and most Asian, Middle Eastern, and African countries, with the exception of South Africa.
Inoculations: (p. 44). No inoculations are required by the Chilean government.
Work Permit (p. 37). Required for all foreigners planning to work in Chile.

EMBASSIES AND CONSULATES

CHILE CONSULAR SERVICES ABROAD

Australia: Consulate: Melbourne, level 43, 80 Collins Street, Melbourne, 3000 (☎03 9654 4479; fax 03 9650 8290; cqmelbourne@chile.com.au; www.chile.com.au).

Canada: Consulate: Toronto, 2 Bloor Street West, Oficina 1801, Toronto, Ontario M4W-3E2 (☎416-924-0106; fax 416-924-2627; consulate@conquechiletoronto.com; www.congechiletoronto.com).

UK: Embassy: 12 Devonshire Street, London W1G 7DS (☎00 44 020 7580 6392; fax 00 44 020 7436 5204; embachile@embachile.co.uk; www.echileuk.demon.co.uk).

US: Embassy: Washington, D.C., 1734 Massachusetts Avenue, N.W., Washington D.C. 20036 (☎202-530-4104; fax 202-530-4145; www.embassyofchile.org); Consulate General of Chile in New York, 866 United Nations Plaza, Suite 601, 1st Ave. and 48th St., NYC 10017 (☎212-980-3366; fax 212-888-5288; recepcion@chileny.com; www.chileny.com). Consular services also available in Chicago, Houston, Los Angeles, Miami, Philadelphia, San Francisco, and San Juan, Puerto Rico.

CONSULAR SERVICES IN CHILE

Australia: Embassy: Isidora Goyenechea 3621, 12th and 13th fl., Las Condes Santiago de Chile (☎56 2 550 3500; fax 56 2 331 5960; consular.santiago@dfat.gov.au; www.chile.embassy.gov.au).

Canada: Embassy: Nueva Tajamar 481, 12th fl., Edificio World Trade Center, Torre Norte, Santiago (☎56 2 362 9660; fax 56 2 362 9663; www.dfait-maeci.gc.ca/santiago).

UK: Embajada Británica, Santiago de Chile, El Bosque Norte 0125, Santiago (☎56 2 370 4100; fax 56 2 335 5988; www.britemb.cl).

US: Embassy: Andrés Bello 2800, Las Condes, Santiago (☎56 2 232 2600; fax 56 2 330 3710; www.usembassy.cl).

TOURIST OFFICES

With representative offices in almost all cities and smaller towns across Chile, the National Tourism Board, **Sernatur,** is a particularly helpful resource for travelers. The head office of Sernatur located in Santiago offers an additional facility specializing in adventure tourism and ecotourism.

Sernatur (National Tourism Board): Providencia 1550, Santiago (☎56 2 731 8300; fax 56 2 251 8469; www.sernatur.cl).

DOCUMENTS AND FORMALITIES

PASSPORTS

REQUIREMENTS. Citizens of Australia, Canada, Ireland, New Zealand, South Africa, the UK, and the US need valid passports to enter Chile and to re-enter their home countries. Chile does not allow entrance if the holder's passport expires in under six months; returning home with an expired passport is illegal, and may result in a fine.

NEW PASSPORTS. Citizens of Australia, Canada, Ireland, New Zealand, the UK, and the US can apply for a passport at any post office, passport office, or court of law. Citizens of South Africa can apply for a passport at any office of Foreign Affairs. Any new passport or renewal applications must be filed well in advance of the departure date, although most passport offices offer rush services for a very steep fee.

PASSPORT MAINTENANCE. Be sure to photocopy the page of your passport with your photo, as well as your visas, traveler's check serial numbers and any other important documents. Carry one set of copies in a safe place, apart from the originals, and leave another set at home. Consulates also recommend that you carry an expired passport or an official copy of your birth certificate in a part of your baggage separate from other documents.

If you lose your passport, immediately notify the local police and the nearest embassy or consulate of your home government. To expedite its replacement, you will need to know all information previously recorded and show ID and proof of citizenship. In some cases, a replacement may take weeks to process, and it may be valid only for a limited time. Any visas stamped in your old passport will be irretrievably lost. In an emergency, ask for immediate temporary traveling papers that will permit you to re-enter your home country.

VISAS AND WORK PERMITS

VISAS. As of August 2002, citizens of Poland, New Zealand, Russia, and most Asian, Middle Eastern, and African countries, with the exception of South Africa, need a visa in addition to a valid passport for entrance to Chile; citizens of Australia, Canada, Ireland, South Africa, the UK, the US, and most Western European countries do not need visas. Foreigners traveling without a visa for pleasure or on business trips are allowed to enter Chile for a period of 90 days. A fee must be paid in cash by such travelers at the immigration booth upon entrance to Chile, at which point a tourist card will be issued. The fee is US$30 for Australian citizens, US$55 for Canadian citizens, US$15 for Mexican citizens, and US$61 for citizens of the United States. This administrative fee is paid only once and is valid until the expiration of the passport.

Double-check on entrance requirements at the nearest embassy or consulate of Chile (listed under **Embassies and Consulates Abroad,** on p. 36) for up-to-date info before departure. US citizens can also consult the website at www.pueblo.gsa.gov/cic_text/travel/foreign/foreignentryreqs.html.

WORK PERMITS. Admission as a visitor does not include the right to work, which is authorized only by a work permit. Entering Chile to study requires a special visa. For more information, see **Alternatives to Tourism** chapter (see p. 78).

IDENTIFICATION

When you travel, always carry two or more forms of identification on your person, including at least one photo ID; a passport combined with a driver's license or birth certificate is usually adequate. Never carry all your forms of ID together, split them up in case of theft or loss, and keep photocopies of them in your luggage and at home.

TEACHER, STUDENT, AND YOUTH IDENTIFICATION. The **International Student Identity Card (ISIC),** the most widely accepted form of student ID, provides discounts on sights, accommodations, food, and transport; access to 24hr. emergency helpline (in North America call ☎877-370-ISIC; elsewhere call US collect ☎+1 715-345-0505); and insurance benefits for US cardholders (see **Insurance, p.** 48). The ISIC is preferable to an institution-specific card (such as a university ID) because it is more likely to be recognized and honored abroad. Applicants must be degree-seeking students of a secondary or post-secondary school and must be of at least 12 years of age. Because of the proliferation of fake ISICs, some services (particularly airlines) require additional proof of student identity, such as a school ID or a letter attesting to your student status, signed by your registrar and stamped with your school seal. Sample discounts in Chile include 10-20% off at most car rental agencies, 15% off all bus tickets from Tas Choapa, free admission to the Museo de Arte Precolumbino, Santiago (☎56 2 638 3502), and 10% off meals at the Café Las Urbinas, Santiago (☎56 2 232 8303).

The **International Teacher Identity Card (ITIC)** offers teachers the same insurance coverage as well as similar but limited discounts. For travelers who are 25 years old or under but are not students, the **International Youth Travel Card (IYTC;** formerly the **GO 25** Card) also offers many of the same benefits as the ISIC.

Each of these identity cards costs US$22 or equivalent in other currencies. ISIC and ITIC cards are valid for roughly one and a half academic years; IYTC cards are valid for one year from the date of issue. Many student travel agencies (see p. 61) issue the cards, including STA Travel in Australia and New Zealand; Travel CUTS in Canada; **usit** in the Republic of Ireland and Northern Ireland; SASTS in South Africa; Campus Travel and STA Travel in the UK; and Council Travel and STA Travel in the US. For a listing of issuing agencies, or for more information, contact the **International Student Travel Confederation (ISTC),** Herengracht 479, 1017 BS Amsterdam, Netherlands (☎+31 20 421 28 00; fax 421 28 10; istcinfo@istc.org; www.istc.org).

CUSTOMS

Upon entering Chile, you must declare certain items from abroad and pay a duty on the value of those articles if they exceed the US$1500 allowance established by Chile's customs service. The import of firearms, seeds, plants, and most foodstuffs is prohibited, although up to two liters of alcohol and 400 cigarettes may be brought in. Note that goods and gifts purchased at **duty-free** shops abroad are not exempt from duty or sales tax; "duty-free" merely means that you need not pay a tax in the country of purchase. Upon returning home, you must similarly declare all articles acquired abroad and pay a duty on the value of articles in excess of your home country's allowance. In order to expedite your return, make a list of any valuables brought from home and register them with customs before traveling abroad, and be sure to keep receipts for all goods acquired abroad.

An **International Airport Tax** of US$18, payable in dollars or Chilean pesos, is required upon departure from Chile. For internal flights, there is a tax of US$5.

In addition, Chile has an 18% **Value Added Tax (VAT or IVA),** resembling the sales tax paid in the United States, on merchandise.

MONEY

CURRENCY AND EXCHANGE

The currency chart below is based on August 2002 exchange rates between local currency and Australian dollars (AUS$), Canadian dollars (CDN$), New Zealand dollars (NZ$), South African Rand (SAR), British pounds (UK£), US dollars (US$), and European Union euros (EUR€). For the latest exchange rates, check the currency converter on financial websites such as www.bloomburg.com and www.xe.com, or a large newspaper.

CHILEAN PESOS (CH$)		
AUS$1 = CH$379.49		CH$1 = AUS$0.003
CDN$1 = CH$444.54		CH$1 = CDN$0.002
NZ$1 = CH$326.10		CH$1 = NZ$0.003
SAR1 = CH$65.91		CH$1 = SAR0.015
US$1 = CH$698.60		CH$1 = US$0.001
UK£1 = CH$1067.27		CH$1 = UK£0.001
EUR€1 = CH$682.17		CH$1 = EUR€0.001

As a general rule, it's cheaper to convert money in Chile than at home. While currency exchange will probably be available in your arrival airport, it's wise to bring enough foreign currency to last for the first 24 to 72 hours of a trip. The most popular place for exchange agencies in downtown Santiago is on Agustinas, between Ahumada and Bandera. In addition, several hotels offer competitive exchange rates.

When changing money abroad, try to go only to banks or *casas de cambio* that have at most a 5% margin between their buy and sell prices. In Chile, *casas de cambio* have longer hours and generally offer better exchange rates than banks. Since you lose money with every transaction, **convert large sums** (unless the currency is depreciating rapidly), **but no more than you'll need.** US dollars are widely accepted as well.

If you use traveler's checks or bills, carry some in small denominations (the equivalent of US$50 or less) for times when you are forced to exchange money at disadvantageous rates, but bring a range of denominations since charges may be levied per check cashed. Store your money in a variety of forms; ideally, at any given time you will be carrying some cash, some traveler's checks, and an ATM and/or credit card. All travelers should also consider carrying some US dollars (about US$50 worth).

TRAVELER'S CHECKS

Traveler's checks are one of the safest and least troublesome means of carrying funds. **American Express** and **Visa** are the most widely recognized brands. Many banks and agencies sell them for a small commission. Check issuers provide refunds if the checks are lost or stolen, and many provide additional services, such as toll-free refund hotlines abroad, emergency message services, and stolen credit card assistance. Traveler's checks are widely accepted across Chile. Ask about toll-free refund hotlines and the location of refund centers when purchasing checks, and always carry emergency cash.

American Express: Checks available with commission at select banks and all AmEx offices. US residents can also purchase checks by phone (☎888-887-8986) or online (www.aexp.com). AAA (see p. 71) offers commission-free checks to its members. Checks available in US, Australian, British, Canadian, Japanese, and Euro currencies.

Cheques for Two can be signed by either of 2 people traveling together. For purchase locations or more information contact AmEx's service centers: in the US and Canada ☎800-221-7282; in the UK ☎0800 521 313; in Australia ☎800 25 19 02; in New Zealand ☎0800 441 068; in Chile ☎56 26 369 100; elsewhere US collect ☎+1 801-964-6665.

Visa: Checks available (generally with commission) at banks worldwide. For the location of the nearest office, call Visa's service centers: in the US ☎800-227-6811; in the UK ☎0800 89 50 78; elsewhere UK collect ☎+44 020 7937 8091. Checks available in US, British, Canadian, Japanese, and Euro currencies.

CREDIT, DEBIT, AND ATM CARDS

Where they are accepted, credit cards often offer superior exchange rates—up to 5% better than the retail rate used by banks and other currency exchange establishments. Credit cards may also offer services such as insurance or emergency help, and are sometimes required to reserve hotel rooms or rental cars. **MasterCard** and **Visa** are the most welcomed; **American Express** cards work at some ATMs and at AmEx offices and major airports. In case you lose a credit card in Chile, call: Visa International (☎56 2 631 7003); Mastercard International (☎56 2 631 7003); Diner's International (☎56 2 232 0000); or American Express (☎800 201 022).

ATMs are widespread in Chile. Depending on the system that your home bank uses, you can most likely access your personal bank account from abroad. ATMs get the same wholesale exchange rate as credit cards, but there is often a limit on the amount of money you can withdraw per day (around US$500), and unfortunately computer networks sometimes fail. There is typically also a surcharge of US$1-5 per withdrawal.

Debit cards are a relatively new form of purchasing power that are as convenient as credit cards but have a more immediate impact on your funds. A debit card can be used wherever its associated credit card company (usually Mastercard or Visa) is accepted, yet the money is withdrawn directly from the holder's checking account. Debit cards often also function as ATM cards and can be used to withdraw cash from associated banks and ATMs throughout Chile. Ask your local bank about obtaining one.

The two major international money networks are **Cirrus** (to locate ATMs US ☎800-424-7787 or www.mastercard.com) and **Visa/PLUS** (to locate ATMs US ☎800-843-7587 or www.visa.com). Most ATMs charge a transaction fee that is paid to the bank that owns the ATM.

GETTING MONEY FROM HOME

If you run out of money while traveling, the easiest and cheapest solution is to have someone back home make a deposit to your credit card or cash (ATM) card. Failing that, consider one of the following options.

WIRING MONEY. It is possible to arrange a **bank money transfer**, which means asking a bank back home to wire money to a bank in Chile. This is the cheapest way to transfer cash, but it's also the slowest, usually taking several working days or more. Note that some banks may only release your funds in Chilean pesos, potentially sticking you with a poor exchange rate; inquire about this in advance. Money transfer services like **Western Union** are faster and more convenient than bank transfers—but also much pricier. Western Union has many locations in most cities and major towns in Chile. To find one, visit www.western-union.com, or call in the US ☎800 325 6000, in Canada ☎800 235 0000, in the UK ☎0800 83 38 33, in Australia ☎800 501 500, or in New Zealand ☎800 27 0000, or in South Africa ☎ 0860 100031. In Chile ☎ 56 2 335 5433 for the Western Union at Correos de Chile, Avenida 11 de Septiembre, Santiago, or toll-free for Chilexpress (☎ 800 200 102).

US STATE DEPARTMENT (US CITIZENS ONLY). In emergencies only, the US State Department will forward money within hours to the nearest consular office, which will then disburse it according to instructions for a US$15 fee. If you wish to use this service, contact the Overseas Citizens Service division of the US State Department (US ☎ 202 647 5225; nights, Sundays, and holidays ☎ 202 647 4000).

COSTS

The cost of your trip will vary considerably, depending on where you go, how you travel, and where you stay. The most significant expenses will probably be your round-trip **airfare** to Chile (see **Getting to Chile: By Plane,** p. 59) and bus tickets. Before you go, spend some time calculating a reasonable per-day **budget** that will meet your needs.

STAYING ON A BUDGET. To give you a general idea, a bare-bones day in Chile (camping or sleeping in hostels/guesthouses, buying food at supermarkets) would cost between US$15-25. A slightly more comfortable day would run between US$25-45 (sleeping in hostels/guesthouses or the occasional budget hotel, while eating one meal a day at a restaurant and going out at night). However, for a luxurious day, the sky's the limit. Also, don't forget to factor in emergency reserve funds (at least US$200) when planning how much money you'll need.

TIPS FOR SAVING MONEY. Some simpler ways include searching out opportunities for free entertainment, splitting accommodation and food costs with other trustworthy fellow travelers, and buying food in supermarkets rather than eating out. You may also decide to do your **laundry** in the sink (unless you're explicitly prohibited from doing so). With that said, don't go overboard with your budget obsession. Though staying within your budget is important, don't do so at the expense of your health or a great travel experience.

TIPPING, BARGAINING, AND TAXES

Although it is not necessary to tip when using taxis, a small gratuity may be expected with other services. It is customary to tip 10% at restaurants, even at smaller, more casual establishments. When staying at upper-range accommodations, a CH$500 tip will suffice for porters and bell-boys, but the hotel maid should be tipped between CH$1500-2000 for a two-night stay. Meanwhile, bargaining is not only permissible, but is expected in markets and fairs throughout Chile. Most foreigners will initially be told the *gringo* price for goods, so bargain with vendors in open markets where the price of merchandise is not displayed, particularly in the case of *artesanías* and *ferias*. The same rules apply with tour operators and taxi drivers—try and shop around to get an estimate of current price ranges, haggle for the best value, and always agree upon an amount before embarking on a trip. Bargain at hotels and hostels, especially if traveling during the off-season. Travelers should remember to account for Value Added Tax, commonly known in Chile as IVA, *impuesto valor añadido*, applied at a rate of 18% to merchandise across the country (see p. 38). IVA/VAT refunds are not granted in Chile, however, most hotels, and many other establishments, including restaurants and tour guides, allow foreigners to circumvent the IVA tax by paying for stays or other services in cash, or specifically, US dollars—remember to ask for the IVA discount for foreigners when checking in. Finally, make sure to save some money for the airport departure tax of US$18.

SAFETY AND SECURITY

PERSONAL SAFETY

EXPLORING. To avoid unwanted attention, try to blend in as much as possible. Respecting local customs (in many cases, dressing more conservatively) may placate would-be hecklers. Familiarize yourself with your surroundings before setting out, and carry yourself with confidence; if you must check a map on the street, duck into a shop. If you are traveling alone, be sure someone at home knows your itinerary, and never admit that you're traveling alone. When walking at night, stick to busy, well-lit streets and avoid dark alleyways. If you feel uncomfortable, leave as quickly and directly as you can.

SELF DEFENSE. There is no sure-fire way to avoid all the threatening situations you might encounter when you travel, but a good self-defense course will give you concrete ways to react to unwanted advances. **Impact, Prepare, and Model Mugging** can refer you to local self-defense courses in the US (☎ 800-345-5425). Visit the website at www.impactsafety.org for a list of nearby chapters. Workshops (2-3hr.) start at US$50; full courses run US$350-500.

DRIVING. If you are using a **car,** learn local driving signals and wear a seatbelt. Children under 40lbs. should ride only in a specially-designed carseat, available for a small fee from car rental agencies. Study route maps before you hit the road, and if you plan on spending a lot of time on the road, you may want to bring spare parts. If your car breaks down, wait for the police to assist you. For long drives in desolate areas, invest in a cellular phone and a roadside assistance program (see p. 71). Be sure to park your vehicle in a garage or well traveled area. **Sleeping in your car** is one of the most dangerous (and often illegal) ways to get your rest.

TERRORISM. Due to the presence of suspected terrorist organizations in the Tri-Border Area (Argentina, Brazil, and Paraguay), activities related to terrorism are of concern to the entire region. However, there have been no reports that suggest that terrorism is a credible threat directed at tourists. Traditionally, September 11th-18th is an active period for public demonstrations. Political, labor, and student protests can occur at other times as well, usually near government buildings in Santiago and Valparaíso. Tourists are advised to avoid demonstrations and protest gatherings of any kind.

In addition, land mines may pose a threat to hikers in less-traveled, remote sections of national parks. Specifically, in northern border areas, Parque Nacional Lauca, Monumento Natural Salar de Surire, and Reserva Nacional Los Flamencos are at risk, while in southern Chile, demarcated land mine fields in Parque Nacional Torres del Paine and Parque Nacional Tierra del Fuego are to be avoided. Check with park authorities before wandering into less frequented areas and always heed warning signs. For up-to-date information about potential threats to tourists, consult the Consular Information Program of the US Department of State at http://travel.state.gov or www.usembassy.cl. In addition, the box on **travel advisories** (see below) lists offices to contact and websites to visit to get an updated version of your home country's government's advisories about travel.

FINANCIAL SECURITY

PROTECTING YOUR VALUABLES. There are a few steps you can take to minimize the financial risk associated with traveling. First, **bring as little with you as possible.** Second, buy a few combination **padlocks** to secure your belongings either in your pack or in a hostel or train station locker. Third, **carry as little cash as possible.** Keep

TRAVEL ADVISORIES. The following government offices provide travel information and advisories by telephone, by fax, or via the web:

Australian Department of Foreign Affairs and Trade: ☎ 1300 555135; faxback service 02 6261 1299; www.dfat.gov.au.

Canadian Department of Foreign Affairs and International Trade (DFAIT): In Canada and the US call ☎ 800-267-6788, elsewhere call +1 613-944-6788; www.dfait-maeci.gc.ca. Call for their free booklet, *Bon Voyage...But.*

New Zealand Ministry of Foreign Affairs: ☎ 04 494 8500; fax 494 8506; www.mft.govt.nz/trav.html.

United Kingdom Foreign and Commonwealth Office: ☎ 020 7008 0232; fax 7008 0155; www.fco.gov.uk.

US Department of State: ☎ 202-647-5225, faxback service 202-647-3000; http://travel.state.gov. For *A Safe Trip Abroad,* call ☎ 202-512-1800. For *Tips for Travelers to Central and South America,* visit www.access.gpo.gov/su_docs.

your traveler's checks and ATM/credit cards in a **money belt**—not a "fanny pack"— along with your passport and ID cards. Fourth, **keep a small cash reserve separate from your primary stash.** This should be about US$50 (US dollars are well-known and widely accepted in Chile) sewn into or stored in the depths of your pack, along with your traveler's check numbers and important photocopies.

CON ARTISTS AND PICKPOCKETS. In large cities, **con artists** often work in groups, and children are among the most effective. Beware of certain classics: sob stories that require money, rolls of bills "found" on the street, or mustard spilled (or saliva spit) onto your shoulder to distract you while they snatch your bag. **Don't ever let your passport or your bags out of your sight.** Street crime is a problem in metropolitan Santiago, and reports of the theft of purses, wallets, backpacks, and briefcases are increasing. Beware of **pickpockets** in city crowds, especially on public transportation—petty crime is prevalent at Metro stations. Also, be alert in public telephone booths: if you must say your calling card number, do so very quietly; if you punch it in, make sure no one can look over your shoulder. Other than in Santiago, crime is most frequent in the Viña del Mar and Valparaíso areas, which are increasingly crowded during the height of the Chilean summer season.

ACCOMMODATIONS AND TRANSPORTATION. Never leave your belongings unattended; crime occurs in even the most demure-looking hostel or hotel. Bring your own **padlock** for hostel lockers, and don't ever store valuables in any locker.

Be particularly careful on **buses;** horror stories abound about determined thieves who wait for travelers to fall asleep. Carry your backpack in front of you where you can see it. When traveling with others, sleep in alternate shifts. If traveling by **car,** don't leave valuables (such as radios or luggage) inside.

DRUGS AND ALCOHOL

Although Chilean wines are considered South America's finest, don't get carried away. Foreigners are subject to Chilean laws and regulations that may differ from those of their home country and may not extend expected protections to the individual. Persons violating Chilean law, even unwittingly, may be expelled, arrested, or imprisoned. Only travelers over the age of 18 may imbibe alcohol. Driving under the influence of alcohol is severely penalized in Chile, and may lead to incarceration if the driver is involved in an accident. Similarly, the possession, use, or trafficking of illegal drugs is strictly prohibited, and convicted offenders can expect heavy fines and imprisonment.

HEALTH

Common sense is the simplest prescription for good health while you travel. Drink lots of fluids to prevent dehydration and constipation, and wear sturdy, broken-in shoes and clean socks.

BEFORE YOU GO

In your **passport,** write the names of any people you wish to be contacted in case of a medical emergency, and list any allergies or medical conditions. In general, pharmacies in Chile are reliable and can be counted upon for all your prescription and over-the-counter drug needs. However, pharmacists cannot dispense prescription medication without authorization from a doctor, and matching a prescription to a foreign equivalent is not always easy, safe, or possible, so carry up-to-date, legible prescriptions or a statement from your doctor stating the medication's trade name, manufacturer, chemical name, and dosage. While traveling, be sure to keep all medication with you in your carry-on luggage. For tips on packing a basic **first-aid kit** and other health essentials, see p. 49.

IMMUNIZATIONS AND PRECAUTIONS

Although Chile does not maintain any vaccination requirements for international travelers, those over two years of age should make sure that the following vaccines are up to date: MMR (for measles, mumps, and rubella); DTaP or Td (for diphtheria, tetanus, and pertussis); OPV (for polio); HbCV (for haemophilus influenza B); and HBV (for hepatitis B). Adults traveling to the developing world on trips longer than four weeks should consider the following additional immunizations: Hepatitis A vaccine and/or immune globulin (IG); an additional dose of Polio vaccine; and typhoid and cholera vaccines, particularly if traveling off the tourist path. For those planning to venture into the wild, where an exposure to animals is likely, a rabies vaccination is recommended as well. While a yellow fever vaccination is recommended if you are traveling in rural areas in Argentina, a certificate of yellow fever vaccination is not required for entry into Chile. There is no risk for malaria in Chile, so don't worry about taking malaria prevention medication.

USEFUL ORGANIZATIONS AND PUBLICATIONS

The US **Centers for Disease Control and Prevention** (**CDC;** ☎877-FYI-TRIP; toll-free fax 888-232-3299; www.cdc.gov/travel) maintains an international travelers' hotline and an informative website. The CDC's comprehensive booklet *Health Information for International Travel,* an annual rundown of disease, immunization, and general health advice, is free online or US$25 via the Public Health Foundation (☎877-252-1200). Consult the appropriate government agency of your home country for consular information sheets on health concerns, entry requirements, and other issues for various countries (see the listings in the box on **Travel Advisories,** p. 43). For quick information on health and other travel warnings, call the **Overseas Citizens Services** (☎202-647-5225; after-hours 202-647-4000), or contact a passport agency, embassy, or consulate abroad. US citizens can send a self-addressed, stamped envelope to the Overseas Citizens Services, Bureau of Consular Affairs, #4811, US Department of State, Washington, D.C. 20520. For information on medical evacuation services and travel insurance firms, see the US government's website at http://travel.state.gov/medical.html or the **British Foreign and Commonwealth Office** (www.fco.gov.uk).

For detailed information on travel health, including a country-by-country overview of diseases try the **International Travel Health Guide,** by Stuart Rose, MD (US$19.95; www.travmed.com). For general health info, contact the **American Red Cross** (☎800-564-1234; www.redcross.org).

MEDICAL ASSISTANCE ON THE ROAD

Generally, medical care in Chile is good, although it may not always meet US standards, particularly in remote areas. Doctors and hospitals often expect immediate cash payment for services and medication, and US medical insurance is not always valid outside the United States. If your regular **insurance** policy does not cover travel abroad, you may wish to purchase additional coverage (see p. 48).

Travelers should consider supplemental medical insurance from their insurance companies or travel agents with plans that include special coverage and provisions for medical evacuation—in-country medical evacuations to Santiago cost US$2000 or more, while international evacuations begin at US$10,000. Pharmaceutical drugs are readily available, and Farmacia Ahumada, (Av. Portugal 155, Santiago ☎56 2 222 4000; open 24hr.), and Farmacia Salco are both reliable pharmacy chains. However, English-speaking staff is limited, so it is advisable to bring enough medication to last through your trip.

If you are concerned about obtaining medical assistance while traveling, you may wish to employ special support services. The *MedPass* from **GlobalCare, Inc.**, 2001 Westside Pkwy., #120, Alpharetta, GA 30004, USA (☎800-860-1111; fax 770-677-0455; www.globalems.com), provides 24hr. international medical assistance, support, and medical evacuation resources. The **International Association for Medical Assistance to Travelers** (**IAMAT**; US ☎716-754-4883, Canada ☎416-652-0137, New Zealand ☎03 352 20 53; www.sentex.net/~iamat), has free membership, lists English-speaking doctors worldwide, and offers detailed info on immunization requirements and sanitation.

Those with medical conditions (such as diabetes, allergies to antibiotics, epilepsy, or heart conditions) may want to obtain a **Medic Alert** membership (first year US$35, annually thereafter US$20), which includes a stainless steel ID tag, among other benefits, like a 24hr. collect-call number. Contact the Medic Alert Foundation, 2323 Colorado Ave, Turlock, CA 95382, USA (☎888-633-4298; outside US ☎209-668-3333; www.medicalert.org).

ONCE IN CHILE

ENVIRONMENTAL HAZARDS

Heat exhaustion and dehydration: Heat exhaustion can lead to fatigue, headaches, and wooziness. Avoid it by drinking plenty of fluids, eating salty foods (e.g. crackers), and avoiding dehydrating beverages (e.g. alcohol and caffeinated beverages). Continuous heat stress can eventually lead to heatstroke, characterized by a rising temperature, severe headache, and cessation of sweating. Victims should be cooled off with wet towels and taken to a doctor.

Sunburn: When in Chile, apply sunscreen generously, especially if you are planning on spending time near water, in the desert, or in the snow—you are at risk of getting burned, even through clouds. If you get sunburned, drink more fluids than usual and apply an aloe-based lotion.

High altitude: Allow your body a couple of days to adjust to less oxygen before exerting yourself. If you visit the Andes Mountains, ascend gradually to allow time for your body to acclimatize to prevent insomnia, headaches, nausea, and altitude sickness. Note that alcohol is more potent and UV rays are stronger at high elevations.

Hypothermia and frostbite: A rapid drop in body temperature is the clearest sign of overexposure to cold. Victims may also shiver, feel exhausted, have poor coordination or slurred speech, hallucinate, or suffer amnesia. *Do not let hypothermia victims fall asleep.* To avoid hypothermia, keep dry, wear layers, and stay out of the wind. When the temperature is below freezing, watch out for frostbite. If skin turns white, waxy, and cold, do not rub the area. Drink warm beverages, get dry, and slowly warm the area with dry fabric or steady body contact until a doctor can be found.

E S S E N T I A L S

INSECT-BORNE DISEASES

Many diseases are transmitted by insects—mainly mosquitoes, fleas, ticks, and lice. Be aware of insects in wet or forested areas, especially while hiking and camping; wear long pants and long sleeves, tuck your pants into your socks, and buy a mosquito net. Use insect repellents such as DEET and soak or spray your gear with permethrin (licensed in the US for use on clothing). **Ticks**—responsible for Lyme and other diseases—can be particularly dangerous in rural and forested regions throughout Norte Chico and Norte Grande. Taking precautions against insect bites can prevent the contraction of the following diseases.

Dengue fever: An "urban viral infection" transmitted by *Aedes* mosquitoes, which bite during the day rather than at night. Dengue has flu-like symptoms and is often indicated by a rash 3-4 days after the onset of fever. Symptoms for the first 2-4 days include chills, high fever, headaches, swollen lymph nodes, muscle aches, and, in some instances, a pink rash on the face. If you experience these symptoms, see a doctor, drink plenty of liquids, and take fever-reducing medication such as acetaminophen (Tylenol). **Never take aspirin to treat dengue fever**.

Tick-borne encephalitis: A viral infection of the central nervous system transmitted during the summer by tick bites (primarily in wooded areas) or by consumption of unpasteurized dairy products. The risk of contracting the disease is relatively low, especially if precautions are taken against tick bites.

Other insect-borne diseases: Filariasis is a roundworm infestation transmitted by mosquitoes. Infection causes enlargement of extremities and has no vaccine. **Leishmaniasis,** a parasite transmitted by sand flies, can occur in Central and South America. Common symptoms are fever, weakness, and swelling of the spleen. There is a treatment, but no vaccine. **CHAGAS** disease (American trypanosomiasis) is another relatively common parasite transmitted by the cone nose and kissing bug, which infest mud, adobe, and thatch. Its symptoms are fever, heart disease, and later on an enlarged intestine. There is no vaccine and limited treatment.

FOOD- AND WATER-BORNE DISEASES

Prevention is the best cure: be sure that your food is properly cooked and the water you drink is clean. While tap water in Chile is safe to drink, unaccustomed travelers with delicate dispositions are advised to drink mineral water. Buy bottled water or purify your own water by bringing it to a rolling boil or treating it with **iodine tablets;** note, however, that some parasites such as *giardia* have exteriors that resist iodine treatment, so boiling is more reliable. Consequently, avoid anything washed in tap water, like salad, and remember to peel fruits and veggies. Watch out for food from markets or street vendors that may have been cooked in unhygienic conditions. Other culprits are raw shellfish (generally, the consumption of fish and shellfish during hot summer months is discouraged), unpasteurized milk, and sauces containing raw eggs. Always wash your hands before eating or bring a quick-drying purifying liquid hand cleaner.

Traveler's diarrhea: Results from drinking untreated water or eating uncooked foods. Symptoms include nausea, bloating, and urgency. Try quick-energy, non-sugary foods with protein and carbohydrates to keep your strength up. Over-the-counter anti-diarrheals (e.g. Imodium) may counteract the problems. The most dangerous side effect is dehydration; drink 8 oz. of water with ½ tsp. of sugar or honey and a pinch of salt, try uncaffeinated soft drinks, or eat salted crackers. If you develop a fever or your symptoms don't go away after 4-5 days, consult a doctor. Consult a doctor immediately for treatment of diarrhea in children.

Dysentery: Results from a serious intestinal infection caused by certain bacteria. The most common type is bacillary dysentery, also called shigellosis. Symptoms include bloody diarrhea (sometimes mixed with mucus), fever, and abdominal pain and tenderness. Bacillary dysentery generally only lasts a week, but it is highly contagious. Amoebic dysentery, which develops more slowly, is a more serious disease and may cause long-term damage if left untreated. A stool test can determine which kind you have; seek medical help immediately. Dysentery can be treated with the drugs norfloxacin or ciprofloxacin (commonly known as Cipro). If you are traveling in high-risk (especially rural) regions, consider obtaining a prescription before you leave home.

Cholera: An intestinal disease caused by a bacteria found in contaminated food. The disease has recently reached epidemic stages in Central and South America. Symptoms include diarrhea, dehydration, vomiting, and muscle cramps. See a doctor immediately; if left untreated, it may be deadly. Antibiotics are available, but the most important treatment is rehydration. Consider getting a (50% effective) vaccine if you have stomach problems (e.g. ulcers) or will be living where the water is not reliable.

Hepatitis A: A viral infection of the liver acquired primarily through contaminated water. Symptoms include fatigue, fever, loss of appetite, nausea, dark urine, jaundice, vomiting, aches and pains, and light stools. The risk is highest in rural areas and the countryside, but it is also present in urban areas. Ask your doctor about the vaccine (Havrix or Vaqta) or an injection of immune globulin (IG; formerly called gamma globulin).

Parasites: Microbes, tapeworms, etc. that hide in unsafe water and food. **Giardiasis,** for example, is acquired by drinking untreated water from streams or lakes. Symptoms include swollen glands or lymph nodes, fever, rashes or itchiness, and digestive problems. Boil water, wear shoes, and eat only cooked food.

Schistosomiasis: Also known as bilharzia; a parasitic disease caused when the larvae of flatworm penetrate unbroken skin. Symptoms include an itchy localized rash, followed in 4-6 weeks by fever, fatigue, painful urination, diarrhea, loss of appetite, and night sweats. To avoid it, try not to swim in fresh water; if exposed to untreated water, rub the area vigorously with a towel and apply rubbing alcohol.

Typhoid fever: Caused by the salmonella bacteria; common in villages and rural areas in Central and South America. While mostly transmitted through contaminated food and water, it may also be acquired by direct contact with another person. Early symptoms include fever, headaches, fatigue, loss of appetite, constipation, and sometimes a rash on the abdomen or chest. Antibiotics can treat typhoid, but a vaccination (70-90% effective) is recommended.

OTHER INFECTIOUS DISEASES

Rabies: Transmitted through the saliva of infected animals; fatal if untreated. By the time symptoms (thirst and muscle spasms) appear, the disease is in its terminal stage. If you are bitten, wash the wound thoroughly, seek immediate medical care, and try to have the animal located. A rabies vaccine, which consists of 3 shots given over a 21-day period, is available but is only semi-effective. Plan for the rabies vaccination 4-6 weeks before departing for Chile if planning to hike through national parks or reserves.

Hepatitis B: A viral infection of the liver transmitted via bodily fluids or needle-sharing. Symptoms may not surface until years after infection. A 3-shot vaccination sequence is recommended for health-care workers, sexually-active travelers, and anyone planning to seek medical treatment abroad; it must begin 6 months before traveling.

Hepatitis C: Like Hepatitis B, but the mode of transmission differs. IV drug users, those with occupational exposure to blood, hemodialysis patients, and recipients of blood transfusions are at the highest risk, but the disease can also be spread through sexual contact or sharing items like razors and toothbrushes that may have traces of blood on them.

AIDS, HIV, AND STDS

For detailed information on **Acquired Immune Deficiency Syndrome (AIDS)** in Chile, call the **US Centers for Disease Control's** 24hr. hotline at ☎ 800-342-2437, or contact the **Joint United Nations Programme on HIV/AIDS (UNAIDS),** 20 Appia, CH-1211 Geneva 27, Switzerland (☎ +41 22 791 3666; fax 22 791 4187). Note that Chile screens incoming travelers for HIV, primarily those planning extended visits for work or study, and may deny entrance to those who test HIV-positive. Contact the consulate of Chile for more information (see p. 36).

Sexually transmitted diseases (STDs) such as gonorrhea, chlamydia, genital warts, syphilis, and herpes are easier to catch than HIV and can be just as deadly. **Hepatitis B** and **C** can also be transmitted sexually (see **Other Infectious Diseases**, above). Though condoms may protect you from some STDs, oral or even tactile contact can also lead to transmission. If you think you may have contracted an STD, see a doctor immediately.

WOMEN'S HEALTH

Women traveling in unsanitary conditions are vulnerable to **urinary tract** and **bladder infections,** common and very uncomfortable bacterial conditions that cause a burning sensation and painful (sometimes frequent) urination. Over-the-counter medicines can sometimes alleviate symptoms, but if they persist, see a doctor. Those women prone to urinary tract infections should consider bringing an antibiotic with them.

Vaginal yeast infections may flare up in hot and humid climates. Wearing loose-fitting trousers or a skirt and cotton underwear will help, as will over-the-counter remedies like Monostat or Gynelotrimin. Bring supplies from home if you are prone to infection, as they may be difficult to find on the road.

Since **tampons, pads,** and reliable **contraceptive devices** are sometimes hard to find when traveling, bring supplies with you unless you're spending most of your time in major cities. **Abortion** is illegal in Chile, except when the pregnant woman's life is in danger. **Emergency contraception** is also illegal.

INSURANCE

Travel insurance generally covers four basic areas: medical/health problems, property loss, trip cancellation/interruption, and emergency evacuation. Although your regular insurance policies may well extend to travel-related accidents, you may consider purchasing travel insurance if the cost of potential trip cancellation/interruption or emergency medical evacuation is greater than you can absorb. Prices for travel insurance purchased separately generally run about US$50 per week for full coverage, while trip cancellation/interruption insurance may be purchased separately at a rate of about US$5.50 per US$100 of coverage.

Medical insurance (especially university policies) often covers costs incurred abroad; check with your provider. **US Medicare** does not cover foreign travel to Chile. **Canadians** are protected by their home province's health insurance plan for up to 90 days after leaving the country; check with the provincial Ministry of Health or Health Plan Headquarters for details. **Homeowners' insurance** (or your family's coverage) often covers theft during travel and loss of travel documents (passport, plane ticket, etc.) up to US$500.

ISIC and **ITIC** (see p. 38) provide basic insurance benefits, including US$100 per day of in-hospital sickness for up to 60 days, US$3000 of accident-related medical reimbursement, and US$25,000 for emergency medical transport. Cardholders have access to a toll-free 24hr. helpline (run by the insurance provider **TravelGuard**) for medical, legal, and financial emergencies overseas (US and Canada ☎ 877-370-

4742, elsewhere call US collect ☎ +1 715-345-0505). **American Express** (US ☎ 800-528-4800) grants most cardholders automatic car rental insurance (collision and theft, but not liability) and ground travel accident coverage of US$100,000 on flight purchases made with the card.

INSURANCE PROVIDERS. Council and **STA** travel agencies (see p. 61) offer a range of plans that can supplement your basic coverage. Other private insurance providers in the US and Canada include: **Access America** (☎ 800-284-8300); **Berkely Group/Carefree Travel Insurance** (☎ 800-323-3149; www.berkely.com); **Globalcare Travel Insurance** (☎ 800-821-2488; www.globalcare-cocco.com); and **Travel Assistance International** (☎ 800-821-2828; www.europ-assistance.com). Providers in the **UK** include **Columbus Direct** (☎ 020 7375 0011). In **Australia,** try **AFTA** (☎ 02 9375 4955).

PACKING

Pack lightly: Lay out only what you absolutely need, then take half the clothes and twice the money. The less you have, the less you have to lose (or store, or carry on your back). Extra space will be useful for souvenirs or items you might pick up during your travels. If you plan to do a lot of hiking, also see the section on **Camping and the Outdoors,** p. 52.

LUGGAGE. If you plan to cover most of your itinerary by foot, a sturdy **frame backpack** is unbeatable. (For the basics on buying a pack, see p. 54.) Toting a **suitcase** or **trunk** is fine if you plan to live in one or two cities and explore from there, but a very bad idea if you're going to be moving around a lot. In addition to your main piece of luggage, a **daypack** (a small backpack or courier bag) is a must.

CLOTHING. No matter when you're traveling, it's always a good idea to bring a **warm jacket** or wool sweater, a **rain jacket** (Gore-Tex® is both waterproof and breathable), sturdy shoes or **hiking boots,** and **thick socks. Flip-flops** or waterproof sandals are must-haves for grubby hostel showers. You may also want to add one outfit beyond the jeans and t-shirt uniform, and maybe a nicer pair of shoes if you have the room. If you plan to visit any religious or cultural sites, remember that you'll need something besides tank tops and shorts to be respectful.

CONVERTERS AND ADAPTERS. In Chile, electricity is 220 volts AC, enough to fry any 110V North American appliance. **Americans** and **Canadians** should buy an **adapter** (which changes the shape of the plug) and a **converter** (which changes the voltage; US$20). Don't make the mistake of using only an adapter (unless appliance instructions explicitly state otherwise). **Europeans, New Zealanders** and **South Africans** (who all use 220V at home) as well as **Australians** (who use 240/250V) won't need a converter, but will need a set of adapters to use anything electrical.

TOILETRIES. Toothbrushes, towels, soap, talcum powder (to keep feet dry), deodorant, razors, tampons, and condoms may be available, but can be difficult to find, so bring extras along. If you wear **contact lenses,** traveling with enough lenses and solution for your entire trip is essential, as they may be expensive and difficult to find. Also bring your glasses and a copy of your prescription in case you need emergency replacements. If you use heat-disinfection for contacts, either switch temporarily to a chemical disinfection system (check first to make sure it's safe with your brand of lenses), or buy a converter to 220/240V.

FIRST-AID KIT. For a basic first-aid kit, pack: bandages, pain reliever, antibiotic cream, a thermometer, a Swiss Army knife, tweezers, moleskin, decongestant, motion-sickness remedy, diarrhea or upset-stomach medication (Pepto Bismol or

ESSENTIALS

Imodium), an antihistamine, sunscreen, insect repellent, and burn ointment. Be sure to check expiration dates before leaving home. In order to avoid hassles at security checkpoints, any sharp objects that you include in your kit should be packed in the luggage that you will check rather than in your carry-on.

FILM. Film and developing in Chile are fairly reasonable (about US$5 to purchase and US$7 to develop a roll of 36 exposures). Less serious photographers may want to bring a **disposable camera** or two rather than an expensive permanent one to avoid the risk of it being lost or stolen. Despite disclaimers, airport security X-rays *can* fog film, so buy a lead-lined pouch at a camera store or ask security to hand-inspect it. Always pack film in your carry-on luggage, since higher-intensity X-rays are used on checked luggage.

OTHER USEFUL ITEMS. For safety purposes, you should bring a **money belt** and small **padlock.** Basic **outdoors equipment** (plastic water bottle, compass, waterproof matches, pocketknife, sunglasses, sunscreen, hat) may also prove useful. **Quick repairs** of torn garments can be done on the road with a needle and thread; also consider bringing electrical tape for patching tears. If you want to do laundry by hand, bring detergent, a small rubber ball to stop up the sink, and string for a makeshift clothes line. **Other things** you're liable to forget: an umbrella; sealable **plastic bags** (for damp clothes, soap, food, shampoo, and other spillables); an **alarm clock;** safety pins; rubber bands; a flashlight; earplugs; garbage bags; and a small **calculator.**

IMPORTANT DOCUMENTS. Don't forget your passport, traveler's checks, ATM and/or credit cards, and an adequate ID (see p. 38). Also check that you have any of the following that might apply to you: a Hosteling International (HI) membership card (see p. 50); driver's license (see p. 38); travel insurance forms; and/or rail or bus pass (see p. 66).

ACCOMMODATIONS

HOSTELS

Hostels are generally laid out dorm-style, often with large single-sex rooms and bunk beds, although some offer private rooms for families and couples. They sometimes have kitchens and utensils for your use, bike or moped rentals, storage areas, Internet access, and laundry facilities. There can be drawbacks: some hostels close during certain daytime "lockout" hours, have a curfew, don't accept reservations, impose a maximum stay, or, less frequently, require that you do chores. In Chile, a bed in a hostel will average around US$10-$20.

HOSTELLING INTERNATIONAL

Joining the youth hostel association in your own country (listed below) automatically grants you membership privileges in **Hostelling International (HI)**, a federation of national hostelling associations that guarantees a certain level of quality in terms of cleanliness, comfort, and friendliness. There are 13 participating hostels scattered through Chile, in locations including Ancud, Chillán, Frutillar, Isla de Pascua, Pucón, Puerto Montt, Punta Arenas, Salto de Laja, Santiago, Temuco, Valdivia, and Viña del Mar. HI's umbrella organization's web page (www.iyhf.org), which lists the web addresses and phone numbers of all national associations, can be a great place to begin researching hostelling in a specific region.

Most student travel agencies (see p. 61) sell HI cards, as do all of the national hostelling organizations listed below. All prices listed below are valid for **one-year memberships,** unless otherwise noted.

Australian Youth Hostels Association (AYHA), 10 Mallett St., Level 3, Camperdown NSW 2050 (☎02 9565 1699; fax 9565 1325; www.yha.org.au). AUS$52, under 18 AUS$16.

Hostelling International-Canada (HI-C), 400-205 Catherine St., Ottawa, ON K2P 1C3 (☎800-663-5777 or 613-237-7884; fax 237-7868; info@hostellingintl.ca; www.hostellingintl.ca). CDN$35, under 18 free.

An Óige (Irish Youth Hostel Association), 61 Mountjoy St., Dublin 7 (☎830 4555; fax 830 5808; anoige@iol.ie; www.irelandyha.org). €13, under 18 €5.

Youth Hostels Association of New Zealand (YHANZ), P.O. Box 436, 193 Cashel St., 3rd Floor Union House, Christchurch 1 (☎03 379 9970; fax 365 4476; info@yha.org.nz; www.yha.org.nz). NZ$40, under 17 free.

Hostels Association of South Africa, 73 St. George's St. Mall, 3rd fl., P.O. Box 4402, Cape Town 8000 (☎021 424 2511; fax 424 4119; info@hisa.org.za; www.hisa.org.za). SAR45.

Scottish Youth Hostels Association (SYHA), 7 Glebe Crescent, Stirling FK8 2JA (☎01786 89 14 00; fax 89 13 33; www.syha.org.uk). UK£6.

Youth Hostels Association (England and Wales) Ltd., Trevelyan House, 8 St. Stephen's Hill, St. Albans, Hertfordshire AL1 2DY, UK (☎0870 870 8808; fax 01727 84 41 26; www.yha.org.uk). UK£12.50, under 18 UK£6.25, families UK£25.

Hostelling International Northern Ireland (HINI), 22-32 Donegall Rd., Belfast BT12 5JN, Northern Ireland (☎02890 31 54 35; fax 43 96 99; info@hini.org.uk; www.hini.org.uk). UK£10, under 18 UK£6.

Hostelling International-American Youth Hostels (HI-AYH), 733 15th St. NW, #840, Washington, D.C. 20005 (☎202-783-6161; fax 202-783-6171; hiayhserv@hiayh.org; www.hiayh.org). US$25, under 18 free.

HOTELS, RESIDENCIALES, AND HOSPEDAJES

The terms hotel, *residencial*, and *hospedaje* are sometimes used ambiguously to refer to similar establishments in Chile. **Residenciales,** sometimes called *hostales*, however, are the most common accommodations—they are usually established businesses offering simple, short-term lodging, often with shared bathrooms and up to four beds in a room. A bed in a *residencial* tends to cost US$10-20 a night, although single rooms and rooms with special amenities such as television cost slightly more. **Hospedajes,** which run about US$10-$15 per night, are modest accommodations with shared bathrooms and are usually family-run and located in a few spare rooms of the family's home. **Hotels** are generally more expensive than *residenciales* and *hospedajes*, offering more amenities, especially in the larger cities. Hotels are rated on a scale of one to five stars by the Chilean national tourist board, **Sentaur** (see p. 36), but the rating system is based on facilities and not upkeep; ask to see a room before you spring for a pricey four-star. **Hotel singles** in Chile cost about US$20-40 per night, **doubles** cost slightly more. You'll typically share a hall bathroom; a private bathroom will cost extra, as may hot showers. Some hotels offer "full pension" (all meals) and "half pension" (no lunch). If you make **reservations** in writing, indicate your night of arrival and the number of nights you plan to stay. The hotel will send you a confirmation and may request payment for the first night. Not all hotels take reservations, and few accept checks in foreign currency. Enclosing two International Reply Coupons will ensure a prompt reply (US$1.05 each; available at any US post office).

CAMPING AND THE OUTDOORS

Camping is one of the most accessible and enjoyable outdoor activities in the many **parques nacionales** and **reservas nacionales** in Chile. Sites vary from the most rustic grounds to swankier private-owned venues offering restrooms, water supply, cooking facilities, and hot showers. Official campsites charge about US$10-15 per tent, although it is more economical to look for the occasional grounds that charge US$10-15 for an entire site and share the cost with a few other campers. Private campgrounds in and around smaller towns offer more services and are generally cheaper than official **Conaf** administered campsites (see p. 52). Most national parks prohibit camping outside of designated areas, and camping in the wild is not suggested except for the most experienced campers with their own transportation and a knowledgeable guide.

Spanish-speakers planning on camping and trekking should check out the Chilean **Turistel** website (www.turistel.cl) for information about *Turistel's* meticulous maps of camping spots and comprehensive camping guides such as *Guía Turística Turistel: Rutero Camping*. Another excellent general resource for travelers planning on spending time in the outdoors is the Great Outdoor Recreation Pages (www.gorp.com). This site includes a section entitled *Chile: 20 Best Adventures* (www.gorp.com/gorp/location/latamer/chile/top_twenty.htm), with some useful information about outdoor activities in Chile. Gochile.com also has detailed descriptions of most parks in both English and Spanish (www.gochile.com).

USEFUL PUBLICATIONS AND RESOURCES

A variety of publishing companies offer hiking guidebooks to meet the educational needs of novices or experts. For a free catalog about camping, hiking, and biking, contact the publishers listed below.

Sierra Club Books, 85 Second St., 2nd fl., San Francisco, CA 94105, USA (☎415-977-5500; www.sierraclub.org/books). Publishes general resource books on hiking, camping, and women traveling in the outdoors.

The Mountaineers Books, 1001 SW Klickitat Way, #201, Seattle, WA 98134, USA (☎800-553-4453 or 206-223-6303; fax 223-6306; www.mountaineersbooks.org). Over 400 titles on hiking, biking, mountaineering, natural history, and conservation. Check out *Mountaineering in Patagonia* (Mountaineers Books, US$22.95) for information about outdoor adventures in Chile and Argentina.

NATIONAL PARKS

The system of national parks in Chile is controlled by the **Corporación Nacional Forestal, Conaf,** a government-run corporation that aims for responsible use of resources while preserving the country's flora, fauna, and spectacular natural environments. Conaf runs administration offices in Chile's national parks and national reserves, offering information, maps, and rescue services for hikers and other visitors. The conserved spaces in Chile—totalling a whopping 14 million hectares, 18% of the country's territory—include 31 *parques nacionales* (national parks), 48 *reservas nacionales* (national reserves), and 15 *monumentos naturales* (natural monuments). The difference between **parques nacionales** and **reservas nacionales** is subtle. The *parques* are extensive areas generally used only for recreation and study, and are intended to preserve Chile's threatened or endangered plants, creatures, and environments. The *reservas* are meant to ensure the country's proper use of essential natural resources, but are also used for recreational purposes. **Monumentos naturales** tend to be smaller areas set aside to preserve specific native species of flora and fauna or geological sites that have

GET CARD.

TRAVEL HARD.

SCENIC DRIVE
FOOD + GAS
LOOKOUT

There's only one way to max out your travel experience and make the most of your time on the road: The International Student Identity Card.

 Packed with travel discounts, benefits and services, this card will keep your travel days and your wallet full. Get it before you hit it!

Visit **ISICUS.com** to get the full story on the benefits of carrying the ISIC.

90 minutes, wash & dry (one sock missing).
5 minutes to book online (Detroit to Mom's)

Save money & time on student and faculty
travel at **StudentUniverse.com**

ENVIRONMENTALLY RESPONSIBLE TOURISM. The idea behind responsible tourism is to leave no trace of human presence behind. A camp stove is the safer (and more efficient) way to cook than using vegetation, but if you must make a fire, keep it small and use only dead branches or brush rather than cutting vegetation. Make sure your campsite is at least 150 ft. (50m) from water sources or bodies of water. If there are no toilet facilities, bury human waste (but not paper) at least four inches (10cm) deep and above the high-water line, and 150 ft. or more from any water supplies and campsites. Always pack your trash in a plastic bag and carry it with you until you reach the next trash receptacle. For more information on these issues, contact one of the organizations listed below.

Earthwatch, 3 Clock Tower Place #100, Box 75, Maynard, MA 01754, USA (☎800-776-0188 or 978-461-0081; info@earthwatch.org; www.earthwatch.org).

International Ecotourism Society, 28 Pine St., Burlington, VT 05402, USA (☎802-651-9818; fax 802-651-9819; ecomail@ecotourism.org; www.ecotourism.org).

National Audubon Society, Nature Odysseys, 700 Broadway, New York, NY 10003 (☎212-979-3000; fax 212-979-3188; webmaster@audubon.org; www.audubon.org).

Tourism Concern, Stapleton House, 277-281 Holloway Rd., London N7 8HN, UK (☎020 7753 3330; fax 020 7753 3331; info@tourismconcern.org.uk; www.tourismconcern.org.uk).

ESSENTIALS

particular cultural or scientific relevance. Chile's preserved areas are representative of the extreme natural environments of the country, including the towering volcano of the **Parque Nacional Lauca** in Norte Grande; the scenic waterfalls and pools of the **Reserva Nacional Radal Siete Tazas** in Middle Chile; and the striking granite pillars and glaciers of **Parque Nacional Torres del Paine** in the far south.

Parques nacionales, reservas nacionales, and *monumentos naturales* are often accessible by inexpensive public transportation from nearby cities or towns. Some charge no entrance fee, while others charge as much as US$15 during peak season. Visitors to both *reservas nacionales* and *parques nacionales* should start by checking out the **Centro de Información Ambiental** run by Conaf for maps, educational talks and other orientating information—ask for suggestions about hiking routes and local guides. Conaf also often runs campsites for approximately US$10-15 per tent (see **Camping,** above).

CONAF, Bulnes 285, Oficina 501, Santiago, Chile. (☎56 2 390 0000 or 56 2 390 0208; consulta@conaf.cl; www.conaf.cl). Contact the central office for general information; see individual parks for information about Conaf services.

WILDERNESS SAFETY

THE GREAT OUTDOORS. Stay warm, stay dry, and **stay hydrated.** The vast majority of life-threatening wilderness situations can be avoided by following this simple advice. Prepare yourself for an emergency, however, by always packing raingear, a hat and mittens, a first-aid kit, a reflector, a whistle, high energy food, and extra water for any hike. Dress in wool or warm layers of synthetic materials designed for the outdoors; never rely on cotton for warmth, as it is useless when wet.

Check **weather forecasts** and pay attention to the skies when hiking, since weather patterns can change suddenly. Always ask Conaf officials and/or park rangers whether hiking trails are passable before embarking on your trek (erratic weather patterns can suddenly and drastically alter the condition of trails in national parks, especially those in Chiloé and the Far South). Whenever possible, let someone know when and where you are going hiking, either a friend, your hostel, a park ranger, or a local hiking organization. Do not attempt a hike beyond your ability—you may be endangering your life. (See **Health**, p. 44, for information about outdoor ailments and basic medical concerns.)

Earthquakes are not uncommon in Chile. Although the possibility of natural disasters should not keep you away, it is a good idea to be informed before heading out into Chile. Consult the website for the **Oficina Nacional de Emergencia de Chile (ONEMI)** for information on Chilean earthquakes (www.angelfire.com/nt/terremotos2). For more general information about earthquake awareness, check out the **US Federal Emergency Management Agency** site at www.fema.gov.

WILDLIFE. Lucky for travelers in Chile, there are no poisonous snakes or insects in the country that pose a threat to humans. The **puma**, or mountain lion, is the only large feline in the country, but it generally avoids humans and is elusive in its natural habitat. Nevertheless, travelers should always be cautious of fauna in the wild and should not disturb their natural environments. For more information, consult *How to Stay Alive in the Woods*, by Bradford Angier (Macmillian Press, US$8).

CAMPING AND HIKING EQUIPMENT

WHAT TO BUY...

Good camping equipment is both sturdy and light. Camping equipment is generally more expensive in Australia, New Zealand, and the UK than in North America. While high-quality camping equipment is readily available in larger Chilean cities such as Santiago, Arica, and La Serena, the merchandise is no cheaper than in other countries, as there are no reputable, local Chilean companies distributing camping equipment.

Sleeping Bag: Most sleeping bags are rated by season ("summer" means 0-5°C at night; "four-season" or "winter" often means below -18°C). They are made either of **down** (warmer and lighter, but more expensive, and miserable when wet) or of **synthetic** material (heavier, more durable, and warmer when wet). Prices range US$80-210 for a summer synthetic to US$250-300 for a good down winter bag. **Sleeping bag pads** include foam pads (US$10-20), air mattresses (US$15-50), and Therm-A-Rest self-inflating pads (US$45-80). Bring a **stuff sack** to store your bag and keep it dry.

Tent: The best tents are free-standing (with their own frames and suspension systems), set up quickly, and only require staking in high winds. Low-profile dome tents are the best all-around. Good 2-person tents start at US$90, 4-person at US$300. Seal the seams of your tent with waterproofer, and make sure it has a rain fly. Other tent accessories include a **battery-operated lantern,** a **plastic groundcloth,** and a **nylon tarp.**

Backpack: Internal-frame packs mold better to your back, keep a lower center of gravity, and flex adequately to allow you to hike difficult trails. **External-frame packs** are more comfortable for long hikes over even terrain, as they keep weight higher and distribute it more evenly. Make sure your pack has a strong, padded hip-belt to transfer weight to your legs. Any serious backpacking requires a pack of at least 16,000cc (4000 in.^{3}), plus 8200cc (500 in.^{3}) for sleeping bags in internal-frame packs. Sturdy backpacks cost anywhere from US$125-420—this is one area in which it doesn't pay to economize. Fill up any pack with something heavy and walk around the store with it to get a sense of how it distributes weight before buying it. Either buy a **waterproof backpack cover,** or store all of your belongings in plastic bags inside your pack.

Boots: Be sure to wear hiking boots with good **ankle support.** They should fit snugly and comfortably over 1-2 pairs of wool socks and thin liner socks. Break in boots over several weeks first in order to spare yourself painful and debilitating blisters.

Other Necessities: Synthetic layers, like those made of polypropylene, and a **fleece jacket** will keep you warm even when wet. A **"space blanket"** will help you to retain your body heat and doubles as a groundcloth (US$5-15). Plastic **water bottles** are virtually shatter- and leak-proof. Bring **water-purification tablets** for when you can't boil water. Although most campgrounds provide campfire sites, you may want to bring a small **metal grate** or **grill** of your own. For those places that forbid fires or the gathering of firewood, you'll need a **camp stove** (the classic Coleman starts at US$40) and a propane-filled **fuel bottle** to operate it. Also don't forget a **first-aid kit, pocketknife, insect repellent, calamine lotion,** and **waterproof matches** or a **lighter.**

...AND WHERE TO BUY IT

The mail-order/online companies listed below offer lower prices than many retail stores, but a visit to a local camping or outdoors store will give you a good sense of the look and weight of certain items.

Campmor, 28 Parkway, P.O. Box 700, Upper Saddle River, NJ 07458, USA (US ☎888-226-7667; elsewhere US ☎+1 201-825-8300; www.campmor.com).

Discount Camping, 880 Main North Rd., Pooraka, South Australia 5095, Australia (☎08 8262 3399; fax 8260 6240; www.discountcamping.com.au).

Eastern Mountain Sports (EMS), 1 Vose Farm Rd., Peterborough, NH 03458, USA (☎888-463-6367 or 603-924-7231; www.shopems.com).

L.L. Bean, Freeport, ME 04033 (US and Canada ☎800-441-5713; UK ☎0800 891 297; elsewhere, call US ☎+1 207-552-3028; www.llbean.com).

Mountain Designs, 51 Bishop St., Kelvin Grove, Queensland 4059, Australia (☎07 3856 2344; fax 3856 0366; info@mountaindesigns.com; www.mountaindesigns.com).

Recreational Equipment, Inc. (REI), Sumner, WA 98352, USA (☎800-426-4840 or 253-891-2500; www.rei.com).

YHA Adventure Shop, 14 Southampton St., Covent Garden, London, WC2E 7HA, UK (☎020 7836 8541; www.yhaadventure.com). The main branch of one of Britain's largest outdoor equipment suppliers.

ORGANIZED ADVENTURE TRIPS

Organized adventure trips offer another way of exploring the wild, placing individual travelers or small groups on trips with other adventurers of similar experience levels. Tours usually offer all necessary equipment and meals; always bring your own water. Activities include hiking, biking, skiing, canoeing, kayaking, rafting, climbing, photo safaris, and archaeological digs. There are many agencies that organize adventures abroad, but if you'd rather arrange trips once you've arrived in Chile, local tourism bureaus can often suggest parks, trails, and outfitters. Look for local tour operators in the Practical Information section of all cities under Tours. Local operations are generally reliable, and provide a safer and cheaper means of seeing the best of the Chilean outdoors than going it alone. Most operations are staffed with helpful, experienced, English-speaking guides and include equipment and/or meals within the price of the tour. The supervision of a trained tour guide is often a good idea in remote, possibly unchartered, terrain in many parts of Chile including Norte Grande, Chiloé, and the Far South—remember, solo attempts to traverse trails or ascend peaks that require you to be accompanied by a guide is not only unnecessarily reckless; it is illegal and potentially fatal.

Bío bío Expeditions Worldwide, P.O. Box 2028, Truckee, CA 96160, USA (☎800-246-7238; US fax 530-550-9670, Chile fax 011-56-2-334-3012; H2OMarc@bbxrafting.com; www.bbxrafting.com/adventure/chile). Kayaking and whitewater rafting expeditions in Chile.

Expediciones Chile, (☎888-488-9082; office@exchile.com; www.exchile.com). Offers kayaking, fly fishing, and multi-sport trips in Chile.

GORPtravel, P.O. Box 1486, Boulder, CO 80306, USA. (US ☎877-440-GORP; international calls 1+720-887-8500; http://gorptravel.gorp.com). Adventure tours to Chile and Argentina include mountain biking, hiking, walking, whitewater rafting, and kayaking.

Specialty Travel Index, 305 San Anselmo Ave., #313, San Anselmo, CA 94960, USA (☎800-442-4922 or 415-459-4900; fax 415-459-9474; info@specialtytravel.com; www.specialtytravel.com). Listings for tours worldwide, including Chile.

KEEPING IN TOUCH

BY MAIL

SENDING MAIL HOME FROM CHILE

Airmail is the best way to send mail home from Chile. Write airmail or "por avión" on the front. Regular mail takes between two and three weeks to reach Europe or the US, whereas Chile Express is the most common, reliable, and inexpensive way to send mail within a few days.

Post offices in larger cities tend to have the quickest and most consistent service —if you need something to reach its destination in a reasonably short time period, don't send it from a tiny post office in a remote town.

SENDING MAIL TO CHILE

Mark envelopes "air mail," "por avión" to ensure their delivery. In addition to the standard postage system whose rates are listed below, **Federal Express** (Australia ☎13 26 10; US and Canada ☎800-247-4747; New Zealand ☎0800 73 33 39; UK ☎0800 12 38 00; www.fedex.com) handles express mail services from most home countries to Chile—a fairly pricey but efficient service. For example, a Fed-exed letter from New York to Chile would typically take 1-3 business days and cost US$45; one from London to Chile would average 1-3 days for UK£37. DHL is less common in the US, but offers similar rates and services and has more locations in Chile than FedEx, making it a more convenient alternative.

Australia: Allow 6-7 days for regular **airmail.** Postcards and letters up to 20g cost AUS$1; packages up to 0.5kg AUS$9, up to 2kg AUS$46. EMS can get a letter to Chile in 4-5 days for AUS$32. www.auspost.com.au/pac.

Canada: Allow 6-10 days for regular **airmail.** Postcards and letters up to 30g cost CDN$1.25; packages up to 0.5kg CDN$10, up to 2kg CDN$46.30. www.canada-post.ca/CPC2/common/rates/ratesgen.html#international.

Ireland: Allow approximately one week for regular **airmail.** Postcards and letters up to 50g cost €0.65. www.anpost.ie.

New Zealand: Allow approximately one week for regular **airmail.** Postcards NZ$1.50. Letters up to 200g NZ$2.00; small parcels up to 0.5kg NZ$8.51, up to 2kg NZ$21.70. www.nzpost.co.nz/nzpost/inrates.

UK: Allow 5-8 days for **airmail.** Letters up to 20g cost UK£0.65; packages up to 0.5kg UK£4.55, up to 2kg UK£8.22. **UK Swiftair** delivers letters a day faster for UK£2.85 more. www.consignia-online.com.

US: Allow 5-7days for regular **airmail.** Postcards/aerogrammes cost US$0.70; letters under 1 oz. US$.80. Packages under 1 lb. US$17; larger packages US$20-30. **US Express Mail** takes 2-5 days and costs US$22.25/24.75 (0.5/1 lb.). **US Global Priority Mail** delivers small/large flat-rate envelopes to Chile in 4-7 days for US$5/9. http://ircalc.usps.gov.

RECEIVING MAIL IN CHILE

General Delivery: Mail can be sent to Chile through **Lista de Correos** (or by using the international phrase **Poste Restante**) to almost any city or town with a post office. Address *Poste Restante* letters to: Pablo NERUDA, Lista de Correos, Town, CHILE. The letter should also be marked *Favor de retener hasta la llegada* (please hold until arrival). The mail will go to a special desk in the central post office, unless you specify a post office by street address. It's best to use the largest post office, since mail may be sent there regardless. Bring your passport (or other photo ID) for pick-up; there may be a small fee (if there is, it should not exceed the cost of domestic postage). If the clerks insist that there is nothing for you, have them check under your first name as well. *Let's Go* lists post offices in the **Practical Information** section for each city and most towns.

American Express: AmEx's travel offices throughout the world offer a free **Client Letter Service** (mail held up to 30 days and forwarded upon request) for cardholders who contact them in advance. Address the letter in the same way shown above. Some offices will offer these services to non-cardholders (especially AmEx Travelers Cheque holders), but call ahead to make sure. *Let's Go* lists AmEx office locations for most large cities in **Practical Information** sections; for a complete, free list, call US ☎ 800 528 4800.

BY TELEPHONE

CALLING HOME FROM CHILE

A **calling card** purchased before you leave for Chile is probably your cheapest bet. Calls are billed collect or to your account. You can frequently call collect without even possessing a company's calling card just by calling their access number and following the instructions. **To obtain a calling card** from your national telecommunications service before leaving home, contact the appropriate company listed below. To **call home with a calling card,** contact the operator for your service provider in Chile by dialing the appropriate toll-free access number. Ireland and New Zealand do not have direct calling plans to South America.

COMPANY	TO OBTAIN A CARD, CONTACT:	TO CALL ABROAD FROM CHILE, DIAL:
AT&T (US)	www.consumer.att.com/prepaidcard/	800 225 288
British Telecom Direct	0800 34 51 44; http://www.payphones.bt.com/2001/phone_cards/globalcard/globalcard.html	123 00208 401
Canada Direct	800 668 6878; http://www.mts.mb.ca/	800 360 280 or 800 800 226
MCI (US)	800-955-0925; http://www.mci.com/calling_cards/	800 207 300
New Zealand Direct	www.telecom.co.nz	800 800 693 or 800 360 160
Sprint (US)	https://prepaid.sprint.com/	800 360 777
Telkom South Africa	10 219; http://www.telkom.co.za/products/worldcall.shtml	123 003 271

ESSENTIALS

You can usually also make direct international calls from pay phones, but if you aren't using a calling card, you may need to drop your coins as quickly as your words. Where available, prepaid phone cards purchased in Chile (see **Calling within Chile** p. 58) and occasionally major credit cards can be used for direct international calls. (See the box on **Placing International Calls** p. 58 for directions on how to place a direct international call.)

Placing a **collect call** (*llamada con cobro revertido*) through an international operator is even more expensive, but may be necessary in case of emergency. You can typically place collect calls through the service providers listed above even if you don't have one of their phone cards

In order to dial out from any phone in Chile, you can choose a **carrier service** by dialing one of the numbers below. To call within Chile, dial the carrier code and then the regional area code and number; for international calls, dial the carrier code followed by a 0 and the country code and phone number. If you wish simply to use the default carrier for the phone you are using, for calls within Chile, dial zero followed by the area code and phone number; for international calls, dial 00 followed by the country code and phone number.

CARRIER	DIAL
Bell South	181 + 0 + Country Code + Area Code + Number
Chilesat	171 + 0 + Country Code + Area Code + Number
CNT Carrier	121 + 0 + Country Code + Area Code + Number
Entel	123 + 0 + Country Code + Area Code + Number
Manquehue LD	122 + 0 + Country Code + Area Code + Number
Telefónica (CTC)	188 + 0 + Country Code + Area Code + Number
Transam Comunicaciones	113 + 0 + Country Code + Area Code + Number
VTR	120 + 0 + Country Code + Area Code + Number

PLACING INTERNATIONAL CALLS. To call Chile from home or to call home from Chile, dial:

1. The **international dialing prefix**. To dial out of out of **Chile,** dial 00 or specific carrier number (see above chart); **Australia,** dial 0011; **Canada** or the **US,** 011; the **Republic of Ireland, New Zealand,** or the **UK,** 00; **South Africa,** 09.

2. The **country code** of the country you want to call. To call **Australia,** dial 61; **Canada** or the **US,** 1; the **Republic of Ireland,** 353; **New Zealand,** 64; **South Africa,** 27; the **UK,** 44; **Chile,** 56.

3. The **city/area code.** *Let's Go* lists the city/area codes for cities and towns in Chile opposite the city or town name, next to a ☎. If the first digit is a zero (e.g., 02 for Santiago), omit the zero when calling from abroad (e.g., dial 2 from Canada to reach Santiago).

4. The **local number.**

CALLING WITHIN CHILE

The simplest way to call within the country is to use a phone at a **locutorio,** a grouping of phones, which enables you to pay after you have made your calls. **Prepaid phone cards** (available at newspaper kiosks and tobacco stores) carry a certain amount of phone time depending on the card's denomination, and usually save time and money in the long run. The computerized phone will tell you how much time, in units, you have left on your card. Another kind of prepaid telephone card comes with a Personal Identification Number (PIN) and a toll-free access number. Instead of inserting the card into the phone, you dial the access number and follow the directions on the card. These cards can often be used to make international as well as domestic calls. International calling cards from Entel or CTC offices (generally in denominations of CH$1000-3000, CH$5000, and CH$10,000) tend to be cheaper than using *centro de llamados* services, which in turn are cheaper than public pay phones. Phone rates typically tend to be highest in the morning, lower in the evening, and lowest on Sunday and late at night.

TIME DIFFERENCES

Greenwich Mean Time (GMT) is five hours ahead of New York time, eight hours ahead of Vancouver and San Francisco time, two hours behind Johannesburg time, 11 hours behind Sydney time, and 12 hours behind Auckland time. Chile falls 4 hours behind **GMT**, and ignores **daylight savings time.**

The following chart is applicable from **late October** to **early April**.

4AM	6AM	7AM	8AM	NOON	10PM
Vancouver Seattle San Francisco Los Angeles	Galapagos Chicago	Toronto New York Boston Chile	New Brunswick	London (GMT)	Sydney Canberra Melbourne

Chile **ignores daylight savings time**, as does Australia. The following table is applicable from **early April** to **late October.**

4AM	5AM	6AM	7AM	8AM	NOON	9PM
Vancouver Seattle San Francisco Los Angeles	Galapagos Denver	Chile Chicago	New York Toronto Boston	New Brun- swick	London (GMT)	Sydney Canberra Melbourne

BY EMAIL AND INTERNET

Internet cafes are the easiest and most reliable way to access the Internet in Chile. You can find them in every major city and even in most smaller cities and towns. Rates are generally US$2-4 per hour, with other services such as printing and sometimes CD burning provided for an extra charge. Though in some places it's possible to establish a remote link with your home server, in most cases this is a much slower (and thus more expensive) option than taking advantage of free **web-based email accounts** (e.g., www.yahoo.com).

GETTING TO CHILE

BY AIR

When it comes to airfare, a little effort can save you a bundle. If your plans are flexible enough to deal with the restrictions, courier fares are the cheapest. Tickets bought from consolidators and standby seating are also good deals, but last-minute specials, airfare wars, and charter flights often beat these fares. The key is to hunt around, to be flexible, and to ask persistently about discounts. Students, seniors, and those under 26 should never pay full price for a ticket.

AIRFARES

GATEWAYS. Although Chile has a number of international airports, almost every flight from outside of South America has a connection in Santiago. From there travelers can hop a flight to any of the country's dozen airports. **Fares** for roundtrip flights to Santiago from the US cost US$600-1300, from Canada CND$900-2100, from the UK UK£900-1200, from Australia AUS$3000-5000.

TIMING. Airfares to Chile peak between July and August and December and January, with fares often soaring to US$1200 and up; holidays are also expensive. The cheapest times to travel are February to May and September to November. Midweek (M-Th morning) round-trip flights run US$40-50 cheaper than weekend flights, but they are generally more crowded and less likely to permit frequent-flier upgrades.

ROUTES. Round-trip tickets are usually the cheapest way of flying. Not fixing a return date ("open return") or arriving in and departing from different cities ("open-jaw") can be much pricier. Patching one-way flights together is the most expensive way to travel, especially within Chile where internal one-way flights are often more expensive than round-trip flights.

If Chile is only one stop on a more extensive globe-hop, consider a round-the-world (RTW) ticket. Tickets usually include at least five stops and are valid for about a year; prices range US$1200-5000. Try **Northwest Airlines/KLM** (US ☎ 800-447-4747; www.nwa.com) or **Star Alliance,** a consortium of 22 airlines including United Airlines (US ☎ 800-241-6522; www.star-alliance.com).

BUDGET AND STUDENT TRAVEL AGENCIES

While knowledgeable agents specializing in flights to Chile can make your life easy and help you save, they may not spend the time to find you the lowest possible fare—they get paid on commission. Travelers holding **ISIC** and **IYTC cards** (see p. 38) qualify for big discounts from student travel agencies. Most flights from budget agencies are on major airlines, but in peak season some may sell seats on less reliable chartered aircraft.

usit world (www.usitworld.com). Over 50 **usit campus** branches in the UK, including 52 Grosvenor Gardens, **London** SW1W 0AG (☎0870 240 10 10); **Manchester** (☎0161 273 1880); and **Edinburgh** (☎0131 668 3303). Nearly 20 **usit NOW** offices in Ireland, including 19-21 Aston Quay, O'Connell Bridge, **Dublin** 2 (☎01 602 1600; www.usit-now.ie), and **Belfast** (☎02 890 327 111; www.usitnow.com). Offices also in Athens, Auckland, Brussels, Frankfurt, Johannesburg, Lisbon, Luxembourg, Madrid, Paris, Sofia, and Warsaw.

Council Travel (www.counciltravel.com). Countless US offices, including branches in Atlanta, Boston, Chicago, L.A., New York, San Francisco, Seattle, and Washington, D.C. Check the website or call ☎800-2-COUNCIL (226-8624) for the office nearest you. Also an office at 28A Poland St. (Oxford Circus), **London,** W1V 3DB (☎0207 437 77 67). As of May, Council had declared bankruptcy and was subsumed under STA. However, their offices are still in existence and transacting business.

CTS Travel (www.ctstravelusa.com). Offices across Italy, in Paris, London, and now in New York. Call toll-free ☎877-287-6665. In UK, 44 Goodge St., London W1T 2AD (0207) 636 0031; fax 637 5328; ctsinfo@ctstravel.co.uk).

STA Travel, 7890 S. Hardy Dr., Ste. 110, Tempe AZ 85284, USA (24hr. reservations and info ☎800-781-4040; www.sta-travel.com). A student and youth travel organization with over 150 offices worldwide (check their website for a listing of all their offices), including US offices in Boston, Chicago, L.A., New York, San Francisco, Seattle, and Washington, D.C. Ticket booking, travel insurance, railpasses, and more. In the UK,

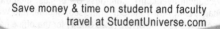

walk-in office at 11 Goodge St., **London** W1T 2PF (☎0207 436 7779). In New Zealand, Shop 2B, 182 Queen St., **Auckland** (☎09 309 0458). In Australia, 366 Lygon St., **Carlton** Vic 3053 (☎03 9349 4344).

Travel CUTS (Canadian Universities Travel Services Limited), 187 College St., **Toronto,** ON M5T 1P7 (☎416-979-2406; fax 979-8167; www.travelcuts.com). 60 offices across Canada. Also in the UK, 295-A Regent St., **London** W1R 7YA (☎0207-255-1944).

✈ **FLIGHT PLANNING ON THE INTERNET.**
Many airline sites offer special last-minute deals on the Web. American Airlines (www.aa.com), British Airways (www.britishairways.com), Delta Airlines (www.delta.com), Lan Chile (www.lanchile.com), Lufthansa (www.lufthansa.com) and Swiss (www.swiss.com) are just a few. Other sites do the legwork and compile the deals for you—try www.bestfares.com, www.flights.com, www.hotdeals.com, www.lowestfare.com, www.onetravel.com, and www.travelzoo.com.

■ StudentUniverse (www.studentuniverse.com), STA (www.sta-travel.com), Council (www.counciltravel.com), and **Orbitz** (www.orbitz.com) provide quotes on student tickets, while **Expedia** (www.expedia.com) and **Travelocity** (www.travelocity.com) offer full travel services. **Priceline** (www.priceline.com) allows you to specify a price, and obligates you to buy any ticket that meets or beats it; be prepared for antisocial hours and odd routes. **Hotwire** (www.hotwire.com) is a happy medium offering ultra-cheap fares with the benefit of seeing price estimates without making a purchase commitment (flight schedule and airline info withheld until after purchase). **Skyauction** (www.skyauction.com) allows you to bid on both last-minute and advance-purchase tickets.

An indispensable resource on the Internet is the *Air Traveler's Handbook* (www.cs.cmu.edu/afs/cs/user/mkant/Public/Travel/airfare.html), a comprehensive listing of links to everything you need to know before you board a plane.

COMMERCIAL AIRLINES

The commercial airlines' lowest regular offer is the **APEX** (Advance Purchase Excursion) fare, which provides confirmed reservations and allows "open-jaw" tickets. Generally, reservations must be made seven to 21 days ahead of departure, with seven- to 14-day minimum-stay and up to 90-day maximum-stay restrictions. These fares carry hefty cancellation and change penalties (fees rise in summer). Book peak-season APEX fares early; by May you will have a hard time getting your desired departure date for summer travel. Use **Microsoft Expedia** (msn.expedia.com) or **Travelocity** (www.travelocity.com) to get an idea of the lowest published fares, then use the resources outlined here to try and beat those fares.

A number of major airlines fly into **Aeropuerto Comodoro Arturo Merino Benitez** (SCL), the international airport in Santiago. From North America, the most convenient and generally the cheapest is the **American Airlines/Lan Chile** alliance (American ☎800-433-7300, www.aa.com; Lan Chile US☎800-735-5526, www.lanchile.com). **Delta Airlines** (☎800-221-1212; www.delta.com), **United Airlines** (☎800-241-6522; www.united.com), and **US Air** (☎800-428-4322; www.usair.com) all have routes from the US to Chile, but tend to be slightly more expensive. From the UK and Western Europe, **Lufthansa** (UK ☎0845-7737-747, Germany 49 (0)1803-803-803; www.lufthansa.com) generally has the best prices. In France and Spain, **Air France** (☎0820 820 820; www.airfrance.com) and **Iberia** (☎93 401 3131; www.iberia.com) respectively have cheaper fares. Except for a few of the above listings, most major airlines have partnerships with some of the Latin American airlines listed below and connect through US hubs such as Miami and Atlanta or through Latin American hubs like São Paulo, Buenos Aires, and Lima. This is also true for **South African Airlines** (☎0861 359 722; www.flysaa.com) in South Africa; **Qantas Airlines** (☎1300 650 729; www.qantas.com.au) in Australia; and **Air New Zealand** (☎0800 737 000; www.airnz.com.nz) in New Zealand.

You will probably find flying on one of the following Latin American airlines a better deal, if any of their limited departure points is convenient for you.

LanChile (US ☎800-735-5526, Santiago 600 526 2000; www.lanchile.com) is one of the largest airlines in Latin America. Partnered with some of the largest international airlines, including American Airlines, it serves six continents.

Varig Airlines (US ☎800-990-5534, Brazil 55 11 3119 7007; www.varig.com) is another one of the larger airlines. Part of the Star Alliance, a conglomerate of 14 international airlines, Varig has flights from almost every part of the world.

Aero Continente (US ☎877-482-2501; www.aerocontinente.com.pe). A Peruvian airline that mostly serves Latin America, Aero Continente is rapidly becoming Chile's second most dominant airline.

Avianca (US ☎212-399-0858; www.avianca.com.co) is a Colombian airline with flights to major cities throughout Latin America. Most flights connect through Bogotá.

Grupo TACA (US ☎800-535-8780; www.grupotaca.com) is an alliance of several Central American airlines with TACA Peru. With direct flights from most major cities in the US, Grupo TACA is one of the more convenient airlines for flying within the Americas.

AIR COURIER FLIGHTS

Those who travel light should consider courier flights. Couriers help transport cargo on international flights by using their checked luggage space for freight. Generally, couriers must travel with carry-on luggage only and deal with complex flight restrictions. Most flights are round-trip only, with short fixed-length stays (usually one week) and a limit of a one ticket per issue. Most of these flights also operate only out of major gateway cities, mostly in North America. Round-trip courier fares from the US to Chile run about US$300 to US$500. Most flights leave from New York, Los Angeles, San Francisco, or Miami in the US; and from Montreal, Toronto, or Vancouver in Canada. Generally, you must be over 21 (in some cases 18). In summer, the most popular destinations usually require an advance reservation of about two weeks (you can usually book up to two months ahead). Super-discounted fares are common for "last-minute" flights (three to 14 days ahead). See www.aircourier.org or www.courier.org for more information.

STANDBY FLIGHTS

Traveling standby requires considerable flexibility in arrival and departure dates and cities. Companies dealing in standby flights sell vouchers rather than tickets, along with the promise to get to your destination (or near your destination) within a certain window of time (typically 1-5 days). You call in before your specific window of time to hear your flight options and the probability that you will be able to board each flight. You can then decide which flights you want to try to make, show up at the appropriate airport at the appropriate time, present your voucher, and board if space is available. Vouchers can usually be bought for both one-way and round-trip travel. You may receive a monetary refund only if every available flight within your date range is full; if you opt not to take an available (but perhaps less convenient) flight, you can only get credit toward future travel. It is difficult to receive refunds, and clients' vouchers will not be honored when an airline fails to receive payment in time. Carefully read agreements with any company offering standby flights, as tricky fine print can leave you in a lurch. To check on a company's service record in the US, call the Better Business Bureau (☎212-533-6200).

TICKET CONSOLIDATORS

Ticket consolidators, or **"bucket shops,"** buy unsold tickets in bulk from commercial airlines and sell them at discounted rates. The best place to look is in the Sunday travel section of any major newspaper (such as the *New York Times*), where many bucket shops place tiny ads. Call quickly, as availability is typically extremely limited. Not all bucket shops are reliable, so insist on a receipt that gives full details of restrictions, refunds, and tickets, and pay by credit card (in spite of the 2-5% fee) so you can stop payment if you never receive your tickets. For more info, see www.travel-library.com/air-travel/consolidators.html.

TRAVELING FROM THE US AND CANADA

Travel Avenue (☎ 800-333-3335; www.travelavenue.com) searches for best available published fares and uses several consolidators to beat that fare. Other consolidators worth trying are **Interworld** (☎ 305-443-4929; fax 443-0351); **Pennsylvania Travel** (☎ 800-331-0947); **Rebel** (☎ 800-227-3235; travel@rebeltours.com; www.rebeltours.com); **Cheap Tickets** (☎ 800-377-1000; www.cheaptickets.com); and **Travac** (☎ 800-872-8800; fax 212-714-9063; www.travac.com). Yet more consolidators on the web include the **Internet Travel Network** (www.itn.com); **Travel Information Services** (www.tiss.com); **TravelHUB** (www.travelhub.com); and **The Travel Site** (www.thetravelsite.com). Keep in mind that these are just suggestions to get you started in your research; *Let's Go* does not endorse any of these agencies. As always, be cautious, and research companies before you hand over your credit card number.

TRAVELING FROM THE UK, AUSTRALIA, AND NEW ZEALAND

In London, the **Air Travel Advisory Bureau** (UK ☎ 0207 636 5000; www.atab.co.uk) can provide names of reliable consolidators and discount flight specialists. From Australia and New Zealand, look for consolidator ads in the travel section of the *Sydney Morning Herald* and other papers.

BY LAND

In 1925, a multinational coalition initiated a project that would make the road tripper's ultimate fantasy come true, the Pan-American Highway, more commonly known as the Panamericana. Running from Alaska to Chile, the route was supposed to connect an entire hemisphere. Unfortunately, the underdeveloped and highly dangerous Panama-Colombia border proved too much to overcome. Nevertheless, road warriors can still embark on a shorter version from almost anywhere in South America and arrive in Chile.

BORDER CROSSINGS

Border crossings in Chile range in their quality and accessibility. Except in the far south, most crossings are high up in the Andes. Accessibility is dependent in all cases on the weather, since heavy snow can close many of the passes. To travel into Peru and Bolivia, Arica is the best city from which to leave. There are several more routes to Bolivia farther south, but they tend to be less well-maintained and service is not as regular. Options for entering Argentina abound; the most popular route is from Santiago to Mendoza. Buses run frequently to Mendoza, and from there, service extends to locations throughout South America, including Buenos Aires, São Paulo, and Río de Janeiro. Farther south, passes become more common as the Andes descend. However, snow and ice also become more of a problem. Some of the more popular routes to Argentina are from Puerto Montt to Bariloche, Puerto Ingeniero Ibáñez to Calafate, Puerto Natales to Tierra del Fuego, and Puerto Williams to Ushuaia.

ESSENTIALS

INTO ARGENTINA

Visitors from English-speaking countries do not need to obtain a visa ahead of time. Free tourist visas are issued upon arrival for 90 days and can be extended for another 90 days. Numerous border crossings interrupt the long border between Argentina and Chile. The most commonly used route runs between Mendoza and Santiago (see p. 147), where thousands of buses and cars pass through the renown mile long tunnel through the Andes. Crossings in the north include the route from Copiapó through Paso San Francisco (see p. 248) and from La Serena through Paso de Agua Negra (see p. 237). Boats between Puerto Williams and Ushuaia (see p. 494) are a popular choice among locals and tourists alike. The roads from Osorno to Bariloche (see p. 394), Chile Chico to Los Antiguos (see p. 458), Puerto Natales to Cerro Castillo (see p. 475), and Porvenir to Río Grande (see p. 487) also see heavy tourist traffic, and are the most frequently used routes in the south.

INTO BOLIVIA

Except for citizens of Ireland, travelers from English-speaking countries do not need to pay for a visa for stays shorter than 90 days. However, tourist visas (issued upon arrival) generally expire after 30 days and can only be renewed in La Paz (see p. 329). There is a US$25 airport fee when flying out of the country. The most common crossing to Bolivia is from Arica to La Paz (see p. 329). The road over the Andes has recently been renovated and makes for a fairly comfortable trip. Many travelers also cross from San Pedro de Atacama through Hito Cajón, on their way to see the spectacular Salar de Uyuni (see p. 285).

INTO PERU

Visas are not required for stays shorter than 90 days for travelers from English-speaking countries. However, there is a US$25 airport fee when flying out of the country. The easiest and most common Chile-Peru border crossing is between Arica and Tacna (see p. 317). The road is well maintained and heavily traveled by buses and cars.

GETTING AROUND CHILE

BY PLANE

Although flying is generally not the cheapest manner of traveling, Chile does have one of the best air transit systems in South America. Dominated by LanChile, a former state-owned enterprise that has become one of the most successful international airlines in Latin America, service between major cities is frequent and competitively priced when purchased in advance.

From Santiago, you can almost always fly direct to most of the major cities including Antofagasta, Iquique, Arica, La Serena, Copiapó, Concepción, Temuco, Puerto Montt, and Punta Arenas; those that aren't direct may include intermediary touch-downs that do not require switching planes. Other smaller cities such as Calama, El Salvador, Valdivia, Osorno, Coyhaique, and Balmaceda can be reached with a local connecting flight. **LanChile** (Chile ☎ 600 526 2000; www.lanchile.com), its subsidiary **LanExpress** (formerly Ladeco; Chile ☎ 600 526 2000; www.lanexpress.com) and, to a lesser extent, **Aero Continente** (Chile ☎ 600 242 4242; www.aerocontinente.com.pe) are the major domestic airlines. **Avant Airlines**, once Lan Chile's biggest competitor, has recently suspended its service. All three of the above airlines have offices in major cities and have online reservation services.

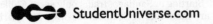

Airfares vary depending on how far in advance you purchase your tickets and where you are going. Buying tickets three to seven days in advance is almost always cheaper than buying last minute, saving you US$30-40. Purchasing tickets more than a week in advance can be even cheaper. However, LanChile often does have special last-minute fares available that can often be up to 50 percent off. They publish drastically discounted *"último minuto"* fares every Tuesday evening for flights departing on the following three days. Round-trip tickets are also much cheaper than two one-way tickets. If you are traveling from anywhere in central or northern Chile to the southern regions around Punta Arenas and Tierra del Fuego, air travel is always the most economical way of arriving there.

For multiple internal flights, a **Visit Chile Pass** is definitely your best option. **Lan-Chile** (see above) offers a very good package. For US$250 you receive three flight coupons that allow you to fly anywhere within the country as long as your international flight was with LanChile. You can also purchase up to three more coupons for US$60 each. The pass is more expensive if you do not use LanChile as your international carrier; US$350 for the first three and $80 thereafter.

BY BUS

Buses are the cheapest and most convenient way of traveling. The quality of buses varies depending on the route, but the system as a whole is one of the best in Latin America and, by US and European standards, is fairly inexpensive. All of Chile's major roads are paved and in good condition with the exception of the Camino Austral in the southern region of Aisén—the road is rough and, in many places, incomplete. Secondary roads in rural areas tend to be gravel and sometimes dirt.

The bus system in cities and large towns is generally very well organized. Most buses leave from central terminals at regularly scheduled times. For common routes, you can simply show up and purchase tickets from the offices at the time you wish to travel; you may, however, want to call in advance during holidays and some summer weekends. Smaller towns without specific bus terminals often have a central street or block with bus company offices where passengers are picked up. In rural areas, bus stops are generally along the road, and travelers must flag down the bus they want and purchase tickets on board.

Fares depend on how far you go as well as how you travel. Buses in Chile have several different classes. For major routes, the norm is **pullman,** a standard 44-seat bus similar to those used in the US and Europe. For longer routes, **semi-cama** is a more comfortable but more expensive option. These buses have partially reclining seats and serve drinks and snacks. **Salón cama** is the most luxurious, with fully reclining seats (that are nearly bed-like) and meal service. Although this costs considerably more than the standard service, it can be worth the expense for long trips. Shorter routes tend to use smaller buses and sometimes oversized vans. Fares are generally fixed when departing from a station or a company's office, although there are occasionally student discounts for longer trips. In more rural areas, when catching buses from a road-side bus stop, fees are up to the discretion of the driver, so there is often room for negotiation.

BY TRAIN

Chile's train service is very limited. Starting in Santiago, trains only serve Chillán, Concepción, and Temuco. Rates are moderate (US$15-18 one-way) for tourist class. However, the late-night schedule of many trains can make a sleeping compartment (US$35-50 one-way) worth the money. Round-trip fares are cheaper, as well. In general, though, buses are more frequent and less expensive.

BY CAR

Despite the quality of Chile's bus system, travelers may find that, at times, having a car can be a good option. Especially in the desert areas of the north and the Lakes District in the south, a car may be the only way to reach some remote sites. Driving in Chile is not as much of a challenge as you might think. Road conditions are very good on main roads, and four-wheel-drive vehicles are available to rent for people headed into more rural areas. Chileans also drive on the right side of the road and follow similar traffic laws to those of the United States (although they are known for changing lanes without signaling).

Technically, the only thing a tourist needs to drive in Chile is a valid license from their home country. However, it is highly recommended that travelers obtain an International Driving Permit (see p. 71). Although car rental companies do not require it, *carabineros* (police) in rural areas have been known to detain drivers who do not have one. (Unlike in some of its neighboring countries, Chile's *carabineros* strictly enforce traffic laws such as speed limits and cannot be bribed.) Drivers should also double check that their insurance will cover them while abroad, as many companies have special rules concerning the developing world.

RENTING

A rented car can be invaluable if you are planning on spending a significant amount of time in some of Chile's more rural or underdeveloped areas. However, rentals are not cheap and the various costs of renting, insuring, and operating a car add up quickly. In most cases, negotiating a deal with a taxi service or local tour agency is more economical and much less hassle. If you are going to rent, keep in mind the region in which you will be driving. Most rural areas have roads in good enough shape that a normal sedan can handle them. However, in the desert area of the north, the Camino Austral, and many of the national parks, a four-wheel-drive vehicle is strongly recommended, if not necessary. Also, when negotiating with rental agencies, remember that cheaper cars tend to be less reliable and harder to handle on difficult terrain. Less expensive four-wheel-drive vehicles in particular tend to be more top heavy, and are more dangerous when navigating particularly bumpy roads.

RENTAL AGENCIES. Almost every major city in Chile has at least a few car rental companies. Arrangements can be made the day of, although during the Chilean summer it is often necessary to call ahead in order to guarantee you get the type of car you want. Arrangements for many rental companies can now be made over the Internet, and all places accept advance reservations over the phone. For major international renters like Hertz, you can also call the office in your home country and have them make the reservation, but prices and availability can vary greatly. Numbers for these local offices are included in town listings; for home-country numbers, call your toll-free directory.

To rent a car from most establishments in Chile, you need to be at least 25 years of age with a valid license or International Drivers Permit. However, many agencies will rent to travelers as young as 23 or 21, although there is sometimes an additional charge or insurance fee.

Large national and international chains often allow one-way rentals, picking up in one city and dropping off in another. There is usually a minimum hire period and sometimes an extra drop-off charge that varies with the distance between the two points. Major rental agencies in Chile include:

Hertz (Santiago ☎2 420 5200; www.hertz.com) has locations in almost every major city in Chile.

Budget (Santiago ☎2 362 3200; www.budget.com) is another international rental agency in Chile.

Thrifty (Santiago ☎ 2 225 6328; www.thrifty.com) is more limited in its coverage, serving only a few cities.

COSTS AND INSURANCE. Rental car prices start at around US$50 a day from national companies, US$40 from local agencies, with significant discounts when renting for six days or more. Expect to pay US$30-50 more for larger cars and for four-wheel-drive vehicles. Cars with **automatic transmission** can cost up to US$10 a day more than standard manuals (stick shift), and in some places, automatic transmission is hard to find in the first place. It is virtually impossible, no matter where you are, to find an automatic four-wheel-drive vehicle.

Most rental packages offer unlimited mileage, although smaller businesses tend to give you a certain allowance per day. Return the car with a full tank of gas to avoid high fuel charges at the end. Be sure to ask whether the price includes **insurance** against theft and collision. Remember that if you are driving on an **unpaved road** in a rental car, you are almost never covered by insurance; ask about this before leaving the rental agency. Beware that cars rented on an **American Express** or **Visa/Mastercard Gold or Platinum** credit cards in Chile might *not* carry the automatic insurance that they would in some other countries; check with your credit card company. Insurance plans almost always come with an **excess** (or deductible) of around US$350-500 for conventional vehicles; excess can be higher for younger drivers and for four-wheel-drive vehicles.

ON THE ROAD. Driving in the populated areas of Chile is not difficult. All the main roads are paved and generally well-maintained. More rural areas, however, tend to have gravel and dirt roads. Drivers should be extra-cautious when traveling through the mountains and parks area, as roads are generally narrow and winding and are often covered by fog. The strictly-enforced speed limit is generally 50km/hr. in towns and cities and 100km/hr. on the highway. **Petrol (gasoline)** prices vary, but average about US$0.50 per liter in cities and US$0.60 per liter in outlying areas; gas stations generally sell unleaded (*sin plomo*), leaded (*con plomo*), and diesel fuel, so pay attention to what type of fuel your car requires. Also, when traveling through remote areas such as the desert region in the north, be sure to carry an extra container of gas, since stations are few and far between.

> **DRIVING PRECAUTIONS.** When traveling in the summer or in the desert, bring substantial amounts of water (a suggested 5 liters of **water** per person per day) for drinking and for the radiator. For long drives to unpopulated areas, register with police before beginning the trek, and again upon arrival at the destination. Check with the local automobile club for details. When traveling for long distances, make sure tires are in good repair and have enough air, and get good **maps**. A **compass** and a **car manual** can also be very useful. You should always carry a **spare tire** and **jack, jumper cables, extra oil, flares, a torch (flashlight),** and **heavy blankets** (in case your car breaks down at night or in the winter). If you don't know how to **change a tire,** learn before heading out, especially if you are planning on traveling in deserted areas. Blowouts on dirt roads are exceedingly common. If you do have a breakdown, **stay with your car;** if you wander off, there's less likelihood trackers will find you.

CAR ASSISTANCE. The Automóvil Club de Chile (Santiago ☎ 2 431 1000; www.aclub.cl) has locations in most major cities and offers a variety of services, including car insurance and towing. Purchasing coverage from them gives you free towing for up to 120km from anywhere in the country. Some of the larger rental agencies like Hertz also offer roadside assistance.

DRIVING PERMITS AND CAR INSURANCE

INTERNATIONAL DRIVING PERMIT (IDP). If you plan to drive a car while in Chile, you should obtain an International Driving Permit (IDP). While, you can rent a car with only a valid license from your home country, it may be a good idea to get an IDP anyway in case you are in a situation (e.g. an accident or stranded in a small town) where the police do not know English; information on the IDP is printed in ten languages, including Spanish.

Your IDP, valid for one year, must be issued in your home country before you depart for Chile. An application for the permit usually needs to include one or two photos, a current local license, an additional form of identification, and a fee. To apply, contact the national or local branch of your home country's automobile association.

CAR INSURANCE. Most credit cards cover standard insurance. If you rent, lease, or borrow a car, you will need a **green card,** or **International Insurance Certificate,** to certify that you have liability insurance and that it applies abroad. Green cards can be obtained at car rental agencies, car dealers (for those leasing cars), some travel agents, and some border crossings. Rental agencies may require you to purchase theft insurance.

TAXIS AND COLECTIVOS

Taxis can be hired to reach destinations not easily accessible by public transportation. Taxis tend to linger around the Plaza de Armas in cities and large towns, and "radio taxis" can also be called for pick-up at a private residence or hostel. For longer trips, it is advisable to negotiate a price beforehand (feel free to ask around for a driver offering the lowest fares). **Colectivos** are taxis with established routes and prices that are generally shared among several travelers. *Colectivos* tend to be significantly cheaper than taxis and are widespread throughout Chile. See the **Transportation** section in individual cities and towns for more information.

BY BOAT

Ferries are not a very common mode of transportation except in the southern region of Aisén. In this rugged country, the Camino Austral is in rough condition and incomplete. Boats are often the only way to continue moving. The route from Puerto Montt to Puerto Natales has become fairly popular since it avoids the hassle of multiple bus and ferry lines while passing through the islands and fjords that dominate the region (see p. 415 for more information).

BY BICYCLE

For those hard-core travelers who want to set their own pace and keep in shape, bicycling through Chile can be a very rewarding experience. Cyclists should be careful though, as main roads like the Panamericana, although well maintained, have heavy traffic. Secondary and rural roads can also be a problem due to their narrowness and lack of paved shoulders. Travelers should look for a sturdy mountain bike to carry them through these regions.

When traveling by bike, be sure to carry extra supplies. These include tools for bike repairs such as replacement inner tubes for the tires and also food and drink. In remote areas where water is difficult to come by, carrying extra is a necessity. Wind can also be a major problem, especially in the Patagonia region—try and do most of your biking during periods of the day when the wind has subsided.

BY THUMB

> ❗ **HITCHHIKING AND SAFETY** *Let's Go* urges you to use common sense
> if you decide to hitch and to consider all the serious risks before you make that
> decision. The information listed below and throughout the book is not intended
> to recommend hitchhiking.

Hitchhiking in Chile is fairly common. In the summer months, you will actually
see Chileans themselves (generally students) hitting the road with their packs on
and their thumbs out. Truck drivers are the most likely to pick up passengers
and the easiest way to catch a ride is to find a service stop off of a main highway
and ask around. In more rural areas, individuals and families in cars are more
likely to pick you up, however, there is less traffic in general, so be prepared to
wait awhile.

As always, use common sense when hitchhiking. If something does not feel right
then don't do it; you are better off waiting. Women traveling alone should never
hitchhike. Despite the fact that it is a popular mode of travel, because of safety
concerns, *Let's Go* does not recommend hitchhiking and urges you to consider all
possible risks before doing so.

SPECIFIC CONCERNS

WOMEN TRAVELERS

Women exploring on their own inevitably face some additional safety concerns,
but it's easy to be adventurous without taking undue risks. If you are concerned,
consider staying in hostels which offer single rooms that lock from the inside.
Communal showers in some hostels are safer than others; check them before set-
tling in. Stick to centrally located accommodations and avoid solitary late-night
treks or metro rides. Always carry extra money for a phone call, bus, or taxi. **Hitchhiking** is never safe for lone women, and is not even recommended for two women
traveling together.

Chile, like most Latin American countries, is a very *machista* culture. Men will
often make comments about passing women, especially in front of other men,
although public violence against women is rare. To lessen unwanted attention,
dress conservatively, especially in rural areas, and try to blend in. Look as if you
know where you're going and consider approaching older women or couples for
directions if you're lost or uncomfortable. When comments are made, ignore
them and keep moving. The vast majority of men will never go beyond that. If the
man is extremely persistent or you are in a situation where you cannot move
away (i.e. on a bus or metro) then a firm, loud, and very public *"¡Déjame en
paz!"* (DEH-ha-me en pas; "Leave me alone!") or *"¡No me moleste!"* (no me mole-
EST-e; "Don't bother me!") should be enough to dissuade him. If harassment does
not subside, do not hesitate to turn to an older woman for support or seek out a
police officer.

As a general rule, memorize the emergency numbers in places you visit, and consider carrying a whistle on your keychain. A self-defense course will both prepare
you for a potential attack and raise your level of awareness of your surroundings
(see **Self Defense**, p. 42). Also be sure you are aware of the health concerns that
women face when traveling (see p. 48).

TRAVELING ALONE

There are many benefits to traveling alone, including independence and greater interaction with locals. On the other hand, any solo traveler is a more vulnerable target of harassment and street theft. As a lone traveler, try not to stand out as a tourist, look confident, and be especially careful in deserted or very crowded areas. If questioned, never admit that you are traveling alone. Maintain regular contact with someone at home who knows your itinerary. For more tips, pick up *Traveling Solo* by Eleanor Berman (Globe Pequot Press; US$17) or subscribe to **Connecting: Solo Travel Network,** 689 Park Road, Unit 6, Gibsons, BC V0N 1V7, Canada (☎604-886-9099; www.cstn.org; membership US$35). **Travel Companion Exchange,** P.O. Box 833, Amityville, NY 11701, USA (☎631-454-0880, or in the US ☎800-392-1256; www.whytravelalone.com; US$48), will link solo travelers with companions with similar travel habits and interests.

ESSENTIALS

OLDER TRAVELERS

In Chile, senior citizen discounts are not as common as in other countries, but there are some opportunities for discounts on transportation, museums, movies, theaters, concerts, restaurants, and accommodations. The books *No Problem! Worldwise Tips for Mature Adventurers*, by Janice Kenyon (Orca Book Publishers; US$16), and *Unbelievably Good Deals and Great Adventures That You Absolutely Can't Get Unless You're Over 50*, by Joan Rattner Heilman (NTC/ Contemporary Publishing; US$13), are both excellent resources. For more information, contact one of the following organizations:

ElderTreks, 597 Markham St., Toronto, ON M6G 2L7 (☎800-741-7956; www.elder-treks.com). Adventure travel programs for the 50+ traveler in Chile.

Elderhostel, 11 Ave. de Lafayette, Boston, MA 02111 (☎877-426-8056; www.elderhostel.org). Organizes 1- to 4-week "educational adventures" in Chile on varied subjects for those 55+.

The Mature Traveler, P.O. Box 15791, Sacramento, CA 95852 (☎800-460-6676). Deals, discounts, and travel packages for the 50+ traveler. Subscription US$30.

GAY AND LESBIAN TRAVELERS

Like in most of Latin America, the strong Catholic tradition in Chile is still fairly intolerant of homosexuality. The tactile nature of Chilean culture is helpful in some ways, since it is not uncommon for women to hold hands and men to embrace. However, actions beyond that are met with suspicion.

Despite this obstacle, there is a growing, vocal gay, lesbian, and bisexual community, especially in Santiago. There is also a small but thriving gay rights movement led by the Movimiento Unificado de Minorías Sexuales (MUMS; www.orgullo.cl). Their website has links to other gay community resources, including organizations like Lambda News (www.lambdanews.cl) and Gay Chile (www.gaychile.cl). *Let's Go* tries to list gay-friendly nightlife wherever possible.

The are also a number of US and European companies that focus on international issues of homosexuality. Listed below are contact organizations, mail-order bookstores, and publishers that offer materials addressing some specific concerns. **Out and About** (www.planetout.com) is a comprehensive site addressing gay travel concerns that offers a bi-weekly newsletter addressing travel concerns.

Gay's the Word, 66 Marchmont St., London WC1N 1AB, UK (☎+44 20 7278 7654; www.gaystheword.co.uk). The largest gay and lesbian bookshop in the UK, with both fiction and non-fiction titles. Mail-order service available.

Giovanni's Room, 1145 Pine St., Philadelphia, PA 19107, USA (☎215-923-2960; www.queerbooks.com). An international lesbian/feminist and gay bookstore with mail-order service (carries many of the publications listed below).

International Lesbian and Gay Association (ILGA), 81 rue Marché-au-Charbon, B-1000 Brussels, Belgium (☎+32 2 502 2471; www.ilga.org). Provides political information, such as homosexuality laws of individual countries.

> ▼ **FURTHER READING: BISEXUAL, GAY, AND LESBIAN.**
> *Spartacus International Gay Guide 2001-2002.* Bruno Gmunder Verlag (US$33).
> *Damron's Accommodations,* and *The Women's Traveler.* Damron Travel Guides (US$14-19). For more info, call ☎800-462-6654 or visit www.damron.com.
> *Ferrari Guides' Gay Travel A to Z, Ferrari Guides' Men's Travel in Your Pocket,* and *Ferrari Guides' Inn Places.* Ferrari Publications (US$16-20). Purchase the guides online at www.ferrariguides.com.
> *The Gay Vacation Guide: The Best Trips and How to Plan Them,* Mark Chesnut. Citadel Press (US$15).

TRAVELERS WITH DISABILITIES

Traveling with a disability through Chile may be difficult. The more upscale hotels will generally be able to meet your needs, but public transportation and most hostels are ill-equipped. Those with disabilities should inform airlines and hotels of their disabilities when making arrangements; some time may be required to prepare special accommodations. Call ahead to restaurants, hotels, parks and other facilities to find out about the existence of ramps, the widths of doors, the dimensions of elevators, etc., keeping in mind that handicapped-accessible places are scarce.

USEFUL ORGANIZATIONS

Mobility International USA (MIUSA), P.O. Box 10767, Eugene, OR 97440, USA (voice and TDD ☎541-343-1284; www.miusa.org). Sells *A World of Options: A Guide to International Educational Exchange, Community Service, and Travel for Persons with Disabilities* (US$35).

Society for the Advancement of Travel for the Handicapped (SATH), 347 Fifth Ave., #610, New York, NY 10016, USA (☎212-447-7284; www.sath.org). An advocacy group that publishes free online travel information and the travel magazine *OPEN WORLD* (US$18, free for members). Membership US$45, students and seniors US$30.

TOUR AGENCIES

Directions Unlimited, 123 Green Ln., Bedford Hills, NY 10507, USA (☎800-533-5343). Books customized individual and group vacations for the physically disabled; not an info service.

MINORITY TRAVELERS

Nearly all of the Chilean population is white or *mestizo,* having fairer skin than the populations of most South American countries. This general homogeneity means that any minority traveler—regardless of skin color—is bound to stick out, particularly when traveling in rural or less touristed parts of the country. In general, the whiter your skin, the better treatment you'll receive. (Unfortunately, light-skinned travelers are viewed as wealthier and therefore may be more likely to be the targets of crime or subjected to inflated prices at markets.) Travelers of African or Asian descent will likely attract more attention from curious locals and their gawking children, who may point, giggle, and stare. Asians may find themselves called *chinos*, while African Americans may be called *morenos* or *negros*. None of these words are meant to be offensive; to Chileans they are simply descriptive terms and are uttered as expressions of surprise upon sighting someone of a different ethnicity. In many rural areas, non-Spanish speakers may be viewed by some as a threat, and generally, across the country, natives are not accommodating or patient with non-Spanish speakers. It helps to try to speak Spanish and get accustomed with words and phrases particular to Chilean Spanish—it'll put the locals at ease and probably make you many friends. Check out the Spanish Quick Reference in the Appendix for a useful, on the road guide (p. 497).

TRAVELERS WITH CHILDREN

Family vacations often require that you to slow your pace, and always require that you plan ahead. Fortunately, Chile is a child-friendly country, with few health risks. Unless your child is unusually sensitive, Chilean food is easily digestible and the water is almost always drinkable. Ticket sellers and tourist agencies are also partial to families with young children, so when making arrangements as a family always try to negotiate.

Discounts for children vary, so be sure to inquire everywhere you go. Children under 12 get special prices on flights but do not on long-distance bus rides. Nevertheless, city buses generally allow young children on for free. Hostel and hotel owners will often charge one full price for two kids and tourist agencies will sometimes allow young children to go for half price or even for free.

If you rent a car, make sure the rental company provides a car seat for younger children. Also be sure that your child carries some sort of ID in case of an emergency or in case he or she gets lost.

For more information, consult one of the following books:

Backpacking with Babies and Small Children, Goldie Silverman. Wilderness Press (US$10).

How to take Great Trips with Your Kids, Sanford and Jane Portnoy. Harvard Common Press (US$10).

Have Kid, Will Travel: 101 Survival Strategies for Vacationing With Babies and Young Children, Claire and Lucille Tristram. Andrews McMeel Publishing (US$9).

Adventuring with Children: An Inspirational Guide to World Travel and the Outdoors, Nan Jeffrey. Avalon House Publishing (US$15).

Trouble Free Travel with Children, Vicki Lansky. Book Peddlers (US$9).

DIETARY CONCERNS

Vegetarians should not have too much trouble finding decent culinary options in Chile's major cities, especially in Santiago, which has several vegetarian restaurants. It is more difficult in rural areas, however, where meat and fish are major parts of the meal. However, many dishes can easily be altered by asking for them *sin carne* (without meat) or requesting extra vegetables. For more information, check out the North American Vegetarian Society, P.O. Box 72, Dolgeville, NY 13329 (☎518-568-7970; www.navs-online.org), which publishes information about vegetarian travel, including *Transformative Adventures, a Guide to Vacations and Retreats* (US$15). You can also visit your local bookstore, health food store, or library, and consult *The Vegetarian Traveler: Where to Stay if You're Vegetarian,* by Jed and Susan Civic (Larson Publications; US$16).

Jewish travelers keeping Kosher will also have to pay special attention while on the road. Chile has only a small population of Jews, concentrated mostly in Santiago and a few other major cities. There are some Kosher markets and a few restaurants in these cities. However, if you are strict in your observance, you may have to prepare your own food on the road. Check out Kosher Delight (www.kosherdelight.com), Shamash (www.shamash.org/kosher), and the World Jewish Congress (www.wjc.org.il) for more info on Chile's Jewish communities. Another good resource is the *Jewish Travel Guide,* by Michael Zaidner (Vallentine Mitchell; US$17).

OTHER RESOURCES

Let's Go tries to cover all aspects of budget travel, but we can't put *everything* in our guides. Listed below are books and websites that can serve as jumping off points for your own research.

TRAVEL PUBLISHERS AND BOOKSTORES

Hippocrene Books, Inc., 171 Madison Ave., New York, NY 10016, USA (☎718-454-2366; www.hippocrenebooks.com). Publishes foreign-language dictionaries and language learning guides.

Hunter Publishing, 470 W. Broadway, Fl. 2, South Boston, MA 02127, USA (☎617-269-0700; www.hunterpublishing.com). Has an extensive catalog of travel guides and diving and adventure travel books.

Rand McNally, P.O. Box 7600, Chicago, IL 60680, USA (☎847-329-8100; www.randmcnally.com), publishes road atlases.

Adventurous Traveler Bookstore, P.O. Box 2221, Williston, VT 05495, USA (☎800-282-3963; www.adventuroustraveler.com).

Travel Books & Language Center, Inc., 4437 Wisconsin Ave. NW, Washington, D.C. 20016, USA (☎800-220-2665; www.bookweb.org/bookstore/travelbks/). Over 60,000 titles from around the world.

WORLD WIDE WEB

Almost every aspect of budget travel is accessible via the Web. Within ten minutes at the keyboard, you can make a reservation at a hostel, rent a car, or find out exactly how much a train from Santiago to Concepción costs.

Listed here are some budget travel sites to start off your surfing; other relevant web sites are listed throughout the book. Because website turnover is high, use search engines (such as www.google.com) to strike out on your own.

THE ART OF BUDGET TRAVEL

How to See the World: www.artoftravel.com. A compendium of great travel tips, from cheap flights to self defense to interacting with local culture.

Rec. Travel Library: www.travel-library.com. A fantastic set of links for general information and personal travelogues.

Lycos: cityguide.lycos.com. General introductions to cities and regions throughout Chile, accompanied by links to applicable histories, news, and local tourism sites.

INFORMATION ON CHILE

CIA World Factbook: www.odci.gov/cia/publications/factbook/index.html. Tons of vital statistics on Chile's geography, government, economy, and people.

Geographia: www.geographia.com. Highlights, culture, and people of Chile.

Go Chile: www.gochile.cl. A comprehensive source of information for travelers offering detailed facts about cities, national parks, and the amenities available in different parts of Chile.

Atevo Travel: www.atevo.com/guides/destinations. Detailed introductions, travel tips, and suggested itineraries.

AND OUR PERSONAL FAVORITE...

Let's Go: www.letsgo.com. Our constantly expanding website features photos and streaming video, online ordering of all our titles, info about our books, a travel forum buzzing with stories and tips, and links that will help you find everything you ever wanted to know about Chile.

ESSENTIALS

ALTERNATIVES TO TOURISM

Traveling from place to place around the world may be a memorable experience. But if you are looking for a more rewarding and complete way to see the world, you may want to consider Alternatives to Tourism. Working, volunteering, or studying for an extended period of time can be a better way to understand life in Chile. This chapter outlines some of the different ways to get to know a new place, whether you want to pay your way through, or just get the personal satisfaction that comes from studying and volunteering. In most cases, you will feel that you partook of a more meaningful and educational experience—something that the average budget traveler often misses out on.

VISA INFORMATION

US citizens planning on studying or working in Chile need to apply for an appropriate visa before embarking. Check the US Embassy website (www.chile-usa.org) for the consulate that has jurisdiction over your state. The process of collecting the necessary documentation, sending it to your local consulate, and receiving approval may take several weeks, so start far ahead of your expected departure date.

Student Visas require: a) a passport that will be valid until after the expected end date, b) a health certificate stating that you are in good health and have been HIV tested, c) a police certificate confirming that you are a citizen in good standing, d) four recent passport photos, e) US$61 fee, f) proof of acceptance from the university or program you will be attending in Chile, and g) a statement from your bank or parents showing that you are financially solvent.

Temporary Resident Visas require items a) through e) listed above and g) a statement of your financial solvency. If you have been hired by a Chilean company for long-term work, you may have to apply for a **Working Visa**. This requires a contract signed by both you and your employer that is notarized in Chile plus a recommendation from a past employer.

STUDYING ABROAD

Study abroad programs range from basic language and culture courses to college-level classes, often for credit. In order to choose a program that best fits your needs, you will want to find out what kind of students participate in the program and what sort of accommodations are provided. In programs that have large groups of students who speak the same language, there is a trade-off. You may feel more comfortable in the community, but you will not have the same opportunity to practice a foreign language or to befriend other international students. For accommodations, dorm life provides a better opportunity to mingle with fellow students, but there is less of a chance to experience the local scene. If you live with a family, there is a potential to build lifelong friendships with Chileans and to experience day-to-day life in more depth, but conditions can vary greatly from family to family.

Those relatively fluent in Spanish may find it cheaper to enroll directly in a Chilean university, although getting college credit may be more difficult. Some American schools still require students to pay them for credits they obtain elsewhere. Most university-level study-abroad programs are meant as language and culture enrichment opportunities, and therefore are conducted entirely in Spanish. Still, many programs do offer classes in English and beginner- and lower-level language courses. A good resource for finding programs that cater to your particular interests is www.studyabroad.com, which has links to various semester abroad programs based on a variety of criteria, including desired location and focus of study. The following is a list of organizations that can help place students in university programs abroad, or have their own branch in Chile.

AMERICAN PROGRAMS

The following is a list of several US-based programs that organize study abroad opportunities. There also a number of universities that run their own programs in Chile including Clemson University, Farleigh Dickinson University, State University of New York (SUNY), Syracuse University, Tufts University, University of Miami, and University of Wisconsin.

Institute for Study Abroad—Bulter University (IFSA-Butler), Butler University, 1100 W. 42nd Street, Suite 305, Indianapolis, IN 46208-3345 (☎ 888-344-9299; www.ifsa-butler.org), runs programs in conjunction with the **Cooperating Opportunities Program of America (COPA)** in Santiago, Valparaíso, and Viña del Mar.

Council on International Educational Exchange (CIEE), 633 3rd Ave., 20th fl., New York, NY 10017-6706 (☎ 800-407-8839; www.ciee.org/study), sponsors work, volunteer, academic, and internship programs in Chile.

School for International Training, College Semester Abroad, Admissions, Kipling Rd., P.O. Box 676, Brattleboro, VT 05302 (☎ 800-336-1616 or 802-257-7751; www.sit.edu). Semester- and year-long programs in Chile run US$10,600-13,700. Also runs the **Experiment in International Living** (☎ 800-345-2929; fax 802-258-3428; www.usexperiment.org), 3- to 5-week summer programs that offer high-school students cross-cultural homestays, community service, ecological adventure, and language training in Chile and cost US$1900-5000.

State University of New York (SUNY) at Plattsburgh, 101 Broad Street, Plattsburgh, NY 12901-2681 (☎ 518-564-2395; www2.plattsburgh.edu/las), runs study abroad programs in several major Chilean cities.

Institute for International Education of Students, 33 North LaSalle Street, 15th Floor, Chicago, IL 60602 (☎ 800-995-2300; www.iesabroad.org), provides opportunities for course study, internships and service work.

International Partners for Study Abroad (IPSA), 3646 W. Brown Street, Suite A, Phoenix, AZ 85051 (☎ 602-942-6734; www.internationalstudyabroad.com), has a variety of language programs, university courses, and short-term work opportunities.

PROGRAMS IN CHILE

Studying in Chile is common for US students and is easy to arrange. The most convenient way is to apply to a US program like one of those listed above. For a flat fee they will generally take care of enrolling you in your selected university, arrange housing, and provide important resources and support while you are living there. When selecting a program pay attention to what kind of living and studying situation they offer. Depending on your preferences, you will have to decide whether to stay with a family or in a dormitory, to study in the actual university classes or in special program classes, and to have a very supportive program or a

ALTERNATIVES TO TOURISM

more flexible, independent one. This varies greatly from program to program, so be sure to talk with other students who have previously participated in them or with university study-abroad advisors.

If you are looking for a more independent immersion experience, you may want to enroll directly in Chilean universities with international exchange programs. This is a much more difficult task since you have to negotiate your application to the university and arrange housing on your own, but is often more rewarding.

LANGUAGE SCHOOLS

Unlike American universities, language schools are frequently independently-run international or local organizations or divisions of foreign universities that rarely offer college credit. Language schools are a good alternative to university study if you desire a deeper focus on the language or a slightly less-rigorous courseload. These programs are also good for younger high school students that might not feel comfortable with older students in a university program. Some good programs include:

Facultad de Filosofía de la Universidad de Chile, Paraguay 265, office 1712 (☎678 7040), in Santiago. Offers semester-long Spanish courses for foreigners. Semesters run from late Aug.-early Dec. and from Mar.-July (US$600). Monthly homestays available (US$350 per month). Open M-F 9am-6pm.

Instituto de Letras (☎354 7882), on the San Joaquín campus of the Universidad Catolica in Santiago. Offers shorter Spanish language courses and arranges homestays. Private lessons US$25 per hr., group courses US$17 per hr. Open M-F 9am-6pm.

Natalis Language Center, Vicuña Mackenna 6, 7th fl. (☎222 8721; www.natalislang.com), in Santiago. Customized course offerings available, ranging from 20-25hr. per week with up to 5 students. 3-week, 75hr. courses are the most popular offering (US$330), and private lessons are available as well (US$13 per hr., US$600 per 100hr.).

Universidad Austral de Chile, Casilla 567 (☎213 911), in Valdivia. Students interested in learning Spanish can enroll directly in the university and take special courses offered by the language department in addition to or instead of regular classes. Many professors also offer private lessons for about CH$7000 per hr.

¡école!, General Urrutia 592 (☎441 675; ecole@entelchile.net; www.ecole.cl), in Pucón, offers Spanish classes starting at CH$9000 for a 2hr. class. with 4 people. Up to CH$14,000 for one-on-one instruction. Package rates available for long-term study.

WORKING

There are two main schools of thought about working abroad. Some travelers want long-term jobs that allow them to get to know another part of the world in depth (e.g. teaching English or working in the tourist industry). Other travelers seek out short-term jobs to finance their travel. They usually seek employment in the service sector or in agriculture, working for a few weeks at a time to finance the next leg of their journey. This section discusses both short- and long-term opportunities for working in Chile. Make sure you understand Chile's **visa requirements** for working abroad. See the box on p. 78 for more information.

To find casual, private employment, it helps to post an ad in a local store or pay for an advertisement in the classified sections of newspapers such as *El Mercurio* (☎56 2 330 1111) or *La Tercera* (☎56 2 550 7000). *El Rastro* (☎56 2 672 2051), a paper that publishes free advertisements, is also a good resource.

For US college students, recent graduates, and young adults, the simplest way to get legal permission to work abroad before leaving home is through **Council Exchanges Work Abroad Programs.** Fees are from US$300-425. Council Exchanges can help you obtain a three- to six-month work permit/visa and also provides assistance finding jobs and housing. To acquire an official work permit once in Chile, visit the *Extranjeria* section of the State *Intendencia* (☎56 2 676 5800), on the corner of Calle Moneda and Morande in Santiago, for information about applying for a one-year work permit. The permit can usually be updated later with little difficulty to a *visación de residencia*, which allows an unlimited stay in Chile.

LONG-TERM WORK

If you're planning on spending a substantial amount of time (more than three months) working in Chile, search for a job well in advance. International placement agencies are often the easiest way to find employment abroad, especially for teaching English. **Internships,** usually for college students, are a good way to segue into working abroad, although they are often unpaid or poorly paid (many say the experience, however, is well worth it). Be wary of advertisements or companies that claim the ability to get you a job abroad for a fee—often the listings are out of date or readily available online or in newspapers. It's best, if going through an organization, to use one that's reputable. Some good ones include:

GoAbroad.com, 8 East First Avenue, Suite 102, Denver, CO 80203, USA (☎720-570-1702; fax 720-570-1703; Info@goabroad.com; www.goabroad.com). Lists jobs in Chile and has specific sites for teaching, interning, and general working abroad.

Internships International, LLC, 1612 Oberlin Rd, Raleigh, NC 27608, USA (Dec.-May ☎919-832-1575; June-Nov. 207-443-3019; fax June-Nov. 207-442-7942; intintl@aol.com; www.rtpnet.org/~intintl). Offers unpaid internships and connections to language schools in cities around the world, including Santiago. Fee of US$800 guarantees placement in an internship.

TEACHING ENGLISH

Teaching jobs abroad are rarely well-paid, although some elite private American schools can pay somewhat competitive salaries. Volunteering as a teacher in lieu of getting paid is also a popular option, and even in those cases, teachers often get some sort of a daily stipend to help with living expenses. In almost all cases, you must have at least a bachelor's degree to be a full-fledged teacher, although college undergraduates can often get summer positions teaching or tutoring. There are a wealth of jobs available teaching English in Chile—it is perhaps the most accessible employment for those looking to work in the country for an extended period of time.

Many schools require teachers to have a **Teaching English as a Foreign Language (TEFL)** certificate. Not having one does not necessarily exclude you from finding a teaching job, but certified teachers often find higher paying jobs. Native English speakers working in private schools are most often hired for English-immersion classrooms where no Spanish is spoken. Those volunteering or teaching in public, poorer schools, are more likely to be working in both English and Spanish. Placement agencies or university fellowship programs are the best resources for finding teaching jobs in Chile. The alternative is to make contacts directly with schools or just to try your luck once you get there. If you are going to try the latter, the best time of the year is several weeks before the start of the school year. The following organizations are extremely helpful in placing teachers in Chile.

Bridge-Linguatec International, 915 South Colorado Blvd., Denver, CO 80246, USA (☎303-777-7783, toll-free in the US and Canada 800-724-4210; www.bridgelinguatec.com). Places chosen applicants in positions teaching English to business people in Santiago. Certification is required for all teachers; preference given to those who certify with Bridge-Linguatec. Pay starts at US$7 an hour. Contact Eugenia at teachers@linguatec.cl (cc:rbrown@bridgelinguatec.com) with an email expressing interest; attach resume.

International Schools Services (ISS), 15 Roszel Rd., Box 5910, Princeton, NJ 08543-5910, USA (☎609-452-0990; fax 609-452-2690; www.iss.edu). Hires teachers for more than 200 overseas schools including in Chile; candidates should have experience teaching or with international affairs; 2-year commitment expected.

TeachAbroad.com, 8 East First Avenue, Suite 102, Denver, CO 80203, USA (☎720-570-1702; fax 720-570-1703; Info@goabroad.com; www.teachabroad.com). Part of the umbrella company **GoAbroad.com,** this service allows you to search listings for teaching positions around the world, and has numerous listings for Chile.

Teaching English in Chile (http://lauca.usach.cl/~mfarias/index.html). Website offers links to resources and opportunities for English teachers in Chile.

English First (☎56 374 2180) is probably the best place in Chile to start seeking for a job teaching English as a foreign language. The establishment is well respected, and prefers to hire candidates with a TEFL certificate and/or prior teaching experience. Compensation begins at an hourly rate (around CH$3000-7000 per hr.). Also provides information on other programs hiring teachers.

Wall Street Institute for English, Caupolicán 299 (☎41 910 791; www.wsi.es; wsiconce@chilesat.net), in Concepción. Seeks part- or full-time English instructors year-round. Pay is CH$3000-3500 per hour. Contact the director, Patricia Pinto, or manager Katherine Maidstone for more information. Open M-F 8am-9:30pm, Sa 10am-2pm.

AU PAIR WORK

Au pairs are typically women, aged 18-29, who work as live-in nannies, caring for children and doing light housework in foreign countries in exchange for room, board, and a small spending allowance or stipend. Most former au pairs speak favorably of their experience, and of how it allowed them to really get to know the country without the high expenses of traveling. Drawbacks, however, often include long hours of constantly being on-duty and the somewhat mediocre pay. Much of the au pair experience really does depend on the family you're placed with. The agencies below are a good starting point for looking for employment as an au pair.

Au Pair Chile (www.aupairchile.cl/HomeEnglish.htm; agencies@aupairchile.com). Interviews women wishing to travel to Chile to work as an au pair; also matches Chilean au pairs with foreign families.

Great Au Pair Enterprises, contact InteliMark Enterprises, LLC, 21001 San Ramon Valley Blvd., Suite A4-326, San Ramon, CA 94583, USA (☎925-361-0800; fax 925-551-8484; info@greataupair.com; www.greataupair.com). Become a registered au pair and search for families in countries worldwide, including Chile.

SHORT-TERM WORK

Traveling for long periods of time can get expensive; therefore, many travelers try their hand at odd jobs for a few weeks at a time to make some extra cash to carry them through another month or two of touring around. Although a notarized contract of employment and contract visa is required to remain legally employed in Chile, since short-term placements usually offer free or discounted room and/or board in exchange for work, a work permit is not required. Other short-term work opportunities like fruit-picking, bartending, and waitressing abound, and the small amount of cash earned usually absolves the traveler from legal mandates. Short-term job opportunities are occasionally listed at www.gonomad.com/alternatives. Most often, these short-term jobs are found by word of mouth, or simply by talking to the owner of a hostel or restaurant. Many places, especially due to the high turnover in the tourism industry, are always eager for help, even if only temporary. *Let's Go* tries to list temporary jobs like these whenever possible; check the practical information sections in larger cities, or check out the list below for some of the available short-term jobs in popular destinations.

Ancud: Fundación Con Todos, Eleutario Ramírez 207, 2nd fl. (☎65 622 604; contodos@entelchile.net). The Fundación deals with projects available among a growing network of farmers in Chiloé making individual farms available for accommodations under the premise that visitors will participate in farm activities. Longer-term volunteer projects can be arranged. **Agroturismo** (☎65 628 333; www.portalsur.cl), operating out of the same office, handles the marketing and tourist side of the corporation.

Chillán: Hostal Canada, Libertad 269 (☎42 234 515), hires one English-speaking tour guide to take hostel guests on 4hr. excursions on bicycle around the Chillán area, from Dec. to Mar. Trips include visits to the city's historic neighborhoods and parks. Guide must lead two 4hr. tours every weekday, and one 4hr. tour on Saturday. Compensation includes a minimum-wage salary (CH$105,000 per month) and lunch; great compensation possible for experienced candidates. Contact Mariela Albornoz, the hostel's owner, for more information.

Concepción: Restaurant Da Giovanni, Caupolicán 346, Local 3 (☎41 241 936), hires up to two waiters for work in Dec. and Jan. Work is M-F 48 hours per week, with a salary of CH$120,000 per month, plus tips. Contact the owner, Gilda Carnese, for information. **Havana Club,** Barros Arana 1356 (☎41 224 006), hires up to 5 waiters and 4 bouncers during Jan.-Mar. to work 8 hours per day W-Sa. Pay is CH$100,000 per month. Call the office during business hours for more information.

Los Angeles: Restaurant El Alero, Colo Colo 235 (☎43 320 058), hires waiters and kitchen helpers, usually between Nov. and Mar. Pay is CH$110,000 per month plus tips for a 48-hr. work week (12hr. shifts). Contact the administrator for more information. **Hotel y Hostería Salto del Laja** (☎43 321 706 or 43 313 956; fax 43 313 996), in Salto del Laja, 27km north of Los Angeles. Needs waiters, cooks, receptionists, laundry washers, and other staff for its hotel and restaurant during the summer. Monetary compensation. Contact Martinentel Puff, the general manager, by the beginning of Dec. for the following summer.

Pucón: Hostería y Restaurant Mill-Rahue, O'Higgins 460 (☎45 441 610), between Ansorena and Panguín, hires three or more waiters and three or four cooks for summer-time work Jan.-Mar. Employees must work 10hr. per day, 7 days a week. Waiters receive about CH$110,000 per month, plus tips, while cooks make CH$300,000 per month. Talk with manager for more information. **Turismo M@yra,** O'Higgins 447 (☎45 444 514; myhostel@hotmail.com), hires secretaries and salespeople to work in their office Dec.-Feb. Pay is CH$110,000 per month plus a 3% commission, with lodging provided. Employees work 6 days per week 10-12hr. per day. Talk to owners for more information.

Rancagua: Max Sabor. Hires 3-4 waiters and other workers for 2-3 month periods, especially when business picks up in Nov. Drop in or phone and speak to the manager. Monetary compensation. **Granja Amanda** (☎72 198 2346) on Carrelea de la Fruta, El Manzano. Needs up to 10 people at a time with training in (or a keen desire to learn) landscaping and tree care, year-round, for long-term, full-time work. Housing, meals, and salary available. Contact Juan Enrique (☎099 536 6050) for more information. **Hotel Termas de Cauquenes** (☎72 899 010; fax 72 899 009; termasdecauquenes@terra.cl), Termas de Cauquenes, Machalí. Hires people to work at the reception desk and in the dining room in Feb. for one month. 8hr. per day, with a salary of CH$120,000 per month. Contact the manager of the hotel, Sabine Acklin, for more info.

San Fernando: Hotel Termas del Flaco (☎711 832) needs as many as 70 seasonal workers in various hotel jobs from Dec. to Apr. Monthly salary of CH$110,000. Contact Dan Miguel Gúzman (☎711 832) for more information.

Villarrica: Politur Villarrica, Camilo Henríquez 475 (☎/fax 72 414 547; foresta007@hotmail.com; http://politurvillarrica.enynter.net or www.politur.com), looks for up to 2 guides or office workers to help out Dec.-Feb. and possibly at other times of the year. Candidates must speak English and Spanish. Duties range from leading tours in parks or on river rapids to regular office tasks. The position pays CH$35,000 per month and is geared towards university students doing 3-month *practicums*. Contact Erna Avello Aedo.

VOLUNTEERING

Volunteering can be one of the most fulfilling experiences you can have, especially if you combine it with the wonder of travel in a foreign land. Since Chile has low volunteer statistics in comparison with other countries (a meager 4% of the adult Chilean population volunteers, against 56% in the US, 34% in Germany, and 34% in neighboring Peru that leads in the region), there are endless volunteer programs in Chile. Many of these services charge a fee to participate in the program and to do work. These fees can be surprisingly hefty (although they frequently cover airfare and most, if not all, living expenses). Try to do research on a program before committing—talk to people who have previously participated and find out exactly what you're getting into, as living and working conditions can vary greatly. Different programs are geared toward different ages and levels of experience, so make sure that you are not taking on too much or too little. The more informed you are and the more realistic expectations you have, the more enjoyable the program will be.

Most people choose to go through a parent organization that takes care of logistical details, and frequently provides a group environment and support system. There are two main types of organizations—religious (often Catholic), and nonsectarian—although there are rarely restrictions on participation for either. For a list of organizations that offer volunteer opportunities in Chile visit www.chilevoluntario.cl.

Earthwatch, 3 Clocktower Pl., Suite 100, Box 75, Maynard, MA 01754, USA (☎800-776-0188 or 978-461-0081; www.earthwatch.org). Arranges 1- to 3-week programs in Chile to promote conservation of natural resources. Costs average $1700 plus airfare.

Elderhostel, Inc., 11 Avenue de Lafayette, Boston, MA 92111-1746, USA (☎877-426-8056; fax 877-426-2166; www.elderhostel.org). Sends volunteers age 55 and over around the world to work in construction, research, teaching, and many other projects. Costs average $100 per day plus airfare.

Fundación Chol-Chol, Casilla 14, Nueva Imperial, Novena Region, Temuco, Chile (☎56 45 197 4864; www.volunteerabroad.com/listings). Offers volunteer opportunities for a minimum of 3 months to Spanish speakers possessing an undergraduate degree to work in local health clinics, in the field of agricultural development, within the forestry program, and as grant writers or computer programmers.

Habitat for Humanity International, 121 Habitat St., Americus, GA 31709, USA (☎229-924-6935 ext. 2551; www.habitat.org). Volunteers build houses in over 83 countries for anywhere from 2 weeks to 3 years. Short-term program costs range from US$1200-4000.

Hogar de Cristo (www.hogardecristo.com) selectively recruits volunteers to work in branches scattered throughout Chile. Volunteers can be assigned to one of several programs, among them, working with street children, orphans, or pre-schoolers; monitoring the organization's Chile-wide crisis hotline; and ministering to the elderly, sick, and dying. The organization is predominantly Catholic in membership as well as mission. Consult the bilingual website to apply.

Outreach International: Community Volunteers Program, P.O. Box 59065, Birmingham, AL 35259, USA (☎205-871-1552; fax 205-933-6133). In Chile, Galvarino Gallardo 2155, Providencia, Santiago (☎/fax 56 2 209 5295). Offers young adults (18+) an opportunity to participate in international social development, eco-conservation, and poverty alleviation projects. Volunteers take part in a 2-day orientation in Chile and spend 10 days doing development work. They live with host families in the community where they work. Other cultural activities and field trips are organized for volunteers, and they have the option of studying Spanish under the guidance of local qualified tutors. Approximately US$1850 per project, including airfare, cost of living, daily excursions, social activities, and 10hr. Spanish tutoring.

Raleigh International, 27 Parsons Green Lane, London SW6 4HZ, UK (☎+44 20 7371 8585; fax +44 20 7371 5116; international@raleigh.org.uk; www.raleighinternational.org). Prince William spent his gap-year working on sustainable environmental and community projects in Tortel, Chile through Raleigh. If that doesn't commend it enough, surf the website to learn more about the 3-month expeditions that are part of a longer program including training weekends and workshops. With an emphasis on personal development and cultural awareness, Raleigh volunteers in Chile track endangered species with the financial support of Chilean government ministries, international development groups, and the Millennium Commission.

Volunteers for Peace, 1034 Tiffany Rd., Belmont., VT 05730, USA (☎802-259-2759; www.vfp.org). Arranges placement in work camps in Chile. Membership required for registration. Annual *International Workcamp Directory* US$20. Programs average US$200-500 for 2-3 weeks.

FOR FURTHER READING ON ALTERNATIVES TO TOURISM

Alternatives to the Peace Corps: A Directory of Third World and U.S. Volunteer Opportunities, by Joan Powell. Food First Books, 2000 (US$10).

How to Live Your Dream of Volunteering Oversees, by Collins, DeZerega, and Heckscher. Penguin Books, 2002 (US$17).

International Directory of Voluntary Work, by Whetter and Pybus. Peterson's Guides and Vacation Work, 2000 (US$16).

International Jobs, by Kocher and Segal. Perseus Books, 1999 (US$18).

Overseas Summer Jobs 2002, by Collier and Woodworth. Peterson's Guides and Vacation Work, 2002 (US$18).

Work Abroad: The Complete Guide to Finding a Job Overseas, by Hubbs, Griffith, and Nolting. Transitions Abroad Publishing, 2000 (US$16).

Work Your Way Around the World, by Susan Griffith. Worldview Publishing Services, 2001 (US$18).

SANTIAGO

Founded as an obscure colonial outpost devoid of the protracted, often bloody clashes typical of its neighbors, Santiago has evolved into one of South America's most impressive metropolises and has established itself as Chile's dynamic liaison with the outside world. Once barely able to sustain its founders, the city has experienced an explosive growth rate over the last few decades, and is now home to over 5 million Chileans, a third of the nation's populace. This expansion has sent the capital sprawling across the Maipo Valley, threatening to infiltrate the farmlands and vineyards that tenuously skirt Santiago's suburban strip development.

In the heart of the city, an impressive subway system, large plazas, stalwart cathedrals, and recently renovated colonial facades give downtown an unmistakably European feel. And while the cobblestone pedestrian walkways of *el centro* teem with businesspeople, adjacent neighborhoods beat to the syncopated pulse of student and artistic tastes. In niches around the city, Chilean tradition meets international variety in the culinary, theatrical, musical, and nocturnal offerings that greet the curious visitor.

Nevertheless, with the rewards of growth come significant environmental and social costs. In winter, a brilliant white blanket of snow coats the Andes mountains surrounding the city—Santiago is denied this alpine view as a layer of smog settles over the city. A similar psychological cloud casts a dark shadow on the minds of the *Santiaguinos*—the memory of Pinochet's military dictatorship (1973-1989). The impacts of one of South America's most brutal and oppressive regimes is still a subject of heated debate in both universities and cafes in the city. The soaring skyscrapers, wide boulevards, and modern metro of downtown Santiago testify to the economic stability forged by Pinochet. Yet, the legacy of a high unemployment rate, an ineffective social support system, and a divided, highly unequal society have tainted this success, leaving the new democracy the unenviable task of balancing continued growth with rising social demands.

For those seeking a sojourn from such serious matters, however, Santiago offers a collection of idyllic daytrips perfect for travelers who prefer Sauvignon Blanc, surfboards, or ski boots to politics and pollution. And although residents of Santiago frequently spend their weekends away, they'll be the first to extol the virtues of their city and its economy. After all, Santiago has weathered strong earthquakes, fierce floods, and financial crises to emerge as a beacon of civil order, economic success, and cultural vibrancy on a struggling continent.

HIGHLIGHTS OF SANTIAGO

GORGE on fresh seafood and juicy fruit in the wrought-iron Mercado Central (p. 102).

PARTY till the sun comes up. From the ultra chill **Pub La Boheme** (p. 117) to the posh **Tantra** (p. 118), you'll be jumping all night.

GASP at the view of Santiago and the Andes atop **Cerro San Cristobal** (p. 107).

WONDER about the origins of Pablo Neruda's eccentric collection of odds and ends in the **Museo La Chascona** (p. 109).

FLY on skis or with the aid of a hang-glider over **Valle Nevado** (p. 111).

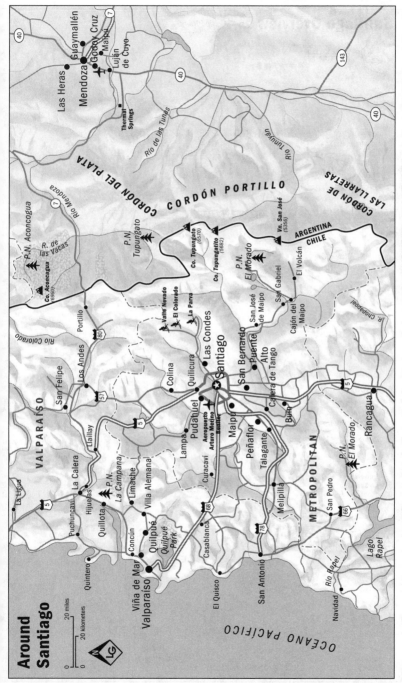

Around Santiago

SANTIAGO

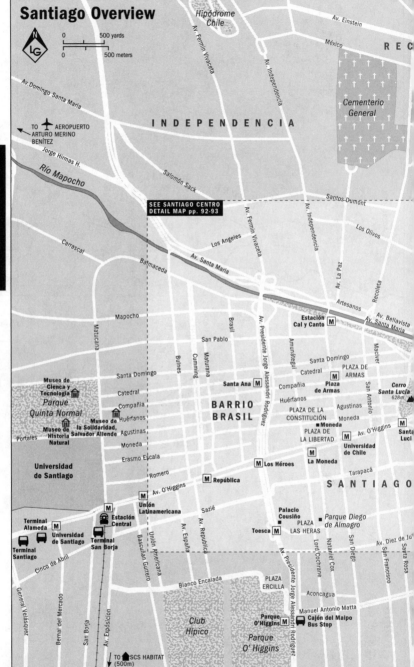

Santiago Overview

N LG

0 — 500 yards
0 — 500 meters

Hipódrome Chile

Av. Einstein

México

R E C

Cementerio General

Av. Domingo Santa María

TO ✈ AEROPUERTO ARTURO MERINO BENÍTEZ

Av. Fermín Vivaceta

Av. Independencia

I N D E P E N D E N C I A

Jorge Hirmas H.

Río Mapocho

Salomón Sack

Santos-Dumónt

SEE SANTIAGO CENTRO DETAIL MAP pp. 92-93

Av. Fermín Vivaceta

Av. Independencia

Los Olivos

Carrascal

Los Angeles

Av. Santa María

Av. La Paz

Recoleta

Balmaceda

Artesanos

Av. Bellavista
Av. Santa María

Mapocho

Brasil

Av. Presidente Jorge Alessandri Rodríguez

Estación Cal y Canto M

Macher

Matucana

San Pablo

Amunátegui

Santa Domingo

Bulnes

Cumming

Maturana

Santa Domingo

Catedral

PLAZA DE ARMAS

Cerro Santa Lucía 628m

Museo de Ciencia y Tecnología 🏛
Parque Quinta Normal

Santa Domingo

Santa Ana M

Compañia

Plaza de Armas M

San Antonio

Catedral

B A R R I O
B R A S I L

Huérfanos

Agustinas

Compañía 🏛

PLAZA DE LA CONSTITUCIÓN

Moneda

M
Santa Lucí

Museo de la Solidaridad, Salvador Allende

Huérfanos

■ Moneda

Av. O'Higgins

Portales

Museo de Historia Natural 🏛

Agustinas

PLAZA DE LA LIBERTAD

M
Universidad de Chile

Santa Luci

Moneda

M La Moneda

Universidad de Santiago

Erasmo Escala

Romero

M Los Héroes

Tarapacá

Av. O'Higgins

M República

S A N T I A G O

Unión Latinamericana

Sazié

Palacio Cousiño

■ *Parque Diego de Almagro*

M
Estación Central

PLAZA LAS HERAS

Terminal Alameda M

Universidad de Santiago

Av. España

Av. República

Toesca M

Lord Cochrane

Nataniel Cox

San Diego

Av. Diez de Ju

Terminal Santiago

Terminal San Borja

Unión Americana

Basculian Guerrero

Av. Presidente Jorge Alessandri Rodríguez

San Francisco

Santa Rosa

Cinco de Abril

Blanco Encalada

PLAZA ERCILLA

Aconcagua

General Velásquez

Bernal del Mercado

San Borja

Av. Exposición

Club Hípico

Parque O'Higgins M

Parque O' Higgins

Manuel Antonio Matta

Cajón del Maipo Bus Stop

Av. Presidente Jorge Alessandri Rodríguez

TO 🏠 SCS HABITAT (500m)

OLETA

SEE PROVIDENCIA & LAS CONDES
DETAIL MAP pp. 105

ementerio
Católico

Canal El Cármen

Parque
Metropolitano

Jardín
Botánico
Mapulemo

LAS
CONDES

Av. Santa María

Nueva Costanera

Vitacura

Av. Presidente Kennedy

Club de Golf
Los Leones

Presidente Riesco

El Cerro

Av. Pedro de Valdivia N

Los Conquistadores

Río Mapocho

Andres Bello

Vitacura

Av. Apoquindo

M Tobalaba

M
El Golf

Estadio
Francés

Av. Tobalaba

Cerro San Cristóbal
880m ▲

M Los Leones

Lota

Av. Perú

Dominica

Jardín
Zoological

Av. Providencia

M
Pedro de Valdivia

PROVIDENCIA

Carlós Antúnez

Av. Los Leones

PLAZA
LORETE
COUSIÑO

M
Manuel Montt

Eliodoro Yáñez

PLAZA
RIO DE JANEIRO

BARRIO
BELLAVISTA

M Salvador

Parque Gran
Bretaña

Pocuro

Colegio
San Ignacio

Parque
Forestal

PLAZA
BAQUENDA

Alfaréz Real

PLAZA DE LA
ALCALDESA

PLAZA
EL BOSQUE

M
Bellas Artes

M Baquedano

PLAZA P.
DE VALDIVIA

M
U. Católica

Parque
Bustamante

Rancagua

Parque Inés
de Suárez

Av. Pedro de Valdivia

Campus
Oriente U.
Católica

Parque
Bustamante M

Av. Francisco

Salvador

Bilbao

Av. José Infante

Av. José Miguel Claro

Av. Manuel Montt

Av. Antonio Varas

Doctor Ferrer

Sen J. Guzmán E

Curicó

Av. Vicuña Mackenna

M Santa Isabel

TO PARQUE POR LA PAZ,
BARRIO ECOLÓGICO

Santa Isabel

Av. Bustamente

PLAZA
FRANCKE

Simón Bolívar

Lira

M
Irárrazaval

SEE ÑUÑOA DETAIL
MAP pp. 106

amachuco

Carmen

Av. Portugal

Irarrázaval

Dublé Almeyda

José Domingo Cañas

Eduardo Castillo Velasco

ÑUÑOA

PLAZA
ÑUÑOA

Manuel Antonio Matta

Av. Vicuña Mackenna

San Eugenio

Av. Grecia

Campos de Deporte

Av. Pedro de Valdivia

Av. Josee Pedro Alessandri

Sierra Bella

TO VIÑA
SANTA CAROLINA ▼ M Ñuble

Av. Grecia

Estadio
Nacional

S
A
N
T
I
A
G
O

✈ INTERCITY TRANSPORTATION

Airport: Aeropuerto Arturo Merino Benítez (☎ 601 9709, flight info 690 1900 and 690 1706, tourist info 601 9320) is the well-maintained hub for all international and domestic flights. **Taxis** from the airport to Santiago Centro cost CH$6000-8000. A cheaper alternative is **Transfer** (CH$3200 to Santiago Centro; CH$3700-4500 to Providencia, Ñuñoa, and Las Condes), which acts like a *colectivo* but offers door-to-door service. Find its booth near the baggage terminal. **Tur Bus Aeropuerto** drops off at M: Los Héroes (every 15min., CH$1200). To get to the airport, **TransVip** (☎ 677 3000) will pick you up 3hr. before flight departure (CH$3200). You can also take the metro to Los Héroes and take **Tur Bus** from there, or go to the shuttle's headquarters on Moneda, just west of San Martín.

International and Domestic Airlines:

AeroContinente, Huérfanos 935 (☎ 242 4242), in Santiago Centro. Open M-F 9am-6pm. Flies to: **Arica** (3½hr., CH$175,000) via **Iquique** (2½hr., CH$170,900); **Calama** (3hr., CH$I96,000) via **Antofagasta** (2hr., CH$160,000); **Guayaquil, Ecuador** (2¼hr., CH$174,000); **La Paz, BOL** (1½hr., CH$174,000); **Lima, PER** (1½hr., US$114,000); **Quito, Ecuador** (2¼hr., CH$174,000). Fares can be significantly lower in winter.

LanChile, Huérfanos 926 (☎526 2000; www.lanchile.com), in Santiago Centro, is generally more expensive than AeroContinente but offers special last-chance fares for flights within 4 days. Some fares drop dramatically in winter. Flies to: **Arica** (CH$130,000); **Buenos Aires, ARG** (2hr., CH$168,000); **Mendoza, ARG** (2hr., CH$75,000); **Puerto Montt** (2hr., CH$100,000). Open M-F 9am-6pm, Sa 9am-12:30pm.

American Airlines, Huérfanos 119 (☎679 0000 or 601 9272), in Santiago Centro. Open M-F 9am-6:30pm.

British Airways, Isidora Goyenechea 2934, office 302 (☎330 8610), in Santiago Centro.

Continental (in alliance with **Copa**), Fidel Oteíza 1921, 7th fl. (☎200 2101 or 200 2101), in Santiago Centro.

Delta, Fidel Oteíza 1971, office 201 (☎274 1819).

Taca, Dr. Barros Borgoño 105, 2nd fl. (☎235 5500).

United, El Bosque Norte 0177, 19th fl. (☎632 0279 or 632 0280). Tickets must be purchased 7 days in advance with at least a 4-day stay, including Sa.

Trains: Metro Estación Central (☎376 8500 or 376 8312), next to the Alameda bus station, west of downtown on the main Metro line. **EFE** trains only run south, and the line terminates at Temuco. Goes to **Chillán** (5hr.; 7:45am, 1:45, 6:45pm; CH$5000) and **Temuco** (13hr., 8 and 9pm, CH$8400) via **Concepción** (9hr., CH$6800); all trains via **Rancagua** (1¼hr., CH$2100). Fares are for standard seats; bunks available for about twice the price.

Buses: The four main bus terminals in Santiago are located on the southwestern side of the city. Beware of super cheap tickets—they might be missing the space, comfort, and quality that make 25hr. bus rides such a joy. For those willing to spend a few bucks, the luxury coaches with "beds" are worth it on longer journeys. **Tur Bus** is the largest and most reputable company in Chile, but is often slightly more expensive. **Pullman** is the second largest company, with numerous individual, regional-based franchises. These two companies have frequent and regular departures to most locations. **Buses Ahumada** and **Tas Choapa** are two other sizeable companies. All fares are quoted one-way, but slight discounts can usually be gained by purchasing round-trip tickets.

Terminal San Borja, Alameda 3250, Santiago Centro (☎776 0645). M: Estación Central. The largest in Chile and a hub of activity for the **central** and **northern zones**. The higher the ticket booth number, the farther north that bus goes. **Tur Bus** (☎778 7836 or 270 7500) goes to: **Arica** (29hr.; 10:30am, 4, 10:30pm; CH$16,000); **Copiapó** (12hr., CH$7200); **Iquique** (24hr., CH$15,000); **Valparaíso** and **Viña del Mar** (1¾hr., every 15min., CH$2600). **Pullman Bus** (☎778 7086 or 778 8230) has regional lines to: **Arica** (CH$22,000); **Calama** (CH$24,500); **Copiapó** (CH$10,000); and **Iquique** (CH$25,000).

Terminal Alameda, Alameda 3712. M: Universidad de Santiago. **Tur Bus** (☎270 7500 or 270 7425) and **Pullman** (☎778 1185 or 776 2424) depart from here. Buses run both **northern** and **southern routes**. **Tur Bus** goes to **Viña del Mar** and **Valparaíso** (2hr., every 30min., CH$2800). **Pullman** only goes to **Viña del Mar** (CH$2600).

Terminal Santiago (Terminal Sur), Alameda 3850 (☎376 1755 or 376 1750). M: Universidad de Santiago, next to Terminal Alameda. Trips to **southern Chile** and **international destinations**. This is the largest col-

Santiago Centro

See map p. 92-93

SANTIAGO

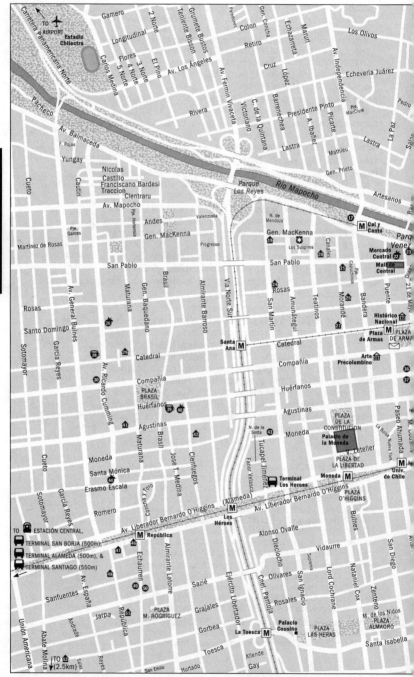

SANTIAGO

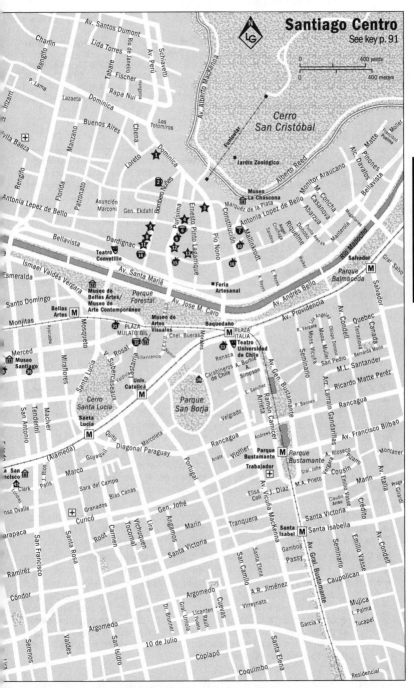

Santiago Centro
See key p. 91

S A N T I A G O

lection of independent and small-scale companies outside of the San Borja terminal. **Tur Bus** is conspicuously absent.

Terrapuerto Los Héroes, Tucapel Jiménez 21 (☎420 0099). M: Los Héroes. **Pullman International** goes to **Buenos Aires** (20hr., CH$30,000). **Pullman del Sur** has overnight coaches to **Temuco** (9hr., 10pm, CH$5500) and **Valdivia** (12hr., 9:30pm, CH$5800). **Buses Ahumada** (☎696 9798 or 696 9799) goes to **Los Andes** and **San Felipe** (every 30min., CH$1800 each), and to **Mendoza, ARG** (9:30am and 1pm, CH$7000). **Tas Choapa** (☎696 9326 or 697 0062) goes to several destinations in the north and south, including **Antofagasta** (6pm, CH$13,000) and **Puerto Montt** (4 per evening, CH$6000).

ORIENTATION

Alameda, Santiago's main street, runs southwest to northeast; it is called **O'Higgins** to the west and **Providencia** to the east. When visible, the Andes are a good directional reference to the east and southeast. The city itself has clusters of interesting districts, interspersed amongst bland residential areas and bleak, sooty commercial strips.

Policemen (clad visibly in green) are stationed prominently throughout the city, making the streets very safe in daylight and relatively safe at night. Of course, as in any major city, it pays to exercise caution and guard possessions closely. Stay out of the parks (especially Cerro Santa Lucia and San Cristobal) after closing time, as muggings have occurred there.

Walking the city can be quite tiring, especially without direction or proper cartographic guidance. Each major neighborhood near the center warrants a day or half-day's exploration, time permitting.

Barrio Brasil is an inexpensive area replete with small universities, institutes, and cafes that lend it an authentic, bohemian feel. Although the streets themselves aren't much to look at, seek out good restaurants on Ricardo Cummings. **Internet access,** especially south of Alameda, offers a useful diversion.

Santiago Centro sets a high standard and an ambitious daytime pace for Chile's capital. This central tourist district harbors the nation's governmental and commercial lifeblood. Museums, expansive plazas, pedestrian walkways, and *sandwicherías* come together to constitute this people-watching mecca. On the east side of Centro, **Plaza Italia** forms the crossroad from which the many buses headed to various destinations in the city and surrounding suburbs depart.

Barrio Bellavista is the most vibrant gay and lesbian district in all of Chile. As the hotspot of Santiago's art and entertainment world, Barrio Bellavista is notorious for the late-night revelry that ensues here year-round. Ignore the somewhat scuzzy appearance of the neighborhood—instead, enjoy the cheap food and good times that abound here.

Providencia stretches east toward the Andes and encompasses **Barrio Suecia,** the snazzier, more upscale version of Bellavista. Fancy hotels and cafes abound, and the urge to go on a shopping spree will inevitably hit in one of many commercial complexes.

Las Condes, a well-to-do residential zone with interesting colonial architecture, features several large shopping malls and premier hotels at the foot of the Andes.

Barrio Ñuñoa, unlike its neighbors, does not lie on Alameda. Situated several kilometers south of Las Condes and Providencia along Los Leones, it is quiet and residential, with the exception of the periodically raucous *Estadio Nacional* and the weekend crowds that gather at Plaza Ñuñoa for an assortment of bars, cafes, and theatrical performances. All this plus nice views of the peaks will draw many visitors despite its distant from the convenient curves of the Metro schema. For information on transport to Plaza Ñuñoa, see the Insider's City sidebar (p. 116).

▐ LOCAL TRANSPORTATION

Buses: Known as *micros*, these can be boarded anywhere, especially along **Av. O'Higgins/Alameda/Providencia.** Bus routes are marked on the windshield, with most buses traveling along part of Alameda and passing **Plaza Italia.** Bus riding is not for the meek; energetically flagging one down and declaring your desired destination (if you are not sure the bus is headed that way) is known to work quite well. Make sure you watch for your stop and head for the doors or ring the buzzer, as the bus only stops when dropping off or picking up passengers. Buses run M-F until 1am, Sa-Su 24hr. along Alameda (CH$290). Bright blue **Metrobuses** depart from the end of metro lines or the busiest metro stops (CH$250). **Colectivos** have neon signs on the roof and run fixed routes. They cost less than regular taxis, but more than buses (CH$500-800).

Taxis: Metered taxis are black with yellow roofs. Standard rate CH$150, plus CH$150 every 200m, CH$180 at night. **"Radio taxis"** are a good choice at night: **Alto Kennedy** (☎246 3082), **Arauco** (☎246 1114), and **Nuevo Flash** (☎247 2727) each charge CH$500 per km, CH$1500 minimum.

Metro: Carrying "more than 800,000" passengers per day, the modern, French-designed subway runs M-Sa 6:30am-10:30pm, Su 8am-10:30pm. The **red line** (línea 1) travels roughly east-west, following **Providencia/Alameda/O'Higgins** from the eastern edge of **Pudahuel** to **Las Condes.** The **yellow line** (línea 2) runs north-south, beginning near **Río Mapocho,** cutting into the red line at its northernmost stop, **Los Héroes,** and ending in the suburb of **La Cisterna.** The **green line** (línea 5) also runs north-south, beginning east of the yellow line, intersecting the red line at **Baquedano,** and extending south to the community of **La Florida.** Individual fares oscillate between rush hour (6-7:30pm, CH$370) and all other times (CH$290). If planning to travel much during commuting hours, it's best to buy a **multiviaje** ticket good for 10 trips (CH$3300). During off-peak times, the **valor** ticket (CH$3300) is a better deal, subtracting the value of each trip at the time of travel, thus allowing penny-pinchers to eke out 11 rides.

Car Rental: Most branches are represented at the airport. National chains allow drop-off flexibility, but for those returning to Santiago, local companies are cheaper. **Avis,** Guardia Vieja 255, office 108 (☎600 601 9966). **Budget,** Fidel Oteíza 1439, office 201 (☎381 1500). **Dollar,** Kennedy 8292 (☎202 5510). **Hertz,** Zurich 221, office 11 (☎520 5800). **Diagonal Rent-A-Car,** Diagonal Oriente 1648 (☎225 1737; dwdiagonal@entelchile.net), has rates from CH$20,000 per day including free mileage and VAT. **Costanera Rent-A-Car,** Av. Padre Hurtado Central 1205 (☎235 7835; info@costanerarent.cl), has cars from CH$19,000 with free mileage and free pickup.

▐ PRACTICAL INFORMATION

TOURIST AND FINANCIAL SERVICES

Tourist Offices: Sernatur, Providencia 1550 (☎731 8336 or 731 8337), in a large brown-brick building, serves as the National Tourism Board of Chile and provides good maps and detailed brochures. Pick up a complimentary copy of *Santiago Alive* for practical info and descriptions of sights in and around Santiago. Open Apr.-Nov. M-F 9am-6:30pm, Sa 9am-2pm; Dec.-Mar. daily 9am-6:30pm. **Municipalidad de Santiago,** Merced 860 (☎632 7783 or 632 7785), a block from the Plaza de Armas in historic Casa Colorado, provides lots of maps and guides to the city's sights. They also have an office on Cerro Santa Lucia. Open M-Th 10am-6pm, F 10am-5pm.

Tours: LanChile (see **International and Domestic Airlines,** p. 90) has package deals to **Easter Island** and other places. The **Isla de Pascua** tours start from about US$800 for

SANTIAGO

Santiago Metro

Linea 1
Linea 2
Linea 5

5 days and 4 nights, but prices are lower for shorter visits and for last-minute purchases, sometimes available within 4 days of departure.

Adventure Tours: Altue, Encomenderos 83, 2nd fl. (☎233 2964; www.chileoutdoors.com), offers sea kayaking, trekking, and horseback riding trip deals, as well as day tours to the ancient forests of **Parque Nacional la Campaña** (US$90) and rafting down the wild **Maipo River** (US$35). More hard-core, 9-day expeditions attempt the summit of the formidable Aconcagua (from US$1500, 10% ISIC discount). **Cascada Expediciones,** Orrego Luco 019, 2nd fl. (☎234 2274 or 232 7214; www.cascada-expediciones.com), runs an all-inclusive Maipo rafting trip (US$70), a 6-day sea kayaking trip in the southern fjords (US$990), a 6-day nature tour of Easter Island (US$608), and mountaineering trips to Volcán Parinacota in **Parque Nacional Lauca** and Aconcagua (US$1500-2000 each). **KL Chile,** Av. Las Condes 12207 (☎217 9101; www.klchile.com), has backcountry skiing, trekking, and serious mountaineering trips, crowned by its **Aconcagua** expedition (US$3200 includes plane ticket from US or Europe). **Yak Expediciones,** Nocedal 7135 (☎227 0427; www.yakexpediciones.cl), offers whitewater kayaking (CH$24,500) and rafting (CH$13,900) on the Maipo.

Embassies and Consulates: Argentina, Miraflores 285 (☎633 1076); **Australia,** Gertrudis Echeñique 420 (☎228 5065); **Bolivia,** Santa María 2796 (☎232 8180 or 232

4997); **Brazil,** Alonso Ovalle 1665 (☎698 2486); **Canada,** Nueva Tajamar 481, 12th fl. (☎362 9660); **Ecuador,** Providencia 1979, 5th fl. (☎231 5073); **Ireland,** Isidora Goyenechea 3162, office 801 (☎245 6616); **New Zealand,** El Golf 99, office 703 (☎290 9802); **Peru,** Andres Bello 1751 (☎235 6451 or 235 2356); **South Africa,** 11 de Septiembre 2353, 16th fl. (☎231 2862); **UK,** El Bosque Norte 0125, 3rd fl. (☎370 4100); **US,** Andrés Bello 2800 (☎232 2600; www.usembassy.cl). Open M-F 8:30-11:30am.

Immigration Office: Extranjería, Teatenos 950 (☎688 1590 or 674 4000). Open M-F 9am-noon. Report lost tourist cards (☎737 1292).

Currency Exchange: Casas de cambio are scattered throughout the city, especially along Augustinas and Huérfanos. Hotel exchange rates tend to be the lowest.

Banks: Widespread and easily accessible, most banks have **24hr. ATMs.** Many banks cluster in the city center along O'Higgins, to the east of M: Baquedano. **Banco de Chile,** O'Higgins 140 (☎638 5102 or 637 1111), and **Banco del Estado de Chile,** O'Higgins 1111, Santiago Centro (☎670 7000), are the largest. Banks operate M-F 9am-2pm.

ATM: Called **Redbanc,** these are found mostly in supermarkets, malls, bus stations, and along the busiest pedestrian stretches. MC/V.

American Express: Andrés Bello 2711, 9th fl. (☎350 6700). M: Tobalaba. Open M-Th 9am-6:30pm, F 9am-5pm.

Western Union: Providencia 2309 (☎231 8969). Open M-F 9am-2pm and 3:30-7pm, Sa 10am-1pm. Branches also available in **Correos de Chile** locations (see **Emergency and Communications,** p. 98).

Teaching English: English First (☎374 2180) is probably the best place to start if seeking a job teaching English as a foreign language. For more information see **Alternatives to Tourism,** p. 82.

Language Schools: Facultad de Filosofía de la Universidad de Chile (☎678 7040); **Instituto de Letras** (☎354 7882); **Natalis Language Center** (☎222 8721; www.natalislang.com) offer a variety of Spanish-language courses. For details on course offerings see **Alternatives to Tourism,** p. 80.

LOCAL SERVICES

Luggage Storage: (☎589 2354), in the Estación Central terminal. CH$600 per piece per day for normal-sized backpacks. Open daily 7am-10:30pm. Most hotels and hostels will also store bags.

Outdoor Equipment: Outdoors and Travel, Encomenderos 206 (☎335 5710), Las Condes, has shoes, clothing, packs, bags, tents, climbing equipment, and info on tour companies. Open M-F 10am-7pm, Sa 10am-6pm. **Rod & Gun,** Kennedy 9001 (☎215 4464), Alto Los Condes, sells boots, pads, packs, fishing equipment, and 9mm berettas. Open M-F 10am-10pm. **Patagonia,** Helvecia 210 (☎335 9796), has clothing, water bottles, gloves, shoes, and packs. Open M-F 10am-8pm, Sa 10am-7pm.

English Bookstore: Books, Providencia 1670B (☎235 1205), in Galería el Patio, lives up to its name selling a range of used material in English, from trashy romance novels to fallen travel guides. Book exchange. Open M-F 11:30am-8pm, Sa 11:30am-3pm. **Librería Inglesa,** Huerfanos 669, local 11 (☎632 5153, 638 7118), sells new books at exorbitant prices, about twice the cover price. M-F 10am-7:30pm, Sa 10am-2pm.

Library: Biblioteca Nacional, Alameda 651 (☎260 5200), has English-language books and magazines housed in its impressive stone and marble quarters. While visitors can't check anything out without a library card, they can read in the library if they show passport ID. Open M-F 9am-8pm, Sa 9am-2pm.

Cultural Center: Instituto Chileno Norteamericano Cultural, Moneda 1467 (☎677 7000). Has a library with info on Chile. Open M-F 9am-8pm.

Bi-Gay-Lesbian Organizations: Librería Lila, Providencia 1652 (☎236 1725), next to **Books** (see above). This Spanish-language bookstore focuses on women's issues, sexuality, gender, and new age philosophy. The management has its finger on the pulse of local gay and lesbian life. There are a host of websites on this subject, but **www.gay-chile.com,** in three languages, provides good recommendations for gay travelers regarding safety and gay-friendly establishments in Santiago and elsewhere. Open M-F 10am-8pm, Sa 10am-2:30pm. **Radio Tierra** (AM1300) has a gay and lesbian radio show (Sa 6:30-8pm).

Public Market: Mercado Central is one of Latin America's most elegant, despite the overwhelming odor of fish. Built in 1872, it now harbors small seafood joints, a few fruit and veggie stands, plenty of fishmongers, and some classier restaurants. Open M-Th 9am-4pm, F 9am-6pm, Sa 7am-6pm, Su 7am-5pm.

Laundromat: Lavandería Echaurren, Echaurren 164 (☎671 3420), Barrio Brasil, is the de facto choice for travelers and students in that area. Wash or dry CH$1000, both CH$1690. Open M-Sa 9am-8pm, Su 11:30am-2pm and 3-8pm.

EMERGENCY AND COMMUNICATIONS

Emergency: Ambulance ☎131. **Fire** ☎132. **Police** ☎133. **Information** ☎103.

Police: General Mackenna 1314 (☎544 5000). Open 24hr.

Crisis Hotlines: Fonosida (☎800 202 120). A confidential, anonymous, and free AIDS hotline. Su-Th 2pm-midnight, F-Sa 2pm-9am. **Domestic Violence Hotline** (☎800 220 040).

24-Hour Pharmacy: Farmacia Ahumada, Providencia 2132 (☎222 1121), is one of several 24hr. pharmacies on the main drag of Providencia.

Medical Services: Recommended by the US embassy for quality and service are the **Clínica Alemana,** Vitacura 5951 (☎212 9700), and the **Clínica Las Condes,** Lo Fontecilla 441 (☎210 4000). Both open 24hr.

Telephones: Card- and coin-operated **Entel** phones are everywhere, but users report that these phones often don't accept coins, or worse, eat them.

Internet Access: Cyber cafes have popped up all over Santiago, especially in Barrio Brasil south of Alameda, in Providencia, and throughout Santiago Centro. **Red Café,** Eschauren 127, Barrio Brasil. CH$500 per hr. Open M-Th 9:15am-11:30pm, F 10am-11:30pm, Sa 10:30am-11:30pm. **Biblioteca Nacional,** Alameda 651, Santiago Centro (☎260 5200). CH$600 per hr. 18+. Passports are sometimes required. **Internet,** República 16, Barrio Brasil. CH$600 per hr. Open M-Sa 9am-10pm.

Post Office: Empresa Correos de Chile (☎274 7799 or 269 2866), has several locations, including the Plaza de Armas. Open M-F 8:30am-7pm, Sa 8:30am-2pm. **Branch** on Providencia 1466 (☎235 7086) has Federal Express. Open M-Sa 9am-6:30pm, Su 9am-12:30pm. Another Providencia **Branch,** Av. 11 de Sept. 2092. Open M-F 9am-7pm, Sa 9am-1pm. **Federal Express** main office, Providencia 1951 (☎361 6000). Open M-F 9am-1:30pm and 2:30-7pm.

▛ ACCOMMODATIONS

As a large, sprawling city, Santiago offers a range of accommodations, from *residenciales* to hotels, that vary greatly in quality and price. Truly budget accommodations are clustered southwest of the Mercado Central, in the neighborhoods of Santiago Centro, and in Barrio Brasil. Carefully evaluate the security of these establishments before paying, as reassuring safety signs like locked doors at night can be few and far between. Providencia teems with snazzier, higher-priced hotels. Prices are listed in US currency when payment is accepted in US dollars in order to circumvent the 18% VAT (see Essentials, p. 41). For longer stays, check out the newspaper *Mercurio*, which has a section on rooms for rent (around CH$80,000-100,000 per month).

SANTIAGO CENTRO AND PROVIDENCIA

Budget accommodations in the center tend to be the cheapest in town, but with few perks or amenities. Very little English is spoken in these establishments. Cheaper hotels are ideal for saving some cash, but can become inconvenient and inhospitable during longer stays.

Residencial Londres, Londres 54 (☎ 638 2215). The courtyards, colonial furniture, high ceilings, elegant salons, and gorgeous rooms in a quiet neighborhood populated with high-end hotels seem worth more than you actually dish out. Breakfast CH$700. Luggage storage CH$300 per day per piece. Singles CH$6500; doubles CH$13,000, with bath CH$15,000; triples CH$19,500, CH$22,500. ❷

Hotel Olicar, San Pablo 1265 (☎ 698 3683), 2 blocks from the Mercado Central. This spacious, high-ceilinged, charming hotel is kept very clean by an attentive staff. A sense of security is maintained due to the conscientiously locked front door. Lounge in the common area, which includes a kitchen and TV. Can get a little chilly in winter. 6-bed dorms CH$3000; doubles CH$8000, with bath CH$10,000; triples CH$10,000. ❶

Residencial José Estay, Ramón Corvalán 37, local 112 (☎ 247 2272; joseestay@hotmail.com), in the "Don Bernardo" building. Offers 2 rooms in a comfortable, secure, and well-decorated apartment, located conveniently by Plaza Italia. Check out the amazing collection of Coca-Cola merchandise and paraphernalia that crowds the kitchen. English-speaking José is a great source of info on Santiago and Chile. Both rooms have a private bath. Breakfast included. Free Internet M-F after 8pm, Sa after 2pm, and Su all day. Must contact José by email or phone at least 5-7 days before arriving in Santiago; no walk-ins accepted. CH$11,000, discounts on longer stays. ❸

Hotel Diego de Velazquez, Diego de Velazquez 2141 (☎ 234 4400; hvelazquez@ia.cl). In a classy Providencia neighborhood. The impeccable interior is marked by adobe themes. Ask for a new room, as the most recently renovated units are less run-down and much brighter, but cost the same as old rooms. Cable TV, A/C in every room. Breakfast included. Pricey Internet (CH$35 per min.). Singles US$65; doubles US$75. ❺

Hotel España, Morandé 510 (☎ 696 6066). With a central location and a friendly staff, this is the perfect refuge in which to lap up luxury for a day. Recently refurbished with oil paintings, leather couches, and a beautiful marble lobby. 24hr. staffed front desk. Free Internet, cable TV, and luggage storage available. Breakfast included. Singles US$40; doubles US$60; triples US$85; rates US$10-20 less in winter. ❺

Hotel Indiana, Rosas 1339 (☎ 688 0008; hostal_indiana@hotmail.com). Pleasant common rooms, accessible kitchen facilities, and public telephone take the edge off the saggy mattresses. Basic shared bathrooms and storage. Laundry CH$1500 per 5kg. Internet CH$1000 per hr. Dorms CH$3000-4000. ❶

Hotel Caribe, San Martín 851 (☎ 699 6661), has clean double, twin, and dorm rooms with shared baths off a pleasant open-air courtyard. Front door not kept locked. Kitchen available. Internet access CH$500 for 30min. Rooms from CH$4500 per person. ❷

Hotel Cervantes, Morandé 631 (☎ 696 7966). While not the best deal in town, Hotel Cervantes offers nicely painted rooms with large cabinets and antique furnishings that line the squeaky, rubberized hallway. The plush, comfortable living room is ideal for lounging, and the atmosphere is safe and quiet. Most rooms have private baths and cable TV. Singles CH$14,000; doubles and twins CH$17,000; triples CH$22,000. ❸

SANTIAGO

THE LOCAL STORY

RED, RED WINE

Rodrigo, a manager at Vinoteca, the wine specialty store in Las Condes, has worked in the Chilean wine industry for six years. He took some time out to give *Let's Go* the lowdown on Chile's vineyards and vintages.

Q: How do Chilean wines stack up against the rest of the world? What are their strengths and weaknesses?

A: The character of Chilean wines has changed a lot over the past 10 years; many vineyards have spent a lot of money on technological advances, and there has been an increase in the number of little wineries, "boutique" wineries, producing really good wine.

Q: What are the strongest types of wine? Has that changed as well?

A: Without a doubt, the Cabernet Sauvignon has the best reputation among Chilean wines, although boutique wineries are producing interesting, good wines of all sorts.

Q: And of white wines, are there any that Chile specializes in, generally speaking?

A: Some of the Sauvignon Blancs are quite good, more so than the Chardonnays.

Q: So can you recommend a Cabernet that is both reasonable and of good quality?

A: Well, I don't think I can single out a specific label, because there are so many complex yet reasonable wines that sell for maybe US$3-4—we are talking *really good* wines for that price.

Hotel Nuevo Valparaíso, Morandé 791 (☎671 5698). Ultra-simple rooms with nice mattresses. Kitchen available. Cable TV in the common area. Satisfied visitors have left notes in various languages on the walls. Singles CH$3000; doubles CH$6000. ❶

BARRIO BRASIL AND THE SOUTHWEST

Student-friendly Barrio Brasil is full of universities, institutes, good cafes, and nice restaurants. Thanks to the collegiate population, there is more nightlife here than in Santiago Centro, but it's also a bit more expensive.

La Casa Roja, Agustinas 2113 (☎696 4241; info@lacasaroja.tie.cl). Australian backpacker extraordinaire Simon is in the process of transforming the "Big Red" into a tried-and-true international backpackers haven. Stunning bathrooms, large common spaces, impromptu barbecues, ping pong tournaments, and jam sessions are the norm here—if you're not in the mood for thumping Saturday nights, schmooze with a chiller crowd at the SCS Habitat (see below). Breakfast CH$1500. Internet free for 20min., then CH$600 per hr. CH$2000 key deposit. Checkout 1pm. 6- or 8-bed dorms CH$3500; doubles CH$9000.❶

SCS Habitat, San Vicente 1798 (☎683 3732; scshabitat@yahoo.com). From Estación Central, take buses 335, 358, or 360 for 18 blocks (3-5min.) and get off before the underpass; walk to the end of Exposición, turn left on Subercaseaux, and go east 3 blocks to San Vicente. If you don't mind the small commute, this place is definitely worth it. Scott, the friendly and super-helpful American owner, has covered all his bases, offering camping equipment, trekking maps, bike rental, a food store, and the nicest kitchen in town. Great source of information about Chile for independent, resourceful backpackers. Internet CH$600 per hr. Free phone for receiving long-distance calls. Breakfast CH$1000 includes fresh fruit and occasional baked goodies. Dorms CH$3000-4000. Camping CH$2500. ❶

Residencial Mery, Pasaje República 36 (☎696 8883 or 699 4982; m.mardones@entelchile.net). Bright hallways and lacquered wood add to the pleasant atmosphere of this beautiful *residencial*. Firm beds and the quiet back-alley location ensure a good night's sleep. Clean rooms come with towels. Common areas have cable TV. Reservations recommended in the summer. Shared baths. Singles CH$8000; doubles CH$15,000; triples CH$19,000; quads CH$23,000. ❸

Hotel Conde Ansúrez, Av. Republica 25 (☎696 0807 or 671 8376). The good Count A. certainly picked a good piece of real estate for his hotel—the liveliest corner of Barrio Brasil. Quiet but central, near M: República. Cable TV available. Security boxes in every room. Breakfast included. Singles US$60; doubles US$70; triples US$80. ❺

Hostelling International, Cienfuegos 151 (☎671 8532; histgoch@entelchile.net). Everything about this place is clinical, but the hostel boasts friendly international clientele. Cafeteria, patio, lockers, off-street parking, and luggage storage (CH$500 per day per piece) all available. Breakfast CH$500. 3-bed dorms CH$7950; 2-bed dorms CH$8950; singles CH$9950. CH$1500 discount with ISIC. ❸

Hotel Residencial, Catedral 2235 (☎671 9045 or 695 4800). Don't worry, the exuberant kids you may run into sleep upstairs, and the owner is accommodating. Oddly placed windows give guests a great view of the hallway. Although rooms are a bit dingy, bright lighting, cable TV, private baths, and heaters are compensation enough. The guests' "kitchen" is in a courtyard, under a fiberglass roof. Decide to treat yourself to breakfast in bed. Singles CH$5000, with breakfast CH$6000; doubles CH$12,000. ❷

Residencial Metro República, Alameda 2248, 3rd fl. (☎695 6509), right by the metro. Open building with securely locked apartments. Small, cozy residence with some noise coming in off the street. Clean rooms come with color TV. Breakfast included. Singles CH$7000, with bath CH$10,000; doubles CH$14,000; triples CH$18,000. ❸

Residencial Alemana, República 220 (☎671 2388; ralemana@entelshile.net). This antique house across from Universidad Nacional Andrés Bello presents a nice façade while hiding a disappointingly cold interior. A popular choice for European travelers. Clean, shared baths. TV available. Breakfast included. Singles and twins CH$8000 per person, with bath CH$10,000. ❸

🖸 FOOD

If you're in the mood to cook, get food at **Santa Isabel,** Providencia 2178 (☎233 0092; open M-Sa 9am-10pm, Su 10am-8pm), or **Almac,** 11 de Septiembre 2249, local 52 (☎251 3196; open M-Sa 8am-10pm, Su 9am-9pm), in Plaza Lyon. In Santiago Centro, **Montserrat,** 21 de Mayo 819 (☎638 4339; open 8am-10pm), does the honors. In Barrio Brasil, it's **Economax** (open 8:30am-10pm), at the corner of Ricardo Cumming and Compañía. For **fruits and veggies** on the cheap, try the low-lying corrugated-roof **market** across the river from the Mercado Central via the footbridge from 21 de Mayo. Open 7am-9am.

Q: Where do people generally buy their wine here, at a bottle shop or a wine store? What is your clientele like?

A: Generally, for everyday consumption, people go to the supermarket and purchase an ordinary label for very reasonable prices, whereas the people who come to a place like this are looking more to buy a really special wine—maybe a reserve or an older vintage—to take home with them or give as a present.

Q: If somebody wants to visit a vineyard in Santiago, what do you think the best tour and tasting packages are?

A: Several vineyards now have interesting tours, but I think Concha y Toro is definitely a good value. A really nice location with a really old *bodega* that is a little bit more expensive is Santa Rita.

Q: Finally, considering Santiago's air quality problems and the proximity of many vineyards in the Maipó Valley to the city, can you notice a difference in taste between wines that are grown in urban or suburban settings as opposed to rural ones?

A: Well, there are definitely distinctive tastes and different characteristics of wines in the Maipó area, but it's hard to generalize, because grapes grown near the mountains have a different flavor from grapes grown further west. There are many factors involved, including soil and individual microclimates, moisture levels, and sun angles in different locations. I think it is very hard to generalize what makes grapes taste the way they do.

THE BIG SPLURGE

AKARANA

Reyes Lavalle (☎ 231 9667). M: El Golf. Stationed strategically across from the new Ritz-Carlton, this sparkling white, mediterranean-style trans-Pacific import claims to offer the finest of New Zealand's cuisine. Which begs the question: what is Kiwi cuisine and what is it doing in Santiago, Chile? Well, the owner hails from Auckland, and according to the menu, New Zealand chefs assimilate culinary ideas and inspirations from all over the world. Although this may sound like a less pretentious moniker for "fusion" or "Pan-Asian" cuisine, it's not so simple. The menu makes particularly good use of fresh Chilean seafood. Appetizers include nearly-raw oysters with caviar, fried leeks, and lemon (CH$3000). Entrees span the range from a gourmet version of fish'n'chips (CH$6000), a true New Zealand staple, to the delicious Easter Island Yellowfin Tuna dish (CH$7800). Finish up with Pavlova (a type of meringue, CH$2600), the most identifiably Kiwi item on the menu, and a tasty espresso (CH$800). A testimony to Santiago's cosmopolitan flair, this establishment has impeccable service, and the candle-lit ambience is lovely, especially out on the patio. You will hear lots of English, but whatever language other diners speak, nobody will be saying anything disparaging about Akarana. Open noon-midnight. ❹

SANTIAGO CENTRO

Seafood, fast food, and ice cream offerings proliferate here. Very few restaurants remain open beyond 9-10pm.

Mercado Central, on the corner of Paseo Ahumada and San Pablo, is the best place in town to get that seafood fix. Stands offer delicacies ready for slurping—fresh *erizo* (sea urchin; CH$500) can be cut right from the shell. It goes great with a squirt of lemon, as do half-shell oysters (25 for CH$1500). If you are planning to cook your own, the huge chunks of salmon (CH$3000 per kilo) and albacore tuna ($CH3600) are barely samplings of the impressive smorgasbord of marine carcasses. Hawking for both stands and restaurants is aggressive. Sit-down restaurants offer similar seafood delights (although they are forbidden by health codes from serving them raw), including popular *mariscal* (mixed fish and shellfish broth; CH$1700), *pescado frito* (fried fish; CH$1500), and *ceviche* (CH$3000). Open M-Th 7am-4pm, F-Sa 7am-6pm, Su 7am-5pm. ❶

Donde Augusto (☎ 698 1366), in the center of the Mercado Central. Offers everything the market stands have, plus more variety, style, ambience, and cost. Celebrity diners, whose photos line the walls, recommend it highly. Regulars love the staple bass, salmon, or albacore served under *salsa de mariscos*, a creamy, chowder-like shellfish sauce (CH$6980). It would almost be criminal to enjoy the seafood paella *especial* (CH$12,000) and other high-end entrees without a glass of fine Chilean white wine (CH$1800). Open M-Th 7am-4pm, F 7am-8pm, Sa 7am-6pm, Su 7am-5pm. ❹

Bravissimo Gelateria, Providencia 1406 (☎ 235 2511), Paseo Estada 333, and other locations. The funky geometric storefront and loud colors of this quality chain scream "EAT HERE!" Munch on healthy, conscience-pleasing salads and then indulge yourself with a cone of homemade ice cream, hailed as the best in Santiago. Plenty of cakes and shakes served up as well. Chicken salad CH$2200, single-scoop ice cream cone CH$550, shakes CH$1100. Open Su-Th 8am-11pm, F-Sa 8am-2am. ❷

Fuente Alemana, Alameda 58 (☎ 639 3231), near M: Baquedano. The place for *comida típica* in the center. Hunt down a seat at the quadrilateral bar or stand along the walls. Then gape at the skilled assembly of your chosen *churrasco*. Cheap options include the range of *completas* (CH$1500-2300). Open 9:30am-11:30pm, later on weekends. ❶

Les Assassins Restaurant, Merced 297B (☎ 638 4280). Dine on well-executed French food chosen from an outstanding menu selection. The *locos salsa de* *jaida fresca* (abalone in crab sauce) adds a Chilean seafood *sabor*. French onion soup CH$3100, French-style scallops CH$4600. Open M-Sa 7-11pm. ❸

BARRIO BRASIL AND WEST SANTIAGO

Packs of ravenous college students attest to Barrio Brasil's good, cheap, accessible eats. More refined ethnic and seafood restaurants also infiltrate the neighborhood. The thoroughfare of Ricardo Cumming, north of Alameda, hosts clusters of quality eateries, all the way north to Santo Domingo.

▨ **Las Vacas Gordas,** Cienfuegos 280 (☎697 1066 or 673 3962), at Huérfanos, Barrio Brasil. A pervasive aroma from the open grill warns visitors this place has meat, and lots of it. The atmosphere is cozy, clean, and new-looking. The asparagus salad (CH$1590), *brocheta de lomo* (grilled pork; CH$2390), chicken breast with lemon (CH$2390), and steak (CH$2890) are all notably succulent. Wash it all down with a stiff pisco sour (CH$850). Open M-Sa 12:30pm-midnight, Su 12:30-4pm. ❸

Makalu Kebab, Salvador San Fuentes 2249 (☎698 4956). A favorite hangout for university students for its casual, hip atmosphere and bargain food. The jukebox plays familiar English songs. Kebab and fries (CH$650), 6 *empanadas* with drink (CH$1000), *churrasco* (CH$850), and beer (CH$900) are all good deals. Open M-Th 10am-12:30am, F 10am-2:30am, Sa noon-8pm. ❶

El Citte Restaurante, Ricardo Cumming 635 (☎698 4877). The *a la carte* menu is intriguing. Among the fish options (CH$3000-4000), the *corvina* (sea bass) is especially good, but choose your sauce (CH$1100-1300) wisely. Set back off the street, the open dining room draws mainly locals. Open M-Sa 11am-midnight, Su 11am-4pm. ❸

Gran Taipei Bella City, Ricardo Cumming 78 (☎699 1809). Chefs from Shanghai, Guangdong, and Taiwan ensure an authentic culinary experience. They also accommodatingly cook by request. 4-course *menú* (CH$5250) available. Sautéed bamboo and mushroom CH$2980. Special lunch menu CH$1350. Sushi menu includes 6-piece salmon plate CH$2500. Open daily 11am-1am. ❸

BARRIO BELLAVISTA

For a little extra money, you can treat yourself to a memorable meal in Bellavista. This bohemian *barrio* features many specialty restaurants that prepare dishes with an artistic flair commensurate with the multicultural surroundings. The best culinary strip resides on **Constitución.**

▨ **Como Agua para Chocolate,** Constitución 88 (☎777 8740). Beware: the menu prepared in the "magic kitchen" and a Mexican villa interior combine to make an irresistible aphrodisiac. Date-friendly dishes include *Salad Seducción* (CH$3900) and *Ave de la Pasión* (CH$5900). Romantic meals for 2 CH$13,000. The namesake dessert (CH$3000) may seem like a chocolate overload, but will certainly take its consumer to decadent heights. Open Su-Th 1-4:30pm and 7:30-11:30pm, F-Sa 1-4:30pm and 7:30pm-1am. ❸

Tasca Mediterránea, Purisima 161 (☎735 3901). The Mediterranean menu is fashioned after some of Pablo Neruda's favorite recipes, illustrating the icon's impeccable taste. The ambience follows suit, with a decisively poetic and alluringly romantic flavor. A slightly more economical choice for those on an artist's budget is the grilled fish with vegetables (CH$4500). 3-course lunch CH$3500. Theater and live music W-Sa. Open daily noon-2am. ❸

Azul Profundo, Constitución 111 (☎738 0288). Locals say it serves some of the best seafood around, and that's saying a lot. Sink into its specialty, grilled fish (CH$5600-6200), amidst mastheads, portholes, and other trinkets from the deep blue sea. A la carte sauces CH$1700-1900. Reservations recommended on weekends. Open Su-F 12:30-4pm and 7:30pm-midnight, Sa 7:30pm-1:30am. ❸

PROVIDENCIA & LAS CONDES

The Suecia strip just north of the **Los Leones** metro station delivers chow at tourist prices, drawing more of an expatriate crowd to its bar scene. Various lunch spots and eateries are scattered around and along the main drag, the dynamic Ave. Providencia.

■ **Casa de la Cultura de Mexico,** Bucarest 162 (☎334 3848), attached to the Mexican Cultural Center. The charming waitstaff serves Mexican favorites in the bright, homey dining room. For a more romantic atmosphere, dine on the greenery-lined patio. Best of all, a delightful ambience doesn't mean they skimp on portions. *Enchiladas* CH$2500, *arroz con leche* CH$1100. The *pollo con mole verde* (CH$4500) is highly recommended. Open M-Sa noon-11pm. ❷

El Huerto/La Huerta, Orrego Luco 054 (☎233 2690). This two-pronged establishment serves up greens and more greens. The patio cafe and lunch establishment, La Huerta, offers fine soup and salad deals (CH$2000), as well as an "American breakfast" (CH$1900). Portions, however, are not huge (maybe because the corporate clientele doesn't have time to really dig in?). El Huerto serves dinner inside, across the hall from new-age bookstore Gaia. La Huerta open M-Sa 8am-4pm; El Huerto open M-Sa noon-midnight, Su 7pm-midnight. ❶

BARRIO ÑUÑOA

Although Ñuñoa lies far from the city center, it rewards with reasonably priced restaurants and excellent ambience. Virtually all of the neighborhoods cluster around Av. Irarrazaval, especially in Plaza Ñuñoa.

El Amor Nunca Muere, Humberto Trucco 43 (☎274 9432). A pleasant dinner and late-evening snack locale with passionate French dishes (at least in name), mainly consisting of savory and sweet crepes. *Desnudo* (pancakes with green beans, cheese, tomato, and curry sauce) CH$2000, apple crepes CH$1200. Pisco sour CH$1600. Open M-Th 5pm-1:30am, F-Sa 5pm-4am. ❶

Las Lanzas, Humberto Trucco 25 (☎225 5589). The local favorite for good *comida típica* at reasonable prices. Popular choices include *lomo completo, churrasco* (meat, *not* on a bun), and *chacarero* (meat with green beans and tomatoes) for CH$1300 each. Ribs CH$1300. Open M-Th 9am-2am, F-Sa 9am-3am. ❶

La Tecla, Doctor Johow 320 (☎274 3603). A keyboard marks the entrance of this distinctive restaurant, while collages and murals flank the walls of the interior. Diners in the main room are treated to *panqueques* like the Brutus (spinach, meat, and cheese in a white sauce; CH$2500) and a variety of pizzas (from CH$2500) while taking in a unique, black-and-white Santiago skyline. Open M-Th noon-1am, F-Sa 7pm-2am. ❷

⊞ CAFES

Although a stroll through Santiago won't deliver up an abundance of cafes, as a bustling metropolis the city harbors a fair share of establishments complete with typical cafe atmospheres and chain-smoking en masse. Barrio Brasil is the best place to go for artsy cafes, although some may be hard to find.

On the other end of the cafe spectrum, Santiago Centro's pedestrian walkways are littered with establishments like **Café Caribe** and **Café Haiti.** These cafes draw an ogling, suit-clad corporate clientele with young, busty female waitstaff decked out in slinky evening wear. Known widely as *"Cafés con piernas"* (coffee with legs), these establishments may seem scandalous or indecent, but the high-quality coffee tends to lure even those with objections to the objectification. Tinted and blacked-out windows on other "cafe" fronts indicate that even more is revealed inside. Make no bones about it, however; the only stimulation you'll be getting

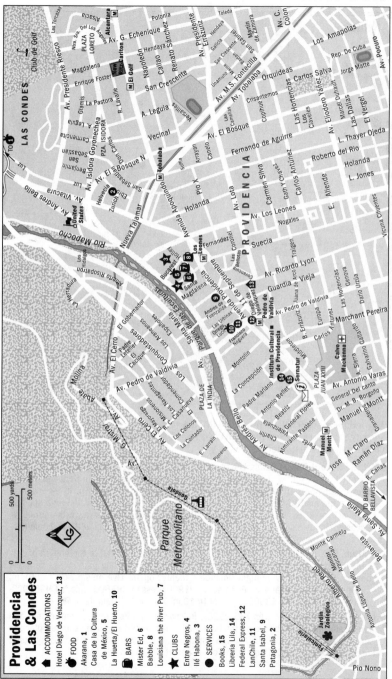

SANTIAGO

Providencia & Las Condes

▲ ACCOMMODATIONS
Hotel Diego de Velazquez, 13

🍴 FOOD
Akarana, 1
Casa de la Cultura
de México, 5
La Huerta/El Huerto, 10

🍺 BARS
Mister Ed, 6
Babble, 8
Louisiana the River Pub, 7

★ CLUBS
Entre Negros, 4
Ilé Habona, 3

● SERVICES
Books, 15
Librería Lila, 14
Federal Express, 12
LanChile, 11
Santa Isabel, 9
Patagonia, 2

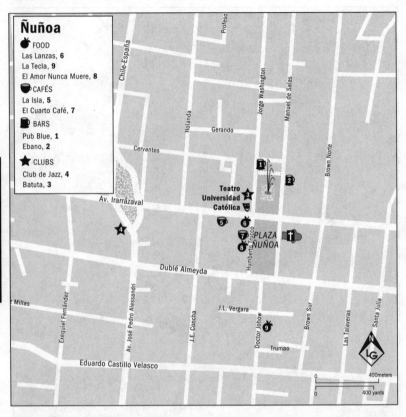

Ñuñoa

🍅 **FOOD**
Las Lanzas, **6**
La Tecla, **9**
El Amor Nunca Muere, **8**

☕ **CAFÉS**
La Isla, **5**
El Cuarto Café, **7**

🍺 **BARS**
Pub Blue, **1**
Ebano, **2**

⭐ **CLUBS**
Club de Jazz, **4**
Batuta, **3**

(beyond the visual) will be from the caffeine—absolutely no alcohol is served, and security stands ready to ensure that you behave in that sedate, so-what-if-she's-half-naked, cafe customer kind of way.

🟦 **Off The Record Cafe,** Antonia Lopez de Bello 0155 (☎777 7710), Bellavista. Whether the mic is on or not, we can safely say this is one of the best cafes in Santiago. All-day *huevos rancheros* (CH$2500) go well with a cappuccino (CH$1100). In the evening, share a tiramisu (CH$1900) and a scandalous conversation with someone special, because, you know, it's..."*off the record.*" Decorated almost exclusively with portraiture. Occasional movie screenings, poetry readings, and exhibitions. Open Su-Th 10am-midnight, F-Sa 10am-2am. ❷

N'Aitun, Ricardo Cummings 453 (☎671 7837), Brasil. Dedicated to the fine art of *descansar* (rest), the upstairs venue boasts soft lighting, dangling plants, and candlelit beams. Live shows every night, including theater on Th. Live music F-Sa 10:30pm. Cover varies for musical acts. Pisco sour CH$900, dessert CH$600, salads CH$550. 3-course lunch menu CH$3000. Open M-Th 10am-2am, F-Sa 10am-4am. ❶

Libro Café, Purísima 165 (☎735 0928), Bellavista. With its candle-lit red interior and large selection of old books on the back wall, this is a perfectly sophisticated place to sip a glass of wine (CH$1500) and listen to the jazz that plays in the background. *Tapas* CH$2500-3850. Open M-Th 7pm-midnight, F-Sa 7pm-4am. ❷

La Isla, Irarrazaval 3465 (☎341 5389), Ñuñoa. A smaller cafe in front; a larger, more formal dining area in back. Chic clientele common on weekend nights. Excellent fruit shakes CH$1300, *café de la isla* CH$1200, piña colada CH$2700. Open M-Th 10am-1:30am, F 10am-3am, Sa 7am-3am. ❷

R. Restaurant and Café, Lastarria 307 (☎664 9844), Santiago Centro. Located in Plaza Mulato Gil with the Museo de Artes Visuales, the big "R" might stand for "rejuvenation," "recaffeination," or maybe even "ridiculous shovels" (which line some of the walls). Whatever the meaning, this "refuge" is great for coffee and dessert, but a bit overpriced for dinner. Espresso drinks about CH$800. Dinner pastas from CH$5000. Cafe open M-Sa 10am-midnight, Su noon-11pm; restaurant open M-Sa noon-3:30pm and 7:30pm-midnight. ❸

Peperone Empanadas Café, Huerfanos 1954 (☎687 9180), Brasil. The name is a turn-off for cafe connoisseurs, but this cafe is well-endowed with superior *empanada* fare (CH$850-1000), good cappuccino (CH$850), and an interior plastered with a portrait of Dalí, poetry by Borges, and more. Open M-Th noon-11pm, F noon-midnight, Sa noon-5pm. ❶

El Cuarto Café, Humberto Trucco 35 (☎225 1495), Ñuñoa. This unpretentious cafe keeps prices down and quality up. Scope out the wide selection of pies and cakes in the display case. Caramel-orange pancake CH$1200, hot chocolate CH$700, banana milk frappe CH$900. Open daily 1:30-11:30pm. ❶

◙ SIGHTS

PLAZA DE ARMAS. The traditional center of municipal life still exhibits the city's vitality, especially on weekdays during a late 6-7pm rush hour, when *Santiaguinos* flood the square and linger to watch **street performers,** survey the displays of landscape and portrait **art,** and meet on benches with friends and **lovers.** Save for the visual intrusion of a monstrous TV screen and the occasional auditory annoyance of fire-breathing religious fanatics, the square is a delightful place in Santiago Centro to relax and **people-watch.** To the west of the plaza, the hulking brown **Cathedral de Santiago** is as imposing and solid as the religious foundation of Chilean society. The church offers visitors a beautiful (if dim and chilly) interior with an impressive collection of ecclesiastical art. *(In the center, located between the two north-south pedestrian walkways. M: Plaza de Armas. Cathedral open Tu-F 10:30am-1:30pm and 3:30-6pm.)*

PARQUE METROPOLITANO DE SANTIAGO. A green escape from urban smog and noise, this park offers over seven square kilometers of sharp hills and breathtaking views of Santiago below. When weather permits, you can also catch spectacular views of the Andes in the background (the best time to visit the park is after heavy rain). The main entrance to the park at the end of **Pío Nono** (Barrio Bellavista) houses the base of a **funicular** (cable railway) that sends you to the top of **Cerro San Cristobal,** 250m above the surrounding urban environs. From there you can take the **teleférico** (cable car) to explore **giant swimming pools** and botanical **gardens.** If you get hungry, the park has restaurants, coffee shops, and snack stands—but make sure not to feed the animals in the **zoo.** The highest point, Cerro San Cristobal, is topped by an immense statue of **Virgin Mary** and the immaculate conception. Made in Paris and installed in 1908, the statue weighs a hefty 36,610kg and stands 35m high. It can be seen from virtually anywhere in Santiago, especially when lit up at night. *(☎777 6666, ext. 131. Open daily 8am-10pm. Funicular open M 1-8pm, Tu-Su 10am-8pm; round-trip CH$1200, children CH$700. Cable car open M-F 2:30-6:30pm, Sa-Su 10:30am-7:30pm. Zoo open Tu-Su 10am-6pm; CH$1500. Combined funicular, cable car, and zoo CH$3700; children CH$1600.)*

CERRO SANTA LUCIA. Santiago spent a lot of time trying to solve the ever-elusive question: what can you do with a pile of rock and dirt in the middle of the cap-

NAKED LUNCH

What started with a bang ended with a whimper in the case of the now famous "Baby Vamp," 17-year-old Lucia Fernanda Flores and her artistic partner and agent, Luizo Vega. The project "Bad Girl," masterminded by some combination of Flores and Vega, involved Flores going through the routine of her daily life in Santiago naked, with Vega documenting the reactions of observers in a collection of photos that he would present at the end of the 7-10 day project. The co-conspirators claimed that the project intended to expose the contradictions of Chilean society: the tension between conservative Catholic values and the licentious offerings of pop culture.

And so she walked, naked. Her first walk on June 10, 2002 led through Barrio Bellavista, inspring applause from a group of construction workers and some dismay from more prudish passersby. The walks continued the next day with a stroll through Providencia, a haircut there, and a thwarted attempt to ride naked in the city Metro. On June 12, the stunned authorities finally found a way to impede the project, hauling the Argentinian Luizo Vega into immigration for questioning regarding his tourist visa. He responded to the "oppression" by saying "I don't understand why whenever there is an artistic project, it is cut short by the artist's imprisonment."

ital? The answer: Cerro Santa Lucia, Santiago's first observatory. In 1872, Santiago's mayor **Benjamin Vicuña Mackenna** decided to transform the immovable eyesore into a public park, decorated with turrets, plazas, fountains, and 1000 different species of trees. The result was an enduring success; hundreds of locals continue to take midday strolls amidst the park's lovely man-made and natural formations. Complete with a **Japanese garden,** imported **French fountains,** and **great views** of the city, Cerro Santa Lucia is graced with a romantic ambience (and thus utilized both at midday and in the evenings). In honor of Mackenna's visionary improvement to city life, he was buried in the park, in the **Capilla La Ermita** chapel near the summit. Visitors' daily respite is broken at noon by a traditional **cannon blast** in the direction of the Plaza de Armas. *(M: Santa Lucia. ☎664 4216. Open Mar.-Dec. daily 9am-6pm; Jan.-Feb. 9am-7pm. 2hr. tours available Th 11am. Sign-in required. Free.)*

PLAZA O'HIGGINS AND PALACIO DE LA MONEDA. Though it lacks activities and is not particularly visitor-friendly, Plaza O'Higgins does feature the **Altar de la Patria,** a statue of celebrated Chilean liberator Bernardo O'Higgins. His **tomb** lies beneath the altar, accompanied by an eternal flame titled "Llaman la Libertad" that is guarded 24 hours. At 6pm, the national band plays the **Chilean anthem** in O'Higgins's honor at the military building to the east of the plaza. *(Just south of Palacio de la Moneda, near Estación Moneda. Open daily 10am-5pm. Free.)* North of Alameda, the **Palacio de la Moneda** might just be the most impressive building in Santiago. The host of alert, sharply dressed *carabineros* probably doesn't hurt. Ignore the rifle-bearing guards and walk through the fountained courtyard to get a real "insider's" perspective on Chilean history and government. The changing of the guard every 48 hours is worth seeing. *(Courtyard open to the public daily 10am-6pm. Changing of the Guard every other day 10am.)*

IGLESIA DE SAN FRANCISCO. This ancient of Chilean architecture hails from a simpler time, when rough-hewn rock could be exposed on a cathedral's interior walls. As the oldest building in Santiago, dating from 1628, it warrants a peek before proceeding to the **Museo Colonial,** a worthy exhibit of ecclesiastical art and objects from the preceding two centuries. *(Bernardo O'Higgins 834. M: Universidad de Chile. ☎639 8737. Museum open Tu-Sa 10am-1pm and 3-6pm, Su 10am-2pm. Museum CH$1000; children CH$300.)*

PALACIO COUSIÑO. To see the influence of old European money on Chilean society and history, one need look no further than this colonial mansion. The ornate, stately decorations inspire more than a few gawks. *(Dieciocho 438. M: Toesca.* ☎ *698 5063. Required tours Th-F 9:30am-12:30pm and 2:30-4pm, Sa-Su 9:30am-12:30pm. CH$1500, children CH$500.)*

PARQUE QUINTA NORMAL. Encircled by clouds of exhaust and run-down storefronts, this pleasant 16-acre park is perfect for bike rides, strolls, picnics, and summer boating on the **pond.** Those seeking some more intellectual stimulation can find it at the various **museums** (see below) nearby. *(Four blocks north of M: Estación Central. Open summer Tu-Su 8am-8:30pm; winter 8am-7pm. Free.)*

🏛 MUSEUMS

Although the art collections in Santiago are somewhat diffuse and disappointing, the cultural and historical museums are quite impressive. If short on time, stick to the center or examine a particular sliver of Chilean culture (i.e. Neruda's house or Matta's works), but avoid the Quinta Normal museums, as they offer less payback for the time and energy invested. **Sernatur** (see **Tourist Office,** p. 95) provides a complete listing of museums in central Santiago.

MUSEO LA CHASCONA. While the name refers to the unruly hair of Pablo Neruda's widow, Matilde Urrutia, it could just as easily refer to the eccentric and sprawling design of the famed poet's house. La Chascona is one of three Neruda houses that have been turned into museums (see **Valparaíso,** p. 123, and **Isla Negra,** p. 134). The blue exterior pays homage to Neruda's obsession with the sea, while the design motifs of the premises' two main buildings represent a ship and a lighthouse. Pre-Columbian pottery, a slew of Russian dolls, and wooden African statues reflect his diplomatic and personal world travel. *(Fernando Marquéz de la Plata 0192, Barrio Bellavista.* ☎ *777 8741. Open Tu-Su 10am-6pm. Required tours in English CH$3000, in Spanish CH$1800, students and seniors CH$900.)*

MUSEO HISTÓRICO NACIONAL. Though the exhibit ends with a surprisingly poignant display of Allende's broken glasses, the years after 1973 are conspicuously absent. The Spanish-only, text-heavy displays of economic, agricultural, and political change in Chilean society would satisfy the most rigorous historian, but the scale model of Santiago and illustrative photos make for an entertaining shorter and less comprehensive visit. *(Plaza de Armas 951, on the north side of the plaza to the right of the post center. M: Plaza de Armas.* ☎ *638 1411; www.museohistoricona-cional.cl. Open Tu-Su 10am-5:30pm. CH$600, ages 8-18 CH$300, seniors free.)*

But the detainment was short-lived—the freed Vega quickly stirred up more controversy by getting in a spat with the mayor of Ñuñoa, Pedro Sabat, on the TV talk show, *El Thermamador.* The row turned into a pushing match, which the show's producer had to break up. But while the combatants were waging a petty war of words, SENAME, the Chilean child welfare department, began investigating alleged past and present pedophilic transgressions of Mr. Vega. And with the artist in prison, "Baby Vamp" was forced to curtail project "Bad Girl."

Although the project was eventually brought to a halt, in light of this controversy, one has to wonder; are exhibitionism, sensationalism, and a reliance on shockvalue the only avenues left for artistic expression in post-Pinochet Chile? Or does Vega's project indicate an adolescent phase in the Chilean art scene that will soon give way to other profound, and hopefully more sustainable, projects? In the end, Baby Vamp's experience during the summer of 2002 shows that streaking through the Plaza de Armas is probably not the best way to get a handle on Chilean jurisprudence.

MUSEO DE BELLAS ARTES AND MUSEO DE ARTE CONTEMPORANEO. This gorgeous Neoclassical monument, built in 1910 to commemorate Chile's first centenary, houses these two museums, the largest concentration of collected art in all of Chile. The Museo de Bellas Artes displays classic and contemporary artwork by Chilean and international artists. While the Museum of Contemporary Art sits in the shadow of its more formidable twin, the rotating exhibits will impress. Call ahead for current exhibits; international-caliber work does occasionally hang here. *(M: Bellas Artes, near Parque Forestal. The Bellas Artes is located on the east side of the building, with the Arte Contemporaneo on the west. Bellas Artes ☎ 638 4060. Open Tu-Su 10am-6:30pm. Free tours Sa-Su 12:30 and 4:30pm. CH$600, students CH$300, but prices vary per exhibition. Arte Contemporaneo ☎ 639 5486 or 639 6488. Open Tu-Sa 11am-7pm, Su 11am-4pm. CH$300, students CH$200.)*

MUSEO DE ARTE PRECOLOMBINO. Well-organized and informative, this museum showcases indigenous artwork from all over Latin America. Highlights include 7000-year-old mummies from Arica (whose soft parts have been replaced with branches, plants, and mud) and a large wooden statue crafted by the Mapuche people to commemorate their dead. Be sure to check out the Mayan artifacts. *(Bandera 361, 1 block west of the southwest corner of Plaza de Armas. ☎ 688 7348. Open Tu-Sa 10am-6pm, Su 10am-2pm. Free tours in English and Spanish Tu-Sa 1 and 5pm. CH$2000, students free; free on Su.)*

MUSEO DE LA SOLIDARIDAD, SALVADOR ALLENDE. Built in 1971, the museum showcases art donated by international artists who first expressed solidarity with President Allende and later supported Chile's return to democracy. The seven rooms of art center around a peaceful courtyard and are only partially political in nature. Especially impressive are the downstairs "Finnish room" and the "Spanish room" upstairs. *(Herrera 360A. From Estación Central, walk 6 blocks north to Compañía, then 2 blocks east to Herrera. ☎ 681 7542. Open Tu-Su 10am-7pm. CH$500, students CH$250.)*

MUSEO DE SANTIAGO. From Santiago's beginnings as a colonial outpost to the building of the Puente Cal y Canto, this modest museum outlines the history of the city. It takes note of some interesting phenomena, like the development of the tram and the building of Cerro Santa Lucia, while leaving out modern developments in the city's landscape and culture. The Casa Colorada building, which shelters the museum's halls, is a historical artifact of its own, having been the site of the first government *junta* of 1810-11. *(Merced 860, just east of the southeast corner of the Plaza de Armas. ☎ 633 0723. Open Tu-F 10am-6pm, Sa 10am-5pm, Su 11am-2pm. CH$500; free on Su.)*

MUSEO DE ARTES VISUALES. One of Santiago's newest museums, it features six floors of modern art produced by Chilean artists since the 1960s. The mural outside was created by Roberto Matta, a popular poet and painter. *(Lastarria 307, in the Plaza del Mulato Gil. From M: U. Católica, walk up Lastarria 3 blocks; the plaza is on the right. ☎ 638 3502. Open Tu-Su 11:30am-7:30pm. CH$1000, students CH$500; free Tu after 3:30pm.)*

MUSEO NACIONAL DE HISTORIA NATURAL. The museum is antiquated, but it still has a handful of worthy sights, especially the blue whale and mastadon skeletons. The most modern exhibit is run by Procobre, the copper industry's non-profit public relations branch, and seems to be designed to transform school children into copper-loving fanatics. *(Parque Quinta Normal. ☎ 680 4631 or 680 4600. Open Tu-Sa 10am-5:30pm, Su noon-5:30pm. CH$600, students CH$300.)*

SMALLER MUSEUMS. Museo Ralli rewards the public transportation pilgrimage with a solid collection of Latin American and European contemporary art, including works by Dalí, Miró, and Matta. *(Alonso de Sotomayor 4110, at the intersection with Candelaria Goynechea, in Vitacura. ☎ 206 4224. From M: Los Leones, take any bus headed up Av. Vitacura, get off right after Alonso de Cordova, and go 3 blocks north on Candelaria Goynechea. Open May-Sept. Tu-Su 10:30am-4pm; Oct.-Apr. Tu-Su 11am-5pm. Free.)* **Museo de**

Ciencia y Tecnología has interactive astronomy, geology, and multimedia exhibits. *(Parque Quinta Normal. ☎681 8808. Internet CH$500 per hr. Open Tu-F 10am-5:15pm, Sa-Su 11am-5:15pm. CH$800, students CH$600.)* Mummy lovers should check out **Museo Arqueológico de Santiago.** *(Lastarria 321, next to Museo de Artes Visuales. ☎638 3502. Open M-F 10am-2pm and 3:30-6:30pm, Sa 10am-2pm. Free.)* Children's museum junkies will want to make the trek all the way to La Florida for the ultra-modern **Museo Interactivo Mirador (MIM),** a huge chunk of geometrically sculpted cement on an expansive esplanade. Everything in this museum turns, twists, opens, reveals, and demonstrates, and will consequently please visitors of all ages. *(Punta Arenas 6711. From M: Mirador, follow Mirador Azul 3 blocks west to Punta Arenas, go left, then immediately right, and follow the signs into the park. ☎294 3955. Open in summer 10am-7pm, in winter 9:30am-5:30pm. CH$3000, children CH$2000.)*

⛷ SKIING

Perched only 90 minutes up an extremely curvy road from Las Condes, the ski resorts of **Valle Nevado, El Colorado/Farellones,** and **La Parva** beckon from above the smog. In the winter, from mid-June to mid-October, snow collects in thick layers, pleasing ski bums and daytrippers alike. During the summer months, these stark ski villages draw mountain bikers and trekkers with their convenient access to the high Andes peaks. During the ski season, **SkiTotal,** Apoquindo 4900 (☎246 6881; www.skitotal.cl), three blocks east of M: Escuela Militar, offers equipment rental and transport to any of the ski resorts. (Buses depart from Las Condes daily 8:15am; depart ski areas 5pm. Skis, boots, and pole rental CH$13,000 per day. Transport to Nevado CH$6500; El Colorado/Farellones and La Parva CH$6000.) **KL Chile,** Av. Las Condes 12207 (☎217 9101; www.klchile.com), offers similar services on a more limited scale. To get there, take buses #229, #637, or others going up Av. Las Condes to Cantagallo; the office is across from IMAC. (Transport leaves daily 8:30am, returns 5:30pm. Complete rentals US$15-20. Transport US$10.) **Ski Van,** Nicholas Gogol 1483 (☎219 2672), in Vitacura, also runs vans. For avid skiers, a **combined lift ticket** is available from any of the four resort sites, as trails and lifts can be linked. Inquire at the ticket office.

VALLE NEVADO. Generally acclaimed by beginning and intermediate skiers as the best ski area in Central Chile, Nevado doesn't disappoint with a huge, contiguous patch of skiable terrain. Lodging is quite expensive here during the peak season, but the best bet if you're desperate is **Hotel Tres Puntas ❺** (over US$200). In summer, the lifts carry hang-gliders up to their point of departure, and mountaineers can use the resort as a staging ground of their own. *(55km up the road from La Barneachea. ☎206 0027; www.vallenevado.com. 11 lifts service 34 trails totalling 23 miles: 12% beginner, 29% intermediate, 41% advanced, 18% expert. 22,239 skiable acres. Elev. 2860-3670m. Rentals available. Tickets in July CH$18,000, children CH$12,000; June, Aug., and Sept. M-F CH$14,500/CH$9500.)*

EL COLORADO/FARELLONES. These resort towns offer visitors two separate base towns, but the lifts and trails are all interconnected and inseparable. *(36km up the valley road. ☎246 3344; www.elcolorado.cl. 18 lifts service 20 trails totalling 23½ miles. 2471 skiable acres. Elev. 2430-3333m. Tickets in July CH$17,000, children CH$10,000; June, Aug., and Sept. M-F CH$13,000/CH$8000.)*

LA PARVA. Higher than El Colorado and generally considered to be better for experts, La Parva is situated immediately below the impressive Cerro Parva and Cerro Pintor. Summer brings great trekking opportunities. *(40km up the valley road. ☎264 1466; www.laparva.cl. 14 lifts service 30 trails totalling 23½ miles: 15% beginner, 45% intermediate, 30% advanced, 10% expert. 1730 skiable acres. Elev. 2670-3630m. Tickets in July CH$17,000, children CH$12,500; June, Aug., and Sept. M-F CH$13,500/CH$9800.)*

THE TIMES, THEY ARE A-CHANGIN'
Conflicting Social and Political Mores in Santiago's La Victoria

"*Y por qué vives allá?*" The taxi driver had been unwilling to drive me home until I convinced him that if I could live in Santiago's infamous *barrio*, La Victoria, he could certainly take me there. This initial reluctance to venture towards La Victoria is not unusual, however. Many Chileans have a similarly strong visceral reaction to the mere mention of the neighborhood's name. Sentiments towards La Victoria range from extreme glorification to scathing condemnation. An examination into prevailing attitudes towards La Victoria and the history that informs those attitudes provides an interesting segue to the sharp political divisions of Chile's past, the changing social landscape of its present, and the vast uncertainty of its future.

Communism in Chile has had a controversial history. Marxist ideologies pouring out of Europe at the turn of the century galvanized mine workers and by 1922, the Communist Party was thriving. The Great Depression further strengthened the radical left, increasing tension with the ruling elite and provoking widespread social turbulence. The presidential victory of the middle-class Radical Party seemed to announce a new era of social reform, until the advent of the Cold War sparked a backlash against the left. Nevertheless, the Communists were back on the streets, initiating nearly two decades of protest that grew in intensity until its fateful end in the bloody coup of 1973.

During this tumultuous period, La Victoria became a symbol of popular struggle. Founded by *pobladores* (loosely, colonizer) in 1957 through a *toma de terreno* (land takeover), La Victoria became a model for *tomas* throughout Chile as well as a touchstone for popular leftist action. In the months leading up to the *toma*, members of Chile's Communist Party and students from the University of Chile successfully organized hundreds of homeless families who had become resigned to squatting on the banks of a river on the periphery of Santiago. Under the guidance of a member of the Communist Party, the group identified a few large plots of land held by wealthy landowners and planned their future community. The present-day site of La Victoria was to be developed into a self-sufficient commune including roads, a school, a health clinic, and a home for every family. On the night of October 30th, 1957, the group seized the land and immediately began preparing to defend themselves against police officers who would doubtless try to expel them from the property. However, the *pobladores* stalwartly stood their ground, and after several days of resistance, declared victory, naming their new community La Victoria in honor of the occasion.

The taxi I'm in turns onto 30 de Octubre, a street whose name commemorates the date the *poblacion* was founded. On this same street several months earlier, I witnessed the annual reenactment of the *toma*, as a few hundred *victorianos*, marching to chants of "*El pueblo unido jamás será vencido*" (the people united will never be conquered), proudly followed in the steps taken by their parents and grandparents 44 years before. Under the watchful eye of a police escort, the crowd, comprised mostly of adult women, elderly men and women, and children under the age of 15, stopped pointedly in the middle of the main thoroughfare Avenida La Feria to block traffic before triumphantly continuing into the *población*.

However, this historical celebration of La Victoria's founding was dwarfed by the cultural celebration that followed a few evenings later, when over a 1000 residents and visitors from other *barrios* crowded the street for a festive night of musical and dance performances. The program was an eclectic mix of traditional Chilean music, including homages to legendary folk singers Victor Jara and Violeta Parra. More trendy groups such as Amerikan Sound, a long-haired Chilean version of the Backstreet Boys, were also represented.

The obvious distinctions between these two events are a good representation of the competing social and cultural traditions of La Victoria. Considering the youthful crowd's frenzied response on the latter occasion to the heartthrobs who comprise Amerikan Sound, one might conclude that the direction of the *población's* future is clear.

However, as we pass the Communist Party building, I catch a glimpse of a group of middle-aged men deep in discussion under the intense gaze of Che Guevara. Two black-and-white murals of the communist revolutionary in his trademark beret and a conspicuous color mural of Salvador Allende, the first and only declared Marxist to rule Chile before the coup, preside over the room as if to urge their disciples to continue the Communist struggle. The murals hint at the brutal struggle that has defined the Communist movement in Chile, a struggle in which many residents of La Victoria have played a central role. In 1983, when *victorianos* took to the streets in the first massive protest against the Pinochet regime in Chile, they set off a series of nationwide protests that began the eventual decline of the military government's iron-tight regime. For years, the residents of La Victoria suffered the consequences of their bravery—detention, torture, and several deaths—but they remained resolute in their opposition.

Ironically enough, present-day democracy has done for the neighborhood what those years of repression could not—fractured La Victoria's social solidarity and ideological homogeneity. Without a unifying force to oppose, the residents of La Victoria remain primarily preoccupied with economic pressures of providing for their families in one of the world's most liberal free-market systems. Within this social and political vacuum, other forces have begun to take control of the streets as well—at night, drug dealers stand on the corner of 30 de Octubre and brazenly hawk their wares to passersby, causing the controversial district's reputation to devolve from famous to infamous in recent years.

We pull in front of the house, which appears from the outside to be little more than a ramshackle pile of wood, plastic cartons, and scrap metal, where I live with an extended Chilean family of ten. The taxi driver has already asked me to have exact change ready so that he can speed off. I open the door and enter the living room where I find the eldest daughter patiently copying a Pablo Neruda poem to distribute at an event commemorating the Communist poet's birthday the following day. Her younger sister mimics the suggestive movements of scantily clad Brazilian dancers on TV. The conflicting social, cultural, and political mores of La Victoria are so patently manifest in these sisters, I can't help wondering which foresees La Victoria's future.

Brian Milder was a Researcher-Writer for Let's Go: New Zealand 2000. He has spent the past year in Chile as a Rockefeller Fellow living in La Victoria and volunteering at the Nonprofit Enterprise and Self-sustainability Team (NESsT).

PORTILLO. A bit further from the city of Santiago, northeast past the city of Los Andes, Portillo probably gets the most attention abroad for its fabulous location and dry snow. The catch is that you have to cash in all your earthly possessions to ski here. Daily lift tickets may or may not be available, but the facilities are gorgeous. (☎361 7000; www.skiportillo.com. *12 lifts serve a variety of terrain: 18% beginner, 25% intermediate, 35% advanced, 22% expert. 145km from Santiago. Open mid-June to mid-October. Tickets CH$17,000, children CH$12,000.)*

🎬 ENTERTAINMENT

SPORTS

FÚTBOL. Some argue that the advertising campaign *"Piensa Positivo"* ("Think Positive") aims to treat public depression regarding the national team's poor performance, rather than depression about Chile's current recession. The earth comes to a proverbial grinding halt when the capital's three most popular clubs— **Club Colo Colo,** Cienfuegos 41 (☎695 2251); **Universidad Católica,** Andrés Bello 2782 (☎231 2777), Las Condes; and **Universidad de Chile,** Campos de Deportes 565 (☎239 2793), Ñuñoa—play each other in what are called "classics". *(Tournaments take place in the Estadio Nacional, Grecia 2001, Ñuñoa. ☎238 8102 for tickets. Seats from CH$4000.)*

HORSE RACING. Hipódromo Chile, Hipódromo Chile 1715, Independencia, hosts races at 2pm on Saturdays and alternate Thursdays. *(To get there, take an Independencia-Plaza Chacabuco bus from the Mapocho station or the #303 bus from Bandera St. in town.* ☎270 9200.) **Club Hípico,** Blanco Encalada 2540, also has races at 2:30pm on Mondays and alternate Wednesdays, and offers great views of the Andes. *(☎693 9600; 7 blocks south of M: Union Latinoamericana on Union Americana.)* If you prefer to watch from a screen, there are several tele-tracks throughout downtown and in Barrio Brasil that satiate betting appetites.

RODEO. Rodeo, the proclaimed "national" sport (some soccer fans would debate this point), is especially popular during the month of September when the season coincides with other national festivities. The season continues into May, but the most important event, the **Campeonato Nacional de Rodeo,** takes place out in Rancagua on the last weekend in March. *(Call the Federación de Rodeos de Chile for more information. ☎699 0115. Tickets CH$5000-40,000.)*

PERFORMING ARTS

Bellavista has the highest concentration of theaters in the city, many offering avant-garde productions (Th-Su, tickets CH$4000-8000). While most theaters tend to be pricier on weekends, they offer student discounts on Thursday and Sunday. **Teatro Municipal,** Agustinas 794 (☎369 0282), is Chile's official artistic center and features concerts, ballets, and operas by prestigious national and international groups. Unfortunately, only those fluent in Spanish may delve into the Santiago art scene, as performances are rarely staged in English.

Teatro Conventillo, Bellavista 173 (☎777 4164), Bellavista. One of the oldest in Santiago and credited by many with making theater more accessible to the masses. CH$3000-7000.

Teatro Universidad de Chile, Providencia 043 (☎634 5295), by M: Baquedano. Houses the national Chilean ballet company and hosts world-renowned Latin American musicians for weekly concerts. Shows from CH$1000.

Teatro Universidad Católica, Jorge Washington 24 (☎205 5652), Plaza Ñuñoa, is the hub of artistic life in the southeastern suburb. Shows W-Su. Weekend public admission CH$7000.

CINEMA

Hollywood films, rivaled by an excellent collection of independent films, come to Santiago a few weeks after their US release. Most films are in their original language with Spanish subtitles. (Tickets CH$1600-2800; nearly all theaters give student discounts.)

Cinema Hoyts, Huérfanos 735 and San Antonio 144 (☎664 1861 or 632 9566), features mainstream US, art house, and Chilean flicks. CH$2600-2800.

Centro de Extensión Universidad Católica, Alameda 390 (☎686 6516), offers country- and director-specific film showings in conjunction with local embassies. Call ahead for schedule. CH$2000.

Cine Arte Alameda, O'Higgins 139 (☎664 8890), features international art house films. CH$1800.

CULTURAL INSTITUTES

Santiago's cultural institutes offer the Chilean artistic and creative community a number of smaller venues for exhibiting and performing their work. Activities include plays, workshops, exhibitions, film screenings, readings, and more. The largest and most significant institutes are the old train station **Centro Cultural Estación Mapocho** (☎361 1761), M: Puente Cal y Canto, and **Plaza Central Centro de Extensión Universidad Católica,** Alameda 390 (☎686 6518 or 222 0275), M: U. Católica. Smaller ones include **Biblioteca Nacional,** O'Higgins 651 (☎360 5200), M: Santa Lucia, and **Instituto Cultural del Banco Estado del Chile,** Alameda 123 (☎639 2624 or 639 7785), M: Baquedano.

🛍 SHOPPING

Santiago has many shopping options, from **department stores** to **flea markets** to **craft fairs.** Makeshift stands and merchandise-covered blankets filled with inexpensive goods can be found all along **Alameda.**

MALLS AND COMMERCIAL GOODS

Alto Las Condes, Kennedy 9001 (☎299 6999), in Las Condes. Catch a bus along Alameda or take a cab from Escuela Militar. The biggest and most modern mall in Chile, with 240 shops and department stores. Open 10am-10pm.

Mall del Centro (☎361 0011), 2 blocks north of the Plaza de Armas. Smaller than Las Condes, but more conveniently located. Open 10am-10pm.

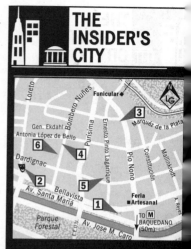

THE INSIDER'S CITY

MIDNIGHT IN BELLAVISTA

In fact, midnight is the only gathering time in this, the youngest and hippest nightlife neighborhood in Santiago. The crowds begin to mull among the street vendors and hawkers as the clock strikes 12, clubs and pubs get going a short time later, and the party rides on 'til morning light. Stay somewhat sober and secure when away from the busy Pío Nono strip.

1 Table-shop for souvenirs at Parque Gomez Rojas late into the night.

2 Enjoy nifty student discounts—catch a cool show at Teatro Conventillo.

3 Get a spicy taste of salsa music and dancing at the hippest *salsoteca,* La Maestra Vida.

4 Or join Bob Marley's faithful posse at the reggaed-out Jammin' Club.

5 Gawk at Santiago's bold, beautiful, rich, and famous at the hottest spot in town, the elusive Tantra.

6 But if you don't get in there, which you might not, don't dismay because Bunker pumps the best techno and house in Bellavista and stays thumping into the wee hours.

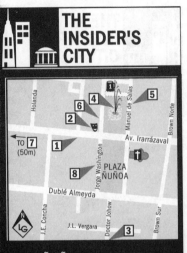

THE INSIDER'S CITY

ÑUÑOA AT NIGHT

Removed from the main axis of Santiago's cultural life, the cluster of cafes, bars, restaurants, and a theater around Plaza Ñuñoa is an artistic island in this residential desert. The variety of establishments here lend themselves to a well-rounded evening. Take any bus south from Los Leones that says "Irarrazaval" on it. Thursday through Saturday nights are always the most vibrant.

1 Begin the evening with a fruit smoothie or coffee at the chic La Isla Café.

2 Cruise on over to the Teatro Universidad Católica and catch a show before dinner.

3 Follow the curious keyboard into unassuming La Tecla, the perfect eatery for a light dinner of pizza or *panqueques*.

4 Walk off that mozzarella with a stroll on Plaza Ñuñoa's paths to the fountain, a favorite among amorous couples.

Mercado Persa, near Estación Central. One of the largest and best organized flea markets in Santiago. Open 9am-9pm.

Mundo de Vino, Isadora Goyenechea 2931 (☎244 8888). Has the largest selection of Chilean wines on the planet (from CH$2700), as well as some international brands. Open M-Sa 10:30am-8:30pm, Su 10:30am-8pm.

La Vinoteca, Isadora Goyenechea 2966 (☎334 1987). Right down the road from the more comprehensive and overwhelming "Mundo," this wine boutique shop gives customers a bit more personal attention. Open M-F 10am-9pm, Sa 10am-5pm, Su 11am-2pm.

LOCAL CRAFTS

Ferias artesanales (craft fairs) are ubiquitous in Santiago, and feature everything from lapiz lazuli jewelry to llama wool sweaters. The *artesanal's* well-endowed wooden figurines are a tourist favorite. Bellavista's **Parque Gomez Rojas,** at the corner of Pío Nono and Santa María, has a permanent, convenient *feria artesanal.* Another *feria* sits across from the **Biblioteca Nacional,** on Alameda 672. (Open 10am-9pm.) **Pío Nono** also erupts at night to become its own *artesanía* bazaar. A bit farther out is **Pueblito de los Dominicos,** Apoquindo 9085 (☎245 5142), in Las Condes next to the Cathedral of the Dominicans, which features some handicrafts that you might not see elsewhere—don't miss the intricately carved matchsticks. For a more laid-back (and pricey) craft-shopping atmosphere, try **Artesanias de Chile,** Lastarria 305, #107 (☎633 0081), in Plaza Mulato Gil, next to Museo de Visuales Artes.

■ NIGHTLIFE

Though possibly disappointing compared with other major South American cities, Santiago holds its own when it comes to livin' *la vida loca.* Virtually every establishment in barrios **Bellavista** and **Suecia** turns into a pub, disco, or both at night, and still struggles to contain the throngs of party-seekers who come looking for the ultimate weekend beat. **Vitacura** and **Ñuñoa,** though a bit farther away, are also crowd-pleasers. Festivities start between 11pm and midnight, and crowds usually spill onto the street until 5am. Bohemian Bellavista hot spots are the cheaper (and thus more popular) choice for locals, especially for teenagers and university students; most of these are near **Av. Pío Nono.** Suecia's more expensive nocturnal delights, clustered around **Suecia,** have a more commercial appeal and attract an older, more international crowd.

BARS

🖫 **Pub La Boheme,** Bombero Nuñez 336 (☎737 4110). An elite scene, frequented by a young, good-looking crowd. Various depictions of bodies and body parts adorn the tastefully stark walls. Techno weekends, softer stuff on weekdays. Not hopping until late. Pisco sour CH$1300, Margarita CH$2700, Amaretto coffee CH$800. Minimum consumption on weekends CH$1500. Open Tu-Th 8:30am-1am, F-Su 8:30am-5am.

Babble, General Holley 2337 (☎223 8433), in Suecia. A festive atmosphere is optimal for the many bachelor parties thrown here. Features celebrity impersonators and karaoke contests. Beers from CH$1900. Cover F-Sa CH$3000. Open Tu-Th 6pm-1am, F-Su 6pm-4am.

Pub Blue, 19 de Abril 3526 (☎223 7132), Plaza Ñuñoa. The tiki torches outside don't lead you to a tribal council, and no, this pub will most definitely not be voted off Plaza Ñuñoa's island of nightlife. The blue interior is all-consuming while pisco sours (CH$1800) are all consumed. Happy hour F-Sa 7-10pm, M-Th 5-7pm. Open M-W 4pm-1am, Th 4pm-2am, F-Sa 6pm-3am.

Mr. Ed, Suecia 0152 (☎231 2624). While the talking horse may now only exist in re-runs, his popularity still lives on. A barn-like pub packed with dancing locals who make the tabletop candles look a little out of place. Live rock on weekends. Beer CH$1600-2000. Happy hour 7-10pm. Open M-W 7-11pm, Th-Sa 7pm-5am.

Ebano, Manuel de Salas 123 (☎209 5220). Although this *"cocina soul"* (soul kitchen) is technically a restaurant, the menus clearly show an emphasis on wine and mixed drinks. Quiet ambience and 70s soul music. A "large portion" of sushi CH$4000. Assortment of glasses of wine CH$1500-2000. Half-price mixed drinks during happy hour (M-Sa 7-9:30pm). Open M-Th 7pm-1am, F-Sa 6pm-3am.

Louisiana the River Pub, General Holley 2308 (☎242 8077), in Suecia. This neon river-boat is hard to miss. 2 floors, each with a live band playing 80s music and salsa at 8:30pm. Lots of seating accommodates the older crowd that frequents the River Pub. Kitchen open late. Beer from CH$1100. Open M-Th 8am-1am, F-Su 8am-5am.

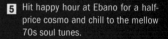

5 Hit happy hour at Ebano for a half-price cosmo and chill to the mellow 70s soul tunes.

6 Turn it up a notch by meandering over to Batuta, which rocks out to live music nightly.

7 If the loud music leaves you frazzled, move along to Club de Jazz, where the live Big-Apple-esque tunes might just rejuvenate you and get you in the mood for...

8 A late-night snack of crepes of all kinds at El Amor Nunca Muere, a French-styled eatery that'll send you and your stomach home smiling.

CLUBS AND DISCOS

Rule of thumb: the cheaper the cover, the less mature the crowd. Bellavista is hipper and more happening, but packed dance floors are the norm in Suecia. If you want to avoid the pretenses and just dance Latin-style, try the **Asociación Cristiana Feminina,** Moneda

1640, Santiago Centro. Mondays feature tantalizing tango classes with the talented Vania Montecinos, Thursdays are salsa nights, and there's samba, merengue, and more throughout the week. (☎ 696 1608. Classes CH$1000 per session, CH$4000 per month. Open daily 5-11pm.)

■ **Tantra,** Ernesto Pinto Lagarrigue 154 (☎ 732 326 or 735 5535). Elegant salons with white couches and South Asian accents add a touch of VIP to the air, as do the glamorous celebrity guests. Open to the public only when not booked for a private function. Dress to impress and don't look intimidated by the black facade, the bouncer with his multiple piercings, or the bronze "protrusions" that straddle the entry. Fusion restaurant open Tu-Sa 8pm-midnight. Happy hour Tu-Th 6pm-midnight. Weekend cover CH$8000-10,000. Club open Th-Sa midnight-5am.

Ilé Habana, Bucarest 95 (☎ 231 5711), in Suecia. Classy Afro-Cuban atmosphere with an energetic dance floor. Live Cuban bands Tu-Sa. Mambo, cha-cha-cha, and bacheta classes, as well as other cultural programs. Tends to get going earlier than surrounding locales. Cuban drinks CH$3200. Weekend cover up to CH$5000. Open M-Th 7:30am-3:30am, F-Sa 7:30am-5am.

Entre Negros, Suecia 0188 (☎ 334 2094). 2 floors of mixed crowds and mixed music, including pop, salsa, merengue, and techno. Live music daily 10pm-1am. Open 'til the wee hours, well beyond most other establishments in Suecia. Cover CH$4000. Open M-Sa 9pm-late.

Batuta, Jorge Washington 52 (☎ 274 9432), at Plaza Ñuñoa. Good live acts grace this nightlife standout in the Ñuñoa area. Acts vary from rock to funk and everything in between. Cover CH$2000-4000. Open W-Th 9pm-late, F-Sa 10pm-late.

Jammin' Club, Antonia López de Bello 49, in Bellavista. The spot for reggae, incense, and unkempt rastafarian hair. Plenty of red, yellow, and green decor and clothing, not to mention the Bob Marley memorabilia. Cover CH$2500. Open F-Sa 11pm-5am.

Club de Jazz, Alessandri 85 (☎ 274 1937), in Ñuñoa, behind the big palm tree. This mansion features local and foreign musicians playing—you guessed it—jazz. A nice escape from the rest of Santiago's salsa- and cover-heavy live music scene. Cover CH$3000, students CH$2500. Open Th-Sa 10:30pm-2am.

Maestra Vida (Salsoteca), Pío Nono 380 (☎ 777 5325), in Bellavista. This raging salsa machine is probably the pinnacle of Pío Nono's salsa establishments. Cover CH$2500. Open Tu-W 10:30pm-2am, Th-Sa 10:30pm-5am.

Havana Salsa, Dominica 142 (☎ 737 1737 or 777 5829), in Bellavista. Behind a Potemkin storefront facade, gorgeous professional Cuban dancers gyrate to merengue, salsa, hip-hop, tango, flamenco, and more. Drink yourself silly and try it yourself. Show midnight-1am. CH$7500 includes buffet dinner before 11:30pm and 1 drink after. This is only the spot to come if you want to make an evening of it. Open W-Sa 8:30pm-5am.

Drag Queen, Bombero Nuñez 169 (☎ 738 2314 or 738 2301). The most flamboyant dining experience in Santiago serves dishes from a seafood-strong list of mains (CH$5000). Drag show every night (1am). Also has a bar and disco. Pisco sours CH$1900-2500. CH$3000 minimum consumption. Open Tu-Sa 8:30pm-5am.

GAY AND LESBIAN FOOD AND NIGHTLIFE

Although Santiago still has a great deal of discrimination against homosexuals, the gay and lesbian community does have access to a vibrant nightlife, primarily in Barrio Bellavista. Establishments can be unmarked and inconspicuous from the outside, but inside, they host some of the city's best parties.

■ **Bunker,** Bombero Nuñez 159 (☎ 737 1716). The premier gay and lesbian club, and one of the best clubs in the city. Great house and techno, 3 bars, deck, catwalk, and plenty of cages. Black-lit spectres on the walls and dismembered parts of anatomically-correct mannequins adorn the bars and walls. Sells its own CD mix. The only club with its own cabaret drag show (2:30am). Pricey mixed drinks from CH$3000, beers CH$1500-2000. Cover CH$5000-7000. 2-for-1 before 1am. Open F-Sa midnight-6am.

Capricho Español, Purísima 65 (☎777 7674). This attractive restaurant has an intimate yet festive atmosphere, as seen in the wall design—it's lined with modern paintings, hot peppers, and garlic. *Tapas* CH$3500, crab pie CH$3800, *paella* for 2 CH$9600, omelette CH$1900. Whiskey sour CH$2500. Open M-Th 8pm-1am, F-Su 8pm-3am.

Farinelli Café, Bombero Nuñez 68 (☎732 8966). A twist on the infamous *cafes con piernas*, with lots of *pierna*. Well-toned waiters flaunt tight shirts and thong underwear. Indulge in the tea, coffee, and cakes (CH$800-1200) among deep purple environs. Open M-Th 5pm-midnight, F-Sa 5pm-2am and 3-9am, Su 5pm-2am.

Mascara, Purísima 129 (☎737 4123). This upscale disco draws a lesbian crowd and is run mostly by women. Music from salsa to pop to techno. Internet, darts, and pool. Cover CH$4000. Open Th-Sa 9pm-5am.

Bar Dionisio, Bombero Nuñez 111 (☎737 6065), marked by red doors and a blue pillar. Bare torsos on the walls make for good conversation at the bar. Weekends feature comedians and drag queens (12:30-3am). Latin, Anglo, funk, and pop music abound. Beer from CH$1500. Cover CH$1000. Open Tu-Th 9pm-2:30am, F-Sa 9pm-4:30am.

▶ DAYTRIPS FROM SANTIAGO

CONCHA Y TORO

To get to Concha y Toro, take M: Baquedano (near Plaza Italia) line 5 south to Bellavista de la Florida. From there, take Metrobuses 72, 73, 74, 80, or 85, which emerge from the suburbs into more verdant terrain to stop at Concha y Toro (40min.). Tours 1hr.; Spanish M-F 10:30am and 4pm, Sa 11am; English M-F 11:30am and 3pm, Sa 10am and noon. CH$2600 per person.

Chile is a rising star in the world of wine exporters, thanks to the success of brands like **Concha y Toro** (☎821 7069 or 821 1063; www.conchaytoro.cl), the country's largest wine producer. The mere scale of the nationwide operation is impressive—Concha y Toro vines cover 3800 hectares over six valleys of central Chile, producing grapes for 100 million liters of finished product. Concha y Toro has won international recognition for its products and proudly offers tours of its Maipo Valley vineyard to show how it's all done. From the vineyards, tours continue through wine cellars and end in the tourist shop, where you can purchase discounted wines. Enjoy the three complimentary wine tastings in your free souvenir glass.

CAJÓN DEL MAIPO

*To get to Cajón del Maipo, take Metrobus #72 from M: Bellavista de la Florida to San José del Maipo. Going up the canyon beyond San José, the more convenient blue-and-white **Buses Cajón de Maipo** (☎850 5769) leave from just east of the M: Parque O'Higgins exit. Buses to: Baños Morales (2hr.; Jan.-Feb. daily, Oct.-Nov. and Mar. 7:15am; CH$2000); San Alfonso (1hr., every 30min. 7am-10pm, CH$1500); San José (45min., every 10min. 7am-10pm, CH$1200). For tourist information, visit **Municipalidad de San José de Maipo** (☎861 1275) or **Sernatur**, in Santiago.*

Cajón del Maipo is inundated in the summer with *Santiaguinos* escaping their urban environs for a refreshing breath of mountain air. For visitors to Santiago, this area merits a look. In summer, services and outfitters are more conveniently geared for visitors, but the lack of crowds make a fall or winter visit more peaceful. Without a doubt, the most popular activity in Cajón del Maipo is **rafting** down the Maipo River. A host of Santiago outfitters operate daytrips from the city that range US$25-70, depending on the duration of the tour and perks (e.g. lunch) included (see **Adventure Tours**, p. 96). Quite near the town of San Alfonso, the retreat of **Cascada de las Animas** (☎861 1303; www.cascadadelasanimas.cl) draws hordes of summer recreationalists. Its **rafting** (CH$14,000) and **horseback riding** (CH$15,000 for 2hr.) trips, proximity to the adjacent mountains, affordable cabins (from CH$30,000), and camping (CH$2500 per person) ensure a memorable stay. Possibly the most beautiful area of the canyon is the head of the right fork of the canyon, near **Baños Morales.** From the baths, an 8km trail (3hr.) leads up through **Monumento Natural El Morado** (CH$1200), offering views of **Laguna El Morado** and the **San Francisco Glacier.** The left fork of the road, departing from San Gabriel, is quite rough, but leads to the trailhead for **Termas del Plomo,** a collection of remote hot springs in the valley at the foot of mighty Tupungato.

MIDDLE CHILE

Superlatives abound in describing Middle Chile, the heart of the nation—it is the richest, most populated, most developed region in the country. Home to some of the wildest cities and ritziest resorts in South America, Middle Chile has a very different flavor than its more rugged and rural neighbors to the north and south. Sporadically warm and rainy, rolling hills and farmlands cover the fertile valley that begins just north of Santiago and sinks slowly deeper as it heads south to the Lakes District. The region isn't entirely bereft of natural attractions either. Several magnificent parks feature lush forests, thundering waterfalls, and incredible vistas. On the cultural front, a rich history ferments as the southern edge of the region delineates the battle lines for centuries of ethnic war, colonial battles, and indigenous struggle, and has become the center of cultural *mestizaje*.

Middle Chile is home to Chile's largest urban metropolises and all the comforts and conveniences that they offer. The Pacific coast to the west is lined with ritzy beach resorts interspersed with hip surfer communities, while the Andes to the east offer some of the best skiing on the continent. The verdant farmlands give way to vineyards that produce Chile's world famous wines and forested foothills offer the weary road warrior a chance to unwind in soothing spas and hot springs.

The jewels of Middle Chile are the sister cities of **Valparaíso** and **Viña del Mar,** west of Santiago on the Pacific Coast. Valparaíso, the older sibling, is a venerable port city with a complicated maze of narrow streets that wind through the picturesque hills that surround its center. Viña, the younger, wilder sibling, has developed into one of the premiere beach resorts in South America both for its beaches speckled with the bold and the beautiful, and its oh-so-trendy nightclubs. To the west of the capital, just over the Argentine border, the open and relaxed city of **Mendoza** has become a popular getaway for many Chileans and is a great base for excursions in to the Andes' many ski resorts. Heading into the Central Valley, **Rancagua** is the major transportation center of the region and a perfect jumping-off point for exploring the surfing haven of **Pichilemu** or the prolific wineries surrounding **Curicó** and **Talca.** No one should miss **Chillán,** with its monumental cathedral and proximity to the posh Termas de Chillán. In the southern reaches of the region sits one of Chile's largest cities, the bustling, modern **Concepción.** The gravity of history shrouds this city, the former site of bloody battles between the Mapuche and Spanish colonizers, and home to the plaza where Chile's Declaration of Independence was signed.

HIGHLIGHTS OF MIDDLE CHILE

WANDER through the eclectic collections of famed poet Pablo Neruda at **La Sebastiana** (p. 129) in Valparaíso and his house on **Isla Negra** (p. 134).

ZOOM down the slopes of **Volcán Chillán** or relax in the **Termas de Chillán** (p. 186).

FLOAT in a lovely teacup pool in **Parque Nacional Radal Siete Tazas** (p. 173).

HANG TEN on "big breakers" at the Surfing Championship held in **Pichilemu** (p. 165).

CATCH a view of the whole breadth of Chile from the rocky Andes to the shimmering Pacific on top of Piedra del Aguila in **Parque Nacional Nahuelbuta** (p. 207).

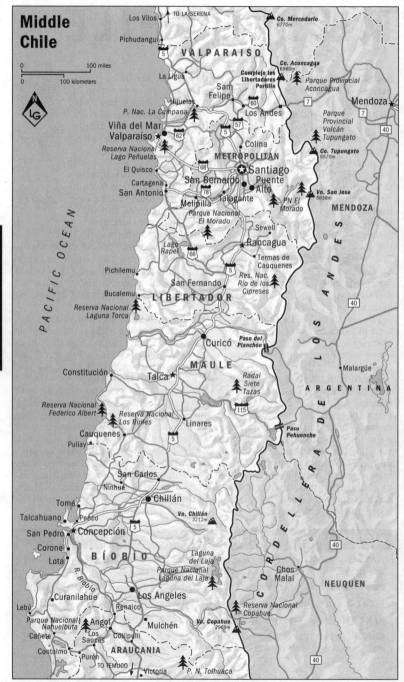

Middle Chile

THE COASTAL RESORTS

VALPARAÍSO ☎ 32

Valparaíso (pop. 300,000), Chile's second largest city and its main port, is a city of contrasts: old and new, high and low, rich and poor. At first glance, Valpo (as it is commonly called) looks like a jumble of buildings and ships haphazardly thrown together. Houses cling precariously to the hillsides, offices and museums crowd the narrow flatland, luxurious hotels surround el Congreso, back-alley brothels line the port, and small fishing boats fight for harbor space between looming Chilean naval vessels. *Porteños*, Valparaíso's residents, are proud of their city's heritage and work hard to preserve its diverse cultural monuments.

Discovered by the Spanish in 1536, Valparaíso was quickly colonized and named by Spaniard Juan de Saavedra. The city became a major port for ships making the long trip around Cape Horn, the southernmost tip of South America, from the Atlantic Ocean. During the California Gold Rush of 1849, up to 800 ships simultaneously dropped anchor en route to find their fortunes, and despite the opening of the Panama Canal in 1914, the port city has remained vibrant and bustling—Valparaíso is the proud home of Chile's navy and the keeper of its naval history.

At least eight major earthquakes have taken their toll on Valparaíso. The worst of these quakes devastated the city in 1906, leaving every major structure, except some old mansions such as Lyons Palace, which holds the natural history museum, flattened or burned to the ground. Another feature that managed to remain intact is the system of *ascensores*, or lifts, which shuttle people between the city's two levels. All these lifts were placed on a 1996 list of the world's most endangered sites by the World Monument Fund.

⊠ INTERCITY TRANSPORTATION

Flights: There is no airport in Valparaíso, but **LanChile** has an office at Esmeralda 1048 (☎251 441). Open M-F 9am-6:30pm and Sa 10am-1pm.

Trains: The train station is at Muelle Prat, facing the Plaza Sotomayor. Open 6:30am-10:30pm. Trains go to **Viña del Mar** (15min., every 10-30 min., CH$280) en route to **Limache.**

Buses: Estación Rodoviario, Pedro Montt 2800 (☎939 646), Valparaíso's main terminal, is at the edge of town across from the Congreso Nacional. A second **bus station,** Molina 366 (☎216 568), serves the northern towns of **La Ligua** and **Los Vilos.**

International: For those wishing to go to **Argentina, Bolivia,** or **Brazil,** most buses leave from the Estación Rodoviario around 8am and can cost up to US$100.

Long-Distance: Most long-distance buses connect through Santiago, so travelers should check before boarding a bus to see if a shuttle to the capital might be cheaper. The following leave from the main terminal. **Tur Bus** (☎212 028) goes to: **Antofagasta** (15hr., 2 per day, US$30); **Arica** (24hr., US$40); **Chillán** (8 hr., 3 per day, US$12); **Concepción** (10 hr., 3 per day, US$16); **Iquique** (20hr., 2 per day, US$35); **Osorno** (14hr., 3 per day, US$24); **Puerto Montt** (16hr., 3 per day, US$25); **Talca** (6hr., 3 per day, US$8); **Temuco** (11hr., 3 per day, US$18). Other companies serving the northern cities include: **Buses Zambrano** (☎268 986), with daily departures at 8am; **Pullman Bus** (☎256 898), with several daily departures; **Flota Barrios** (☎253 674), with 3 departures daily. Southern buses also include: **Buses Norte** (☎258 322), running nightly; **Tas Choapa** (☎252 921); **Buses Alsa** (Formerly Buses Lit, ☎237 200); **Intersur** (☎212 297).

Regional: Buses to **Santiago** come and go in a steady stream. **Tur Bus** (☎212 028) departs more frequently than the others (2hr., every 15min. 6am-10pm, US$4). Other companies include: **Condor Bus** (☎212 927); **Sol del Pacifico** (☎212 927); **Sol del Sur** (☎252 211); **Buses Alsa** (For-

MIDDLE CHILE

MIDDLE CHILE

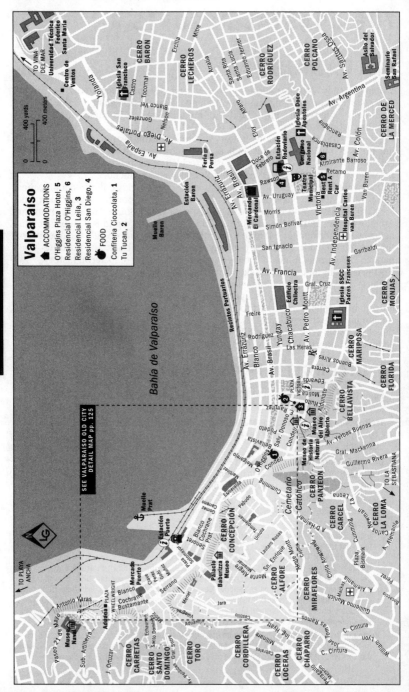

Valparaíso

■ ACCOMMODATIONS
O'Higgins Plaza Hotel, 5
Residencial O'Higgins, 6
Residencial Leila, 3
Residencial San Diego, 4

● FOOD
Confitería Cioccolata, 1
Tu Tucan, 2

SEE VALPARAISO OLD CITY DETAIL MAP pp. 125

Bahía de Valparaíso

Valparaíso Old City

🏠 ACCOMMODATIONS
B&B Brighton, 9
Casa Latina, 6
Hotel Reina Victoria, 4

🍴 FOOD
Bote Salvavidas, 2
Café Brighton, 10
Café Turri, 7
Confitería Cioccolata, 11
La Columbina, 5
La Casteñita, 1
Neptune, 3
Valparaíso mi Amor, 8

merly Buses Lit, ☎237 290). **Transportes Lasual** (☎214 915) goes to regional cities in Norte Chico including **Ovalle** (4hr., US$12) and **La Serena** (6hr., US$14). Northern beaches are served by several carriers. **Condor Bus** (☎212 927) goes to **La Ligua** (1hr., every 30min. 6:45am-9:15pm, US$2). **Buses JM** (☎256 581), **Pullman Bus** (☎256 898), and **Buses Dhino** (☎221 298) all go to: **Los Andes** (2hr., every 30min. 6am-10pm, US$4) via **Limache, Quillotab,** and **San Felipe.** To head to the southern beaches, take the pink **Pullman buses** (☎224 025), leaving every 15 minutes 6am-10pm, for: **Algarrobo; Cartegena** (2hr., US$3.50); **El Quisco** (1¼ hr., US$3); **Isla Negra** (1½ hr., US$3).

🔛 ORIENTATION

Getting around the confusing streets of Valparaíso can initially be a bit intimidating. Valpo is wedged between the hills and the ocean, so the easiest way to stay oriented is to find one or the other. The bus station sits at the eastern edge of town, on Av. Pedro Montt. From the main entrance to the terminal, turn right and walk down Montt to **Plaza Victoria.** The streets begin to converge here in a bottleneck between hill and sea but generally run parallel to the water. Av. Errázuriz follows the curve of the shore all the way through the city. The western edge of town is marked by **Plaza Wheelwright,** where the red Aduana sits. All of the city's downtown hills can be reached by *ascensores* or winding roads. Cerros Alegres and Concepción are the most centrally located *ascensores*.

STAIRWAY TO HEAVEN

Valparaíso is made up of over a dozen hills covered by steep, twisting roads and long, grueling stairways. However, before throwing yourself at these insidious inclines, you may want to consider another way of surmounting these peaks—sailing slowly over them! The hills around downtown Valpo are served by 15 different *ascensores*. Built around the turn of the century, these lifts have survived floods and earthquakes to become one of Chile's most eccentric sights. The following is a list of the *ascensores* and the Cerros they serve.

Ascensor Barón (1906) - Cerro Barón	Ascensor Reina Victoria (1902) - Cerro Concepción
Ascensor Lecheros (1906) - Cerro Lecheros	Ascensor Concepción (1883) - Cerro Concepción
Ascensor Larraín (1909) - Cerro Larraín	Ascensor El Peral (1902) - Cerro Alegre
Ascensor Polanco (1915) - Cerro Polanco	Ascensor San Agustín (1913) - Cerro Cordillera
Ascensor Monjas (1912) - Cerro Monjas	Ascensor Cordillera (1887) - Cerro Cordillera
Ascensor Mariposa (1904) - Cerro Mariposa	Ascensor Artillería (1893) - Cerro Artillería
Ascensor Florida (1906) - Cerro Florida	Ascensor Villaseca (1907) - Cerro Playa Ancha
Ascensor Espíritu Santo (1911) - Cerro Bellavista	

⊡ LOCAL TRANSPORTATION

Buses: Valparaíso is small enough to walk around, but **local buses** are plentiful. Many have service between Valpo and neighboring **Viña del Mar** (10min., CH$500). These are easy to catch from Errázuriz, which runs along the ocean; look for a sign reading "Viña" in the front window. All buses have labeled routes. Buses labeled "Puerto Montt" or "Rodoviario" pass by the bus terminal; those also saying "Aduana" will pass through downtown all the way to the red customs house; Green "Verde Mar" buses labeled D or O will head up Alemania to La Sebastiana, Pablo Neruda's house.

Taxis: Taxis are often idling at Valparaíso's many plazas. **Taxi colectivos** have set routes and take several passengers at once but are cheaper than individual taxis. Taxis can also be called for service; try: **Plaza Aduana** (☎256 215), **Plaza Sotomayor** (☎213 265), or **Terminal** (☎253 451).

Ferries: Boat tours of the bay leave from Muelle Prat. Schedules vary depending on the weather and the season. 30min. tours can go for as little as US$2 in the winter and as much as US$20 in the summer; bargaining may be possible. Taking a boat ride over to Viña del Mar may also be negotiable.

Car Rental: Best Rent A Car, Victoria 2681 (☎212 885 or 250 868). Open M-F 8:30am-7:30pm, Sa 9:30am-6pm, Su 10am-1pm.

⊡ PRACTICAL INFORMATION

Tourist Office: The **main office** is at Condell 1490. Open M-F 8:30am-2pm and 3:30-5:30pm. There are also several tourist kiosks and small offices in convenient locations. Look for one at **Terminal de Buses** (☎213 246). Open daily in summer 10am-7pm, in winter Tu-Su 10am-6pm. A kiosk in **Plaza Victoria** is open daily 10am-7pm in the summer, closed in winter. A small office on **Muelle Prat** (☎236 322) is open daily 10am-7pm.

Tours: Ask at the tourist office at Muelle Prat for a listing of tour operators.

Bank: There is no shortage of banks in Valparaíso; many lie on Prat near Plaza Sotomayor. **Banco Estado de Chile,** Prat 659, has good exchange rates and a 24hr. **ATM.** Open M-F 9am-6pm.

Market: Santa Isabél, at the corner of Bellavista and Brazil. Open M-Th 8:30am-10pm, F-Sa 8:30am-11pm, Su 9am-10pm.

Laundry: Lavacentro Servicio, Donoso 1450 (☎230 522). Open M-F 9:30am-1pm and 4pm-8:30pm, Sa 9am-2pm.

Emergency: ☎131 (ambulance).

Police: ☎ 133

24-Hour Pharmacy: Cruz Verde, Pedro Montt 1902 (☎212 777). **Farmacia Ahumada,** Pedro Montt 1881 (☎215 524).

Hospital: Hospital Carlos van Buren, Colón 2454 (☎254 074).

Fax Office: Office Center, Cochrane 841 (☎254 717). Open M-F 8:30am-7:30pm and Sa 10am-1pm.

Internet: Ciber Internet, Communicaciones y Servicios Ltda., Pedro Montt 2209 (☎745 435). Open 24hr.

Post Office: Correos de Chile (☎211 260), Plaza Sotomayor. Open M-F 8:30am-6pm.

ACCOMMODATIONS

Valparaíso is not the cheapest city in Chile for the budget-conscious traveler, but it is far from outrageous. Some of the nicest hotels, catering to visiting government officials, can be found near the **Congreso** (and the bus terminal) or in fashionable **Cerro Concepción.** Cheaper options are spread out all over town. The **tourist offices** have some brochures. Staying on one of the *cerros* is a good idea for anyone interested in a quieter, more scenic setting.

O'Higgins Plaza Hotel, Retamo 517 (☎235 616), off Parque O'Higgins. The 10 rooms in this upscale hotel are a retreat for weary travelers looking to splurge. Businessmen and government officials like its convenient location near the Congreso. The fully carpeted rooms are huge and furnished with a table, a couch, cable TV, and phone. Breakfast included. Reserve ahead in summer. Singles CH$25,000; doubles CH$35,000. ❺

B&B Brighton, Paseo Atkinson 151-153 (☎223 513; brighton-valpo@entelchile.net; www.brighton.cl). Overlooking downtown and away towards Viña del Mar, the Brighton is an excellent choice for an upscale splurge. The six rooms each feel welcoming and relaxed, most with views of the ocean. Head to the cafe below for dinner or a late night drink. Reservations Dec.-Feb. are a good idea. Singles with shared bath US$28; doubles or *matrimonios* with private bath US$48. ❹

Casa Latina, Papudo 462 (☎494 622), on Cerro Concepción near the *ascensor.* Simple, clean rooms on the scenic *cerro* make Casa Latina a beacon for backpackers. The house is full of echoes but there is a nice space for hanging out and a kitchen for guest usage. Breakfast included. Singles CH$8000; doubles CH$12,000. ❸

Residencial O'Higgins, Victoria 2792, behind the Congreso Nacional near the bus terminal. This large, open building escapes the claustrophobic feel of downtown Valpo. It has a big lobby and a green interior. The 30 rooms are a little musty, but are large and come with a private bath. Singles CH$10,000; doubles CH$16,000. ❸

Residencial Leila, Donoso 1430 (☎252 898). Good sized rooms with private baths can be a bit dim at night. There is a lobby with a comfortable couch and the *dueña* is very friendly. Convenient for downtown activities. Singles CH$8000; doubles CH$12,000. ❸

Hotel Reina Victoria, Plaza Sotomayor 190 (☎212 203), across the plaza from the post office. The Victoria is an exception to the rule that beauty is on the inside. Its dignified exterior hides dark rooms that echo the noise from the traffic below. Breakfast included. Second floor singles CH$10,000; doubles CH$13,000. Upper floors cheaper. ❸

Residencial San Diego, Rawson 276 (☎251 218), behind the bus terminal. This hostel is very basic, with peeling walls and a dark interior. Its only merit is its proximity to the bus terminal. Singles CH$4000; doubles CH$6000. ❷

◘ FOOD

It may not be haute cuisine, but visitors won't go hungry in Valparaíso; restaurants are everywhere. Exploiting the available resources, most mid- and upper-range restaurants specialize in seafood. Even the most basic establishments carry their fair share of clams "*a la macha.*" The best views come with more expensive meals on the surrounding hills. Cerros Alegre and Concepción are good places to splurge. At the opposite end of the spectrum, fresh vegetables and cheap seafood are easily found at the Mercado Puerto past Plaza Sotomayor.

Valparaíso mi Amor, Papudo 612 (☎749 992), on Cerro Concepción. If you've never heard "Girl from Ipanema" sung in three different languages, then you've never spent an evening here. Art gallery, bookstore, Internet cafe, bar—this place does it all with a bohemian charm. Veggie sandwich and fries CH$2400. Wednesday evenings at 9pm the owner, an amateur cinematographer, shows foreign films (Spanish subtitles). Beatles nights Thursdays. F and Sa live music. Open Su-W 10am-2am, Th-Sa 10am-3am. ❷

La Columbina, entrances on Pasaje Apolo 77-91 or Paseo Yugoslavo 15 (☎236 254 or 236 226), across from the Museum of Fine Arts. This 3-story cafe built into the hillside is one of Cerro Alegre's gems. Taking a cue from the neighboring Museo de Bellas Artes, it has an art gallery on its first floor and a relaxing, artsy theme throughout. Oysters with olive oil, garlic, and goat cheese will cost you CH$7400, but a post-museum coffee is only CH$500. Head chef Iván Aray is especially helpful with useful info about the city. F and Sa live music. Open M-Sa 9am-midnight, Su noon-5pm. Pub F-Sa until 2:30am. Cash only. ❹

Cafe Brighton, Paseo Atkinson 151-153 (☎223 513), on Cerro Concepción, is doing its part to improve local color with its shocking yellow paint job. Perched at the edge of Cerro Concepción, it looks majestically down over the lower part of the city. The cafe has a comfortable, informal feel. If you sneak in during a quiet moment, you might find the staff in the corner, playing cards to pass the time. *Menú del día* is CH$6200; a cheaper *menú turistico* is available for CH$4200. F bolero nights, Sa tango; both start around midnight. Open Su-Th 11am-midnight, F-Sa 11am-3am. ❸

Tu Tucan, Pedro Montt 1639 (☎596 163). Despite the cheesy name, this restaurant is one of the least gimmicky around. Each intimate booth is adorned with a stained glass hanging lamp. If conversation eludes you, pick an outdoor table and watch the families stroll by. Open Su-Th 9am-1am, F-Sa 9am-2am. ❷

La Casteñita, Blanco 86 (☎591 946), near the Mercado Puerto on the corner of Blanco and Valdivia. Chefs prepare the seafood here in a palm-covered *cabaña* in the center of the room. Eel soup CH$3200. Open daily noon-11pm. ❷

Neptune, Blanco 558 (☎224 761 or 250 134), just off Plaza Sotomayor across from the backside of Hotel Reina Victoria. The nautical theme at Neptuno beats out the tired ambience of its neighbors. Duck in for lunch after cruising the plaza. Pitchers of beer CH$3000. Open M-Th 9am-1am, F-Sa 9am-7am.

Cafe Turri, Templeman 147 (☎252 091), on Cerro Concepción, directly to the left of the exit of Ascensor Concepción. Turri is a lively place to take *onces* after a day walking the hills. The attentiveness of the officious waiters corresponds to the price tag on some of the meals (a whopping CH$23,200 for lobster), but you can get a sandwich and coffee for CH$4000 and concentrate on the great views of the port. ❺

Restaurante Bote Salvavidas (☎251 477), on Muelle Prat at the end of the pedestrian walkway. If you can stand the menu's kitschy subtitles—"ready to loosen moorings"—you can enjoy your eel (CH$6000) and watch the fishermen and naval vessels at the same time. This upscale restaurant is built to look like a boat itself. Open Tu-Sa noon-1pm, Su-M noon-5pm. 10% discount with MC. ❸

Puerta de Alcalá, Pirámide 524 (☎227 478), on the corner of Condell, has bright watermelon-colored table clothes and tinted glass that shields patrons from the bustle outside. Vegetarian plate CH$1500. *Menú (*including a pre-dinner drink and coffee) CH$3500. Open daily 8am-11pm. ❷

Confetería Cioccolata, Condell 1235 (☎214 240). The soft yellow lighting and pastoral murals on the walls of this dessert cafe will lure you in after a long afternoon pounding the pavement. *Onces,* with a sandwich, costs about CH$2500. The desserts are too enticing to pass up. Open M-F 9:30am-8:30pm, Sa 10am-2pm and 5-7:30pm. ❷

◎ SIGHTS

Conforming to Valparaíso's haphazard sprawl, the city's attractions are randomly arrayed throughout the town. An interested visitor could spend several days wandering through the winding streets and steep hills, which have surprises at every turn. The houses hanging from the *cerros* are a sight in themselves, as are the 15 *ascensores* rising among them. Not to be overshadowed by these encroaching hills, the port is an area of constant activity.

The city's tourist attractions are bounded on the east by the hulking and modern **Congreso Nacional,** where the government conducts official business, and on the west by the working relic of the **Aduana,** the port's customs office. In between these two contrasting monoliths are a number of interesting museums, including the **Museum of Natural History** and the landmark **Plaza Sotomayor.** Looking down on downtown Valparaíso from their hilltop perches are some of the more thought-provoking sights such as **La Sebastiana,** one of Pablo Neruda's three homes, on Cerro Florida; the **Museo de Bellas Artes** in **Palacio Barburriz** on Cerro Alegre; and the **Naval Museum,** surveying the port from Cerro Artilleria. These museums are accessible from rickety *ascensores* that have survived more than a century of development and natural disasters.

◪ LA SEBASTIANA. Pablo Neruda's *casa en el aire* sits high above the city on Cerro Florida. From here, the grime and noise of downtown melt away and what remains is the essence of Valparaíso's colorful architecture and sprawling port. Neruda moved here in 1961 and named his home after the architect who built it. Although he spent more time at his other homes (see Isla Negra p. 134 and La Chascona p. 109), La Sebastiana is filled with his odd collections and eclectic furniture. A life-sized poster of Walt Whitman, whom Neruda admired greatly, is framed into a door on the third floor. There are no guided tours, but ask at the entrance for an English explanation of the rooms. *(Ricardo Ferreri 692, off the 6900 block of Alemania. Take Verde Mar bus D or O from Plaza Sotomayor or a taxi colectivo and ask to be let off at the Casa de Neruda. ☎256 606. Open Mar.-Dec. Tu-F 10:30am-2pm and 3:30-6pm, Sa-Su 10:30am-6pm; Jan.-Feb. Tu-Su 10:30am-7pm.)*

◪ NAVAL MUSEUM. This former school sits atop Cerro Artilleria at the western edge of town, surveying the port. Valparaíso places great importance on its naval history and this self-serious museum attempts to explain the most important moments in that long history. The plaque at the museum entrance entreats visitors to meditate on the meaning of heroics. Many of the displays are dedicated to the Battle of Iquique on May 21, 1879, in which the Chilean ship Esmeralda was sunk by Peruvian ships. Admiral Arturo Prat, along with his crew, went down with their vessel. One of Prat's early uniforms lies in state under a giant Chilean flag. Some of the displays have signs in English. *(At the top of Cerro Artilleria. Take Ascensor Artilleria to get there. Open Tu-Su 10am-6pm. CH$500; children and seniors CH$200.)*

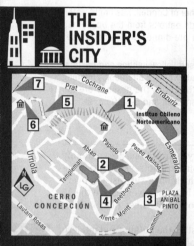

THE INSIDER'S CITY

A WALK IN THE CLOUDS

One of Valparaíso's most picturesque and interesting neighborhoods is the area spanning Cerros Concepción and Alegre. Hotels cling to hillsides, streets wind down steep hills, and at night the surrounding countryside sparkles. Many people choose to stay here, but the area also makes for a good afternoon walk.

1 **Ascensor Concepción**. Begin by riding up Valpo's oldest *ascensor*. At the top, on **Paseo Gervasoni**, sits the **Museo Lukas**, home to the artwork and humor of the famed Chilean cartoonist, and **Cafe Turri.**

2 **Valparaíso mi Amor** is a great place to drop in for a bite or to catch an art house flick on Wednesday nights.

3 **Paseo Atkinson.** Just down the street begins this checkerboard walkway. Navigate your way through the enraptured couples as you head towards **Cafe & Hotel Brighton.** With an incredible view of the sea, this is a great place get a bite to eat or even a room for the night.

MUSEO DE BELLAS ARTES. Valparaíso's Museum of Fine Art was founded by painter Alfredo Valenzuela Puelma in 1893. When the original building was destroyed in the 1906 earthquake, the museum began several decades of homeless wandering. In 1971, it moved into its present home, the former residence of Croatian philanthropist Pascual Baburizza. The house, **Palacio Baburizza,** was declared a national monument in 1979. The museum's collection includes paintings of Valparaíso's history. The sculpture is particularly intriguing. Check out Iván Cabezón's simultaneously erotic and uninviting piece "Sex-Eclair"—an iron torso partially unzipped. The museum has been undergoing renovations for some time, but should be open by 2003. Call for details. *(Paseo Yugoslavo on Cerro Alegre, next to Ascensor el Peral.* ☎ *252 332. Free.)*

PLAZA SOTOMAYOR. This plaza is probably Valparaíso's most recognizable tourist destination and one of the most open spots in the city. Since the cars that used to cover it have been moved to a subterranean lot, the plaza has a vaguely empty feeling. The arresting blue facade of the ex-Intendencia of Valparaíso (now the naval headquarters) encloses one end of the plaza. Facing it is the plaza's main attraction, the **Monumento a los Heroes de Iquique.** The statue is dedicated to the martyrs of the War of the Pacific and pays particular homage to Arturo Prat, whose remains are interned beneath the statue. An eternal flame is burning at all times along with a plaque that reads "This flame symbolizes the spirit of Prat and the heroes who offered their lives for the greater good of Chile. May their resplendence give you pause to think and feel the pride of being Chilean." The statue was dedicated on May 21, 1978, 99 years after the battle of Iquique. *(There is a daily flag lowering ceremony at 6pm.)*

PLAZA DE LA JUSTICIA. Located at the base of the hills, just south of the Plaza Sotomayor, the Plaza de la Justicia is an often overlooked quick visit. The lower entrance for **Ascensor el Peral** is here, but more impressive in its grandeur is the dark stone edifice enclosing the **Tribunals of Justice.** A bronze statue portrays Justice as a woman gazing towards the sea with the scales at her side. The inside is not as imposing, but provides a cool respite on a hot day. Stern-faced guards survey the activity from the second and third floor balconies. *(Tribunals open for viewing M-F 8am-2pm, Sa 8am-noon. Free.)*

MUSEO LUKAS. It's a good thing this cartoonist changed his name: Renzo Antonio Giovanni Pecchenino Raggi would never fit on the sign over the door to his museum. The building houses the art of renowned newspaper satirist and cartoonist LUKAS, who moved from Italy to Valpo at age one and remained here for most of his life. If you understand any Spanish, the cartoons displayed here will make you smile, but even without the words they are entertaining. There is a helpful book in English and Spanish that can be purchased for CH$5000. If you don't want to buy it, ask to look through it before you head into the museum. *(Paseo Gervasoni 448. Turn right when exiting Ascensor Concepción. ☎ 221 344. Open Tu-Su 10:30am-2pm and 3-6pm. CH$500.)*

MERCADO PUERTO. The two-story market is a great place to grab a cheap lunch at one of the seafood restaurants upstairs or to ogle the variety of shellfish and fish culled from the bay that sit glistening in beds of ice. There are also stalls with other foods like cheeses and fresh vegetables. *(Entrance on Cochrane or Blanco between San Martín and Valdivia. Open M-Th 8am-7pm, F-Sa 8am-7:30pm, Su 8am-5pm).*

ASCENSOR CONCEPCIÓN. Also known as Ascensor Turri, this is the oldest of the city's 15 lifts. Inaugurated on December 1, 1883 by then mayor Liborio Brieba, it was operated by filling and emptying water buckets. Always slightly behind technological advances, it has been upgraded several times over the years, first to a steam-powered motor and then finally to an electric one. Despite its rickety appearance, it carts residents and tourists alike from *el plan* to Cerro Concepción and back down again with grace. *(Accessible from the corner of Prat and Almirante Carreño on the bottom, across from the clock tower, and at the top from Paseo Gervasoni. Open daily 7am-11pm. CH$120 up, less to go down.)*

ASCENSOR ARTILLERIA. At the northwest edge of town, this *ascensor* was built in 1893 to ferry naval students from their school on the hill to the customs house below. Wood beams help to support the 175m track up the hill. The car allows wide views of the town and naval docks from its large windows. *(The ascensor is attached to the Aduana building. Follow Errázuriz, keeping the ocean on the right. Open daily 7am-11pm. CH$120, pay at the top.)*

LA ADUANA. This long, low-slung red building was built in the colonial era in the Spanish style to serve as the customs office for the burgeoning port city. It seems amiss now among the tall port buildings—one would almost expect that a horse and buggy should be waiting in the plaza instead of a gas-spewing *micro*. Despite its antique appearance, it still functions quite efficiently. A peek inside proves its modern activity. *(The Aduana rests at the northwest edge of town. From the Plaza Sotomayor walk along Errázuriz, keeping the ocean to your right until you come to the Plaza Aduana.)*

4 **The Churches.** Up the hill from the Brighton sits the somber **Lutheran Church.** Just two blocks away, in stark contrast to this gravity, is the **Anglican Church.** Palm trees flourish in its yard and the building itself is white stucco with yellow trim.

5 **Pasaje Apolo.** Down the hill from the churches is the base of the Pasaje Apolo, a breathtaking (literally!) staircase to the top of Cerro Alegre. Take a rest part way up at **La Columbina,** a three story restaurant built into the hillside.

6 **Paseo Yugoslavo.** Running from the top of the Pasaje, this walkway will lead you directly to the lovely **Palacio Baburriza,** home of the **Museo de Bellas Artes.**

7 **Heading Home.** Just beyond the museum is the **Ascensor El Peral,** which will carry you back down to **Plaza Sotomayor.**

ASCENSOR EL PERAL. This *ascensor*, built with German machinery in 1902, runs between two sections of town most interesting to visitors: Plaza Sotomayor on the bottom and Cerro Alegre at the apex. Windows on all sides make the short trip scenic. *(Lower entrance adjacent to the Tribunals of Justice in Plaza de la Justicia. High entrance next to the Museo de Bellas Artes on Paseo Yugoslavo. Open daily 6am-11pm. CH$70 up, CH$60 down.)*

MUSEO DE HISTORIA NATURAL. This odd little museum in the beautiful mansion **Palacio Lyon** in the center of downtown is a good excursion for a rainy day. Some of the exhibits here look like natural history themselves. Still, they are entertaining, and some, such as the exhibits dealing with Chile's early inhabitants, are worth a second look. *(Condell 1546. Downtown near the Plaza Victoria. ☎ 257 441 or 215 330. Open Tu-F 10am-1pm and 2-6pm, Sa 10am-6pm, Su 10am-2pm. CH$600, children CH$300.)*

MUSEO DEL AIRE ABIERTO. Begun by Chilean art students and completed by professional artists over three decades ago, the 20 murals painted on Cerro Bellavista's stone walls have seen better days. The stairways are grimy and detract from the pleasure of the art. *(The murals begin south of Plaza Victoria at Calle Aldunate and continue up Cerro Bellavista. Don't go at night.)*

🎭 ENTERTAINMENT

Neighboring Viña del Mar has a reputation for hot nights that Valparaíso just can't touch, but in summer months this less flashy city manages to hold its own. Clubs are scattered around the downtown area, and can be located by their pulsing music. A few good ones include: **Club Kahuna,** Blanco 552; **Bahia Azul,** Donoso 1423; **Cosmonova,** on Pedro Montt towards the bus station. On Avenida Ecuador, clubs popular with students and foreigners line the hillside.

    Cine Hoyts, Pedro Montt 2111 (☎594 709), shows American movies (with Spanish subtitles) on its five screens. Not far from the bus station on Plaza O'Higgins, the **Teatro Municipal** frequently has shows and live music.

    Valparaíso's soccer team, the **Santiago Wanderers,** play in the **Estadio Municipal** in Playa Ancha west of town. Any fan in town is more than happy to tell a stranger the schedule, but the office, Independencia 2061, is a close second with information.

🏖 DAYTRIP FROM VALPARAÍSO: QUINTAY

Buses to Quintay leave from Valparaíso's central terminal, but their times are irregular. The most convenient option is to squeeze into a taxi colectivo waiting at the back of the terminal. These fixed-route cabs will leave when there are 3 or 4 passengers. They can drop visitors at any of the town's three sections (1hr., CH$1500).

The small fishing village of Quintay is remote enough to preserve a fairly secluded atmosphere but close enough to Valparaíso to make a good daytrip. The area has three sections. The town center, up from the water, has some restaurants and places to stay, like **Residencial Monica ❸,** (☎362 090). The *caleta*, where fishermen repair their nets on the tiny shore and pelicans bob on the waves, is down from the main square. There are several good restaurants here, including **La Sirena de Miguel ❶,** (☎362 117), where old timers will tell you about the old whaling station farther down the shore. (Open daily 10am-9:30pm.) The Playa Grande, Quintay's third section, is a 25-minute walk from the Plaza or hike from the *caleta*, but the reward is a beautiful sandy beach surrounded by hills falling directly into the ocean. There are many restaurants and possible hostel options here, but it is easily seen as a daytrip from Valparaíso.

NEAR VALPARAÍSO

ALGARROBO

During summer months, this town swarms with visitors from all over Chile and beyond, while in winter even the locals seem to have abandoned it. Nevertheless, the beaches—Algarrobo's main attraction—are good for a stroll year-round, with their deep beige color and rocky outcroppings. There's lots of action near **Playa las Cadenas,** including the **tourist center,** Alessandri 1633 (open daily in summer, weekends the rest of the year), and an **ATM** (across from Tourist Center). The better beach, **El Canelo,** is at the town's southern end. **Restaurant Algarrobo ❸,** Alessandri 1505, has well-priced fish in its upscale dining room. Grilled salmon is CH$4600. ☎481 078. (M-F 12:30-9pm, Sa-Su 12:30-midnight.) Lodging opportunities blossom with the summer crowd, but all-seasons options include the simple **Residencial Vera ❸,** Alessandri 1521. (☎481 131. Breakfast included. CH$12,000 summer, much cheaper off-season.) Across the street, at Alessandri 1468, is the considerably dimmer **Residencial Colonial ❷.** (☎482 050. Singles CH$5000; triples CH$12,000.) Mid-range options near the beach include the **Hotel del Pacífico ❺,** Alessandri 1930, where rooms come equipped with private bath, cable TV, and telephones. Guests can take scuba diving lessons or swim in the hotel pool. (☎481 649. Summer singles CH$40,000, doubles CH$48,000; winter prices are half off.) Try renting a **cabaña** in the summer (ask at the tourist center).

Pullman buses leave from the terminal in Valparaíso (1hr., every 20min., CH$1500). From the bus stop, walk downhill on Mücke to the ocean. Av. Carlos Alessandri follows the curve of the water. Buses also go here en route between Valpo and Santiago.

EL QUISCO

El Quisco (3km from Algarrobo) has much the same feel—a town living off its summer tourists. Restaurants and *residenciales* line I. Durbounais, the main road between Algarrobo and Isla Negra. Hostels spread along the road up from the beach. **Alojamiento la Playa ❸,** Durbounais 102, has basic rooms with cable and private bath. (☎471 651. Singles CH$8000; triples CH$15,000.) The **Gran Hotel Costañera ❹,** (☎471 242), sits on the edge of the beach and has slightly more upscale rooms with TV, phone, and private bath for CH$20,000 to CH$28,000, depending on the view. The comfortable **El Cordones ❷,** Durbounais 296d, across from the Pullman bus station, has grilled chicken and salad for CH$2350. (☎471 573. Open Su-Th 1pm-midnight and F-Sa 1pm-1am.)

Pullman buses leave Valparaíso and stop in El Quisco between Algarrobo and Isla Negra (1hr., every 15min., CH$1500).

PUNTA DE TRALCA

Strewn like Incan ruins on a hillside near Isla Negra are several large **stone faces.** These blocks of granite were carved by Chilean sculptors in honor of Pablo Neruda and serve as lonely witnesses to the flow of the tide. Unfortunately they have been defaced by graffiti. Just as interesting is the rocky outcropping extending into the ocean. The rocks are great to climb around when you want to feel wonderfully removed from civilization. With almost no sign of human disturbance, there is no one out here except the resting sea birds. Take a water bottle and a snack and spend a few hours here exploring.

Pullman buses leave Valparaíso for Punta de Tralca (1¼hr., every 15min., CH$1500). Ask the bus driver to tell you when to get off. From the bus stop, walk down Punta de Tralca. Bear left where the road splits. From here you can see the rocky outcropping and the headland where the faces sit. To get to the faces, follow the road around to the left to its end and head up the hill. It is a 20min. walk from the bus stop to the headland.

ISLA NEGRA

Isla Negra, 1½hr. from Valparaíso, is known for one thing: it is the home of Chile's patron saint of poetry, Pablo Neruda. The small town has remained largely under-developed since Neruda bought his house overlooking the ocean in 1939. The same cannot be said for the home. Neruda's collections of shells, ashtrays, ship figureheads, and even insects are crammed into every corner. He spent much of his later years writing here, and its easy to see why: the view is inspiring, with white-capped waves crashing into dark rocks on the beach. Tours of the house are required but visitors can sit outside and compose their own odes for as long as they wish. (Museum ☎461 284. Open Tu-Su 10am-2pm and 3pm-6pm in winter, 10am-8pm summer. CH$2400. Call ahead for tours in English.)

Most visitors move on after visiting the museum and the trinket shops above it. Those who, like the poet, are lured to stay can find cheap rooms harboring other wandering souls at the **Casa Azul ❷,** a 10min. walk from the museum. Azul fea-tures a communal kitchen, a nice sitting room, and space for camping. To get there from the museum turn left onto the road the buses run along Santa Luisa 2. Take the first right onto Central and bear right onto Santa Luisa. (☎461 154. CH$6000.) **Cabañas Curi Huapi ❹,** (☎461 574 or 461 846), are tucked into the trees off Central and rent for CH$15,000-25,000, depending on the season and the num-ber of guests (up to 6). Call ahead for reservations. The **Hotel Restaurante La Can-dela ❺,** down the hill from the museum, is overpriced. (Doubles CH$38,000.) **Café Calú ❶,** across the street from the path to the museum, is a good spot for a snack. A large *empanada de mariscos* runs CH$1000. (☎462 400. Open M-F 9am-6pm, Sa-Su 8am-9pm.)

Pullman buses leave from the terminal in Valparaíso (1½hr., every 20min., CH$1500), en route to Santiago. Passengers are dropped at the path to the museum, just past Central.

CARTAGENA

Cartagena, equidistant from Santiago and Valparaíso (100km), is a lovely seaside resort—especially lovely in winter, when the boulevard is deserted and the waves crash upon the beach unobstructed by bathing beauties. During the summer months *Santiaguinos* (from Santiago) crawl all over Cartagena, filling the multi-tude of hostels that cling to the hills overlooking the sea. The resort became stylish at the end of the 19th century as a summer retreat for wealthy Santiago families. The town is still popular among central Chile's elite, but with so much affordable lodging, it is equally popular with families and backpackers.

Visitors gravitate to the two beaches, but the town's central plaza is between them and slightly uphill. The **tourist center** is located in the basement of the Municipalidad flanking the plaza. The helpful staff can provide brochures and listings of accommodations (☎200 736. Open M-F 9am-2pm and 2:30-6pm, until 8pm in summer.) Straight down from the Plaza de Armas is a rocky point, crowned by a statue of the **Virgen del Suspiro,** who overlooks the town and beaches on either side. To her right, in the south, lies the **Playa Chica.** To sleep close to the waves, try the slightly upscale **Hotel Bellavista ❷,** Ricardo Santa Cruz 216 (☎451 216). Spacious, light rooms with private bath and TV are CH$6000. Sev-eral older hotels and restaurants keep an eye on the shell-covered beach, Playa Chica. Lunch is good at **El Fafra ❶,** Playa Chica 136. (☎854 8960. Open M-F 10am-9pm, Sa-Su 10am-2am.)

NERUDA'S LEGACY
Demythologizing Chile's Mythical Icon

The name Pablo Neruda is the stuff of legend and lore from Mexico to Myanmar, but nowhere is his memory as revered as in his native Chile. From his racy love life to his Nobel Prize, his senatorial stint to his flirtation with communism, few figures stir such a sense of pride and national identity in the Chilean people as that of Pablo Neruda. Born Neftalí Ricardo Reyes Basoalto in 1904 to a modest family in the town of Parral, Neruda spent most of his childhood in Temuco. He began his career as a writer at the tender age of thirteen, publishing his first poem in the daily paper. After studying French and pedagogy at the Universidad de Chile in Santiago, Neruda began his career in politics in his mid-twenties. However, literature, politics, and women would occupy the next five decades of his life.

Neruda's twenties were marked by two of his most widely read publications, *Crupusculario (Dusk)* and *Veinte poemas de amor y una canción desesperada (Twenty Love Poems and a Song of Despair)*. These poetry anthologies were both published by the time Neruda was 20, and while they are not regarded as his highest literary achievements, they are remarkable works that established him as a major literary force. They also earned him the reputation as a hopeless romantic that followed him to his grave.

In the years between 1927 and 1935, the Chilean government appointed Neruda to several honorary consulships, which took him first to Burma (now Myanmar), and later to Spain. At this time, Neruda also ended a torrid love affair to marry Maria Antoineta Hagenmaar, a Dutch woman who did not speak Spanish. Despite Neruda's amorous disposition, love could not conquer this formidable linguistic divide, and the couple divorced in 1936. Maria Antoineta is the only one of Neruda's wives not to be labeled with an odd, diminutive nickname, perhaps because she is rarely mentioned at all in his letters and writing.

The years Neruda spent in Madrid and Barcelona launched him into one of the most eccentric and ground-breaking artistic circles of the 20th century, the *Generación de '27* (Generation of 1927). While rubbing shoulders with painter Salvador Dalí, filmmaker Luis Buñuel, and such great poets as Federico García Lorca, Luis Cernuda, and Vicente Aleixandre, Neruda produced one of his more esoteric publications, the surrealist masterpiece *Residencia en la tierra (Residence on Earth)*, in 1933.

Neruda not only fit into this group of friends and artists, he lorded over it. Weekly *tertulias* (artsy-intellectual chat rooms) around the kitchen table of his Madrid apartment were the central social activity of the *generación*, since, besides being a talented writer himself, Neruda could bring out the best in those around him. One evening, while walking through the streets of Madrid, Neruda stumbled across an illiterate Andalucian sleeping on a park bench; under the tutelage of Neruda and company, this unlikely protégé, one Miguel Hernández, became one of the most mesmerizing Spanish poets of the 20th century.

With the onset of the Spanish Civil War in 1936 and the subsequent murders of his friend Federico García Lorca and his protégé Miguel Hernández, Neruda fled to France. There, he dabbled in communism while working as a consul for Spanish emigration, and published *España en el corazón (Spain in the Heart)* before being transferred to Mexico. There he penned one of his greatest works, *Canto general (Common Song)*.

In 1943, Neruda entered into his second marriage with the Argentine painter Delia del Carril. She is rarely referred to by her name in Chile, and is known instead as *la Hormiguita* (the little ant; Neruda's nickname for her), or, more commonly and more derisively, as "the poet's second wife." Although the couple returned to Chile that same year, their marriage was never officially recognized there, and they separated in 1955, in part due to Neruda's copious carrying-on with his soon-to-be third wife.

Returning to Chile a full-blown literary celebrity after 15 years of government service put Neruda in a prime position to run for office. In 1945, he was elected senator of the Republic, and publicly joined the Communist Party. He served as senator until 1949, although he had to live in hiding in his own country from 1947 to 1949 due to political differences with then-president González Videla.

Although they had been involved for many years, it was not until 1966 that Neruda married his third wife, *la Chascona* (the messy-haired), his affectionate nickname for Chilean singer Matilde Urrutia. His constant companion in their homes in Valparaíso at La Sebastiana, on La Isla Negra, and in Santiago, Matilde was the inspiration for some of his most famous love sonnets, including *Cien sonetos de amor (100 Love Sonnets)*, which he published in 1959. Matilde is respectfully acknowledged as the love of Neruda's life and the woman to whom we, the tourists of the world, are greatly indebted—only through her generosity are we able to visit all three of the couple's homes to gain an insight into Neruda's lifestyle.

Literature never took complete precedence over politics in Neruda's life. Under president Salvador Allende, Neruda served as an ambassador to France beginning in 1970. However, this tenure as ambassador was short-lived due to Neruda's own failing health as well as a declining political environment. According to legend, Neruda lost his battle against leukemia on September 23, 1973, the same night Augusto Pinochet's forces were making their way to his home at La Isla Negra to arrest him.

Indeed, the violence that defined recent Chilean history is brutally manifest in Neruda's homes. After his death, Pinochet's forces raided and robbed his house at La Isla Negra, as well as in Santiago. The smashed grandfather clock that Matilde chose to leave standing in the study of La Chascona is but one of the visceral reminders of the many faces of civil war that fringed Neruda's life. These troubling traces of past violence are juxtaposed against his numerous awards and honors, including his Nobel Prize for Literature, which he won in 1971. Still, what makes Neruda's homes such remarkable places is neither the political nor the glorious artifacts from his life on display.

A stroll through one of Neruda's residences produces an almost indecent feeling of intimacy and familiarity with this iconic bastion of Chilean culture. Perusing Neruda's eclectic collection of miscellaneous objects gives one an insight into the literary giant's personal idiosyncrasies and endearing eccentricities. Odd splotches of green ink that he so loved to write with; profiles of himself embedded within Matilde's wild hair in sketchy portraits of her; altar-like shrines to Walt Whitman, his literary father; the intentionally squeaky floors, intended to remind Neruda of the sea (although he preferred to be on land)—these quirky relics from an artist's life bring to life the man behind the myth.

Neruda attempted his whole life to do what was right, although he may not be exempt from moral criticism in politics or his personal life. In literature, he represented both the ecstasy and the despair of love, as well as the divinity of something as mundane as an artichoke. It is this duality and cascading complexity that make Neruda accessible to all, and getting better acquainted with him could be the pinnacle of any jaunt through Chile.

Sarah Kenney was the editor of Let's Go: Barcelona 2002. *She is now working in publishing.*

From the Virgen's left side extends **Playa Grande,** which, as its name suggests, is the larger beach. It's also more suitable for sunbathing and swimming. Of the many hostels up the hill from the beach, the **Residencial Orianita ❷,** Ignacio Carrera Pinto 12A, in back of the Shell Station, is a cheerful choice. With walls the color of the sea. (☎094 353 246. CH$6000.) Only a step from the sand is the **Restaurante Pato Santis ❷,** (☎450 147), where its possible to watch the fishermen cast into the waves while enjoying a heaping bowl of *paila marina* (CH$2500).

If you would rather be closer to the Plaza but still want an ocean view, check out the **Residencial Santis ❶,** Suspiro 211. This large yellow compound is roomy and the proprietor maintains a quiet family atmosphere. (☎452 787. CH$3000 per person, CH$4600 with meals.)

Pullman Bus leaves from the terminal in Valparaíso. (2hr., every 15min., CH$1900). The driver can drop passengers at Playa Grande or close to the tourist office in the Plaza de Armas. From either stop, both the town and the sea are accessible. Be aware that *residenciales* fill up quickly in the summer—it's good to call ahead.

VIÑA DEL MAR ☎32

Blue skies, crashing waves, bronze beauties in bikinis on the beach—no, this isn't Miami Beach, the Riviera, or Rio de Janeiro—it's Viña del Mar (pop 304,203), Valparaíso's sister city. Sometimes called the "Garden City" because of the exotic trees in its Quinta Vergara, Viña is best known as one of the hottest coastal resorts in South America, and it lives up to its reputation with gusto. Luxury condominiums tower over streets bustling with people day and night—from the families who crowd the coastline at mid-day, to couples strolling arm-in-arm along white-sand beaches at dusk, to the young and hip who pack the *discotecas* all night long. Even outside the crazy months of high-season, most establishments remain open, making the spring and fall, when the weather is pleasant and the crowds aren't so thick, idyllic times to visit.

Viña del Mar (Vineyard of the Sea) takes its name from the vineyard stretching out from the Quinta Rioja at one of the city's two original *haciendas*, which were united by engineer Don José Francisco Vergara in 1855 to form the town. The city was officially founded in 1874, and the population exploded with the advent of the railway, which brought many *porteños* from neighboring Valparaíso. Between the turn of the century and the 1930s, many of Viña's finest buildings were constructed, including the Teatro Municipal, the Palacio Rioja, and the Casino. The "Reloj de Flores," a large working clock with a face made entirely of blooming plants, has only added to Viña's reputation as a beautiful and unique city.

▐▀ TRANSPORTATION

Trains: Viña's **main terminal** is just 1 block off the Plaza Vargara at Bohn. Trains run to **Valparaíso** (15min., every 10-15min, CH$280).

Buses: The **bus terminal** is at Valparaíso and Quilpué. Schedules and prices are almost identical to those in Valparaíso, as most northbound buses stop in Viña on their way from Valparaíso.

International: Most originate in Valparaíso. To get to **Mendoza, Argentina,** and **Buenos Aires, Argentina,** try **Tas Choapa** (☎752 023), **El Rapido** (☎752 013), **Buses Ahumada** (☎752 005), or **TAC** (☎752 070). Note that to get to international destinations, it is often easier and cheaper to take a separate to Santiago and go from there.

Long-Distance: Heading north, **Pullman Bus Norte** (☎752 021) has six departures daily to: **Antofagasta** (CH$16,000); **Arica** (CH$22,000); **Copiapó** (CH$10,000); **Iquique** (CH$20,000); **La Serena** (CH$7000); and intermediaries. Other companies heading north include: **Tur Bus** (☎750 203) with 2 daily departures; **Fenix Pullman Norte** (☎752 007) with 3 daily; **Flota Barrios** (☎752 024) with 1 daily. Heading south, **Tur Bus** goes daily to: **Chillán** (5:40pm, CH$5100); **Concepción** (7 per day 8am-9pm, CH$16,100); **Osorno** (7pm, CH$15,600); **Temuco** (4 per day 7am-9pm; CH$13,300, *salon cama* CH$26,800); **Valdivia** (7:40pm, CH$14,400). Other buses going south include **Condor Bus** (☎752 028) and **Buses Alsa** (formerly **Buses Lit;** ☎752 001).

Regional: Try **Pullman Bus** (☎752 028) for trips to **Santiago** (every 10min. 5:30am-10:30pm, US$5). Other companies include **Buses Alsa** (formerly **Buses Lit;** ☎752 001), **Condor Bus** (☎752 028), and **Tur Bus** (☎752 200). **Buses Intercomunal** (☎752 003) goes to **Los Vilos** (every 3 hr. 7:15am-6:30pm, US$8).

Micros: *Micros* labeled "Puerto" or "Aduana" go to **Valparaíso**; those labeled "Libertad" run to **Mall Arauco Marino**. Local buses on Av. Libertad running to **Reñaca** and **Concón** are clearly labeled.

Taxis: *Colectivos* and taxis wait at the train station, Plaza Vergara, and the Casino. Call **Radio Taxi** (☎993 420) for a pickup.

Car rental: Bert Rent A Car, Alvarez 762 (☎685 515).

■ ▐ ORIENTATION AND PRACTICAL INFORMATION

Viña is an easy city to navigate. The river **Estero Marga Marga**, a muddy eyesore, runs east to west, bisecting the city. South of the river, the commercial section of town stretches from the **Plaza Vergara** to **Von Schroeders** on Arlegui and Valparaíso. The **bus station** is 3 blocks east of the plaza. North of the Marga Marga, the streets are ordered in a regular grid pattern. This section consists mainly of private homes and condominiums, except on San Martín and near the beach areas. **Libertad** is the main thoroughfare for buses and *colectivos* heading to the neighboring beaches of Reñaca and Concón.

Playa Abarca is the only beach south of the Marga Marga and is easily reached on Av. Marina. The northern beaches extend beyond a rocky sea wall and are accessible from Av. Peru or San Martín.

Tourist Office: The **main office** is just off Plaza Vergara, next to Puente Libertad. Helpful staff has an abundance of information, including lists of accommodations. Open M-F 9am-2pm and 3-7pm, Sa-Su 10am-2pm and 3-7pm. There is also a **tourist kiosk** at the bus station. The **tourist hotline** ☎800 800 830, is toll-free.

Tours: Tours of Viña del Mar are possible in **horse-drawn carriages** leaving from Plaza Vergara or the Casino.

Bank: Banks and exchange houses line Arlegui and Av. Valparaíso. **Santander,** on Plaza Vergara, has a 24hr. **ATM.** Open M-F 9am-6pm.

Cultural Center: Libertad 250 (☎972 972), in Palacio Carrasco.

Market: Santa Isabel, on Valparaíso, just east of Plaza Vergara. Open M-Th 8:30am-10:30pm, F-Sa 8:30am-11pm, Su 9am-10pm.

Emergency: ☎131

Police: ☎133. *Carabineros* at 4 Norte 320 (☎689 268).

Pharmacy: Cruz Verde, Valparaíso 404 (☎714 044).

Hospital: Hospital Gustavo Fricke, Alvares 1532 (☎675 067).

Internet: Cafe Alavista, Valparaíso 196 (☎690 529). CH$500 per hr. Open M-Sa 10am-1am, Su noon-1am.

Post Office: Next to the tourist office, near Puente Libertad. Open M-F 9am-6pm, Sa 9:30am-1pm.

MIDDLE CHILE

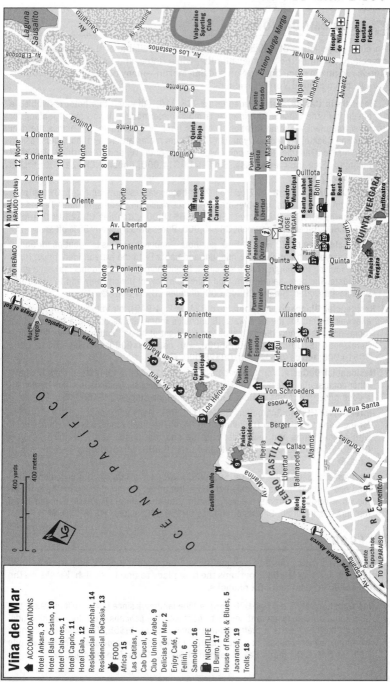

MIDDLE CHILE

Viña del Mar

▲ ACCOMMODATIONS
Hotel Ankara, 3
Hotel Balia Casino, 10
Hotel Calabres, 1
Hotel Capric, 11
Hotel Gala, 12
Residencial Blanchait, 14
Residencial DeCasia, 13

● FOOD
Africa, 15
Las Cañtas, 7
Cab Ducal, 8
Club Union Arabe, 9
Delicias del Mar, 2
Enjoy Café, 4
Fellini, 6
Samoiedo, 16

🏠 NIGHTLIFE
El Burro, 17
House of Rock & Blues, 5
Jacarancá, 19
Trolls, 18

▐ ACCOMMODATIONS

An eight-page listing of Viña's accommodations, available at the tourist office, is especially useful in the summer months, when hotels and hostels fill up quickly. Hotels ranging in price line Arlegui and San Martín—many of the cheaper *residenciales* crowd around Von Schroeders.

Hotel Balia Casino, Von Schroeders (☎978 310). Although this hotel resembles a castle from the outside, the interior is much more modest. If you aren't looking for royal treatment, its ideal location, 2 blocks from Av. Valparaíso and across the river from the Casino, should suit you just fine. Some rooms are better than others; ask to see what is available. Rooms come with private bath, TV, and a hair dryer. Breakfast included. Free Internet access. Singles CH$14,000; doubles CH$21,000; triples CH$26,000. ❹

Hotel Calabres, 7 Norte 627 (☎973 215; hotelcalabres@hotmail.com). Owned by a friendly Argentine man, Calabres has small but welcoming rooms. All have TV and private baths. Breakfast included. Singles CH$18,000; doubles CH$23,000; triples CH$28,000; 6-person apartment CH$40,000. Prices drop by nearly 50% off-season. ❹

Hotel Gala, Arlegui 273 (☎321 500; galahotel@webhost.cl). This is about as far from a *hostal* as you can get, from the mini-bar and cable TV to the extraordinary price. But if you're looking to splurge, Gala's spacious, bright rooms and bathrooms make it a great candidate. The pool, sauna, gym, and incredible view of the city only add to the luxury. Breakfast included. Singles CH$45,000; doubles CH$51,000. ❺

Residencial Blanchait, Av. Valparaíso 82A (☎974 949), off Valparaíso, down a tiny alleyway. Except for the bare walls, Blanchait's rooms are as cozy as a friend's guest room—and the friendly *dueña* makes you feel right at home. Mattresses vary in quality. Breakfast CH$1000. Singles CH$6000, with bath CH$9000; doubles CH$12,000/CH$14,000; triples CH$18,000/CH$20,000. ❷

Residencial DeCasia, Von Schroeders 151 (☎971 861). Setting itself slightly above other comparable lodging with its comfortable mattresses, DeCasia is a fine choice for a good price. The rooms share a bath on a long hall. Singles CH$4000. ❷

Hotel Capric HI, Von Schroeders 39 (☎978 295). Many backpackers make a beeline for the Capric, one of few HI members in Chile. The small rooms are quiet and bright, with private baths and low beds. Located near the beach and downtown. Singles CH$8000; doubles CH$12,000; triples CH$16,000. CH$5000 per person with HI card. ❸

Hotel Ankara, San Martín 476 (☎ 692 085; www.hotel-ankara.co.cl). Conveniently situated near the beach and nightlife hot spots, but prices are rather steep for those traveling on a budget. Rooms are very comfortable but small. Breakfast in the hotel restaurant is included. Singles or doubles CH$59,800; suites CH$78,000. ❺

▐ FOOD

Viña is loaded with cafes and top-quality seafood restaurants. **Av. Valparaíso** is lined with cafes, and **San Martín** is perhaps the best place to find fresh fish. Kiosks on the beach sell ice cream and other snacks.

Cap Ducal, Av. Marina 51 (☎626 655). A Viña landmark since it was built in 1936, this ship-shaped hotel/restaurant seems to float with the pelicans atop the incoming tide. Though the hotel costs a pretty penny (rooms start at CH$55,000), the restaurant is worth the few extra pesos. In winter months, the warm stove provides a welcome respite from the brisk sea breeze. Baked salmon CH$4500. Open 7am-midnight. ❸

Samoiedo, Av. Valparaíso 637 (☎684 610). Sit inside for a little calm in the midst of the city, or grab a table outside to watch the bustling crowd. The awning and menu scream chain restaurant, but it's a good place to rest and enjoy a cup of coffee. *Onces* CH$4700. Open daily 7:30am-11pm, later in the summer. ❸

Club Unión Arabe, Av. Marina 50 (☎667 190), between Playa Abarca and Castillo Wulff. Housed in a sea-front mansion, this restaurant strives to bring together all types of Arab customs. The *menú* (CH$4500) includes Middle Eastern specialties, but more typical Chilean fare is available. Live show F and dance classes 3 nights a week. Open 11am-midnight. ❸

Delicias del Mar, San Martín 459 (☎901 837). This restaurant wants to be taken seriously, with its extensive wine list and featured creation by the chef (conger eel "*apasionado*" CH$6500). But it's hard not to laugh when the mounted plastic fish, "Big Mouth Billy Bass," is crooning in the lobby. The seating area is more dignified—a pleasant place for dinner. Open Su-F noon-4pm and 7pm-midnight, Sa noon-midnight. ❸

Fellini, 3 Norte 88 (☎975 742), close to the casino. Tired of seafood? Fellini's creative Italian menu will make your mouth water for lasagna in no time. The extensive menu is a little pricier than you might expect. *Filetes* CH$6100. Open M-Th 11am-4pm and 8pm-midnight, F-Su 11am-4pm and 8pm-1am. ❸

Africa, Av. Valparaíso 324 (☎711 698). Of the two "Africas" in Viña (the other is on Plaza Vergara), this one boasts a better location. Nearly life-sized sculptures of elephants and other wild animals look ready to plunge down from the second-story balcony out front—don't get too excited, however, the inside is much less decorative. Nevertheless, the restaurant draws crowds and the food is cheap. *Mariscos* CH$3250, *filetes* CH$3930, *pescado* CH$3500. Open M-Th 8am-2am, F-Sa 8am-4am. ❷

Las Catitas (☎699 802), on the corner of 1 Norte and 5 Poniente. The sign on the window of this corner restaurant advertises it as a cure for the common hangover. Open until 6am, it also caters to local workers coming off late shifts. Sandwiches CH$1500, entrees CH$2500. Open 11am-4pm and 7:30pm-6am. ❶

Enjoy Café (☎690 855 or 884 492), on Peru near the casino. Vest and button-bedecked waiters scamper around taking orders for ice cream and banana splits (CH$2000) at this cheery dessert cafe. If you're feeling like a kid after your ice cream, the playground next door offers pony rides. Open 10am-11:30pm. ❶

🅖 SIGHTS

▨**MUSEO FONCK.** If the US$1000 ticket to Easter Island breaks your bank, head to the Museo Fonck for the next best thing. A large stone *moai* (native sculpture transported from Easter Island) looms over the lawn, and inside the museum is a thorough exhibit on the island and its culture. Other rooms include displays of Chilean natural history, including fascinating mummies. *(4 Norte 784, around the corner from Palacio Carrasco. ☎686 753. Open Tu-F 9:30am-6pm, Sa-Su 9:30am-2pm. CH$1000.)*

QUINTA VERGARA AND PALACIO VERGARA. The beautiful woodsy paths of the Quinta Vergara are some of Viña's hidden treasures. In the heart of the city's urban sprawl, this impressive expanse of exotic and native trees feels like another world entirely. If you stroll the easy paths to the top of the hill, the vista over the entire town is stunning.

The **Palacio Vergara,** a beautiful mansion near the entrance to the Quinta, houses the **Museo de Bellas Artes.** A look at the palace itself is almost worth the entrance fee, but the art collection inside makes it a must-see. In one room dedicated to religious images, Gabriel Guay's *El Martirio de Sta. Paulina* dominates an entire wall, drawing the eye to the rising figure that it depicts.

Beyond the mansion, a path leads to the park's amphitheater, where occasional concerts are played. The largest of these is the "Festival Internacional de Canción," held every year in February, which draws popular international stars like Julio Iglesias. *(Entrance to Quinta Vergara at Quita and Errázuriz. Park open 7am-6pm. Free. Palacio Vergara and museum ☎ 680 092 or 684 137. Open Tu-Su 10am-1:30pm and 3-5:30pm. CH$500, children CH$300.)*

RELOJ DE FLORES. No tour of Viña would be complete without the requisite photo beside the exquisite "flower clock," whose face is made entirely of carefully arranged blooming plants. Perhaps the photos on display of women posing in bikinis, pointing to the clock Vanna White style are a little tacky, but the enormous clock is the quintessential Viña landmark and at least deserves a surreptitious look. *(Behind Playa Abarca, where España meets Marina.)*

PALACIO RIOJA. Declared a historic monument in 1985, the Palacio Rioja retains the grandeur of its origins. The French neo-classic mansion was built between 1906 and 1910 for Don Fernando Rioja, a Spanish banker and tobacco investor who lived and worked at the palace with his wife, their eight children, and as many as 40 servants. Now owned by the city, the palace's main floor has been preserved in its original style, and all visitors are forced to don ridiculous felt booties to protect the floor. The curved marble staircase leads to a large entrance hall where private city functions are still held—the orchestra balcony in the dining hall is also worth a look. A conservatory in the basement houses a classical concert series; check with the tourist office for schedules. *(The Palacio sits on large grounds covering a whole block at Quillota 214. Entrance is on 3 Norte. ☎ 689 665. Open Tu-Su 10am-1:30pm and 3-5pm. CH$200, children CH$100.)*

CASINO VIÑA DEL MAR. Think Viña's too hot? Want to lose your shirt? Then head over to the Casino, where they'll be more than happy to strip you of whatever you've got. The pink romanesque building dominates the block, inviting adventurous gamblers up its stairs into the arms of its many slot machines. There are also bingo parlors and card games. Meals here are definitely not a bargain, and drinks are expensive. A five-star hotel, Viña's first, should be completed on site at the beginning of 2003. *(On San Martín, near the mouth of the Marga Marga. ☎ 500 600. Open M-Th noon-4am, open continuously F noon to M 4am.)*

CASTILLO WULFF. Strolling along Marina, you may wonder why a castle with boarded-up windows and graffitied walls stands before you. In 1880 this striking turreted castle was built on a rocky promontory jutting into the sea. The castle's namesake died in 1946, and the property passed into municipal hands 13 years later—the Chilean navy used it as a museum for many years, but abandoned it in 1980. A decade later it was transformed into the **Museo de la Cultura del Mar,** dedicated to the writer Salvador Reyes. The castle now lies dormant again, but is still quite a sight, with the waves crashing just beneath it. *(Follow Av. Marina along the seashore from the mouth of the Marga Marga.)*

MUELLE VERGARA. Viña's only pier has outlived its usefulness to industry— today, it caters to tourists and fishermen. When viewed from a distance, the structure's bright blue paint and stained-glass windows make a lovely picture—up close it's more tacky, dotted with little ice cream stands and restaurants. Fishermen charmingly cast their lines from the pier's end in the evenings. *(The pier separates Playa Acapulco and Playa El Sol from Playa Blanca and Los Marineros.)*

PALACIO CARRASCO. Carrasco was one of several mansions built in Viña during its heyday at the beginning of the 20th century. Its architect, resident Frenchman Alfredo Azancot (also responsible for nearby Palacio Rioja), built this large 4-story mansion in French renaissance style, complete with a mansard roof. A sculpture by Rodin, "La Defensa," decorates the entrance. The Palacio was the home of the *municipalidad* for 40 years mid-century, but is now the **Centro Cultural,** as well as the resting place of the city's historical archives and the Benjamin Vicuña Mackenna library. Check at the tourist office or inside the palace for details on classes and concerts offered at the Centro Cultural. *(Libertad 250. ☎972 972. Open daily M-F 9:30am-1pm and 2-7pm, Sa 10am-1pm.)*

🎭 🎶 ENTERTAINMENT AND NIGHTLIFE

The **Marina Arauco Mall,** on Libertad and 4 Norte 1, is popular among teenagers. The mall seems to have every department store imaginable, and on the top floor **video games, bowling** (☎388 282), and an eight-screen **movie theater** (☎688 188) provide great diversion. (Open M-Th 10am-9pm, F-Sa 10am-9:30pm, Su 11am-9pm.)

More cultured entertainment is available at the **Teatro Municipal** (☎681 739), on Plaza Vergara. Check at the tourist office for schedules of concerts and ballets at the *teatro,* and for offerings at the **Centro Cultural** in Palacio Carrasco (see **Sights,** p. 142). **Cine Arts,** 142 Plaza Vergara (☎882 798), shows one artsy flick at a time. If all else fails, there's always money to be spent at the **Casino** (see **Sights,** p. 142).

Viña's nightlife can be raucous in the summer, but it quiets down as the crowds disperse. San Martín is packed with pubs, as is Av. Valparaíso. On weekends throughout the year the **Paseo Cousiño,** off Av. Valparaíso, shakes to the beat of its discos, including **El Burro, Trolls,** and **Jacarandá.** Special kudos go to 🗹**House of Rock and Blues,** 100 Peru (☎683 139), where the Marga Marga meets the sea. This hot spot offers live music, and in warm weather visitors can dance to the tunes alongside the crashing waves.

NEAR VIÑA DEL MAR

REÑACA
☎32

Just a few miles north of Viña del Mar, Reñaca is its main suburb, offering the same bodaciousness you've come to expect of Viña. Smooth beaches, numerous touristy shops and restaurants, and a blight of condominiums rising into the hills are common sights here as well. The plethora of stores and discos suggest that this beach is especially popular among teenagers evading the watchful eyes of their parents for the afternoon. Easy-to-spot **discos** are open in the summer and during long weekends. **Cine Plaza Reñaca,** Borgoño 14580, in Plaza Reñaca, shows one new movie at a time.

It is easiest to get to Reñaca from Viña del Mar by frequent **micros** traveling down Libertad—the beige-colored **Sol de Reñaca** *micros* are the easiest to spot (CH$250). Once in Reñaca, Borgoño is the main street, where buses turn right and head uphill onto Calle Angamos. To get to the beach, ask to be let off after the turn, before the bus heads up the hill. **Banco de Chile,** Borgoño 14675, has an **ATM.**

Reñaca is more of a daytrip than an overnight destination for budget travelers—hotels are pricey, and there are no hostels or *residenciales* to be found. The Best-Western affiliated **Hotel Piero ❺,** Segundo 89, off Borgoño, has standard rooms with nice balconies that overlook the ocean. Entertainment at Piero includes a pool and pool tables. (☎830 280 or 832 926. Doubles CH$50,000; triples CH$60,000.) **Holiday Hotel and Cabañas ❺,** Angamos 367, up the hill from Borgoño, has private two- or four-person *cabañas.* Nicer than hotel rooms, the cabins come with a porch, living room, and kitchenette. (☎830 005. Doubles CH$57,500; quads CH$95,500.) The best deal on food is at the rustic-style 🗹**Entre Masas ❷,** 75 Central (☎839 888), just across from Hotel Piero. With adobe walls, a bookshelf of old magazines, and a tree growing up through the stone floor, the restaurant has character—a much needed change of pace from the sterile restaurants nearby. Try the **Disco Entre Masas** (CH$10,000), a huge plate of meats, shrimp, cheese, and stuffed artichokes that serves four—or choose from the large selection of *empanadas.*

THE NORTHERN BEACHES

North of Viña del Mar, the *litoral central* is characterized by scrubby hillsides and rocky coastline punctuated by enclaves of civilization, which are actually some of Chile's finest resorts. Its hard to go wrong with any beach you choose, but each town has its own take on oceanfront life. From Viña, the *litoral central* goes through Reñaca, Concón, Quintero, Maitencillo, and Zapallar, ending in Papudo, about 100km north.

CONCÓN

Fifteen kilometers from Viña del Mar, Concón follows Reñaca in the string of beach towns climbing up the coast. Concón's major beaches are **Playa Las Bahamas,** not so much a beach as a pile of slick rocks worn smooth by the ebbing tide; **Playa Negra,** a pile of larger rocks; and **Playa Amarilla,** the prime spot for swimming and sunbathing. Near Amarilla, new-age condominiums are built into the hill like stairs, and during the summer, kiosks selling snacks are all around. At the southern end of Concón is the **Higuerillas Yacht Club** (☎816 831), on Borgoño, where sailboat rental is possible in the summer. The yacht club is part of **Caleta Higuerilla,** where fishermen bring in their catches.

There are two roads from Viña to Concón—one follows the coast on Borgoño, and the other, more frequently traveled by **buses,** heads inland from Reñaca, behind large rolling dunes. **Micros** leave Viña on Libertad on a regular basis and say "Concón" in the window. At the northern edge of Concón, at Caleta La Boca, there is a **rotary.** Buses circle here before returning to Viña or crossing Río Aconcagua to head north to other beaches. If you arrive here, follow the coastal road away from the river, and you will reach **Playa Amarilla.**

If you want to spend the night in town, try the waterfront **Hostel Taitao ❺,** Borgoño 23100, on the Playa Amarilla. (☎816 611 or 816 029. Large bathrooms. Breakfast included. Doubles CH$30,000, quads CH$40,000.) Otherwise, the better lodging deals in Viña are worth the trip back.

Two good restaurants serve the catch of the day on the Caleta Higuerilla. At **Aquí Jaime's ❸,** Borgoño 21303, the menu itself is a work of art, decorated with shells and starfish. Entrees are a little pricey, but the grilled sea bass with capers (CH$5000) is awfully tempting. (☎812 042. Open Tu-Sa noon-2am, Su-M lunch only 2-4pm.) Other great eats can be found past the Caleta, at **Restaurant Bellamar ❸,** Borgoño 21550. The eclectic restaurant has Egyptian queens painted on the walls, fish gurgling in the tanks, and pelicans sunning themselves on the rocks outside the window. (☎811 351. Children's menu available. Shrimp salad CH$3850. Open 10:30am-2am.) Beyond Playa Amarilla, the **Caleta La Boca** houses some ramshackle restaurants and *pescaderías* selling fresh fish.

QUINTERO

Quintero stands out from the other beach towns in the *litoral central* because of its beautiful path along the water and its tiny, sheltered beaches. This is a great town to visit off-season, when the paths aren't crowded and the beaches feel like your own private getaway.

Quintero's famous path begins from the pier at the end of the main road, 21 de Mayo. The unmistakable **Waikiki Disco** is at the beginning of the path, as well as a small beach, but keep going, as there are better stretches of sand farther along. As you follow the path, your surroundings become woodsy—birds (sounding remarkably like wild pigs) call from the tall cypress trees and sea lions sometimes sun themselves on nearby stones. Small white-sand beaches, sheltered by rocky outcroppings, also line the path until it comes to an end at the **Cueva del Pirata,** where graffiti paintings on the rocks depict Ghandi, Pablo Neruda, and Bob Marley, among others. Walking the full path takes less than an hour if you resist the temptation to wander off onto the rocks or one of the beaches—but why resist?

Buses leave from Viña del Mar on Libertad or from the terminal. From Concón, you can grab a bus to Quintero at the rotary (US$2). If you meander away the hours and decide to stay in Quintero, two inexpensive hostels on 21 de Mayo are happy to oblige. **Hotel Monaco ❶**, 21 de Mayo 1530, is worn but decent. Try to get the pretty wood-paneled room near the balcony. (☎934 690. Doubles CH$3000, with private bath CH$10,000.) Closer to the pier, **Residencial Brasilian ❸** has big rooms with private baths. The owner here also offers "therapeutic baths" called *talasoterapía* which, according to her advertisement, cure everything from asthma to the common cold. (Breakfast included. Singles CH$12,000; doubles CH$20,000; triples CH$28,000.) There are several unspectacular **pubs** along 21 de Mayo serving seafood and beer.

ZAPALLAR   ☎33

Zapallar's neighbors to the north and south (Maitencillo and Papudo, respectively) are more developed, with hostels and unsightly condominiums, but Zapallar has avoided such development. Somehow, it has managed to remain a quiet residential neighborhood with turn-of-the-century mansions and tall groves of trees—in fact, walking around Zapallar feels a little like trespassing in a gated community. The major tourist activity here is to stroll along Zapallar admiring the homes or to enjoy the coastal paths and sheltered beach.

There are no real tourist accommodations in the town proper (although in summer it may be possible to rent rooms in private homes), but a couple of upscale hotels are on the highway where buses pass, such as the pricey **Hotel Isla Seca ❺**. (Singles US$95; doubles US$135; 4-person suites US$270.) A great restaurant by the tiny *caleta* is **Restaurant Cesar ❸**, where the locals descend from their holiday homes to dine on entrees such as grilled sole with shrimp (CH$6000), right on the beach. (☎099 875 4842. Open daily noon-midnight.)

MIDDLE CHILE

PARQUE NACIONAL LA CAMPANA

Declared a national park in 1967, La Campana has been well-known since 1834 when Darwin scaled the park's namesake mountain and admired the views that extend as far as Valparaíso. Following in Darwin's footsteps, thousands of visitors make the ascent every year for a glimpse of the sea to the west and the high *cordillera* of the Andes to the east.

The park's 8000 hectares enclose stands of *roble* (the northern-most growth of this tree in Chile) and forests of native Chilean palms, considered a "vulnerable" species. Campana's animals are mostly small, but visitors occasionally see foxes and mountain cats. Eagles, hawks, and the giant hummingbird number among the birds, and small lizards, toads, and the *rana grande* hide among the rocks.

AT A GLANCE	
AREA: 8000 hectares.	**HIGHLIGHTS:** La Campana mountain, forests of *roble* and Chilean palm. Diversity of flora and fauna.
CLIMATE: Moderate climate; average of 800mm of precipitation annually, mostly between May and Sept. Mean temperature 13.8°C.	**FEES:** CH$1500, children CH$500.
GATEWAYS: Olmúe (Granizo and Cajón Grande sector), Hualcapo, and Escuela Las Palmas (Ochoa sector).	**CAMPING:** Free campsites in each of the three sectors—Segundo Puente in Granizo, El Belloto and El Arenal in Cajón Grande, and La Buitrera in Ochoa.

TRANSPORTATION. Buses stop in Olmúe, about 1km from the Granizo entrance and 3km from the Cajón Grande entrance. *Colectivos* sometimes take passengers to the Granizo entrance. **Buses Ciferal Express** makes the two-hour trip from Viña del Mar. To get to sector Ochoa, take a bus to **La Calera** or **Quillota** and pick up a *colectivo* from there. *Colectivos* drop passengers at Hualcapo and the Escuela Las Palmas, 4km and 2km from the park entrance.

ORIENTATION AND PRACTICAL INFORMATION. The park has three sectors, each with a **Conaf** administration station, potable water, and camping areas. During summer months, all 3 sectors of the park are open daily for visitors (CH$1500, children CH$500). From May to August, Granizo is the only sector that admits visitors, and on Saturday, Sunday, and holidays there is no camping allowed. Winter months can bring heavy rains, so it's a good idea to check with **Conaf** (☎441 342; www.conaf.cl), in the park at Sector Granizo, before heading out. In Viña del Mar, Conaf's office is at 3 Norte 541. (☎970 108 or 689 267. Open M-Th 8:45am-5:45pm, F 8:45am-4:45pm.) There are few accommodations other than camping options available within the park, but pricey *hosterías* (and grocery stores) are located in Olmúe, near sector Granizo.

HIKES. Sector Granizo contains the main entrance and is the only sector open in winter months. The campsite, **Segundo Puente,** is 700m from the park entrance. Its 22 sites have bathroom facilities and drinking water available. Two main trails leave from this area; the shorter trail, "La Canasta," is a nice walk through the forest, but the trail of most interest to the serious climber is "El Andinista," which leads to the 1900m peak of **Cerro La Campana.** Those planning to attempt the climb should check with Conaf before going—it's steep, and only climbers with previous experience are encouraged to try for the summit. The climb takes about 4 hours to the top and another 3 hours to get back down.

In **Sector Cajón Grande,** the camp sites **El Belloto** and **El Arenal** are 100m and 200m respectively from the Conaf office at Cajón Grande. "Sendero El Plateau" heads west from here and offers some lovely forest views. Of special interest in this sector are the natural pools formed by the *estero* **Cajón Grande.** "Pozo El Coipo," 800m from the park administration, is suitable for bathing.

Sector Ochoa, Campana's third sector, noted for its forests of Chilean palm, is on the northern edge of the park. The campsite **La Buitrera** lies 1km from the park administration, next to the river Rabuco. A path labeled "La Cortadera" leads 6km to the waterfall of the same name and then loops back around.

LA LIGUA   ☎33

A detour off the Panamericana will land you in La Ligua (pop. 33,974), a dusty agricultural town. In the main square, men and women wearing long white jackets loiter around with baskets filled with *dulces de La Ligua,* the powdered-sugar-coated sweets for which the town is famous. Other than sweets, La Ligua's other principal attraction is the archaeological **Museo La Ligua,** a 10min. walk downhill past the post office towards the outskirts of town on Prat. Small but well-organized, the museum is dedicated to regional history. One of its best displays consists of artifacts discovered between 1977 and 1989 by a group of local teens who called themselves "Yacas" and traveled through the countryside in search of archaeological remains. The eclectic highlights of this museum include the recreated Diaguita burial site, a whale skeleton that discoverers in Papudo initially believed was a dinosaur, and old *escudos*—the original Chilean currency. (Open Tu-F 9:30am-1pm and 3:30-6:30pm, Sa 10am-2pm. CH$400, children CH$100.)

Frequent **buses** run from Santiago and Viña del Mar to La Ligua, stopping at the main square or a block uphill on Polanco. It is also possible to take a **taxi** to the Panamericana and grab a bus there. There's no need to stay, but **Residencial Aconcagua ❶,** Esmeralda 173 (☎711 145), offers family-style rooms with colorful bedspreads and shared baths. Breakfast is available for CH$3000. There are several cafes on the Plaza de Armas—try **Café Macalú** on Polanco for ice cream or sandwiches. (Open M-Sa 9am-9:30pm.)

WEST TO ARGENTINA

BORDER CROSSING INTO ARGENTINA: MENDOZA
Crossing between Chile and Argentina, especially between Santiago and Mendoza, is done by hundreds of people every day and has become nearly routine. The long, twisting road that runs between the cities is paved, well-maintained, and heavily traversed by cars and buses alike. The border crossing itself occurs at the center of a renown mile-long tunnel bored through the heart of the Andes. **Customs** is rigorous but not difficult. Buses and cars are stopped just before the tunnel and passengers must disembark and claim their luggage. All items are briefly searched for contraband and various food products. Passports are also checked and stamped (see **Essentials: Border Crossings,** p. 65, for info on visas and fees).

MENDOZA, ARGENTINA   ☎0261

PESOS (ARGS)		
CH$1 = ARG$0.0051		ARG$1 = CH$196.5
US$1 = ARG$3.610		ARG$1 = US$0.277
UK£1 = ARG$5.529		ARG$1 = UK£0.181
EUR€1 = ARG$3.537		ARG$1 = EUR€0.283

Ever since the city was founded in 1561 by a Chilean troupe sent over from Santiago by Garcia Hurtado de Mendoza, this town has had a fundamental association with Chile. Nowadays, increased purchasing power is inspiring throngs of Chileans to recreate Mendoza's original trans-Andean journey—this million-strong suburban city is a trendy vacation destination of late, in vogue with fashionable and adventurous Chileans alike. Visitors frequently endure the seven-hour bus ride from Santiago to see and be seen, but mostly to enjoy cheap outdoor excursions, savory steak dinners, and raging nightlife. The pedestrian crowd rubs shoulders with mountain climbers on their way to Aconcagua who in turn mingle with vineyard-hopping wine connoisseurs on their way south. Mendoza's wide, welcoming avenues offer plenty of room for all, and its enviable alpine views will keep Chileans coming back for more each year.

▇ TRANSPORTATION

Flights: All flights land at **Aeropuerto El Plumerillo** (☎448 7128), only 10min. northeast of Mendoza proper. **Buses** from the airport run to the Omnibus terminal on the southeast side of town (every 30min., ARG$1.30; purchase a *tarjeta* at the airport info booth). **Taxis** to the city center ARG$8-10. **LanChile,** Rivadavia 135 (☎425 7900), and **Southern Winds** (☎0810 777 7979) are the two airlines that connect directly with Santiago and offer unrestricted round-trip fares for US$120-200. Fares are much lower with 3 weeks advance notice.

Buses: The **local Omnibus** system operates throughout Gran Mendoza. The **two numbers** in each window indicate the bus route—the top number indicates the general area of town serviced and the lower number indicates the specific route. Consult locals or bus stop maps for details. Crosstown fares generally run ARG$1.30. Buy magnetic swipe cards at kiosks or tourist information centers. **Regional** and **international** buses leave from the **Terminal del Sol.** Numerous companies run buses to **Santiago** (7hr., ARG$20-25). Check with: **Tur Bus** (☎431 1008; 3 per day); **Tas Choapa** (☎431 2140; 2 per day); **O'Higgins Internacional** (☎431 5946; 3 per day); **CATA Internacional** (☎431 0782; 3 per day); **TAC** (☎431 1039; 2 per day); **AndesMar** (☎432 2641; 11:15am); **ChileBus** (☎434 9596); and **El Rapido Internacional** (☎431 5271). Direct buses to **Viña del Mar** and **Valparaíso** run only once a day with such companies as Tur Bus and TAC (ARG$20-25). **Minibuses** operated by **Chi-Ar** (☎431 1736) and **Nevada Internacional** (☎431 2908) regularly go to Santiago (ARG$25). Connections to **Buenos Aires** (15hr., ARG$50-65) are available with TAC, AndesMar, and **Central Argentino** (☎431 3112; 6:45pm). **Ski shuttles** are not commonplace, as various tour agencies organize transportation to the slopes, but **Expreso Uspallata** (☎431 3309) sends a daily bus to Penitentes (6 and 10:15am, ARG$11). To get to **Las Leñas,** try TAC buses (6am, ARG$24).

Taxis: Fare from the bus terminal to the airport in metered taxis is ARG$8.50. **Radio taxis** with pick-up service include **Coria Taxis** (☎445 5855) and **Teletaxi** (☎448 4444).

Car Rental: Several agencies operate at the airport, but tend to be expensive. **Andina Rent-A-Car,** Paseo Sarmiento 129 (☎438 0480), in town, has more reasonable rates (from ARG$25-35 with insurance).

✦ 🛈 ORIENTATION AND PRACTICAL INFORMATION

Mendoza is a big, sprawling city in which streets, especially the east-west boulevards, change names with alarming frequency. However, the well-laid-out grid and park system gives disoriented tourists a sporting chance. All street signs in the city's boundaries have a **number** and **direction,** indicating the distance from the central intersection of **San Martín** and **Colón.** San Martín, with its abundance of shops, banks, amenities, and agencies, serves as the functional thoroughfare of the downtown area. **Las Heras,** eight blocks north of Colón, is a historically important byway that boasts an assortment of shops and restaurants. **Paseo Sarmiento,** only four blocks north of Colón and east of the Plaza Independencia, has a bevy of attractive sidewalk cafes. Aside from the city's shifting network of wide streets, the system of **parks** can be used for orientation purposes. **Plaza Independencia** is the ad hoc center of town, as outlying mini-parks surround it within a two-block radius: **Chile** to the northwest, **San Martín** to the northeast, **España** is to the southeast, and **Italia** to the southwest. **Parque General San Martín** borders central Mendoza to the west.

ARGENTINA COUNTRY CODE ☎54

Tourist Offices: Mendoza's information network is very visible, but make sure you are getting *all* the information, since the tourism industry here is very focused on the sales aspect of things. A **tourist stand** at the **airport** (☎448 0017) and one at **Terminal del Sol** (☎431 3001) greet incoming visitors. However, the best place for comprehensive information and reliable advice is the central office of the **Subsecretaria de Turismo,** San Martín 1143 (☎420 2800), between Garibaldi and Catamarca. Open M-F 8am-10pm, Sa-Su 9am-10pm. Nearby, on the northeast corner of San Martín and Paseo Sarmiento/Garibaldi, a small stand-apart **info shack** is more crowded but also very helpful. Open 9am-9pm.

Mendoza Centro

ACCOMMODATIONS
Apart Hotel del Sol, 2
Campo Base, 6
Hospedaje Zamora, 4
Hostelling International, 14
Petit Hotel, 1
Savigliano Hostel, 13

FOOD
Azafran, 8
Facundo, 5
Las Tinajas, 3
Los Tres Mosqueteros, 12
Naturata, 10

NIGHTLIFE
Apeteco, 15
Drugstore Most, 9
El Cuervo Pub and Pool, 11
Por Acá, 7

MIDDLE CHILE

Tours: The plethora of tour companies makes it hard to distinguish between them. **South American Explorers** (☎429 9638 or 156 564 863; www.saexplorers.com) has one of the most complete lineups of adventure excursions, including everything from sandboarding and hiking to climbing and whitewater kayaking. For river-specific tours, **Betancourt Rafting,** Lavalle 35 (☎429 9665; www.betancourt.com.ar), offers a fine selection of trips varying in difficulty and duration (from ARG$30 for 1hr. trip). Several companies compete for the tamer and more conventional bus-tour market, as well as within the ski rental and alpine transport pool. **Turismo Mendoza,** Las Heras 543 (☎429 2013); **Turismo Sapean,** Primitivo de la Reta (☎420 4162; mendoza@sepean.com); and **Saint Germain Tours,** Colón 126 (☎429 620; sgtours@lanet.com.ar) all specialize in city circuits (ARG$15), mountain tours to the **Penitentes** and **Aconcagua** area (ARG$35), and most importantly, wine tours (ARG$16). All three can accommodate English speakers, although the first two companies are more geared to that market. **Hostelling International** and **Campo Base** have a range of activities and outings for guests (see **Accommodations,** p. 150).

Embassies and Consulates: Chile, Paso de los Andes 1147 (☎425 5024). The office stays busy, as many people come here to renew Chilean visas.

Banks and Currency Exchange: Banks are peppered along San Martín and near the Plaza Independencia. Most have functional **ATMs.** The best spot for changing currency is the corner of San Martín and Catamarca. Of the three *cambios* here, **Cambio Santiago** has the latest hours. (Open M-F 8am-8pm, Sa 8:30am-1:30pm and 4:30-8:30pm.) **Western Union,** España 1152 (☎420 5070). Open M-F 9am-7pm, Sa 9:30am-1:30pm. Services available also at the **post office.**

Laundry: Try the self-service **Lava Center,** Mitre 1623 (☎423 4509), or **Lave Mas,** Garibaldi 142 (☎420 3960).

Emergency: ☎101.

Police: Salta 672 (☎449 9000), in Godoy Cruz.

Hospital: Medical emergency ☎107. **Central** (☎420 0600 or 429 7100), at the corner of Alem and Salta, just across from the bus terminal.

Internet: Rates are usually ARG$1 per hr. **Internet Webhouse,** 219 Paseo Sarmiento (ARG$1 per hr.), and **LaRed Ciberbar,** at the corner of Alem and San Juan (ARG$1 per hr.), are open 24hr.

Post Office: Correo Argentino, at the corner of Colón and San Martín. Open M-F 8am-8pm, Sa 9am-1pm.

Postal code: 5500.

ACCOMMODATIONS

The decline and fall of the Argentine *peso* has made accommodations in Mendoza quite affordable, but in the mid- and upper-ranges, there is very little worth shelling out for.

Savigliano Hostel, Pedro B Palacios 944 (☎423 7746; savigliano@hotmail.com), just west of the bus terminal, through an underpass below Palacios. A quiet Mediterranean-style house with a pleasant common room, TV, and über-helpful, dedicated owners who somehow manage to defy Mendoza's hectic pace. Private and shared baths and kitchen facilities available. Breakfast ARG$1. 4-6 bed dorms ARG$10; singles ARG$15-20; doubles ARG$25-30; triples ARG$35-40. ❶

Campo Base, Mitre 946 (☎429 0707; www.cerroaconcagua.com.ar; info@campo-base.com.ar), just south of Plaza Independencia, 7 blocks from the bus terminal either by foot or on the #20 bus. This zany, cramped locale is definitely packed with both character and guests. Management caters to the outdoorsy crowd and has an Aconcagua guiding service; they also run a sister hostel up at Penitentes. 15min. free Internet for guests. Kitchen facilities and laundry service available. 4-8 bed dorms and doubles ARG$9-11 per person. ❶

Hostelling International, España 343 (☎424 0018; info@hostelmendoza.net), 8 long blocks south of Paseo Sarmiento and 2 west of San Martín. A bit set back from the center, but compensates with lots of amenities, a friendly staff, and a large sleeping capacity. Free parking, book exchange, kitchen facilities, laundry services, TV, a climbing wall, and lots of fun events and BBQs are part of the deal. Breakfast included. Bike rental ARG$9 per day. Full-day adventure excursions ARG$55-80. Dorms ARG$12; doubles ARG$32. ❶

Hospedaje Zamora, Perú 1156 (☎425 7537), just north of the intersection with Sarmiento. This central yet quiet location with basic beds has rooms off an interior courtyard. Climbers have been known to patronize this accommodation. Breakfast included. 2-4 bed rooms ARG$18 per person. ❷

Hotel Petit, Perú 1459 (☎425 0682; petit@slatinos.com.ar), just south of Las Heras and north of Plaza Chile. This hotel really isn't as mini as the name suggests. All rooms have phones, private baths, heat, and A/C. Internet access available. Breakfast included. Doubles ARG$35; triples ARG$50; ARG$5 less off-season. ❸

Apart Hotel del Sol, 202 Las Heras (☎ 438 0218), on the southwest corner of the intersection with España. A pink-and-white theme reigns in the halls here, which sport pristine marble-like flooring and worn carpets. Rooms are spacious and come with TV, A/C,
and private baths. Breakfast included. Singles ARG$42; doubles ARG$55; triples
ARG$80. ❹

⬛ FOOD

Unleash the carnivore within—most visitors who journey to Mendoza will want to
feast on various cuts of juicy, cheap Argentine beef. The abundance of *parrillas*
(grill-type restaurants) testifies to this culture's meat-eating, high-cholesterol braving propensities.

▨ **Las Tinajas,** Lavalle 38 (☎ 429 1174), just east of San Martín. The king of Mendoza's
tenedor libre (all-you-can-eat) joints, with a splash of sophistication. The eclectic buffet
includes a huge selection of vegetables, shellfish, various hot dishes, and a whole table
devoted to cuts of meat and rotisserie-roasted carcasses. The gastronomically adventurous can experiment with peculiar, but always tasty, delicacies. Top it all off with delicious custom-made fruit crepes. Lunch M-F ARG$7; lunch Sa and dinner Su-Th ARG$9;
lunch Su and dinner F-Sa ARG$11. Open noon-3:30pm and 8pm-1:30am. ❶

Azafran, Aristides Villanueva 287, west on the way to Parque San Martín. Less a restaurant than a combination wine-bar and South American "deli," this place is a tastebud-
tickler. A platter of olives, cheese, crackers, and other relishes (ARG$10) goes down
well with a 300-label selection of wines, conveniently sold by the glass (ARG$3). Tradi-
tional *tapas* sold in the evenings. Open M-Sa 10am-2pm and 6pm-1am. ❷

Facundo, Sarmiento 641 (☎ 420 2866), west of Plaza Independencia. A good date spot
that combines ambience, a good selection of meat and fish, and a hefty wine list. Salad
bar ARG$4 per plate. Open noon-3pm and 8pm-1:30am. ❶

Naturata, Vincente López 177 (☎ 420 3087), near Plaza Carlos Pelligrini, 2 blocks east
on Alem from San Martín. Although it's only open for lunch, the assortment of bean-
based dishes, salads, fresh fruits, and veggie *empanadas* proves a good antidote to
Mendoza's prevalent meat culture. *Tenedor libre* ARG$7. Open M-Sa noon-3pm. ❶

Los Tres Mosqueteros, Costanera 980 (☎ 423 2633), right near the corner of Alem and
Palacios, near the bus terminal. While this joint won't blow your mind, its convenient
location and the representative *comida típica* are definite pluses. Unfortunately, neither
the cement and cinder-block construction nor the food is dressed up. *Menú* ARG$3.80.
Open 9am-11pm. ❶

⬤ SIGHTS AND OUTDOOR ACTIVITIES

ÁREA FUNDACIONAL. History buffs will want to make this area, 15 blocks north
of the bus terminal west of Palacios, their first stop in Mendoza. **Plaza Pedro del
Castillo** was the site of Old Mendoza, the first location of the city's government and
markets before the devastating earthquake of 1861, which leveled nearly every
building in the city. The city shifted foci to its current layout, but two sights preserve remnants and historical fragments from Old Mendoza. The ▨**Museo del Área
Fundacional** shows the active excavation of Old City Hall, which was buried by the
earthquake, then covered over by a slaughterhouse, and finally by a market. One of
the most fascinating elements of this brilliant archaeological project is the buildup
of fluvial sediments between the historical layers. The sheer amount of dirt illustrates the dynamism of Mendoza's periodic floods and explains the construction of
the city's open drainage system in the 1980s. *(Beltran and Videla Castillo, on the Plaza
Pedro del Castillo. ☎ 425 6927. Open Tu-Sa 8am-8pm, Su 3-8pm. ARG$1.50, students ARG$1.)*

On the northwest side of the plaza, the **Ruinas de San Francisco** are the only pieces of Old Mendoza left standing 150 years after the earthquake, and even then, the rock and mortar is heavily scaffolded and covered with wood and metal support beams. *(On Beltran and Itunaingo. Call the museum to set up guided visits M-F 9am-4pm.)*

PARQUE SAN MARTÍN. A popular weekend getaway for picnic-toting *Mendocinos*, the large park at the western limits of the city has lots of attractions. **Biking** the road system of the park is a good way to see more of the park than is possible by foot. *(Rentals available at second roundabout from the eastern park entrance on Emilio Civit; follow the road south then southwest to the first roundabout, and make a left to the second. The rentals are near the northern end of the concrete rowing lake. Open Sa-Su. ARG$4 per hr.)* **VIP buses** offer a short tour of the entire park, stopping for panoramic views and photos at the top of **Cerro de la Gloria,** an impressive statue-bearing hill on the west side of the park. *(Buses a short walk into the park from the Emilio Civit entrance. ☎ 428 4515. 1hr. tours ARG$3.50.)* The **zoo** is also a popular stop for daytrippers and is acclaimed for its spacious habitats and nice views. *(3km from the east entrance. Take the #110 bus from the city center that says "zoológico" in the front window. Open daily 9am-5pm. ARG$3.)* Regardless of how you decide to spend your day in the park, the **information center** can handle all your recreational queries. *(☎ 420 5052. Open 8am-6pm.)*

BODEGAS. While they're not much to look at, bold, fruity, and flavorful Argentine wines will flirt with your palate; visiting wineries can make for a wonderful afternoon when in Mendoza. Up to 70% of Argentina's wine is produced at the abundant vineyards in this area. Moreover, the fall of the Argentine *peso* has resulted in amazing values in current inventory. Hard-core wine tasters should rent a car and seek maps and guidance at the **visitor information centers** of vineyards they deem worthy of a visit. Those tourists who taste wine more for the flair of the action than the flavor of the product might appreciate the three-per-week, half-day tours of an assortment of *bodegas* that include an ever-important tasting or two (see **Tours,** p. 149). Apart from well-organized tours, **La Rural** is known to have one of the largest and best facilities for independent visitors, including an intriguing museum, tours, and tastings. *(☎ 497 2013. From the terminal, take the bus with #170 on the top and #173 on the bottom; 30-45min. to the location in Maipú. Open M-F 9am-5pm, Sa-Su 9am-1pm.)* Also notable for its proximity and charming staff and ambience is the smaller facility, **Bodegas Lopez.** *(Carril Ozamis 375, in Maipú. ☎ 497 2406. Bilingual tours M-F 9, 11am, 2, 4pm; Sa 9:30, 10:30, 11:30am.)* Other vineyards to consider are **Bodega Salentein** *(☎ 424 1845)*, with its breathtaking location in Godoy Cruz, and boutique-sized **Viña el Cerno** *(☎ 439 8447)*, in Maipú.

SKIING. In the winter, loads of folks hit the eastern slopes of the Andes for first-rate skiing. Farthest from the city of Mendoza, **Las Leñas** has the best ski facilities in the country, but is prohibitively expensive by Argentine standards. Opened in 1983, the resort has over 65km of trail and nearly 200,000 hectares of off-trail skiing. It also has facilities for snowboarders and cross-country skiers. To add to its impressiveness, Las Leñas can hold over 3000 guests in lodgings that are all "ski in, ski out," within 200m of a lift. *(☎ 546 277 1100; www.laslenas.ar. Vertical drop 1230m. 11 lifts serve 55 trails. 5% beginner, 30% intermediate, 25% advanced, 40% expert. Open June-Nov. 9am-5pm.)* In contrast, the nearby **Vallecitos** offers a short season and affordable lift tickets. Despite its smaller size, the mountain does offer trails suited for both skiers and boarders. *(☎ 54-6 250 972. Vertical drop 1320m. 7 lifts serve 16.5km of trail. Open June-Sept.)* **Penitentes** is the unanimous choice for value, with a longer season, more snow, and stunning views of Aconcagua. *(☎ 546 123 4049. Vertical drop 2023m. 5 lifts serve 23.5km of trails. Open June 15-Oct. 15.)* Also at Penitentes is the HI-run **Hostel Refugio Penitentes ❶**, the cheapest lodging option in any of the Mendoza-area resorts. *(☎ 429 0707; info@campo-base.com.ar.)*

FINE ARGENTINE WINE Victor Hugo once noted that while God only made water, man made wine. Unfortunately, he didn't complete his observation by noting that the Argentines made particularly fine wine (and then made this attribute of humanity available to all in copious quantities at reasonable prices). With the economic situation in Argentina causing chaos in the wine industry by shifting relative prices and changing demand, wine is more readily available to budget tourists than in the past—so indulge freely in this most healthful of beverages. Although the best way to appreciate the vintages is to experiment, sampling from the wide array of nuanced options, it does pay to follow some guidelines. First of all, the most acclaimed grapes grown in this region are the **Cabernet Sauvignon** and the **Malbec,** the former also being well-regarded in Chile. An extensive yet fair list of high-quality, good-value labels is impossible to assemble, but some amateur wine drinkers recommend the **Trapiche** and **Peñaflor** wines among the moderate ARG$10-20 per bottle price range. **Flichman** is purportedly the way to go for a more expensive treat. **Azafran** (see **Food,** p. 151) is a great spot to get a sense of your taste buds' fancy while you savor wines of disparate calibers with a partner. Supermarkets and bottle shops supply most of the city's wine.

OTHER SIGHTS. Maybe the best unsung sight in Mendoza is the plaza system of the symmetrical city layout. The fountains and manicured gardens of **Plaza Independencia** are a superficial attraction, but the theater and the **Museo de Arte Moderno** with its three-week exhibition rotation add depth to the visual appeal and make a day spent strolling through the city more substantive. (☎425 7279. Open M-Sa 9am-1pm and 4-9pm, Su 4-9pm. Free.) The most intriguing of the smaller plazas is the heavily-tiled **Plaza España,** which also hosts an impressive monument and a collection of peddling *artesanos* on the weekends.

FESTIVALS. Mendoza's biggest event, the sparkling **Fiesta de la Vendimia,** during the first weekend of March, would make even Dionysus proud. Marking the grape harvest for autumn wine production, the three-day party is distinguished by its wine paraphernalia, lavish food displays, and zany song-and-dance routines. Accommodations fill up well in advance, so plan ahead if you want to participate in the merriment.

◖ NIGHTLIFE

Just because the wine's divine doesn't mean *Mendocinos* don't just knock back for the buzz of it. Mendoza parties hard, and locals don't get their party started till most everyone in Santiago's been asleep for a while. Dinner hours in the city extend past 11pm; clubs don't open their doors until midnight or later. Although the central area of Gran Mendoza near San Martín and Sarmiento has some pubs, the greatest concentration of centrally-located nightlife is on **Aristides Villanueva,** the western extension of Colón. The dress code is fairly lax, but nice shoes and a somewhat spiffy attire will get you in anywhere (while dramatically improving your chances with the ladies). Jeans are fine except in particularly upscale joints.

▨ Por Acá, Villanueva 567, at the corner of Granaderos. A crowd of beautiful young people clink glasses on swanky staircases and lounge in inviting corners—who could ask for more. Chill, jazzy music and dim lighting make the atmosphere smart and sociable. *Empanadas* ARG$0.50, individual pizzas ARG$5-8. Liter of beer ARG$2.50. Open F-Sa 8pm-6am, Su-Th 8pm-4:30am.

Apeteco, San Juan and Barraquero (☎424 9220), on the southeast corner about 8 blocks southwest of the bus station. The curious bi-stickfigured logo may hint at illicit behavior encouraged on far-flung corners of the dance floor, but it's hard to tell through the smoky fog. The energy will escalate as disco, dance, and pop emanate. Cover F-Sa ARG$7, Tu-Th and Su ARG$3. Open Tu-Th and Su midnight-4am, F-Sa midnight-7am.

Drugstore Most, Montevideo and 9 de Julio (☎420 1954), on the northeast corner across from Plaza España. Nominally involved with real pharmaceuticals, Most also supplies beer in copious quantities. A great place for a chill *cerveza* with friends in a brightly-lit fishbowl room with stool seating—just don't reach for codeine instead of your cocktail. Beers ARG$2. Open 24hr.

El Cuervo Pub and Pool (☎425 1892), at the corner of Pedro Molína and San Martín. Cafe by day, this street-level pool hall morphs into a lively pub and disco on weekends. Pool ARG$2.50 per game. Expect a long wait during peak hours. Pub cover ARG$7. Pool hall open Th-Sa 24hr., Su-W till late. Pub open F-Sa midnight-7am.

THE CENTRAL VALLEY

RANCAGUA   ☎72

In the early half of the 18th century, Rancagua was a waystation for priests making the trek from Santiago to Concepción. The city has since developed into a vital resource for the regional economy, functioning as a market for the produce of the outerlying countryside and as the source of much of the labor that keeps the nearby El Teniente copper mine humming. Rancagua, however, is not much to look at—modern shopping centers, graffitied adobe buildings, and local complaints of crime in the dimly lit streets make it a more ideal stopover than a destination. The city is most popular among tourists as a jumping-off point for excursions to the Termas de Cauquenes, Chapa Verde ski center, Reserva Nacional Río de los Cipreses to the east, and Lago Rapel to the west.

The capital of Chile's sixth region, Rancagua gained its glory as the place where independence leader Bernardo O'Higgins and his fellow Chilean patriots valiantly met the Royalist army in battle in 1814. The rebels suffered a crushing defeat, O'Higgins fled to Argentina, and the battle became known as the "Desastre de Rancagua." For many travelers, the past may prove a sufficiently cautionary prologue, and Rancagua will be just a place for pilgrimage, eating, and sleeping. But for those more willing to dig a little deeper, Rancagua can offer a happy medium— less hectic than Santiago, but bigger and badder than the sleepy countryside.

▐ TRANSPORTATION

Trains: Rancagua Station (☎230 361 or 238 530), on Estación between O'Carrol and Pinto, on the western edge of the city. Trains go to: **Chillán** (4hr.; 8:45am, 2:45, 7:45pm; CH$4200); **Concepción** (8hr., 10:53pm, CH$5800); **San Fernando** (50min.; M-F 6 per day 7:55am-10:30pm, Sa-Su 5 per day 11:15am-10:30pm; CH$630); **Santiago** (1¼hr.; M-F 20 per day 6:05am-10pm, Sa-Su 16 per day 7:15am-10pm; CH$1100); **Temuco** (11½hr., 9:09pm, CH$8000).

Buses: Tur Bus leaves from its terminal at O'Carrol 1175 (☎241 117), on the northeast corner of O'Carrol and Calvo, going to: **Santiago** (1½hr., M-F every 15 min. 5:50am-9:45pm, CH$1500); **San Fernando** (50min., M-Sa 6:20am, CH$1200); **Temuco** (8hr., 5:45am and 11:20pm, CH$5900). Other bus companies leave from the **Centro Comercial Rodoviario,** on Doctor Salinas between Av. Viña del Mar and Calvo. **Buses al Sur** (☎222 669 or 230 340) goes to **Santiago** (1½hr., M-Sa every 30min., CH$1000) and **Temuco** (9hr.; 9:10pm; M-Th CH$4300, F-Su CH$9000). **Via-Tur/Jet Sur Rutamar**

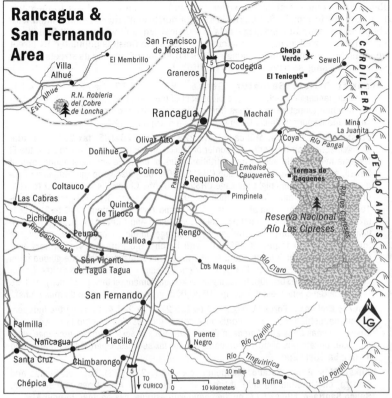

Rancagua & San Fernando Area

San Francisco de Mostazal
El Membrillo
Villa Alhué
R.N. Robleria del Cobre de Loncha
Est. Alhué
Graneros
Codegua
Chapa Verde
Sewell
El Teniente ■
Rancagua
Machalí
Mina La Juanita
Olival Alto
Coya
Río Pangal
Doñihue
Coinco
Embalse Cauquenes
Termas de Cauquenes
Requinoa
Pimpinela
Coltauco
Las Cabras
Quinta de Tilcoco
Reserva Nacional Río Los Cipreses
Río los Cipreses
Pichidegua
Río Cachapoal
Peumo
Malloa
Rengo
San Vicente de Tagua Tagua
Los Maquis
Río Claro
San Fernando
Palmilla
Puente Negro
Río Clarillo
Nancagua
Placilla
Santa Cruz
Chimbarongo
Río Tinguiririca
Chépica
TO CURICO
La Rufina
Río Portillo
CORDILLERA DE LOS ANDES

0   10 miles
0   10 kilometers

MIDDLE CHILE

(☎234 502) goes to **Santiago** (7½-8hr.; 10am and 9:50pm; M-Th, Sa-Su CH$4000, F CH$4500). **Gal-bus** (☎240 579) goes to **El Manzano** (3hr., every 8min. 6am-9pm, CH$1100) and **San Fernando** (1¼hr., every 16min. 6:08am-6:40pm, CH$600). **Sextur** (☎231 342) goes to **Pichilemu** (3-4hr., 6:34am, CH$2000) and **Lago Rapel** (2½hr.; 8, 9:20, 10:20am; CH$1000). **Hotel service,** Gate 15 (☎899 010), goes to **Termas de Cauqueres** (6:30, 9:40am, 1:45, 6:30pm; CH$800).

Taxis: Rancagua is small enough to walk to most places, but try **Radio Taxi Arides** (☎216 175 or 219 728; fax 219 728) for cheap, reliable service. Taxi fare from the train station to city center CH$500-1000. A trip to Machalí, 7km east of Rancagua, will cost CH$3500. **Colectivos** cost CH$300 for trips within Rancagua.

ORIENTATION AND PRACTICAL INFORMATION

Eighty-seven kilometers south of Santiago on the Pan-american Highway, Rancagua was originally designed as an 8-by-8 block chessboard extending from **Av. San Martín** to **Av. Freire,** and from **Av. Libertador Bernardo O'Higgins** to **Millán.** At the center of the grid is **Plaza de Los Héroes,** where you can find Rancagua's City Hall, the provincial government office, and regional capital building. The city's cultural sites can be found on **Estado,** running from the plaza, including the **Iglesia de La Merced,** a block north, and the **Casa de la Cultura** to the south near Millán. Most of

Rancagua's commercial life, however, has shifted to the west, closer to the city's train and bus terminals. **San Martín** is a major north-south thoroughfare, lined with shops and restaurants. **Independencia** is a pedestrian mall where you'll find street performers as well as most of the city's banks, while **Brasil** is populated by street vendors. Keep in mind that Rancagua does a poor job of labeling its streets—many signs are missing, so navigation can be difficult.

Tourist Office: Sernatur, Germán Riesco 277 (☎/fax 230 413; sernatur_rancag@entelchile.net), a block east of the Plaza de los Héroes. This branch of the national tourist service offers free maps of the city and brochures detailing Rancagua and its surroundings. Open M-F 8:30am-5:15pm.

Tours: Turismo Dakota, Mújica 605 (☎228 166 or 228 165; fax 228 165; tdakota@cmet.net), on the northwest corner of Mújica and Asterga. Arranges tours of the El Teniente mine, which include transportation, tours of the mine and neighboring town of Sewell, and lunch (half-day excursion CH$18,000). Tours also go to the Termas de Cauquenes resort (day-and-night package CH$25,000), the Chapa Verde ski center (daytrip CH$10,000), and other locales. Open M-F 9am-1:45pm and 3:15-7:30pm, Sa 10am-1pm. A variety of tours are also offered by **Turismo Terrasur,** Astorga 230 (☎229 161; fax 229 149; terrasur@chilesat.net), between Mújica and Cuevas. Besides its international and cross-country tours, Terrasur sells packages in the Rancagua area: a highlights tour of the rodeo region (CH$3000, with lunch); the Ruta del Vino winery tour (CH$66,000, including lunch and a short course in wine tasting); separate guided tours of El Teniente and Sewell (CH$30,000 for each excursion, including lunch); the Chapa Verde ski resort (CH$66,000, including lift ticket, equipment rentals, and lunch); and the Termas de Cauquenes resort (daytrip CH$30,000, including a dip in the thermal baths).

Currency Exchange: Forex, Astorga 369 (☎235 273; fax 244 499). From the Independencia pedestrian mall, walk north on Astorga—the *casa de cambio* is on your left. Cashes Thomas Cook and American Express traveler's checks. Currency exchange, courier, wire, private postal box, photocopying, and fax services. Open M-F 9am-2pm and 4-7pm, Sa 10am-2pm.

Banks/ATMs: Banco Estado, Independencia 666 (☎239 823), between Bueras and Astorga, on the southern side of the street. Has a 24hr. ATM. Open M-F 9am-2pm. **Banco Santiago,** Mújica 577, on the corner with Astorga, has another 24-hour ATM.

Market: On Brasil, between Santa María and Independencia, a long line of street vendors have set up shop. In their stalls you can find just about anything—from fruit to handbags to L.A. Lakers headbands. Open 9am-10pm.

Sports Complex: Patricio Mekis Sports Complex (☎253 088), just north of the *medialuna,* is a public facility that includes soccer fields, tennis courts, and a pool. Call one week ahead to reserve one of its 4 soccer fields. Open 8:30am-8:30pm. Free.

Work Opportunities: Max Sabor, hires waitstaff in Nov. **Granja Amanda,** Carrelea de la Fruta, El Manzano (☎198 2346), hires long-term, full-time workers in landscaping. **Hotel Termas de Cauquenes,** Termas de Cauquenes, Machalí (☎899 010; fax 899 009; termasdecauquenes@terra.cl). Hires people to work at the reception desk and in the dining room in February, for one month. See **Alternatives to Tourism,** p. 83, for more information.

Emergency: ☎131; **fire** ☎132.

Police: The *carabineros* have their **central office** (☎222 382), at the corner of O'Carrol and Bueras, and a branch office at San Martín 174 (☎221 122), between Cáceres and Mújica on the eastern side of the street.

Late-Night Pharmacy: Farmacia Ahumada, Independencia 799 (☎228 342). Open 8:30am-midnight. **S y B Farmacéutica,** Independencia 784 (☎231 785). Open 9am-midnight.

Rancagua

▲ ACCOMMODATIONS
Hotel Aguilar Real, **9**
Hotel Camino del Rey, **6**
Hotel España, **7**
Hotel Palace, **12**
Hotel Rancagua, **1**
Hotal Turismo Santiago, **10**
Motel Peatonal, **2**

🍴 FOOD
Bavaria, **3**
Centro Chung Hwa, **5**
Dahy, **8**
La Carpa, **4**
Max Sabor, **11**

MIDDLE CHILE

Hospital: Hospital Regional Rancagua, O'Higgins 611 (☎200 200; emergency 207 253), where Astorga meets Alameda.

Fax/Photocopying: Forex, Astorga 369 (☎235 273; fax 244 499). See **Currency Exchange,** above.

Telephones: Telefónica Mundo 188, San Martín 440 (☎227 595). Open M-F 9am-6pm, Sa 10am-1pm.

Internet Access: Servi@net, Centro Comercial Rodoviario Local 58-59 (☎220 814 or 099 226 4972; servi01@hotmail.com). M-F 9am-noon CH$600 per hr., all other times CH$800 per hr., students CH$700. Open M-Sa 9am-10pm. **On-Line Express**, Astorga 230 L-6 (☎246 268; www.online-express.ol), between Mújica and Cuevas. CH$800 per hr. Bottled drinks and snacks also for sale. Open M-Sa 10am-9pm.

Post Office: Correos is at Campos 322 (☎222 898 or 230 927), on the eastern side between Cuevas and the Independencia pedestrian mall, near the Plaza de los Héroes. Open M-F 9am-1:30pm and 2:30-6pm, Sa 9am-12:30pm.

🏠 ACCOMMODATIONS

🏨 **Hotel Rancagua,** San Martín 85 (☎232 663; fax 241 155; hotelrancagua@123click.cl), on the northwest corner of Cáceres. This hotel has the homey feel of a bed and breakfast. The flowers that line the outdoor walkway and decorate the foyer seem to match the sunny disposition of owner Elba Farjas Correa, who works hard at making you comfortable in her family's distinctive orange-and-green lodging. Cable TV and Internet access. Breakfast included. 24hr. reception. Singles CH$16,900; doubles CH$21,600; triples CH$28,100. ❹

Hotel Aguilar Real, Brasil 1045 (☎222 047; fax 223 002; Hsamour@ctcinternet.cl). This upscale hotel, located halfway between the train station and city center, is rather sterile (both aesthetically and hygienically), but it makes up for its lack of pizzazz with an outdoor pool, ping-pong and billiards tables, private parking, and adequate (if somewhat small) mattresses dressed in plaid comforters. Cable TV. Breakfast and laundry service included. 24hr. reception. Singles CH$22,000; doubles CH$31,500; triples CH$37,000; quads CH$48,000. ❹

Hotel Turismo Santiago, Brasil 1036 (☎230 860 or 230 855; fax 230 822; h.santiago@entelchile.net; www.gochile.cl). Head down Brasil to the city center; the hotel is on your right, between Santa María and Portales. In this stately (if somewhat faded) hotel, rooms are so cramped that it's hard to turn around with a full pack on—but it has large, comfy beds, a full-service restaurant, and an outdoor pool. Be aware that in winter, there is barely any hot water for showers. Cable TV. Breakfast included. 24hr. reception. Singles CH$23,500-37,500; doubles CH$35,500-50,900. ❹

Hotel España, San Martín 367 (☎230 141; fax 234 196), several steps north of the intersection of Brasil, Independencia, and San Martín. This century-old hotel has seen better days, as evidenced by the chipped paint on its walls and the ancient wooden doors that are difficult to lock. Nevertheless, Hotel España has a pleasant atmosphere, with its cozy inner courtyard. Cable TV. Breakfast included. 24hr. reception. Singles CH$15,000; doubles CH$20,000. ❹

Hotel Palace, Calvo 635 and Estación 628 (☎224 104). Leaving the train station, head straight down O'Carrol and turn right on Calvo; the hotel is on your left. The sign out front announces "Atención Las 24 Hrs," and red hearts flank the hotel's name—two hints at Hotel Palace's reputation as a place where couples come for a night. Amply spacious beds. 24hr. reception. Matrimonials CH$9000, with space heaters and cable TV CH$11,000. ❸

Hotel Camino del Rey, Estado 275 (☎ 232 314 or 239 765; fax 232 314; hotelcaminodelrey@terra.cl), a block north of the Plaza de los Héroes. The hotel has an elegant, colonial-style facade, and inside its white adobe walls are pleasant enough accommodations. Cable TV, minibar, security safe, hair dryers, private parking, central heating, and A/C. Breakfast included. 24hr. reception. Flexible check-out. Singles CH$32,500; matrimonials CH$45,500; doubles CH$48,750; triples CH$65,000; suites CH$58,500. Foreigners are excused from the 18% IVA tax. AmEx/MC/V. ❹

Motel Peatonal, Cáceres 824 (☎234024), across from Hotel Rancagua, in an inconspicuous white-walled house without any sign. Motels in Chile tend to cater to couples (or couples-to-be) more than to weary motorists. This motel, run by the owners of Hotel Rancagua, has clean and functional rooms, but a drab aesthetic further diminished by the poor insulation that makes the rooms a veritable freezer in winter. Cable TV and space heaters. 24hr. reception. Singles CH$9900; doubles CH$10,800. MC/V. Payment requested up front. ❸

🍴 FOOD

Max Sabor, San Martín 412, 2nd fl. (☎220 088), between O'Carrol and Independencia, on the eastern side of the street. A picture of a smiling waiter dressed in green directs you into the eating area of this second-story establishment, where you'll find cheap specials, such as *pollo asado* (comes with soup, beverage, and a cup of diced fruit; CH$1600). Vegetarians can try the pizza with tomato, cheese, asparagus, and paprika (CH$850). Sandwiches CH$500-1600. Open 9am-2am. Cash only. ❶

Bavaria, San Martín 255, 2nd fl. (☎233 827; www.bavaria.cl), between Mújica and Cuevas, down the street from La Carpa. Locals say that this branch of the popular national chain offers some of the best dining in Rancagua. One of its specialties is a leg of lamb, slowly roasted in a special oven (CH$2700). To balance out its delightfully unhealthy array of barbecue (CH$11,900), there is a variety of salads (CH$850-1950). Open noon-4pm and 7pm-midnight. ❹

Centro Chung Hwa, Cuevas 559 (☎244 705), between Astorga and Campos. As Chinese restaurants in foreign lands go, this one is tastefully appointed, with velvet-lined chairs and crimson tablecloths, and Chinese characters and watercolors decorating the walls. The same cannot be said of the dishes, which range in authenticity and quality, and won't impress patrons used to bona fide Chinatown cuisine. Still, try the *camarón mandarín* (fried shrimp pancakes; CH$2680) or the chow mein noodles (with beef and vegetables; CH$2100). Open 11:30-4:30pm and 7:30pm-12:30am. ❷

La Carpa, San Martín 299 (☎230 285), at the northwest corner of San Martín and Cuevas, on the block next to Hotel España. An unadorned eatery popular with locals, who stop in to watch the ever-droning TV and listen to the Spanish rock piped over the speakers. Serves up basic Chilean meat-and-potatoes—try the filling, if boring, version of *pollo grillé* (CH$2290). The menu is chock-full of different salads and sandwiches, including a *vegetariano* of cheese, avocado, green beans, and tomato (CH$1490). Free salsa and bread. Open daily 10am-3am. Credit cards accepted. ❷

Dahy, San Martín 340 (☎243 813), across from Hotel España. The Budweiser babe meets the Cristal chick at this salt-of-the-earth *fuente de soda* downtown, where the pin-up pictures vie for your attention with equally glamorous photos of cheeseburgers and hot dogs. But forget the aesthetics—you can get a giant jug of Cristal beer for CH$1500. Open daily 6pm-3am. ❷

⊙ SIGHTS

PLAZA DE LOS HÉROES. At the center of the city, in the **Plaza de los Héroes,** a bronze likeness of Chilean independence leader Bernardo O'Higgins leads a charge, his rearing horse trampling a hapless bronze Royalist soldier. As if the bravado of that scene were not enough, words inscribed on the statue's pedestal proclaim manly dicturns like "Live with honor or die with glory." On the western edge of the plaza stands the expressionless stone statue of José Antonio Manso de Velasco, the 1743 founder of La Villa Santa Cruz de Triona, which would later become Rancagua. A wooden carving of Mapuche chieftain Tomás Gauglén, who defied the Spanish invaders, glares back from the east. Rancagua's dubious glory was secured just a block north, at the **Iglesia de la Merced,** Cuevas 399. In October 1814, the church (then a convent), was Rancagua's tallest building, and from its 30m high bell tower O'Higgins kept close watch of the Spanish army as it crossed the Cachapoal River and headed north to smash the rebel movement. When the Royalist troops surrounded Chile's patriots and demanded their surrender, O'Higgins had a black priest's robe hoisted out the tower window to signal his defiance. Ask the church staff nicely, and they'll let you climb to the top of the belltower; alternatively, take a stroll through the church's peaceful inner courtyard. *(Iglesia de la Merced ☎221 456. Open 9am-1pm and 4-7:30pm. Free.)*

On the southern edge of the plaza sits the **Iglesia Catedral.** Originally built in 1775, the church was left in ruins after Spanish soldiers unleashed cannon fire upon the defiant city in 1814. Five decades later, it was rebuilt by an Italian architect, who added its two Doric spires. Though small compared to the Catholic flagships in larger cities, the cathedral can be magnificent on a sunny day, its walls a gleaming gold. *(☎230 048. Open M-Sa 9am-1pm and 4-8pm, Su during mass at 8, 11am, 12:30, 8pm. Free.)*

ALONG CALLE ESTADO. Heading down Estado, the street next to the cathedral, you'll reach the **Museo Regional,** Estado 685, to your right, and the **Casa del Pilar de Esquina,** Estado 682, on your left. These two white adobe buildings are the only structures still standing from the time of Santa Cruz de Triana, the village that later became Rancagua. The two museums have small, rather tedious collections: the Museo Regional showcases rooms with furniture and decorations from the 19th century, while the Casa del Pilar de Esquina features exhibits on aboriginal tribes, Spanish conquistadors, and the mining industry of the sixth region in Chile. *(Museo Regional ☎ 221 524; fax 221 524; museo@chilesat.net. Both Museo Regional and Casa del Pilar open Tu-F 10am-6pm, Sa-Su 9am-1pm. CH$600 includes both museums. Tu free.)*

After leaving the twin museums, head farther south to where Estado meets Millán, and the **Casa de la Cultura,** on Cachapoal, will be across the street, on the left. When the land north of the Río Cauqueres was a huge estate by the name of Los Cipreses, stretching out to the national reserve out east, this was the masters' **casa patronal.** All that remains from that day are portions of the original wall, thick adobe some 300 years old; the sienna-red roof slates and mixed-stone patio have been reconstructed. In addition to its tranquil groves of palm and pine trees, the Casa showcases local art and houses a music school. *(☎ 230 976. Open M-Sa 9am-8pm. Free.)*

RODEO. The Central Valley is known as the *tierra huasa*—cowboy country—and Rancagua is the place where Chile's *huasos* gather for the national **rodeo championships,** which take place every year at the end of March or during the first week in April. The event is held at the city's grand **medialuna,** about a kilometer north of the city center. Here, rows of wooden benches ring a half-moon-shaped dirt space, framed in the distance by towering mountains. Even when the *huasos* aren't in action, however, they impress crowds with their splendid costuming—colorfully woven ponchos (*chamantos*), wide-brimmed hats (*bonetesas huicanos*), and silvery steel spurs. *(To get to the medialuna, follow San Martín, which becomes España, and keep walking north until you hit Germán Ibarra—the yellow adobe complex is on your left across the street. Rodeo season begins after Independence Day, September 18. Call the Federación de Rodeos office in Rancagua, ☎ 221 286, for the dates of local rodeos.)*

▐ DAYTRIPS FROM RANCAGUA

EL TENIENTE COPPER MINE

Codelco arranges tours through several local travel agencies; call the Codelco offices (☎ 292 367 or 292 748; fax 292 795) for the most up-to-date list. Tours generally cost CH$7000 per person, last from 9am-3pm, and include excursions to the mine, the abandoned company town of Sewell, and the mine's smelter. See Travel Agencies p. 156 for a listing of Rancagua agencies that offer El Teniente packages.

The largest underground mine in the world, El Teniente is the flagship of Chile's mammoth copper industry, a 1500km maze of tunnels burrowed into the spine of the Andes, some 50km northwest of Rancagua. Legend has it that in the mid-18th century, a Spanish lieutenant fled across the Andes, headed for Argentina to escape charges of treason. He took refuge in a cave on the mountain, and discovered its secret treasure. The harvesting *en masse* of the mountain's copper began in 1905, and in 1968 Chile's government took over the copper industry. Today, 6300 workers are employed in El Teniente, producing some 350,000 metric tons of fine copper per year—almost a third of the country's entire output. El Teniente's miners these days no longer live in the company town of **Sewell,** near the mine; many commute from Rancagua or Machali. They have, however, retained their tight-knit, ultra-masculine culture. The old saying was that women could not enter the mine, or the mountain would get jealous, raining rocks on the miners' heads. Today, women work in the administration offices and kitchens of the mine complex, but still not in the shafts themselves.

Tourists can visit the mine and even walk through tunnels—with a guide, of course, and wearing the standard protective equipment (plastic helmet topped with flashlight, reflective jacket, long rubber boots, ventilator, safety belt, and goggles).

CHAPA VERDE SKI CENTER

The road to Chapa Verde is blocked to anyone without a permit (CH$80,000 per year), so catch a bus at the supermarket Hiper Independencia, Miguel Ramírez 665, east of the Plaza de los Héroes. ☎217 651. Buses leave M-F 9am and Sa-Su 8am-9:30am. M-F CH$4000, Sa-Su CH$4200. Ski center ☎294 255, www.chapaverde.cl. Fully-appointed cabañas alongside the slopes CH$50,000 per day. Open June-Sept. 9am-5:30pm. Lift tickets M-F CH$11,000, students CH$9500; Sa-Su CH$14,300/CH$11,500. Rentals available for skis, boots, and poles (CH$12,600) or snowboards and boots (CH$18,000).

While outclassed by other ski resorts in the Andes, Chapa Verde offers a respectable array of 22 slopes, less than an hour by bus from Rancagua. Codelco, the government-owned corporation in charge of the nearby El Teniente copper mine, originally established the ski center for its workers, but the public is now welcome. The ski center offers slopes at all difficulty levels, serviced by five lifts (three 1200m, two 300m). There are restaurants at the top, middle, and bottom of the mountain.

NEAR RANCAGUA

LAGO RAPEL

Chile's largest artificial lake, Lago Rapel is a haven for backpackers looking for a not-so-wild wilderness experience and water sport enthusiasts seeking a place to take their jetskis out for a spin. The 40km long lake emerged in its present form in 1968 with the damming of the Cachapoal and Tinguiririca Rivers. For an impressive view, head north along the Carretera de la Fruta—a good 30min. walk—to a bridge that spans the lake. If you can find a spot in the grass along the highway, you will see the lake stretching before you and the Santa Ines hills on the horizon.

Most buses run along the Carretera de la Fruta to **El Manzano,** a village on the southern shore of the lake's upper arm. If you need help, visit the El Manzano *carabineros* east of the town center, on the carretera. A list of campsites and a map of the lake are available at **Las Cabras,** the nearby municipality that has jurisdiction over the lake area (☎501 028 or 501 250). Dozens of campgrounds and *cabañas* festoon the *lago's* shores—one of the campsites closest to El Manzano is **Granja Amanda ❷,** on the southeastern edge of the lake's upper arm, alongside the *carretera* as it heads north. Amanda has 66 sites—10m by 10m spaces along the lakeshore with thatched-roof huts for picnicking under—and a separate shower and bathroom facility. (Dec.-Mar. 5-person campsites CH$25,000, each additional person CH$2500; Apr.-Nov. CH$10,000. Free use of windsurfing equipment, sailboats, and catamarans.)

TERMAS DE CAUQUENES

Squatting on a high bluff alongside the winding Río Cachapoal is the Hotel Termas de Cauquenes, a hot springs resort where Chilean patriot Bernardo O'Higgins once rested and that continues to draw weary travelers looking for some pampering. The thermal baths are housed in the hotel's *sala de baños,* a huge, high-ceilinged wooden hall decorated with stained glass and fresco paintings of international scientists who expounded on the therapeutic qualities of mineral water. There are 26 private stalls, each with a small marble tub (the originals were installed in 1856) or a modern jacuzzi, each running the same pungent waters infused with magnesium, potassium, lithium, and other natural minerals. For some, the experience may seem no more than a hot bath in smelly water, but it certainly soothes a weary back. (CH$3000 for marble baths; CH$5000 for jacuzzi. Massages CH$12,000.) In addition to the hot spring, the resort offers peaceful views of the Andes and the surrounding wilderness. A rickety wooden bridge stretched between two stone arches leads across the river's small, rumbling rapids and into a park, where *cachi* grow alongside towering trees.

Swiss chefs serve up fine meals in the hotel's pink-abode **dining hall ❹**, which also provides a view of the snow-dusted Andes in the distance. (Breakfast CH$4500; lunch CH$9950; dinner CH$11,450.) The **hotel ❺** has rooms that are nothing special, and ironically, seem to be lacking in hot water. (☎ 899 010; fax 899 009; termasdecauqueres@terra.cl. Breakfast included. CH$17,000 extra for three meals per day. Singles CH$52,650, for foreigners with IVA tax excluded US$67; doubles CH$28,570-37,250/US$37-48 per person; triples CH$29,380/US$38 per person; quads CH$26,670/US$34 per person.) The hotel also offers daytrip tours to the nearby **Reserva Nacional Río de los Cipreses,** a vast stretch of wilderness which offers scenic hikes past waterfalls, lakes, and valleys wrought by glaciers.

SAN FERNANDO ☎ 72

On March 3, 1985, an earthquake ripped through this quiet city nestled among the hills, demolishing some of its oldest buildings and crippling many others. Culturally and aesthetically speaking, San Fernando still has not fully recovered. Two national monuments—the Iglesia de San Francisco and the Capilla San Juan de Diós, both dating from the 19th century—crouch forlornly on street corners, their hulking structures in danger of collapse and closed to the public. It doesn't help the tourist industry that such a sizeable city as San Fernando lacks both a Sernatur branch and a municipal tourist office. San Fernando is, however, ringed by scenic hills and a host of resorts, including the well-preserved Hacienda Los Lingues to the northeast and Termas del Flaco thermal baths to the east, which ensure that tourists will continue passing through on their way to more appealing attractions.

TRANSPORTATION

Trains: The **train station** (☎ 711 087) is on Quechereguas. Trains go to: **Chillán** (3½hr., 5 per day 9:30am-11:55pm, CH$2500-3700); **Concepción** (10hr., 10:14 and 11:57pm, CH$3900-5000); **Rancagua** (45min.; M-F 7 per day 6am-9pm, Sa-Su 7am-9pm; CH$630); **Santiago** (2¼hr.; M-F 7 per day 6am-9pm, Sa-Su 7am-9pm; CH$650); **Temuco** (12hr., 10:14pm, CH$4600-7000).

Buses: Terminal de Buses, Manso de Velasco 1009 (☎ 713 912), at the end of the street. Information booth open 6am-10pm. **Buses Nilahue,** Oficina 15 (☎ 711 937), goes to **Pichilemu** (2hr., 23 per day 8am-9:40pm, CH$2000) and **Termas del Flaco** (4hr.; Dec.-Apr. 3, 3:30, 3:45pm; CH$4000). **Tur-Bus,** Oficina 19 and 20 (☎ 712 929), goes to **Concepción** (5hr., 6 per day 7:10am-12:30am, CH$3000) and **Temuco** (7hr., 8 per day 9:30am-12:45am, CH$3900). **Andimar** (☎ 711 817) goes to: **Pichilemu** (2½hr., 7:30am and 8:20am, CH$1500); **Rancagua** (45min., M-Sa 40 per day 5am-10pm, CH$500); **Santiago** (2hr., M-Sa 40 per day 5am-10pm, CH$1500); **Termas del Flaco** (4hr., Dec.-Mar. 3:30 and 4pm, CH$4000).

Taxis: Catch a *colectivo* on the street (they look like cabs except they're painted black). CH$200 to anywhere in the city.

⚡ 🗂 ORIENTATION AND PRACTICAL INFORMATION

San Fernando sits alongside Río Tinguiririca, 51km down the Panamericana from Rancagua. **Manso de Velasco** marks the northern boundary of the city center, ending at the city's hospital and two of its national monuments—the Casa Lircunlauta and the Capilla San Juan de Diós. **Manuel Rodríguez** runs through the heart of the city, from west to east, and is lined by shops, banks, and another national monument, the Iglesia de San Francisco. The city's **Plaza de Armas,** which includes the city hall and provincial government building, lies two blocks from the church.

Tourist Office/Tours: There's no **official tourist office** in San Fernando, but a good bet for basic information is one of the city's private travel agencies. One of the best is the tiny **Turismo Carretel,** Manuel Rodríguez 860 (☎712 895; fax 712 895; turismocarretel@terra.cl), just to the right of Banco de Chile. The gregarious **Sabina Acevedo** is a reservoir of local street wisdom, and can hook you up with transport to the Chapa Verde ski center (CH$5500) or tours of the Ruta del Vino, Termas del Flaco, and Hacienda los Lingues. Open M-F 9am-2pm and 3:30-6:30pm. For a detailed, unwieldy map of San Fernando (CH$600), head to the **Centro de Fotocopiado PSC,** Valdivia 754 (☎713 072), between Cardenal Caro and España. Open M-F 9am-8pm, Sa 10am-1pm.

Banks: Banco de Chile, Manuel Rodríguez 864 (☎712 033), at the southwest corner of O'Higgins and Manuel Rodríguez. Open 9am-2pm.

San Fernando

🏨 ACCOMMODATIONS
Hotel Diego Portales, **1**
Hotel Español, **5**
Hotel Imperio, **6**
Hotel Marcano, **7**

🍴 FOOD
Café Roma, **4**
Rigoletto, **3**
La Posada, **2**

MIDDLE CHILE

ATM: There's a 24hr. Redbanc at **Banco de Chile,** Manuel Rodríguez 864 (☎712 033).

Work Opportunity: Hotel Termas del Flaco (☎711 832), needs 70 seasonal hotel workers. See **Alternatives to Tourism,** p. 84.

Police: ☎133. **Carabineros** are at Manuel Rodríguez 625, right across from the Iglesia de San Francisco, beside the plaza.

Late-night Pharmacy: Farmacia Ahanada, Manuel Rodríguez 902 (☎729 895), across from Banco de Chile.

Hospital: Hospital San Juan de Diós, Negrete 1401 (☎209 400), at the northwestern end of Manso de Velasco, a block south of the corner of Negrete and Carelmapu.

Telephones/fax: Entel, Manuel Rodríguez 999 (☎715 941), to the right of Hotel Español. Public telephones and fax services for CH$350 per page in Chile, CH$990 per page international. Open 8:30am-9pm.

Post Office: Correos, Bernardo O'Higgins 545 (☎711 051), just south of Banco de Chile. Open M-F 9am-1pm and 2:30-5:30pm, Sa 9am-12:30pm.

◪ ACCOMMODATIONS

Hotel Marcano, Manuel Rodríguez 968 (☎714 759; fax 713 943), across from Hotel Español. Rooms vary greatly in price and quality, but tend to be clean and heated with gas-burning stoves. Breakfast included. TV. 24hr. reception. For stays on weekdays, make a reservation a day or two in advance. Singles with shared bath CH$24,000-31,300; triples with private bath CH$35,300. ❺

Hotel Español, Manuel Rodríguez 959 (☎711 098), between O'Higgins and Rancagua. The old world-style hotel has faded somewhat over the last 50 years, but nonetheless offers plump beds and tastefully decadent rooms. There's red carpeting and leafy ferns in the inner patio, and plaster sculptures of nymphs all over. Breakfast included. TV. 24hr. reception. Singles CH$16,520; doubles CH$23,600. ❹

Hotel Imperio, Manuel Rodríguez 770 (☎714 595), just east of the Iglesia de San Francisco, on the other side of the street, on 2nd fl. The space is clean and the furniture simple. Heaters are non-existent, making it a less-appealing option during the winter months. Private baths. Breakfast included. 24hr. reception. Singles CH$13,000; doubles CH$18,000. Cash only. ❸

Hotel Diego Portales, O'Higgins 701 (☎714 696), on the corner of España and O'Higgins (enter through the hotel restaurant). Clean and serviceable, if you don't mind saggy mattresses and chipped paint in the bathroom—or the absence of television and telephones. Private baths. Breakfast included. 24hr. reception and restaurant. Flexible check-out. Singles CH$7000; doubles CH$14,000. Cash only. ❷

◪ FOOD

▨ **Café Roma,** Manuel Rodríguez 815 (☎711 455), between Chillán and O'Higgins. Inside, Roma is spotless and new, with wallpaper and Diego Rivera paintings on the walls. Great sandwiches (CH$1300-1750), including the *sandwich naturista,* with cheese, hard-boiled eggs, tomatoes, and cucumbers (CH$1300). A full meal with salad or soup, an entree, a drink, dessert, and coffee CH$2500. Desserts like the *copa italia* sundae (CH$1650) or orange cheesecake (CH$700) can't be missed. Open 9am-midnight. ❷

Rigoletto, Manuel Rodríguez 751 (☎711 396), between Chachabuco and Chillán, across from Hotel Imperio. The *escalopes kaiser* (deep-fried steak wedged between two slices of ham; CH$3590), is sure to fill you up or give you instant heartburn, whichever comes first. For the more health conscious, there's pizza (CH$1400-1700) or a *plato* *vegetariano* of cooked veggies that somehow includes both cheese and ham (CH$2690). Open M-Sa 8:30am-1am, Su 8:30am-midnight. ❷

La Posada, O'Higgins 651 (☎723 398), between Hotel Diego Portales and Manuel Rodríguez. Posada has the feel of a diner, right down to the formica bar and cheap leather stools. Serves up sandwiches (CH$350-1650), including a hot cheese one for CH$1100. Beer CH$400-1200. Open 8:30am-1am. ❶

🅢 SIGHTS

The **Casa Lircunlauta,** Juan Jímenez 1595 (☎713 326), whose name in Mapuche means "beautiful entry," is a good place to start any cultural tour of San Fernando—mainly because it's the only site that actually lets visitors walk inside. The white adobe *casa patronal* was the home of wealthy landowner Juan Jímenez de Léon y Mendoza, who in 1742 donated 450 *cuadras* (blocks) of his *hacienda* to the Chilean governor for the formation of San Fernando. Today, it is a museum that includes exhibits on *huaso* life, Chile's railroads, and a grim local tale of survival and cannibalism best known through Frank Marshall's 1992 film *Alive!* (Open Tu-Su 9am-1pm and 4-7pm; CH$200, students free.)

Leaving the Casa Lircunlauta, head down Manso de Velasco and make the first right onto Negrete. On your right, you'll pass by the **Capilla San Juan de Diós**—once a pretty red-brick extension of the adjacent Hospital San Juan de Diós but now, thanks to the 1985 earthquake, an abandoned husk, its stained-glass windows punched out and trash piled on its doorstep. Seven blocks farther down on the city's broadway, Manuel Rodríguez, on the corner with Valdivia, is another earthquake-shattered church—the **Iglesia de Don Francisco,** Manuel Rodríguez 620 (☎714 488), whose neo-Romantic/neo-Gothic style of construction features a 32m high tapered minaret with a still-functioning clock.

PICHILEMU ☎72

The brainchild of the half-Scottish businessman Agustín Rous Edwards, Pichilemu emerged in the late 19th-century as a European-style luxury resort with a grand hotel, casino (Chile's first), and palm-studded park. The casino is now closed and the luxury has all but faded away, ever since classy seaside spas elsewhere in the country started out-competing Pichilemu for the high rollers' business. Today, Pichilemu draws a younger, hipper crowd—surfers hailing from the United States, Brazil, Australia, and elsewhere now pack the hotels and *cabañas* in Pichilemu and nearby Punta de Lobos (6km south) during the summers, raising rents and also quite a bit of ruckus. A little more than a decade ago, the seaside city dipped its big *puntilla* into the international surfing world, kicking off an annual championship that draws surfers and spectators from around the globe. The excellent waves aren't the only draw to Pichilemu—its beautiful vistas and *tranquilo* way of life also attract plenty of middle-class Chilean families looking to spend their vacation time on reasonably priced relaxation. Even so, the *surfistas* insist you won't get to know Pichilemu until you've taken a good headlong plunge just beyond the rocks of the Puntilla—so don't forget your wetsuit.

⌸ TRANSPORTATION

Buses: Buses stop along Pinto, near its intersection with Ortúzar; also at a bus stop on the corner of Ángel Gaete and Santa María. Separate booths on Pinto sell tickets for each line. **Nilahue,** Pinto 108 (☎842 138), goes to: **Rancagua** (2½hr.; M-Sa 30 per day 4:40am-6:40pm, Su 24 per day 5am-6:40pm; CH$2000); **San Fernando** (2hr.; M-Sa 30 per day 4:40am-6:40pm, Su 24 per day 5am-6:40pm; CH$1500); **Santa Cruz** (1¼hr.; M-Sa 30 per day 4:40am-6:40pm, Su 24 per day 5am-6:40pm; CH$1500); **Santiago** (4½hr.; M-Sa 30 per day 4:40am-6:40pm, Su 24 per day 5am-6:40pm; CH$2500). **Andimar,** Pinto 166 (☎842 756), goes to: **Curicó** (2½hr., Dec.-Mar. 10am and 10pm, CH$2500); **Rancagua** (3hr.; every 20min. Dec.-Mar. 7:20am-9pm, Apr.-Nov. 10am and 6pm; CH$2000); **San Fernando** (2hr.; 6:20am, 3:20, 4:30pm; CH$1500); **Santiago** (2½-4hr.; 6:20am, 3:20, 4:30pm, more frequent during the summer; CH$2500). **Pullman del Sur** (☎843 118), at Pinto and Ángel Gaete, goes to **San Fernando** (2½hr.; M-Sa 8 per day 5:15am-6:30pm, Su 16 per day 6:30am-6:30pm; CH$2000) and **Santiago** (3½-4½hr.; M-Sa 18 per day 5:15am-6:30pm, Su 16 per day 6:30am-6:30pm; Dec.-Feb. CH$3500, Mar.-Nov. CH$3000).

▪️🔋 ORIENTATION AND PRACTICAL INFORMATION

Once in town, surfers make a beeline for the Puntilla, or "foe," where Pichilemu pricks the rough hide of the Pacific. It is connected to the city's downtown by both **Costanera** and **Ross,** the former of which rides along the beach and the latter of which dives right into **Pinto,** the main commercial strip.

Tourist Office: Oficina de Turismo Ángel Gaete 365 (☎841 257 or 842 532; fax 841 102; infopichilemu@entelchile.net; www.pichilemu.cl.), in the Municipalidad building. Supplies maps of the city and coastal region. There is at least one English speaker among the helpful staff; ask for María Elena Arraya. Open M-F 8am-1pm and 2-5:30pm.

Bank: Banco Estado, Errázuriz 397 (☎841 091 or 841 447; fax 841521), across from Restaurante Donde Pin-Pon. Open 9am-2pm. Or try **Banco del Desarollo,** Ortúzar 472 (☎842 858), between O'Higgins and Prat. Has a **24hr.** Redbanc **ATM.** Open 9am-2pm.

Rentals: Surf Shop, Ortúzar 305 (☎841 236), is a small boutique inside the Farmacia Nacional at the intersection of Ortúzar and Pinto. Buy surf gear here, or rent a surfboard for CH$6500 per day. Open in summer 9:30am-1am, in winter 9:30am-1:30pm and 4-9:30pm. A tiny shop to the left of the **Balaustro** restaurant, Ortúzar 289A (☎842 458 or 099 359 7584; meliapavez@latinmail.com), also sells surfing and skating gear and beach wear. Discount of 7% on cash purchases for *Let's Go* readers.

▨ **Surfing School: Lobos Del Pacífico** (☎099 9773 9580 and 099 9718 0255; lobosdel-pacifico@hotmail.com), on Costanera. With the ocean on your right, walk down Costanera toward the Puntilla; once you pass Merino, you'll see a wooden shack with an "*Escuela de Surf*" sign. Learn to ride the waves, Chilean-style, from the laid back instructors at Lobos del Pacífico—they guarantee you'll be slicing up the sea with your own *cortes* (sharp turns, sans wipeout) in no time—or your money back. Private lessons CH$10,000 for 3hr.; group lessons CH$10,000 but discounted for multiple lessons. Open 9am-7pm, group classes W 4-7pm. *Let's Go* readers get a 20% discount.

Police: The *carabineros* have an office at Ortúzar 609 (☎841 034 or 841 939), at the intersection of Ortúzar and O'Higgins.

Late-Night Pharmacy: Farmacia Nacional, Ortúzar 305 (☎841 236; fax 841 236), at the intersection with Pinto. Open in summer 9:30am-1am, in winter 9:30am-1:30pm and 4-9:30pm.

Hospital: The local hospital (☎841 022) is on Jorge Errúzuriz, between Valderrama and Jaramillo.

Telephone/fax: Centro Communicaciones Punto Com, Ortúzar 349 (☎842 627). Come here for a *centro de llamados,* **Western Union** money wiring service, and fax service (international CH$500 per page, domestic CH$300 per page). Open 9am-10:30pm.

Post Office: Correos (☎842 131), on Ortúzar, near the Hotel Asthur.

ACCOMMODATIONS

Because of Pichilemu's century-old tradition as a vacation spot, there are plenty of options for lodging here—and thanks to the recent infusion of price-conscious surf nomads, the rates can be quite reasonable, too. Many decent hotels are clustered along the shore's wide strip, and enjoy (somewhat distant) views of the glistening Pacific. Another option, popular among foreigners, is renting a *cabaña*. According to locals, many surfers from abroad eschew Pichilemu altogether and head out to Punta de Lobos, 6km south on the shoreline, where they build their own *cabañas* and surf from dawn to dusk.

Hotel Bar Rex, Ortúzar 034 (☎841 003). Nestled alongside Pichilemu's shoreline, Hotel Rex makes a jaunt to the beach all but effortless. But with its plump new mattresses, perpetually hot water, and fine (if pricey) dining, you might be inclined to spend the day lazing at the hotel instead. Surfers descend on Hotel Rex from Dec.-Mar., so reservations are recommended at least 2 days in advance during the high season. Rooms have TV but no telephone. Breakfast included. Reception 8am-midnight. Singles in summer CH$9000, in winter CH$7000; doubles CH$18,000/CH$16,000. ❸

Hotel Asthur, Ortúzar 540 (☎841 072 or 841 495; fax 842 545; asthur@starmedia.com; www.lapaginaweb.de/hotelasthur), down the street from Banco del Desarollo. The main hall at this 70-year-old hotel is quite impressive, featuring a high ceiling, support beams and split staircase made from eucalyptus wood, and a log-burning *sulumandra* fashioned from ceramic bricks. The hotel's rooms radiate off this main hall, with decent beds and some ocean views. The bathrooms have wilted wallpaper and rusty piping. Small outdoor pool. Television. Breakfast included. Call 1 week in advance to reserve a room during Jan. and Feb. Doubles Jan.-Feb. CH$19,000; Mar.-Dec. CH$7000 per person. ❹

Hotel Chile España, Ortúzar 255 (☎841 270; fax 841 314), toward the ocean, under the hot-pink neon sign and various country flags. As you might guess from the framed posters hanging in the hallways—one of Waikiki beach in Hawaii and several from Pichilemu's past international surfing championships—Hotel Chile España is a top lodging choice among wandering wave-seekers. The hotel caters to local and international surfers with simple, smallish accommodations and offbeat furnishings. TV. Some English spoken. Breakfast included. Dec.-Mar. reservations should be made one week in advance. Singles with shared baths CH$7000; doubles and triples with private baths CH$9500 per person. ❷

Cabañas: Marcelo Pérez Rodríguez rents *cabañas* from his real estate agency within **Farmacia Nacional ❷,** Ortúzar 305 (☎841 236; fax 841 237). 8-person *cabañas* along Costanera CH$25,000 per day; reserve 4-5 days in advance. *Cabañas* are also available through the owner of the restaurant **Marixell ❷,** Ortúzar 392 (☎841 990). The cabins are located much more inland, at Millaco 726. Jan.-Feb. 6-person *cabañas* CH$20,000, Mar.-Dec. CH$15,000.

FOOD

Restaurant Donde Pin-Pon, Ross 96 (☎842 820), on the corner of Ross and Errázuriz, across from Banco de Chile. This is the consummate seafood restaurant—right down to the seashell necklaces hanging from the ceiling and the flies buzzing over your salsa. Try the *paila marina* (CH$2200) for a real shellfish rush—a savory, soupy blend of clams, mussels, crab, fish, cilantro, and other secret ingredients. Open 9am-midnight. ❷

Hotel Bar Rex, Ortúzar 034 (☎841 003). The napkins are crisply folded, wine bottles are displayed artistically, and an old black piano from Berlin stands in the corner—but the Victorian air is partially deceptive. As the plates hanging on the walls—earthenware engraved with smiling fishes—attest, this is also a surfers' hangout, specializing in seafood. Try the speciality, a *congrío* dish (conger eel broiled with stuffed tomatoes, cheese, and *choricillo*; CH$2900). Open 8am-midnight. ❷

Balaustro, Ortúzar 289 (☎842 458 or 099 359 7584; info@balaustro.cl). This restaurant, on the fancier side of Pichilemu's offerings, comes highly recommended by locals. It specializes in seafood entrees, including seasoned wine-marinated clams (CH$2500), Ecuadorian shrimp (CH$5500), and the much sought-after *locos* (cousin of the abalone; CH$3500). English menus and live music on some nights. Discount of 7% for *Let's Go* readers paying in cash. ❸

Marixel, Ortúzar 392 (☎841 990), on the block across from Farmacia Nacional. This combination of a restaurant, *fuente de soda*, bar, and pastry shop serves up cheap beers (CH$500) and sandwiches (CH$600-1200)—that is, if you're willing to brave the grimy counters and (equally grimy) rowdies who frequent it late at night. Open Jan.-Feb. 24hr.; Mar.-Dec. 6pm-6am. ❶

◔ SIGHTS

🖾 LA PUNTILLA. Pichilemu's seaward-pointing toe, **La Puntilla,** is a wide, downward-slanting beach ringed with squat black rocks, which has become one of the surf crowd's favorite spots for setting out into the Pacific (the other is Punta de Lobos, an even rockier spot some 6km south). Waves here swoop down upon bathers with relentless force—to place yourself between a rock and that hard fist of water you'd have to be as crazy as...well, a surfer. *(Go down the long set of stairs to the bluff's edge and you will hit Costanera; turn left and follow Costanera down for a few minutes to reach La Puntilla. Beach is public and open 24hr.)*

PARQUE MUNICIPAL AUGUSTÍN ROSS EDWARDS. Originally built and planted by Pichilemu founder Agustín Ross Edwards, the namesake **Parque Municipal,** on a bluff overlooking the sea, retains some of its original palms, as well as a host of smaller trees pruned in the shape of mushrooms. From the park's edge you can see the ocean stretching out before you. On one end of the park is the once-grand casino, the first such gambling operation in the country. The card sharks have long since gone elsewhere, and nowadays the casino is just a historical monument in a sad state of disrepair. The municipality, in fact, is seeking sponsors to fund its renovation. *(Gates heading out to Ross open 9am-6pm; stone steps to the beach open at all times. Free. Casino open middle of Dec. to end of Feb. 10am-11pm. Free, donations suggested.)*

PLAZA ARUTURO PRAT CHACÓN. The **Plaza Arturo Prat Chacón** is dedicated to one of Chile's great naval heroes, who died in a battle with much larger and more heavily armed Spanish ships during Chile's struggle for independence. The Plaza's history is commemorated with a statue of an iron anchor set on a star of white rocks. The plaza is a good place to sit back and watch Pichilemu's signature *puestas de sol* (sunsets), in which the afternoon sun lights a glistening bronze path from the shore to the horizon. *(From La Puntilla, go along Costanera toward the city center; at the intersection with Ortúzar, you will arrive at the plaza.)*

CURICÓ

☎ 75

Founded in 1743, Curicó (pop 104,000) has become a center for communications and agricultural commerce. It does not, however, have much in the way of a tourist industry, unless you count the perpetual throng of bleary-eyed business travelers passing through. Outside its peaceful Plaza de Armas, Curicó tends to appear small and ugly, a city with much commotion but little spirit. That said, the view of the city from the hill nearby is impressive, proving the point that anything, from a distance, can seem worthwhile. Even though it is not much of a tourist hot-spot, Curicó is a convenient jumping-off point to enjoy the nearby wineries and the coveted Reserva Nacional Radal Siete Tazas.

▐▀ TRANSPORTATION

Buses: Terminal de Buses, on the Plaza de Terminal, with entrance to ticket booths at the corner of Maipú and Prat. **Automotores** (☎312 000) goes to **San Fernando** (55min., every 30min. 5:25am-8:25pm, CH$800) and **Santiago** (2¾hr., every 30min. 5am-9pm, CH$2000). **Andimar** goes to **San Fernando** (40min., every hr. 5:30am-9pm, CH$800). **Talmocur** (☎311 360) goes to **Molina** (30min., every 30min., CH$250) and

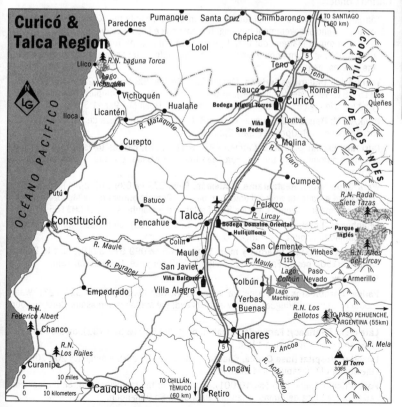

Curicó & Talca Region

Talca (1¼hr.; M-F every 15min. 6:30am-9:30pm, Sa-Su every 30min. 7:15am-9am and every 15min. 9am-9:30pm; CH$1100).

Trains: Estación Curicó, Maipú s/n (☎310 028), at the western end of Prat, where it meets Maipú. Trains go to: **Chillán** (2¾min., 5 per day 10:07am-12:36am, CH$2100-2900); **Concepción** (6½hr., 12:30am, CH$3600-4400); **Rancagua** (1¼hr.; 5 per day 5:37am-7:09pm; CH$1500-1900); **San Fernando** (40min., 5:37am-7:09pm, CH$1100-1500); **Santiago** (2½hr., 5 per day 5:37am-7:09pm, CH$1900-2600); **Talca** (45min.; 5 per day 10:07am-12:36am; CH$1100-1400); **Temuco** (10hr., 10:54pm, CH$4200-6300).

ORIENTATION AND PRACTICAL INFORMATION

Curicó is situated just beyond the arterial flow of the Panamericana, almost 200km south of Santiago. Its downtown is a 7x7 grid of city blocks, with the **Plaza de Armas** at the center square. **Av. Bernardo O'Higgins** marks the western edge of the grid, and one block farther west are the train and bus terminal, along **Maipú** and **Arturo Prat. Av. San Martín** lies on the southern edge of the grid; **Av. Camilo Henríquez** on the north; and the huge promenade of **Av. Manso de Velasco** delineates the eastern boundary. Beyond the downtown grid, the city stretches farther south along the banks of the Río Guaiquillo and east around the gently-curving spine of Cerro Carlos Condell.

Tourist Office: There's no real tourist office in Curicó despite the "Oficina Turismo" sign on the provincial government building. The post office has a section that is supposed to deal with tourist matters, but they'll likely tell you to buy the Turistel travel guide rather than supplying information themselves. For basic info, hotel or hostel staff are generally the greatest help.

Tours: Eden Undurraga Turismo, Merced 225, Oficina 203 (☎313 126 or 320 292; fax 315 181; aeben@entelchile.net), in the Edificio La Merced complex, upstairs and to your left. No regional tours offered. English spoken. Open M-F 9am-1:30pm and 3-7pm.

Bank/ATM: Banco BHIF, Yungay 655 (☎310 036), near the Plaza de Armas, has a 24-hr. Redbanc **ATM.** Open M-F 9am-2pm.

Currency Exchange: Forex, Carmen 497 (☎311 518), cashes traveler's checks and changes currency from the US, European Union, Australia, Canada, Japan, and South America.

Work Opportunity: Restaurante El Alemán, Peña 879 (☎099 262 2441). Needs 6-7 cooks and a waiter to work full-time, 9hr. per day. Contact owner Regina Muñoz Abello for more information. Workers receive 5% of sales and a monthly salary of CH$105,000.

Telephones: Entel, Av. Camilo Henríquez 414 (☎317 415), on the southwest corner of Av. Camilo Henríquez and Yungay. Open 8:30am-10pm.

Internet Access/fax: Internet y m@s, Yungay 665 (☎099 979 3719), next to Banco BHIF. CH$500 per hr. Faxes within Chile CH$350 per page. Open 10am-1am.

Emergency: ☎133

Police: Carabineros have a central office at Av. San Martín 610 (☎324 123). Walk south on Manuel Rodríguez all the way to its end; the station is across the street on your right.

Late-night Pharmacy: Farmacia Salcobrand, at Prat 500 (☎329 732), on the corner of Prat and Peña. Open 9am-11pm.

Hospital: Hospital Base Curicó, Chacabuco 121 (☎206 200, emergency 206 206), at the corner of Chacabuco and Buen Pastor.

Post office: Carmen 556 (☎310 001), to the left of the municipalidad, on the eastern edge of the Plaza de Armas. Open M-F 9am-6pm, Sa 9am-noon.

ACCOMMODATIONS

Curicó is filled with budget hotels and *residenciales*, but mid- to upper-range options are harder to find. Many of the accommodations are clustered in the street surrounding the Plaza de Armas.

Hotel Comercio, Yungay 730 (☎312 443 or 310 014; hotelcomercio@curicochile.cl; www.curicochile.cl/hotelcomercio), two blocks north of the Plaza de Armas on the right. With its no-frills decor and competent service, Comercio makes a strong case for comfort over aesthetics. Hot water and hard-to-come-by radiators in the winter. Breakfast included. Cable TV and Internet access (CH$600 per hr.). Car rental available for CH$23,000 plus CH$300,000 deposit. Free parking. Reservations suggested at least 3 days before arrival. Singles with shared baths and no heater CH$13,000, with private bath CH$19,000; doubles with private bath CH$28,000; triples with private bath CH$36,000. Cheaper prices in US$ without IVA for foreigners. AmEx/MC/V. ❹

Hotel Turismo, Carmen 727 (☎310 823; fax 314 527; htursimo@tnet.cl; www.chilehotels.com), on northwest corner of Prat and Carmen. Hotel Turismo is one of Curicó's ritzier offerings, with huge palm trees flanking a brick walkway that leads to the entrance doors, and a lush garden in the interior courtyard. The hotel's 24 rooms have spotless private bathrooms, with balconies that look onto the garden or street below. Cable television and radiator heating. Breakfast included. Reservations recommended Jan.-Mar., one week before arrival. Singles CH$25,000-34,000; doubles CH$33,000-39,000; triples CH$46,500; quads CH$56,000. AmEx/MC/V. ❺

Hotel Prat, Peña 427 (☎311 069), across from Residencial Ruhue, between Estado and Argomedo. The dining room's tacky painting of a treasure chest and skull with a pirate's galleon sailing in the distance sums up the situation at Hotel Prat—not much in the way of classy comfort, but an idiosyncratic charm nonetheless. Rooms are high-ceilinged with skylights, though gloomy at night; the singles have huge, if sagging, mattresses. Space heaters. 24hr. reception. Singles CH$4000; doubles CH$10,000. Rooms with private bath, cable TV, and breakfast included CH$7000 per person. ❷

Residencial Rahue, Peña 410 (☎312 194), across from Hotel Prat, between Estado and Argomedo. You can't miss this conspicuously cheerful green-and-yellow building on the street, but inside, the lodging is rather grim, with cramped rooms and two shared bathrooms so old that toilets don't flush toilet paper. Breakfast included. Cable TV and space heaters. 24hr. reception. Singles CH$4000 with shared bath; one roomier single with a private bath CH$13,000. ❷

FOOD

Curicó is no culinary capital, but you can easily find decent meals at bargain prices here. Even the upscale restaurants won't charge you your firstborn to dine well (unless, of course, you wish to sample the region's fabled export wines.)

Nuevo Fogón Chileno, Montt 399 (☎325 592 or 099 874 1048), between Yungay and Carmen. A down-to-earth restaurant that really knows its meat. While you admire the pictures of *huasos* spread across the walls, the cook grills your steaks (CH$2800) within view. There are plenty of sandwiches (CH$600-1450), but not much in the way of veggies. Live music on F and Sa nights. Open noon-midnight. ❷

Club de la Unión, Merced 341 (☎310 026; fax 328 843; restaurant@rubentapia.cl; www.rubentapia.cl), on the northern end of the Plaza de Armas. You too can eat with Curicó's high society at this social club/restaurant housed in a white building with elegant pillars and balconies. The salon and dining hall have high ceilings, with numerous windows to illuminate the luxurious furnishings—or your equally luxurious glass of Chilean wine (CH$3800-42,000). Most of the dishes are not terribly expensive. Grilled chicken breast CH$1800, fish dishes CH$2000-6000. Open 10am-midnight. ❸

Restaurante El Alemán, Peña 879 (☎099 262 2441), between Av. Camilo Henríquez and Montt. Except for the stout Aryan in overalls and a feathered cap on the restaurant's storefront sign, this restaurant is not so much German as it is a cholesterol-saturated excess. Try the *lomo a la plancha,* a slab of beef draped in sunny-side-up eggs and sauteed onions (CH$2500). For those with a less-than-Bavarian palate, there is a selection of pizzas, including a vegetarian one for CH$2500. Open 9am-4am. ❷

🔵 SIGHTS

When not populated by shrieking, uniformed teenagers just unleashed from school, Curicó's **Plaza de Armas** is a tranquil place to spend an afternoon. Located at the center of the city, it features several fountains amid ancient palms and pines that soar into the sky. On the plaza's eastern end is an elegantly wrought New Orleans style bandstand, decorated with flourishes of iron petals and flower stems, that must have been magnificent when it was constructed in 1905 but now looks forlorn with its green paint peeling and dead leaves ringing its crown. Near the southern edge of the park is a tree trunk carved into the likeness of **Toqui Lautaro,** the Mapuche leader who finally rid the land of conquistador Pedro de Valdivia and his scourge of terror. Created by a Mapuche sculptor, it depicts the indigenous warrior as a vision of indignant rage, with his brow arched in anger as he throws a spear.

The **Iglesia Matriz** sits in ruin on the northwestern corner of the plaza, its huge wooden doors closed ever since a 1985 earthquake devastated the building. The city is in the process of reconstructing it, but for the time being it remains desolate, its stained-glass windows punched out and graffiti all over its walls. The fluted white pillars and balconies of the **Club de la Unión,** Merced 341, on the other hand, survived the earthquake intact. You can still enter the 120-year-old building, which houses a social club and upscale restaurant (see **Food,** p. 171).

To escape the heavy urban air for a bit, take a walk down Prat heading east, and cross the grand avenue of Manso de Velasco. You'll find a path leading up to the top of a small hill, **Cerro Carlos Condell.** Enjoy the view of the city from its 99m summit or walk around the hill's western ridge, along the Avenida, to find the local swimming pool, tennis courts, and playground. Avoid this area after dark.

🔳 DAYTRIP FROM CURICÓ

LA RUTA DEL VINO

To schedule an organized wine-tasting tour, contact La Ruta del Vino Valle de Curicó, Merced 341, on the northern edge of the Plaza de Armas. ☎328 972 or 328 976. Open M-F 9am-1:30pm and 3-7:30pm. The Miguel Torres bodega is located off km 195 on the Panamericana; take the bus from Curicó to Molina and ask to be left off at the bodega. ☎564 100; fax 564 115; mgarcia@migueltorres.cl.

One of the activities that draws the most tourists to Curicó is **La Ruta del Vino Valle de Curicó.** At the Ruta del Vino **office,** you can schedule trips to 17 wineries, including the renowned **Bodega Miguel Torres** just outside the city limits. A half-day walking tour of two bodegas, with wine tasting and transportation included, costs US$23 and up.

It is also possible to drop in at the Bodega Miguel Torres on your own for a free 30min. tour of their operation. The grapes in the Torres vineyard start growing in September and ripen in March, so it's best to visit during the harvest, which lasts until the end of April.

RESERVA NACIONAL RADAL SIETE TAZAS

The jewel in central Chile's verdant crown, the Reserva Nacional Radal Siete Tazas is best known for the otherworldly beauty of its "seven teacups"—a tightly linked chain of silver-blue mountain pools punctuated by short waterfalls descending like stairs into the depths of a narrow canyon. A steep wood and stone walkway meanders around the lip of the mostly submerged teacups, From it you can view almost the entirety of the Siete Tazas' churning course: water from melting glaciers pouring out of holes in the rock face, cascading downward and then disappearing around a cavernous bend in the cliff wall. During hot summer days visitors leap into the teacups to cool off, and some intrepid kayakers even bounce their way through to the very bottom.

AT A GLANCE

AREA: 7645 hectares.

HIGHLIGHTS: The 7 teacup-shaped pools connected by waterfalls, including Velo de la Novia fall (the Bride's Veil).

GATEWAYS: Molina.

CAMPING: Sites at Camping los Robles.

FEES: CH$1000, children CH$250.

CLIMATE: Warm climate with a prolonged dry season. Coldest temperatures are in July, reaching 8.4°C; the warmest are in January at 22°C. Annual rainfall is 980mm, falling mostly between Apr. and Feb.

WILDLIFE: Forests of cypress trees; many species of singing birds, including zorzal and tenca; pumas.

TRANSPORTATION

To get to RN Radal Siete Tazas, take a bus from Curicó or Talca to **Molina**, a small town along the Panamericana highway. Then catch a bus at the terminal headed for Radal. **Buses Hernandez** (☎75 491 607) in Molina has frequent service to the park entrance during January and February (2½hr.; M-Sa 7 per day 8am-7pm, Su 5 per day 9am-6:30 pm; CH$1000). From March to December, there is only a 5:30 shuttle that takes workers in Molina back to their homes in Radal, and it doesn't go all the way to Parque Inglés (see **orientation,** below). Be forewarned—it's a 60km journey over rock-covered dirt roads from Molina to Parque Inglés, and you will have to cross many narrow wooden bridges that seem less than sturdy for motor vehicles.

Rather than braving the park in a rental car during the off-season, a good option is to call **guide** Juan Anival Ganga, (☎099 692 3077), a Molina taxi driver who grew up in the hills near Radal. For CH$20,000-30,000 Juanito will take you around to the major waterfalls and even give you a walking tour of the scenic trail, pointing out various kinds of flora and the occasional puma footprint.

ORIENTATION AND PRACTICAL INFORMATION

The reserve itself is open year-round, but during the winter months snowfall often blocks the dirt roads leading up to it. At its entrance you must stop at a control post overseen by *carabineros* wanting to see your **identification** (i.e. passport). For safety reasons, they will ask how long you intend to stay in the reserve.

About 4km past the Siete Tazas vista (see **Sights,** below) is **Parque Inglés,** a tranquil camping area nestled between the snow-dusted peaks of the Andes. Here you'll find an information center run by **Conaf,** which occasionally arranges free educational talks and guided walks for visitors. (Open daily Jan.-Feb. 9am-11pm; Mar.-Dec. 9am-1pm and 2-6pm.) For information about the reserve, call the Conaf office in **Talca,** at 3 Sur 564, which oversees all of the region's state-owned forest. Groups can arrange free guided tours of the reserve. (☎228 029; ccarreno@conaf.cl; www.conaf.cl. Open M-F 8:30-5:30 pm.)

MIDDLE CHILE

FROM THE ROAD

CHILEAN MYTH #1: IT'S ALWAYS WARMER INDOORS

A word to the wise budget traveler: southern Chile can be a cold place to spend the summer (that is, the summer for those in the northern half of the planet—dead of winter for Chileans). This is an obvious point in the parts of southern Chile that lie near the icy cap of the Antarctic, but it also is true in the central and lakes region, more often associated with verdant fields and sunny skies. The temperatures here are not particularly frigid—in the coldest months, May and June, they rise up to 16°C and drop a few degrees below the freezing point. The problem is that the great outdoors have a knack of finding their way inside and under your bedsheets. Hardly any buildings outside of Santiago have central heating, much less carpeted floors, and certainly none of the low-budget hotels or hostels do. Sometimes you'll find *salamandras*, stand-alone brick fireplaces whose smoke billows through a long, copper pipe, in a hotel lobby or dining hall—but, unfortunately, never next to your bed. So, for the most part, you may find yourself tiptoeing over icy wooden floors, huddling in front of space heaters, and praying for the shower water to turn warm (a truly miraculous event in many of southern Chile's hotels). Fortunately, on clear days the shining sun helps keep temperatures rather comfortable until they plunge again after sunset.

A word about space heaters: these handy devices are ubiquitous in the region's hotels (or they should be: don't risk staying somewhere without

🏨 🍴 ACCOMMODATIONS AND FOOD

There are two kinds of **camping** available at the **Camping Los Robles ❶** site—choose from sites with showers, hot water, and lighting (CH$8000 per site, up to 6 people) or more basic backwoods living with bathrooms but perpetually cold showers (CH$1000 per person). The price of camping gets you into the Siete Tazas Circuit.

For those who don't particularly enjoy the "rustic" in rustic living, there is also a privately run inn, **Hostería La Flor de Canela ❹**, at the very end of Parque Inglés. The *hostería* burned down in 2001, but now brand new rooms, accompanied by gleaming toilets and sinks, are ready for reluctant campers. (☎ 491 613. English-speaking staff in summertime. 24hr. reception. Reservations recommended 10-15 days before arrival in Jan. and Feb. Singles with shared bath CH$15,000, with private bath CH$20,0000; doubles with private bath CH$25,000. US dollars accepted.) The *hostería* also has a minimarket that sells toiletries, food, drinks, and other necessities. The on-site **restaurant ❶** is housed at one end of the *hostería* in a small wooden hall with sliding-glass doors and plastic lawn chairs. The selection includes pizzas (CH$1500-3000), sandwiches (CH$800-1800), and a surprising assortment of wines, from an individual-sized portion of Leon de Tarapaca (CH$1800) to a bottle of Miguel Torres (CH$8000). (Open 7am-11pm.)

👁 SIGHTS

SIETE TAZAS CIRCUIT. The **Siete Tazas vista** is the first stop on a 1000m circuit (a 30-45min. walk) through an oak- and araucania-laden patch of forest in the heart of the reserve. The path also leads by the **Salto de Leona**, a waterfall that jets from a marbled cliff wall. Sometimes park rangers give free tours of the Siete Tazas circuit if they can spare the personnel. (*Circuit open Jan.-Feb. 9am-11pm; Mar.-Dec. 9am-1pm and 2-6pm. CH$1000.*)

VELO DE LA NOVIA. As for waterfalls, more are spread throughout the 7645 hectares of the reserve, including the majestic **Velo de la Novia** (Bride's Veil), a 50m tower of foam and mist perched against a sheer cliff edge. The falling water untangles into a fine mist much like bridal lace, shrouding the receiving pool. (*The fall is located a short distance beyond the carabinero post at the entrance of the reserve, 7km before the Siete Tazas circuit. Free.*)

TALCA ☎71

Talca is the Mapuche word for "thunder"—and the name aptly describes the bustling chaos of the streets surrounding the city's bus terminal, which on a typical afternoon are jam-packed with buses, taxis, and *colectivos*. Thunder might also describe the startling stroke of good fortune that landed upon the city's scrappy soccer team, the Talca Rangers, who fought their way into the finals of the national championship against heavily favored Universidad Católica in 2001. But beyond its newfound glory, Talca has little excitement going on within its city limits. It is the rather soporific capital city of the even sleepier Region VII of Maule, with a few scattered museums and historic monuments and an uncommonly non-descript (for a city of 200,000) Plaza de Armas. Talca does provide easy access to the region's more interesting points of interest: The Reserva Nacional Radal Siete Tazas, the Villa Cultural Huilquilemu, and some of the country's finest wineries. If you're lucky, you might also find some vendors in the markets who sell delicate works of art woven from *crin*—a material made from horse hair boiled and tinted with dyes and then sewn into dolls, hats, or flowers.

▐ TRANSPORTATION

Buses: Terminal Rodoviario, 12 Oriente 900 (☎243 270), at the intersection of 2 Sur and 12 Oriente. **Pullman del Sur** (☎243 431) goes to: **Constitución** (2hr., every hr. 10:15am-11:30pm, CH$1300); **Curicó** (1hr., every 15min. 5:30am-8:45pm, CH$800); **Santiago** (3½hr., every 15min. 5:30am-8:45pm, CH$3000). **Tur-Bus** (☎245 029) goes to **Santiago** (3½hr., every hr. 7am-8:30pm, CH$2800). **Talmocur** (☎243 467 and 262 038) goes to **Curicó** (1¼hr., every 15min. 6:30am-9:30pm, CH$1100) and **Molina** (1¼hr., every 30min. 6:30am-9:40pm, CH$900). **Tur-Bus** goes to **Chillán** (2hr., every hr. 8am-11:40pm, CH$2000). **Agmital** (☎241 353) goes to **San Clemente** (30min.; every 5min. M-Sa 6am-10pm, Su 7am-10pm; CH$350).

Trains: Estación Talca, 11 Oriente 1000 (☎226 254), at the intersection of 11 Oriente and 2 Sur. Trains go to: **Chillán** (2hr., 5 per day 10:53am-1:25am, CH$1500-2100); **Concepción** (5½hr., 1:25am, CH$2600-3200); **Constitución** (2½hr.; M-F 7:30am and 4:10pm, Sa 7:30am, Su 7:30am and 4:15pm; CH$1250); **Curicó** (1hr., 5 per day 9:35am-5:48am, CH$1100-1400); **Rancagua** (2-3hr., 5 per day 9:35am-5:48am, CH$1800-2500); **Santiago** (3-4hr., 5 per day 9:35am-5:48am, CH$2100-3500); **Temuco** (9hr., 11:43pm, CH$3400-5000).

them, or by daybreak you'll be a popsicle). They come in two varieties, electric and gas. Generally speaking, electric ones are weak, emitting just enough heat to thaw the tips of your fingers and toes. Gas heaters tend to produce an impressive amount of heat, although it is limited to a small radius surrounding the machine. Also, you'll probably drive yourself nuts trying to light your feeble Chilean matches without singeing any vital parts of your face.

Which brings us to the matter of safety (if such a word can apply when discussing a tank of flammable gas): make sure to turn off the space heater whenever you leave the room or go to bed. And keep any ignitable objects away from its scalding-hot metal grill. One unfortunate Let's Go Researcher-Writer (who will remain nameless) nonchalantly tossed his jacket on the edge of his hotel room bed, next to the blazing *estufa;* a few minutes later the acrid smell of charred cotton assailed his nostrils. (Luckily, he was able to extinguish the burning garment in his bathroom sink without setting off any of the room's non-existent smoke alarms.)

Take it from this chagrined traveler: be careful—only YOU can prevent *estufa* fires.

—*Victor Chen*

Taxis: Taxis (black cars with yellow-painted tops) cost CH$400, plus CH$80 for every 200km or 60sec. You can find them ready to pounce on tourists outside the bus terminal and train station, or on the perimeter of the Plaza de Armas. Call **Taxi Plaza de Armas** (☎231 231), on the corner of 1 Sur and 1 Oriente, any time of day for an out-of-the-way pickup. A trip from the bus terminal to the Plaza de Armas costs CH$1500.

Colectivos: *Colectivos* (all black cars) cost CH$250 for anywhere in the city, though you might have to share the ride with other passengers. Generally, you can catch colectivos headed east on 1 Norte to get to the bus terminal or train station (look for ones that say "Terminal" on top of their roofs). *Colectivos* headed west on 1 Sur and along 12 Oriente at the bus terminal say "centro" or "plaza."

Car Rental: Rentacar Rosselut, Av. San Miguel 2710 (☎247 979 or 800 021 298; rentacar@rosselot.cl; www.rosselot.cl), along Panamericana highway. Rentals start from CH$16,900 per day including basic insurance. Must be older than 22 and have a passport/identity card and credit card (AmEx/MC/V).

ORIENTATION AND PRACTICAL INFORMATION

In a rare decision for a Chilean city, the urban planners of Talca designed the city with a numbered grid—a godsend to any clueless tourist who happens to roll into town for a night. It's this simple: the grid starts at the **Plaza de Armas** in the western half of town, and the four streets bordering the plaza are labeled 1 Sur (south), 1 Norte (north), 1 Oriente (east), and 1 Poniente (west), respectively. Numbers increase with each block farther away from the Plaza.

The **train** and the **bus terminal** sit alongside 12 Oriente, which itself runs parallel to a huge concrete overpass as well as railroad tracks that head north to Santiago (250km) and south to Chillán (157km). The city's two main thoroughfares, **1 Sur** and **1 Norte,** both pass through the concrete overpass—1 Sur heads west to the Plaza de Armas, 10 blocks downtown, while 1 Norte runs in the opposite direction back toward the eastern side of the tracks, near the hospital and bus terminal.

Tourist Office: Sernatur, 1 Poniente 1281 (☎233 699; fax 226 940; sernatur_talca@entelchile.net), just north of the Plaza de Armas, in a blue and white building. Offers maps and a multitude of brochures about the Maule region. Open Jan.-Feb. M-F 8:30am-6:30pm; Mar.-Dec. M-F 8:30am-5:30pm.

Currency Exchange: Forex, 2 Oriente 1133 (☎210 838), a block east of the Plaza de Armas. Open M-F 9am-2pm and 3:30-6:30pm, Sa 10:30am-1:30pm.

Banks: Banco de Chile, 1 Sur 998 (☎206 215), between 2 Oriente and 3 Oriente, a block east of the Mercado Central. Open M-F 9am-2pm. Also **Banco del Desarollo,** 1 Norte 901 (☎223 086), down the street from the Museo O'Higginiano. Open M-F 9am-2pm. Both branches have 24hr. Redbanc **ATMs.**

Police: The **carabineros** have their central office at Av. Bernard O'Higgins 687 (☎226 246 and 226 915), on the corner with 1 Poniente.

Late-night Pharmacy: Salcobrand, 1 Sur 1188 (☎229 032), across from the Mercado Central. Open M-Sa 9am-10pm. You'll find a host of other pharmacies at the intersection of 5 Oriente and 1 Sur, as well.

Hospital: Hospital Regional, 1 Norte 1990 (☎209 100), on the eastern side of the railroad tracks, along 12 Oriente.

Telephones/fax: Entel, 1 Sur 908 (☎230 728), on the same block as Banco de Chile. Open M-F 8:30am-9pm, Su 9am-2pm and 4-8pm. International faxes CH$990 per page, within Chile CH$350 per page. Also try **Telefónica CTC,** 1 Sur 1156 (☎229 862), across from Mercado central. Open M-F 9am-10pm, Sa 10am-3pm.

Internet Access: Cibercafé Punto Com, 2 Sur 1014 (☎218 205), a block west of the firehouse, inside the courtyard and to your left. CH$400 per hr. Open M-F 9am-midnight, Sa 10:30am-midnight, Su 3pm-midnight.

Post Office: The city's **Correos** is located at 1 Oriente 1150 (☎227 122), on the eastern edge of the Plaza de Armas. Open M-F 9am-1pm and 3-6pm, Sa 9am-1pm.

ACCOMMODATIONS

Most of Talca's hotels can be found along the length of **1 Sur.** Unfortunately, there aren't many options near the bus and train terminals, which means that travelers have to shell out money for cab fare downtown. Incidentally, it's dark and dangerous at night around the bus and train terminals, so take care and don't walk alone.

Hostal del Puente, 1 Sur 407 (☎/fax 220 930; hostaldelpuente@terra.cl), at the very western end of 1 Sur. Set alongside a murmuring stream with a tiny footbridge, Hostal del Puente offers tidy quietude just a few blocks from the Plaza de Armas. One half of the couple that runs the hotel speaks fluent English, and both are glad to provide tourist brochures and other useful information. Breakfast CH$500-1500. Interior parking, cable TV, space heaters. 24hr. reception. Singles with private bath CH$11,800; without IVA tax for foreigners CH$10,000; doubles CH$18,880/CH$16,000; triples CH$21,240/CH$18,000. Cash only; Euros and US dollars are welcome. ❹

Hotel Terranova, 1 Sur 1026 (☎/fax 29 60239 618; hotelterranova@entelchile.net). Formerly known as the **Inca del Oro,** this hotel changed ownership and now caters mostly to businesspeople passing through town. You can stay in its drab but surprisingly comfy rooms for much less than you'd pay for similar accommodation in a larger city. Cable TV, central heating (radiators), and well-scrubbed private bathrooms. Breakfast included. Singles CH$23,000-26,500, without IVA for foreigners CH$19,492-22,458; doubles CH$31,500/CH$26,695; triples CH$34,500/CH$29,237). AmEx/MC/V. ❹

Hostal Victoria, 1 Sur 1737 (☎/fax 212 074), between 10 Oriente and 11 Oriente. With only 5 rooms and 2 shared (and dark) bathrooms, this family-run hostel offers tight but adequate lodging within a short walk of the train station. The beds aren't the firmest you'll find, and the furniture consists mainly of plastic lawn chairs, but it's hard to beat the price. Cable TV and space heaters. 24hr. reception. Singles CH$11,000; doubles CH$16,000; triples CH$21,000; quads CH$25,000; quints CH$30,000. IVA tax deducted for quads and quints. ❸

Hotel Terrabella, 1 Sur 641 (☎/fax 226 555; terrabella@hotel.tie.cl), between 2 Poniente and 1 Poniente. This upscale hotel caters to an older crowd—as evidenced by the stereo system that pipes mellow mood music into the rooms, featuring an assortment of your favorite English and Spanish crooners (sorry, there's only one channel). Radiators in every room and spotless bathrooms with gleaming tiles. Cable TV, personal safes, small outdoor pool, and free parking inside the hotel. Breakfast included. 24hr. reception. Reservations should be made 1 week in advance. Singles CH$32,580-38,000; doubles CH$42,650-44,780; triples CH$49,990; matrimonial suite CH$55,100. AmEx/MC/V. ❺

FOOD

Cafeterías and *fuentes de soda* dominate the storefronts of 1 Sur, and for the most part you won't be disappointed with the large portions for low prices. Fine dining is also possible in Talca, though the finery has its limits in a small city such as this, and you might pay more than the food deserves. For especially cheap eats, head to the Mercado Central, on 1 Sur between 4 Oriente and 5 Oriente. There you'll find a medley of meat and produce markets, as wells as numerous hole-in-the-wall eateries.

MIDDLE CHILE

MIDDLE CHILE

🞧 **Restaurant Chilote,** 1 Sur 706 (☎215 267), on the southwestern end of the Plaza de Armas. This is one of the classier seafood restaurants in town, as you can tell from the attentive service, the selection of fine wines, and the napkins folded into the shape of seashells. When you try the insanely flavorful house specialty, you'll know why they call them *"locos"* (shellfish in a salsa verde; CH$6000). Wines range from the house table wine (flask, CH$800) to fine bottles of Miguel Torres' creations (CH$11,000). Open M-F 10am-midnight, Su 10am-4pm. Cash only. ❸

Casino Cuerpo de Bomberos, 2 Sur 1160 (☎212 903), inside of the firehouse. This casino is a canteen for firefighters, but lots of young locals hang out here for its laid-back ambience. You can sit in its plastic lawn chairs and fill up on Chilean staples like *pollo asado* (with a side dish, CH$1500) and *lomo a lo pobre* (CH$2500). Beer CH$500-$700. Live music at lunchtime and on F nights. Open M-Sa 10am-midnight, Su 10am-6pm. ❷

Fuente de Soda Germana, 3 Oriente 1105 (☎221 689), two blocks east of the Plaza de Armas. This small eatery proves that Chileans have a hearty appetite for sandwiches. Order a *hamburguesa italiana* (CH$2600) and you'll get a heaping portion of ground beef, slathered with mayo, tomatoes, and guacamole, wedged between two plate-sized pieces of bread. The *cocodrilo* is even bigger, with beef, tomato, guacamole, green beans, ham, melted cheese, and mayo (CH$3200). Wash it all down with a liter of beer (CH$1200). Open 9am-1am. ❷

Bavaria, 1 Sur 1330 (☎227 088; www.bavaria.cl). This local franchise of the popular Chilean restaurant chain has the same tacky decor and American bubble-gum-pop music you've grown to love. Bavaria offers plenty of choices in sandwiches (CH$1350-2550), salads (CH$950-1850), and potatoes—ask for yours french-fried, mashed, sautéed, boiled, or *duquesa* (CH$600-1200). On weekdays, there is a fixed-menu lunch special including salad, entree, and dessert (offered 12:30-3pm; CH$3000). Open M-Sa 9am-11pm, Su noon-10pm. AmEx/MC/V. ❷

🕑 SIGHTS

PLAZA DE ARMAS. The city's rather lackluster Plaza de Armas is dedicated to Colonel Carlos Spano, the "hero of Talca," who died in combat in 1814 with the Chilean flag in his hands. Nowadays, the only action you're likely find here is the noisy enthusiasm of the gaggles of children who pedal through the park in steel-frame race cars. A bandstand topped with iron spikes sits on the plaza's eastern edge, while graffitied white-stone statues—the spoils of war in Peru two centuries ago—line the tree-shaded walkways. In the northwest corner of the Plaza de Armas, a stone statue of one of Talca's past bishops stares toward his old cathedral, the **Catedral de Talca.** The impressive red-brick structure, built in 1954, features a long, dagger-like belltower. *(Cathedral at 1 Norte 650. ☎231 412. Open M-Sa 8:30am-1:30pm and 3:30-9:30pm, Su for mass 10:30am-1pm and 6-8pm. Free.)*

MUSEO BOMBERIL BENITO RIQUELME. Talca's cultural offerings are rather slim, but for those who love a museum, the Museo Bomberil Benito Riquelme is something a bit different. A single room within the city's fully functioning firehouse, this "museum" gives visitors a taste of the history of Talca's bravest. Three antique fire engines, complete with carriage wheels and red-painted water buckets, are crammed together in the room's center. On the walls you'll find ancient fire extinguishers, faded photos, and firefighter-inspired artwork. Just show up and ask the firefighters on duty to unlock the museum room. *(2 Sur 1160, between 4 Oriente and 5 Oriente. ☎231 599 or 232 222. Open 8am-midnight. Free.)*

MERCADO CENTRAL. The city's hulking Mercado Central once had a resplendent fountain at its center. Now there's just a circle of mossy, crumbling, worn stones in the fountain's place. Business, however, goes on as usual—you'll find fruit, meat, and fish for sale alongside stands hawking bags, wallets, and other handicrafts. *(On 1 Sur between 4 Oriente and 5 Oriente. Head north one block from the Museo Bomberil. Open M-F 8:30am-5:30pm, Sa-Su 8:30am-2pm.)*

MUSEO O'HIGGINIANO. The Museo O'Higginiano y de Bellas Artes de Talca is housed in a colonial-style house two centuries old. There are a number of paintings by Chilean and foreign artists here, dating back to the 19th century. A portrait of **Bernardo O'Higgins** hangs in one room, depicting the independence hero as rather plump and dignified in his full military regalia. There are other paintings of various genres, including *Caupolicán Prisionero*, a striking oil painting of an Indian *cacique* about to be executed by Spanish soldiers. *(1 Norte 875, toward the Plaza de Armas. ☎ 227 330. Open Tu-F 10am-6pm, Sa-Su 10am-2pm. Voluntary donation.)*

🔲 DAYTRIPS FROM TALCA

🔲 VILLA CULTURAL HUILQUILEMU

Huilquilemu is 10km east of Talca. Board a micro to San Clemente and ask to be dropped off at the villa. ☎/fax 242 474. Open Jan.-Feb. Tu-F 9am-6pm, Sa-Su noon-6pm; Mar.-Dec. Tu-F 9am-1pm and 3-6:30pm, Sa-Su noon-6pm. CH$500, children and students CH$200.

In Mapuche, the name Huilquilemu means "forest of the *zorzal* bird," but this former *casa patronal* has known little sylvan tranquility over the last few decades. Constructed in 1850 as the home of one of Chile's most influential dynasties, the Donoso family, it was once the base of operations for their huge agriculture enterprise. However, in 1966, when the country was in communist-inspired political upheaval, the **campesinos** seized the house and its surrounding lands and divvied it up among themselves. Finally, in 1974, the **Universidad Católica del Maule** purchased the property and began restoring the old estate.

The villa now has a new life as a **museum** showcasing the university's collection of religious art. Within a grand hall supported by oak pillars you can find a wide array of oil paintings and sculptures of devotional inspiration, including a huge wooden carving of Christ crucified. Elsewhere in the hall is a cracked marble basin that was used to re-baptize Bernardo O'Higgins in 1783.

Other rooms exhibit religious and secular **handicrafts** from all over South America, including vividly painted dragon masks from Bolivia, Peruvian cloth dolls depicting the three kings, and flowers made out of dyed horse hair from the Maule region. You can watch artisans at work on clay, wool, and wicker crafts in the workshop in the *villa* and purchase their works (CH$200-20,000).

The **estate** itself features a majestic brick walkway shaded with a thick covering of *flor de la pluma*, and a number of peaceful tree-lined courtyards hemmed in by the oak pillars and white adobe walls. Walk along the path marked out by pruned shrubs and you'll come across towering sequoias and pines alongside more delicate specimens of flora, such as vibrantly colored camelias.

If you want to dine inside the adobe walls of a real *casa patronal*, try the **Mesón de Rugendas ❷**, an upscale restaurant within the *villa* complex. Entrees include crunchy, fried *congrio* (conger eel) with *papitas* and a salad (CH$3000) and *chupe de locos* (shellfish baked in a clay pot; CH$3500). Try the asparagus and ham pancakes (CH$1500) for something out of the ordinary. (☎245 355 or 245 350. Open for lunch 12:30-3pm, for dinner F-Sa 8pm-midnight.) Also in the *villa* you'll find the office of the **Ruta del Vino Valle del Maule** (see below).

LA RUTA DEL VINO

To plan a wine-tasting tour, contact Ruta del Vino del Valle del Maule, at their Huilquilemu office. ☎ 246 460; wineroute@entelchile.net; www.chilewineroute.com. Open M-F 9am-6pm, Sa-Su noon-6pm. To get to Domaine Oriental Winery on your own from Talca, take the road to San Clemente for 2.4 km until you reach the only intersection, which is just past the Pro Terra building on your right. Turn right onto the dirt road and follow it 3.5km until you see grape fields and the red-adobe hacienda. ☎ 242 506; fax 242 091; courrier@casadonoso.cl; www.domaineoriental.cl. Open W-Su 8am-6:30pm.

Renowned as Latin America's finest wine producer, Chile ships the vast majority of its aged stock overseas. Strangely, you can't find the better brands of *vino* in Chile's own supermarkets, as many Chileans favor beer and various kinds of sugar water to wine. Other than fancy hotels and restaurants, the best place to go to get your hands on the stuff is the bodegas themselves, which dot the countryside just south of Santiago. In recent years, organizations have sprung up to cater to foreign tourists who want to visit the region's wineries, sample their selection, and (hopefully) pack up some bottles to take home.

Near Talca, the **Ruta del Vino del Valle del Maule,** which offers tour packages at 10 wineries in the Maule Valley, has its office in the Villa Cultural Huilquilemu (see p. 179 for directions to the *villa*). Although you can sample the region's wines at the office bar for CH$300-500, actually going to the wineries is much more fun. Tour packages start at US$22 per person for a half-day guided tour of two wineries, with wine tasting and transportation included. Two-person minimum for tour. Make reservations 48hr. in advance.

Of course, you don't have to shell out money for a decadent tourist package to sample the country's fine wines. Many of the **bodegas** allow you to stop by, even without notice, for a brief tour, a wine tasting, and the obligatory walk past the shelves of bottles for sale. Near Talca, a grand red-adobe hacienda once owned by the powerful Donoso family now houses the **Domaine Oriental Winery,** specializing in Cabernet Sauvignon. The free 30min. tour will take you past huge steel wine vats and through many hectares of leafy grape fields.

CHILLÁN   ☎ 42

Known as *"la ciudad de la cuatro fundaciones"*—the city of the four foundings—Chillán first appeared in 1580 as a fort and religious sanctuary planted at the confluence of two rivers, the Río Hatu and the Río Ñuble. Over the next few centuries the town skipped around the river banks in various attempts to escape floods and earthquakes. Finally, in 1835, in what seemed like the end to its troubled history, the town settled at its present location. A century later, however, it would be rocked by its worst natural disaster ever—the earthquake of 1939 which decimated large swaths of the city and killed countless people. Even today, modern Chillán still bears the mark of that catastrophe in its striking modern facade. Previously an aesthetically uninspired cityscape, the razing of the city in 1939 led to the construction of Chillán's prominent cathedral. This imposing construction is fashioned out of a series of huge concrete arches and features a mammoth concrete cross that commemorates those who died in the disaster. Culturally speaking, Chillán is renowned as the birthplace of many of the country's greatest leaders and artists—the liberator Bernardo O'Higgins, the naval hero Sargento Aldea, and the pianist Claudio Arrau all hail from here. Although the city itself is rather small, most travelers will find themselves stopping here on account of its use as a central hub for bus and train lines and because of its proximity to the luxurious Termas de Chillán, considered among the country's finest mountain resorts.

Concepción, Chillán, & Los Angeles Area

TRANSPORTATION

Trains: Estación Chillán (☎222 424), on Brasil, at the western end of Libertad. Trains to: **Concepción** (3½hr., 3:20am, CH$1500-1700); **Santiago** (5hr., overnight 6hr.; 2:35, 3:58, 7:45am, 1:45, 4:30pm; CH$3200-5000); **Talca** (2hr., 5 per day 1:45am-4:30pm, CH$1500-2100); **Temuco** (6½hr., 1:42am, CH$2300-3400).

Buses: Tur-Bus (☎212 502) and **Linea Azul** (☎211 192) run similar routes at comparable rates from the following three bus terminals:

Terminal de Buses Interregionales, Constitución 1 (☎221 014), at the western edge of downtown, south of the train station and across Brasil. Buses to: **Concepción** (1½hr., 16 per day 11am-10:45pm, CH$1000); **Santiago** (5hr., 21 per day 7am-11:49pm, CH$3400); **Talca** (2hr., 14 per day 7am-6:30pm, CH$2000).

Terminal de Buses Paseo La Merced, Maipón 890 (☎223 606), at the corner of Sargento Aldea and Maipón, services rural locations around Chillán. Linea Azul runs buses to the **Termas de Chillán** from Oct. to Mar. (the rest of the year, buses only go as far as **Las Troncas,** 9km from the ski center). Catch the bus from the Keymarket supermarket across the street from the bus terminal (1hr.; 8:15am, 4:25, 8:15pm; CH$1500).

Terminal de Buses de Maria Teresa, Panamericana Norte 010 (☎212 149 or 231 119), just north on O'Higgins. Long distance buses depart from here—call for info, as schedules vary.

Taxis/Colectivos: *Colectivos* cost CH$250 throughout the city center. Taxis from the train station/Terminal De Buses Interregionales to the Plaza de Armas run CH$500-1000. **Radiotaxi Libertador,** Claudio Arrau 809 (☎212 020), and **Radiotaxi Familiamigo,** La Espiga 745, Jardines de Ñuble (☎277 070 or 217 070), offer call-based service.

■* 🛈 ORIENTATION AND PRACTICAL INFORMATION

The city is centered around its peaceful **Plaza Bernardo O'Higgins** and adjacent cathedral, flanked by the two main thoroughfares, **Libertad** and **Constitución.** The train station is on the western end of Libertad and the Terminal de Buses Interregionales is at the western end of Constitución. The downtown forms a 12 x 12 grid, with the plaza at its center; **Av. Argentina** forms the eastern boundary and **Av. Collín** is to the south.

Tourist Office: Sernatur, 18 de Septiembre 455 (☎223 272; infochillan@sernatur.cl), just north of the central plaza. Open M-F 8:30am-6pm. The Municipalidad has a friendly and helpful **tourist office** at its Teatro Municipal building, 18 de Septiembre 590 (☎200 334; dicturchillan@yahoo.es). Brochures and small maps of the city available. English spoken. Open M-F 9am-1pm and 3-7pm, Sa 9am-1pm.

Currency Exchange: Money Exchange, Constitución 608 (☎238 638), at the southeastern end of the Plaza Bernardo O'Higgins. Cashes traveler's checks and exchanges US, Canadian, Australian, British currencies and the Euro. Some English spoken. Open Dec.-Feb. M-F 10am-2pm and 4-7pm, Sa 11am-2pm; off-season M-F 10am-2pm and 4-6pm, Sa 11am-2pm.

Banks/ATM: Banco de Chile, Constitución 580 (☎219 434), at southern edge of Plaza Bernardo O'Higgins. Open M-F 9am-2pm. **24hr. ATM.**

Work Opportunity: Hostal Canada, Libertad 269 (☎234 515), hires one English-speaking tour guide to take hostel guests on 4hr. excursions around the Chillán area. For details, see **Alternatives to Tourism** (p. 83).

Luggage Storage: At the Terminal de Buses Interregionales, Constitución 1 (☎221 014). 24hr. storage CH$500 for a backpack, CH$600 for a hiking pack or suitcase. Open 24hr.

Emergency: ☎133

Police: Carabineros, 27 de Abril (☎211 118). Other offices are situated in the block bounded by Vegas de Saldra and Bulnes, between Claudio Arrau and Carrerra.

Late-Night Pharmacy: Farmacias Ahumada, 5 de Abril 702 (☎216 984), on the corner of Robles and 5 de Abril, near the Mercado Central. Open 8am-midnight. **Redbanc ATM** available.

Hospital: Hospital Herminda Martín, Francisco Ramírez (☎203 000, emergency 208 221, ambulance 212 205), at the intersection of Libertad and Argentina.

Telephones/Fax: Telefónica CTC, Arauco 625 (☎215 443), a block south of the Plaza Bernardo O'Higgins. International faxes CH$1500 per page, local faxes CH$330. Open M-Sa 9am-9pm, Su 10am-9pm.

Internet Access: Nethouse Cibercafé, Constitución 637 (☎246 712), across from Hotel Las Terrazas. CH$500 per hr. Open M-F 10am-11pm, Sa 11am-11pm, Su 4-11pm.

Post Office: Correos, Libertad 501 (☎222 388), at the northern edge of Plaza Bernardo O'Higgins. Open M-F 9am-1pm and 3-6pm, Su 9am-1pm.

🏠 ACCOMMODATIONS

You can't throw a stone from Chillán's train station without hitting a brightly lit "hotel" sign. "Chillán is the place where Chilean travelers stop and spend the night en route to other destinations," says one local hostel owner. Consequently, you'll

find a multitude of accommodations that boast quality far surpassing that of the string of other would-be truck stops north of the Panamericana.

Hostal Canada, Libertad 269 (☎234 515), through a small white doorway on the second floor. Other than the bold red maple leaf on the sign, there's actually nothing Canadian about this small hostel—the owner hasn't been there and there's no Molson in the fridge. Nevertheless, Mariela Albornox proves to be a charming host, and the slightly crowded rooms are a great deal. The shared bathrooms are clean, rooms have cable TV and gas-burning space heaters, and private parking and laundry service are available. Between Dec. and Mar., guides will take you and all the stout-legged mounties you can find on 4hr. bicycle excursions in the Chillán area (CH$3000). Bike rentals CH$1500. Breakfast CH$1000. Check-out noon. Reservations recommended in the summer. Singles, doubles, triples CH$4000 per person; IVA tax deducted for foreigners. Cash only, US dollars accepted. ❷

Hotel Las Terrazas, Constitución 644, 5th floor (☎227 000; fax 227 001; www.lasterrazas.cl; lasterrazashotel@entelchile.net), one block east of the Plaza Bernardo O'Higgins. From its 5th-story perch near the central plaza, Las Terrazas offers remarkable far-reaching vistas of the surrounding city, which in Chillán's case amount to rusty rooftops, trash-strewn lots, and tacky signs. Still, the hotel provides decadent comfort for a decent price: sunny rooms with polished wooden furniture have cable TV, central heating, and well-stocked minibars. Breakfast included. Check-out 1pm. Reservations recommended one week in advance. Singles CH$40,300, with IVA discount for foreigners CH$34,000; doubles CH$44,500/CH$37,000; triples CH$59,000/CH$50,000. AmEx/MC/V. ❺

Hotel de la Avenida Express, O'Higgins 398 (☎230 256), on the corner of O'Higgins and Bulnes, down the street from Ficus. With 8 rooms set in an intimate bungalow, Hotel de la Avenida feels like home—if your home happens to have lovingly polished wooden night stands and headboards. Unfortunately, this home can get cold during the winter. Electric fans available for summertime use. Cable TV, private parking, and laundry service available. Breakfast included. Check-out noon. Reservations recommended. Singles CH$19,800; doubles CH$23,000; triples CH$35,400. IVA tax deducted for foreigners; off-season prices 10-15% lower. AmEx/MC/V. ❹

🍴 FOOD

Chillán's culinary specialty is its plump, juicy *lananizas* lathered up in caramelized onions or peppers, and served with *paps cocidas* (boiled potatoes). For food with a distinctly local flair, head to the **Feria de Chillán**, where small eateries cram the pedestrian mall and surrounding sidewalks. Grab a hot dog, *papas fritas*, and a coke for CH$1190. (Open M-Sa 9am-7pm, Su 9am-4pm.) For a tamer, more touristy scene, go north one block to the **Mercado Techado,** where restaurants are a bit swankier. (Open M-Sa 8am-6pm, Su 8am-2pm.)

🍽 **Café Paris,** Arauco 666 (☎223 881; fax 225 495), just south of Plaza Bernardo O'Higgins. The leafy balcony is a good place to sip a *café irlandés* (CH$2000) or a *Nescafé con leche* (CH$600) while watching the world drift by on Chillán's streets. Besides the snack bar downstairs, a classy 2nd fl. restaurant offers reasonably priced lunch specials (CH$2800-3500), including a vegetarian option that consists of hard-boiled eggs doused in mayo, a vegetable tortilla, and *leche asada* (flan) for CH$3200. Snack bar open Th-Su 24hrs., M 9am-2am. Restaurant open noon-midnight. AmEx/MC/V. ❷

Ficus, Rosas 392 (☎212 176 or 233 522), on the northwest corner of Rosas and Bulnes. Paper napkins in a table dispenser are set down by vested waiters in black bow ties. Locals recommend Ficus for its filling meat portions (CH$2000-3400) and pastas (CH$1600-3000). Open 12:30pm-2am. AmEx/MC/V. ❷

Fuente Alemana, Arauco 661 (☎212 720), a block south of Plaza de Bernardo O'Higgins. If you want to see Chileans dressed up in bright red-and-greed bonnets and aprons like washerwomen from an earlier Teutonic age, visit this cafeteria-style diner near the central plaza. Choose from a range of meats and salads showcased behind the counter (CH$1500-3000) or order sandwiches (CH$1000-2000). Open 8:30am-11:30pm. ❷

Restaurant Boulevard, Arauco 407 (☎245 679 or 099 747 1936), a block north of Plaza Bernardo O'Higgins. A bare-bones eatery with clean tables and floors. Lunch special including a soup, entree, and dessert CH$1250-1390. Open M-Sa 9am-2am, Su 9am-10pm. ❶

👁 SIGHTS

🏛 **IGLESIA CATEDRAL DE CHILLÁN.** Chillán's massive concrete cathedral is the aesthetic centerpiece of the city. Its predecessor was leveled by the 1939 earthquake, and the grieving city set about with determination to commemorate the dead of that catastrophe. A huge **cross** of concrete and iron—36m, 11cm in height—stands to the left of the new cathedral. Like a stone sequoia, its simplicity of form is a surprisingly moving reminder of the city's incalculable loss six decades ago. The church itself is a wonderfully realized combination of form and function: its concrete arches, built to represent two hands curled in prayer, actually descend deep into the ground to complete their arc and thus form a structurally sound foundation to prevent high death-tolls in future emergencies. Inside, the worship space is austere and largely unadorned: small windows filter sunlight onto the marble floors and a huge crucifix, carved from Italian wood with the image of Christ nailed to its trunk, hangs at the far end of the hall. The cathedral faces the city's spacious **Plaza de Armas,** where a statue of Bernardo O'Higgins watches over the city with a knowing expression while tiny Chilean soldiers scamper about the base of his pedestal. *(Arauco 503, on the eastern edge of central plaza.* ☎ *212 071. Open 8am-9pm, closed Tu, W, Su 1-3pm for lunch. Mass M-F 12:15pm, Sa 12:15 and 7pm, Su 8:30, 10am, 12:30, 8pm. Free.)*

ESCUELA MÉXICO. For one of Chile's more off-beat tourist attractions, stop by a local high school, Escuela México. Built with money donated by the Mexican government, the school was erected in the aftermath of the earthquake as a gift recognizing the bond between the two nations. At the urging of Pablo Neruda, two Mexican artists, **David Alfaro Siqueiros** and **Xavier Guerrero,** came to Chillán and decorated portions of the school with striking **murals.** Siquieros's masterpiece is located in the school's library on two opposing walls—the north wall (Mexico) and the south wall (Chile). To the north, the mighty form of the Aztec emperor Cuauthémoc rises from a pyramid, shooting arrows at a cross symbolizing the faith that came to destroy his own; to the right is a fallen Spaniard soldier, his bloody hands symbolizing the cruelty unleashed by his conquest. The left-hand side depicts Mexican leaders like José Maria Morelos, founder of the nation's first congress, and Emiliano Zapata, leader of a *campesino* uprising. On the southern wall, the Mapuche chief Gavarino screams a cry of defiance, the head of Chilean writer and polemicist Francisco Balboa suspended at his side. The two-headed apparition represents the dual struggles, with sword and pen, for freedom from oppression. To the left is Caupolicán raising his spear against the conquistadores, and Bernardo O'Higgins stands to the right, waving a Chilean flag. Guerrero's murals are emblazoned on the walls of the stairwell and entry hall, and include an image of a Mexican woman caring for a Chilean child injured in the great earthquake. Ask at the office labelled *"secretería"* to have the library doors unlocked for a tour of Siqueiros' mural. *(O'Higgins 250, across from Plaza Los Héroes de Iquique.* ☎ *212 012. Open 10am-noon and 3-5pm. Free, donations accepted.)*

IGLESIA SAN FRANCISCO. The pale adobe facade of the Iglesia San Francisco features a **mural** of Saint Francis tending to various farm animals. Built in 1903 for the Franciscan order, the church miraculously survived the 1939 earthquake with the loss of only its once-towering dome, which toppled to the ground. The church houses a religious museum, the Museo San Francisco, which features 19th-century devotional paintings from Italy and Spain, a collection of candelabras and church vestments, an assortment of Mapuche-made clay pots and pitchers, and some Chilean art, including an 18th-century wooden carving of the archangel Michael slaying a demon. *(Sargento Aldea 265, east on Vegas De Saldras on the eastern end of the Plaza General Pedro Lagos M.* ☎ *211 634. Open Tu-Sa 9am-1pm and 3-6pm, Su 1-2pm. CH$500.)*

FERIA DE CHILLÁN. The Feria de Chillán, the city's ancient and ever-bustling locale, is a mecca for bargain shoppers. Also known as the **Mercado Descubierto,** the *feria* sprawls over an entire block, with stores and carts lined up along an X-shaped walkway with its center at the tiny Plaza Sargento Aldea. Kiwis sell for

CH$100 per kilogram at the fruit stands, while boisterous vendors at the multitude of cheap, hole-in-the-wall eateries and craft shops hawk *empanadas, huaso* outfits, and wool scarves. *(Open 9am-7pm.)*

CHILLÁN VIEJO. A tour of the stately **Parque Monumental Bernardo O'Higgins** in the old part of town is a worthwhile excursion. The park features a **mosaic** depicting the life and wondrous deeds of the Liberator. This is the site of the house where O'Higgins was born. Nearby, you'll find the chapel where O'Higgins's mother, Isabel Riquelne, and his sister, Rovita, are buried. *(On O'Higgins. Take a colectivo (CH$250) or bus (CH$200) from the Plaza de Armas. Open 8am-7pm.)*

NEAR CHILLÁN: TERMAS DE CHILLÁN ☎ 42

Eighty kilometers east of Chillán, Volcán Chillán, a 3122m peak shrouded in snow and ice, squats among the Andes. Along its slopes, a Chilean resort company has built two luxury hotels and a mammoth ski center, collectively knows as the **Termas de Chillán** for the sulphur and iron-infused thermal baths that lie at the heart of the resort complex. The skiing here is some of South America's finest, with 29 runs and a 1100m (3600 foot) vertical drop. Nine lifts service the slopes; a snowboarding park, snowmobile circuits, and Alaskan Malamute dog-sledding are also available. Heli-skiing is another option for the those willing to splurge for a helicopter. The lifts are only open during the winter; the rest of the year, skiers must walk up the slope.

The two hotels on the slopes offer extravagantly priced accommodations, with access to a comprehensive spa that is focused around the open-air thermal pools but also includes natural steam baths, hot mud baths, and a wide array of massage services. Even if you can't stay here, it's fun to take a peek at the way stylish Chileans vacation—**Gran Hotel Temas de Chillán ❺** is the ritzier option, a five-star monstrosity that offers squash courts, an indoor swimming pool, an outdoor swimming pool, a fitness gym, a ski shop, and day-care facilities. **Hotel Pirigallo ❹**, a three-star hotel, is barely cheaper, with a ski shop, hot springs pool, and day care facilities. Condominiums are also available for rental, located in a resort village with a clubhouse, mini-market, and even its own chapel.

Public transportation to the Termas is difficult except during the summertime, when buses run directly to the resort (see **Transportation,** p. 181). There are no buses to the Termas during the winter, and the *carabineros* only let cars with chains up to the resort when road conditions get icy. It's usually better to arrange transport through the hotels. Mauricio Lagos (☎ 220 093 or 099 970 8371) will take you up to the resort (CH$25,000 roundtrip)—remind him to put on his tire chains.

To reserve a room in the resort's hotels, contact **Hotelera Somontar** in Chillán, Libertad 1092 (☎ 223 887; open M-F 9am-1pm and 3-7pm, Sa 9am-1pm) or Santiago, San Pío X 2460, Apt. 508. (☎ 233 1313; www.termaschillan.cl or www.skichillan.com; opera@termaschillan.cl. Open M-F 9am-7pm, Sa 10:30am-1pm.) The hotel chain offers transport to and from the resort in their packages.

Those who want to try the slopes without shelling out wads of cash for the hotel packages can do so—separate rates are available for non-guests. Alternatively, much cheaper lodgings are available near the Termas through the host of *cabaña* rental operations along the road to the resort. One *cabaña* site, **Aguas del Fuego ❸** (☎ 197 3610), at the 68km marker on the left side of the road heading toward the Termas, offers a range of options, from matrimonial doubles (CH$10,000-20,000) to four-bed, six-person cabins (CH$20,000-40,000). Kitchens with fridges and gas stoves, TV, and a wood-burning heating stove are available in all rooms. Breakfast in the on-site restaurant is CH$1000.

CONCEPCIÓN ☎41

For centuries, Concepción was the final frontier of Spanish rule—ferocious and unrelenting bands of Mapuche warriors held back the colonizers time and again. The conquistador Pedro de Valdivia founded Concepción in 1550 as a way station on his journey south, but even he could not stake claim south of the Río Bíobío. Instead, he met his grisly end at the hands of Mapuche *cacique* Lautauro, who in 1553 ambushed and captured Valdivia near the settlement, and tortured him to death. Centuries later, Lautauro's people have been uprooted and all but decimated, and a statue of Valdivia in the central plaza still gloats over his conquest.

Concepción today is Chile's third largest city and remains an outpost of sorts. It is the gateway to the still inscrutable south, and an oasis of high culture and art amid the rough *pampa*. Throughout its history, Concepción has remained at the center of the nation's political upheavals: Bernardo O'Higgins signed the Declaración de la Independencia in its central plaza (now named after that seminal event in 1818), and almost a century and a half later, the Movimiento de Izquierda Revolucionaria (Movement of the Revolutionary Left), or Mir, was born in its university. A group of student radicals promoted land seizures and fought for Mapuche rights during the turbulent 60s—only to be all but exterminated by Pinochet after the coup in the 1970s.

Concepción today stands at a cultural crossroads, as the proud Chilean city where O'Higgins announced a new country's independence, and the gateway to the still-untamed south, the heart of the country's indigenous culture.

The historical importance of this city is somewhat obscured by the fact that, because of frequent and sometimes devastating earthquakes, almost all of Concepción's older shell has toppled to the ground, leaving ugly steel and concrete modernity in its place. Nevertheless, Concepción beats with a strong, often frenzied pulse, the mixture of students and workers, artists and businesspeople, creating an atmosphere that thrills in both determined commerce and wild nightlife. At the same time, it is also a mire for the region's poor, with inveterate homelessness, a multitude of street urchins, and rampant (if relatively low-grade) drug use.

MIDDLE CHILE

■ INTERCITY TRANSPORTATION

Flights: Aeropuerto Carriel Sur (☎732 005), in Talcahuano, 16km (15min.) northeast of Concepción. **Taxis** available from the airport to the Plaza de la Independencia (CH$5000). **F&S Transit** (☎935 083 or 099 799 9801), a van shuttle service, charges CH$3000 per trip. You can call up to two hours before your flight, but it's recommended that you make a reservation one day in advance. **LanChile,** Barros Arana 600 (☎229 138 or 600 526 2000; www.lanchile.com), on one corner of the Plaza de la Independencia. Open M-F 9am-6:15pm, Sa 10am-1:15pm. Flies to: **Arica** (3½hr.; 7:30am, 2:40, 8:20pm; CH$132,000); **Puerto Montt** (1¾hr., 5:15pm, CH$27,000); **Punta Arenas** (6hr., 5:15pm, CH$113,000); **Santiago** (1hr., 9 per day 8am-9:30pm, CH$69,000); **Temuco** (40min., 5:15pm, CH$22,000).

Trains: Estación Concepción (☎226 925), on Prat at the western end of Barros Arana, across the Plaza España. Trains to **Santiago** (10pm; economy class CH$5400, first class CH$8800, beds CH$17,000-42,000).

Buses: Tur-Bus (☎315 555), **Bíobío** (☎310 764), **Igi Llaima** (☎312 498), **Eme Bus** (☎312 610), and **Linea Azul** (☎311 126) buses depart from the two bus terminals in town.

Terminal de Buses Camilo Henríquez, Camilo Henríquez 2565 (☎315 036). Catch a Rengo Lientur bus, which makes a circuit on Rengo, Chacabuco, and Lientur, and then shuttles back to the city center (every 5min, CH$250). To: **Chillán** (1½hr., every 30min. 7am-midnight, CH$1300); **Los Angeles** (2hr., 4 per day 7:45am-11:15pm, CH$1800); **Santiago** (6 hr., every 30min. 7am-midnight, CH$5000).

Terminal de Buses Collao, Tegualda 860 (☎749 000). Catch either a Riviera de Bíobío or Hual-pencillo bus with the sign *"A la puertas de terminal"* or "Terminal Callao" from San Martín (every 3-5 min., CH$250). The same buses head back to the city center. To: **Chillán** (1½hr., every 30min. 6:40am-9pm, CH$1800); **Los Angeles** (1¾hr., 31 per day 6:30am-8:45pm, CH$1850); **Puerto Montt** (11hr., 6 per day 10am-9pm, CH$6000); **Santiago** (6hr.; 12 per day 8am-11:45pm; CH$5000, executive CH$7000); **Temuco** (4½hr.; Su-Th 18 per day 6:30am-8:15pm, F and Sa 21 per day 6:30am-9:15pm; CH$3700).

■ ORIENTATION

Concepción centers around its grand **Plaza de la Independencia** which is flanked by its cathedral, government offices, and banks. The plaza is often the site of demonstrations and street theater. Meanwhile, Concepción's layout itself is symbolic of its hybrid and contentious past: many northwest and southeast downtown streets are named after Mapuche chieftains—Caupolicán, Colo-Colo, and so on—while the streets that they cross bear the names of Chilean independence fighters including O'Higgins and San Martín. Important battles in the nation's birthplaces—Maipú and Chacabuco—also make an appearance.

A pedestrian mall heads east on **Barro Arana,** ending two blocks later at Castellón; **Aníbal Pinto** north of Barro Arana is similarly blocked to cars until it reaches Maipú. This extensive pedestrian walkway is always bustling with activity from street performers dancing the *cueca,* to vendors who lay down blankets full of wares and hawk them (illegally) until the *carabineros* walk by. The **Mercado Municipal,** another good place for bargain shoppers, lies two blocks north of the plaza, between Rengo and Caupolicán. If you follow Burnos Arana southwest you'll eventually reach the train station and the **Barrio Estación,** a lively neighborhood devoted to bars, clubs, and vice. On the opposite end of downtown lies the **Universidad de Concepción** and its Barrio Universitario, where you'll find the city's bohemian scene amid a smattering of bars and cafes. At the southeastern edge of the city is a tree-topped ridge, the **Cerro Caracol;** at its foot is a pleasant park.

▐ LOCAL TRANSPORTATION

Buses: City buses cost CH$300 and stop anywhere—flag them down. CH$100 for students with an ISIC card. They run throughout the city and suburbs, but stop late at night.

Taxis/Colectivos: Taxis congregate around the Plaza de la Independencia and train and bus stations. A taxi from the central plaza to the Terminal Collao or Terminal Camilo Henríquez runs CH$2500. A taxi to the airport is CH$5000. Try **Taxi Catedral** (☎236 241) or **Taxi O'Higgins** (☎234 394) for call-based service. **Colectivos** can be found around Freire, Roosevelt, and Chacabuco (CH$300, CH$500 between 9pm-7am).

Car Rental: Econorent, Castellón 134 (☎225 5377 or 600 200 0000; ecorent@chile-sat.net; www.econorent.net), or at Aeropuerto Carriel Sur (☎732 2121). Rentals start at CH$20,000 per day, including insurance. 24+. Concepción office open M-F 9am-1pm and 3-7pm. Airport office open 8am-10pm.

▐ PRACTICAL INFORMATION

TOURIST AND FINANCIAL SERVICES

Tourist Office: Sernatur, Aníbal Pinto 460 (☎227 976; fax 229 201; infobiobio@serna-tur.cl), on the northeastern edge of the Plaza de la Independencia. The professional staff is friendly and will pass along free maps of the city. Open Dec.-Feb. M-F 8:30am-8pm, Sa 10am-2:30pm; off-season M-F 9am-1pm and 3-6pm. **Conaf,** Barros Arana 215 (☎238 504), near Barrio Estación, offers info about the region. Open M-F 9am-

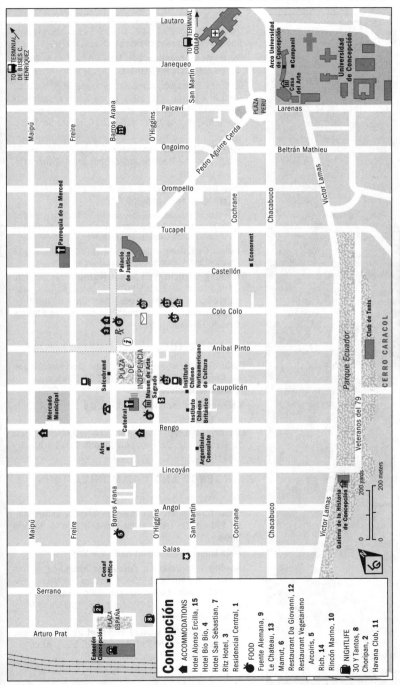

MIDDLE CHILE

TO TERMINAL DE BUSES C. HENRIQUEZ

Lautaro

TO TERMINAL COLLAO

Janequeo

Paicaví

San Martín

PLAZA PERU

Arco Universidad de Concepción

Campanil

Casa del Arte

Universidad de Concepción

Larenas

Maipú

Freire

Barros Arana

O'Higgins

Ongolmo

Beltrán Mathieu

Parroquia de la Merced

Orompello

Cochrane

Chacabuco

Pedro Aguirre Cerda

Victor Lamas

Tucapel

Palacio de Justicia

Econorent

Castellón

Colo Colo

Aníbal Pinto

Parque Ecuador

CERRO CARACOL

Club de Tenis

Salcobrand

PLAZA DE INDEPENCIA

Museo de Arte Sagrado

Instituto Chileno Norteamericano de Cultura

Caupolicán

Mercado Municipal

Catedral

Instituto Chileno Británico

Rengo

Afex

Argentinian Consulate

Lincoyán

Veteranos del 79

Barros Arana

Angol

San Martín

Cochrane

Chacabuco

Galería de la Historia de Concepción

Maipú

Freire

O'Higgins

Salas

Victor Lamas

Conaf Office

Serrano

PLAZA ESPAÑA

Estación Concepción

Arturo Prat

0   200 yards
0   200 meters

Concepción

▲ ACCOMMODATIONS
Hotel Alonso Ercilla, 15
Hotel Bío Bío, 4
Hotel San Sebastian, 7
Ritz Hotel, 3
Residencial Central, 1

🍴 FOOD
Fuente Alemana, 9
Le Chateau, 13
Mamut, 6
Restaurant Da Giovanni, 12
Restaurant Vegetariano
Arcoiris, 5
Rich, 14
Rincón Marino, 10

🎵 NIGHTLIFE
30 Y Tantos, 8
Choripan, 2
Havana Club, 11

FROM THE ROAD

STRANGER IN A STRANGE LAND

Mexican educator José Vasconceles once called Latin America the birthplace of *la raza cósmica*, the "cosmic race." Emerging from the fusion of Spanish and indigenous cultures, the people of Latin America were the future of humanity, wrote Vasconceles—a beautifully mongrel mixture of physiognomy and folklore that represented a world steadily losing all boundaries. I was hoping to find such forward thinking about race when I came to Chile. Instead, I encountered a disturbing amount of racial intolerance and ignorance.

With some exceptions, the Chilean propensity for xenophobia was commonplace. Wherever I went, from small towns to large urban centers, I ran into stares, heckling, and aggressive harassment, prompted by the mere sight of a person of East Asian descent. In Rancagua, a boy popped his head out of a car to shout *"chino!"* In Curicó, a man started making "kung-fu" yelps and shrieks when I approached. Concepción turned out to be the worst place for racial harassment—I was often accosted by men chanting "China! China!" Well, at least they got the ethnicity somewhat right: most would-be bigots would throw out *"japonés"* or *"correano."*

In profound moments of self-pity, I talked to some of the more understanding locals, and they had theories about my problems. Some believed that Chileans were just not used to foreigners. After all, those tall mountains to the east kept out visitors. And the Pinochet regime had not exactly been a wellspring of progressive, cosmopolitan thought. One Chilean ventured that Asians were singled out

1pm and 3-5pm. **Copias Casanueva,** San Martín 663 (☎244 093 or 234 049; fax 230 149), sells maps of the city and its surrounding suburbs (CH$780).

Consulates: Argentina, San Martín 472, Piro 5, Depto. 52 (☎230 257; fax 910 183).

Currency Exchange: Afex, Barros Arana 565, Local 57 (☎239 618; fax 210 590), in the Gutería Internacional. Exchanges currency and cashes traveler's checks. Open M-F 9am-2:30pm and 3:30-6:30pm, Sa 10am-1:30pm.

Bank/ATM: Banco Santander, O'Higgins 560 (☎264 800), near the Plaza de la Independencia. **24hr. ATM.** Open M-F 9am-2pm.

Work Opportunities: For details on all positions, see **Alternatives to Tourism** (p. 83).

> **Restaurant Da Giovanni,** Caupolicán 346, Local 3 (☎241 936), hires up to 2 waiters for work in Dec. and Jan. Contact the owner, Gilda Carnese, for information.
>
> **Havana Club,** Barros Arana 1356 (☎224 006), hires up to 5 waiters and 4 bouncers during Jan.-March.

Teaching English: Wall Street Institute for English, Caupolicán 299 (☎910 791; www.wsi.es; wsi-conce@chilesat.net), seeks part-time or full-time English instructors year-round. For details see **Alternatives to Tourism** (p. 82).

LOCAL SERVICES

Cultural Centers: Instituto Chileno Norteamericano de Cultura, Caupolicán 315 (☎225 506). **Instituto Chileno Británico,** San Martín 531 (☎234 044).

Market: Mercado Municipal, on the corner of Freire and Caupolicán.

Laundry: Lave.rap, Caupolicán 334 (☎234 826), next to Restaurant Da Giovanni. Wash CH$1500, dry CH$1500.

EMERGENCY AND COMMUNICATIONS

Emergency: ☎133

Police: *Carabineros* have their central office at San Martín 171 (☎235 011), at the corner of San Martín and Salas.

Crisis Lines: Drugs addict hotline ☎135.

Late-Night Pharmacies: Farmacias Ahumada, Barros Arana 726-740 (☎255 540), next to the Mamul restaurant. Open 8am-midnight. **Salcobrand,** Barros Arana 611 (☎227 477), along the Plaza de la Independencia. Open 24hr.

Hospital: Hospital Clínico Regional de Concepción, San Martín 1436 (☎237 445 or 208 500), at corner of San Martín and Janequeo.

Telephones/Fax: Entel, Barros Arana 541 (☎911 449), near the Plaza de la Independencia. International faxes CH$1600 per page, local faxes CH$350 per page. Receiving faxes CH$200 per page. Open M-F 8:30am-10pm, Sa 9am-9:30pm.

Internet Access: El Portal, Caupulicán 314 (☎748 986), up the flight of stairs next to the sex shop. CH$600 per hr. Printing CH$50 per page. **Cyber Café,** Caupulicán 588 (☎238 394), between Freire and Barros Arana. CH$500 for 30min. Printing CH$30 per page. Open M-Sa 9am-11:30pm, Su 11am-11:30pm.

Post Office: Correos, Colo-Colo 417 (☎235 666), a block away from the Plaza de la Independencia. **Western Union** wire service available. Open M-F 8am-7pm, Sa 8am-1pm.

ACCOMMODATIONS

Concepción is a little low on rock-bottom budget accommodations; the norm in this big city is glittering luxury guaranteed to leave you in lifelong debt. That said, it's still possible to find a place to hang your hat for a less painful price, even in the heart of the city's madly busy center.

Hotel Alonso de Ercilla, Colo-Colo 334 (☎227 984; fax 230 053; www.hotelalonsodeercilla.co.cl; HAlonsoE@entelchile.net), to the right of the Le Chateau restaurant. If you're willing to pay a little bit more, this hotel offers pleasant modern rooms without the intimidating excess of the priciest establishments. The owner of the hotel, Luz Sobrino, has decorated some of the rooms with his own paintings and pencil sketches—maybe not Van Gogh, but better than most hotel-room wall coverings. Cable TV, radiator heating, free private parking, laundry services, and Internet access (CH$1000 per hr.) available. Breakfast included. Reservations recommended. Singles CH$19,900-25,900; doubles CH$32,900; triples CH$45,000. IVA discount available to foreigners who pay in US dollars. AmEx/MC/V. ❹

Ritz Hotel, Barros Arana 721 (☎226 696 or 243 248; fax 243 249; www.cepri.cl/ritz; ritz@ctcinternet.cl), on the pedestrian mall near the central plaza. Its ritzy days are long over, but the Ritz Hotel offers accommodations right in the high energy heart of the Barros Arana pedestrian mall. The rooms are drab, but you might like the old-fashioned elevator operated by hotel staff. Cable TV, radiator heating, laundry service, and parking (CH$1770 per day) available. Breakfast included. Check-out 2pm. Reservations recommended 3-4 days in advance. Singles CH$14,000; doubles CH$19,000; triples CH$25,000. AmEx/MC/V. ❸

reputed for mistreating Chilean employees who worked in the ubiquitous *chifas*. It probably doesn't help that the average Chilean's knowledge of Asian culture comes from martial arts flicks—the most vivid image I had of Asians during my stay came from an antiperspirant commercial in which an Asian dude karate chops his way through a slew of bad guys only to marvel at the lack of sweat collected under his arm.

As a first-generation Taiwanese American, I began reverting to my North American identity. I imagined myself wearing a sign that read, *"Yo soy un gringo."* But whenever I told a curious Chilean I was from the US, the strange looks and skepticism I got were even more frustrating. Then again, I wasn't sure that being labeled a *gringo* would make matters better: a student from Minnesota told me that early in her stay in Concepción, people would randomly point at her and shriek, *"gringa!"*

After mulling over the issue myself, I realized that I shouldn't be so hard on Chileans for being ignorant about my race or culture. It's not like bigotry is unique to Chile, for as Juan, a waiter in Pichilemu observed, "To a Chilean, your eyes say *japonés*. People here don't know the difference between Japanese and Chinese. But it's the same thing in the US. If North Americans saw a Chilean, they won't think "Chilean," rather, they'd think in generalities like South American or Hispanic." I guess things are difficult for all strangers in strange lands, not just Asians in Chile. And there is something to be said for keeping a thick skin and not letting scattered ignorance make you close yourself to a whole society.

—Victor Chen

Residencial Central, Rengo 673 (☎227 309), across from the Mercado. One of Concepción's cheapest options, Residencial Central is housed in a building dating back to 1811, with high ceilings and wooden floors. Of course, the rock-bottom rates mean the the building is not in tip-top shape—the chandelier chains now hold up ordinary light bulbs, the wall are rather dirty, and the small beds sit on non-orthopedic bamboo or metal frames. TV, gas-burning space heaters, on-site restaurant, and free private parking available. Breakfast included. Reservations recommended 1 day in advance. CH$6500 per person. ❷

Hotel San Sebastian, Rengo 463 (☎910 270 or 243 412; fax 243 412), between Barros Arana and O'Higgins, up a flight of stairs. Nondescript but clean rooms, with carpeting and comfy beds. Cable TV, private parking, radiator heating, and laundry service available. Breakfast included. Reservations recommended 3-4 days in advance from Dec.-March. Singles CH$15,950, with bath CH$19,980; doubles CH$21,960/CH$25,950; triples CH$27,960; quads CH$34,630. AmEx/MC/V. ❹

Hotel Bío Bío, Barros Arana 751 (☎228 018; www.contactoconce.cl), at the end of a long mall corridor off the pedestrian walkway's northern edge. The flashing red neon sign presides over the entrance to this once luxurious, now somewhat seedy, lovers' lodge. Dark hallways lead to run-down bathrooms. Cable TV, laundry services, and electric space heaters available. Breakfast included. Reservation recommended. Singles CH$10,000, with private bath CH$13,000; doubles CH$14,870/CH$20,830; triples with private bath outside room CH$19,980. IVA discount for foreigners. US dollars accepted. AmEx/MC/V. ❸

◘ FOOD

Concepción doesn't have much in the way of local specialties, but as the only big city around, it boasts a wide range of culinary options. You'll find lots of great seafood here, as well as a host of decent burger and sandwich shops.

Le Chateau, Colo-Colo 340 (☎/fax 229 977; lechateau@dipal.cl), next to Hotel Alonso de Ercilla. Dine in style at this upscale French restaurant, where the wine-red tablecloth has a sheen that matches that of the silverware. The flowers along the window might be fake, but the wine in the rocks spaced strategically throughout the restaurant is intoxicating. Pick from various excellent fish and meat dishes, including *corvina con salsa marisco*, a filet of fish drenched in a cream sauce of baby shrimp and *locos* (CH$5310). *La tulipa*, a bud of ice cream topped with orange and chocolate sauce and planted amid petals of house-baked bread crisp (CH$1560), is almost too pretty to eat. Open M-Sa 12:30-2pm and 6-11:30pm. AmEx/MC/V. ❸

Rich, Colo-Colo 325 (☎245 829), across from Hotel Alonso de Ercilla, in the pink building. Locals say this place serves up the best burgers in Concepción. That's actually all they serve—if you don't count their half-hearted *papas fritas* (CH$600) or marmalade pancakes (CH$1000). Rich's burgers (CH$900-1800) come with a wide range of toppings, from avocado pureé (*palta*) to sunny-side-up eggs. Try the "Promoción Rich," a value meal including a hamburger, *papas fritas*, and a soft drink (CH$2800). The lunch counter and tiny tables in the eating space are packed during mealtimes. Open M-Sa 10am-10pm. ❶

Restaurant Da Giovanni, Caupolicán 346, Local 3 (☎241 936), just south of the central plaza. This small, yet excellent, Italian restaurant serves up pastas—lasagna, raviolis, *panzotti, canelones, penne al scampi*, and, of course, spaghetti—in a medley of sauces (CH$2700-2900). Try the tiramisu or *panna cota* for an after-meal infusion of sugar. Open M-F 9am-11pm. ❷

Fuente Alemana, O'Higgins 630 (☎228 307), across from Banco Santander. There are no tables here—just a long counter that stretches along the entire length of the wall. True to the no-nonsense style of the decor, Fuerte Alemana serves up simple but righteous sandwiches (CH$680-2500) to eat there or take away. Look for your favorite Chilean accompaniments: Schop beer (CH$500) and *empanadas* (CH$500 to take out, CH$550 to eat there). Open M-F 8am-11:45pm, Sa 10:30am-11:45pm, Su 12:30-10:30pm. MC/V. ❶

Rincón Marino, Colo-Colo 454 (☎230 311), up the stairs just to the right of the small mall, marked by a small sign for the restaurant. The big model fisherman's boat and the trout-emblazoned sign that reads "Gone Fishing" should tip you off that this is a place that takes seafood seriously. Try the *plato americano* (CH$4500) for a large plate laden with all sorts of maritime mollusks, served cold with a drizzling of *salsa verde* and mayonnaise. Open M-Sa noon-midnight. AmEx/MC/V. ❸

Restaurant Vegetariano Arcoiris, Barros Arana 244 (☎520 300). Go through the walkway with a yellow sign—the restaurant's in a lime-green building with wooden doors. The huge, airy dining space (once a barn) radiates an entirely wholesome ambiance, with unicorn and Earth Day posters on the walls, Mapuche handicrafts hanging from the ceiling posts, and no smoking except on the backyard lawn. The food is prepared in the same conscientious manner, ranging from soy *empanadas* to fresh curry to vitamin-infused fruit drinks. The menu changes daily. All-you-can-eat feast, including dessert (CH$3300). Live music (new age, of course) on Th and F nights. Open M-Sa 8:30am-10pm. MC/V. ❷

Mamut, Barros Arana 744 (☎912 037), on the pedestrian mall right across from the Ritz Hotel. The mammoth menacing its huge tusks on the sign outside might say jungle, but the only savagery going on here is the outrageously tacky decor (plastic jungle ferns included). Mamut has mastered the high-energy banality pioneered by American food chains right down to perky fonts and vivid color photos of food in the menu. Locals flock to this place for exotic dishes such as grilled Alaskan Salmon ($2190), New Orleans steak (CH$2190), and Oriental Chicken Salad (CH$1290). Not very vegetarian friendly, but at least they don't serve mammoth meat. Happy Hour 6-8pm: buy a Schop beer or drink and get another one for free. Open M-Sa 9am-midnight, Su 10am-1am. AmEx/MC/V. ❶

NIGHTLIFE

Laid-back bars vie with throbbing, sardine-packed clubs at the **Barrio Estación,** the city's official hangout for hard drinkers, partyers, and ne'er-do-wells. You'll find whatever poison suits your fancy here—whether it's a smoky bar scene with Eddie Vedder wannabes at the mike, a sweaty dance floor with little wriggle room, or piping-hot *empanadas* oozing oh-so healthy oodles of cheese. Be careful and walk in groups at night, though; the neighborhood is reputed to be the city's most dangerous area. For a more sedate, but still hard-drinking, neighborhood, head to the **Barrio Universitario,** the sector abutting the Universidad de Concepción. You'll find plenty of bars and restaurants, some of which are frequented by the Chilean version of the perpetually sauced frat brother.

The city's most happening (and most exclusive) club is **Katango Planet,** several blocks north of the Barrio Estación, on Arturo Prat after Bulnes. A good choice in the Barrio Estación itself is **Bar del Negro,** Arturo Prat 574 (☎210 905), which on most nights is jam-packed full of young Chileans cradling rum-laced Cokes while they groove (and jostle you) to the beat.

MIDDLE CHILE

⊠ **30 y Tantos,** Prat 402, across from the train station. This is *the* place to go for *empanadas* (CH$980). They serve them in one shape and size, but in 21 different varieties from cheese to apples to *mariscos*. They even have a system of dots on the empanadas to help you remember which one is which variety. Besides the *empanada* offerings, there's a chill atmosphere, as lighting comes from naked light bulbs and candles, old transistor radiators are stacked on the wall shelves, and the piped-in music is loud and lively. Beers CH$850-1200. Mixed drinks CH$900-4800. Open 7pm-2am.

Choripan, Arturo Prat 542-546 (☎253 004), at the eastern end of Plaza España. A mellow bar that features live music on some nights—usually a Chilean rock band trying out your favorite American riffs. Try the *ponche* (red wine mixed with strawberry juices, or white wine mixed with punch juice) to really get that distortion buzzing in your head. (CH$500). Mixed drinks CH$1600-3900. Open 7:30pm-3:30am.

Havana Club, Barros Arana 1356 (☎224 006), four blocks east of the Palacio de Justicia courthouse. It's neither here nor there as far as Concepción's nightlife is concerned, located far away from both Barrio Estación and Barrio Universitario. Still, Havana Club offers two floors of dancing, next to a trickling waterfall and plastic palm trees. Latin dance music and techno keep blasting, while Th is 80s night. Live acts make occasional appearances. Beers CH$500. Mixed drinks CH$1000-2000. Semi-formal dress. 18+ Th, F 9pm-5am, Sa 10pm-5am; cover Th CH$1500, F CH$3000, Su CH$3000. All ages Sa 5-10pm and Su 5-10pm; cover CH$1000, including a soft drink.

◎ SIGHTS

You can get to all of Concepción's major sights by walking. They are clustered around three sectors: the Plaza de la Independencia at the center; the Barrio Universitario to the east; and Parque Ecuador at the southern edge of town, along the hillside.

PLAZA DE LA INDEPENDENCIA. A stone sitting at one end of the central plaza notes the site's chief claim to fame: here, on January 1, 1818, before his Army of the South, Bernardo O'Higgins declared the independence of Chile. The enormous plaza seems a fitting place for such grandiose acts of patriotism: its walkways are thronged with all sorts of trees, shaggy thick and spindly tall, and an elegant fountain, spectacularly lit at night, sits at its center. The metallic column and statue that rise from the **Fountain of Ceres** were forged in Liverpool, England; they are ringed by bare-chested mermaids blowing water out of conches while dragons unfurl from the column to support antique lamps.

IGLESIA CATEDRAL DE CONCEPCIÓN. On the southwestern edge of the plaza, this gray-stone edifice has central doors made of bronze, with scenes from the Old and New Testament counterpoised on either door. Completed in 1964, the cathedral centers around an Italian marble altar, behind which lies a huge, pastel-colored mural, depicting the Holy Trinity, Christ's birth and crucifixion, the Garden of Eden, and the Virgin Mary stamping the head of the serpent. Monvoisin's 19th-century oil painting of Christ hangs on one wall. (*Caupolicán 451.* ☎223 701. *Open M-F 9am-7:30pm, Sa-Su 9am-1pm. Mass M-F 10am; Sa 10am and 7pm; Su 10, 11am, 12:15, 7pm. Free.*)

MUSEO DE ARTE SAGRADO. This museum boasts a repository of religious art owned by the Universidad Católica de la Santísima Concepción. Its collection of objects and ornaments used in Catholic liturgy over the last six centuries includes extravagant amounts of gold, silver, and marble. (*Caupolicán 441, adjacent to the Catedral.* ☎735 060; *gvarela@ucsc.cl. Open Apr.-Oct. Tu-F 10am-1:30pm and 3-7pm, Sa 11am-2pm; Nov.-March Tu-F 10am-1:30pm and 4-8pm, Sa 11am-2pm. CH$300.*)

UNIVERSIDAD DE CONCEPCIÓN. Chile's second largest university, the **Universidad de Concepción** lies in relative seclusion along a forested ridge at the eastern edge of the central city. No trip to Concepción would be complete without a prolonged gaze at the awe-inspiring *Presencia de América Latina,* a huge fiery-red mural by Mexican artist Jorge González Camarena that stretches along the entire back wall of the university's ⬛**Casa del Arte.** Painted in 1965, the mural depicts the whole of Latin America as an organic unity: flags from each country flutter across the top of the mural, while the *pareja original* (the original pair) of an armored conquistador and a naked indigenous woman watch from one end, their joined bodies representing the fusion of native and Spanish blood and destiny. The two look over the fruits of the land—corn and wheat harvested from its soil, and the wealth of gold, silver, iron, and copper buried deep under its skin—represented here by the sleeping figures of metallic-hued women. Along the museum's stairwell runs the serpentine body of Quetzalcóatl, the Mexican symbol of culture. The Casa del Arte also happens to house the country's largest collection of paintings outside of Santiago, including the work of Chileans and foreign artists who painted in Chile, largely from the late 19th and early 20th centuries.

Once you leave the Casa del Arte, turn right and head down Chacabuco until you reach the university's signature **arch.** Situated between the two halves of the university's medical building, the towering arch features a relief by Mario Oímezzano, carved with images out of Greek mythology. The university's elegant **campanil,** a clock tower of pure white stone, sublimely unadorned, lies before the arch. Lovers tend to tryst at the top of its steps, which lead down to the **plaza estudiante,** a space dominated by skateboarders. Around the plaza you'll find a few small lagoons—one of which is frequented by swans—and a wide variety of trees, some exotic. *(On Paicaví, at Chacabuco, on Plaza Peru's eastern end. ☎ 204 290. Open Tu-F 10am-6pm, Sa 10am-4pm, Su 10am-1pm. Free.)*

PARQUE ECUADOR. A quiet park nestled in the shadow of a pine-topped hillside, Parque Ecuador features playgrounds, tennis courts, and benches to sit on and savor a cloudless day. You can climb to the top of **Cerro Caracol** for a resplendent view of the city. Stay clear once the sun sets, though; locals say the hilltop is dangerous at night. At the western edge of the park you'll find the **Galería de la Historia de Concepción,** which features small, but well-crafted, *dioramas* illustrating Concepción's four and a half centuries of history. Recorded audio messages provide an accompaniment to the straightforward museum displays. The Galería also features paintings by local artists on its second floor. *(On Victor Lamas, at the corner of Victor Lamas and Lincoyán. ☎ 231 830. Open M 3-6:30pm, Tu-F 10am-1:30pm and 3-6:30pm, Sa-Su 10am-2pm and 3-7pm. Free.)*

MONITOR HUÁSCAR. Naval buffs and young children will gladly make the trip out to the Talcahuano naval base, 16km northeast of Concepción, to see the (still-floating) ironclad *Huáscar.* Built in England in 1865, with an 11cm thick hull of riveted steel and a double-cannon turret capable of rotating 180 degrees, this Peruvian gunship terrorized the relatively weak Chilean navy for more than a decade, until two Chilean ships snuck up on it on Oct. 8, 1879, and battered it into submission with cannon fire. Before it was finally captured, however, the Huáscar took the lives of Chile's two greatest naval heroes, Captain Arturo Prat and Sergeant Juan de Kios Aldea, the "Heroes of Iquique," saintly figures whose names now bless many a Chilean street sign. In one of history's most courageous (and pointless) acts of heroism punctuating the beginning of the war of the Pacific, Captain Prat leapt from his sinking wooden ship, the *Esmeralda,* onto the deck of the Huáscar, sword in hand (or at least that's how his statue in the plaza of the naval base remembers him). He was promptly shot to death. With such a glorious history, it's no wonder that the Peruvian government is still wrangling with Chileans over the boat which they claim is stolen property. The ironclad ship is kept in a frighteningly meticulous state of preservation; cleaning occurs every morning from 8:30-9am, and all day on Monday. The blue-uniformed sailors on-board will happily explain the intricacies of the ship's turret system, engine room, and portable latrine. *(Talcahuano naval base. ☎ 745 520. Catch the micro run by Buses Base Naval, with a sign that reads "Base Naval" on the windshield from O'Higgins and Castellón, or flag down the bus anywhere on O'Higgins. (45min., every 15min., CH$200). You'll have to leave your passport and any bags at the gate with the guard. Open Tu-Su 9:30am-noon and 2-5:30pm. CH$1000.)*

◻ SHOPPING

The **Mercado Municipal** offers fruits, vegetables, and other foodstuffs, as well as *artesanías* endorsing a variety of wares including fine wooden carvings (as much as CH$40,000), ceramic pitchers and plates (CH$600-3000), vibrant ponchos of natural wool (CH$5000-10,000), wool caps (CH$2000), and even cozy woolen socks. (Open 8am-8pm.) If you're looking for seedier shopping and better bargains, head to the **pedestrian mall** along Barros Arana north of the plaza. You'll find small-time capitalists selling blanketfuls of pirated CDs, socks, and rubber heating pads. The blankets are there so the vendors can gather up their goods and run as soon as green-coated *carabineros* walk by. The mall clears out around midnight.

SOUTH TO THE LAKES DISTRICT

LOS ANGELES   ☎43

A small city with the feel of a small town, Los Angeles (pop. 125,000) may inspire raised eyebrows once travelers realize this is a curious counterpart to the gilded extravagance of its less sensible North American namesake. One similarity may be the two cities' lack of visible history: once a summer camp for the Spanish *Ejercito de la Frontera* (Frontier Army), Chile's Los Angeles was destroyed and rebuilt several times after its first founding as a fort in 1739. In more recent years, it has shunned the cookie-cutter traditionalism of its Chilean peers with shocks of modernity, including a newly renovated steel and concrete Plaza de Armas.

▐ TRANSPORTATION

Buses: Local bus routes are reliable. Hail a bus at Villagrán to get to the bus terminal; they should say "terminal" in the windshield (CH$220). Buses return to the city center on Almagro. The four main bus terminals in town are serviced by **Tur-Bus** (☎363 136), **Buses Bío Bío** (☎363 145), **Buses Igi Llaima** (☎363 100), **Unión del Sur** (☎363 045), **Jote Be** (☎363 037 or 322 881), and **Buses ERS** (☎322 356). Routes and rates are similar, but shop around to find times that best suit your schedule.

Terminal Rodoviario, Sor Vicenta 2051 (☎363 066). *Colectivos* run to the terminal and back from the Plaza de Armas (5-10min., CH$250). Or catch a bus heading north on Villagrán. Buses go to: **Angol** (1¼hr., 9 per day 9am-9:30pm, CH$900); **Chillán** (1¾hr.; M-Sa 13 per day 7:30am-9:30pm, Su 10 per day 8:45am-9:30pm; CH$1600); **Concepción** (1¾hr., 29 per day 7:40am-10pm, CH$1850); **Osorno** (6hr.; 10, 11:45am, 1:50, 11pm; CH$4000); **Puerto Montt** (7½hr.;

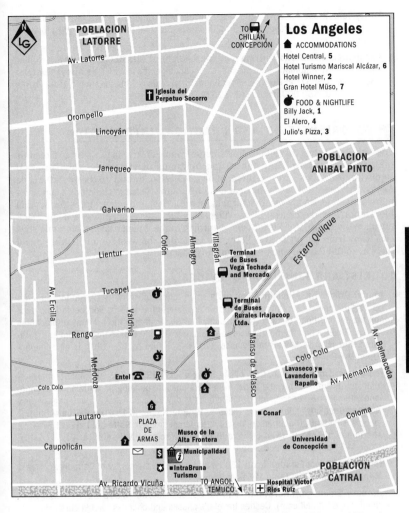

10, 11:45am, 1:50, 11pm; CH$4500); **Santiago** (7hr., every hr. 8am-3:30pm and 11pm-1am, CH$3000); **Temuco** (2½hr., 20-23 per day 7:30am-11pm; CH$2500).

Terminal de Buses Vega Techada, San José 146 (☎324 080), on Villagrán, at the eastern end of Tucapel. Goes to **Salto del Laja** (1½hr., every 30min. 5am-8pm, CH$600). Last bus returns to Los Angeles at 8:10pm.

Terminal de Buses Rurales Islajacoop Ltda., Villagrán 501 (☎313 232 or 315 128; fax 315 128), at corner of Rengo, to the right of the Más supermarket. Buses go to **El Abanico** (1½hr.; M-Sa 8:30, 11:30am, 1:30, 5:30, 7:15pm; Su 8, 10am, 3, 7:15pm; CH$1000) and **Antuco** (1hr.; M-F 8 per day 7:15am-7:45pm, Sa 6 per day 9am-7:15pm, Su 7:15, 10am, 3, 7:15pm).

Tur-Bus Terminal, Sor Vicenta 2061 (☎363 136). Buses go to **Santiago** (8hr.; every 30min. 8:45am-4:15pm, CH$4500-5000; overnight buses 10:45, 11:15, 11:20, 11:30, 11:45pm; CH$9900-16,900) and **Temuco** (2¼hr., every 30min. 6:20am-8:15pm, CH$2500).

Taxis/Colectivos: *Colectivos* and taxis can be found around the bus terminal and the Plaza de Armas. *Colectivos* CH$250 within town. Call **Taxi Rengo** (☎321 226) for door-to-door service.

Car Rental: InterBruna Turismo rents cars starting at CH$30,000 per day, including insurance. No automatic transmission cars. For one of those, call **Luis Arroyo González** (☎099 889 5857) at Nueva Beeper Andes, who rents out his automatic 1992 Toyota Corolla for CH$30,000 per day (CH$25,000 per day if rented out for a week).

■ ■ 🔧 ORIENTATION AND PRACTICAL INFORMATION

Los Angeles sits just off Ruta 5, the Panamericana. **Sor Vicenta** leads away from this major thoroughfare, first depositing busloads of visitors at the Terminal Rodoviario and then carrying them, in bus, *colectivo*, or taxi, to the city's **Plaza de Armas** (the street becomes **Almagro** heading south). **Colón** is the city's main commercial avenue, lined with restaurants, pharmacies, and other stores for several blocks north of the central plaza. **Villagrán,** a block east of Almagro, heads back north, merging into Sor Vicenta and returning to the Panamericana. **Alemania** goes east away from the plaza (it is known as **Lautaro** to the west) and will take you all the way to the Parque Nacional Laguna del Laja.

TOURIST AND FINANCIAL SERVICES

Tourist Office: The **Municipalidad** has a small tourist office at its Libertador Bernardo O'Higgins building, at Caupolicán and Colón. Talk to the staff person behind the desk on the second floor, outside the museum. They supply maps and an array of brochures on Los Angeles and the nearby scenic attractions. Open M-F 8:15am-1:45pm and 2:45-5pm. **Conaf,** José Manso de Velasco 275 (☎321 086 or 321 130), is also helpful. Open M-F 8am-2pm.

Tours: InterBruna Turismo, Caupolicán 350 (☎313 812; fax 325 925; interbruna@hotmail.com), further down the street from the Municipal building. In addition to national and international services, InterBruna offers full-day tours in the region with English- and German-speaking guides. Tours include: **Parque Nacional Laguna del Laja** (min. 2 people; CH$14,000 per person, discount for larger groups); **Salto del Laja** (CH$7000); the mines of **Lota** (CH$24,500); and **Parque Nacional Nahuelbuta** (CH$17,500). Open M-F 9am-1:30pm and 3-8pm, Sa 9am-2pm.

Bank/ATM: BancoEstado, Colón 160 (☎314 120), on the corner of Caupolicán. Has a **24hr. Redbanc ATM.** Open M-F 9am-2pm.

Currency Exchange: InterBruna Turismo, Caupolicán 350 (☎313 812; fax 325 925; interbruna@hotmail.com). Cashes traveler's checks and changes foreign currency.

Work Opportunities: For detailed information on the following positions, see **Alternatives to Tourism,** p. 83.

Restaurant El Alero, Colo Colo 235 (☎320 058), hires waiters and kitchen helpers between Nov. and Mar.

Hotel y Hostería Salto del Laja (☎321 706 or 313 956; fax 313 996), in Salto del Laja, needs waiters, cooks, receptionists, laundry washers, and other staff for its hotel and restaurant during the summer.

LOCAL SERVICES

Library: Biblioteca Pública Roberto Espinoza, Caupolicán 399 (☎408 641), 1st fl. of the Municipalidad building. Open M-F 8am-7:45pm, Su 9am-1pm.

Market: The city's **Mercado,** located around the Terminal de Buses Vega Techada, sells fruit, vegetables, and handicrafts, and houses a range of cheap eateries. Open 8am-8pm. You can find people hawking ultra-cheap caps, candy, and other goods near the intersection of Rengo and Villagrán.

Laundromat: Lavaseco y Lavandería Rapallo, Alemania 355 (☎326 222).

EMERGENCY AND COMMUNICATIONS

Police: The *carabineros* have their office at Colón 108 (☎312 595), near the plaza.

Late-Night Pharmacy: Salcobrand, Colón 412 (☎327 542), near the corner of Colón and Colo-Colo. Open 9am-11pm.

Hospital: Hospital Víctor Ríos Ruíz, Ricardo Vicuña 147 (☎409 600), at the corner of Los Carreras.

Telephones: Entel, Colo-Colo 460-B (☎323 333).

Internet Access: Zona Internet, Colón 482, Local 70 (☎/fax 345 445; www.zonainternet.cl; cybercafe@zonainternet.cl), inside the Edificio España mall, up the ramp walkway to the 2nd fl. and at the end of the hallway. M-F CH$800 per hr., Sa CH$600 per hr. Faxes in Chile CH$250 per page. Open M-Sa 9am-10pm.

Post Office: Correos, Caupolicán 460 (☎321 041), on the southern edge of the Plaza de Armas. **Western Union** wire service available. Open M-F 9am-7pm, Sa 9am-1pm.

▐ ACCOMMODATIONS

In one way, Los Angeles seems to imitate its famous sister on the northern half of the globe: those with thick wallets get to stay at the glitzy hotels where they can guzzle *pisco sours* at the bar, while the rest of the plebeians make do with *residenciales* at a distance from the leafy central plaza. Nevertheless, Los Angeles does have a dearth of mid-range accommodations—and the better hotels are not really worth the prices. In fact, many hotels have sprung up along the Panamericana, ensuring that tourists have a clear path to the Salto del Laja without having to set foot in the city at all.

Gran Hotel Müso, Valdivia 222 (☎313 183; fax 312 768; www.hotelmuso.cl; gerenciap@entlchile.net), on the western edge of the Plaza de Armas. The rooms won't blow you away, but they're perfectly comfortable and you might dig the array of neon in the hotel lounge. Perks include cable TV, laundry service, and free private parking. Breakfast included. Reservations recommended 2 days before arrival during the summer. Singles CH$27,500, for foreigners with IVA discount CH$22,000; doubles CH$36,000/CH$28,800; triples CH$50,500/CH$44,100. Discount for stays on weekend nights: 20% if paying in cash, 5% if paying with credit card. AmEx/MC/V. ❹

Hotel Winner, Rengo 126 (☎343 040 or 099 422 4403), between Villagrán and Almagro on the south side of the street. It's hard to find—look for the salmon-pink building without any signs. For the price, though, it's worth the trouble, with big beds in five spacious rooms and aging but clean bathrooms offering brief spurts of hot water. There is no heating in the rooms, but they face a wood-burning stove in the adjacent TV room. Breakfast included. Reservations recommended 1-2 days before stay. If traveling alone, call ahead to see if they have rooms to spare; you might be able to get a double room for half the price. Doubles CH$14,000, with private bath CH$16,000. ❷

Hotel Turismo Mariscal Alcázar, Lautaro 385 (☎/fax 311 725; www.hotelalcazar.cl; reservasalcazar@hotelalcazar.cl), near the Plaza de Armas. Considering the sparkling finery of the reception area and lounge, the rooms here are a bit of a letdown, with cheap wooden furniture, worn hardwood floors, and small TVs. Still, if comfortable lodging is what you want, this is the place to find it. Along with the well-stocked minibar, guests get a free *pisco sour*, courtesy of the hotel. Central heating, free parking, cable TV, and small fans available in summer. Breakfast included. Reservations recommended 2 days before stay. Singles CH$30,720-34,920 with IVA discount for foreigners; doubles CH$38,640-44,470; triples CH$49,670. AmEx/MC/V. ❺

Hotel Central, Almagro 377 (☎323 381), between Lautaro and Colo-Colo. More than 60 years old, this worn-faced hotel has 25 rooms, all with shared bathrooms. Above the sagging mattresses are kitschy landscape paintings, and the wooden night stands are decorated with stickers. No TV or phones in rooms. Heating available through the paraffin-burning stoves. Laundry services available. Singles CH$5000; doubles CH$7000-8000; triples CH$8000-10,000. ❷

◨ FOOD

Los Angeles prides itself on its hearty traditional fare—*empanadas* stuffed with beef, tenderly grilled *parrilladas*, and *pollonas* (boiled chicken served with *papas fritas* and fried eggs). For cheaper food, head out to the **Mercado,** where you'll find *empanadas* galore (CH$300-400), along with other typical dishes like *porotos* (beans; CH$1200) and various *cazuelas* (stews; CH$1500). The market stays bustling from 8am to 8pm.

▨ **El Alero,** Colo-Colo 235 (☎320 058), between Almagro and Villagrán, with a huge sign protruding into the street. This restaurant serves up hearty *parrilladas* (CH$3050) and *braseros* (CH$3900). If you don't want to gorge yourself on so much red meat, there are smaller (and cheaper) *ofertas*—try the *pollo asado* with a side dish, bread, and a drink (CH$1200). There's not much in the way of vegetarian options, though you could try the cream of asparagus soup (*crema de espàrragos*; CH$500) or the salads (CH$500-1200). Open M-Sa noon-3:30pm and 8pm-1am. ❷

Julio's Pizza, Colón 452 (☎314 530), between Rengo and Mendoza, with a lit-up Cristal Beer sign. This sit-down pizzeria features a variety of delicious, large pies (individual portions CH$2300-4200) including the *Piña* (mozzarella, pineapple, cream, and *marrasquinos*), the *Cabecitas de Espárragos* (mozzarella, ham, asparagus heads, and tomato), and the *Marinera* (mozzarella, *mariscos*, and tomato). The *champiñones* pizza (mushrooms, mozzarella, and tomato) is the one vegetarian option. They also serve sandwiches (CH$600-3000), grilled meat *parrilladas* (CH$3200-8200), and soups (CH$600-650). Open M-Sa 9am-1am, Su 11:30am-midnight. AmEx/MC/V. ❷

Billy Jack, Colón 592 (☎320 594), on the corner of Colón and Tucapel. An intriguing cross between an order-and-go fast-food joint and a sit-down family restaurant. Patrons sit at nicer-than-usual wooden tables and chairs in front of a big-screen TV, but there's no service and they order from a lit-up menu displaying a smiling bull wearing a cowboy hat. Choose from a variety of value meals, as low as CH$890 for a hamburger with mayo and salsa, plus a drink. Or order separately from the three fast-food groups: hamburgers (CH$770-1250), *churrascos* (CH$480-750), and pizzas (CH$980-1400). Open 9am-9pm. AmEx/MC/V. ❶

◎ SIGHTS

In 2000 and 2002, the city of Los Angeles embarked on an ambitious overhaul of its central plaza, whose traditional layout, punctuated by four palm trees, had been the city's public face since the 1920s. Some 533 million pesos later, the Plaza de Armas has been resurrected—this time, as the **Plaza de Armas Libertador Bernardo O'Higgins,** a splendid, strikingly modern space, where the usual army of plaza trees joins broad stone walkways and tall steel arches, elegant in their simplicity. As a nod to the plaza's willed modernity, it even offers wheelchair-accessible ramps—not something often stumbled upon in southern Chile. The very center of the square, where various stone paths cross a ring of water and converge, represents the union and intermingling of the Mapuche and Spanish cultures. The seven fountains that surround it symbolize the seven rivers of the region that have given sustenance to its civilization. At night, some of the arches and palm trees are lit with blue and green Christmas lights—a touch that makes for a pleasant evening stroll.

Other than the plaza, Los Angeles's other attraction is its **Museo de la Alta Frontera,** located on the second floor of the Municipalidad's building at Caupolicán 399, on the northeast corner of the plaza. Along with a disturbing collection of taxidermied animals and a cache of foreign rifles used on the frontier, the museum showcases a resplendent array of Mapuche silver jewelry. The various necklaces, belts, and headbands were all meticulously wrought by hand, with their intricate interlocking loops and decorative tassels forming lustrous scales, almost like armor. A photo on the wall of the exhibition room shows Mapuche women bedecked in the jewelry, looking almost like old-school rap stars. The museum showcases painting and photography by local artists and also has a room devoted to obligatory Bernardo O'Higgins paraphernalia. (☎408 641. Open M-F 8:15am-1:45pm and 2:45-6:30pm. Free.)

NEAR LOS ANGELES

SALTOS DEL LAJA

Crowned by the largest waterfall in Chile, the Saltos del Laja thunder with a vengeance through a tree-ringed gorge 27km north of Los Angeles. Here, the broad width of the Río Laja uncoils from a 50m precipice, its marbled white waters angrily licking the cliff edge until they descend into a torrent of foam and mist. Visitors can walk close to the waterfall on a flat stone plane in front of the Salto Principal right into the churning remnants of its impact (signs pointedly tell you not to bathe in the water, but you can get close enough to feel soft nettles of mist slap you on the cheek). A concrete walkway winds its way along one edge of the waterfall, giving visitors expansive vistas of the wide skirt of cascading water, as well as ring-side seats for an equally entrancing performance: the momentary materialization of the most exquisite rainbows from the cloak of mist that hangs over the water. (Be careful on the concrete steps; the fine mist makes them wet and slippery at all times.)

If you're looking to splurge, a great place to spend that extra cash is at the ◙**Hotel y Hostería Salto del Laja ❸,** at Panamericana Km. 480, situated right on the Isla de la Laja. Many rooms have stunning views of the white-shrouded silhouette of the Salto Principal. The hotel permits horseback riding on its 35 hectares of island property featuring 50 species of trees and a pool with river water in which to bathe. (☎321 706 or 313 956; fax 313 996. Central heating, free parking, TV. Breakfast included. With views of falls: singles CH$32,000-40,000; doubles CH$40,000-48,000; triples CH$49,000; suites for 2 people CH$40,000; 3 people CH$49,000; 4 people CH$56,000. Without views of falls: *cabañas* for 2 people CH$25,000; 3 people CH$32,000; 4 people CH$40,000. IVA tax discounted for foreigners. 25% discount off-season. AmEx/MC/V.) For fine dining, try the **hotel's restaurant ❸.** Feast on salmon (CH$4800) or trout (CH$4200) while taking in the view of the falls. The French onion soup is a savory vegetarian option for CH$2100. (Open 8am-midnight. AmEx/MC/V.)

If you decide not to shell out the big bucks, there are countless **campsites** and *cabañas* along the road that passes by the Saltos del Laja. However, you can save some money and pitch a tent right on the lip of the Salto Principal. **Parque Salto de Laja ❶** offers **camping** with picnic tables, a fire pit, and hot-water baths, at a prime location along the Río Laja before it drops on the rocks. Spacious 5-person **cabañas** with kitchens and private baths are also available here. (From the Salto Principal, walk uphill on the dirt road away from the falls until you see the sign for the campgrounds. ☎ 099 354 1255. Campsites available Dec.-March CH$8000 per site for up to 6 people. CH$6000 per site off-season. Daytrippers can picnic for CH$700 per person. *Cabañas* CH$15,000-20,000. Rental of wooden shacks with 4 mattresses and electricity CH$8000-12,000.)

To get to the Saltos Del Laja, take a Jote Be bus heading north from Los Angeles' Terminal de Buses Vega Techada (see **Transportation,** p. 196). The falls are also easily accessible by car—they're a half-hour drive north on the Panamericana. Take the turnoff that says "Salto del Laja," about 1km before the falls. (Cars CH$400 to enter.) The entrance to the Salto Principal walkway is a bit hidden; it's to the left of the **Feria Artesenal Stall** which sells wooden carvings and other souvenirs.

PARQUE NACIONAL LAGUNA DEL LAJA

As bodies of water go, this one is rather small, but what makes ◼**Laguna del Laja** special is its location—the lake is nestled among prickly Andes peaks at the base of the majestic **Volcán Antuco,** a 2820m slumbering giant wrapped in a mantle of snow. Besides gentle ripples along its surface caused by the wind, the Laguna is eerily motionless, the snow banks on its edges imposing an otherworldly silence. Decades ago, the waters of the lake crept up to a concrete barrier planted a few hundred meters away, but the damming of the Río Laja, which feeds into the *laguna*, has drained away a significant portion of its volume. Still, the paths that run through the surrounding park are long enough to provide a full day of hiking and plenty of visual stimulation.

AT A GLANCE	
AREA: 11,880 hectares.	**HIGHLIGHTS:** Laguna Laja, its namesake river, and Sierra Velluda. Diverse flora and fauna including mountain cypress, *coigüe* trees, and nearly 50 species of birds.
CLIMATE: The temperature tends to be cool, ranging from 13.6°C in Jan. to as low as 0°C in Aug.	
CAMPING: Campsites in Sector Lagunillas (CH$5000 per site). *Cabañas* CH$25,000.	**FEES:** Entrance fee CH$700, children CH$300.

◼ **ORIENTATION.** The two main parts of the park are **Sector Los Pangues, Sector Lagunillas,** and **Sector Chacay.** Popular park activities include skiing on the volcano slopes or climbing the two largest peaks in the vicinity—the volcano itself, a rather straightforward ascent, or the much deadlier **Sierra Velluda,** whose twin peaks measure 3200m and 3500m, respectively. The latter can only be ascended during the winter, when a bridge of ice forms to allow passage up to the mountain summit. However, only 4WD vehicles can reach the *laguna* during the winter, and even with superior traction, there are no guarantees on the treacherous mountain road. Arrive well-prepared for the ascent—several climbers have died on Sierra Velluda's treacherous slopes. Besides the towering peaks of the Volcán Antuco and Sierra Velluda, a series of muscular hills roll out along the lake's perimeter, their slopes bearing a short stubble of pine trees.

⌁ TRANSPORTATION. To get to Laguna del Laja, your best bet is to get your hands on a car—preferably one with sturdy tires and a good set of shocks, as the road becomes a rock-strewn dirt path 5km east of Antuco (23km from the park entrance). Beware of falling rocks and the blinding clouds of dust that form behind passing cars. **Buses** run as far as El Abanico, 8km from the park entrance and a 6km hike from the *laguna* (see **Transportation,** p. 196).

☷ PRACTICAL INFORMATION. At the park entrance, **Sector Los Pangues,** you'll be charged an admission fee of CH$700 for adults, CH$300 for children. (☎ 321 086. Park office open June-Sept. 8:30am-9pm; Oct.-May 8:30am-6pm; last entry 2pm.) **Conaf rangers** offer tours for larger groups from this point. The dirt road from the entrance continues to the volcano and the lagoon, passing by scenic viewpoints and the **information center** at Chacay (3km from the entrance). Here, you can see the sunlight glinting off the silvery skin of the Río Laja, its white foamy rapids just a murmur in the distance. The road then winds its way up along the mountains until it reaches the **Centro de Esquí Antuco,** a small ski center along the northern slope of the volcano. The skiing is pretty basic—drag lifts take visitors 1800m up to an expert slope or 600m up to the beginner's slope. The view is breathtaking, with mountains stretching out on all sides. (Ski Center Office in Los Angeles ☎ 322 651. Open end of June/beginning of July until mid-Sept. Lift tickets weekends CH$10,000, weekdays CH$7000. Ski rental CH$10,000. Ski lessons CH$12,000 per hr. No snowboard rentals, although snowboards are permitted on the slopes.)

⌂ ACCOMMODATIONS. A kilometer from the dirt road you'll find **Sector Lagunillas,** where campsites and *cabañas* are located. There are 22 **campsites ❷** in a tree-shaded valley near the Río Laja, which offer electricity, grills, and bathrooms with showers. Hot water only available during the summer; the rest of the year it's "tepid." (Camping CH$5000 per site.) Four double-level *cabañas,* each with five beds (1 matrimonial), kitchens with fridges and stoves, and bathrooms with hot-water showers, are available. They are heated by wood-burning stoves or gas-burning space heaters. (Reservations recommended a week in advance between Jan. and Mar., 1 day in advance in July. 6-person *cabañas* CH$25,000.) The campgrounds also have a **24hr. market,** which stocks food, drinks, toiletries, and other basic goods. For information or reservations, call **Conaf** (☎ 321 086).

⌗ HIKING. One of the most popular treks is the circuit from the western edge of the *laguna* along its rock edge to its southern tip in **Sector Los Barros,** 32km from the park entrance (5-8hr.). But don't plan on staying there—the military base at Los Barros is not particularly hospitable and the soldiers will only lend you a cot if you get stranded there because of heavy snow. From there, the path around the *laguna* continues onto a mountain pass into Argentine Paso Pichachén, another 29km down. It's too cold to swim in Laguna del Laja, even in the summertime, but you'll probably feel inclined just to sit down at its rocky edge and absorb the beauty of the landscape.

For those looking for something a little less rigorous than the full loop, there are several shorter hikes that follow the Río Laja up to the majestic falls of Chilcas and Torbellinos (2-4hr.). Of course, there is the opposite extreme, which includes the ascents of Volcán Antuco and Sierra Velluda.

MIDDLE CHILE

ANGOL   ☎ 45

Although it is the capital of the province of Malleco, Angol (pop. 50,000) has the feel of a sleepy border town, where on any given Sunday the only souls you'll find on the streets are shaggy stray dogs. The city was founded by Pedro de Valdivia in 1553, and was razed six times by disgruntled Mapuche before the settlement finally took root. Most people here work in the forestry industry, exploiting the region's sprawling forests of pine trees, and most tourists come here (if they come at all) to bike on the *araucaria*-lined trails of Parque Nacional Nahuelbuta, three kilometers to the west.

▐ TRANSPORTATION

Buses: Terminal Rodovario, Caupolicán 200 (☎ 711 854), a block north of the Plaza de Armas, is owned by Buses Thiele, so don't be surprised when they answer the information number. **Tur-Bus** (☎ 711 655) goes to: **Los Angeles** (1¼hr.; 8:30am, 10, 11pm; CH$900, 10pm bus CH$1200); **Puerto Montt** (8hr., 8am and 10:55pm, CH$4800); **Santiago** (8hr.; 8:30am, 10, 11pm; CH$4800, with bed CH$8000); **Temuco** (2¼hr., 8am and 10:55pm, CH$1400). **Buses Bío Bío** (☎ 711 777) goes to: **Concepción** (3¼hr.; 16 per day 6:30am-7:30pm; CH$2500, students CH$2100); Los Angeles (1¼hr.; 7per day 7am-7pm; CH$900, students CH$700); **Temuco** (2¼hr.; 26 per day 6am-8pm; CH$900, students CH$700).

Taxis/Colectivos: Taxis anywhere in the city cost CH$1500. *Colectivos* run throughout the city, many of them passing down Lautaro, by the central plaza, along O'Higgins and then back again. CH$200, 9pm-midnight CH$250, midnight-7am CH$300.

Car Rental: Turismo Christopher (see **Tours,** below) rents cars starting at CH$25,000 per day. Insurance included. Must be 18+ and show valid driver's license. Jeeps CH$60,000. Manual transmission only.

✦ ⁊ ORIENTATION AND PRACTICAL INFORMATION

Angol is located between Los Angeles (60km) and Temuco (145km), 34km down a turnoff on the Panamericana. It is split in two by the **Río Vergara,** and across its muddy expanse is a sturdy bridge (Puente Vergara) connecting the city center with the outerlying stretches of the city. Surrounding the heart of the city, around the **Plaza de Armas Benjamín Vicuña Mackenna,** and especially along **Lautaro,** you'll find many of the city's shops, banks, and restaurants.

Tourist Office: Oficina de Turismo, Lado Puente Vergara 1, Edificio Cena Chile (☎/fax 201 571; contactour@hotmail.com), next to O'Higgins, on the end furthest from the Plaza de Armas. The helpful staff offers maps of the city and brochures for tourist sites throughout the region. Some English spoken. Open M-F 8:30am-1pm and 2:30-6:30pm. **Conaf,** Prat 191 (☎/fax 711 870 or 712 328; hlucero@conaf.cl), 2nd fl. of the Ministerio de Agricultura building, southeast corner of the Plaza de Armas. Provides glossy maps of Parque Nacional Nahuelbuta and other information about the region's parks. Open M-F 9am-2pm.

Tours: Turismo Christopher, Ilabaca 421 (☎ 715 156; christop@entelchile.net), down the street from Banco de Chile. Offers tours of local sites, including Parque Nacional Conquillío, the Siete Lagos, and various indigenous locales (starting at CH$35,000 per person). Open M-F 9:30am-2pm and 4-9pm.

Currency Exchange: Turismo Christopher (see **Tours,** above) cashes traveler's checks and changes US, Argentine, Australian, Canadian and European currencies.

Bank/ATM: Banco de Chile, Lautaro 02 (☎712 746), on the corner with Ilabaca, has a **24hr. Redbanc ATM.** Open M-F 9am-2pm.

Police: Dieciocho 340 (☎711 124), between Tucapel and Coihüe.

Pharmacy: Farmacia Ahuile, Lautaro 20 (☎711 828), between Sepúlveda and Ilabaca. Open M-F 9:30am-9pm, Sa 9:30am-1:30pm. If they are not open, a sign on the door will tell you where to go.

Hospital: Hospital Mauricio Heyerman, Ilabaca 752 (☎711 001), between Covadonga and Jarpa.

Internet Access: ISS Computación, Ilabaca 347 (☎718 330), between Prat and Lautaro. CH$800 per hr. Open 9:30am-1:30pm and 3:30-10:30pm.

Post Office: Lautaro 202 (☎716 232), alongside the Plaza de Armas. Open M-F 9am-1pm and 3-6:30pm, Sa 9am-12:30pm.

■ ACCOMMODATIONS

Decent accommodations are, for some reason, hard to find in Angol. Some of the city's more luxurious hotels have faded in recent years, becoming quite bland, and the smaller establishments, while cheap, tend to have a rather dismal appearance. There are, however, a few options that rise above the sea of mediocrity.

Hotel Restaurant Club Social Angol, Caupolicán 498 (☎711 103; fax 712 269; csahotel@entelchile.net), down the street from the Municipalidad. This building is actually devoted to the city's exclusive social club, but it has 9 rooms that it lets out to the public. The rooms are quite comfortable, if somewhat sterile, with decent beds and hot-water showers. Plus, you're welcome to shoot some pool in the game room or even enjoy a round of bowling. Cable TV, laundry, outdoor pool, private parking. Breakfast in bed included. Reservations recommended during summer. Singles CH$15,900, with larger beds CH$19,200; doubles CH$19,900/CH$23,500. AmEx/MC/V. ❹

Hostal El Vergel (☎712 103), on the grounds of the agricultural institute of El Vergel, 5km south of downtown. At the entrance to the school grounds, go down the dirt road and turn left at the fork; the hostel is on your left after a sharp bend in the road. This old house set within Vergel's leafy shade is more than a century old. Among the hostel's 7 rooms, the singles are cramped—there's barely enough space for the bed, much less you—but the larger doubles are quite pleasant, with views of the extensive grounds. TV, laundry, private parking. Breakfast included. Reservations recommended during summer. Singles CH$8000, Apr.-Oct. CH$6000; doubles CH$16,000/CH$14,000, with private bath CH$18,000/CH$16,000; suites with private bath CH$22,000/CH$20,000. Dec.-Feb. MC/V; off-season cash only. ❸

Residencial Olimpia, Caupolicán 625 (☎711 162), down the street from the Club Social, heading away from the bus terminal. The owner of this 9-room *residencial* once ran the Hotel Angol, near the Plaza de Armas, during its more luxurious days. Now however, her lodgings are much more modest—spartan rooms within hardwood floors and spongy mattresses, lit by naked light bulbs and tiny lamps. The bathrooms are a bit dismal and there's no heat in the rooms themselves, but the budget price should warm you up. Private parking and kitchen access. Breakfast included. Singles, doubles, and triples with shared bath CH$6000 per person. ❷

◗ FOOD

You'll find quite a few hole-in-the-wall restaurants along the main streets around the Plaza de Armas, but don't expect much in the way of fine dining.

Hotel Restaurant Club Social Angol (see **Accommodations**, p. 205). This small dining room tucked in Angol's social club makes a half-hearted attempt at elegance—the brass chandeliers have mismatched bulbs, while the oil paintings on the walls look somewhat out of place above a floor of drab wooden tiles. Still, the food here is quite decent and just down the hall is a pleasant, softly-lit bar. The specialties include a hearty *filete a la plancha* (CH$3950) and *guatitas a la española* (beef tripe doused in a tomato sauce; CH$2200). Soups CH$750-3200, salads CH$500-2450, fish and shellfish CH$2900-9900, *carne* CH$1900-5950. Open noon-3pm and 8pm-midnight. Bar open M-Sa noon-1am, Su noon-midnight. ❸

Hostería El Vergel (☎712 103), on the grounds of the Institute near the Hostal Vergel (see **Accommodations**, p. 205). The sunny dining room has a bank of windows that overlook a garden. Here you'll find your usual Chilean staples of meat and fish, simply but deliciously done; lunch specials are a good value (soup, entree, and dessert CH$1800). The chocolate flan, topped with Oreo cookie bits, is especially scrumptious (CH$400). Open 9:30am-7:30pm. Dec.-Feb. MC/V; Mar.-Nov. cash only. ❶

Lomito'n, Lautaro 145 (☎717 675), between J. Sepulveda and Chorrillos. The bolted-down chairs and tables and photos of smiling customers may be a little tacky, but the food is reasonable for lack of more gourmet options. All of the sandwiches are smeared with *palta*, the mashed avocado sauce that Chileans are so crazy about. Combination meals CH$1290-1990. Open M-Th 10am-8pm, F-Sa 10am-8:30pm, Su noon-8:30pm. AmEx/MC/V. ❶

🄶 SIGHTS

Angol's most beautiful locale **El Vergel,** is actually 5km from the city center. The thickly wooded campus of an agricultural institute is run by the Methodist Church. Spread across the peaceful grounds are an array of trees from all across the Americas, including various species of *araucaria* (the Monkey Puzzle tree), cypress, and conifers. Down a short dirt road from the entrance are El Vergel's *hostal* and *hostería* (see **Food** and **Accommodations,** above); a little further down you'll find the **Escuela Agrícola El Vergel,** across a grove of towering pines. Inside the school is the **Museo Dillman Bullock,** a museum dedicated to a US-born agricultural specialist who settled down in Chile and served as director of the school. Bullock's eclectic interests in anthropology and archaeology are reflected in the museum, which features fascinating exhibits on the Kofkeche indigenous people who lived in the region more than 800 years ago. The other exhibits range from Mapuche artifacts to a taxidermy display with preserved animals and an authentic mummy. *(To get to El Vergel, take colectivo no. 2 from the Plaza de Armas or from anywhere along Lautaro or O'Higgins heading across Puente Vergara away from the city center—the last stop is El Vergel. Museum ☎711 142 or 712 395; fax 719 303; elvergel@ctcinternet.cl. Open M-F 9:30am-7pm, Sa-Su 10am-7pm. CH$450, children 6-12 CH$200.)*

There's rather little to see or do in downtown Angol, but you might want to take a stroll in the city's rather attractive **Plaza de Armas Benjamín Vicuña Mackenna.** The cosmopolitan selection of trees include a magnolia, a Lawson cypress, and a Lebanese cedar, and there is a lovely pool at the center, surrounded by four marble statues. These four statues are supposed to symbolize the four continents of Asia, Europe, Africa, and the Americas, but instead are hilarious, stereotypical representations of those cultures. If you've had enough of the grass-skirted, feather-headdress-wearing American statue and her iguana, move on to **Parroquía y Convento Buenaventura,** Vergara 825, on the corner of Vergara and Covadonga. Built in 1863 by the Franciscan Order, it is the oldest surviving church in the area. The light pink exterior is topped by a soft yellow wooden steeple bearing a metal cross. The interior is filled by worn pews, stained-glass windows and carved wooden saints. *(☎711 216. Church office open Tu-Sa 9:30am-2:30pm and 3:30-7pm. Free.)*

PARQUE NACIONAL NAHUELBUTA

As Chile's parks go, Parque Nacional Nahuelbuta is one of the smallest, a mere 6832 hectares of land, whose longest hike takes just two and a half hours to complete. But therein lies its advantage—it's only an hour to the **Piedra del Aguila**, a 1379m high granite hilltop where you can take in the whole breadth of Chile, from ocean to Andes, and even glimpse the snow-capped peak of Volcán Villarrica to the far south. Nahuelbuta boasts vast stretches of *araucaria*, the Monkey Puzzle Tree, which are curious, disheveled-looking columns of living wood that sport spiky wigs of bristles. Their English name supposedly derives from the apparent difficulty any monkey would have climbing them. The oldest of these are said to have lived over two millennia. These trees used to cover all the coastal mountains, but most of the population has been all but decimated by the region's timber industry. Nahuelbuta is a good place to relax, savor nature's beauty, and avoid the stampeding hordes of tourists at other, larger parks during the summer.

AT A GLANCE	
AREA: 6832 hectares. **CLIMATE:** Temperate; visit between Nov.-May for optimal conditions. **FEATURES:** Piedra del Aguila and Cerro Anay. **FEES:** Entrance fee CH$2000.	**HIGHLIGHTS:** A view of the whole breadth of Chile from Piedra del Aguila. Diverse flora and fauna including Monkey Puzzle and *coigüe* trees, and the *chilote* fox. **CAMPING:** At the Centro de Información (CH$5500 per site).

ORIENTATION. The warmer months from Nov. to May are the best times to visit Nahuelbuta, and in Nov. and Dec. the forests are alive with blooming flowers. The best place to get info on the park is at the **Conaf office** in Angol (see **Practical Information,** p. 204), though there is also a **Centro de Información** about 5.5km inside the park (turn left at the fork when walking from the entrance). The Centro is also the main **campground** ❷ for the park and has hot-water showers and toilets. (6-person site CH$5500. Park entrance fee CH$2000, children CH$500.)

TRANSPORTATION. Parque Nacional Nahuelbuta is located 35km west of Angol, up a dirt road. There is public transportation to the park itself only in January and February when **Buses Angol** offers Sunday full-day tours from the Terminal Rural, at the corner of Ilabaca and Lautaro (☎712 021; 1½hr.; 6:45am, returns 6pm; CH$1150, round-trip CH$2300). The buses drop off at the Conaf station where one of the park rangers leads a tour of the park. Visitors should bring food, as there is none available within the park.

Another option is to take a bus from Angol to the town of Vegas Blancas and walk the remaining 7km to the park entrance. Two companies run buses out of the Terminal Rural in Angol: **Buses Angol** (☎712 021; 1hr.; M, W, F 6:45am and 4pm, returning 9am and 6pm; CH$1000) and **Buses Nahuelbuta** (☎714 611; 1hr.; Tu, Th, Sa 6:45am and 4pm, returning 9am and 6pm; CH$1000).

HIKING. The two most popular viewpoints at Parque Nacional Nahuelbuta are the **Piedra del Aguila** (Eagle's Stone) and the **Cerro Anay,** further to the south. A trail leads from the Centro de Información around and up the granite hill known as Piedra del Aguila, passing by ancient *araucaria* and *coigüe* trees before looping back to its point of origin (4.5km, 2hr.). Along the way you should pass by some of the park's larger Monkey Puzzle Trees, more than 50m in height and covered in rich green moss. Their trunks are so thick that it requires eight people clasping hands to encircle just one tree. **Cerro Anay** (1402m) is another hilltop with breathtaking views of the country, and is reached by two trails in succession—**Sendero Estero Los Gringos** (5km, 2½hr.) and then **Sendero Cerro Anay** (0.8km, 30min.), passing through pure forests of *araucaria* and *lenga* trees. If you're lucky on these trails, you might spot one of the park's several species of fox, including the *chilote*, a species from the island of Chiloé that inexplicably found its way here. There are also plenty of woodpeckers to observe along the way.

NORTE CHICO

Lying between the desolate, yet beautiful landscapes of Norte Grande and the bustling urban centers of Middle Chile, Norte Chico is often overlooked by thrill-seeking travelers. Those travelers are missing out. The southern extent of the Atacama desert, vast scrub plains, and a sandy, moist coastline combine to form a fascinating mix of terrain. Pristine white-sand beaches lie surrounded by eerie, rugged landscapes, cloudforests hide amidst rolling fog banks in the barren plains, and soaring volcanoes hurl themselves skyward at the edges of glistening-white salt plains.

Travelers who skip over this region also bypass an intriguing fusion of human influences. The scrawled remnants of ancient peoples who inhabited the land thousands of years ago can still be found on cave walls and rocky outcroppings. More recently, Norte Chico has been home to the celebrated poet and its Nobel Laureate, Gabriela Mistral. The region is equally famed for its potent *pisco* and crystal clear skies that have inspired the construction of some of the largest observatories in the world. This mixture of ancient prowess and booming modernity has created a quirky, yet spiritual way of life in tune with both the technological developments and the balance of energies in the region.

Ovalle is the first major city north of Santiago; most travelers, however, tend to head right to **La Serena.** More than just a convenient jumping-off point replete with amenities, the city offers some of the most inspiring churches in Chile and an up-and-coming beach resort strip. **Vicuña,** to the west, is the home town of Gabriela Mistral. The vast plains around this town are populated by several enormous international telescopes and the largest *pisco* plant in Chile. To really see the true home of *pisco*, though, you have to head to its namesake, **Pisco Elqui.** For a slightly more spiritual experience, trek out to the tiny town of **Cochiguaz** and search out some holistic healing. The little town of **Bahía Inglesa** and **Parque Nacional Pan de Azúcar** harbor stunning beaches, while **Parque Nacional Pingüino de Humboldt** offers a rare opportunity to play with friendly penguins.

HIGHLIGHTS OF NORTE CHICO

GASP in awe at the rare transformation of the desert around **Vallenar** into a striking, flower-filled eden (p. 239).

PILGRIMAGE to the immense **Cross of the Third Millenium** (p. 222) in **Coquimbo** (p. 219) and marvel at this starkly modern religious icon.

CONQUER the grueling slopes of the highest active volcano in the world, **Ojos del Salado,** just outside **Parque Nacional Nevado Tres Cruces** (p. 247).

WANDER through the majestic cloudforests of **Parque Nacional Fray Jorge,** mysteriously nourished by a coastal fog (p. 216).

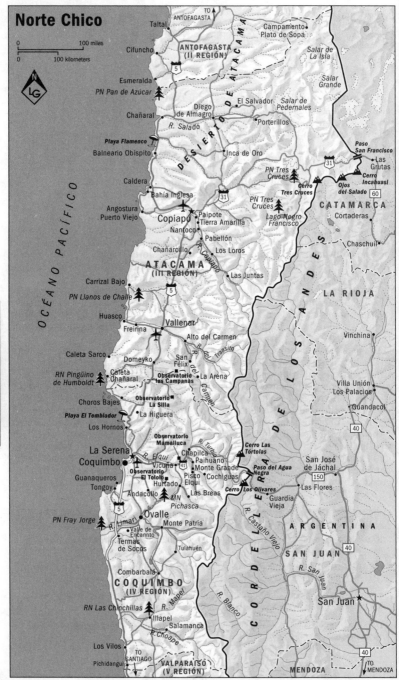

Norte Chico

0 _____ 100 miles
0 _____ 100 kilometers

OCÉANO PACÍFICO

TO ANTOFAGASTA
Taltal
Cifuncho
ANTOFAGASTA (II REGIÓN)
Campamento Plato de Sopa
Salar de La Isla
Salar Grande
Esmeralda
PN Pan de Azúcar
Diego de Almagro
El Salvador
Salar de Pedernales
Chañaral
R. Salado
Porterillos
Playa Flamenco
Balneario Obispo
Inca de Oro
Paso San Francisco
Las Grutas
Cerro Incahuasi
Caldera
PN Tres Cruces
Bahía Inglesa
Cerro Tres Cruces
Ojos del Salado
CATAMARCA
Angostura Puerto Viejo
Copiapó
Paipote
Tierra Amarilla
PN Tres Cruces
Lago Negro Francisco
Cortaderas
Nantoco
Pabellón
Chaschuil
Chañarcillo
Los Loros
ATACAMA (III REGIÓN)
R. Copiapó
Las Juntas
LA RIOJA
Carrizal Bajo
PN Llanos de Challe
Huasco
Freirina
Vallenar
Alto del Carmen
Vinchina
Caleta Sarco
Domeyko
San Félix
R. del Tránsito
La Arena
Villa Unión
Los Palacios
RN Pingüino de Humboldt
Caleta Chañaral
Observatorio las Campanas
R. del Carmen
Guandacol
Choros Bajos
Observatorio La Silla
Playa El Temblador
La Higuera
40
Los Hornos
Observatorio Mamalluca
R. Turbio
Cerro Las Tórtolas
CORDILLERA DE LOS ANDES
La Serena
Coquimbo
Chapilca
Paihuano
San José de Jáchal
Observatorio El Tololo
Vicuña
R. Elqui
Monte Grande
Cochiguas
Paso del Agua Negra
Guanaqueros
Pisco Elqui
150
Tongoy
Hurtado
Las Breas
Cerro Los Olivares
Las Flores
Andacollo
MN Pichasca
Guardia Vieja
PN Fray Jorge
Ovalle
R. Limarí
Monte Patria
ARGENTINA
Valle de Encanto
Termas de Socos
Tulahuén
R. Castaño Viejo
SAN JUAN
Combarbalá
R. San Juan
COQUIMBO (IV REGIÓN)
San Juan
RN Las Chinchillas
R. Mapel
Illapel
Salamanca
R. Choapa
R. Blanco
Los Vilos
TO SANTIAGO
Pichidangui
VALPARAÍSO (V REGIÓN)
MENDOZA
TO MENDOZA

**La Serena &
Ovalle Region**

0   10 miles

0   10 kilometers

NORTH TO LA SERENA

LOS VILOS

About a third of the way up the coast from Viña del Mar towards La Serena, Los Vilos is a nice place to stop for a night or two. There is plenty of affordable lodging, and artisans set up shop in the summer. Like most coastal cities, Los Vilos gets crammed in December and January, but outside of the peak season the town seems to roll happily along.

⌗⑦ TRANSPORTATION AND PRACTICAL INFORMATION. The **bus terminal** is on Allende, by the water. **Buses** arrive from Santiago, Viña del Mar (3 per day), and La Serena. Buses following the Panamericana can drop passengers nearby on the highway, where *colectivos* wait to take passengers to the town center for CH$350. In summer the *municipalidad* runs a **tourist office** on Caupolicán, the main street, near the pier. A **bank** and **pharmacy** are in close proximity.

⌂▢ ACCOMMODATIONS AND FOOD. There are plenty of inexpensive places near the beach to lay your head. The cream of the crop is ▨**Hostal El Conquistador ❸**, Caupolicán 210, at the end of the street near the water, where the pleasant rooms are almost like *cabañas*. The owner makes his guests feel very comfortable, allowing them to cook and do laundry on the premises and even spend time in his home. (☎541 663. Rooms come with private baths and TV. Breakfast included. Singles CH$12,000; doubles CH$18,000; triples CH$24,000.) Cheaper digs are available at **Hotel Bellavista ❷**, Rengo 20, above the *caleta*. Bellavista is near enough to the beach that you can hear the waves crash from the rooms, which are bright if unimaginative. (☎541 073. Breakfast included. Rooms CH$4000 per person, CH$6000 with private bath and TV.) The **Residencial Vienesa ❷**, located in an old home, is also a good deal. (CH$4000, with TV CH$5000.) For a group of four, the best deal is **El Pelusa ❹**, Caupolicán 411, which provides *cabañas* with sea views, living rooms, and kitchenettes. (☎541 041. Breakfast included. One person CH$20,640; two people CH$23,600; three people CH$27,200; four people CH$35,200.) **Hostería Lord Willow ❸**, Hostería 1444, features a pool, parking, and crisp white bedspreads, but it's a tight fit in the rooms for three people. (☎ 541 037. TV and private baths. Singles CH$12,000; doubles or triples CH$18,000.) **Residencial Turismo ❷**, Caupolicán 437, is part of a string of *residenciales* on Caupolicán. There's nothing particularly special about rooms here, but they are a solid option if other places are full. (☎541 176. Singles with shared bath CH$5000; triples with TV and private bath CH$6000 per person.)

There are several good fish restaurants in town. The local favorite is **Alisio ❸**, Caupolicán 298. It is upscale by the town's standards, but the fish is excellent and creatively presented, and the blue walls make the bustle of the street feel far away. (☎542 173. Open M-Sa noon-4pm and 8pm-midnight.) Another local favorite, **El Faro ❷**, Colipí 224, up from the beach off Lautaro, is more down-to-earth. Families sit together here, watching TV. (☎541 190. Entrees average CH$3000. Open daily 10am-10:30pm.) Closer to the waves is **Restaurant Costanera ❶**, Puren 80 (☎541 257). Costanera's wide-open dining area overlooks the *caleta*. (*Menú* CH$1800, conger eel with butter and lemon CH$2600. Credit cards accepted.)

⑤🎵 SIGHTS AND ENTERTAINMENT. Los Vilos has a very small **aquarium** near the sea at Allende 131. It only takes about 10 minutes to peruse the fish swimming in their hazy tanks, but the mounted shellfish are interesting and the guide to the shoreline fauna is instructive. (Open Tu-Su 10:30am-1pm and 3:30-7pm. Free.) In summer, *lanchas* leave from the *caleta*, taking **tours** around the bay to see penguins and sea lion colonies. **El Bodegón** and its attached cafe, **La Bodeguita**, at the end of Caupolicán, have art and music exhibitions and Internet access. There are several pubs and nightclubs in town along Caupolicán and down towards the *caleta*. Try **El Faro** *discoteca*, on Rengo near the beach, or **Barbacos Pub** on the corner of Hostería and Av. Los Vilos, where they advertise all drinks for CH$1000.

OVALLE   ☎53

Perched on the banks of the vigorous Limarí River and calling itself the "Pearl of Limarí," Ovalle (pop. 97,514) is the capital of Limarí province. For a pearl, however, Ovalle is lacking some luster. There isn't much to do in Ovalle itself, but it is a good base from which to explore the surrounding idyllic countryside consisting of fertile valleys overflowing with fruits and vegetables. Produce growers congregate in Ovalle four times a week to sell their crops in the colorful Feria Modelo.

▐ TRANSPORTATION

Buses: Terrapuerto Limarí, on the corner of Maestranza and Balmaceda, services all bus routes through Ovalle. Buses en route to or from **La Serena** stop here. **Tur Bus**

NORTE CHICO

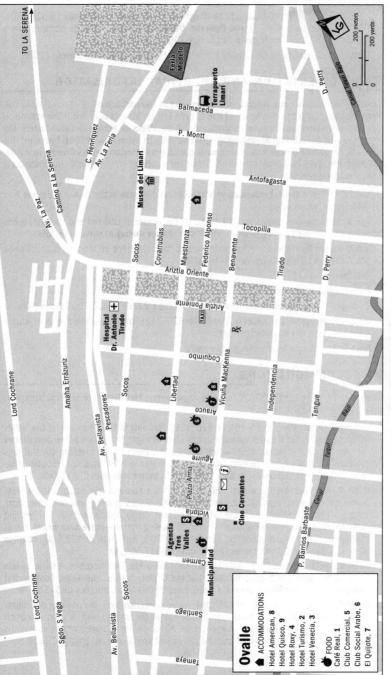

TO LA SERENA

Feria Modelo

Terrapuerto Limari

Balmaceda

P. Montt

C. Henriquez

Av. La Feria

Av. La Paz

Camino a La Serena

Museo del Limari

Antofagasta

9

Socos

Covarrubias

Maestranza

Federico Alfonso

Benavente

Tocopilla

Tirado

D. Perry

Ariztía Oriente

Ariztía Poniente

Hospital Dr. Antonio Tirado

TAXI

Rx

Coquimbo

Vicuña MacKenna

Independencia

Tangue

Lord Cochrane

Amaha Errázuriz

Av. Bellavista

Pescadores

Socos

Libertad

Arauco

4

6

7 8

3

5

Aguirre

Plaza Arma

Victoria

Cine Cervantes

$

i

$

Agencia Tres Valles

2

1

Carmen

Municipalidad

Santiago

Socos

Av. Bellavista

Lord Cochrane

Sgdo. S. Vega

Tamaya

P. Barrios Barbaste

Canal

Tugui

Ingo

Canal Tugui Bajo

D. Perry

N

200 meters
200 yards

Ovalle

ACCOMMODATIONS
Hotel American, 8
Hotel Quisco, 9
Hotel Roxy, 4
Hotel Turismo, 2
Hotel Venecia, 3

FOOD
Café Real, 1
Club Comercial, 5
Club Social Arabe, 6
El Quijote, 7

(☎623 659) has several buses to Santiago (US$7), as does **Tas Choapa** (☎626 820). **Pullman Bus** (☎626 825) and **Pullman Carmelita** (☎631 698) go north to **Arica** (CH$14,500) and **Antofagasta** (4 per day, CH$10,000).

Taxis: Taxi *colectivos* wait on Ariztia Poniente and go frequently to La Serena (1½hr.).

✳ ❷ ORIENTATION AND PRACTICAL INFORMATION

Ovalle's bus station, the **Terrapuerto Limarí,** sits at the eastern edge of town near the **Feria Modelo.** To get to the heart of town, turn left on Maestranza from the entrance to the *terrapuerto* and continue until you hit the **Plaza de Armas.** Several hotels are conveniently located on **Maestranza.** Most activity in town can be found around the plaza or on **Vicuña Mackenna,** which runs parallel to **Libertad. Ariztía Oriente** and **Ariztía Poniente,** two one-way streets divided by a grassy strip, bisect the town in a north-south direction.

Tourist Office: A **tourist information kiosk** sits on the plaza at the corner of Aguirre and Mackenna. Hours vary.

Tours: Agencia Tres Valles (☎629 650), on the corner of Libertad and Carmen, leads trips into the surrounding areas. They also **exchange money** at reasonable rates.

Bank: Banco Santander, on the plaza, next to the post office on Mackenna and **Banco de Chile,** on Victoria, both have **24hr. ATMs.**

Emergency: ☎131.

Police: Aguirre 641 (☎133).

24-Hour Pharmacy: Farmacia Ahumado, Mackenna 73-90 (☎630 720). Open 24hr.

Hospital: Hospital Dr. Antonio Tirado (☎620 042), on the northern end of Ariztia Poniente, near the Museo de Limarí.

Post Office: Vicuña Mackenna, on the plaza.

⌂ ACCOMMODATIONS

Lodging in Ovalle is an underwhelming experience, but there are several inexpensive choices near the plaza.

El Quisco Hotel, Maestranza 161 (☎620 351). Not only is El Quisco one of the better deals in Ovalle, but if you're rolling into town late at night, this is one of the best places to stay because of its proximity to the bus station. Don't let the clashing colorful rugs and bedspreads strain your eyes too much. All rooms with TV. Singles CH$5000; doubles CH$10,000; doubles with bath CH$12,000; triples with bath CH$18,000. ●

Hotel Roxy, Libertad 155 (☎620 080). Although the name of this establishment resonates strongly with hopping clubs rather than with places to hang your hat, Hotel Roxy is a quiet hotel built around a big sunny courtyard. Some people consider it refreshing that getting to the shared bathrooms involves walking outside—make sure you're one of those people before checking in. Singles CH$6500, with bath CH$13,000; doubles CH$10,000/CH$13,000; triples CH$12,000/CH$17,500. ●

Hotel Venecia, Libertad 261 (☎620 968), near the plaza. This inexpensive hotel boasts reasonable rates and a good location, but the brightly colored checkered floor cannot compensate for the Roxy's pleasant patio. Singles CH$4000; doubles CH$7500. ●

Hotel Turismo, Victoria 295 (☎623 258; www.hotelturismo.cl), overlooking the plaza. Turismo is Ovalle's nicest hotel—too bad it knows this all too well. A prime location allows Turismo to get away with higher prices. All rooms are equipped with private baths and TV, but triples are crowded and the prices just aren't worth it. Singles CH$19,500; doubles CH$28,000; triples CH$33,000. ❹

Hotel American, Mackenna 169 (☎620 159; www.hotelamerican.cl). The only thing that stands out about the American is the cutesy toilet cover in the bathroom. The dark rooms, while cool in the summer, are gloomy in colder weather. Big TVs in all the rooms to compensate for the lackluster views. Breakfast included. Singles CH$17,500; doubles CH$25,000; triples CH$29,950. ❹

🍴 FOOD

Ovalle's few restaurants are scattered around the Plaza de Armas and on Mackenna. The regional speciality, river prawns, are worth a try when in season. Fresh fruits and vegetables are abundantly available at the Feria Modelo (farmer's market) near the bus station.

Café Real, Mackenna 419b (☎624 526), just off the plaza, around the corner from Hotel Turismo. Coffee shop serving up real ground beans by day, pub by night, and movie theater on the weekend, Café Real is certainly Ovalle's hippest spot. Slide along the shiny blue floors to a secluded table and let one of the waitresses in matching geometric-print shirts serve you a *leche con fruta* or a sandwich while George Michael croons on the stereo. Movies are shown on the screen at the back of the cafe on weekends. Open M-Th 9am-8:30pm, F 9am-1:30am, Sa 10am-1:30am. ❷

Club Social Arabe, Arauco 225 (☎620 015 or 632 155), off Mackenna, offers standard Chilean fare and spicier, more interesting Middle Eastern food in a spacious room. The cupola on the top is enclosed by windows, lighting up the peach-colored walls. It's a nice setting for some *kuppe* (CH$3000). Open M-Sa 10am-1am, Su 10am-4pm. ❸

El Quijote, Arauco 284 (☎620 501), on the corner of Mackenna. Stepping into Quijote feels like stepping into a 1960s commune. Politically-themed posters and iconic images line the walls, towering over tables tucked into shady corners (don't mind it if Pablo Neruda or Salvador Allende oversee your meal). On weekdays, it's a little gloomy and the service can be painfully slow, but it's a great weekend meeting spot. The mixed drinks are a better bet than the food itself. Open M-Th 9am-1am, F-Sa 9am-3am. ❷

Club Comercial, 244 Manuel Aguirre (☎620 141). This run-of-the-mill establishment with a large room full of metal tables and a big TV offers standard food for standard prices in an austere setting. *Biffe a lo pobre* CH$2800. Open M-Sa 10am-midnight. ❷

👁 SIGHTS

Stroll over to the **Museo del Limarí** on Covarrubias, at the northern end of Antofagasta. This archaeological museum, located in an old train station, has fastidious displays of Diaguita pottery in a slick museum setting, complete with track lighting, darkened rooms, and lots of glass. It's a small collection, but worth a look. There is a helpful timeline of life in the region, commencing with the paleoindians and ending with the Spanish, illustrated with artifacts from each era. (☎620 029. Open Tu-F 9am-1pm and 3-7pm, Sa-Su 10am-1pm. CH$600, children CH$300. Free on Su.) Then walk down a couple of blocks to the **Feria Modelo,** behind the bus station, at the end of Maestranza. The fertile fields around Ovalle offer up all the fruits and vegetables imaginable and they're all available at the local farmer's market that takes place in a huge train hanger. A literal cornucopia of colors and flavors, the market is replete with piles of oranges and lemons, carts bursting with long strands of garlic cloves, and deep tanks of black olives. In addition to the food, there is also a miscellaneous "goods" section where vendors sell everything from pots and pans to watch bands and baby pacifiers. (Open M, W, F 8am-5pm.) If a day at the market isn't thrilling enough, catch the latest American action flick at **Cina Cervantes,** on Mackenna, near the plaza, right next to the post office.

NORTE CHICO

NEAR OVALLE

PARQUE NACIONAL FRAY JORGE

A World Biosphere Reserve since 1977, Parque Nacional Fray Jorge is renown for its most unique section: 400 hectares of Valdivian cloudforest, where the fauna common to the cool, rainy regions of Valdivia and Patagonia in the south are surrounded by the cacti and sand more typical of the semi-arid desert conditions of Norte Chico. The cloudforest is sustained by the *camanchaca*, the dense fog that descends over the tress and provides nearly 10 times the average annual rainfall for the region (which averages around 100mm). Most visitors come to see the bizarre cloudforest. Although scientists have not been able to explain fully the presence of southernly plant species such as *Canelo* and *Olivillo*, it is suspected that this forest was at one time larger than its current 400 hectares and has disappeared due to either climate change or human interference. The coastal park consists of 10,000 hectares in total, 90km from Ovalle and 110km from La Serena; altogether, the park extends from sea level up to 600m. Temperatures average between 7°C in July and 23°C in February at the coast. The cloudforest is cooler and quite wet—warm waterproof clothing is essential when traipsing through the park. Although it was deemed a national park in 1941, its namesake, Fray Jorge, was a Fransiscan friar from La Serena who visited the park in the 1600s.

AT A GLANCE	
AREA: 10,000 hectares. **CLIMATE:** Temperate; Feb. average 7°C; July average 23°C; annual rainfall 100mm, rainier in the cloudforest. **CAMPING:** *Cabañas* and camping sites available at El Arrayancito (CH$8000 per site).	**FEATURES:** 400 hectares of Valdivian cloudforest sustained by the mysterious *camanchaca*. **HIGHLIGHTS:** Hiking Sendero el Bosque. **FEES:** CH$1600, children CH$600. **GATEWAYS:** Ovalle, La Serena.

Sendero el Bosque, a 1km trail through the forest speckled with labeled trees, is accessible just past the park administration. Although this is not a particularly exciting route, it can be completed in 40min., giving visitors a taste of the cloudforest climate and forest.

Although there is no public transportation to get you to Fray Jorge, taxis offer fixed rates to and from the park. More conveniently, several travel agencies in La Serena lead daytrips to the park. If you're driving yourself, the turn-off for the park is at 389km on the Panamericana. From the turn off, it's another 22km west to the park entrance.

Camping is possible at **El Arrayancito ❷,** consisting of 13 sites administered by **Conaf.** There are bathroom facilities and potable water at the campsite 5km from the **info center** (CH$8000 per site). A **cabaña ❷** that houses five people is also operated by Conaf. (CH$22,000; off-season CH$18,000. Park open Jan.-Mar. F-Sa 9am-4:30pm; Mar.-Dec. Sa-Su 9am-4:30pm. CH$1600, children CH$600.)

VALLE DEL ENCANTO

From Ovalle, Route 43 heads northeast 88km to La Serena through endless fields of grapes, artichokes, and mandarine orange groves interspersed with flat scrubby land dotted with cacti. Twenty kilometers from Ovalle is a sign for Valle del Encanto, a remote archaeological monument. It's a dusty 5km walk from Route 43 to the park entrance, but it's often possible to get a ride with other visitors. The park is comprised of about three hectares of **petroglyphs** (images carved into stone) and **pictographs** (images painted onto stone) dating back at least 2000 years to the pastoral Molle people. The images are best observed on sunny afternoons and appear to depict religious images—it is thought that the valley held spiritual significance for its original inhabitants. *Guardaparques* Salvador Araya and Clemen Pizarro are happy to explain prevailing archaeological theories. Visitors are able to scramble around the boulders while seeking out the ancient images which are helpfully pointed out by white arrows.

From Ovalle, ask any **bus** heading to La Serena to drop you at the turn-off for Valle del Encanto, 19km north on Route 43. (Do the same if heading out from La Serena. The 5km walk to the park is flat. Alternatively, it is possible, but expensive, to hire a **cab** in Ovalle (CH$15,000).

Free **camping** is permitted at three spots within the park. The sites are marked with picnic benches and signs. Ask at the entrance for a map. (Park open 8:15am-8:30pm, off-season 8:15am-6pm. CH$300.)

TERMAS DE SOCOS

Thirty-four kilometers from Ovalle, where Route 43 meets the Panamericana, lies the **thermal spa** known as Termas de Socos. The thermal baths are famed for their theraputic healing properties and have consequently become a sacred retreat for the weary. **Hotel Socos ❺** monopolizes the spot, managing the baths and providing luxurious accommodations along with an **on-site camping area ❷**. Although a stay at the hotel is an expensive option, a night here is worth every penny. The warm **thermal baths** are really just glorified bathtubs, but the heat is immediately soothing. The hotel **pool** is at air-temperature and filled with the magical water for those who need miracle healing in the summertime. Bottled water from the thermal baths is available at the hotel reception. Non-guests are welcome to take a dip in the thermal baths as well. (☎ 982 505, in Santiago 2 363 336. Singles with full board, thermal baths, and access to the pool CH$40,000; doubles CH$74,000; triples CH$105,000. **Camping** with pool access and services CH$4500. 30min. soak in thermal baths CH$3700. Pool access CH$3600.)

The turn-off for the Termas de Socos is at 370km on the Panamericana. **Buses** on the Panamericana heading to La Serena from Ovalle can drop off or pick up passengers. From the turn off, it's another kilometer to the spa. Hotel staff will pick up and drop off guests who call ahead.

BETWEEN OVALLE AND LA SERENA

ANDACOLLO ☎ 53

The small mining town of Andacollo lies in a dramatic gorge midway between Ovalle and La Serena. The ride there is an adventure in itself on a road that makes hairpin turns through the undulating foothills. As the road dips towards the entrance to the town, the white peaks of the *cordillera* emerge menacingly in the distance. However, the visitor's eye is quickly drawn from the jagged peaks to the pointed spires of Andacollo's two central churches.

Numerous abandoned pits and mineral deposits tell the story of Andacollo's history as a copper and gold mining town. Today, these closed mines mean rampant unemployment, a depressed economy, and increasing problems with alcoholism. Despite its problems, Andacollo remains a heavily visited town, attracting over 100,000 tourists every Christmas.

NORTE CHICO

LA VIRGEN DE ANDACOLLO According to local history, Andacollo's small statue, the Virgen del Rosario, was found in the mid-1500s by a local Indian who was out chopping wood. The Virgen had most probably been abandoned by Spanish soldiers from La Serena who feared that she would be stolen by pirates. When the *indígena* cut the tree in which the Virgen was hidden, he grazed her cheek with his ax, leaving a small scar. He brought her back to the village and there she remained until 1672, when she was suddenly and inexplicably lost. The creation of a new statue was commissioned from Lima, Peru, and was eagerly awaited until its successful arrival in 1676. This latter reproduction now resides in Andacollo's Iglesia Chico until the annual Fiesta Grande, when she is paraded around the plaza and into the enormous Basílica. The Virgen's healing powers are legendary, moving 100,000 people to make the yearly pilgrimage to Andocollo. Evidence of the icon's largesse are displayed in the museum adjacent to the Iglesia Chico: discarded wheelchairs and crutches and expensive jewels given in gratitude lie among other tributes to this small but powerful idol.

This influx of visitors is explained by the town's main attraction: the 103cm wood statue of the Virgen de Andacollo. For close to five centuries, the virgin has been hearing prayers and curing illnesses. During the annual **Fiesta Grande**, December 23-26, the town swells with devout pilgrims. The **Fiesta Chica**, held on the first Sunday in October, was implemented to give the locals their own celebration, but this latter celebration draws in quite a crowd as well.

⌨️📞 TRANSPORTATION AND PRACTICAL INFORMATION. Catch a **colectivo** on Domeyko in La Serena (1½hr., CH$1500). **Urmaneta** is the main thoroughfare through town. A **bank** and a *discoteca* called Inexcess are located on Urmaneta.

🏠 ACCOMMODATIONS AND FOOD. Andacollo is best as an easy daytrip from La Serena, but if you decide to stay on in town, there are several decent *residenciales* on Urmaneta, the only main street in town. During Fiesta Grande there is **camping** across the bridge from the plaza and several homes become short-term hotels as they open their doors and rent out beds. Year-round, try **Residencial Las Vegas ❶**, close to the plaza on Urmaneta. Although it is a little dark and dusty, it's a good budget option. (Rooms CH$2000 per person.) The best restaurant in town is the striking red adobe **La Casona De Tomás ❶**, a block up Urmaneta from the plaza. The high-ceilinged green dining room with stained-glass windows looks like it could almost be another church. (*Menú* CH$1500.)

◉ SIGHTS. The small town is centered around its beautiful **Plaza Pedro Nolasco Videl** and the two churches flanking it. The national monument **Iglesia Chica** was built in the 1600s and protects the Virgen de Andacollo for most of the year in an ornate silver-plated altar. The rest of the church is much more modest, with simple wooden benches and three small chapels off to the side. Attached to the church is a small **Museo de Ofrendas a la Virgen**, where many of the gifts the Virgen has received over the years, including baby clothes, jewels, and diplomas, are kept. (Open Sa-Su 9am-6pm.) Around the corner, also on the plaza, is the huge **Basílica**, a Byzantine-style wood church covered with galvanized steel and painted a bright salmon-pink. Two tall, imposing towers out front balance the interior of the church that reportedly has seating room for 10,000 people. Spiral staircases lead to the balcony of the church, while huge wooden pillars, impressively painted to resemble marble, hold up the entire structure.

TONGOY ☎ 51

Not far from the busy cities of La Serena and Coquimbo, the small village of Tongoy sits languidly by the sea, inviting visitors to take breaks from their hectic itineraries and sunbathe on its sandy beaches instead. Not exactly a hotbed of activity, the town remains quiet, except for during the summer months, and is a peaceful alternative to city life.

◨◪ TRANSPORTATION AND PRACTICAL INFORMATION. Serenamar Buses leave frequently from **Coquimbo's** main bus terminal throughout the day (1hr., CH$800). **Taxi colectivos** also run to and from Coquimbo for CH$1600. The main road into town is called **Fundición** (Sur heads into town, Norte heads back to La Serena). A **bank** and the **post office** are on the grassy strip between Fundición Sur and Norte, by the bus stop. Tongoy's small beach, **Playa Socos,** is at the end of Fundición Sur, on the right. During the tourist season, artisans set up a row of kiosks and sell trinkets. The larger beach, **Playa Grande,** stretches north along the peninsula beyond Fundición Norte and is an excellent spot for a long walk. A hill rises over the southern end of the peninsula, affording a nice view.

◪ ACCOMMODATIONS. In the off-season, you may have to hunt around for a budget option that remains open, but if you don't mind splurging a bit, there are numerous hotels and *residencials* spread throughout town that stay open year-round. The nicest place to stay is **Hostería Tongoy ❹,** Costanera 10, on Playa Socos, with bright rooms boasting pink stucco walls, cable TV, and pretty sea views. A good restaurant is attached to the hotel as well. (☎391 203. Breakfast included. Doubles CH$32,000; extra beds CH$6000.) On the sandy streets near Playa Grande, try the modest no-name **residencial ❷,** Av. La Serena 58. The beachfront location, family environment, and private baths compensate for the slightly run-down interior with saggy beds. (☎392 953. Rooms CH$4000 per person.) Up the hill on the end of the peninsula is the boxy, bare-walled, and overpriced **Hotel la Bahía ❸,** Urmaneta Sur 95. (☎391 244. Breakfast included. Doubles CH$18,000; triples CH$21,000.)

◖ FOOD. There are many good seafood restaurants on Playa Grande. **El Rey II ❸** is at Lord Cochrane 47, at the southern edge of the peninsula, right below the hill. The large bay windows provide diners with a good view of the hustle and bustle along the curve of Playa Grande. The tasty entrees are worth the price. (Entrees CH$3500-6000. Open 9:30am-10pm.) On Playa Socos, head for the restaurant at **Hostería Tongoy ❸.** In town, on Fundición where the buses drop off and pick up, the **Restaurante Sin Rival ❷** has gaudy fluorescent tablecloths and a huge screen TV where loyal fans gather to watch soccer games.

COQUIMBO ☎ 51

Coquimbo is one of many coastal cities with a fairytale history of conquistadors, pirates, and buried gold. Sir Francis Drake made a pit stop here in the 16th century and many other adventurers, nefarious and otherwise, have followed suit throughout the centuries. These days, visitors to Coquimbo tend to have less menacing intentions. Some make the short trek over from La Serena for Coquimbo's bargain accommodations. Others journey from inland cities to catch an ocean breeze and a glimpse of the many naval vessels in the harbor. And still others have begun to make the pilgrimage from even farther distances to see Coquimbo's newest attraction, the enormous Cruz del Tercer Milenio, a gigantic cement cross that towers over the city and can be seen for miles from incoming buses.

Coquimbo can still have a slightly menacing feel, especially down in the harbor area where the city drunks congregate. A large blue and black ship, the Margot Maria Stengel, used to lie out on the sand, but has been pulled to the shore and tethered along the seawall near the bus terminal. Rumor has it the ship may be turned into a disco, but it seems that's just an old drunk's tale. Coquimbo is not a must-see for a time-conscious traveler, but it makes a colorful blue-collar contrast to resorty La Serena and is a good spot for harbor boat trips.

TRANSPORTATION

Within Coquimbo, *colectivos* and local buses labeled *"parte alta"* head to the upper part of town, while those sporting a picture of the cross or labeled *"cruz"* take pilgrims to the Cruz del Tercer Milenio (CH$250).

Buses: The **Terminal de Buses** is on Varela, facing the shore from the corner of Garriga. Long-distance buses stop in Coquimbo on their way to and from La Serena. Prices and times are nearly identical to those in **La Serena** (see **Transportation**, p. 223).

Colectivos: Hail *colectivos* to **La Serena** at the bus terminal (CH$450).

ORIENTATION AND PRACTICAL INFORMATION

Coquimbo sits on the northern edge of a wide peninsula and looks out over the **Bahía de Coquimbo.** There are two levels to the city, the *parte alta* and the main part of town, down by the water. White stone staircases zigzag up and down the hillside, connecting the two levels. The bus station is close to water and is in the same vicinity as many hotels. To reach the shore, head down the hill from the terminal. **Malgarejo** and **Aldunate** both run parallel to the shoreline and bound the **Plaza de Armas.** The **tourist office** lies on Malgarejo on the corner with Las Heras. To orient yourself in town, look for the towering monument, the **Cruz del Tercer Milenio,** which is on the opposite side of town from the ocean.

ACCOMMODATIONS

Although Francis Drake probably got a steal when he visited Coquimbo, you don't have to be a pirate to get a good deal in town these days. Most hotels and hostels are reasonably priced, and it might be worthwhile to upgrade the standard of your housing options to get the most bang for your buck. Many good options cluster on or around Aldunate. From the bus station, head away from the shore and go towards the Plaza de Armas.

Hotel Ibérica, Lastra 400 (☎312 141). Overlooking the plaza on Aldunate, this old, colonial-style hotel is a great deal in an even better location. Rooms include TV, a view, and overwhelmingly pink walls. Singles CH$4000, with bath CH$6500; doubles CH$8000/CH$10,000; triples with bath CH$15,000. ❷

Hotel Lig, Aldunate 1577 (☎311 171), at the northern end of town where Aldunate splits. Don't be dissuaded by its slightly tattered outside appearance—if you've got a few extra pesos, this place is a gem. Plants blooming in the courtyard and sun from the skylights falling onto yellow walls give it an airy, bright, and lively feel. Amenities include TVs, phones, mini-fridges, and private baths. Breakfast included. Singles CH$11,300; doubles CH$18,500; triples CH$23,100. ❸

Hotel Restaurant Bilbao, Bilbao 471 (☎315 767), off Aldunate. It may seem romantic to stand on the balcony in front of your room and look down the sweep of narrow stairs to the restaurant below, but the romance is short-lived: clinking glasses and merry chatter lose their charm when they're keeping you awake at 1am. However, if you don't mind staying up late, this could be a good choice. Rooms have TVs and private baths. Breakfast included. CH$6000 per person. ❷

Residencial Rincón de Mamá, Alcadela 226 (☎315 609). This hostel and restaurant is nothing spectacular, but boasts a great location—it's close to the bus station, shore, and plaza. Shared bathrooms are small and cramped but the rooms are airy. An especially good deal if you're traveling in a group of 3. Tours of Coquimbo and the surrounding area can be reserved here. Singles CH$6000; doubles and triples CH$10,000. ❷

🍴 FOOD

Food in Coquimbo, particularly coveted seafood, is generally fresh, tasty, and fairly inexpensive, but not very flashy or cosmopolitan. It can be difficult to find one establishment that stands out from the rest. The **Feria del Mar** is the most interesting culinary experience in the city, offering a variety of possibilities. Many of the hotels near the Plaza de Armas also have decent options.

Feria del Mar, in front of the bus terminal on the shore. The freshest fish in town is down in the *caleta* at the Feria del Mar. Want proof? They'll gut and fillet your fish right in front of you. Dozens of stalls and small restaurants operate here, and if you're willing to brave the over-zealous vendors eager to woo you by any means possible to their doorstep, it's fun to stroll through the market. All the fish and shellfish here are fresh, well-prepared, and pretty cheap. Open dawn to dusk. ❷

Restaurante El Callejón, Pasaje los Artesanos 21 (☎315 765), a few blocks from the Plaza de Armas and not far from the bus terminal off Malgarejo. The chairs, tables, and walls are painted in bright primary colors, giving Callejón a nursery school feel. The big screen TV at the back is more likely to show riveting *fútbol* matches than Sesame Street. The *"ckrepes de mar"* taste better than they're spelled. Open 10am-3am. ❷

Hotel Restaurant Bilbao, Bilbao 471 (☎315 767). Down the narrow hallway, Bilbao's tables are set into a sunken indoor courtyard that becomes lively at night. The *parillada* for CH$7500 is a little pricey, but everything else is cheaper. Try the *sopa marinero* (CH$3500) if you're in the mood for seafood. Open 1-3pm and 8:30pm-1:30am. ❸

👁 SIGHTS

PLAZA DE ARMAS. Sights are limited for those looking for museums and other high-brow experiences—but this should not prevent area visitors from exploring around the city. The Plaza de Armas, a few blocks from the bus terminal on Aldunate, is filled with palm trees, old folks sharing gossip while enjoying the breeze, and pre-teens strutting around in their school uniforms. An **artisan's fair** resides across the street on Aldunate.

COQUIMBO'S CALETA. Heading towards the shore, away from the bus station, lands you at the *caleta,* one of the more interesting parts of town. To the right, the beach stretches across to La Serena, and while this spot isn't as nice as La Serena's beaches, it's pleasant, with local kids playing soccer games in the sand. To the left, on the **boardwalk,** the energy is palpable. Watch as the fishermen repair their nets upon the dock, or head on to the **Feria del Mar** (see **Food,** p. 221) where vendors will tempt you with fine fresh fish. Even farther along are the hulking profiles of **naval vessels.** It's a little hit-or-miss, but occasionally the sailors will allow guests to tour the ships (locals say a little flirting goes a long way with the sailors). **Harbor tours** leave from this area as well. These 30min. or hour-long tours circle around the harbor and pass a sealion and penguin colony.

CRUZ DEL TERCER MILENIO. Towering over Coquimbo and the surrounding towns is a giant new monument. Called the Cruz del Tercer Milenio, it has become an imposing presence in the community. The 93ft. tall cement cross is a Catholic memorial commemorating the 2000th birthday of Jesus Christ. Construction began in May of 2000 and the ambitious project aims to be completed in seven years. As of June 2002 it is only 25% done, but when finished it will include large parks for meditation, groups of confessionals, vivid depictions of the Ten Commandments, and, according to the signs at its base, "a whole change of the quality of living of the people surrounding the cross." Even with so much remaining to do, the cross is an amazing, if somewhat bizarre, sight and well worth a visit. There are galleries in the base of the cross and an elevator that takes visitors up to the third-floor viewing area (CH$250). From there, a second elevator (CH$1000) goes straight up the center column of the cross into the glass-enclosed arms. The view from here is truly awe-inspiring—whether infused with a religious dimension or not. The iron port of Guayacan is visible sitting in its sheltered horseshoe bay; La Serena shows off its glitter in the opposite direction; and in the hazy distance to the east the plains stretch to the Elqui Valley's hills.

The administrators of Coquimbo hope to make the cross one of the major pilgrimage sites in the Southern Hemisphere, rivaling the most important monuments and cities in Catholic culture. However, it doesn't exactly inspire reverence as much as bafflement. The new age structure, with a cement spiral staircase and three columns leading to the arms, looks more like the realization of a science fiction novella than religious icon. And the regular but invisible banging of hammers adds to the surreal atmosphere. The spirituality of the structure isn't exactly enhanced by the teenagers run around taking pictures of themselves or the tour guides walking backwards, leading groups of tourists around the galleries. The whole scene is an odd cross between a holy pilgrimage and a Catholic-themed Disney World. *(Take a #10 colectivo from the bus terminal (CH$250), or any colectivo or bus labeled "cruz." Drop-off near the entrance. Open M-F 9:30am-8pm, Sa-Su 10:30am-9pm. Ground-level pavilion free.)*

■ NIGHTLIFE

Most of the area's club scene takes place next door in La Serena, but for those looking for action in Coquimbo, there are a couple of exciting options. The **Lusitania Salon de Pool,** Borgoño 254, is good for a few games. Try tangoing at the **Club Social,** Aldunate 631, or tap your way into the **Club de Jazz de Coquimbo,** Aldunate 739, near the Plaza de Armas. Coquimbo can feel a little threatening at night, so it's advisable to spend a night on the town in a group of friends—women especially should not go solo on this one.

LA SERENA   ☎51

As the capital of Region IV and the second oldest city in Chile, La Serena is one of nation's up-and-coming tourist cities. Its pristine beaches, stately churches, and tree-lined avenues are impressive draws, and have made the city one of the most popular destinations in Norte Chico. Despite this newly acquired reputation, it has managed to retain much of its relaxed feel and old-world charm, something that can only be found in a city as old as La Serena.

Founded by the Spaniard Juan de Bohón in 1544, the city was burned down by Diaguita Indians and had to be reconstructed five years later. Like its southern neighbor Coquimbo, La Serena played host to Sir Francis Drake and a string of other treasure-seekers. City growth was slow until the 1940s, when Don Gabriel Gonzalez Videla, the much revered governor and then president, instituted a "Plan Serena,"

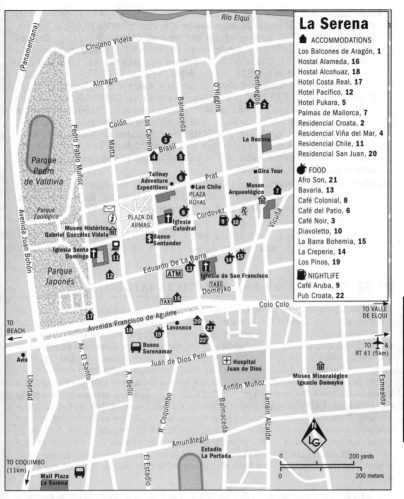

La Serena

🏠 ACCOMMODATIONS
Los Balcones de Aragón, **1**
Hostal Alameda, **16**
Hostal Alcohuaz, **18**
Hotel Costa Real, **17**
Hotel Pacífico, **12**
Hotel Pukara, **5**
Palmas de Mallorca, **7**
Residencial Croata, **2**
Residencial Viña del Mar, **4**
Residencial Chile, **11**
Residencial San Juan, **20**

🍴 FOOD
Afro Son, **21**
Bavaria, **13**
Café Colonial, **8**
Café del Patio, **6**
Café Noir, **3**
Diavoletto, **10**
La Barra Bohemia, **15**
La Creperie, **14**
Los Pinos, **19**

🍸 NIGHTLIFE
Café Aruba, **9**
Pub Croata, **22**

NORTE CHICO

aimed at boosting the economic and cultural significance of La Serena. Today, the city is once again visited by treasure-hunters. However, this time the treasure is a little more cultural, including the city's museums, churches, and peaceful plazas, and, in the case of the clubs and discos that line the shores, a little commercial as well.

TRANSPORTATION

Flights: Aeropuerto La Florida (☎200 900), 5km east of town by way of Juan de Díos Peni. **Lan Chile** has offices at the airport (☎200 993 or 200 904), downtown at Balmaceda 406 (☎221 531; fax 219 496), and in the mall. **American Airlines** is downtown at Cordovez 672, #290 (☎211 724). Frequent and regular service to **Santiago** and most other Chilean cities available.

Buses: Long-distance buses stop at the **Terminal de Buses** (☎224 573), on the corner of Amunategui and El Santo. **Pullman Bus** (☎225 152) to: **Arica** (6:45am, 3:45pm, 12:15am; CH$20,000) via **Antofagasta** and **Iquique; Calama** (3 per day); **Copiapó** (6hr., 10 per day, CH$4500); **Ovalle** (every hr., CH$1500); **Santiago** (*semi-cama* CH$9000, *salon cama* CH$14,000); **Valparaíso** and **Viña del Mar** (7am and midnight, CH$7000). **Tur-Bus** (☎218 786) to: **Arica** (6 per day 2-11:40pm, CH$25,000) via **Antofagasta** and **Iquique; Calama** (3 per day); **Copiapó** (6hr., several per day); **Ovalle** (every hr., CH$1500); **Santiago** (*semi-cama* CH$9000, *salon cama* CH$14,000); **Valparaíso** and **Viña del Mar** (7am and midnight, CH$9900). **Flota Barrios** (☎213 394) to: **Arica** (5:30pm, CH$13,000) via **Antofagasta** and **Iquique; Calama** (3 per day); **Ovalle** (every hr., CH$1500); **Santiago** (*semi-cama* CH$9000, *salon cama* CH$14,000); **Valparaíso** and **Viña del Mar** (7am and midnight, CH$4500). **Tacc Expreso Norte** (☎224 857) also goes to **Copiapó** (6hr.) and **Valparaíso** and **Viña del Mar** (CH$6000).

Taxis/Colectivos: The easiest way to get around the area is with *colectivos*. Most *colectivos* line up on Domekyo, off Balmaceda, and these go to **Andacollo, Ovalle, Vicuna,** and intermediaries for CH$1500. **Taxis** to Coquimbo leave frequently from Aguirre and Los Carrera (CH$250).

Rental Car: Budget, Balmaceda 3820 (☎297 916; fax 290 241; budgetlsr@entelchile.net). **Avis,** Aguirre 63 (☎227 171; fax 227 049; laserena@avischile.cl).

■ 🛈 ORIENTATION AND PRACTICAL INFORMATION

While not a perfect grid, La Serena is a fairly easy city to navigate. Sights are scattered in a radius around the **Plaza de Armas,** where the streets are very regular. The main areas of interest are bordered by the Panamericana (which runs parallel to the ocean and is called **Juan Bohón**) on the western edge, **Francisco de Aguirre** to the south, **Colón** to the north, and **Benavente** to the east. Aguirre is also the main avenue to the beach, a 40min. walk along the picturesque palm-lined street.

The bus terminal is south of town, down by the Panamericana. Downtown is a 25min. walk from the bus station, but there are lots of *colectivos* and taxis outside the terminal. Exit the main doors of the terminal and turn left to get to Amunategui. Turn right onto Amunategui, walking away from the bus terminal and the Panamericana. Cross the street and take the first left onto El Santo. Follow El Santo to Aguirre, which is recognizable by the grassy median. Across Aguirre, any of the intersecting streets will lead into downtown. The most direct access is on Matta. Turn left from Aguirre onto Matta and walk two blocks to reach the Plaza de Armas.

Tourist Office: Sernatur, Matta 461 (☎225 138 or 226 199), on the Plaza de Armas, is extremely helpful with information. Open M-F 8:30am-6pm.

Tours: There are numerous organized tour companies in La Serena. Guides take tourists to Parque Nacional Fray Jorge and Reserva Nacional Pingüino de Humboldt, as well as through the Elqui Valley and to the world renowned astronomical observatories. In summer, tours run all week, but in the off-season, most tours run only on weekends. Call ahead for updated information. Quality tour companies include **Gira Tour,** Prat 689 (☎223 535; giratour@tie.cl), and **Talinay Adventure Expeditions,** Prat 470 (☎218 658; extimfun@yahoo.com), in the same building as Café del Patio (see **Food,** p. 227).

Banks: Banco Santander, on the Plaza de Armas, has a **24hr. ATM.** Tour agencies often exchange traveler's checks, as well.

Market: Mercado La Recova, at Cienfuegos and Cantournet, has some goods. Or try the larger **Santa Isabel** next door.

Laundromat: Lavaseco La Universal, Aguirre 411 (☎222 845). CH$1200 per kg. Same-day service. Open M-F 9am-1pm and 4-8:30pm, Sa 9am-1:30pm.

Emergency: ☎131

Police: ☎133. *Carabineros,* Larrain Alcalde 700 (☎224 488). **International Police** (☎229 394 or 229 389).

Pharmacy: Farmacia Ahumada, Cordovez 651 (☎218 065).

Hospital: Hospital Juan de Díos, Balmaceda 916 (☎225 569).

Internet Access: Net Café, Cordovez 285 (☎212 187), a block off the Plaza de Armas. Pricey but hip. A giant latte or fruit smoothie and an hour of Internet access cost CH$2300. Open M-Sa 10:30am-1am, Su noon-10pm.

Post Office: On the corner of Prat and Matta in the Plaza de Armas. Open M-F 8:30am-6:30pm, Sa 9:30am-1pm.

▌ ACCOMMODATIONS

La Serena has become something of a resort town in recent decades and beach-side accommodation prices reflect the change. Visitors who want to be pampered should skip the city hostels and head straight to the beach, where they have their choice of hotels along the strip of sand between Coquimbo and La Serena. However, more budget-conscious travelers will have no trouble finding satisfactory accommodations in town. There are many reasonable hotel and *hostal* choices in close proximity to the Plaza de Armas. Aguirre has the closest hostels for those who want to be near the bus terminal. Though most hostels aren't dirt cheap, they are generally good quality, and worth the extra thousand pesos.

Residencial Croata (HI), Cienfuegos 248 (☎216 994), is La Serena's only Hosteling International member. Outdoorsy types, backpackers, and budget travelers flock here and the owner, an outdoorsy type himself, advertises his *residencial* as a welcoming community for travelers. It's a little pricey for those on a very tight budget, but it's worth paying a little more for a place where Internet access is free, the rooms are sunny, the baths private, and bikes can be rented on site. Cable TV and breakfast included. Singles CH$8000; doubles CH$12,000; triples CH$15,000. ❸

Hotel Pacífico, Barra 252 (☎225 674). The Pacífico's regal façade encompasses a bizarre pocket of space that appears to be firmly stuck in the 1950s. Old, faded maps of Chile and the US peel from the wall in the lobby. The rooms are airy and large, especially those on the upper floor, and though they don't come with a lot of amenities, they are a great deal so close to the town center. Breakfast included. Singles CH$6000, with private bath CH$10,000; doubles CH$12,000; triples CH$19,000; quads CH$24,000. ❷

Hotel Los Balcones de Aragón, Cienfuegos 209 (☎211 982), 2 blocks past the Mercado La Recova. Despite its highbrow name, Los Balcones is more campy than classic. The upholstery in the hallways is overwhelmingly brown, from the carpets to the leather chairs. In each room the color of the bedspread changes slightly, but beside each bed sits a brass lamp whose base is in the shape of a child reading a book. The rooms have pristine bathrooms, alarm clocks (a first!), heat, and TVs. Breakfast included. Singles CH$26,000; doubles CH$43,000; triples CH$49,500. 20% off-season discount. ❺

Hostal Alcohuaz, Aguirre 307 (☎099 726 0406), on the corner with Andrés Bello. Named after the last town in the Valle de Elqui, Alcohuaz is a warm, new hostel run by a friendly family. Its location is conveniently near the bus station, but the street is noisy. High ceilings, TVs, and small marble bathrooms give it a homey touch. Laundry service and parking are available. 4- to 6-bed dorms CH$3500; singles CH$4000-5000; doubles CH$10,000. ❷

IN RECENT NEWS

ART "BUFF"

When Brazil won the World Cup in June 2002, three thousand naked Chileans in the streets of Santiago cheered. No, this is not some bizarre South American soccer (ahem, fútbol) custom, although Chile certainly has its fair share of these. In this case the rampant exhibitionism was explained away as cheering nudes making "art." American photographer Spencer Tunik, known for his photos of large numbers of nudes in various cities around the world, had set his sights on Santiago.

Nudity has been in the news a lot recently. Stories of Baby Vamp, a 17-year-old who went about her business—shopping, eating lunch, riding the bus—in the buff, except for a pair of shoes, a carryall, and a pair of earphones, were plastered all over the newspapers (see p. 108). This too was ostensibly art although TV talk shows in Chile were more skeptical and argued that Baby Vamp's nudity was either exploitative or offensive.

Enter Spencer Tunik. The hoopla had barely died down over Baby Vamp when the news began flashing photos from Tunik's repertoire of work in other cities. Full frontal nudity on the nightly newscast was juxtaposed with concerned Catholic bishops denouncing Tunik's impending appearance in Santiago. The exact location where the photo would take place was kept a secret and speculation ran from presidential palace La Moneda to a gypsy hang out, Cerro Santa Lucía.

Palmas de Mallorca, Cordovez 750 (☎224 072), near the archaeological museum on the eastern side of town. How many times have you arrived in a hotel only to find that they don't have a stereo system in your room? The nerve of those places. Well, Mallorca feels your pain. Their rooms not only have cable TV but stereos as well, clearly a hotel necessity. The color scheme is overwhelmingly yellow, but there is a nice sitting room with wood columns. Inexpensive breakfast included. Singles CH$8000; doubles CH$10,000; triples CH$15,000. ❸

Hotel Costa Real, Aguirre 170 (☎221 010; www.regiondecoquimbo.cl/costareal). If you're into fancy-schmancy hotels, head to the Costa Real. It doesn't have much character, but who cares when you can shell out money in the bar or boutique? Terrace with a lovely pool. All rooms are large and modern. Breakfast included. Singles US$63; doubles US$69. ❺

Hotel Pukara, Balmaceda 319 (☎211 933). A decent mid-range hotel. Seventies-style furnishings will appeal to those with a retro groove going on. Rooms come with cable TV and private baths, but there are better options around town. Breakfast included. Singles CH$16,000; doubles CH$20,000. ❹

Hostal Alameda, Aguirre 452 (☎213 052). Rooms are small but likeable and travelers making an early-morning exit to the bus station might want to stay here. There is a porch swing in the entrance and faded wallpaper—it has a sort of dilapidated charm. Breakfast included. Singles CH$6000, with private bath CH$9000; doubles CH$13,000/CH$15,000; triples CH$18,000; quads CH$22,000. ❷

Residencial Chile, Matta 561 (☎211 694). An eclectic *residencial* near the plaza, the Chile sports an anchor clock on the wall, MC Escher-esqe decorations, and chirping parakeets in the courtyard. The singles are tiny boxes but the owner is welcoming to foreigners. Singles CH$6000; doubles CH$10,000; triples CH$15,000. ❷

Residencial San Juan, Balmaceda 827 (☎212 794). Though not particularly noteworthy, the San Juan is surprisingly quiet for its location. On the plus side, the headboards on the beds have wings, so you can float off to dreamland. All rooms come with shared baths and desks. Rooms CH$4000 per person. ❷

Residencial Viña del Mar, Brasil 423 (☎212 349), a block off the plaza. If nothing else strikes your fancy, this *residencial* is decent enough. The striped and diamond wallpaper is a little dizzying. Breakfast is not included, but the rooms are big. Singles CH$6000, with private bath CH$8000; doubles CH$12,000/CH$15,000; triples CH$15,000/CH$18,000. ❷

◖ FOOD

A little sleuthing can lead discerning eaters to the riches in La Serena. Standard cafes and restaurants abound in the center of town near the Plaza de Armas, but the real treasures are farther afield, mostly to the east. Seafood is fresh and excellent in La Serena, particularly in the **Mercado La Recova.** Papaya is a regional specialty and can be consumed in many creative ways.

La Creperie, O'Higgins 635 (☎219 214; lacreperie@123.cl). From the moment you walk through the huge swinging doors at the entrance, La Creperie exudes hipness. The courtyard has slatted floors and is lit by streetlamps and occasionally spiced up with live music. The interior has a sort of spare art-deco feel. The list of crepes is long and includes both sweet and savory varieties, all of which are very tasty and quite reasonably priced. There are also pizzas and sandwiches for the less adventurous and a full bar to wet the whistle. Open 11am-midnight, closed Su in the winter. ❸

Café del Patio, Prat 470 (☎212 634). Located in the same building as Talinay Adventure Expeditions, this cafe is a great meeting and hangout spot. The fare is good for bar food and the atmosphere is laid back. On weekend nights there is often live jazz and blues. Popular among visiting students and bohemian wannabes. Open M-Sa 11am-midnight, Su 4-10pm. ❷

Café Noir, Brasil 426. A gem of a find, this tiny family-run cafe is a relaxing alternative to the downtown restaurants. The prices are great and breakfast is delicious. Along with lots of fresh juice and *leches,* there are many interesting hot drinks, including the *Submarino,* a chocolate bar melted into a cup of steaming milk (CH$580). The atmosphere is nice, clean, and attractive with light-colored wood everywhere. Open 10am-9pm. ❶

Diavoletto, O'Higgins 560 (☎224 850). After a day of wandering around town, sometimes a good ice cream really hits the spot, and Diavoletto is the perfect place to go when the urge hits. The "artesanal" gelato is made in-house and is excellent. The friendly staff also serves sandwiches and *onces,* but the gelato is the real draw. 2 scoops CH$400. Open 9am-10:30pm. ❶

La Barra Bohemia, O'Higgins 624 (☎219 682). The corner doorway opens into a dark room lit by green light bulbs hanging in copper pots, and a long strip of green neon lighting illuminates the underside of the bar. Black-and-white pictures adorn the balcony, where there is live music Th-Sa nights. Good sandwiches and a wide range of drinks complement the atmosphere. Open 6pm-2am. ❸

In the end, Tunik chose the Museum of Modern Art in Bellavista. The streets surrounding the museum were cordoned off and in the cold dawn hours Tunik prepared his equipment. While much of the rest of the world was focused on the match-up of Germany and Brazil in the final game of the World Cup, 3000 people in Santiago stripped down to their birthday suits and posed for the camera.

The news was inundated with bare flesh once again, but oddly enough, the reaction was predominantly one of pride. "3000 people? That's more than he had in Paris!" someone said in La Serena. Even a hermetic zen master in the heart of the Elqui Valley incorporated Tunik's feat into his spiritual readings. "Everyone wants to be free," he said in a soothing tone. "Those people taking off their clothes in Santiago. It's an expression of free will."

While it doesn't appear that nudity will become the status quo in Santiago (well, at least not in June when temperatures often dip below freezing), it's interesting to know that free will is a tangible experience for 3000 people in Santiago.

Afro Son, Balmaceda 824 (☎229 344), south of Aguirre. The room here is as flavorful as the menu. Located in the Centro Latinoamericano de Arte y Cultura, Afro Son is a great place for a quiet lunch or a raucous Saturday night. There is live Latin music on weekends and occasional puppet shows or other exhibitions. Lunch *menú* CH$1500. Open M-Sa 10am-2am. ❷

Café Colonial, Balmaceda 475. Why colonial? Perhaps it's the wooden tables and pastoral paintings on the wall. Otherwise, it's a pretty standard cafe, with pizzas, sandwiches, and 2-for-1 drinks during Happy Hour. One noteworthy standout is the Australian manager who goes out of his way to help overwhelmed tourists. Open M-Th 9am-10pm, F-Sa 9am-midnight. ❷

Los Pinos, Los Carrera 831. The sign advertises friendly, home-cooked meals, and indeed it is like home cooking—there's no menu, just the fixed lunch, which locals devour on their lunchbreak. Check out the bar lined with beer cans or sit in either of the other two big rooms. *Menú* CH$1200. Open 10am-9:30pm. ❶

Bavaria, Barra 489 (☎228 894), on the corner with Balmaceda. Hungry patrons are drawn in by the soft yellow glow like moths to a flame. Bavaria is a chain restaurant, but this one can look so welcoming in the evening that it's hard to resist. The entrance is through swinging Old West-style wooden doors, and the chairs look strangely like donuts. Though Bavaria is better known for its *parilladas* (CH$7900 for 2 people), vegetarians should check it out for its long list of salad options. Rotating lunch *menú* CH$2900. Open 11am-4pm and 6pm-midnight. ❸

👁 SIGHTS

MUSEO ARQUEOLÓGICO. The first exhibit in the city's archaeological museum begins ambitiously with the start of life on earth and takes off from there. Visitors walk around the horseshoe-shaped museum traveling through time. The museum supports the theory that humans arrived in Chile from North America across the Bering land bridge. Cultural artifacts from Chilean ancestors are displayed throughout the halls. A sea lion hide boat is well preserved and an Easter Island Moai is strikingly presented. Other highlights include mummies and shrunken heads. The museum does not have English translations, but the artifacts themselves are intriguing—the museum is enjoyable for all ages and linguistic abilities. *(Cordovez on the corner with Cienfuegos, 3 blocks east of the Plaza de Armas. Open Tu-F 9:30am-5:50pm, Sa 10am-1pm and 4-7pm, Su 10am-1pm. CH$600, children CH$300.)*

IGLESIA SANTO DOMINGO. This is one of the most beautiful of La Serena's many churches. First built in 1673, Santo Domingo had to be reconstructed after being sacked by pirates a century later. There is no fanfare here; contrasting with the norm, the chapel is plain and simple. Natural light streams through stained glass windows onto the beautiful stone walls. On the right hand side, climbing vines and red flowers are visible, as tinted shadows dance upon the opaque glass. One can see why this place would be called a sanctuary. *(Located on the corner of Cordovez and Muñoz, a block west of the plaza.)*

LA RECOVA. This large market and artisan's fair in La Serena is a must-see. It is an excellent place to go to get acquainted with the regional specialties in food and handicrafts. Sweets made from papaya are especially popular, but there are also musical instruments, alpaca clothing, and all sorts of edible delicacies. Artists set up kiosks outside of the market, making this a perfect place to bargain for gifts. Upstairs in the marketplace are dozens of seafood restaurants. Beware the hawkish waiters who come close to forcing passersby into their restaurants. If you don't mind the aggressive advertising, this is a great place for lunch—the freshest seafood is here. *(Cienfuegos on the corner of Cantournet, on the eastern side of town. Follow Prat from the Plaza de Armas. Open daily until 8pm.)*

NORTE CHICO

CASA GABRIEL GONZÁLEZ VIDELA. Off the plaza by the same name, this national monument, built in 1894, has been the home for La Serena's main historical museum since 1984. The museum exhibits displays of regional historical artifacts upstairs and has several rooms dedicated to Chilean art, but the front of the house is reserved for homage to **González Videla.** Videla was a La Serena native who served as President of Chile from 1946 to 1952. The tribute to his life in this museum includes everything from his desk and old radio to life-sized models wearing his and his wife's clothing. One of the more interesting museums in La Serena, it's worth a trip. *(The museum is on the plaza at Matta 495. ☎215 052. Open M-F 10am-6pm, Sa 10am-1pm. CH$600, children CH$300.)*

IGLESIA CATEDRAL DE LA SERENA. Built in 1844 in the neoclassical style and now a national monument, the redundantly named "church cathedral" lords over the other single-named *iglesias* from its prime location on the Plaza de Armas. Inside the cool stone building, the soft songs of pious monks can usually be heard from deep inside the cloisters—but don't be fooled, it's on stereo. Still, the mood inside is somber. Eyes are drawn from the checkered marble floor, up the stone columns, and towards the magnificent curved ceiling. Through a door on the left near the altar is the **Sala de Arte Religioso,** where serious-looking faces peer from classic paintings. The highlights here are the emerald and amethyst colored slippers, reminiscent of the Wizard of Oz, worn by the Bishop. *(The catedral is on Los Carreras at the corner with Cordovez, on the Plaza de Armas. The sala is open M-F 10am-1pm and 4-7pm, Sa 10am-1pm. CH$400.)*

PARQUE JAPONÉS. Also known as the **Jardín del Corazón,** this enclosed Japanese garden boasts over 80 species of plants, including bamboo groves and many exotic flowers. Bridges traverse still pools and lovers cuddle on the benches. It would be nicer if it were free, but nonetheless this is a perfect spot to take an afternoon stroll or read a book. *(Along the western side of town, past Pedro Pablo Muñoz. From the plaza, walk down Cordovez towards the ocean until the road ends at the park. The garden is on the left hand side. Open 10am-6pm. CH$600, children CH$300.)*

IGLESIA DE SAN FRANCISCO. This was the first stone church in La Serena and remains a fine example of colonial architecture. It has been restored in the past few years so that visitors can now explore the interior, where multi-tiered chandeliers hang from wooden beams and the altar, backlit in blue, has an eerie glow. Ominous music completes the mood. *(Balmaceda 640, on the corner of de la Barra, southeast of the Plaza de Armas.)*

MUSEO MINERALÓGICO IGNACIO DOMEKYO. The Museo Mineralógico has a comprehensive collection of mineralogical specimens, but if you're not a geologist, it kind of looks like a pile of rocks. Ignacio Domekyo, the museum's namesake, is considered the father of Chilean mineralogy. His collection rests here within the halls of the Universidad de la Serena. Unfortunately, the importance of this collection will be lost on all but the most rock-oriented visitors and is probably worth skipping in favor of less eclectic museums. *(In the University of La Serena's engineering school at Anfion Muñoz 870. ☎204 096. Enter the building, go up the stairs, turn right and walk through two sets of doors. Ask a passing student if lost. Open M-F 8:30am-12:30pm, Sa 8:30am-6pm. CH$500.)*

PARQUE ZOOLÓGICO. The city zoo is a depressing grouping of holding pens displaying a few despondent animals, many of which are not even exotic enough to merit display. For example, there is a chicken pen with an informative sign explaining that the domesticated chicken can be seen "from Asia throughout the rest of the world." A beautiful gray eagle seems desperate to escape, the rabbits have mange, and the giant turtle is decorated with graffiti. But the llamas have a

NORTE CHICO

knack for getting out of their pens and can often be joined for a picnic on the grass. *(In Parque Pedro de Valdivia, on the western edge of town. Across from the entrance to the Japanese Garden. Walk down Cordovez towards the ocean. The zoo is on the right. Open Tu-Su 10am-6pm. Free.)*

⚡ ENTERTAINMENT

There are several options for nightlife in La Serena. **Afro Son** (see **Food**, p. 228) has live Latin music on weekends and sometimes holds other cultural events. On a more family-oriented note, the **Mall Plaza La Serena,** next to the bus terminal down by the Panamericana, has a **Cinemark** movie theater (☎600 600 2463), a **LanChile** office, and all of the typical designer stores. (Open 10:30am-11:30pm.)

■ **Pub Croata,** Balmaceda 871, south of Aguirre, gets a major *Let's Go* thumbs up for creativity and variety. A cut above the rest, Pub Croata has one room romantically lit with candles, while another has a large blacklight painting glowing on the wall. Then there is the bar area, with a full range of drinks. Plus they serve dinner. But the best part is all the way in the back: two large illuminated soccer fields where men, women, and children play pick up games all day and night. Did we mention that there are also pool tables? Thursday nights there is live blues, F nights are live classic rock, and Sa turn the pub into a DJ-style discotheque. Cover on Sa-Su is CH$3000 for men, includes 1 drink; women free. Soccer fields open all day. Pub open M-Sa 7pm-3am.

Café Aruba, O'Higgins 529. A stop for the more daring tourist who'd be interested in seeing live nude dancers shake their stuff for visiting sailors. It's too bad this *sala de espectaculos* isn't more universally appealing—the lounge area is scattered with very comfortable couches and chairs, plus it's open late on weekends with dancing in the evenings. Cover CH$4000; drinking required. Open F-Sa 11am-5pm.

NEAR LA SERENA

RESERVA NACIONAL PINGÜINO DE HUMBOLDT

Spanning the border between regions III and IV, Reserva Nacional Pingüino de Humboldt is a 859 hectare reserve consisting of a number of islands which are home to nesting Humboldt penguins. Daytrippers from La Serena take tours of the two main islands, **Isla Choros** and **Isla Damas,** to see the **penguins, sea lions,** and **bottle-nose dolphins** who often follow the boats, playfully jumping and frolicking in the waves.

In the **Caleta de Choros,** it is possible to hire local **fishing boats** to take sightseers around the islands (US$10 per person for a 7-person boat). Boat tours generally circle around Isla Choros and Isla Damas. This latter isle has a **beach** where it is possible to swim, sunbathe, picnic, or clamber around the rocks. From December 15 to March 15, **camping ❷** is permitted on Isla Damas at Playa la Poza. Payment and permission should be taken care of at the park administration at Caleta de Choros. Campers need to bring their own equipment, food, and water, and make sure to take their trash with them when they leave (CH$12,000 per site).

There is no public transportation to Caleta de Choros, but many travel agencies in La Serena, 120km away, lead daytrips that include transportation to the reserve and island tours. If you're driving, the turn-off for the town of Choros is 70km from La Serena on the Panamericana. From here, it's another 45km to the Caleta. Entrance to the reserve is at Caleta de Choros, 44km off the Panamericana from the turn-off for Choros. Here visitors register with **Conaf** and pay the entrance fee (CH$1600, children CH$600). Although the park is open year-round, boats don't run to the islands in rough seas. (Open 9am-6pm.)

VICUÑA ☎ 51

Located in the heart of the Elqui Valley and surrounded by fertile hills and clear skies, Vicuña is one of Chile's most attractive cities. Teenagers breakdance in the evenings in the Plaza de Armas, artists sell their crafts in the *pueblito de artisanos*, and the well known face of Gabriela Mistral is lovingly displayed throughout this town that claims her as their own.

Vicuña was founded in 1821 under a mandate from Bernardo O'Higgins. Its construction was directed by the *intendente* of the province, Coronel Joaquin Vicuña Larrain, and the city took his name in homage. Its most famous citizen, Nobel prize winning poet Gabriela Mistral was born in a small house on the edge of the city, now a museum, and a large replica of her funeral mask forms the center of the Plaza de Armas. The city has never been a bustling center, but its appeal lies in its peacefulness. The hills encircling the city look chalky white at dusk, and it's hard not to feel at peace as the sun sets on the hazy, grape-filled valley.

Vicuña is also an excellent base for excursions into the Elqui Valley. Several major astronomical observatories are most easily accessible from Vicuña, and a smaller amateur observatory overlooks the city. *Pisco*, the most traditional Chilean drink, is made regionally and several interesting production plants are a good daytrip from Vicuña. But the city itself, with its charming hotels and wonderful climate, makes for a relaxing visit on its own.

▐ TRANSPORTATION

Vicuña's **bus terminal** is on Prat, on the corner with O'Higgins. There are several buses to **La Serena** and **Coquimbo** (1hr., CH$1000). There are also a couple of buses to **Santiago** on Pullman Bus, Expreso Norte, and Diamantes de Elqui. It's probably better to catch long distance buses in La Serena, where there are more choices, destinations, and departures.

The terminal for **taxi colectivos** is directly across from the bus station. *Colectivos* go frequently to La Serena (CH$1000), as well as to other towns in the Elqui Valley, including Monte Grande and Pisco Elqui. *Colectivos* are usually the most efficient method of transportation to La Serena. Local **taxis,** and the men who drive them, lounge on the north side of the Plaza de Armas.

▐ ▐ ORIENTATION AND PRACTICAL INFORMATION

Vicuña sits on the northern bank of the **Río Elqui** and is constructed in an easy grid pattern centered on the **Plaza de Armas. Mistral** runs east-west and is the major thoroughfare and a good reference point. The Río Elqui borders the city to the south and access to the city from Ruta 41 is across two narrow bridges. Both roads lead to the plaza.

The municipal **tourist office,** San Martín 275, is in the Torre Bauer on the corner on the plaza. The helpful staff is happy to give away their many pamphlets. (☎ 209 125. Open M-Sa 8:30am-9pm, off-season M-Sa 8:30am-5:30pm.) **Banco del Estado,** Chacabuco 384, on the plaza, has an ATM but it does not give cash for foreign cards, so visitors should plan to use traveler's checks or exchange money in a larger city. The **Casa de Cultura,** Chacabuco 334 (☎ 411 283), on the plaza, has a library and seasonal exhibitions. The **pharmacy Cruz Verde** (☎ 411 223) is on Prat between the bus terminal and the plaza. **Hospital San Juan de Dios** (☎ 411 263) is at Prat and Independencia, a few blocks north of the Plaza. **Internet access** is slow but available at **Ciberbook,** Mistral 571. The post office, **Correos de Chile,** is on the plaza on the corner of San Martín and Mistral, alongside the **municipalidad.**

FROM THE ROAD

SUNNY SIDE OF THE ROAD

At 10am on a gray Saturday morning in north central Chile I set my pack down on the roadside and sat on top of it to wait for a bus. The long highway known as the Panamericana stretches the length of Chile and you can get almost anywhere once you've made it to the highway, if you're willing to wait long enough.

I am an organized person. I like to know where I'm going and exactly how I'm going to get there. So I was a little surprised at myself when I waved goodbye to the departing van that had just dumped me at the roadside without so much as a bus schedule. Not only was I not nervous, I was, well, gleeful. I sat down to wait for what would surely be a fast approaching bus and couldn't help but smile to myself. I opened my notebook and began to write:

Right now, right this minute, I feel like a wanderer. Sitting on top of my pack waiting for a bus to pass by, humming a little. The birds are twittering in the trees and now and then a rooster crows. Big 18-wheelers rumble by, honking to say "Hey baby, going my way?" I am, as it turns out, but there's no way I'm jumping into the cab with one of them—I've seen enough scary movies. There's no one around and only the donkey in the field across the road looks up when I start singing "Sunny Side of the Street." My hands are cold but I don't care. I'm happy. It feels good to sit out here alone, looking into the hills as the cars pass by too fast. On the road.

ACCOMMODATIONS

For such a small town, Vicuña has a number of fine places to stay in all budget ranges. Many good choices line up on Mistral east of the plaza, but there are a few other budget choices on the western side of town as well.

Hostal Valle Hermoso, Mistral 706 (☎411 206), past the Museo Mistral. Honoring its nearby neighbor, this hostel has portraits of the poet on its wall. Rooms all have showers, TV, and faux roses to make visitors feel at home. The hostel is very quiet and spacious and rooms are off a boxy courtyard. Not the cheapest option for budget travelers, but a nice one. Breakfast included. Singles CH$7000; doubles CH$12,000; triples CH$16,000. ❷

Hotel Halley, Mistral 542 (☎412 060), east of the plaza. This is one of the best hotels in Chile and is a great deal, especially in the off-season, when it's possible to bargain the prices down. The elegant rooms in this beautiful building have antique furniture and lacy doilies covering the bedspreads. Rooms are spaced around a lovely courtyard and have tall wooden doors. TV, private bathrooms, pool. Breakfast included. Singles CH$15,000; doubles CH$26,000; triples CH$35,000; 4-person suite CH$45,000. ❹

Hostería de Vicuña, Aldea 101 (☎411 301; www.hosteriavicuna.cl), on the western edge of town at the end of Chacabuco or O'Higgins. This *hacienda*-like large place is some distance from the rest of the points of interest in town, but it is also the most resort-like. The large, white stucco rooms have TVs and baths, and there is a pool, ping-pong tables, a tennis court, and several large birdcages. Try and stay in the room that was Mistral's when she visited. Singles CH$26,000; doubles CH$33,900; triples CH$44,800; quads CH$54,500. ❺

Hostal Michal, Mistral 573 (☎411 060). A decent hostel, considering Vicuña's high standards. The rooms are reminiscent of dorm rooms, but are quite comfortable, with TV, baths, and a little table. The overrun yard has a swing set. Singles CH$8000; doubles CH$10,000; triples CH$12,000. ❸

Hotel Restaurant los Olmos, Prat 148 (☎411 124). No-frills rooms are kind of dark, not to mention the fact that the hotel is adjacent to a funeral home. All in all, not the most cheerful environment. However, it is right near the bus station and makes a fine place to sleep for those in transit. Rooms have private baths and TVs. CH$3500 per person. ❶

Yunkay, O'Higgins 72 (☎411 593), west of the plaza, rents out *cabañas*. Each *cabaña* has two rooms and a little kitchen. The bathrooms are simple and the little living room has a mini TV. Windows look out onto a rainbow-colored playground and a nice pool. There are also double rooms available for those who don't want a *cabaña,* but both are overpriced. Doubles CH$30,000; *cabañas* CH$49,000. ❹

Residencial la Elquina, O'Higgins 65 (☎411 317), west of the plaza. This *residencial* has a fertile garden with a large orange tree and bright red pepper plants. Quarters are cramped for 3, but it's a decent choice for couples or single travelers. Singles CH$5000, with private bath CH$6000; doubles CH$8000/CH$10,000; triples CH$12,000/CH$15,000. Prices can be bargained. ❷

Residencial Mistral, Mistral 180 (☎411 278), west of the plaza after Infante. There are better options than this in Vicuña, but this *residencial* is nice enough and quite cheap. The building has a low, sagging-wood ceiling and the rooms are typical, offering nothing fancy. Some rooms have a nice balcony. Shared baths are clean. Breakfast included. CH$2500 per person. 15% senior discount. ❶

FOOD

Despite its prime location in Chile's culinary heartland, Vicuña is not known for its food. Choices are limited in such a small city, but it is possible to do better than a sandwich or pizza at some of the nicer restaurants on Mistral. Whatever the meal is, though, the perfect accompaniment is a nice cool *pisco sour.*

Restaurant Yo y Soledad, Los Carrera 320 (☎419 002), a block north of Mistral. Just inside the entrance through the wide doorway is an arresting display of plants and climbing vines. Tables are set down in the slightly sunken center on the stone floor. The blue walls give it a sort of airy feeling. Simple but welcoming, with inexpensive lunch options and a stocked bar. *Menú* CH$2500 for 4 plates or CH$1500 for 2 plates. Open 10am-11pm. ❷

Restaurante Halley, Mistral 404 (☎411 225), on the plaza's northeast corner. This restaurant is run by the same people who run the spiffy Hotel Halley and it is probably the best choice for a splurge in town. The restaurant is large, with several big rooms. One of the sections has a thatched roof as decoration. Nuts hang down in bundles and other odd knickknacks make dining here a visual experience. On the walls of this casual area there are paintings of food with the names above, as if they came out of a children's book—a good lesson

Two hours later: same scene. I was still sitting on the side of the road, and was no longer quite as happy as I had been earlier. Six buses had passed going in the opposite direction, but not one was going my way. It was cold. The birds had stopped singing and the donkey had hunkered down in a cornfield, even the ubiquitous dogs had gone to find a warmer hovel. "Sunny Side of the Street" was certainly not the song I was singing anymore. In fact, when the wind picked up and whipped through my fleece, it started to feel like a cruel irony. Those truckers were starting to look less menacing.

By mid-afternoon, when a bus finally did show up, I had begun trying to warm up my thumb enough to hitch. I had never been so happy to see a big boxy bus before. It wasn't until I was settled back in my seat and beginning to thaw out that I remembered (and appreciated) the saying of a traveling companion I had met in Chile three years ago. Her toast as I took off for this trip now seemed prescient:

"May the weather hold, the showers flow hot, and may the buses come, eventually."

—Jane Lindholm

for those still learning the Spanish words for what they're eating. The other dining room is slightly more fancy. The *pastel de choclo* (CH$2950) is the specialty of the house and is deliciously filling. Rabbit with salad CH$3650. Open 10am-midnight. ❸

Timbao, San Martín 203 (☎412 732), on southern end of the plaza. Although the food is basic, the atmosphere is nice, with soft yellow lighting and a chess game set up in the corner in between two comfortable chairs. The best thing on the menu is the pizza. With a nice cold beer it's a good place to grab a bite and watch the hustle and bustle of the plaza. Open 10am-9pm. ❷

Club Social, Mistral 445 (☎411 853), a block east of the plaza. The Club Social is probably the swankiest restaurant in Vicuña. There are indoor and outdoor tables and a couple of giant wagon wheels for decorative flair. Most meat dishes run CH$3300-5000, a little more expensive than they're worth. Adjacent lounge area has stiff-backed chairs and many landscape paintings for sale. Open 10am-11:30pm. ❸

🎴 SIGHTS

PLANTA CAPEL. After setting down their packs, the first item on many people's must-do list for Vicuña is a trip back across the river for a tour of the Capel *pisco* plant, where much of the nation's *pisco* is made and shipped out. The smell of fermenting grapes envelops visitors as they enter. Those unaccustomed to *pisco* may be reminded of the smell of tequila. Capel stands for Cooperativa Agrícola Piscera Elqui Limitada; it is one of two major *pisco* grower cooperatives (the other being Control). Fifteen-hundred growers from the III and IV regions—the only area where *pisco* can be produced—send their grapes here to be fermented and transformed into *pisco*. At the Planta Capel, a woman dressed head to toe in red leads tours of the factory. Interesting at any time of year, it's probably best from February to May, during the harvest. The tour ends with a *pisco* tasting in the showroom and the opportunity to buy the many products shamelessly promoting Capel. (*Across the river from the main area of Vicuña. Taxis leave from the Plaza de Armas, but the walk is only about 20min. Walk east on Chacabuco, away from the plaza. Eventually the road curves around and crosses the river. After the bridge turn left. The plant will be visible about 300 yards ahead.* ☎411 251. *Open in winter 10am-12:30pm and 2:30-6pm; in summer 10am-6pm. Tours in English Mar.-Dec. Call ahead. Free.*)

PLAZA DE ARMAS. Vicuña's main square is a friendly, palm-filled meeting place for the town. In the evenings, teenagers bring out the boombox and their best breakdancing moves. Jugglers practice here too, on the stage set up for summer performances. In the center of the square, surrounded by a blue pool of water, is a huge stone model of Gabriela Mistral's funeral mask. There are tricycles for rent for little kids. On the northwest side of the plaza the red **Torre Bauer,** built in 1905 in German style for the Mayor Adolfo Bauer, resembles a childlike drawing of a classical tower, and one half expects to see Rapunzel at the top. Instead, it is the home of the municipal information office. Diagonally across from the tower on Mistral is the main church, the **Iglesia Inmaculada Concepción,** also red and built around the same time as the tower. Inside, the ceiling of the nave is painted with religious motifs. Just down from the church is the **Pueblito de los Artisanos,** an ideal spot to shop for high quality Elqui Valley artwork and gifts.

MUSEO ENTOMOLÓGICO E HISTORIA NATURAL. Despite the fact that this museum clearly has no money, it is quite entertaining, especially for kids or adults who are into bugs. The many fossils include Pleistocene horse bones and neat fish fossils. The dinosaur bones are boring, entomologically speaking—luckily there are amateur papier-mâché models showing what the dinosaurs looked like in their entirety. The museum also has great collections of shells, some stuffed birds, and mounted bugs with labels listing the regions in the world where they can be found. There are huge stick bugs, creepy spiders, and beautiful butterflies. Signs and descriptions are in both English and Spanish. *(Chacabuco 334, on the plaza. Open 10:30am-1:30pm and 3:30-6pm. CH$400, children CH$200.)*

MUSEO GABRIELA MISTRAL. Gabriela Mistral, Chile's main mother figure, was the first Latin American author to win the Nobel Prize for Literature, which she received in 1945. In addition to writing several volumes of well-respected poetry, Mistral also served as a diplomat in Europe and traveled throughout the world. She is widely revered in Chilean cities and more so than most in Vicuña, where she was born in 1889. The centerpiece of the Mistral museum is the replica of the humble house she was born in. It consists of just two small rooms, with furniture of the epoch and dirt floors. The rest of the museum is considerably more modern but less interesting. The library has books and photos, as well as Mistral's eclectic keepsakes, including a dried flower arrangement and a bag of dirt from Monte Grande (the nearby town where she spent most of her childhood), which she kept to her death. The museum has a nice back room dedicated to children, with colorful educational displays. *(Several blocks east of the plaza on Mistral 579. ☎ 411 223. Open Oct.-Dec. M-F 10am-1pm and 3-7pm, Sa 10am-1pm and 3-6pm; Jan.-Feb. M-Sa 10am-7pm, Su 10am-6pm; Mar.-Sept. M-F 10am-1pm and 2:30-5:45pm, Sa 10am-1pm and 3-4:45pm. CH$600, children CH$300.)*

MIRADOR LA VIRGEN. An easy walk from the town center is the Mirador la Virgen, which sits upon a tall hill. From the top, the whole valley comes into view, swallowed up by the surrounding mountains, some of which are snowcapped in winter. There is a shrine to the virgin, and visitors trek up to light candles and make small offerings. Unfortunately, the beauty of the hillside is marred by a radio transmission tower. Nonetheless, this quick jaunt out of town gives visitors a chance to enjoy the fresh air and get a new, higher perspective of the town. *(Walk east on Mistral away from town, past the Museo Mistral. At the end of town, when the road ends, turn left. Follow this road as it winds around until you hit a dirt road with a sign indicating the mirador. Turn left here and walk along the road until reaching a path with a handrail. This will wind up the hill to the top. The entire walk, from the plaza to the top takes no more than 45min. at a leisurely pace. It is also possible to drive to the top by following the same directions and continuing along the dirt road.)*

EL SOLAR DE LOS MADARIAGA. The sign outside advertises a glimpse into the past, and the man who runs this small museum seems to come right out of the past himself. The original Sr. Madariaga was a wealthy businessman from Valparaíso who made a home in Vicuña on a friend's recommendation. The 15-room *solar* was his home, and it has been preserved in its original state, with elegant furniture, faded family photographs, and fruit trees blooming in the courtyard. The very old man who oversees this house was married to the granddaughter of the original Madariaga. Dressed impeccably in a pin-striped suit, he is happy to invite visitors to take a seat on one of the antique chairs while he explains the family history. The sign on the front is right; this is less of a museum and more like a step back through time. *(Mistral 683, several blocks east of the plaza. Open 10am-7pm, off-season 10am-1pm and 3-7pm. CH$400.)*

MUSEO HISTÓRICO DE ELQUI. Though it's supposed to be a museum, it looks more like a jumbled antique store pile. Ostensibly this small museum illustrates Vicuña and the Elqui Valley's history, but nothing is very well presented and it can be frustrating to visit. It is sort of a curiosity and perhaps worth a glance for visitors already down by the bus station. Among the heaps of things to see are old furniture, guns, and a row of rusted padlocks. *(Prat 90, between the bus terminal and the plaza. ☎ 099 743 8830. Open 10am-6pm. CH$400, students CH$200.)*

⚡ DAYTRIP FROM VICUÑA: MONTE GRANDE

Buses leave every hr. from Vicuña and drop passengers in the town center (CH$800). Ask the driver to let you know when to get off. Buses continue on to Pisco Elqui before returning along the same road.

Monte Grande is a small town in the Valle de Elqui, less than an hour away from Vicuña. It is the town where Gabriela Mistral spent much of her childhood and where she chose to be buried. The **tumba de la poetisa** rests on a hill at the edge of the village and has become something of a pilgrimage site over the years. Buses let passengers off in the town square before continuing on along the main road. Mistral's tomb is up the hill on the right about 200m from the town square. Visitors climb up a staircase to the simple monument. The inscription reads, "What the soul does for the body, the artist does for the community." The tomb is surrounded by grape fields and hills and is a lovely contemplative spot. Heading downhill from the town square is the small museum **Casa Escuela,** the tiny schoolhouse where Gabriela Mistral lived as a child. Her half-sister was the schoolteacher there. The museum only takes about 5min. to pass through; after all, it was a one-room schoolhouse. But the old desks and maps and the small bedroom where Gabriela slept are interesting artifacts from her life. (Open Tu-Su 10am-1pm and 3-6pm. CH$300.) Across from Mistral's tomb is the **pisco plant** where the *artisanal pisco* **los Artesanos de Cochiguaz** is made. This plant is smaller than the *pisco* plant in Vicuña but also part of the Capel cooperative. (Free tours and tastings. Open 10am-1pm and 2:30-6pm.) Farther down the hill is the eclectic round building called the **Galeria de Arte Zen.** There is a large sand garden, soothing music, and "Zen paintings." In addition to the paintings, candles, and perfumes for sale, there is also a Zen master on hand to give tarot readings (CH$10,000), Zen readings (CH$15,000) and Astrology readings (CH$20,000). Visitors to Monte Grande should check out the gallery whether they desire a reading or not—it's a soothing and unique experience. (Open daily, in Zen style, from morning to evening.)

There are no accommodations in Monte Grande and visitors should plan to either return to Vicuña or travel a few kilometers further to Pisco Elqui to spend the night. There is a restaurant however, across from the Casa Escuela. Called **Méson del Fraile ❷,** it is small but friendly with a good selection of "sandwishes" on the English menu. It also has traditional Elqui beverages papaya sour and *mote con huesillos.* (Open 9am-10pm, off-season 9am-6pm.)

PISCO ELQUI   ☎ 51

Four kilometers deeper into the valley from Monte Grande is the wonderful village of Pisco Elqui. There are no museums, no hectic tours, just peace and quiet and wonderful welcoming people. The plaza is the main point of reference for the small town. A beautiful fountain shoots up in the center and fronts a tall stone church which lies before a beautiful backdrop of deep red mountain peaks. Artisans have set up shop on the outskirts of the plaza and there is a tourist kiosk open in the summertime. Pisco Elqui was originally called La Union but the name was changed to honor the drink that provides so much revenue and fame to the valley.

🚍 TRANSPORTATION. Take a local **bus** from the terminal in Vicuña or pick it up in Monte Grande (CH$800 from Vicuña).

🛏🍴 ACCOMMODATIONS AND FOOD. Near the plaza, farther up on the right, there is a municipal pool and **campground ❷.** (Swimming is CH$1500. Camping CH$5500 per site.) At the top of the hill, this road ends and is intersected by Prat. Turning left on Prat leads to the **Hotel Gabriela Mistral ❷,** which has rustic but very comfortable *cabañas* and rooms off a balcony overlooking the street. (☎ 198 2525. Singles CH$7000; doubles CH$10,000; 3-person *cabañas* CH$15,000; 4-person *cabañas* CH$20,000.) Farther along Prat is the hippie **Hostería los Datiles ❹,** which has a restaurant, pub, *cabañas* (some with kitchens), and holistic healing pyramids. The little garden has mint springs, a lime tree, and lavender. There is also a pool and a little river running through the property. Some of the *cabañas* have beautiful views of the valley and come with kitchenettes. In addition, the *hostería* offers yoga meditation and Maya horoscope charts. (☎ 198 2540. Singles CH$15,000; doubles CH$25,000; *cabañas* CH$40,000-45,000.) Turning right on Prat leads to the **Tesoro de Elqui ❺.** Visitors who like to think they're roughing it but want to rough it in luxury should look no further. The very well-maintained *cabañas* have wood paneling and a soothing feeling. On-site massage and reflexology are available, in addition to a beautiful pool and garden, and the neighbor offers psychic reading. The restaurant is an open windowed affair with books and is probably the best deal in town—the smells wafting from the kitchen are too tempting to resist. (☎ 198 2609. Single *cabañas* CH$9000; doubles CH$22,000; triples CH$24,000; quads CH$27,000-32,000.)

Directly off the plaza, **Los Jugos ❶** is a juice bar under a thatched roof. The delicious fresh juices are only CH$1000 each and come in large steel mugs with a straw. Connected to Los Jugos is the terrific pizza restaurant **Mandarino ❷.** The pizzas are homemade and delicious (CH$2500 for a small, CH$7000 for a large). Try the vegetarian, loaded with local veggies. The owner is friendly and very helpful. Plus, the atmosphere is unique: the restaurant has a dirt floor and the clay benches are strewn with sheepskins as cushions. In the winter, the fireplace gets a warm fire roaring.

 BORDER CROSSING INTO ARGENTINA: PASO DE AGUA NEGRA

East of Vicuña, the hills of the Elqui Valley rise to the snow-covered peaks of the Andes and the mountainous border between Chile and Argentina. True adventurers (with hardy all-weather vehicles) can attempt to traverse the Paseo de Agua Negra, one of the highest and most beautiful passes between the two countries. The pass is speckled with ice sculptures known as **penitentes** and sharp spikes of opaque glacial snow. Halfway between the pass and Vicuña is the little town of Juntas, home to the **Baños del Toro** and the **Mina del Indio,** as well the **Chilean Customs.**

Heading east from Vicuña, the main road to the border pass is 18km out at the town of **Rivadavia,** where the Río Claro meets the Río Turbio. There is no public transportation beyond Rivadavia, so you'll need a 4WD to continue the journey. While the right-hand turn off heads to the Elqui Valley, the left-hand fork, Route 41, winds into the mountains and over the Agua Negra pass. Once over the border follow the road to the Argentine city of **San Juan.**

The pass at Agua Negra is closed all winter due to bitter conditions and, although it is open Dec.-Mar., it's worth your while to double-check with authorities in La Serena or Vicuña before you attempt the ascent. The customs office in Juntas (84km from the border) is open from 8am-5pm. The process is fairly simple and involves no more than a brief search of your luggage for contraband and various food products and a passport stamp (see **Essentials: Border Crossings,** p. 65, for info on visas and fees).

FROM THE ROAD

ME AND ZIGGY: A SHORT HISTORY OF THE UNIVERSE

Some people come to the Elqui Valley in Chile for its unique offerings—the consistently clear sky and fertile valleys overflowing with papayas, artichokes, and rows of Muskatel grapes perfect for *pisco*. Others, particularly astrophysicists, come here for some of the world's foremost observatories. And still others come here to interact firsthand with aliens.

Leave it to me to find myself making spaghetti sauce in a wooden cabin in the valley that is home to a 50-year-old Bavarian who belongs firmly in the third category.

Ziggy lives in the last house in Cochiguaz, an isolated community of hippies and spiritualists, with his partner Ana and their two small children. Residents of Cochiguaz believe that the Elqui Valley is the center of energy and power on earth. According to a peculiar science, the center of energy shifts every 12,992 years from the Himalayas to the Andes, and the current shift to the Andes is due to be complete in 2012, when the planet Kobolus will appear. The Elqui Valley has become a popular destination for those seeking to connect to the magnetism of the earth. Consequently, the valley is dotted with meditation pyramids and the oddly shaped homes in the community display guides for meditation, homeopathy, and chakra cleansing.

According to Ziggy, the magnetism of the area is responsible for the frequent UFO sightings. You see, the wellness of the earth is reflected in this valley, and aliens come to check it out in preparation for landing. Ziggy insists that the scientists in the area

5 SIGHTS. Visitors who wish to honor the spirit of Pisco Elqui can raise a glass after a tour of the **Solar de Pisco Tres Erres,** the *pisco* plant at the edge of the plaza. *(English tours 11:30am-12:30pm and 2:30-6:30pm; off-season closed every alternate Su or M. Free.)* Travelers who want to take advantage of the beautiful surroundings should check out **Rancho Rodríguez.** This ranch offers horseback riding tours into the valley for a reasonable CH$2500 per hour. They also offer 2hr. nighttime stargazing tours (CH$5000), as well as overnight tours. *(Walk up the main road from the plaza, past Mandarino, and take a right onto Prat at the top of the hill. The ranch is down the hill on the left, across from El Tesoro.)*

COCHIGUAZ   ☎51

Just above Monte Grande, the road splits and a windy dirt road crosses the river and cuts into the mountains. This remote stretch of land is known as Cochiguaz and it is one of the most unique towns in all of Chile, although it's not so much a town as a string of campgrounds, *cabañas*, and holistic healing centers. It was founded in its current incarnation in the 1960s by groups of hippies who flocked to the area for its reported healing powers. Despite its decentralization, the local residents have a strong community. Many of them are bonded by their belief in the spiritual power of the valley. According to one commonly held theory, Cochiguaz is the world center of energy and harmony. Believers say that the balance of energy in the world shifts from the Himalayas to the Andes and vice-versa every 12,992 years. The new era of energy in the Andes is just beginning and residents of Cochiguaz want to be right where it all starts. Regardless of your personal belief in these theories, or lack thereof, Cochiguaz is an interesting place to spend a few days. The setting, along the northern banks of the Río Cochiguaz, is breathtaking and the massages are, if nothing else, relaxing and rejuvenating.

There is only one road in Cochiguaz; it threads its way through the mountains for 19km. There are quite a few *cabañas* and campgrounds along the way and visitors need only drive along and find the one that suits their fancy. A couple of examples are the **Alma Zen ❹,** a solar powered inn 11km along the road. Rooms face the river and its gurgling provides a soothing lullaby. The mosquito netting over the bed looks like royal trappings. (☎228 957. Singles CH$20,000, with heat CH$25,000; doubles CH$35,000.) **Río Mágico ❶,** below the Alma Zen, has **camping** for CH$4000 per couple per night, right on the banks of the river. At the end of the road, the **Casa del Agua ❸** is one of the most luxurious options in accommodations. The *cabañas* here resemble a little red-roofed village as you head towards it along the road. Though expensive, the *casa* does provide exceptional service. There is an attractive restaurant, natural and heated pools to bathe in, massage service, and even horseback riding tours led by a very interesting Bavarian named Ziggy. (☎293 798; www.casadelagua.cl. 4-person *cabañas* CH$40,000, 6-person CH$54,000.)

There is no public transportation beyond Monte Grande. It is possible to hike along the main road. And although *Let's Go* does not recommend hitchhiking, there are many people who believe enough in karma to pick up tired backpackers.

VALLENAR ☎ 51

Vallenar takes its name from the hometown of the colonial governor Bernardo O'Higgins, who was from Ballenagh, Ireland. Over time the name was bastardized and now the city of Vallenar doesn't even resemble Ireland in name. Halfway between La Serena and Copiapó, Vallenar is the main city in the Huasco valley. Though not huge, it is a nice enough place to spend a day and makes a good jumping-off spot for daytrips to other villages in the valley.

⬚ TRANSPORTATION

The **terminal de buses** is on the western edge of town at the corner of Prat and Matta. Buses en route to **Copiapó** or **La Serena** stop here several times a day and it is possible to catch a bus to **Santiago** coming from Copiapó or to **Arica** on a bus from La Serena. Not all buses stop in Vallenar however, so it is advisable to check at the ticket booth ahead of time.

Local bus service within the Huasco valley, as well as **taxi colectivo** service, is localized on Maranon between Verdaguer and Ercilla. A couple of buses per day run to **San Felix** and **Alto del Carmen** in the early morning and late afternoon (CH$1000).

⬚ ⬚ ORIENTATION AND PRACTICAL INFORMATION

Buses drop off passengers at the eastern end of town, after descending from the Panamericana. The city is laid out in a very regular grid and navigation is easy. **Plaza O'Higgins** makes a good reference point. The plaza is plopped down in the center of town, interrupting the main thoroughfare, **Prat**. The bus station is several blocks east of the plaza on Prat, and west of the plaza Prat becomes a semi-pedestrian walkway where many of the shops and restaurants are situated. The northern boundary of town is **Maranon**, while **Sargento Aldea** marks the southern edge.

are well-aware of the UFOs but do not have permission to talk about them.

However, news of an alien influx should not worry you for, as Ziggy explains, Darwin was wrong: evolution never happened. Rather, each human race was developed by various types of aliens and then placed on earth.

Ziggy told me that he doesn't remain idle while waiting for his alien ancestors to return to earth. In his past life he was a viking and stayed busy doing viking-like things. In this life, like many people in Cochiguaz, Ziggy leads horseback riding and trekking trips through the valley and the Casa del Agua (www.valledeelqui.cl).

Deciding not to take Ziggy up on a trekking offer, I found myself on the way to Monte Grande the next morning after my night at the Alma Zen (no UFO sightings, unfortunately). A few kilometers on the way to Pisco Elqui, I encountered an animated middle-aged man in a blue jeep who spoke his own mixture of Spanish, English, and German who offered me a ride and a place to stay for the night. Ordinarily not in the habit of accepting kindness from strangers, I accepted this generous offer and got free lodging for the night in addition to having my aura discovered.

I blame the valley's karma for making me so trusting. Or maybe it was Ziggy's insight into my soul and my fears that he discerned from my name and the mystical sense I exuded. Either way, their ideas may not be mainstream, but the people in the Elqui Valley are nothing if not kind, and they open their homes and hearts to visitors willing to open their minds. Drop by to collect some food for thought.

– Jane Lindholm

There is no tourist office in Vallenar, but visitors can ask for information at the bus terminal or at the **municipalidad,** on the northeast corner of the plaza. Several **banks** and **ATMs** are also conveniently located along Prat. The **Centro Cultural de Vallenar,** at the corner of Prat and Colchagua, sometimes offers painting exhibits. **Ahumado** is the 24hr. pharmacy on the corner of Prat and Colchagua, near the Centro Cultural. The **hospital** (☎611 202) is on the northeast side of town, on the corner of Merced and Talca. There is a small **Internet** kiosk located on the southwest side of the plaza, opposite the church that keeps irregular hours (CH$900 per hr.). The **post office** is off the northeast corner of the plaza.

ACCOMMODATIONS

There are no spectacular deals in Vallenar, but everything is pretty acceptable. Most of the budget accommodations are a few blocks off Prat in either direction and there are a couple of upscale locations in the southern part of the town.

Hostal Camino del Rey, Merced 943 (☎613 184), off Santiago. Rooms come with cable TV and some have private baths. Although on the small side, they are brightly lit and have windows onto the courtyard. But the best thing about this hostel is that the breakfast includes two eggs—a far cry from the mere toast and marmalade that most equivalent places serve. Singles CH$7800, with private bath CH$13,000; doubles CH$13,000/CH$18,000. ❸

Hotel Cecil, Prat 1059 (☎614 071), right on the main drag. There are metallic fish on the lobby wall and although this could look cheesy, they fit in well at the Hotel Cecil. Rooms off the courtyard look like a little village of row houses. Inside, they are roomy with chairs and couches. There is also a pool and parking. Breakfast included. Prices are negotiable. Singles CH$18,000; doubles CH$22,000. ❹

Residencial Oriental, Serrano 720 (☎613 889), near the plaza. Sherbet-colored birds cheerily chirp in their courtyard cage. The rooms are similarly cheerful and are a very good deal for the price. All rooms have TVs, some with baths. Singles CH$3500, with private bath CH$6500; doubles CH$7000/CH$12,000. ❶

Hotel Garra de León, Serrano 1052 (☎613 753), is very roomy with huge bathrooms and large bedrooms. Probably the nicest place in town, it's also among the priciest. Still, to have fridges that look as secure as safes justifies the expense. Breakfast included. Singles CH$28,000; doubles CH$34,100; triples CH$38,500. ❺

Hostería de Vallenar, Arcilla 848 (☎614 379), in the southeast corner of town near the Museo del Huasco. This is the one of the ritzier places in Vallenar, and although it's not exceptional, those with money to burn may want to check it out. The beds are extremely high and very comfortable, the bathrooms have big bathtubs for soaking, and there are tempting snacks left out on top of the wet bar. Rooms with 3 beds are a little cramped but the rooms for 4 people have 2 separate sleeping areas. Singles CH$34,650; doubles CH$39,900; each extra person CH$13,650. ❺

Residencial Mary 2, Ramírez 631 (☎610 322), just north of and parallel to the plaza. Not the most attractive place, but inexpensive and friendly. Rooms are decent sized with private baths and the plastic walls are made to look like wood. Enter through the restaurant. CH$5000 per person. ❷

FOOD

Like accommodations, the food in Vallenar is not spectacular but suffices. The **Mercado Municipal** on Serrano and Santiago, below Prat, has some cheap choices.

Café, Prat 874, 2 blocks west of the plaza. This bright pastel building and swirly sign call out to strollers. And what do they say? Come on in and try the excellent ice cream and sandwiches the cafe has to offer. The inside is sleek and outside there are tables set up so diners can watch passersby. Enjoy the full, well-stocked bar. Open M-Sa 10am-7pm. ❷

Bar Bogart, Serrano 975. This 50s style bar lives up to its name. Dark red carpeting and black walls are accented by hanging posters of Marilyn Monroe and James Dean. The sandwiches are cheap and the drinks are not, but of all the gin-joints in the world, this is the one to check out. Open M-Sa 10am-4am, Su 7pm-2am. ❷

Il Boccato, Prat 750, on the plaza. Basic but good for sandwiches and pizzas, Boccato also has an extensive menu of pastas. There's not a lot of character but the waiters are attentive and it's a good place to catch your favorite *telenovela* on the big screen. Open Su-Th 10am-midnight, F-Sa 10am-1am. ❷

Café del Centro, Prat 1121, in the main part of town, feels like a diner and serves good diner food. It's the perfect place to pop in for *onces* when it's not too crowded. Peach Melba CH$1800. Open 10am-3pm and 5-10pm. ❶

🄯 SIGHTS

There's not much to see in Vallenar, although the **Museo del Huasco,** in the southwest corner of town, tries its best to provide an educational resource for tourists and schoolchildren. Financed only by its entrance fees, the museum clearly does not have enough money to update, so it looks as old and dusty as some of its artifacts. Despite its financial difficulties, it remains a good museum. The diagrams of Chilean regions are informative, and it has many interesting exhibits of colonial artifacts, including a stockade used by the Spanish to punish prisoners, as well as some disturbingly toothy porcelain dolls. The recreated burial site and enormous clamshells are also worth a glance. *(Sargento Aldea 742, between Colchagua and Alonzo de Ercilla. ☎ 610 635. Open M-F 9am-1pm and 3-6pm. CH$450, children CH$200.)* The **plaza** is also an entertaining spot to pass the time. The resident church has a distinctive open steeple and copper dome. There is a fountain in the center—by day adults sit around it on the benches and chat; in the evening, teenage bikers take over, riding the benches and taking tremendous falls.

ALTO DEL CARMEN

Deeper into the Huasco valley are the secluded towns of Alto del Carmen and San Felix, 45km and 70km, respectively, from Vallenar. Along the windy but well paved rural route to Alto del Carmen is the huge dam called the **Embalse Santa Juana,** finished in 2000, which plugs up the Río Huasco, making the hills fall straight into the still blue water. Farther along, the road forks just before reaching Alto del Carmen. The right branch leads to the small town of El Transito, but the road is not very well-paved and there is no public transportation. The left hand fork leads right into downtown Alto del Carmen, known mostly for its *pisco* plant, which makes the well-known brand by the same name. There is only one main street, a church, and a small restaurant called **Jorgito.** Tours of the plant are free and run from M-F 8:30am-12:30pm and 2-6pm. There is no place to stay in Alto del Carmen.

SAN FELIX

Another 35km east is the even smaller town of San Felix. The main reason to visit San Felix is to check out the *pisco* plant. There may be other *pisqueras* that are easier to get to, but this is the best tour out of all of them. The plant, which makes the specialty brand Horcón Quemado, is up the hill in San Felix. Ring the doorbell and ask for a tour. The amiable grandson of the original founder still makes *pisco* in the plant attached to his home and he is happy to give a tour for even one person. The equipment is old and interesting and Sr. Mulet spikes his narrative with personal anecdotes. The *pisco* is of the highest quality since it is made in small batches, something of a rarity.

What's more, Sr. Mulet has begun constructing beautiful **cabañas** on his land above the plant. They are built with quality and care and have a very home-like feel. The kitchens are spacious and clean and the bedrooms are airy and bright. The view is incredible, and if you get hungry, there are fruit trees outside the front door. (To be completed by January 2003. 6-person *cabaña* CH$35,000.) San Felix's main plaza is overgrown and jungle-like and on the corner sits the **Residencial San Felix ❶,** run by a very old couple. The rooms are sparse and the bathrooms are extremely rustic but the owners are very nice and also run an attached restaurant. (Rooms CH$2500 per person.)

A couple of regional **buses** leave daily from the terminal on Maranon and head to San Felix by way of Alto del Carmen (CH$1000). There are also **colectivos** that go to the nearer Alto del Carmen and leave from near the bus terminal (CH$2000).

COPIAPÓ ☎ 52

The city of Copiapó, discovered in 1832 by the townsman Juan Godoy, was originally named Copayapu, a Diaguita word meaning cup of gold. But it was silver, not gold, that gave Copiapó its wealth. Godoy's discovery led to several silver booms and a great economic surge for the city, bringing with it, among other things, South America's first railroad. Mining has remained an important part of Copiapó's character and the remnants of old mines are visible in some of the dusty hills that surround the city. Recent years have not been especially kind to the mining industry and the city has begun to feel the pinch. Present-day Copiapó has a bustling city center and a workaday feel, but other than a few museums dedicated to regional history, tourist activities are scarce. Many visitors use the city as a base for exploring nearby national parks like Parque Nacional Nevado Tres Cruces and Parque Nacional Pan de Azúcar.

☐ TRANSPORTATION

Flights: Chamonate Airport (☎214 360) 15km west of Copiapó. **LanChile,** Colipí 484 (☎213 512 or 214 085), just off the plaza. Open M-F 9am-1:30pm and 3-7pm, Sa 10am-1pm. **LanChile Express,** Colipí 354 (☎217 285 or 217 406). Daily flights to **Santiago** on LanChile and LanChile Express (formerly Ladeco) and to **La Serena** on LanChile Express.

Buses: Terminal de Buses, Chacabuco 112 (☎212 577), down by the Panamericana. Though most companies depart from here, several have their own terminals, including **Tas Choapa,** Chañarcillo 631 (☎238 066); **Tur Bus,** Chañarcillo 680 (☎238 612); and **Pullman Bus,** Colipí 109 (☎212 977), a block from the terminal. Pullman Bus hits all northern destinations, including: **Arica** (16hr., CH$20,000); **Iquique** (14hr., CH$18,000); and **Antofagasta** (8hr., CH$14,000). Other buses going north include Tur Bus and Buses Fenix. Heading south, **Pullman Bus, Tur Bus, Flota Barrios** (☎213 645), and **Libac** (213 355) all go to **La Serena** (5hr., several per day, CH$6000), and Santiago (11hr., 2 per day, CH$12,000). **Regional Buses** are across from the Terminal de Buses on the corner of Chacabuco and Esperanza. **Buses Recabarren** (☎216 991) and **Casther** (☎218 889) go to **Caldera** (1hr., CH$1000).

Taxis and Colectivos: Taxis hang out at the Plaza de Armas. *Colectivos* to Diego de Almagro can be grabbed from Chacabuco 151, where the regional buses pull in, across the street from the Terminal de Buses. *Colectivos* to Vallenar, Huasco, Caldera, and Chañaral can be found there or at the Terminal de Buses.

Car Rental: Avis, Peña 102 (☎213 966), off the Panamericana. **Budget,** Friere 466 (☎218 802 or ☎216 030), right on the Panamericana. Both are at the western end of town.

✦ 🛈 ORIENTATION AND PRACTICAL INFORMATION

Copiapó has a central area constructed in a grid pattern. The center of the grid is **Plaza Prat.** Most accommodations and restaurants are within a few blocks of the plaza. To the west, the town squeezes between dusty hills and stretches thin in the area where there are several museums and the university. The southern boundary of the city is the **Panamericana,** alternately called **Copayapu, Kennedy,** or **Freire.** Northern **Infante** has most amenities, and the eastern boundary is at **Henríquez.**

Tourist Office: Sernatur, Los Carrera 691 (☎231 510), on the northeast side of the plaza, is very helpful. English spoken. Open M-F 9am-5:30pm, Sa-Su 9am-5:30pm.

Conaf, Martínez 55 (☎210 282 or 237 104), a 15min. walk west of the plaza, has

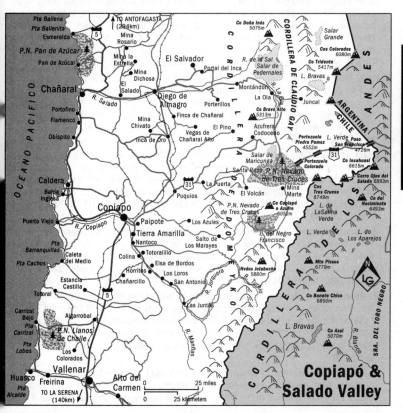

Copiapó & Salado Valley

NORTE CHICO

good information about nearby national parks Nevado Tres Cruces and Pan de Azucar, as well as updates on trail conditions. Open M-Th 8:30am-5:30pm, F 8:30am-4:30pm.

Bank: There are several **banks** and **ATMs** on the eastern side of Plaza Prat.

Market: There is a huge **Deca Supermarket** on Chacabuco between Atacama and Chañarcillo. Open M-F 8am-9:30pm, Sa-Su 9am-7pm.

Emergency: ☎ 131

Police: ☎ 133. *Carabineros,* O'Higgins 753.

Pharmacy: Farmacias Ahumada has two locations, Chacabuco 201 (☎ 231 815) and O'Higgins 561 (☎ 236 712).

Hospital: Hospital San Jose (☎ 212 023), on Los Carreras at the corner with Vicuña, several blocks east of the plaza.

Internet Access: Cyber Chat, Vallejos 431 (☎ 099 553 9139). CH$600 per hr. Open 9am-midnight.

Post Office: Los Carreras 691 (☎ 212 398), behind Sernatur. Open M-F 8:30am-6pm.

ACCOMMODATIONS

Hotel Chagall, O'Higgins 760 (☎ 213 775 or 211 454), one block off the plaza. After stepping off a bus after a long grimy ride, Chagall looks like Shangri-La. Nice big lobby, pastoral paintings on the walls, plush beds, and that "nice hotel" smell. The suites are beautiful—large and elegant. Singles are roomy and luxurious. Warm in winter; A/C in the summer. Breakfast included. The only kicker? You guessed it, the price. Singles CH$37,640; doubles CH$41,180; triples CH$46,000; suites CH$46,020. ❺

Hotel Montecatini I, Infante 766 (☎ 211 363). Big, wide doors let in lots of light in this mid-range hotel. The stately courtyard has a pool. Rooms on the opposite sides of the courtyard have different prices. The older rooms on the right are just fine and cheaper, but the newer "VIP" rooms have carpets and cable TV. Private baths. Breakfast included. Singles CH$12,700, VIP CH$17,000; doubles CH$17,500/CH$24,500; triples CH$22,800. ❸

Hotel Copa de Oro, Infante 530 (☎ 216 309). A bright green building that's hard to miss. Many of the rooms here look out over the parking lot and can be a little dark, but they're not gloomy. Fancy lampshades grace the bedside table lamps and the rooms have nice tables, cable TV, and private baths. There are soft leather couches in the lounge. Breakfast included. Singles CH$20,000; doubles CH$25,000; triples CH$30,000. ❹

Residencial Nuevo Chañarcillo, Rodríguez 540 (☎ 217 105). This *residencial* has a green theme with unique rooms and quirky collections in the hallways. Rooms all have flowery wallpaper and some have private baths. Rooms with shared baths are an especially good deal. Singles CH$4720, with bath CH$9440; doubles CH$8260/CH$12,980; triples CH$12,390/CH$15,930. ❷

Residencial Casa Grande, Infante 525 (☎ 244 450), across from Copa de Oro. Fittingly, this *residencial* is located in what appears to be a very big house. At one point it must have been quite nice, but it's a little dilapidated now. Nonetheless, it is a great budget option with airy and bright rooms, some with wood paneling, and a nice courtyard. Some long-term renters stay here, so there is not always room. Rooms CH$3000 per person. ❶

Residencial Chañarcillo, Chañarcillo 741 (☎ 213 281), near the bus station. Not to be confused with the Residencial Nuevo Chañarcillo. Although it's very basic and the rooms are small, it is one of the better choices for lodging near the bus terminal. There

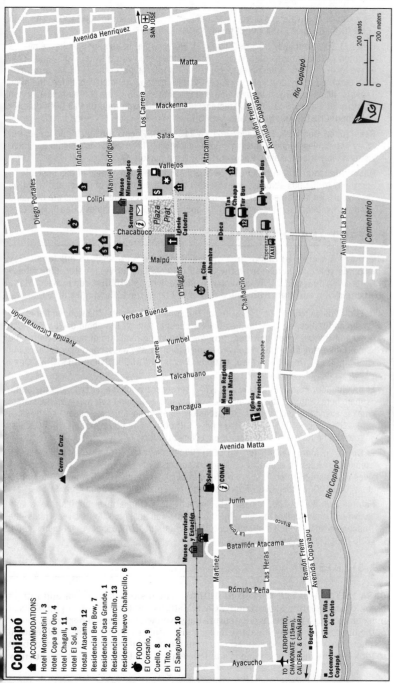

NORTE CHICO

Copiapó

▲ ACCOMMODATIONS
Hotel Montecatini I, **3**
Hotel Copa de Oro, **4**
Hotel Chagall, **11**
Hotel El Sol, **5**
Hostal Atacama, **12**
Residencial Ben Bow, **7**
Residencial Casa Grande, **1**
Residencial Chañarcillo, **13**
Residencial Nuevo Chañarcillo, **6**

♦ FOOD
El Corsario, **9**
Cuello, **8**
Di Tito, **2**
El Sanguchon, **10**

is a choice of private or shared baths. All rooms have TV. Singles CH$4000, with bath CH$7000; doubles CH$12,000; triples CH$15,000. ❷

Hotel El Sol, Rodríguez 550 (☎215 672). Hotel El Sol is as sunny as its name—it's painted yellow both inside and out. Most rooms come with private baths, and some have cable TV. Rooms here are decent but not worth the price—this feels like a *residencial* that tried to up its standings simply by placing the word hotel in its name. The manager is willing to bargain though, and a single with shared baths and no breakfast can cost as little as CH$4000. Breakfast included. Singles with bath CH$13,000; doubles with bath CH$18,000; triples with bath CH$20,000. ❸

Residencial Ben Bow, Rodríguez 541 (☎215 672). Rooms are small and basic, but they are spotlessly clean and the snazzy yellow walls keep everyone's spirits up. There is a restaurant on the side. Rooms CH$3000 per person. ❶

Hostal Atacama, Chanarchillo 620 (☎363 5220). The main appeal of this hostel is its proximity to the bus station. Otherwise this is a last-resort type of place, and when we say resort, we don't mean luxury. Paint peels off the walls, and the rooms are dark and drafty. Private baths. Singles CH$5000; doubles CH$10,000; triples CH$15,000. ❷

🔾 FOOD AND ENTERTAINMENT

There are a couple of discos in Copiapó for those who wish to cut loose. Try **Splash,** Martínez 46, across from the Conaf offices. The movie theater, **Cine Alhambra,** Atacama 455 (☎212 187), downtown, shows a couple of first-run movies. Make an evening of it and start with a nice dinner at one of the following establishments.

Di Tito, Chacabuco 710 (☎244 309), on the corner with Infante. The wooden floors and green and red ceiling give the restaurant a cheerful feeling. The photo of New York City covering the back wall however, provides a haunting reminder of recent events. The smells emerging from the kitchen are enough to make any passersby linger to check out the big list of veggie and meat options. Pizzas CH$2500. Schop CH$1350. Open 10am-4pm and 7pm-2am. ❷

El Sanguchon, Atacama 407 (☎231 872), serves sandwiches with style and the atmosphere here, with red stucco walls, neon lights in the bar, and soft music on the stereo, makes everything taste better. Unfortunately, charm doesn't come cheap—sandwiches are a little pricey (CH$2300). Fresh juice CH$600, *leche con platano* CH$750. Take-out available for lunch or dinner. Open 10am-11:30pm. ❷

El Corsario, Atacama 245 (☎233 659). While it's possible to sit inside, the outside seating is where it's at at this seafood restaurant. Birds chirp blissfully, the water sparkles in a plant-filled pool, and a waiter in a black vest hurries forth with a plate of oysters (CH$4000). Open M-Sa noon-4pm and 7:30-midnight, Su noon-4pm. ❸

Fabrica Helados Cuello, Maipú 519. You may do a double take, but it's true—a soft-serve ice cream maker in Chile. This hole-in-the-wall delights with its sweet treats—the machinery looks like it's straight out of the 50s, but the ice cream still tastes good. CH$200-300 for a swirl. ❶

👁 SIGHTS

CASA MATTA AND THE MUSEO REGIONAL. The historic monument and former home of the wealthy Matta family, Casa Matta is the location of Copiapó's best museum. Though modest, it does surprisingly well with its limited resources. Some of the displays are pretty standard: indigenous history through the ages and regional artifacts like muskets and copper pots from the colonial period. But the room built to look like the inside of a mine is a unique experience that adults just might enjoy as much as kids. A pamphlet (printed partly in English) offers information about the city and its history. The staff is helpful for visitors requesting any more information. *(Atacama 98, on the corner with Rancagua. Open M 2-5:45pm, Tu-F 9am-5:45pm, Sa 10am-12:45pm and 3-5:45pm, Su 10am-12:45pm. CH$600, children CH$300; Su free.)*

PLAZA DE ARMAS "ARTURO PRAT". One of the most beautiful in Chile, Plaza Prat is filled with palm trees, tiled walkways, and a central fountain. On the western side of the plaza is the **Iglesia Catedral.** The church was built between 1840 and 1841 to replace an earlier church that was destroyed in an earthquake. Together the plaza and the church make a lovely town center, a great place to sit with an ice cream or a book.

IGLESIA SAN FRANCISCO. This towering, red-walled church is quite striking as it stands watch over the plaza. If you are in Copiapó on a Friday morning, tear yourself away from the busy center and head over to the *iglesia*, where the **farmers' market** will be in full swing. The church was built in 1872 and was the sight of the first Franciscan convent in the area. *(Near the Panamericana on the western edge of town, between Matta and Rancagua. Market F 7am-3pm.)*

MUSEO MINEROLÓGICO. Although to some it might seem like a glorified rock collection, the mineral displays in Copiapó's Museo Minerológico are well-presented, well-labeled, and well worth a look. Divided by shape and physical make-up, some of the specimens here glow blue and green. Interesting displays compare and contrast minerals in their natural form with polished-up finished products like marble tiles. Old mining photos line the walls, and there are some informational posters in English. *(On the corner of Colipí and Rodríguez, a block from the plaza. ☎ 206 606. Open M-F 10am-1pm and 3:30-7pm, Sa 10am-1pm. CH$500, children CH$200.)*

ESTACIÓN FERROCARRIL. As the original train station in Copiapó, it must have been fabulous when first built—a beautiful wide building with tall windows and a low slung colonial style. The station itself is closed now, but it's still a nice place to sit for a while. Kids play on the on the old model trains that sit in front. *(On Martínez at the corner with Batallon Atacama, in the town's west end.)*

UNIVERSIDAD DE ATACAMA. On the western edge of town, across the Panamericana, the Universidad de Atacama serves the region's higher educational needs while preserving some of the city's historical artifacts. The **Palacete Viña de Cristo** used to be an elegant mansion, but now the walls are peeling and it's sort of run down. Visitors can walk right in and head up the elegant spiral staircase to the cupola. From the top there is a nice view of the barren hills behind the town. The University is also the final resting place of the **Locomotura Copiapó,** the first railcar in South America and one of the oldest steam engines in the world. Built by Norris Brothers in Philadelphia in 1850, it was the inaugural car on the first railroad in South America, which went from Copiapó to Caldera. *(The Palacete is on University grounds at the end of Romulo Peña. Open Mar.-Dec. M-F 9am-6pm. The Locomotura is outside, a few blocks further on, also within the school grounds. Ask for directions if lost.)*

EAST OF COPIAPÓ

PARQUE NACIONAL NEVADO TRES CRUCES

Parque Nacional Nevado Tres Cruces, 180km from Copiapó, is fast becoming one of Chile's most desired new adventure destinations. Founded in 1995 on 59,000 hectares of land deep in the *cordillera* of the Atacama region, it is known for the large numbers of flamingos that feed in the saline waters of its several lakes. The park consists of two main sections.

NORTE CHICO

The larger sector of the park comprises the Laguna Santa Rosa and the Salar de Maricunga. The **Salar de Maricunga** is a large, brilliant-white salt flat surrounded by tall mountains. Stretching across the barren, isolated land with its odd, flamingo-filled pools, it is the most southernly salt flat of the Atacama region. The blue waters of **Laguna Santa Rosa** begin in the southeast end of the Salar de Maricunga and help sustain a population of *guanacos* and other Chilean flora and fauna.

The smaller sector of the park, a few hours south of the larger sector, encircles the **Laguna del Negro Francisco,** a striking deep blue-green lake at 4500m above sea level. It actually has an incredible variety of crustaceans and other aquatic organisms due to the variation of salinity levels in different parts of the lake. Flamingos linger in both the salty and freshwater parts, dotting the entire lake with color.

To reach the park from Copiapó, drivers should take International Highway 31 east out of the city. At Sector de la Puerto, take the east fork, Route C-341, to get to Laguna Santa Rosa. Allow several hours for the trip. Laguna Del Negro Francisco is another 85km south of this sector. Visitors should be sure to have good 4WD vehicles to drive anywhere in the park or if crossing into Argentina (see **Border Crossing,** p. 248). For detailed instructions and information, contact Conaf or Sernatur in Copiapó. Entrance to the park is CH$2500 for nationals and CH$3500 for foreigners; children are CH$500/CH$1000.

OJOS DEL SALADO

Volcán Ojos del Salado lies just outside of Parque Nacional Nevado Tres Cruces, and the volcano is rivaling its neighbor as one of the "hottest" regional destinations for adventurous travelers. It is the Chilean Andes' tallest peak at somewhere around 6890m (the exact height is disputed) and is considered the world's highest active volcano, with two eruptions in the 20th century. It derives its name from the large salt deposits, once saline lakes, that are scattered throughout the area. At the base of the volcano sits the emerald **Laguna Verde,** a lake which seems to contain no living organisms. The climb up Ojos del Salado is not particularly technical, but can be difficult at the top, and is cold year-round. Climbers wishing to try it should go between October and April—Conaf recommends seven days to attempt the climb. There are two *refugios* along the way: the **Universidad de Atacama** has a small basic *refugio* at 5100m and **Refugio Cesar Tejos,** at 5750m, is larger and somewhat better equipped. Because the volcano straddles the border with Argentina, hikers must obtain special permission to attempt the trek. The Conaf offices in Copiapó and Santiago have more information on this process.

 BORDER CROSSING INTO ARGENTINA: PASO DE SAN FRANCISCO

To the north of Volcán Ojos del Salado is Paso de San Francisco, the route from Chile into Argentina. Several *ripio* roads from Copiapó and the surrounding area meet in PN Nevado Tres Cruces, passing by stretches of salt flats, flocks of flamingos, and high barren peaks. **Chilean customs** is at the Salar de Maricunga, 105km from the pass. The route continues across the border to **Tinogasta** in Argentina.

The pass can be closed in winter due to inclement weather, so it's worth your while to double-check with Conaf before attempting the crossing. The customs office at Maricunga station is open from 8:30am-6:30pm. The process is fairly simple and involves no more than a brief search of your luggage for contraband and various food products and a passport stamp (see **Essentials: Border Crossings,** p. 65, for info on visas and fees).

To get to Ojos del Salado, continue along the international highway from Parque Nacional Nevado Tres Cruces. From Copiapó, it is about 260km to the base of the mountain. The highway ultimately unites Copiapó with the province of Catamarca in Argentina.

WEST OF COPIAPÓ

CALDERA   ☎52

Unlike many of its industrial neighbors, Caldera (pop. 12,000) is deceptively unscathed—the sun is plentiful on the fine sandy beaches here, and the tranquil bays are perfect for a leisurely afternoon of swimming, kayaking, and windsurfing. Although Caldera was developed as a port for the region's silver and copper mines, it still manages to project a relaxed holiday town atmosphere, even on Playa Copiapina, which lies right inside the port.

TRANSPORTATION. Taxi colectivos leave from the Plaza de Armas in Caldera and run between Caldera and **Bahía Inglesa** (5-10min., CH$400) and **Copiapó** (CH$1400). During the summer, **minibuses** run between Caldera (from the Plaza de Armas) and Bahía Inglesa (from Av. Chañaral) for CH$200. **Taxis** cost CH$1500 between Caldera and Bahía Inglesa. **Tur Bus,** Gallo 149 (☎316 832), near Vallejos, departs from its office for: **Antofagasta** (6hr.; 9:15, 11:45am, 5, 8:15, 11:45pm; CH$6600) via **Chañaral** (1hr., CH$1200); **Arica** (18hr., 11:45am, CH$11,200); **Calama** (10hr., 9:15am and 11:45pm, CH$12,400); **Iquique** (12hr., 11:45am and 8:15pm, CH$10,500); **Santiago** (12hr., 9:15pm, CH$7200) via **Copiapó** (1hr., CH$1000), **Vallenar** (3hr., CH$2800), **La Serena** (6hr., CH$5800); **Taltal** (3hr., 5pm, CH$4100). **Pullman Bus** (☎316 585), just across Gallo from Tur Bus on the corner with Vallejos, goes to: **Antofagasta** (7hr., 6 per day 9am-10:30pm, CH$10,000) via **Chañaral** (1hr., CH$1000); **Arica** (16hr., 1:15 and 9:15pm, CH$13,000); **Iquique** (12hr.; 1:15, 8, 10:30pm; CH$12,000); **Santiago** (12hr.; 7, 7:10, 7:30, 9, 10:15pm; CH$8000-12,000) via **Copiapó** (1hr., CH$1000), **Vallenar** (3hr., CH$3000), **La Serena** (6hr., CH$5000).

ORIENTATION AND PRACTICAL INFORMATION. The main streets with most shops and services are **Ossa Cerda, Gana,** and **Cousino** between **Wheelwright** and **Carvallo.** The **Municipalidad** is housed in the **Ex Estación Ferrocarril,** the old train station on the waterfront. This long green building studded with wooden beams has a large hall inside for movie showings and cultural and musical performances, as well as a helpful **tourist information office.** (☎316 891. Open M-Sa 9am-2pm and 6-11pm, Su 10am-2pm; off-season M-F 9am-1:30pm and 3-5pm.)

Caldera has most services, including **Banco Estado** with an **ATM** on Gallo and Tocomal; **El Inca supermarket** at Cousino and Edwards (open 9am-10:30pm); a **police** station, Batallon de Atacama 319 (☎315 237); and **Farmacia Cruz** on Gana and Galo. (☎315 133. Open M-Sa 9:30am-10pm, Su 5pm-10pm.) Internet is available at **CasiCasi,** Ossa Cerda 484, opposite the church. (CH$1000 for 30min. Open 8am-9:30pm.) There is also a **Chile Express,** Ossa Cerda 370 (☎315 707); **Bianchi,** Edwards 520-A (☎315 748), which sells camping gear; and a **post office,** Edwards 325 (☎315 285).

ACCOMMODATIONS AND FOOD. Accommodation options are plentiful in Caldera but it is better to stay in Bahía Inglesa, which has excellent camping and *cabañas* in beautiful surroundings. There are a few places in Caldera that you can try, including **Hotel Costanera ❸,** Wheelwright 543, on Playa Copiapina,

NORTE CHICO

which has decent rooms with TV, baths, and breakfast. (☎316 007. Singles CH$12,000-18,000; doubles CH$14,000-22,000; triples CH$16,000-24,000.) **Hotel Pucara ❸,** Ossa Cerda 460, opposite the Iglesia, is another option with its self-serve kitchen and clean rooms with baths, TV, and breakfast. (☎319 886. Singles CH$7000-12,000; doubles CH$10,000-15,000.) Gastronomically, the choices are fairly good in Caldera. **Nuevo Miramar ❷,** on Playa Copiapina, has good service and good fish (CH$3100-4500). (☎315 381. *Carne* CH$2600-3800, sandwiches CH$800-1650. Open M-Sa noon-4pm and 7pm-midnight, Su noon-8pm.) There is also **New Charles Restaurante ❸,** on Ossa Cerda between Gallo and Carvallo, with the canteen-like atmosphere. Entrees CH$3000-4500. (☎315 348. Open 9am-2am.)

🅖 🎵 **SIGHTS AND ENTERTAINMENT.** Just a block away from the Municipalidad is **Ex Aduana** on Wheelwright and Gana, a green neo-classical building which is now the **Centro de Desarrollo Cultural.** (☎316 576. Open M-F 8:30am-1pm, 2:30-6pm, and 7-10:30pm; Sa 10am-2pm and 4-8pm. Free.) Part of **Universidad de Atacama** (☎319 436 or 316 576), the Centro has an exhibition room and a tiny museum in two rooms downstairs, devoted to the region's archeology, history, and geology. A few blocks inland, in the **Plaza de Armas** on Carvallo is the **Iglesia de San Vincente** (built in 1862) with a yellow exterior and a tall gothic bell tower. Although **Playa Brava** lies within Caldera, there are a couple of better beaches ten kilometers north, including **Playa Rodillo** and **Ramada,** both crowded in summer and good for bathing. The best beaches, however, are in Bahía Inglesa. In the summer, there are a couple of **discotecas** open, including **Takeo** and **Loreto,** both on Camino Caldera-Bahía Inglesa between Caldera and Bahía Inglesa.

BAHÍA INGLESA   ☎52

Just five kilometers south of Caldera is the little beach resort of Bahía Inglesa, an unadulterated beach nirvana. Named the "English Bay" due to the landing of British privateer Edward Davis in 1687, the fine sand and azure waters attract more than just lonely sailors. During the summer holiday season, the sweeping coastal desert setting draws vacationers from all over Chile, making advanced reservations for the fabulous camping and *cabañas* a must.

The main reason to be in Bahía is its coastal attractions. Excellent beaches are found at Playas Las Machas, Las Piscinas, and El Chuncho y Blanca. There is also **kayak rental** in the summer on Playa El Chuncho next to Hotel Rocas de Bahía. Farther south of Bahía Inglesa are more fine beaches, such as Playas Chorrillos and Bahía Cisne y Puerto Viejo.

Bahía has incredible accommodations considering its small size. These range from rustic camping and *cabañas* to ritzy hotels. Among the former is **Camping Bahía Inglesa ❶** on 20 hectares of fenced camp ground on Playa Las Machas, which offers 56 excellent *cabañas* all with kitchen facilities, baths, and a living room in addition to 90 campsites with clean communal baths. There is also a swimming pool. (Santiago ☎631 8312 or 631 8317; Bahía Inglesa fax 315 424. 6-person *cabañas* CH$14,000-45,000; 6-person campsite CH$7200-18,000.) There are a couple of other places with *cabañas* nearby. One of them is **El Umbral de Bahía Inglesa.** (☎315 000. 2-3 people CH$60,000, off-season CH$30,000; 4-5 people CH$30,000/CH$15,000; 6 people CH$40,000/CH$20,000.) The other one is **Los Jardines de Bahía Inglesa,** which has 35 *cabañas* and a bar/restaurant. (☎315 359; Santiago 698 2650. 2-3 people CH$42,000, off-season CH$33,000; 4-5 CH$56,000/42,000; 6-7 CH$66,000/47,000; 8 people CH$94,000/59,000.) **Hotel Rocas de Bahía ❺,** El Morro 888, right on Playa El Chuncho, is an exquisite whitewashed 4-star hotel where all rooms, tastefully designed in maritime deco, have a great ocean view.

The pyramid-like building, set against the blue ocean water and the white sand, resembles a Greek Aegean resort. On the top floor are a beautiful swimming pool and a bar/restaurant. (☎316 005; www.depetris.cl/rocasdebahia. Baths, breakfast, TV, and free bike rental. Singles CH$29,300-60,000; doubles CH$39,000-66,600; triples CH$47,000-66,000.) If you need to satiate a grumbling stomach, **Bahía House ❶**, El Morro 1038, on Playa El Chuncho, has filling *empanadas* (CH$500-750) and cheap sandwiches. (☎099 348 7204. Open 8am-10pm.) Or splurge a little at the restaurant in the **Hotel Rocas ❸**. (Pasta CH$2500-3800, fish CH$4200-4800, seafood CH$4000-6800, *lomo* CH$3900-4000. Open 12:30-4pm and 8pm-midnight. AmEx/DC/MC/V.)

Taxi colectivos from Bahía Inglesa to the Plaza de Armas in **Caldera** (5-10min., CH$400). During the summer, **minibuses** run between Bahía Inglesa (from Av. Chañaral) and Caldera (from the Plaza de Armas) for CH$200. **Taxis** cost CH$1500 between Bahía Inglesa and Caldera.

NORTH TO NORTE GRANDE

CHAÑARAL   ☎52

Sitting 400km south of Antofagasta and 165km north of Copiapó, Chañaral is little more than a fishing and mining port of 12,000 inhabitants. Nevertheless, its proximity to Parque Nacional Pan de Azúcar (a spectacular sanctuary of coastal desert wilderness) and easy access to the Panamericana make it a good stopover. The highway divides the town into a small northern section and much bigger southern section. Much of the town is on hilly coastal terrain, rising somewhat sharply from the narrow flat shoreline containing sandy but polluted beaches. Merino Jarpa is the main drag with most shops and services. Decent beaches are found farther south of Chañaral, including Playa Flamenco 15min. by car from downtown.

⛟ TRANSPORTATION. Tur Bus (☎481 012), on the Panamericana opposite the Copec station, departs from its office for: **Antofagasta** (5hr.; 7:45am, 12:45, 9:30, 10:45, 11:55pm; CH$5700); **Caldera** (1hr., 2 and 8pm, CH$1200); **Santiago** (14hr.; 7:20am, 3, 4, 6:50, 8pm; CH$13,700) via **Copiapó** (2hr., CH$1800) and **La Serena** (7hr., CH$6100); **Taltal** (2hr., 1:45 and 6:10pm, CH$1900). **Pullman Bus** (☎480 213), on Los Banos across from Municipalidad, departs from its office for: **Arica** (14hr.; 10:15pm, midnight, 12:15am; CH$10,000); **Calama** (8hr.; 9:30, 10:15am, 12:30, 1, 3:30, 11:45pm; CH$8000); **Iquique** (12hr.; 9am, 2:45, 11:30pm, 3am; CH$10,000) via **Antofagasta** (5hr., CH$5000) and **Tocopilla** (7hr., CH$8000); **Santiago** (14hr., 6 per day 3:45-11:45pm, CH$10,000) via **Caldera** (1hr., CH$1000), **Copiapó** (2hr., CH$2500), **La Serena** (7hr., CH$6000). **Flota Barrios**, Merino Jarpa 567 (☎480 894), opposite the fire station, goes to **Calama** (8hr.; 9, 10am, 2pm; CH$8000) via **Antofagasta** (5hr., CH$5000) and **Santiago** (14hr.; 5, 7:30, 8:30, 11:45pm; CH$9000, *salon cama* CH$15,000) via **Copiapó** (2hr., CH$2000), **Vallenar** (4hr., CH$3500), **La Serena** (7hr., CH$5000).

⛏ PRACTICAL INFORMATION. Chañaral has no tourist office, so inquire at **Municipalidad's Relaciones Publica** on the corner of Merino Jarpa and Los Banos. (In Dec. and Jan., there is a tourist information kiosk right on Panamericana, south of Copec station. ☎480 142 ext.209. Open M-F 8am-2pm and 3-7pm.) There is a **souvenir kiosk** next to Municipalidad on Merino Jarpa, where you may book tours to Parque Nacional Pan de Azúcar run by **Souvenir Tour Chile**. (☎099 555 4454. All-day trip to El Mirador CH$28,000, min. 4 people; full-day trip to Las Lomitas CH$45,000, min. 4 people. Open M-Sa 9am-2pm and 6:30-10pm, Su

6:30pm-10pm.) Souvenir Tour Chile also provides taxis to Pan de Azúcar (CH$8000, min. 4 people for round-trip). In terms of amenities, you'll find a **Banco Estado** with an **ATM** at Buin 801. (☎480 000. Open M-F 9am-2pm.) **Supermercado Zamora** is at Templo and Freire. (Open 7am-11pm.) The **police** station (☎480 133) is on Carrera, and the **Hospital Doctor Luis Herrera** (☎480 107) is at Prat and Carrera. Buy late-night supplies at **Farmacia Varas,** Zuleta 150. (☎481 105. Open M-Sa 10am-10pm, Su 10am-noon.) A **Copec** service station and a **Chile Express** with **Western Union** services are located near the *centro de llamadas,* Los Banos 202, opposite Municipalidad. (☎480 187. Open M-F 9am-2pm and 4-7pm, Sa 10:30am-1pm.) **Internet** access is available at **Servicios Computacionales,** Los Banos 202, opposite Municipalidad. (☎480 187. CH$1000 per hr. Open M-Sa 9:30am-2pm and 4:30-9pm). Bikes and camping and fishing gear are available through **Distribuidor Don Alvaro,** Merino Jarpa 1101. (☎480 083. Open M-Sa 10am-9pm.) Chañaral has a **post office,** Comercio 172. (☎489 041. Open M-F 9am-1pm and 3-7pm, Sa 9am-12:30pm.)

⌂⌂ ACCOMMODATIONS AND FOOD. There are several decent accommodations in town, including **Hostal Los Aromos ❷,** Los Aromos 7, a new setup with the most comfortable rooms in town, all with TV. (☎489 636. Singles CH$5000, with bath CH$7000; doubles CH$10,000/CH$15,000; triples $15,000.) Another good option is **Hostería Chañaral ❹,** Muller 268, which has a nice open-air courtyard with lots of flowers and a beach view from the comfy lounge area. Rooms in this aging building include TV, bath, and breakfast, but are slightly overpriced. (Singles CH$18,000; doubles CH$22,000; triples CH$24,000.) The affiliated **restaurant ❸,** however, is entirely decent. (Sandwiches CH$900-CH$1600, fish CH$3500-CH$6500, steaks CH$3600-CH$5500. Open noon-3pm and 7-11pm. AmEx/DC/MC/V.) More basic accommodations are found at **Hotel Jimenez ❹,** Merino Jarpa 551, with its clean rooms, some with TV. (☎480 328. Singles CH$4000, with bath CH$5500; doubles CH$11,000/CH$12,500; quads CH$16,000.) **Hotel Nuria ❸,** Costanera 300, is a good value for rooms with bath, TV, and breakfast. (☎480 903. Singles CH$9000; doubles CH$15,000; triples CH$22,000.) **Hotel Carmona ❷,** is similar to Nuria for rooms with bath and TV (☎480 522 or 480 367. Breakfast included in summer. Singles CH$6000; doubles CH$12,000; triples CH$15,000; quads and quints room CH$20,000), and **Hotel La Marina ❶,** Merino Jarpa 562, opposite Hotel Jimenez, the most basic choice for clean rooms with shared baths. (☎099 340 8464. CH$3000 per person.) There are a few good seafood restaurants next to one another in the northern part of town, right off the Panamericana opposite the Copec gas station, including **La Querencia ❶,** which serves *congrio* (CH$2500), *paila marina* (CH$2500) and fish sandwiches (CH$700) to a clientele that includes many truck drivers and motorists. (☎480 222. Open 24hr.) Next door, **Los Arbolitos ❷,** next to Tur Bus, also serves *congrio* (CH$2800) and *paila marina.* (CH$2500; Open 24hr.) In downtown proper, you can try **Restaurant Rincon Porteno ❷,** Merino Jarpa 567, a canteen-style set up popular with locals where simple meals cost CH$2200-CH$2800. (☎480 071. Open 9am-10pm.)

PARQUE NACIONAL PAN DE AZÚCAR

Created in 1985 on 44,000 hectares of coastal desert wilderness, including mountains reaching up to 800 meters, Pan de Azúcar is now one of the premier national parks of Chile. During the summer months, tens of thousands of tourists from Santiago and as far as Europe flock here for the pristine white sandy beaches, excellent camping, hiking, and fishing, and the abundant flora and fauna (more than 20 cactus species feeding on coastal fog known as *caman-*

AT A GLANCE

AREA: 44,000 hectares.

CLIMATE: Mediterranean. Hot in the summer with temperatures upwards of 13.8°C. Winters are mild and rainy.

GATEWAYS: Chañaral.

FEES: CH$3500, children CH$2000.

HIGHLIGHTS: Pristine white-sand beaches and desert landscapes. Abundant flora and fauna and lots of hiking, camping, and fishing.

CAMPING: Various *refugios* along the beaches; *cabañas* near Caleta.

chaca, plus seagulls, pelicans, cormorants, sea otters, seals, Humboldt penguins, guanacos, foxes, and condors). The renown beaches are dotted with half-buried rock formations that give the entire scene the feel of a mystical Zen garden. Sunsets here are sublime, as the entire coastline with its barren mountain backdrop glows in the translucent hues of the setting sun. It would be a tough call to find another coastal desert more desolate yet more aesthetically and spiritually appealing.

■ **ORIENTATION.** The park is located 22kms north of Chañaral on a good gravel road. **Playa Refugio,** the beach just before the park's southern entrance, is not suitable for camping, but you can walk on its fine sand and admire the stunning scenery. Enter from the southern entrance to approach **Playa Blanca,** an amazing white sand beach lying adjacent to **Playa Piqueros,** which in turn lies at the base of towering Cerro Soldado and near **Playa Soldado.** A couple of hundred meters away from Playa Piqueros is **Isla Pan de Azúcar,** a small hilly island that is home to 3000 Humboldt penguins in addition to seals, sea otters, pelicans, and cormorants. The Isla is off-limits to visitors, but you can approach it on a boat to observe the animals at close range (see below). Although the beaches in the park are not suitable for bathing due to strong currents, they are great for sunbathing or fishing. You can also bike or drive along the well-maintained gravel roads anywhere in the park (no need for a 4WD, guide, or map on these well-marked roads, unless it rains heavily). Among the more worthwhile vantage points in the park are **El Mirador,** a lookout point 300m high and about eight kilometers from the Conaf office, and **Las Lomitas,** a peak 800m high that is 30km from the office. Both can be hiked without great difficulty. A couple of kilometers farther north of the Conaf office is **Caleta Pan de Azúcar,** a ramshackle village of 20 fishermen. Buy fresh seafood directly from the fishermen or stop in at one of the small stores nearby (other provisions available).

■ **TRANSPORTATION.** The best way to get here is by **biking** the two hours from Chañaral. In the summer, **Turismo Chango,** Comercio 265 (☎ 480 484 or 480 668), in Chañaral, runs a minibus service to and from the park (30min.; 4 per day 8:30-9am, returns 6pm; CH$1000-2000). **Taxis** from Chañaral to Caleta depart from the Municipalidad area (round-trip CH$14,000). See **Chañaral Transportation** (p. 251) for additional transportation information.

■ **PRACTICAL INFORMATION.** The **Conaf office** at the southern entrance is home to a Conaf ranger who collects entrance fees (CH$3500, Chileans CH$2000). and provides maps, brochures, and up-to-date information about the park. (Open 24hr. Copiapó Conaf office ☎ 210 282 ext.33. Open 8:30am-12:30pm and 2-6:30pm.) Rodrigo Carvajal, one of the villagers from Caleta Pan de Azúcar, runs boat trips to Isla Pan de Azúcar. (☎ 480 563 or 099 429 2132; www.galeon.com/pinguitour. CH$25,000 per boat per hr. Tent rental also available.) In the summer months, other fishermen are willing to take out travelers as well. Surprisingly enough for such a small hamlet, there is a satellite telephone in the village (☎ 02 196 5300). There no police in the park.

ſ ACCOMMODATIONS AND CAMPING. There are several Conaf camping **refugios ❶** on Playas Piqueros and Soldado, all with a rock shelter, picnic tables, BBQ equipment, and communal ablution facilities. A restaurant and communal showers are soon to join these amenities when construction is complete. (No hot water. 4-person site CH$6000.) Just north of Caleta in Sector Norte are more Conaf camping *refugios* on the beach. Also close to Caleta are four Conaf **cabañas ❶**, which are excellent values in beautiful settings. Baths, a living room, kitchen facilities, solar power, and hot water are included. Reserve these a month in advance in high season by calling the Copiapó Conaf office (6-person *cabaña* CH$20,000-35,000). Camping in the park is allowed only at the designated Conaf camping *refugios*. Private camping *refugios* are open in the summer just south of the Playa Refugio.

NORTE GRANDE

Norte Grande is more, much more than endless stretches of *altiplano* wasteland in one of the world's driest deserts. This, the northernmost region of Chile, boasts warm, sunny weather year-round, and a amazing range of hidden gems from one end to the other. A microcosm of the best that Chile has to offer, Norte Grande is where the earth breathes deeply and the ancient past inhabits the present.

The world is a painter's palette as sunsets melt into stunning desertscapes across the **Atacama desert.** But the arid clime does not deny Norte Grande the richness of biodiversity inherent to Chile's more fertile valleys. **Parque Nacional Lauca** exists as an elegant synopsis of Chilean wildlife: llamas, alpacas, and vicuñas scamper among soothing thermal baths while flamingos soar towards the peaks of mist-covered mountains. The rumblings of **Volcán Isluga** echo across the undulating sands and endangered *tamarugo* trees persevere to mighty heights in the **Reserva Nacional Pampa del Tamarugal.** The secrets of the earth dance by morning light for mesmerized visitors at **El Tatio Geysers,** while the nectar of the gods, legendary wine from the lush desert oasis, flows freely in **Matilla.** Tourists soak up the sun while languishing on the fabulous beaches of **Iquique** by day, and gorge on shellfish in the coastal town of **Mejillones** by night.

This natural abundance does not distract from the fact that Norte Grande is a land before time. *Mestizaje* here is not simply a fusion of cultures and ethnicities—the prehistoric past and frenzied present converge on the streets in Norte Grande each day. The largest geoglyph in the world, **El Gigante de Atacama,** towers above the Panamericana. Tourists cruise to **Socoroma,** a charming Aymara farming village centered around a traditional Andean bell-tower, in shiny four-wheel-drive vehicles. The sound of clinking glasses from **Arica's** swanky restaurants tinkles over amazing relics from the **Chinchorro** culture in the Museo Arqueológico San Miguel de Azapa. Meanwhile, hip beats emanating from nightclubs and *discotecas* in Iquique and **Antofagasta** threaten to awake carefully preserved **mummies** in the Museo Arqueológico Gustavo le Paige in **San Pedro.** All the amenities and comforts expected of life in the 21st century are provided in five-star hotels down the street from where costumed dancers celebrate ancient rites.

If Chile isn't enough to satisfy you, then Norte Grande is the perfect place to launch yourself into even more adventures. Head north from Arica across the border to the slightly confused former Peruvian, former Chilean, now Peruvian again city of **Tacna.** Or head west into Bolivia to the bustling capital of **La Paz** or the sparkling white plains of the **Salar de Uyuni.**

HIGHLIGHTS OF NORTE GRANDE

STEP into the past with a visit to **Socoroma** (p. 316), a traditional Aymara village.

MINE copper, or learn how it's done, at **Humberstone,** a defunct *oficina* (p. 301).

MOONWALK through the **Valle de la Luna** (Moon Valley), near **San Pedro de Atacama,** where salt pans eerily resemble sunken lunar crater (p. 284).

GYRATE Greek-god-style in Pharos, one of Iquique's hottest nightclubs (p. 301).

LANGUISH under date palms while enjoying the fine wine of lush desert oases **Pica** and **Matilla** (p. 303).

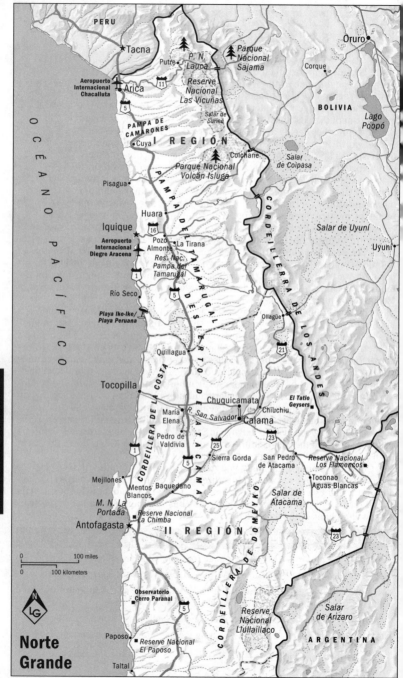

Norte Grande

ANTOFAGASTA   ☎ 55

As the capital of Chile's Region II and the country's fifth largest city, dry and sunny Antofagasta (pop. 230,000) welcomes visitors with its pleasant beaches and enormous, strikingly efficient port, the biggest on South America's Pacific coast. Like Iquique further north, Antofagasta came into its own as a port city during the nitrate boom of the late 19th and early 20th centuries, a legacy reflected in the neo-classical buildings of the waterfront Barrio Histórico. Once part of Bolivian territory, the city was conquered by Chile during the War of the Pacific (1879-1884). Today, Antofagasta still ships goods from Bolivia and remains the main export platform for copper from Chuquicamata and other minerals of the Atacama desert. Although the beaches here are not as warm or suitable for surfing as those in Arica or Iquique further north, and parts of downtown can seem rather gray and unappealing, the traveler will nevertheless find a well-connected transportation hub with all the conveniences of a large city. The proximity of stunning coastal sights such as La Portada, the most photographed site on Chile's northern coast, add beauty to the utility of Antofagasta.

▐ TRANSPORTATION

As the capital of Region II of Chile, Antofagasta is well-connected by air and road to other destinations in Chile.

Flights: Aeropuerto Cerro Moreno, 25km north of downtown off Ruta 1, is connected to downtown by **radio taxis** (CH$6000) and **mini buses** (CH$3000). For mini buses, try **Aerobus,** Baquedano 328 (☎262 727) or **Aeropuerto,** Curicó 2578 (☎372 658), which provide door-to-door service. The main flight provider **LanChile** (☎265 151), on Prat between San Martín and Latorre. Open M-F 9am-7pm, Sa 10am-1pm. Flies to **Santiago** (3hr.; 7 per day 8:30am-8:30pm; CH$100,300, round-trip CH$80,000) via **La Serena** (1hr.; CH$75,000, round-trip CH$87,000) and **Arica** (1½hr., 1 and 9pm, CH$25,400) via **Iquique** (45min., CH$29,400).

Buses: Major intercity bus companies and a regional minibus company have their own offices/terminals from which their buses leave, but a few smaller companies leave from **Terminal de Buses Rurales,** on the corner of Latorre and Riquelme.

Tur Bus, Latorre 2751 (☎220 240), between Bolívar and Sucre, departs for: **Arica** (11hr., frequent departures 3:30am-10:30pm, CH$7000); **Calama** (3hr., frequent departures 5am-9:45pm, CH$2500) via **Baquedano** (1hr., CH$1300); **Iquique** (6hr., frequent departures 2:45am-10:30pm, CH$6000) via **Tocopilla** (3hr., CH$3000); **Mejillones** (1hr.; 11am, 4:15, 5, 9, 11:15pm; CH$1400); **San Pedro de Atacama** (4hr.; 7, 10:45am, 3pm; CH$3000); **Santiago** (20hr., 11 per day 10am-midnight, CH$14,000) via **Chañaral** (5hr., CH$5100), **Copiapó** (7hr., CH$7200), **La Serena** (12hr., CH$11,000); **Taltal** (4hr.; 8, 11:45am, 3, 6:45, 7:30pm; CH$3500).

Pullman Bus (☎268 838), on the corner of Latorre and Bolívar, goes to: **Arica** (10hr.; 8:45, 9:45, 10:30pm; CH$9000); **Calama** (3hr., 7 per day 7:15am-9pm, CH$2500) via **Baquedano** (1hr., CH$1500); **Iquique** (7hr.; 4, 11:15, 8:45pm; CH$6000) via **Tocopilla** (3hr., CH$3000); **Maria Elena** (3hr.; 7:45am, 4:15, 8:45pm; CH$2000); **Santiago** (20hr.; 12 per day 10:45am-midnight; CH$18,000, *salon cama* CH$25,000) via **Chañaral** (5hr., CH$7000), **Caldera** (6hr., CH$8000), **Copiapó** (7hr., CH$9000), **Vallenar** (10hr., CH$10,000), **Ovalle** (13hr., CH$13,000); **Viña del Mar** and **Valparaíso** (20hr.; 4:15, 9:15pm, 12:45am; CH$18,000).

Flota Barrios, Condell 2764 (☎351 410), near Bolívar, leaves for: **Arica** (8hr., 9:15 and 10pm, CH$7000); **Calama** (3hr., 8 per day 7:45am-8:30pm, CH$2500) via **Baquedano** (1hr., CH$1200); **Iquique** (7hr., 10:30pm, CH$5000) via **Tocopilla** (3hr., CH$2500); **Santiago** (20hr.; 11:15am, 7, 10:30pm; CH$13,000. *Salon cama* 18hr., 3 and 6:30pm, CH$22,000) via **Chañaral** (5hr., CH$5000), **Copiapó** (7hr., CH$7000), **Vallenar** (10hr., CH$8000), **La Serena** (12hr., CH$10,000), **Ovalle** (13hr., CH$10,000); **Valparaíso** and **Viña del Mar** (20hr., 11am and 7pm, CH$13,000).

Antofagasta
ACCOMMODATIONS
Hotel Antofagasta, 3
Hotel Brasil, 9
Hotel Capri, 10
Hotel Diego de Almagro, 5
Hotel Puerto Mayor, 16
Hotel San Marcos, 2
Hotel Valdivia, 17
Residencial El Cobre, 15
FOOD
Club de Yates, 1
Don Pollo, 18
El Arriero, 4
Jeitinho, 11
Restaurant Kong Long, 12
Pub Sunrise, 13
Puerto Viejo Restaurant, 14
NIGHTLIFE
Era 2000, 8
Iguana & Disco Box, 7
Kamikaze, 6
LA PORTADA, TOCOPILLA, IQUIQUE, &
Casas ex Anglo Lautaro Nitrate Co (Soquimich)
Avenida Iquique
E Ramírez
Adamson
Caracoles
Muelle Salitrero Melbourne Clark (MN)
Anibal Pinto
Patio Ferroviario Ferrocarril Antofagasta Bolivia FCAB
Avenida Argentina
Covadonga
Ex Resguardo Maritimo (MN)
Ex Gobernación Maritima (MN)
Ex Estación
Ex Aduana (MN)
Terminal de Buses Rurales
Riquelme
Bolívar
Pullman Bus
Serrano
Tur Bus
PLAZA COLÓN
Torre del Reloj (MN)
Teatro Municipal
Megatur
Arturo Prat
Puerto de Antofagasta
Iglesia Catedral San José
Flota Bamos
Intendencia
Balmaceda
Isaac Arce
Washington
San Martín
Municipalidad
Sucre
Avenida Argentina
Condell
Latorre
Baquedano
Bilbao
Uribe
M.A. Matta
Ossa
TO
Maipú
14 de Febrero
(500m), (1KM),
(700m), (100m),
(500m), & (700m)
TO (2km), (2km), (2km),
(1km), 5, & COPIAPO

Megatur, Latorre 2748 (☎450 813), opposite Tur Bus, is a minibus company that departs for **Mejillones** (1hr., every 30min. 7:30am-9pm, CH$1000) via **La Portada** (25min., CH$600). In summer, Megatur also goes to **Juan Lopez** (45min., 4-5 per day, CH$1000).

Local Buses and Colectivos: Buses in town run daily 6am-2am and cost CH$250. *Colectivos* anywhere in town cost CH$250-350. *Colectivos* serving La Portada from Antofagasta depart from corner of Bolívar and Latorre (20min., CH$6000 per person). There is no *colectivo* to Mejillones.

Radio Taxis: There are numerous companies, including **Abece** (☎244 222), **Antofagasta** (☎268 726), **Gran Via** (☎240 505) and **Servitaxi** (☎251 222).

Car Rentals: Hertz, Balmaceda 2492 (☎269 043; www.hertz.cl), and **Budget,** Balmaceda 2584, office 06 (☎225 370 or 251 745; www.budget.cl). For smaller, cheaper companies try **Ballart,** Tarapaca 4469 (☎252 776; ballart@terra.cl), or **Econorent,** Prat 206, Local 5 (☎251 745; ecoantofagasta@entelchile.net).

ORIENTATION AND PRACTICAL INFORMATION

Similar to its northern neighbor, Iquique, Antofagasta sits on a narrow coastal strip surrounded by a backdrop of abruptly rising mountains. The Panamericana passes some 20km further east and is accessed by two paved roads heading north and south. The scenic and coastal Ruta 1 connects the city northward to Iquique,

Calama, and San Pedro de Atacama. While the city itself is a big jumble of neighborhoods sprawling north to south, the downtown area next to the port is a compact rectangular grid bound by **Bolívar** and **Maipú** running northwest to southeast, and **Balmaceda** (which turns into Aníbal Pinto farther north) and **Ossa** southwest to northeast. **Plaza Colón** is the heart of downtown, while **Prat** between San Martín and Matta is the main shopping street.

Tourist Office: Sernatur (☎451 818 or 457 819; www.sernatur.cl), on the corner of San Martín and Prat, on the ground floor inside the Intendencia (Regional Government) building. The helpful staff speaks some English, and photo displays of the region's tourist attractions include explanations in English and Spanish. Open M-F 8:30am-5:30pm.

Tours: Rutas de Sal, Jose Miguel Carrera 1485 c-1 (☎/fax 386 827; www.rutasdesal.cl), south of downtown, is the only operator in town and organizes tours to La Portada and other attractions in and around Antofagasta during the high season.

Consulates: Argentina, Blanco Encalada 1933 (☎220 440; fax 378 707). Open M-F 9am-1pm. **Bolivia,** Washington 2675, Office 1301 (☎259 008; fax 221 403). Open M-F 8:30am-1:30pm.

Banks, ATMs, and Currency Exchange: The densest concentration is on Prat between San Martín and Matta. **BankBoston** is on the corner of Prat and San Martín. Also try **Banco de Chile,** Prat 356 (☎205 712) and **Banco del Estado de Chile,** Prat 400 (☎268 948).

Supermarkets: There are several in town, including the centrally located **Korlaet**, on Ossa between Maipú and Baquedano. Open M-Sa 9am-10pm, Su 9am-3pm.

Pharmacies: These are abundant all over town, especially on Prat between Matta and San Martín. Try **Farmacias Ahumada** (☎285 828), on the corner of Prat and Condell. Open 8:30am-midnight.

Hospital: Hospital Regional de Antofagasta Dr. Leonard Guzman, Argentina 1962 (☎204 648 or 204 571), near the corner with Velásquez, south of downtown.

Emergency: ☎133.

Police: (☎231 209 or 237 681) on Ejercito Parque Croacia, near Universidad del Norte, a few kilometers south of downtown.

Internet Access: Easily available in town. Try **Alf@net,** Prat 785 (☎493 507), between Matta and Ossa. CH$500 per hr. Open 10am-2am.

Courier Services: DHL, Prat 260 (☎252 001; www.dhl.com), between Balmaceda and Washington. Also functions as a **Western Union.** Open M-F 9am-7pm, Sa 10am-1pm. **ChileExpress,** Prat 471 (☎800 200 102), between San Martín and Latorre. Also serves as a Western Union. Open M-F 9am-2pm and 4-7:30pm, Sa 10am-1pm.

Post Office: At Washington 2623 (☎222 089), on Plaza Colón. Also functions as a **Western Union.**

■ ACCOMMODATIONS

Although there is a wide range of options in town, it is a challenge to find good *hostales* or *residenciales*. Inexpensive but quality hotels listed below are your best budget choices. In the summer, free camping on beaches further south of town is popular with independent travelers.

Hotel Brasil, Ossa 1978 (☎267 268), on the corner with Copiapó. Easily the thumbs-up choice in the budget price range. The compulsively clean 38 rooms in the new 2-story building all have TV. The very friendly staff makes a stay here enjoyable. Singles CH$5500, with bath CH$11,000; doubles CH$8500/CH$15,000; triples CH$12000 / CH$18,000. ❷

THE BIG SPLURGE

HOTEL ANTOFAGASTA

Balmaceda 2575 (☎228 811; www.hotelantofagasta.cl), on Aníbal Pinto, on the beach opposite the northern end of Prat. Don't get intimidated by the primarily business clientele at this luxurious establishment—sling your backpack on with pride and graciously part with your money to enjoy some five-star treatment. Located on the beach, Hotel Antofagasta is just a stone's throw away from the city center—but that doesn't matter since there's no reason for you to leave the hotel. You can suntan on the sandy beach, float in the cool swimming pool, or work out in the fitness center before gorging on sumptuous Italian food, or other international cuisine, in the hotel's ritzy restaurants. When evening rolls around, relax in the billiard room or the plush lounge with a swanky piano bar before snoozing, or stroll through the flower shop and jewelry store. In the morning, an elaborate buffet breakfast awaits. This large ship-shaped building has lots of rooms, many with breathtaking ocean views. All rooms have private baths, satellite TV, A/C, phone, fridge, a locked safe, and well-stocked minibars. 24hr. room service is available (order in that caviar!). Breakfast included. Singles CH$55,000; doubles CH$72,450; triples CH$82,450. Member of Panamericana Hoteles chain (www.panamericanahoteles.cl). All major credit cards accepted. ❺

Hotel Capri, Copiapó 1208 (☎263 703), close to Av. Argentina. Similar to Hotel Brasil, but a bit worn-out. The 43 good-value rooms on the 3 floors are equipped with TVs. Breakfast included. Singles CH$5000, with bath CH$7500; doubles CH$10,000/CH$15,000; triples with bath CH$22,500. ❷

Hotel Puerto Mayor, Ossa 2643 (☎410 081 or 410 188), between Prat and Sucre. The new building, motel-like super comfy rooms, and friendly staff make this a great choice. Its central downtown location and free parking perks for guests makes this an even better choice for motorists. Rooms include baths, TV, and breakfast. Singles CH$15,000; doubles CH$18,000; triples CH$25,000. ❹

Hotel Valdivia, Ossa 2644 (☎265 911), between Prat and Sucre, opposite Hotel Puerto Mayor. The small 2-story box-like building with a blue exterior has a number of simple but clean rooms upstairs. TV and baths. Singles CH$8000; doubles CH$12,000. ❸

Hotel San Marcos, Latorre 2946 (☎251 763, 261 543 or 226303), between Serrano and Riquelme. One of the better bets in the lower-middle price range with clean, comfy rooms with baths and TV. Breakfast included. Singles CH$12,000; doubles CH$18,000; triples $21,000. Visa. ❸

Hotel Diego de Almagro, Condell 2624 (☎268 331; fax 251 721), between Prat and Sucre. A little pricier than other options but worth the splurge. The renovated rooms in the old building come with private baths, TV, and fridges. Breakfast included. Singles CH$22,400; doubles CH$30,000. ❹

Residencial El Cobre, Prat 749 (☎225 162), between Matta and Ossa. Very basic rooms in an old blue-painted interior. Singles CH$4000, with bath CH$8000; doubles CH$7000/CH$12,000. ❷

🍴 FOOD

Finding quality restaurants downtown can be surprisingly tricky, but several establishments stand out for vibrant victuals and value. To shop for fresh produce and seafood, try **Mercado Central** on Matta between Maipú and Uribe.

🦐 **Jeitinho,** Copiapó 900 (☎410 780 or 495 851), on the corner with 14 de Febrero. Locals in the know pack this Brazilian joint for the excellent buffet salad bar and the mouth-watering meat dishes. Kick back to the soft serenading of a mellow Bassanova guitar amidst the psychedelic, yet oddly relaxing, decor. The good food, chill atmosphere, and friendly waitstaff make this an unbeatable choice to satisfy your hunger. The lunch special, including two meat entrees, a salad buffet, hot side dishes, and dessert, is a steal at CH$3000. Or indulge yourself and get a *pisco sour* or mango cocktail followed by two meat entrees, a salad buffet, and a dessert (CH$4000). The fixed dinner menus after 9pm are good too (CH$4000-5000). Open noon-1:30am. ❸

Club de Yates (☎ 263 942), on Aníbal Pinto, on the waterfront next to Hotel Antofagasta. Dine in style while taking in the harbor view on the wooden deck next to moored yachts. The maritime deco ranges from white and blue tableware to real, peckish sea-birds. Just be sure not to feed them. 3-course lunch specials CH$4500. Chicken CH$4800-5500, omelets CH$6000, steak CH$7500-12,000, seafood CH$4000-30,000 (that would be for lobster). Open M-Sa 10am-1:30am, Su 10am-4pm. AmEx/DC/MC/V. ❹

Puerto Viejo Restaurant, Copiapó 597 (☎ 252 272), between Esmeralda and 14 de Febrero. One of the best seafood joints in town. Enjoy savory ocean dishes amongst a slightly older clientele in this intimate interior with a seafaring theme that includes ship steering wheels, anchors, and life-savers. Fish CH$4800-8200, *mariscos* CH$3200-6500, *carne* CH$4500-5800. Open M-Sa 8pm-5am. AmEx/DC/MC/V.❸

El Arriero, Condell 2644 (☎ 264 371), between Prat and Sucre. A *parrillada* (grilled steak) eatery that also turns out excellent fish. Patrons gorge on *lomo a las brasas* (CH$6000) and *filete* (CH$7000-8500) in the hearty interior enlivened with dried-up cow legs, rusty gramophones, a squeaky violin, and a cracked bronze bell. Fish CH$6000-7500, salads CH$2000. Live piano music M-Sa. Open M-Sa 11:30am-4pm and 7:30pm-midnight, Su 11:30am-4pm and 7:30-11pm. AmEx/DC/MC/V. ❸

Pub Sunrise, Copiapó 936 (☎ 099 489 8789), between Esmeralda and 14 de Febrero. In the dimly-lit interior reminiscent of a Spanish castle, the sunburst decor with the mellow hues and wooden ceiling calms the nerves of a slightly older clientele. *Empanadas* CH$2000, chicken/meat CH$3500-4000. Beer CH$1500-2000. Soothing live music F-Sa on the small stage. Open Tu-Sa 8:30pm-4am. AmEx/DC/MC/V. ❷

Restaurant Kong Long, Matta 2269 (☎ 495 964), between Uribe and Orella. Agreeable service and good Asian cuisine add to the pleasing nature of this dragon-themed restaurant. Seafood CH$3500-3700, *carne* CH$2400-3200, chop suey CH$2000-3000, chicken CH$2400-3200. Open noon-4pm and 8pm-12:30am. AmEx/DC/MC/V. ❷

Don Pollo, Ossa 2594 (☎ 252 691), on the corner with Prat. Red-uniformed *señoritas* serve grilled chicken with ruthless efficiency on two floors of kitschy parasoled red plastic tables. Good for a quick bite as evidenced by the crowd of locals. Chicken CH$900-1500, with fries CH$1400. Open M-Sa noon-3:30pm and 7-11pm, Su noon-4pm. ❶

SIGHTS AND ACTIVITIES

A walking tour of the historic town center starts on **Plaza Colón,** embellished with sculpted fountains, palm trees, tropical plants, and plenty of benches. In the center is **Torre del Reloj,** a clock tower which is a small-scale replica of the Big Ben in London. This national monument, about 15m tall, indicates the importance of the British role in the city's development during the nitrate boom, a legacy acknowledged by Chilean and British flags painted near the base of the clock tower. On the southeastern side of the plaza near San Martín stands the striking **Iglesia Catedral San Jose** (built 1906-1917) with its tall spires and three Gothic entrances.

One block northeast of the plaza towards the old port is the **Barrio Histórico,** an area replete with Victorian-style buildings, some of which were erected with British financing during the nitrate boom. National monuments here include **Ex Estación,** a rail station built in 1887 with a second floor added in 1892. Originally offering passenger railway service all the way to Bolivia and Argentina, it now only sends cargo trains to Calama. The station, housed in a magnificent building with

NORTE GRANDE

wooden stairways, is a stately open-air museum with well-maintained lawns, where old locomotives and passenger cars stand on tracks next to a platform displaying British clocks, ticket tickers, red phone booths, and pulleys. The offices of **Ferrocarril Antofagasta-Bolivia** (☎206 700) are also housed here. (Enter through the metal gate and tell the guard that you are a tourist; passport or copy required for a guided tour. Open M-F 8:30am-12:30pm and 3-6pm. Free.)

Just across Bolívar from Ex Estación, on the corner with Balmaceda, is **Ex Aduana,** the old customs building. Classified as a national monument, the structure was prefabricated in Valparaíso in 1868 and finally erected on the present site in 1888. A fine example of the architecture of the nitrate epoch, the two-story structure with white beams now houses the **Museo Regional,** which has excellent exhibits on the region's ecology, geology, history, archeology, and paleontology. (☎227 016. Open Tu-F 10am-6pm, Sa-Su 11am-2pm. CH$600, children CH$300.) Opposite Ex Aduana on Balmaceda, sitting along the waterfront, is the **Ex Gobernación Marítima,** the old Port Authority, and the adjacent **Ex Resguardo Marítimo,** the old Coast Guard. Both these national monuments were built around 1910 in the neoclassical style. Unfortunately, visitors are not allowed inside. Next to these two small buildings, **Muelle Salitrero Melbourne Clark,** the nitrate pier, stretches out into the old port. Another relic of the nitrate era, it was constructed in 1872 by Melbourne Clark Company and later used for shipping cargo brought by into town via railway.

After this historical tour of downtown, head south to the **beaches** for a little *descansa* and catch a memorable sunset. The closest is **Balneario Municipal,** the municipal beach a few kilometers from downtown, close to Estadio Regional. With fine sand, a beach promenade, and a protected bathing area flanked by a McDonald's, this is a popular choice among locals. (From downtown, CH$250 by bus or CH$300 by *colectivo*.) Further south are bigger and more natural beaches, like **Balneario El Huascar** and **Playa Amarilla.**

🎵 SHOPPING, ENTERTAINMENT AND NIGHTLIFE

Department stores like **Ripley** and **Falabela** are located close to the corner of Prat and Condell. There is a **Feria Artesanal** (arts and crafts market) in Mercado Central, housed in an impressive building set on the large plaza occupying the block bounded by Matta, Ossa, Maipú, and Uribe. For entertainment and cultural performances, check out the **Teatro Municipal** in the large concrete building, which stages ballet, concerts, plays, and other shows. (☎264 919. Shows usually 9:30pm. Ticket office open M-F 9am-1pm and 3:30-7pm.) For movies, try **Cine Nacional,** Sucre 743, between Matta and Ossa. (☎269 167. Shows 2-9:30pm. Th-Su CH$2600, M-W CH$1700.) In terms of nightlife, Antofagasta rocks on weekends, with a high concentration of bars and clubs lined next to one another on the beach south of downtown. (Taxis CH$3000.)

Kamikaze (☎245 138), on Camino Coloso. Part of a popular chain, this club features an oddly morbid decor using World War II paraphernalia. Yet, the local crowd of 20 to 30-somethings seems oblivious to the kamikaze pilots with their Zero Sen fighters waving goodbye as they dance away the night. Occasional live music. Beer CH$1500. Cover CH$6000 for men, CH$5000 for women, includes 1 drink. Open Th-Sa 11pm-5am.

Iguana Pub and Disco Box (☎289 354), on Camino Coloso, opposite Kamikaze. A little less crowded than its neighbor, Iguana is a lively 2-in-1 deal. The cover gets you inside the bar and the *discoteca*, both featuring energetic dance floors and a happy crowd of young locals. Occasional live band. Beer CH$1500. Cover CH$6000 for men, CH$5000 for women, includes 1 drink. Open Th-Sa midnight-5am.

Era 2000, on Jaime Guzman, next to the Iguana Pub. A poor-man's version of the Iguana Pub, Era 2000 grooves to a mellower vibe offering cheaper prices. Cover CH$2500 per person until 1am; after 1am CH$5000 for men, CH$3000 for women, includes 1 drink. Open F-Sa midnight-5am.

⚄ DAYTRIPS FROM ANTOFAGASTA

From Antofagasta, Ruta 1 extends all the way to Iquique, offering spectacular coastal scenery with white sand beaches below sharply rising mountains, especially between Tocopilla and Iquique. Just north of Antofagasta off Ruta 1 are beautiful natural attractions, including ⚄**Monumento Nacional La Portada,** only 15km away. Managed by Conaf, La Portada is a stunning arch-shaped rock formation sculpted by volcanic flows and the tidal flux of the raging Pacific. The sandy coves surrounded by steep cliffs make for the perfect location for photographers and an afternoon of tanning, fishing, or walks along the lovely beach. Unfortunately, the current is too strong for bathing or surfing but you can lie back and watch the seals and pelicans frolic among the waves. A lookout point with a restaurant and souvenir shops is on top of the cliffs, from which a trail with railings leads down to the beach below. The fine restaurant, **Restaurant La Portada ❸,** is a great place to grab a beer (CH$900-1100) or lunch while savoring the magnificent scenery. (☎226 423. Fish CH$4500-7500, pasta CH$4100, *lomo* CH$4900-6000. Open noon-8pm. Credit cards accepted.) To get to or from La Portada, catch the **bus/minibus** serving the Antofagasta-Mejillones route at the drop-off point on Ruta 1 and walk the one kilometer on the paved road that leads further west towards Juan Lopez (for minibuses between Antofagasta-Mejillones, see **Antofagasta Transportation** p. 257 and **Mejillones Transportation, p. 264).**

From La Portada, it is another 16km west to **Juan Lopez,** a small beach village that is popular in the summer for swimming and fishing. A couple of hotels and restaurants, including **Hostería Sandokan,** are set back from the beach. Megatur runs **minibuses** from Antofagasta in the summer (45min., CH$1000) or jump in a taxi for CH$7000. Another major sight between La Portada and Antofagasta is **Reserva Nacional La Chimba,** some 2500 hectares of coastal wilderness including beaches for swimming and fishing. (Take Micro 2 or 3 for CH$300 from the corner of Sucre and Latorre in Antofagasta. Open in the summer.)

South of Antofagasta, visit the **European Space Organization's astronomical observatory** on Cerro Paranal (2644m), located off a gravel road 130km from Antofagasta. ESO has built four Very Large Telescopes, each 8.2m in diameter. (☎435 000 or 435 001. No public transportation available, but ESO may accept visitors on its own buses. Call ahead.) Not far from Cerro Paranal, off the Panamericana, is **Mano del Desierto,** the 1992 work of Mario Irarrazabal, an Antofagasta-based sculptor. Made of an iron-cement mix, this 11m tall hand half-buried in the desert plain points upwards towards the clear sky (visible as you ride on the highway).

NEAR ANTOFAGASTA

BAQUEDANO   ☎55

If you've ever harbored a burning desire to star as a wild train robber in a Western flick, you can enact your fantasies on the magnificent antique locomotives and rusting passenger railcars sitting in the open-air museum in Baquedano (pop. 2000), a quintessential middle-of-nowhere town about 70km northeast of Antofagasta on the way to Calama. Situated amidst the abandoned *oficinas salitreras,* Baquedano was an important rail junction during the nitrate boom. Although some freight trains still roll through on their way between Antofagasta and Calama, the town is primarily a truck stop for the Panamericana. The museum, **Museo Ferroviario,** in the old train station, has a circular shed enclosing a swanky collection of black steam-engine locomotives that look like something right out of the movies. You can climb in many of them and feel just like John Wayne or Billy the Kid heading out West. There is no ticket office or guide, so just enter anytime for free. Adjacent to the old train station are newer tracks and the offices of **Ferronor** (☎641 966), which has cargo trains chugging all the way to Socompa.

Intercity bus companies have no offices here, so you need to buy tickets from the driver when the bus stops here. **Tur Bus, Pullman Bus,** and **Flota Barrios** stop here daily en route between Calama and Antofagasta. (Frequent buses between 8am and 11pm; Calama CH$2000, Antofagasta CH$1000.) There is no tourist office, so inquire at the **tourism/information** section of the Municipalidad. (☎641 915. Open M-F 8:30am-1:30pm and 3-5:30pm.) The town does, however, have a **police station,** a **paramedic clinic,** a couple of **grocery stores,** a **centro de llamados** with a fax machine (open daily 9am-8pm), and a **post office** (open M-F 8:30am-1:30pm). Baquedano has no lodgings and only a couple of very basic eateries, including **San Miguel ❶,** in the large parking area right on the Panamericana where passing traffic stops for police control. (☎641 997. Lunch CH$1500. Open 7am-midnight.)

MEJILLONES   ☎55

A pleasant port with decent sandy beaches, Mejillones (pop. 5500) makes a good weekend retreat from Antofagasta or a stopover on Ruta 1 between Antofagasta and Tocopilla. An important Bolivian port until its conquest by Chile in the War of the Pacific (1879), Mejillones also served as a shipping outlet during the nitrate boom of the early 20th century and today lives off the main industries of fishing, hydroelectricity, gas, and tourism.

⏚ TRANSPORTATION. Tur Bus (☎622 816), on Latorre between Rodríquez and Las Heras, goes to **Antofagasta** (1hr., 5:30 and 9pm, CH$1400) and to **Iquique** (8hr.; 12:15, 6:15pm, 12:30am; CH$5800) via **Tocopilla** (2hr., CH$2500). **Megatur** (☎621 528), on Latorre between Borgono and O'Higgins, has departures to **Antofagasta** (1hr., every 30min. 7:15am-9:45pm, CH$1000) via La Portada. Located close to Megatur on Latorre, **Fepstur** (☎621 644) also has daily departures to **Antofagasta** (1hr., 7 per day 6:45am-8pm, CH$800). **Corsal** (☎623 110) also provides service to Antofagasta (1hr., every 30min. 6:40am-10pm, CH$1000). **Radio taxis,** including **Radio Taxi Mejillones,** stand on the municipal plaza on the corner of Latorre and Borgono. (☎623 107 or 622 260. CH$500 inside Mejillones, CH$1000 to outskirts of town, CH$12,000 to Antofagasta/La Portada, CH$15000 to Juan Lopez.)

⏚ ORIENTATION AND PRACTICAL INFORMATION. Most shops and services are on San Martín and Latorre, both running east-west parallel to the downtown beach, which has fine sand but is littered in some places. A much better beach is found at **Hornito,** 40km north of Mejillones just off Ruta 1. It is protected by cliffs and is suitable for bathing. Mejillones has most amenities, including **Banco Santander** (☎621 532) with an **ATM;** a **Copec service station;** a **centro de llamados** with **Western Union** services; a **police station** (☎621 516); and a hospital (☎621 575). An Internet cafe, **Cyber Maicol,** is on the corner of Riquelme with Ongolmo. (CH$500 per hr. Open 10am-midnight.) Contact the **post office** at ☎621 510.

⏚ ACCOMMODATIONS AND FOOD. There are a few accommodations and restaurants in town, including **Residencial Dona Juanita ❷,** Latorre 441, which has clean rooms with TV and also serves breakfast (CH$700) and lunch (CH$2000) in its sunny dining area. (☎623 026. Singles CH$5900, with bath

CH$8000; doubles with bath CH$10,000; triples CH$9000.) **Hotel Capitania ❸**, San Martín 410, on the corner with Pinto, with its second floor wooden veranda, is a more upscale establishment. (☎621 542 or 621 276. Bath, TV, phones. Singles CH$15,000; doubles CH$18,000; triples CH$24,000.) The most expensive option is **Hotel Mejillones ❺**, Manuel Montt 86, on the corner with San Martín, which has excellent deluxe rooms with private baths, satellite TV, fridge, phones, and a buffet breakfast. If your room isn't one of those with a great ocean view then head up to the top floor and chill in the plush bar/restaurant which looks out over the entire coast. (☎621 244 or 621 590. Singles CH$33,000; doubles CH$37,000; triples CH$46,000. Major credit cards accepted.) Camping is available at **Camping Toi Thai ❸**, on the beach south of downtown. (☎410 550. CH$8000 per person with bath/shower; 6-person *cabinas* with kitchen and bath CH$18,000.) Next to Toi Thai is **Camping Codelco ❷**, which has similar *cabinas* for CH$30,000.

When hungry, try one of several good seafood restaurants in town, including **Casino Municipal de Mejillones ❷**, in the spacious building on the beach next to Capitania del Puerto. (☎623 113. *Mariscos* CH$3500-4900, *pescados* CH$3800-4500, sandwiches CH$1500-2500, *menú de casa* CH$3500. Beer CH$1000. Open noon-9pm.) Apart from the couple of good seafood joints on Rodríguez between Latorre and San Martín, you can catch a quick bite to eat at the super-friendly **My Family ❶**, Latorre 845, between O'Higgins and Riquelme, which serves good simple meals for CH$1000-1500. (☎623 727. Open 9am-1am.)

◪ SIGHTS. There are a few buildings of historical interest, such as the **Capitania del Puerto** (Port Authority), a waterside Tudor-style two-story edifice built in 1906. **Ex Aduana**, a white wooden building with a red roof built in the same year and style, now houses the **Museo Histórico y Natural de Mejillones** on the corner of Pinto and San Martín. After looking at the interesting exhibits on local history and geology, walk several blocks east on Latorre to the corner with Cataillo to see **Iglesia Corazón de Maria**, a wooden structure with three naves also built in 1906.

TOCOPILLA   ☎55

Sandwiched between the sea and barren mountains on a narrow strip of land covered with shanty dwellings, Tocopilla (pop. 25,000) is not quite the coastal paradise that some of its neighbors are. Weary travelers stumbling into town are greeted by an enormous gray hydroelectric plant in the harbor emitting clouds of smoke from its monstrous stacks. The rusty brown piers jutting out into the polluted port crowded with enormous cranes and nitrate ships complete the scene. Although the beaches downtown are too dirty and rocky for sunbathing, let alone swimming, the sunny climate and the amenities of a sizable town make this transportation hub a pleasant stopover. From here, travelers can easily make their way along the coastal Ruta 1, past some of the most spectacular desert scenery in northern Chile, to Iquique (638km away) or Antofagasta (185km away). Travelers are also well-connected by the paved Ruta 24 to Calama (166km east) and San Pedro de Atacama further on. For anyone needing more than a short break from the road, this industrial port does have some nightlife and interesting historical edifices. A few usable beaches lie south of downtown (including Balneario Covadonga).

▐ TRANSPORTATION. Tocopilla is well-connected by bus to major destinations. **Tur Bus** (☎811 122), on the corner of 21 de Mayo and Bolívar, departs daily for: **Antofagasta** (3hr., 6 per day 7:10am-9:30pm, CH$2500); **Calama** (3hr.; noon, 7:30, 8:30pm; CH$3500) via **María Elena** (1hr., CH$1700); **Iquique** (3hr., 8 per day 7am-

IN RECENT NEWS

PLUNGING PESOS

With the dramatic devaluation of the Argentine peso since the beginning of 2002, the Argentine Republic, once the most expensive Latin American country to travel in, has suddenly become a very affordable place for foreign visitors with dollars to spend. In less than a year, the peso, which had until recently been fixed one to one with the dollar, has depreciated in value to less than 3.5 pesos per dollar. This has meant that even the penny-pinching budget travelers can now afford to eat out at attractive restaurants in Buenos Aires, where a sophisticated three-course meal can be enjoyed for under 3 dollars. While this turn of events has been quite a money-saver for travelers, it has become a serious worry for many of Argentina's neighbors.

Just across the Andes to the west, the Chileans have been fortunate that the ongoing economic crisis has not spilled over into their own country, at least not yet. Two key factors have helped buffer them. Comparatively sound macroeconomic fundamentals have given rise to an incredibly durable stability. Until 1998, Chile had experienced nearly a decade of sustained economic growth at over 6% annually. Their export profile, Chile's main source of revenue, also has low exposure to the Argentine market. The other major factor perpetuating economic durability is the relative political stability maintained by the lack of major elections in 2002.

8:30pm, CH$3100). **Pullman Bus** (☎815 340), on the corner of 21 de Mayo and Baquedano, goes daily to **Antofagasta** (2½hr.; 12:30, 5:30, 6:30, 10pm; CH$2500) and **Iquique** (3hr.; 8am, 2:30, 4:40, 6:30pm; CH$3000). **Flota Barrios** (☎813 224), on 21 de Mayo between Washington and Colón, goes to **Antofagasta** (2½hr.; 7am, 3, 7, 8pm; CH$2200) and **Iquique** (3hr., 1:30am, CH$2500). **Pullman Carmelita** (☎813 269), on 21 de Mayo next to Municipalidad, also goes to **Antofagasta** (2½hr., 11:30pm, CH$2500) and **Iquique** (3hr.; 7, 11am, 2pm; CH$3000). **Buses Camus** (☎813 102), on 21 de Mayo between Freire and Rodríguez, departs daily for **Antofagasta** (2½hr.; 7:20am, 2, 5:50pm; CH$2800); **Calama** (3hr., 7:20am and 4:50pm, CH$3000) via **María Elena** (1hr., CH$1700); **Iquique** (3hr., 7:20am, CH$3000). **Taxi colectivos** depart from Rodríguez and 21 de Mayo for **Calama** (CH$3000 per person) via **María Elena** (CH$1500-2000 per person).

⌨ 🛈 ORIENTATION AND PRACTICAL INFORMATION. Most shops and services are clustered on Prat and 21 de Mayo, parallel streets running north-south. The small **Plaza Condell** is on 21 de Mayo between Pinto and Bolívar. **Torre del Reloj** (erected in 1800), on the corner of Baquedano and Prat, is a pink wooden clock tower with yellow rims, peeling paint, and an onion-shaped dome. Just a block south on the corner of Prat and Serrano is **Iglesia Parroquial Nuestra Señora del Carmen** with its smog-stained exterior. The pink Art Deco-style **Municipalidad** building on the corner of 21 de Mayo and Pinto is the only appealing building in town.

The travel agency, **Travel Pacífico Tour,** 21 de Mayo 1524, serves as an unofficial tourist office with its knowledgeable and helpful staff. (☎811 127. Open M-F 10am-1:30pm and 5-9pm, Sa 10am-noon.) Other amenities Tocopilla offers include: a **Shell service station** at the northern end of town; **Banco Estado**, 21 de Mayo and Freire (☎813 012 or 811 791), with an **ATM;** an Entel **centro de llamados** with **Western Union** services on 21 de Mayo between Rodríguez and Cienfuegos (☎813 015, Open M-F 10am-2pm and 5-9pm); and **Supermercado Colón,** Colón 1311. (Open M-Sa 9am-1:30pm and 4-9:30pm, Su 9am-1:30pm.) The **police station** is at 21 de Mayo 1666 (☎813 202) and **Hospital Marcos Macuada** (☎812 839 or 814 558) is on Santa Rosa. Look for **Farmacia San Luis** at the corner of 21 de Mayo and Colón. (Open 9am-11:30pm.) Internet access is available at **Ultraweb,** 21 de Mayo 1768a. (☎815 923. CH$800 per hr. Open M-Sa 9am-11pm, Su 11am-3pm and 6-10pm.) **Chile Express,** with Western Union, is at 21 de Mayo 1927. (☎813 192. Open M-F 9am-2pm and 4-7pm, Sa 10am-1pm.) The **post office** is on 21 de Mayo. (☎813 257. Open M-F 9am-5pm.)

ACCOMMODATIONS AND FOOD. What it lacks in tourist attractions, Tocopilla tries to make up for by way of offering decent accommodations, eateries, and nightlife. The best hotels in town are next door to each other on 21 de Mayo between Bolívar and Baquedano. **Hotel Atenas ❹**, a modern two-story building, has rooms with baths, TV, phone, fridge, and breakfast. (☎813 651 or 813 652. Singles CH$15,000; doubles CH$20,000; triples CH$24,000.) Its next door neighbor, **Hotel Chungará ❸**, has 22 rooms with private baths and TV enclosing an inner open-air corridor. (☎811 036; fax 812 445. Breakfast included. Singles CH$11,800; doubles CH$14,300; triples CH$15,800.) A step down is **Hotel Vucina ❸**, 21 de Mayo 2069, five blocks north from Atenas, where decent rooms with baths, TV, and phones enclose a pleasant courtyard. (☎813 088 or 812 155. Breakfast included. Singles CH$10,000; doubles CH$14,000.) **Hotel Casablanca ❷**, 21 de Mayo 2054, just across the street from Vucina, has very basic rooms with baths. (☎813 187. CH$5000 per person.)

The restaurant scene is a bit better, with **Casa de Don Julio ❸**, Serrano 1336, topping the list due to its excellent international menu and attentive service. (☎816 129. Soups CH$2500, entrees CH$3000-5000. Open noon-3pm and 8pm-1am.) Also good is **Club de la Union ❷**, on Prat between Baquedano and Serrano, with its spacious interior and hard-to-find street entrance. (☎813 198. Entrees CH$2000-4000. Open noon-4pm and 8:30-11pm.) Other choices include **Restaurant Atenas ❸**, at Hotel Atenas, which has good lunch set menus (CH$2500-CH$3000) and regular entrees (CH$3500-6000) in the pink-painted interior. (☎813 651. Open M-Sa 9:30am-5:30pm and 8:30-midnight, Su 9:30am-5:30pm.) **Restaurant Echikhouse ❶**, 21 de Mayo 2132, in the three-story building, offers a fixed lunch menu (CH$1500) and sandwiches (CH$1000-2000). The third floor of Echikhouse is a bar with a hip DJ. (☎813 172. Beer CH$500-1000, *tragos* CH$1500-2500. Open 10am-3am.) Decent Chinese food is available at **Chifa Jok San ❷**, 21 de Mayo 1488, upstairs. (☎811 458. *Carne* CH$2800-CH$3000, fish CH$2800-4000, soup CH$1300-1500. Open 12:30-3pm and 7:30pm-1am.)

NIGHTLIFE. There are a number of options for nightlife, especially near the corner of 21 de Mayo and Serrano. **Puerto Pelicano,** Serrano 1329, is a combination bar-*salsoteca-discoteca* with a kitschy, bright-colored, palm-studded interior. (☎815 587. Beer CH$2000. Cover with drink CH$4000. Bar open M-Sa midnight-5am, dancing F-Sa midnight-5am.) Nearby are **Lukas** and **Tequila Pub.** Both are open on weekends.

Nevertheless, the Andes may not prove to be as solid a firewall as many Chileans had hoped. Already, signs of an economic slowdown have begun to manifest themselves and, in an effort to stave off a recession and possible currency crisis, the Chilean central bank has lowered interest rates several times since the beginning of 2002. Unfortunately, the fate of Chile's economy depends heavily on world markets and political events beyond their control. Because of Chile's increased trade links with Asian and North American economies and dependence on copper and other commodities for export earnings, the continued instability in these economies has seriously diminished Chile's growth prospects.

Other major events within Latin America could also have a lasting impact. This is especially true of the upcoming general elections in Brazil in October, since foreign investors are notoriously finicky during election periods. The likely shift to the left in this, Latin America's largest economy, almost guarantees nervous investors and volatile foreign exchange markets, a phenomenon all too common but never beneficial. In a year shepherded in by the Argentine debt crisis and a sluggish US economy, the months ahead may witness even more volatility than usual for Chile.

MARÍA ELENA AND THE OFICINAS SALITRERAS   ☎ 55

On the desert pampa between Tocopilla on the coast and Calama in the east are dozens of *oficinas salitreras* (nitrate company towns) scattered as far north as Quillagua and as far south as Baquedano. All of these are now abandoned ghost towns, mostly reduced to mere piles of rubble. María Elena (pop. 14,000) some 70 kilometers east of Tocopilla, is the exception—it is the only one that is still functioning. The last to be abandoned, in 1996, was **Pedro de Valdivia,** 40 kilometers south of Maria Elena. Established by the Guggenheim Brothers in 1931, it reached a production peak of 1,220,000 tons per year in its heyday and is actually still functioning, although no one lives there. One of the most interesting and well-preserved mining towns is **Chacabuco,** near the junction between Ruta 25 and the Panamericana. Built in 1922-1924 and closed in 1940, Chacabuco, now a National Monument, was the last and the biggest *oficina* equipped with the Shanks system. Restoration work was begun in the early 1990s on some of the sites in Chacabuco, including Teatro Filarmonico Chacabuco, a four-story building with interior murals in Art Nouveau style. What makes this *oficina* so distinct is that it was used for two years by the Pinochet regime as a concentration camp housing 3000 prisoners. Roberto Zaldivar, an ex-prisoner, lives here, and offers tours to interested visitors. (Take an intercity bus along the Panamericana or Ruta 25 and ask them to drop you off and walk the one kilometer to town. Tours CH$1000, children CH$500.)

Among the redundant *oficinas*, **María Elena,** founded in 1926, is the most suited for a visit. This laid-back company town comprised of ramshackle houses and dusty grid-ordered streets offers several attractions, including a visit to the **nitrate plant.** (Call Socieda Chemica Minera de Chile ☎ 413 756. Open M-F 9am-6pm.) The **Museo Arqueológico e Histórico,** on the town plaza, is worth a visit for its collection of pre-Hispanic and nitrate-era paraphernalia. (Open M-Sa 8am-noon and 6-9pm, Su 9am-noon, but times can vary. Free.) To pass the time here, linger on the benches of the tree-lined plaza while enjoying the view of the yellow church and abandoned theater.

▣ **TRANSPORTATION.** All bus companies have offices on Balmaceda near the plaza. **Tur Bus** (☎ 639 431) goes daily to: **Calama** (80min.; 1, 8:45, 9:45pm; CH$1900); **Iquique** (5hr.; 8:45am, 6:15, 7:30pm, 1am; CH$5400) via **Tocopilla** (1hr., CH$1700); **Santiago** (22hr., 7am and 11pm, CH$13,700). **Camus** (☎ 413 619) departs daily for **Calama** (1¾hr., 8:50am and 6:15pm, CH$1800) and **Tocopilla** (1hr., 10am and 6:20pm, CH$1700). **Flota Barrios** (☎ 639 153) goes daily to **Antofagasta** (3hr.; 7:30am, 2:30, 6:30pm; CH$2000). **Pullman Bus** (☎ 639 839) also goes to Antofagasta (2½hr.; 7am, 2:15, 8pm; CH$2000). There is a **Budget** car rental office (☎ 633 0031) in town, and **taxis** sit on the plaza. (To Pedro de Valdivia CH$7000, Chug Chug geoglyphs CH$10,000, Tocopilla $15,000.)

◪ **PRACTICAL INFORMATION.** Several efficient amenities are available in María Elena. **Banco Estado,** on the plaza, has an **ATM.** (Open M-F 9am-2pm.) Next door to El Rincon (see below) are a couple of **supermarkets** where you can get provisions for your trips to nearby ghost towns nearby. A **Chile Express** with a *centro de llamados* (☎ 639 284 or 639 420, open 8:30am-11pm), a **gas station,** and a **lavandería,** O'Higgins 280 (open 9am-2pm and 5-11pm) are situated in the vicinity. In case of an emergency, make use of the helpful **police** office (☎ 633 839) and **hospital** (☎ 413 738). You can surf at the fast-connection **Internet cafe** behind the museum. (☎ 099 429 6533. CH$1000 per hr. Open 2pm-midnight.) Or do it the old-fashioned way at the **Entel centro de llamados.** (☎ 410 401. Open M-F 8:30am-11pm, Sa 9am-10pm, Su 10am-1pm and 5-9pm.) The town also has a **post office.** (☎ 639 355. Open M-F 9am-12:30pm and 3-6pm, Sa 9am-noon.)

ACCOMMODATIONS AND FOOD. There are only two accommodations in which to rest your nitrate-weary head—the best is **Residencial Jorquerav ❷**, which has 30 rooms with baths (some with TV), and a communal self-catering kitchen in a rustic, amiable atmosphere (☎639 104. CH$5000; doubles CH$7000-8000. AmEx/DC/MC/V.) The humbler **Residencial Chacance ❷** has 29 rooms, some with TV, in two separate buildings. (☎639 524. CH$3000-4000.) If you get hungry, grab the filling fixed lunch (CH$1900) at **Restaurant El Rincon ❶**, inside the mini-mall on the plaza. (☎639 427. Open 9am-5pm and 7pm-midnight.) Then down a beer (CH$500) upstairs at **Schoperia Scorpions ❶**, on the plaza. (Lunch CH$1500-1700. Open Tu-Su 10am-midnight.)

CALAMA ☎55

Although the high-brow copper mining town of Calama (pop. 123,000) is not much of a tourist hot-spot, it is an important transportation hub for travelers. Much of the tourist traffic that passes through is en route to nearby San Pedro de Atacama, stopping in briefly for the amenities a town this size offers (banks with ATMs, car rentals, and an airport) that tiny San Pedro lacks. Despite the unattractiveness of the town itself, Calama is convenient to San Pedro (only an hour away on the paved Ruta 23) and has spectacular attractions in the surrounding area, including some interesting archaeological ruins, picturesque Andean villages, and the beautiful landscape of the Atacama. If you rest here for a few days, the town is very pleasant to stroll through, especially in and around the tree-lined Plaza 23 de Marzo, with its pink Iglesia Catedral San Juan Bautista. Within the next couple of years, however, Calama anticipates an influx of more than eager tourists—the entire population of neighboring Chuquicamata (see p. 273), a company town of some 15,000 people, is scheduled to relocate here.

TRANSPORTATION

Calama is a major transportation hub in northern Chile with air, bus, and train connections to both domestic and international destinations.

Flights: Aeropuerto El Loa, 5km from downtown, is serviced by **radio taxis** (CH$3500 to town; see **Taxis and Colectivos,** p. 270). **LanChile,** Latorre 1726 (☎341 477), between Sotomayor and Vicuña MacKenna. Open M-F 9am-1pm and 3-7:30pm, Sa 9:30am-1pm. Flies to **Santiago** (3hr.; 7:30, 10:20, 11am, 6:30, 7:40pm; one-way CH$124,400, round-trip CH$134,000) via **Antofagasta** (30min.; one-way CH$20,700, round-trip CH$41,000). **Sky Airline,** Latorre 1497 (☎310 190), on the corner with Leon Gallo, has cheaper flights to **Santiago** (3hr.; M, W, F 6:30pm; one-way CH$109,000, round-trip CH$120,000).

Long-Distance Buses: There is no central bus station in Calama, and the various bus companies leave from their own offices/terminals.

Manchego, Alonso de Ercilla 2142 (☎318 466 or 316 612), leaves from its office for the most popular international destination, **Uyuni, BOL** (change to a Bolivian bus at the border; 15hr., W and Su midnight, CH$7000).

Tur Bus (☎317 699) has a ticket office on the corner of Balmaceda and Ramírez. Its buses leave from the new terminal at Av. Granaderos 3048, several blocks north of downtown. Daily departures to: **Antofagasta** (3hr., every 30min. 7am-10pm, CH$2500) via **Baquedano** (2hr., CH$2300); **Arica** (9hr., 10:15pm, CH$7500); **Iquique** (7hr.; 6:50am, 4:15, 11pm; CH$6000) via **María Elena** (2hr., CH$1900) and **Tocopilla** (3hr., CH$2900); **San Pedro de Atacama** (1¼hr.; 7:45, 10am, 5, 6:20pm; CH$1200); **Santiago** (22hr.; 6 per day 7:45am-9pm; CH$15,000, *salon cama* CH$29,000).

Pullman Bus (☎311 410) leaves from the corner of Av. Balmaceda and Sotomayor. Goes to: **Arica** (8hr., 9:30pm, CH$6000); **Iquique** (7hr., 10:30pm, CH$5000); **San Pedro** (1½hr., 6 per day

8:30am-8:30pm, CH$1200); **Santiago** (22hr., every hour 7:30am-9:45pm, CH$15,000) via **Baquedano** (2hr., CH$1500), **Antofagasta** (3hr., CH$2000), **Chañaral** (8hr., CH$9000), **Copiapó** (10hr., CH$11,000), **Vallenar** (12hr., CH$13,000), **La Serena** (15hr., CH$13,000), **Ovalle** (16hr., CH$14,000); **Valparaíso** (22hr., 1pm, CH$15,000).

Ramos Cholele (☎317 989) departs from the corner of Vargas and Balmaceda. Departures to **Arica** (9hr., 10pm, CH$7000) via **Iquique** (5hr., CH$4000) and **Santiago** (20hr., 11:30am and 10:30pm, CH$15,000) via **Baquedano** (1½hr., CH$1500), **Antofagasta** (2½hr., CH$2000), **Copiapó** (12hr., CH$13,000), **Ovalle** (15hr., CH$14,000).

Flota Barrios (☎341 643) departs from Santa María near the corner with Ramírez daily for: **Antofagasta** (3hr., 9 per day 8am-10pm, CH$2000) via **Baquedano** (2hr., CH$2000); **Arica** (10hr., 9:30pm, CH$5000); **Santiago** (24hr.; 8, 11:30am, 3, 6pm; CH$13,000, *salon cama* CH$22,000).

Pullman Santa Rosa (☎363 080) leaves from its office on the corner of Ramírez and Balmaceda for **Antofagasta** (3hr., Su 6:45pm, CH$2000) and **Iquique** (7hr., daily 11pm, CH$5000).

Regional Buses: Smaller, regional companies serve nearby destinations. **Camus** (☎342 800) departs from its office on Balmaceda between Vargas and Espinoza for **Tocopilla** (3hr., 8am and 4:30pm, CH$3300) via **María Elena** (1½hr., CH$1800). **Atacama 2000** (☎364 295) leaves from the corner of Antofagasta and Abaroa daily to **Peine** (3½hr., 12:30 and 6pm; CH$2300) via **Toconao** (2¼hr., CH$1500) and **San Pedro** (8:30am, 12:30, 6pm; CH$1000). **Buses Frontera** (☎318 543) leaves from its office on Antofagasta between Abaroa and Latorre for: **San Pedro** (1½hr., 7 per day 8:30am-8:30pm, CH$1300); **Socaire** (2½hr., 6pm, CH$2800); **Toconao** (2hr.; 8:30, 11am, 2:30, 6pm; CH$1800).

Train: The **train station** (☎348 900 or 348 902) is on the corner of Balmaceda and Sotomayor. A British company runs a weekly train service to **Uyuni, BOL** (24hr., W 11pm, CH$7000), where you can connect to trains continuing onto **Oruro, BOL** or **La Paz, BOL.** Book a ticket on the day of departure, between 3-10pm. At Ollagüe on the Bolivian border, the train changes to a Bolivian locomotive—a slow, old train with very basic seats (no first class available). Unless you are a railway aficionado, it is better to go with the faster and more comfortable bus service to Uyuni, BOL.

Micros: Micros run daily 7am-10pm (CH$220; CH$270 to outskirts of town).

Taxis and Colectivos: Taxi companies that head to the airport include **Radio Taxi Afluentes del Loa** (☎316 824), **Taxi Abant** (☎346 769), **Radio Taxi Abadia** (☎310 502), and **Radio Taxi Santa Isabel** (☎342 002). **Taxi LM**, Balmaceda 1974 (☎346 069), goes to **Tocopilla** for CH$3500 per person. **Colectivos** cost CH$300-350 in and near downtown. **Colectivo 80** (☎362 523) goes to **Chiu Chiu** (CH$1300 per person).

Car Rentals: Try the reputable **Hertz**, Latorre 1510 (☎341 380; www.hertz.cl), or **Budget**, Granaderos 2875 (☎361 072; airport 346 868; www.budget.cl). For cheaper options, call **Alamo**, Felix Hoyos 2177 (☎364 545), on the corner with Granaderos.

■✦🗾 ORIENTATION AND PRACTICAL INFORMATION

The downtown area is pretty compact, with most shops and services concentrated within a **rectangular grid** bound by Vargas to the north, Vicuña MacKenna to the south, Granaderos to the west and Vivar to the east. **Ramírez** is a pedestrian street between Abaroa and Vivar, and **Sotomayor** is the main banking and commercial street.

Tourist Office: Oficina de Información Turística, Latorre 1689 (☎345 345; calamainfotour@entelchile.net), on the corner with Vicuña Mackenna, is run by Corporación Cultural y Turismo de Calama and has excellent English-speakers on duty. Extremely helpful. Open M-Th 8:30am-1pm and 3-7pm, F 8:30am-1pm and 3-6pm.

Tour Agencies: There are several tour operators in town, but they don't operate during the off-season, so your best bet is to inquire at the **Oficina de Información Turística** (see

Tourist Office, above), which offers guided tours to **El Tatio Geysers** with visits to Chiu Chiu, Caspana, and other villages and archaeological ruins. (Breakfast, lunch, water, and snacks included. Departs 4am and returns 6pm. CH$30,000 per person, min. 6 people.) Trips to **San Pedro de Atacama, Lago Chaxa** in Salar de Atacama, **Toconao,** and **Valle de la Luna** also available. (Lunch, water and snacks included. Departs 7am and returns 10:30pm. CH$30,000 per person, min. 6 people. Entry fee to Lago Chaxa and the museum in San Pedro extra.) The **Chuquicamata Division of Codelco Chile** runs the must-see tour of the Chuquicamata mine (see **Chiquicamata,** p. 273).

Consulates: Bolivian Consulate, Vicuña MacKenna 1984 (☎344 413 or 341 976), on the corner with Latorre. Open M-F 9am-3pm.

Banks, ATMs, and Currency Exchange: There are tons in town, especially on **Sotomayor** between Abaroa and Vivar. For a *cambio,* try **Moon Valley,** Sotomayor 1907 (☎361 423), near Vivar, which cashes traveler's checks and functions as a **MoneyGram.** Open M-F 9am-10pm, Sa 10am-10pm.

Camping and Outdoor Equipment: Mall Calama (☎368 300), on Balmaceda, north of downtown, harbors a few stores that sell camping and outdoor equipment. Try **Ripley** on the second floor for camping gear and **Maui and Sons** on the first floor for surf and skate boards. Open 11am-9pm.

Supermarkets: The biggest is **Lider,** Balmaceda 3242 (☎ 368 200), next to Mall Calama, north of downtown. Lider is also a department store. Open 9am-10pm.

Laundromats: There are several in town, including **Lavandería Gallardo** (☎316 541), on Latorre near the corner with León Gallo. CH$1200 per kg. M-Sa 10am-9pm.

Pharmacies: There are many, especially on Latorre between Ramírez and Vargas, including **Farmacia Ahumada** (☎362 418). Open 8am-midnight.

Hospitals: Hospital Carlos Cisternas (☎342 347 or 310 217) on Carlos Cisternas near the corner with Granaderos.

Internet Access: Moon Valley, Sotomayor 1907 (☎361 423), near Vivar. CH$400 per 30min. Open M-F 9am-10pm, Sa 10am-10pm. Also **Moneygram** (see **Banks,** above). CH$400 per 30min.

Post Office: On the corner of Vicuña MacKenna and Granaderos (☎342 536). Also functions as a **Western Union.**

ACCOMMODATIONS

Due to Calama's mining-derived wealth, accommodation prices are significantly higher here compared to those in Arica or Iquique. Despite a few good values, most middle- and upper-range lodgings are overpriced.

Gran Chile, Latorre 1474 (☎317 455 or 331 829), on the corner with Leon Gallo. Easily the best value in the budget price range. The motel-like concrete building has comfy rooms with private baths and TVs. Singles CH$8000; doubles CH$10,000; triples CH$18,000. ❸

Hotel John Kenny, Av. Ecuador 1991 (☎341 430 or 310 400; fax 340 069), on the corner with Latorre, a 10min. walk south of downtown. The new wing here offers the best mid-priced rooms in town. You can't beat the value of these large, restful rooms, despite the rather run-of-the-mill motel-like atmosphere. Singles with private bath and TV CH$15,000; doubles CH$23,000. ❹

Hostal San Sebastián, Aníbal Pinto 1902 (☎343 810), on the corner with Ramírez. One of the better budget options, San Sebastián has nice rooms with a TV. The super-friendly staff only make a stay here more enjoyable. Rooms enclose a dining area. Breakfast included. Singles CH$5000, with bath CH$8000; doubles with bath CH$10,000; triples with bath CH$15,000. ❷

El Mirador, Sotomayor 2064 (☎/fax 340 329 or 310 294), between Abaroa and Latorre. A worthwhile splurge, El Mirador boasts a charming white-washed inner court-yard ideal for lounging, good personalized service, and the distinctive wooden look-out tower (hence the name "El Mirador") on top. Spacious new rooms with private baths and TVs. Breakfast included. Singles CH$32,000; doubles CH$37,000. All major credit cards accepted. ❺

Hotel Punakora, Santa María 1640 (☎344 955 or 344 958; fax 315 840), close to Vicuña MacKenna. The new 2-story building with an inner atrium has appealing and comfy rooms with private baths, TV, phone, and fridge. Breakfast included. Helpful, accommodating staff. Singles CH$36,500; doubles CH$42,500. AmEx/DC/MC/V. ❺

Hostal El Arriero, Ramírez 2262 (☎315 556), between Granaderos and Santa María. Enter through the red fence with yellow railings. The owner shows videos on the large screen in his living room. Basic rooms with shared bath CH$3500 per person. ❶

Hostal Valle de la Luna, Sotomayor 2326 (☎342 114), between Santa María and Aníbal Pinto. These mediocre rooms don't include breakfast, but the kitchen is open for use. Singles CH$4000, with bath CH$7000; doubles with bath and TV CH$14,000. ❷

Hostal Camino del Inca, Banados Espinoza 1889 (☎349 552), between Vivar and Bal-maceda. Simple, clean, and good—period. This small upstairs set-up has rooms of vary-ing sizes with shared baths for CH$10,000 per person; doubles with bath and TV CH$18,000; quads with bath and TV CH$20,000. AmEx/DC/MC/V. ❹

Oasis Hotel, Vargas 1942 (☎319 075 or 361 157; fax 316 151), near the corner with Vivar. A typical "business" hotel. This new building has spotless, comfortable rooms with private baths, TV, fridge, and phone. Breakfast included. Singles CH$19,000; dou-bles CH$36,000-39,000; triples CH$50,000. AmEx/DC/MC/V. ❹

🔲🔳 FOOD AND NIGHTLIFE

Despite its size and significance for travelers, Calama presents a gastronomical challenge. It takes some effort to find a decent eatery with a good atmosphere. Similarly, the nightlife here is less than hopping, as bars or dance clubs with style are few and far between.

Barlovento, Granaderos 2030-2034 (☎342 848), between Antofagasta and Vargas. With excellent dishes and attentive service, this is one of the best restaurants in town. The plain interior has nicely prepared tables. Seafood CH$3000-6000, *carne* CH$4500-10,000, vegetarian dishes CH$2500-3800, soup CH$1200-4000. Beer CH$500-1000. Open 8am-1am. AmEx/DC/MC/V. ❸

Restaurante Las Brasas de Juan Luis, Balmaceda 1972 (☎344 366), between Vargas and Ramírez. A decent eatery with personal service. A large selection of beers that includes Guinness CH$600-1200. Fish CH$4800-6600, *carne* CH$3600-4800. Open M-Sa 1-4pm and 8:30pm-1am, Su 1-4pm. AmEx/DC/MC/V. ❸

Restaurant La Paila, Vargas 1905 (☎099 394 2795), on the corner with Vivar. Enter the nondescript interior to be greeted by a "welcome" plaque in 7 languages. A good bet for seafood (fish CH$3000-4500, *mariscos* CH$3000-5000), or sandwiches (CH$1000-2000). Beer CH$1000. Open noon-5am. ❷

Club Croata, Abaroa 1869 (☎342 126), on the east side of Plaza 23 de Marzo. With its walls covered by posters and pictures of the Dalmatian coast and Croatian coats of arms, this restaurant pays homage to the homeland. Try the *almuerzo del día* (4-course lunch special; CH$2500) or sample from the Croatian/Chilean international menu that includes sandwiches (CH$1500-2000), *carne,* fish (CH$4000-4800), and salads (CH$1200-1500). Open 9:30am-4pm and 7:30-midnight. ❷

Restaurante Grande Chong Hua, Latorre 1415 (☎363 826), south of Leon Gallo. A fine restaurant with an imposing, glitzy facade. Inside, waitresses clad in red silk attire serve fish (CH$4500-5100), chicken (CH$3500-4000), *lomos* (CH$3700-4200), and soups (CH$1500-3000). Open noon-4pm and 8pm-1am. AmEx/DC/MC/V. ❸

Cuervo, Av. La Paz 988 (☎347 564), east of downtown. A club popular with local yuppies. The vibe is mellow and a happy crowd shakes the night away beneath the straw mat ceiling. Occasional live band. Beer CH$1500. Cover for men CH$7000, women CH$5000; includes 1drink. Open Th-Sa 10:30pm-5am. AmEx/DC/MC/V.

👁 🎵 SIGHTS, ACTIVITIES, ENTERTAINMENT

One of the best things to do in Calama is the highly recommended tour of **Chuquicamata mine** offered by **Chuquicamata Division of Codelco Chile,** the large state-owned copper producer. The three-hour tour starts from **Ayuda Place** on the corner of Tocopilla and Jose M. Carrera in Chuquicamata. To get to Ayuda Place from Calama, take any yellow-covered *colectivo* from the corner of Abaroa and Ramírez (25min., CH$800 per person). The tour starts with presentations, both oral and video (in both Spanish and English), at Ayuda Place, followed by a bus tour of the copper mine (long pants and closed shoes are recommended). If the first bus is full, then another bus is usually organized. (In the peak season, there is sometimes an afternoon tour; ☎321 861 or 322 293; fax 322 795 or 322 302; www.codelco.com. Tours M-F 9am. CH$1000 donation goes toward helping the youth in the villages of the Atacama highlands) There is a small **canteen** ❶ at Ayuda Place, so you can grab a bite to eat before the tour starts. (Sandwiches or snacks CH$500-900. Open 7:30am-5pm.)

On a lazy afternoon, take a stroll on **Plaza 23 de Marzo** and peek into the spacious interior of **Iglesia Catedral San Juan Bautista,** which was built in 1906 and remodeled in 2000. Another spot to visit **Park El Loa,** just south of downtown on Av. O'Higgins next to the Río Loa, which has a riverside swimming pool and *artesanía* stalls. (Open 8am-10pm.) Adjacent to the park is the **Museo Arqueológico y Etnográfico.** The museum features exhibits on the archaeological and cultural heritage of the Atacama altiplano. (Take Colectivo 18 from downtown. ☎316 400 or 340 112. Open Tu-F 10am-1pm and 3-7pm, Sa-Su 3-8pm. CH$400, children CH$200.)

There are numerous **artesanías** selling crafts and souvenirs in town, including Feria Artesanal on Ramírez, but you are better off buying these in San Pedro, which has a better selection. For recent Hollywood movies and other flicks, you can try **Teatro Municipal** on Ramírez between Latorre and Abaroa. (☎342 864. Shows 3-8pm. CH$2000, W CH$1000.) For daytrips from Calama to the Andean villages and **archaeological ruins** between Calama and the El Tatio Geysers, including Chiu Chiu, Caspana, and Pukará de Lasana, see **Between El Tatio and Calama,** p. 274.

NEAR CALAMA

CHUQUICAMATA   ☎55

Superlatives abound in describing the mining town of Chuquicamata, simply called Chuqui by locals—it is the biggest open-pit copper mine in the world, owned and operated by the biggest copper producer in the world, which is the biggest single contributor to Chile's Gross Domestic Product. Chuquicamata is a company town that intends to delve into the mines to increase production for many years to come. As you tour the state-of-the-art facilities that produce refined copper, the vast importance of the mining industry in Chile begins to hit home.

NORTE GRANDE

Codelco, Corporación Nacional del Cobre de Chile, is the world's foremost copper producer, churning out 16% of the total world production, and controlling 20% of the total identified copper reserves worldwide. Despite Codelco's efforts at environmental protection, which include a system of dust control in the environment, and the purifying and recycling of 80% of the water from the Andean highlands used in copper production, the company will be relocating Chuquicamata's resident population to Calama in 2004, partially due to persistent ecological problems, such as air contamination from emissions of sulfur dioxide.

A three-hour tour of Chuquicamata begins in Calama (see **Sights and Activities,** p. 273). This is an informative and entertaining tour, as you visit not only the massive open pit, but also the impressive smelting plant and gigantic refining plant, where you can see the molten copper molded and refined to 99.9% purity. The tour includes a stop at a garage containing enormous trucks where you can take pictures standing next to monstrous tires three meters tall.

Yellow **taxi colectivos** to Calama leave from Ayuda Place and the Plaza de Armas (CH$800 one way) and black *taxi colectivos* going to anywhere in town cost CH$300. At present, Chuquicamata has most of the amenities expected of a large company town of its size, including a **gas station,** an **Internet cafe, banks, supermarkets,** a **paramedic station,** a **police station,** and a **post office.** There are also several places to eat, including **ChileX Club** (☎321 320), on Tocopilla in the western part of the town, which is part of a complex for company employees that includes a swimming pool, a bowling alley, and tennis courts. However, there are no accommodations here, and there is no reason to stay here overnight, given the air pollution and the proximity of Calama with its abundance of accommodations.

EAST TO EL TATIO

A series of Andean villages and pre-Hispanic archaeological ruins dot the rugged landscape between the Calama and El Tatio Geysers. These make for a pleasant daytrip from either Calama or San Pedro; many tour operators in San Pedro include these in full-day tours, beginning at El Tatio at sunrise and ending in either Calama or San Pedro.

CHIU CHIU. Chiu Chiu (pop. 500) is a picturesque village with a pleasant **Plaza de Armas.** On the plaza, a colonial adobe church, **Iglesia de San Francisco,** has a rustic feel. (Open in summer Tu-Su 9:30am-1pm and 3-6:30pm, in winter Tu-Su 9:30am-1pm and 3-5pm.)

There is no bus service between Calama and Chiu Chiu, so grab a **colectivo**—call **Linia 80** in Calama. (☎362 523. 45min; CH$1500.) Chiu Chiu has a few small **grocery stores,** a **centro de llamados** (open daily 9:30am-1pm and 3-5pm), an **artesanía,** and a **paramedic station.** Decent lodgings are available at **Hotel Tujina ❷,** which supplies comfortable rooms with a steady supply of hot water. (☎099 566 4589. Singles with shared bath CH$5000 per person, with private bath and breakfast CH$9000; doubles with private bath and breakfast CH$20,000.) A couple of simple restaurants are also available, including **Muley ❷,** which has a nice atmosphere and garden in the backyard. (☎099 451 7743; muley@chile.com. Meals CH$2000-3000. Open Tu-Su 9am-midnight.)

CASPANA. The most significant among the Andean villages in this area is Caspana (pop. 500), some 40km from El Tatio via a network of gravel roads. In this charming *precordillera* village nestled in a fertile river valley, villagers can be spotted herding sheep on green pastures watered by the Río Caspana. Many of the quaint houses are made of stone, with straw roofs, mud reinforcement, and cactus suspension beams. The rustic town also features the agricultural terraces of pre-Hispanic origins and the whitewashed **Iglesia de San Lucas** (built in 1641). Next to a stone bridge straddling the Río Caspana is the **Museo Etnográfico** (ethnographical museum), which houses a significant collection representing the local cultural and archaeological heritage. (Open Tu-Su 10am-1pm and 2-5pm. CH$500.)

To get here, you need to come with a tour group or drive on your own, as there is no public transportation. The drive from El Tatio has spectacular *altiplano* scenery, with sweeping vistas of snow-capped peaks, herds of llamas and vicuñas on vast *punas*, and steep canyons with scattered petroglyphs.

Very humble accommodations are available in a run-down dorm room at **Comite Artesanas de Caspana ❶**. (No hot water. CH$1500 per person.) The only eatery in town is **Cecimar ❷** (☎851 067), featuring basic meals (3-course lunch CH$2300). The Comite also doubles as a tiny grocery store. (Open 9am-1pm and 5-8pm.) There are no other services in town except for a **posta** (paramedic station) and a **centro de llamados** (open 9am-1pm and 5-8pm).

Near Caspana, heading further north, is the even tinier village of **Toconce** (pop. 100), with a small *iglesia* (church) and agricultural terraces, and the similarly diminutive **Aiquina** (pop. 40), which has a nice lookout point over the Río Salado. Situated between Aiquina and Toconce is **Pukará de Turi,** the ruins of a pre-Inca city, and the nearby **Baños de Turi,** a natural thermal spring. Further west, 33km from Turi, is **Pukará de Lasana,** the ruins of a 12th-century village restored between 1951 and 1953. Built on a hill that rises above the valley of the Río Loa, the longest river in Chile, Pukará de Lasana is an intricate maze of rooms and passages enclosed by gray stone walls. There is an entrance at the foot of the hill with a small exhibition room featuring stone-age tools, pottery, and other archaeological findings. The climb up the hill is an easy five-minute walk—you can tour the whole Pukará in 20 minutes if you are in a hurry. (Open 10am-6pm. CH$500.) The only way to get here is via a tour group or by *colectivo*—try **Linia 80.** (☎362 523. CH$2000 per person for the one-hour ride from Calama; CH$500 from Chiu Chiu.) In the summer, **camping** is possible along Río Loa (if you pay the CH$500 admission fee, you can use the super-clean bath/shower during office hours in the entrance to the Pukará building).

SAN PEDRO DE ATACAMA ☎55

In the past decade, the tiny desert oasis village of San Pedro de Atacama (pop. 1500), with its gravel streets and quaint adobe houses, has been transformed into the tourist mecca of northern Chile. A hip *precordillera* town packed with trendy eateries, bars, and accommodations, San Pedro de Atacama's greatest attraction is the endless possibility for adventure tours into the surrounding Atacama desert, among the driest in the world, and to nearby sites such as the El Tatio Geysers and the Reserva Nacional Los Flamencos.

San Pedro is a village of great historical significance. A center of the local pre-Inca culture, this area was home to the fifteen *ayllos* (kinship-based socio-economic groupings) that cultivated the land with water from the Río Grande. Subjugated by the Incas in 1450 when they erected an administrative center at nearby Catarpe, it was later visited by Diego de Almagro in 1536, and conquered by Pedro de Valdivia in 1540. During the late 19th and early 20th century, the town grew into a transportation hub for commercial and cattle traffic between Salta, Argentina and the nitrate-mining towns further west. Although it declined with the end of the nitrate boom, San Pedro has bounced back in recent years, redefining itself as a tourist destination visited in droves year-round by both foreigners and Chileans.

NORTE GRANDE

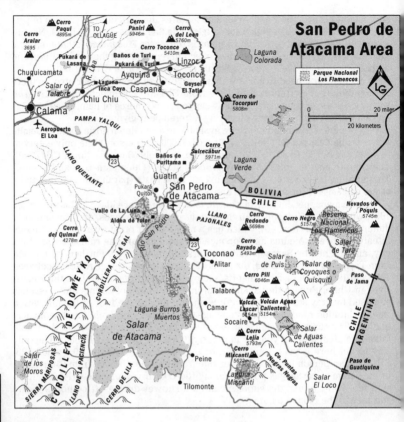

TRANSPORTATION

Flights: Calama airport is the closest airport. **Transfer Licancabur** (☎/fax 334 194) runs a minibus from the airport to San Pedro (1½hr., CH$5000 per person). Call for schedules. There is no *taxi colectivo* between Calama and San Pedro.

Buses: San Pedro does not have a bus terminal, but most buses leave from the area on **Licancabur** between Calama and the Feria Artesanal. **Buses Frontera** (☎851 117), on Licancabur near Tocopilla, goes to: **Calama** (1hr., 7 per day 8am-8pm, CH$1300); **Socaire** (1½hr., 7:30pm, CH$1500); **Toconao** (30min., 4 per day 10am-7:30pm, CH$500). Note: these Frontera buses are often used by **Pullman buses** for the same routes, and tickets can be purchased at the Frontera office for Pullman buses connecting Calama to **Antofagasta, Arica, Iquique, Santiago,** and other cities. **Buses Atacama 2000** (☎851 501), on Licancabur opposite Feria Artesanal, goes to **Calama** (1hr.; 8am, 1:30, 7pm; CH$1200) and **Peine** (1½hr., 2 and 7:40pm, CH$1300) via **Toconao** (30min., CH$500). **Tur Bus** (☎851 549), on the corner of Licancabur with Calama, goes to: **Arica** (11hr., 8:30pm, CH$8500); **Calama** (1hr.; 10:30am, 5:50, 8:30pm; CH$1200); **Santiago** (22hr., 7:30pm, CH$16,000) via **Copiapó** (15hr., CH$11,000), **La Serena** (17hr., CH$14,000), and **Vallenar** (16hr., CH$12,000).

San Pedro de Atacama

▲ ACCOMMODATIONS	Restaurant/Residencial Juanita, 8
Hostaría San Pedro de Atacama, 19	
Hostal Camping Puritama, 10	🍎 FOOD
Hotel Tambillo, 4	La Estaka, 14
Residencial Corvatsch, 2	Café Export, 15
Hotel Tulor, 16	Café Adobe Restaurant, 13
Residencial Chiloé, 1	Restaurante La Casona, 11
Hostal Camping Takha Takha, 9	Restaurante Casa Piedra, 12
Hostal Katarpe, 5	Café Étnico, 7
Residencial Rayco, 3	Restaurant Tulor, 17
Residencial Florida, 6	Restaurant Ayllu, 18

Taxis: Taxis leave from the general bus stop area on **Licancabur,** opposite Feria Artesanal. **Radio taxi** goes to destinations in or near San Pedro, including: **Calama** CH$25,000; **Catarpe** CH$6000; **Pukará Quitor** CH$3000; **Toconao** CH$15,000; **Tulor** CH$6000.

✳ 🛈 ORIENTATION AND PRACTICAL INFORMATION

San Pedro is one and a half hours by bus from Calama on the paved **Ruta 23,** which continues south to Socaire. Most destinations in town are within 10-15 minutes walking distance, and although most addresses are *sin número* (without a number), the village is small enough to navigate easily. The church and many services are on the **Plaza de Armas,** but **Caracoles** is the main drag where most restaurants, tour operators, and shops reside.

Tourist Information Office: Sernatur, on the northeast corner of Plaza de Armas, currently has no English-speaking staff, but does offer decent information and brochures. Open M-W, F-Sa 9:30am-1pm and 2-7pm; Su 9:30am-1pm and 3-7pm.

Tours: Most agencies offer the same tours and will often work together to fill up available slots. The "Big Three" tours are offered daily by every operator, going to: **Valle de la Luna** (includes visit to Valle de la Muerte and other nearby sights; 3pm and evening full-moon trip, CH$4000-5000); **El Tatio Geysers** (breakfast included; 4am, CH$10,000-12,000); and **Laguna Chaxa** in the Salar de Atacama (includes visit to Toconao; 3pm, CH$4000-6000, entrance fee CH$2000). A full-day trip is **Geysers y Pueblos,** which visits El Tatio Geysers and a series of Andean villages and archaeological sites between El Tatio and Calama, including Caspana and Pukará de Lasana (breakfast and lunch included; 4am, CH$20,000). **Lagunas Altiplánicas y Salar de Atacama** covers Laguna Chaxa and a series of *altiplano* lakes further south such as Lagunas Miscanti, Miniques, and Lejia (lunch and snack included; 7 or 8am, CH$20,000-22,000, entrance fee CH$2000). Many operators also offer half-day **archaeological tours** around San Pedro that go to Pukará de Quitor, the ruins in Catarpe, and Tulor (8 and 9am, CH$6000-7000, Tulor entrance fee CH$1000). Full-day trips and archaeological tours usually require a minimum of 4 persons. A few operators offer specialized tours, such as mountaineering trips to nearby peaks and a 3-day trip to **Uyuni, BOL.**

Tour Agencies: The following is a selection of tour operators that are among the more established and better-run. It is important in choosing an operator that you ask specifically what is included in the tour before signing up; it is also helpful to ask for suggestions from other travelers.

Azimut 360 (☎ 851 469; www.azimut.cl), on Caracoles between Calama and Atienza. Azimut is an experienced, well-run mountaineering and trekking tour operator. It is especially proud of its female staff, who in 2001 were the first South American women to reach the summit of Mt. Everest. Along with guided trekking and mountaineering trips (prices depend on number of people and days; also provides transportation and equipment to independent alpinists), Azimut also runs half- and full-day mountain biking trips and the "Big Three" tours (see **Tours,** above). Also rents bikes (CH$5000 per day) and offers horseback riding (CH$3500 per hour). Additional offices in Santiago and Puerto Natales. Open 9am-10pm.

Colque Tours (☎ 851 109; www.colquetours.com), on the corner of Caracoles and Calama. Colque is the best bet for multi-day trips to Uyuni, BOL. (US$80-90 per person; US$100 for the 4-day trip returning to San Pedro. All meals and lodging included. US$85 extra for an English-speaking guide.) The company has offices in Uyuni and La Paz, so you don't need to change to a different Bolivian company when you reach the border. Also offers a half-day trip to Laguna Verde and Laguna Blanca in Bolivia (CH$8000 per person, min. 2 people; US$5 entrance fee) in addition to the usual trips. Open 10am-8:30pm.

Cosmo Andino Expediciones (☎ /fax 851 069; cosmoandino@entelchile.net), on the corner of Caracoles and Tocopilla. "You pay a bit more but you get more" is the motto for this well-organized Belgian-owned operation. English-speaking guides do the usual trips. Open 9:30am-9pm.

Cunza Ecoturismo (☎ 851 183), on the corner of Caracoles and Calama. The English-speaking manager seems to know everyone in town, so he will get you on a tour no matter what. Horseback riding CH$3500 per hr., min. 2hr. (with a guide). Open 9am-9pm.

Desert Adventure (☎ /fax 851 067; www.desertadventure.cl), on the corner of Caracoles and Tocopilla. This is definitely a "what you see is what you get" establishment, with their tours clearly laid out in their English-language brochure. Open M-F 9am-9pm, Sa-Su 10am-9pm.

Corvatsch Expediciones (☎ 851 087), on the corner of Tocopilla with Antofagasta. Also has perfectly-explained English-language brochures. Prices are a bit cheaper than some other agencies. Open 9am-9pm.

Currency Exchange: There are a several exchanges in town, including **Marbumor** (☎ 851 123), on Toconao near Caracoles, which cashes traveler's checks and may also exchange Euros, Bolivian, and other currencies at fairly poor rates. Open M-Sa 10:30am-7pm, Su 10:30am-6pm.

Banks: There are **no banks** in San Pedro. Be sure to carry plenty of money with you.

Rentals: There are no car rental agencies in San Pedro. **Azimut 360** (see **Tour Agencies,** p. 278) sells and rents camping and mountaineering equipment. **H20** (☎ 851 013), on Caracoles between Toconao and Tocopilla, sells mineral water and rents bikes (CH$4000 per day, CH$2500 half-day) and sandboards (CH$3000 for 5hr.). A few tour operators also rent bikes and sandboards at similar prices.

Supermarkets: There are only a few small stores, including the one on the corner of Caracoles and Tocopilla. Open 9am-2pm and 4-9:30pm.

Laundromats: Alaja (☎099 776 9194), on Caracoles between Calama and Atienza. CH$1500 per kg. Open 9am-2pm and 5-9pm.

Police: ☎133. *Carabineros* (☎851 003), on Plaza de Armas opposite the church.

Pharmacies: There are no pharmacies in town, but **Mario Ramos** (☎851 013), next to H2O on Caracoles between Toconao and Tocopilla, has some medication (no antibiotics). Open 9am-10pm.

Hospital: There is only a paramedic clinic, **Posta Médica** (☎851 010), on the Plaza de Armas, next to Sernatur.

Internet Access: There are a few places to connect in town, including **Café Adobe** (See **Food and Nightlife,** p. 280). CH$1000 per hr. Also try **Café Étnico** (☎851 377), on Tocopilla between Caracoles and Le Paige. CH$800 per hr. Open Su-Th 8:30am-1am, F-Sa 8:30am-2:30am or until last customer.

Post Office and Courier Service: The **post office** (☎851 372) is on Le Paige opposite the museum. Open M-F 8:30am-12:30pm and 2:30-6pm, Sa 8:30am-12:30pm. **Chile Express** (☎851 434), on the corner of Calama and Caracoles, also functions as **centro de llamados.** Open M-F 8:30am-10pm, Sa-Su 10am-10pm.

ACCOMMODATIONS

This small town is full of accommodations that run the gamut from simple camping and *residenciales* to posh hotels with jacuzzis and swimming pools. Except for the few upscale hotels that have their own power generators, electricity and hot water are turned off from 1-7am. Most budget and medium-range accommodations don't have heaters, and it can get cold inside these rooms at night, especially in winter.

Hostería San Pedro de Atacama (☎851 011; www.sanpedroatacama.com), south of Caracoles on Toconao. Enter through the open gate with the large sign. The spacious rooms here lack the aesthetic touch of Hotel Terrantai or Hotel Tulor (see below), but the big swimming pool with 3 jacuzzis (two outdoor, one indoor) and view of nearby peaks can't be beat. The large complex of one-story bungalow-style stone buildings with thatched roofs is set on sprawling ranch-like premises. Private baths, TV, 24hr. electricity, and heater upon request. Breakfast included. Singles CH$75,000; doubles CH$82,000; triples CH$95,000; quads CH$103,000. AmEx/DC/MC/V. ❺

Hostal Camping Puritama (☎851 540), on the corner of Caracoles and Atienza, is among the best inexpensive options. Kitchen available. 2-5-bed dorms CH$4000-6000 per person; doubles with bath CH$15,000-18,000. Camping in the backyard (with use of communal bath/shower) CH$3000 per person. ❷

Hotel Tambillo (☎851 078), on Antofagasta between Calama and Atienza. Tambillo is by far the best mid-range accommodation in town. Very comfy rooms, in new buildings. 24hr. lighting available. Private baths. Breakfast included. Singles CH$12,000-18,000; doubles CH$18,000-25,000. ❸

Residencial Corvatsch (☎851 101), on Antofagasta between Calama and Atienza. One of the better bets in town, with a nice yard and self-catering kitchen. The new annex houses a set of deluxe rooms with private baths. Rooms CH$4000-5000 per person; deluxe doubles CH$25,000; deluxe triples CH$30,000. ❷

Hotel Tulor (☎851 063 or 851 027; www.tulor.cl), on Atienza south of Caracoles, features exquisite rooms in a beautiful complex including a swimming pool. All rooms with private bath, breakfast, heaters, telephone, and 24hr. electricity. Restaurant in the hotel (see p. 281). Singles US$76; doubles US$91; triples US$114. ❺

Residencial Chiloé (☎851 017), on the corner of Antofagasta with Atienza, is similar to Residencial Corvatsch but the rooms are not quite as nice. Rooms CH$4000-5000 per person, with bath CH$10,000. ❷

Hostal Camping Takha Takha (☎851 038), on Caracoles near Atienza, has rustic rooms with straw-mat ceilings. Singles CH$7500 per person; doubles with private bath CH$25,000. Camping CH$3500 per person (with use of communal bath/shower). AmEx/DC/MC/V. ❸

Hostal Katarpe (☎851 033), on Atienza between Antofagasta and Cararcoles. Excellent but slightly overpriced rooms reside in a brand-new building. 24hr. hot water. Private baths. Doubles CH$23,000; triples CH$30,000. ❹

Residencial Rayco (☎851 008), at the corner of Antofagasta and Calama. Although clean, the rooms are a bit overpriced and the hot water is irregular. Some rooms have thin glass walls and can get cold at night. Dorms CH$5000 per person; doubles CH$10,000, with bath CH$20,000. ❷

Residencial Florida (☎851 021), on Tocopilla near the corner with Le Paige, has spartan rooms but good rates. Dorms CH$3000-4000 per person; doubles CH$6000. ❶

Restaurant/Residencial Juanita (☎099 441 7663), on the Plaza de Armas next to the Entel office. Juanita is among the humblest in town, but has a nice open-air courtyard. The restaurant/bar serves simple meals (CH$2000) and beers. Very basic rooms CH$4000 per person. ❷

◖◗ ◗ FOOD AND NIGHTLIFE

There are several rustic bar/restaurants with great atmosphere in town, featuring stylish wall-paintings of geoglyphs and petroglyphs, bonfires in their inner courtyards, and thatched ceilings. Most restaurants offer daily **specials** (3- or 4-course meals for CH$2500-4000) and **Happy Hours** (buy one drink, get one free)—nightlife in San Pedro revolves around these trendy eateries. There is no dance club in town, and nights here end early—Sunday-Thursday at 1am and Friday-Saturday at 2am.

▨ **La Estaka** (☎851 201; www.laestaka.cl), on Caracoles near Tocopilla. Easily the best restaurant in town both for its refined cuisine and its imaginative interior deco of adobe walls, colorful tiles, and paper lanterns. The swanky bar plays mellow tunes. Sandwiches CH$1700, *carne* CH$4500. Breakfast CH$2500. ❷

▨ **Café Export** (☎851 547), on the corner of Caracoles and Toconao. With its hip interior, good service, and mouth-watering daily specials, Export is among the best in town. Try the pastas (CH$3000) or pizzas (CH$3000) made with homemade bread (price includes a wine or beer). Salads CH$2000-3000. Breakfast CH$2000-2500. Open Su-Th 8am-midnight, F-Sa 8am-1am. AmEx/DC/MC/V. ❷

Café Adobe Restaurant (☎851 132), on Caracoles between Calama and Tocopilla, has the biggest bonfire in town in its lively open-air seating area. Come here to munch on tasty fare, exchange travel stories, and do a little dancing. Pizzas CH$3000-4300, *carne* CH$4000-5000, sandwiches CH$1200-2800. Breakfast $2500. Coffee CH$500-2000. Open Su-Th 8am-1am, F-Sa 8am-2:30am. ❷

Restaurante La Casona (☎851 004), on Caracoles between Calama and Atienza. One of the bigger eateries in town with a cozy open-air bar. Under the direction of the Finnish owner, the Chilean chefs concoct a wide variety of dishes including pasta CH$2500-4000, vegetarian dishes CH$3000, and sandwiches CH$1000-2300. Breakfast $2000-3000. Beer CH$1000-1500. Open 7am-1am. AmEx/DC/MC/V. ❷

Restaurante Casa Piedra (☎851 271), on Caracoles between Tocopilla and Calama. The large outdoor seating area warms up with a bonfire at night. Come here for Chilean and international fare. Salads CH$2000-3500, pasta CH$3500-4000, vegetarian dishes CH$3800-4800. Open daily 8am-1am. AmEx/DC/MC/V. ❷

Café Étnico (☎851 377), on Tocopilla between Caracoles and Le Paige. Patrons check email (CH$800 per hr.) while munching on excellent sandwiches (CH$1000-1800) or tempting desserts (CH$300-800). Breakfast CH$1500-2500. Also a small book exchange with copies of *Let's Go*. Open Su-Th 8:30am-1am, F-Sa 8:30am-2:30am. ❶

Restaurant Tulor (☎851 063 or 851 027; www.tulor.cl), in Hotel Tulor (see p. 279). The restaurant is in an austere wooden building with a circular thatched roof. Sandwiches CH$1500-3000. Open 7:30am-11:30pm. ❶

Restaurant Ayllu (☎851 814; www.ayllu.cl), on Toconao south of Caracoles. A sports bar/restaurant San Pedro-style. Expats and gringos come to this small joint to cheer their home country's soccer or rugby teams on the large TV screen while chowing down on sandwiches (CH$1000-2700), *carne* (CH$3500-6000), or vegetarian dishes (CH$2000-3000). Milkshakes CH$1500. Open 7am-1am. ❸

🖷 SHOPPING

There are numerous trendy *artesanías* (craft and souvenir shops) all over San Pedro, but the best place to find a bargain is at **Feria Artesanal,** the pedestrian shopping center on the street extending north from Plaza de Armas. Both the Feria and the area north of it on **Licancabur** are full of stalls selling a wide range of memorabilia ranging from wool garments, carved wood, and ceramics to llama dolls, hats, and T-shirts. Some merchandise may be imported from Bolivia.

🖸 SIGHTS

MUSEO ARQUEOLÓGICO GUSTAVO LE PAIGE. A visit to the **Museo Arqueológico Gustavo Le Paige,** on Le Paige diagonally across from Plaza de Armas, is a must-see when in San Pedro. Although this is a regional museum housed in a circular one-story building, the quality of the exhibits is nothing less than world-class—a major reason why San Pedro is dubbed the archaeological capital of Chile. The story of this collection of ancient Atacama culture began in 1953 when Father Gustavo Le Paige, a Jesuit missionary, arrived in Chile from Africa and, two years later, settled in San Pedro. On an excursion to one of the oases near San Pedro, Le Paige accidentally stumbled onto an Indian tomb, which led to a lifetime of work devoted to collecting, cataloging, and preserving what eventually amounted to 380,000 artifacts representing the entire stretch of the Atacama heritage, from about 9000 BC to the 16th century. Administered by the Universidad Católica del Norte, the museum is particularly renowned for its incredibly well-preserved mummies, magnificent ceramics, and displays of ancient instruments, complete with lucid explanations of their use. (Some might find the exhibits on ancient Atacaman hallucinogen-inhalation ceremonies even more intriguing.) The museum also contains a room that is a replica of Le Paige's study and bedroom at the time of his death in 1980. (☎851 002. *Written guide in English available. Open M-F 9am-noon and 2-6pm, Sa-Su 10am-noon and 2-6pm. CH$2000, children and students CH$1000.*)

PLAZA DE ARMAS. On the eastern side of the **Plaza de Armas** is a modest 16th century adobe house known by two names: **La Casa de Pedro de Valdivia,** since it is believed that Valdivia slept here, and **La Casa Incaica,** because of its trapezoidal window with Inca features. Unfortunately, the roof collapsed in 2001, so visits are not possible. Next to the Plaza de Armas is the beautiful, white-washed colonial church, the **Iglesia San Pedro.** Built in the early 18th century, the church, large for a village of this size, has colorful altarpieces and a roof made of wood and cactus tied together with llama leather.

▲ OUTDOORS

San Pedro offers a wide range of outdoor activities, such as biking, hiking, horseback riding, sandboarding and trekking/mountaineering. Numerous tour operators in San Pedro rent outdoor equipment (see **Tour Agencies,** p. 278), including bikes and sandboards. Many also offer **horseback riding** (with a guide; about CH$3500 per hr.). For **mountaineering,** you need to be sufficiently acclimatized to the high altitude of the peaks you want to climb, usually by spending least three days at similar altitudes. **Trekking** trails include half-day trips to the **Valle de la Luna, Mars Valley,** and **Puritama** (see **Daytrips,** below). Among the easier peaks to climb near San Pedro are **Lascar** (5154m), an active volcano, and **Toco** (5604m). More difficult ones include **Sairecabur** (6050m), **Pili** (6040m), **Colorado** (5748m), and **Licancabur** (5916m). **San Pedro** (6150m) and the more distant **Llullaillaco** (6723m) are only for hard-core veterans with special climbing gear (Llullaillaco requires a guide and a permit from Santiago; inquire at **Azimut 360,** see p. 278). All peaks except for Lascar have no marked trails, so it is best to climb with a local guide, even if you are an experienced alpinist. Most peaks can be climbed year-round except in wet weather from January to early March.

▶ DAYTRIPS FROM SAN PEDRO DE ATACAMA

PUKARÁ DE QUITOR AND CATARPE
3km northwest of San Pedro de Atacama. CH$1200 fee at the base of Pukará.

Taken together, the ruins at **Quitor** and **Catarpe** make an excellent half-day trip from San Pedro on foot, bike, or horse. Arrive first at the Pre-Inca hilltop fortress of **Pukará de Quitor,** flanked by two steep gorges, which provides a spectacular view of the surrounding landscape. The climb up the reddish, sun-baked hill takes an easy ten minutes. Next, the Incas await you at **Tambo de Catarpe,** a ruin 8km from Quitor by way of a dried-up river bed involving a few stream crossings. In the wet season, this route is impassable even with a 4WD, so it is better to get here on foot or by bike. Built around AD 1450 on a hill a bit higher than Quitor, this was an administrative center used for the collection of tributes that were sent to Cusco, the Inca capital. Now, piles of stone walls with scattered fragments of Inca ceramics stand against a backdrop of the barren mountain range. The climb up is an easy five minutes from the sign at the bottom.

TULOR
About 5km southwest of San Pedro. Huts open daily 9am-6pm. Free. There is a map of the village at the entrance.

No archaeological tour of San Pedro would be complete without a visit to the prehistoric village of **Tulor,** 10km southwest of San Pedro. Built by the first Atacama farmers between 800 BC and AD 500, this large village, about one square kilometer on an exposed plain, was a web of clay huts inside a walled compound, erected for protection from the gusts of sandy wind. At the entrance to the site are two huts administered by **Conaf** that are reconstructions of the originals, which are now mostly submerged in the earth, with only their top parts visible above the sand. This village, which serves as one of the best examples of how sedentary life emerged in northern Chile, is about 40min. by bike from San Pedro—well worth the ride to see the spectacular view at sunset.

EL TATIO GEYSERS

The best way to get to El Tatio from San Pedro is with a tour group, as the unpaved roads are very hard to follow after dark, and it is best to arrive here by sunrise. If you do go alone, a 4WD is strongly recommended. No camping is allowed here, and the CORFO refugio nearby is not open for travelers; however, you may be able to get help at this refugio in case of an emergency.

The mystically beautiful **El Tatio Geysers** (4321m), located 90km northeast of San Pedro, compose the highest geyser field in the world. Although they have less powerful and less frequent eruptions than the famous geysers in New Zealand's Rotorua or Yellowstone National Park in the United States, the sight of El Tatio's exploding water and vapor set against the pristine *altiplano* is unforgettable, especially at dawn when the fumes are the most visible. Lying between towering peaks on a *puna* (arid, flat stretch of land) marked with yellow-green shrubs and crystal-clear streams, the landscape around El Tatio is similar to the national parks further north. Several hundred meters from the geyser field, there is a sizable thermal pool shielded by a stone fence where you can bathe in the soothing water (about 40°C). Most tours from San Pedro stop here for a dip after serving you breakfast on the geyser field. Be careful when walking around in the field, as some spots have soft surface crust, and cracking into the underlying geyser pool could result in severe burns.

NEAR SAN PEDRO DE ATACAMA

TOCONAO

About 40km south of San Pedro is the idyllic oasis village of Toconao (pop. 550), similar to San Pedro but smaller. The village's brownish-gray volcanic stone houses are less aesthetically appealing than San Pedro's adobe ones, but the surrounding scenery is stunning. The **Río Toconao** flows next to the village, cutting a gorge through the desert and watering an abundance of fruit trees, including apple, pomegranate, and grape. The main sight in Toconao is the trimmed-stone **Iglesia de San Lucas** (built in 1744), on the **Plaza de Armas.** The church has a straw ceiling and a colonial bell tower, which has come to be recognized as the town's symbol. For key to the church, ask at the shop next door.

Buses Frontera goes to **San Pedro** (30min, 6 per day 7am-7pm, CH$500), as does **Buses Atacama 2000** (30min; 7am, 1, 6pm; CH$500). A round-trip **taxi** from San Pedro to Toconao costs about CH$15,000. In town you will find a **police station,** a **paramedic clinic,** a **Conaf office** (open M-F 8:30am-12:30pm and 2-6pm), and a small **grocery store.** There are also several **artesanías** in the village, but you can find better bargains in San Pedro. There is no gas station, bank, or ATM in Toconao.

There are a couple of basic accommodations and restaurants, including **El Valle de Toconao ❶,** which has clean rooms in a new building with shared baths, hot water and electricity until midnight, and a self-catering kitchen. (☎852 009. Singles CH$3000; doubles CH$7000.) Also check out the **restaurant ❷** on the premises, which serves- simple meals. (Lunch menu CH$2500, breakfast CH$1200. Open 7am-1pm and 5-10pm.)

RESERVA NACIONAL LOS FLAMENCOS

The Reserva Nacional los Flamencos is actually made up of seven distinct patches of protected land around the San Pedro de Atacama area, each with a unique landscape and grouping of flora and fauna. The *reserva* encompasses an amazing variety of attractions, including the Valle de la Luna (Valley of the Moon), with its eerie, lunar-looking terrain; the Salar de Atacama, a giant desert salt plain whose micro-organisms sustain three species of flamingos; and the Lago Chaxa, whose lookout points provide vistas of some of the most beautiful sunsets imaginable.

AT A GLANCE

AREA: Total of about 74,000 hectares, in seven separate sectors.

CLIMATE: Each of the 7 areas has a distinct climate; rainy periods from Dec.-Mar.

GATEWAYS: San Pedro, Toconao, Tulor.

HIGHLIGHTS: Valle de la Luna, Salar de Atacama, Lago Chaxa, Lagunas Miscanti and Miñiques; 3 species of flamingos.

FEES: CH$1500, children CH$300.

CAMPING: Official camping not allowed in most places.

⒡ ⒣ TRANSPORTATION AND PRACTICAL INFORMATION

The ride from San Pedro is on a well-maintained gravel road. It is possible to visit on your own in a rented car, but many tour companies also run daytrips to various sites in the reserve (see **Tour Agencies**, p. 278). For up-to-date information on conditions in the Reserva Nacional Los Flamencos, stop in at the **Conaf** office in Solcor, located 10min. south of San Pedro on the way to Toconao, or the Conaf office in Toconao (see p. 283; neither office has a phone). Both offices are open M-F 8:30am-12:30pm and 2-6pm.

◎ SIGHTS

VALLE DE LA LUNA AND VALLE DE LA MUERTE. One of the best and closest daytrips from San Pedro de Atacama is **Valle de la Luna** (Moon Valley), 15km southwest of San Pedro. The valley is one of the seven distinct pockets that make up Reserva Nacional Los Flamencos. Valle de la Luna gets its name from its desolate salt highlands, which feature a circular white salt pan inside what looks like a sunken lunar crater. A climb to the top of the rocky pinnacle (next to the sand dune; more than 100m high) at dusk promises some of the most memorable sunsets in the world.

Near Valle de la Luna is **Valle de la Muerte** (Death Valley), so named because of the lifelessness of its gigantic sand dunes and crystallized salt mines. Most tours from San Pedro take you to the salt mines and a sculpture-like natural salt outwelling called **Las Tres Marías,** which evokes an image of the "Virgen María" (Virgin Mary) standing in prayer, and another of María with a baby. Perhaps the most enjoyable way to take this tour is to visit the Valle de la Luna in the evening, arriving in time to catch the sunset, and then proceed to the salt mines and Las Tres Marías in the moonlight. Bring a flashlight to light up the salt crystals inside the caves and watch them glow. No camping is allowed in this sector of the park.

SALAR DE ATACAMA. South of San Pedro lies the largest salt deposit in Chile, **Salar de Atacama,** in a 3000 square kilometers tectonic basin. Although the *salar* is small in comparison to Bolivia's awesome Salar de Uyuni, it is nevertheless a spectacular natural wonder. The average annual rainfall here amounts to a mere 200-300mm, falling mostly in summer, making for one of the driest desert areas in the world. What little water there is comes from underground sources that evaporate rapidly, leaving shallow scattered ponds filled with salt-saturated waters high in lithium (the *salar's* lithium deposit allegedly makes up 40% of the world reserves). In some of the ponds, there is enough algae and micro-organisms to support breeding colonies of flamingos (thus the name of the Reserva Nacional Los Flamencos). The water in one of the small lakes in the *salar* has enough salt content to produce natural buoyancy, similar to the Dead Sea in Israel.

LAGO CHAXA. Only 4km south of **Toconao** (see p. 283), Ruta 4 meets a turn-off that leads some 28km southwest to **Lago Chaxa** inside the Salar. Here, a marked trail leads into the Salar, with viewing stations along the way for breathtaking vistas of the vast Salar and numerous flamingos of three different species (Chilean, Andean, and James). Like Valle de la Luna, this is the spot for one of the most sublimely beautiful sunsets in the world. The vista inspires poetry: the reflection of the nearby mountains floats on the serene surface of the Lago, as flamingos make faint ripples on this delicate palette shot through with golden sun rays. The fragile desert ecology of the Salar cannot allow for camping, so it is best to come here on a daytrip from San Pedro or from Toconao. *(No public transportation to Lago Chaxa; come with a tour group or in your own car. Park at the entrance to the lake. Open daily 7am-7pm. CH$2000, children CH$500, paid to the Comunidad Atacamena Toconao.)*

LAGUNAS MISCANTI AND MIÑIQUES SECTOR. If you have access to a car, a good daytrip from Toconao is a drive south along Ruta 23 into the Miscanti-Miñiques sector of the reserve. Forty kilometers south along the paved section of the route brings you to the village of **Socaire** (pop. 285), a farming and cattle-breeding community. Thirty-one kilometers south, after **Ruta 23** turns to gravel, is a turnoff that loops east towards **Laguna Miscanti** and **Laguna Miñiques**, two spectacular *altiplano* lakes. Nearby are the lakes' namesake peaks, **Cerro Miscanti** (5622m) and **Cerro Miñiques** (5910m). The loop continues past a few salt pans and small lakes, including the beautiful **Laguna de Tuyajto,** towards **Paso Sico** on the Argentine border. Be careful, as driving on the unpaved roads south of Toconao can be dangerous, if not impossible, in the wet season, when the roads are washed away.

BORDER CROSSING INTO BOLIVIA: HITO CAJÓN
The border crossing between San Pedro de Atacama and the Salar de Uyuni winds its way along the base of the towering **Volcán Licancábur** and down around **Laguna Verde** before heading off to the salt plains. Unfortunately this is not the best of crossings, so it is recommended that you contact a tour agency to arrange good transportation and check weather conditions beforehand. The customs office is in **Hito Cajón** at the border and is open 9am-noon and 2-4pm. The process is fairly simple and involves no more than a brief search of your luggage for contraband and various food products and a passport stamp (see **Essentials: Border Crossings,** p. 65, for info on visas and fees).

WEST TO BOLIVIA

UYUNI, BOLIVIA   ☎ 06

Uyuni (pop. 12,000; 3660m) seems born to be a traveler's hub. Founded in 1889 as an isolated railway station linking coasts in the north, south, and along the Pacific, it won national favor for supporting soldiers who passed through during Bolivia's Chaco War against Paraguay in the early 1930s. For travelers, however, this small, chilly town is little more than a gateway to and from the salt deserts of the **Salar de Uyuni** and lakes to the southwest. Salar tourism has easily replaced *quinoa* grain farming and the locomotive industry as Uyuni's main source of income, and the agencies and restaurants harvesting tourist dollars couldn't be happier.

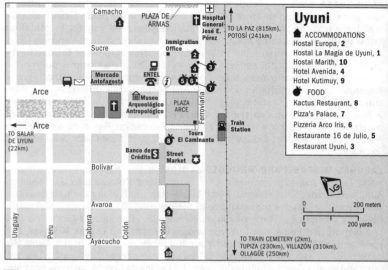

TRANSPORTATION

Trains: Station (☎932 320), at Ferroviaria and Arce. Open M-F 9am-noon and 2:30-5:30pm, Sa-Su 10-11am, and 1hr. before arrivals. Book at least 1 day in advance for **Wara Wara**. To **Oruro** (7hr., M and Th 1:22am, Bs25) and **Villazón** (9hr., F 9:25pm, Bs43) via **Atocha** (2hr., M 5:20pm and F 9:25pm, Bs13) and **Tupiza** (5hr., Bs28).

Buses: Terminal, on Arce between Peru and Cabrera. Open M-Sa 8:30am-noon and 3:30-8pm. To: **Atocha** (3hr., W and Su 9am, Bs20); **La Paz** (12hr.; W 7 and 8pm, Su 6, 7, 8pm; Bs50); **Oruro** (8hr.; M-Sa 8pm; Su 6, 7, 8pm; Bs25); **Potosí** (6½hr., 10am and 7pm, Bs20) via **Pulcayo** (45min., Bs5); **Sucre** (8hr., 10am and 7pm, Bs35); **Tarija** (18hr., 10am, Bs60); **Tupiza** (8hr., W and Su 9am, Bs30).

Taxis: Within the city Bs3.

ORIENTATION AND PRACTICAL INFORMATION

Uyuni's services are closely clustered and the city's gridded streets easy to navigate. At its center is **Plaza Arce**, across from the train station. All important tourist offices, restaurants, and accommodations are within two blocks of the plaza.

Tourist Office: (☎932 400), at Arce and Potosí, in a booth at the end of the plaza. A knowledgeable, English-speaking representative of the **Eduardo Avaroa Reserve**, Georgina González, has tons of information. Open M-F 9:30am-12:30pm and 2-7:30pm.

Tours: It's best to visit the Salar with a tour agency. During high season (June-Sept.) 4-day tours cost up to US$120; low season US$70.

Colque Tours, Potosí 54 (☎/fax 932 199; uyuni@colquetours.com), between Avaroa and Bolívar. The largest agency in Uyuni, with offices in San Pedro and La Paz.

Juliet Tours, at Arce and Ferroviaria. For better or worse, they may be willing to cross a flooded southern Salar when no other tour agency will. Driver **Carlos** is highly recommended.

Tours El Caminante (☎932 920), on Plaza Arce. A new company with well-maintained vehicles.

Toñito Tours, Ferroviaria 152 (☎/fax 932 094; tonitotours@yahoo.com), at Avaroa. Accommodates vegetarians.

! The Uyuni tour agency scene is a nightmare. Stories abound of drunk drivers, vehicle breakdowns, and monotonous meals. When choosing an agency, make sure they can provide a **knowledgeable guide** and a **sturdy Jeep** with a spare tire and salt protection. Ask other travelers for their recommendations. Once you've chosen an agency, ask for a detailed **written itinerary,** including schedule specifics, food, accommodations, and extra fees the night before you leave. Ask how many people will be going in your group; if the agency can't fill the vehicle, they may dump you on a less reliable agency at the last minute. Know the agency's **refund policy** before you go, in case bad weather hits. Even with precautions, things invariably go wrong; agencies lie, tires pop, and food gets served cold. Approach the trip with a touch of humor and lots of patience and you'll have more fun. If a trip goes horribly, the best resource is the Uyuni **police station** (p. 287), which keeps a record on each agency.

Currency Exchange: Banco de Crédito (☎932 050), on Potosí between Arce and Bolívar. Changes cash only. Open M-F 8:30am-12:30pm and 2:30-5pm. Many **tour agencies** and small shops cash traveler's checks for 6% commission.

Immigration Office: (☎932 062), at Sucre and Potosí. Obtain **exit stamps** (Bs15) to cross the border with Chile at Hito Cajón or Avaroa. Open 9am-6pm.

Markets: Mercado Antofagasta, on Arce between Colón and Cabrera. Open 8am-dusk. Open-air markets line Potosí, southwest of the plaza.

Emergency: ☎110.

Police: (☎110), at Ferroviaria and Bolívar. Open 8am-7pm, 24hr. for emergencies.

Hospital: Hospital General José E. Pérez (☎932 081), at Ferroviaria and Camacho.

Telephones: Entel (☎932 111), at Arce and Potosí. Open 8am-10pm.

Internet Access: Mac Internet (☎932 144), on Potosí between Sucre and Arce. Bs10 per hr. Open 9am-midnight.

Post Office: (☎932 146), at Cabrera and Arce. Open M-F 8:30am-7pm and Sa-Su 9am-noon.

▌ ACCOMMODATIONS

No matter what time you arrive, almost all hotel owners will take you in, as long as you knock loud enough to wake them. Most places have hot water. They fill quickly from October to December; it may be a good idea to call ahead. For extra warmth, bring a sleeping bag. Ask in advance about discounts for larger groups.

▨ Hotel Kutimuy, at Potosí and Avaroa (☎932 391). A popular hotel with a sunny terrace, wood floors, and clean rooms. Breakfast Bs10. Dorms Bs20, with bath Bs50; doubles Bs40, Bs70; triples Bs150. MC/V. ❶

Hostal Europa (☎932 752), at Ferroviaria and Sucre. Pink is the color of choice in simple rooms with rosy bedspreads. Hot gas-heated showers. Luggage storage. Laundry Bs15 for 12 items. Breakfast Bs5. Singles Bs15; doubles Bs30. ❶

Hostal La Magía de Uyuni, Colón 432 (☎932 541; magia_uyuni@latinmail.com). Magía's stylishly rustic appeal makes it the nicest (and most expensive) place in town. All rooms have baths, space heaters, and classy wooden beds. Breakfast included. Singles US$15; doubles US$25. Discounts for groups of 8 or more. ❸

Hotel Avenida, Ferroviaria 11 (☎932 078), provides 4-blanket warmth and hot water in an 80-bed behemoth. In the high season, there may be lines for the showers. Free luggage storage. Laundry Bs1 per item. Singles Bs20, with bath Bs40; doubles Bs40, Bs80; triples Bs60, Bs100; quads Bs70. ❶

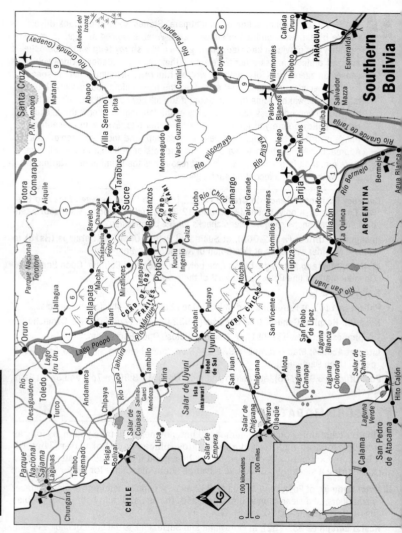

Hostal Marith, Potosí 61 (☎/fax 932 174), has simple, tidy rooms with wood floors. Entel phone and restaurant inside. Continental breakfast Bs10. Laundry service Bs1 per item. Singles Bs15, with bath Bs25; doubles Bs30, Bs50. MC/V. ❶

🍴 FOOD

Uyuni's pricier, gringo-geared restaurants line the plaza, on Arce. The food is nothing to write home about, but this a pizza-lover's paradise (pizzas Bs40-60).

🍴 Pizza's Palace, Arce 7 (☎932 259), off the plaza. This simple diner serves the best and cheapest pizza in town (slice Bs7, large Bs40). Open 9:30am-10:30pm. ❶

Pizzeria Arco Iris, Arce 27 (☎932 517), off the plaza. Tourists chat at black tables surrounded by blue lights and pop music. Pizzas Bs50-60. Open 3pm-midnight. ❷

Restaurante 16 de Julio, Arce 35 (☎932 171), on the plaza. Understaffed, but overflowing with tourists and conversation. Extensive menu. Breakfast Bs7-16. Lunch Bs15. Pizza Bs40-60, pasta Bs20. Open 7am-11pm. ❷

Kactus Restaurant, Arce 45 (☎932 386), off the plaza. A popular traveler joint, thanks in part to lots of beer and a huge sound system. Wagon wheels hang on blue walls. Pancakes Bs10, llama steak Bs24, veggie omelette Bs15. Open 8am-11pm. ❶

Restaurant Uyuni (☎933 036), on Ferroviaria, next to Hotel Europa. The place to go for cheap eats. Breakfast Bs5. Lunch Bs8. Soups Bs3. Entrees around Bs18. Open 7:30am-10:30pm. ❶

📷 SIGHTS

The **Museo Arqueológico Antropológico,** on Plaza Arce, has salt blocks, digging tools, and photos of the Salar; it's a great primer to the natural wonder. The small museum also boasts some well preserved **mummies** and exhibits on the cranial deformations that were a mark of beauty for the area's ancient civilization. (Open M-F 9am-noon and 2-5:30pm, Sa 8:30-noon. Closed during high winds.) About 2km west of Uyuni, along the railway line, tons of orphaned locomotives rust in the **train cemetery.** (Round-trip taxi Bs10 or a 10min. walk.)

SALAR DE UYUNI

The incredible geography of Southwest Bolivia, including its salt deposits and glacial lakes, can be attributed to **Lago Minchín,** which once covered an area of roughly 60,000 sq. km and reached altitudes of 3760m. Minchín dried up about 25,000 years ago, only to be refilled by **Lago Tauca** thousands of years later. Tauca's evaporation 10,000 years ago left behind the two large salt deposits of **Uyuni** and **Coipasa,** as well as **Lago Poopó** and **Lago Uru Uru,** near Oruro to the north. With over 10 billion tons of salt (stretching over 10,000 sq. km) at an average altitude of 3653m, Uyuni's is the **largest and highest salt field in the world.** Deposits in the center can be as deep as 4m.

AT A GLANCE	
AREA: 10,000 sq. km.	**GATEWAYS:** Uyuni (p. 285).
CLIMATE: Rainy season (Oct.-Dec.) makes roads impassable at times.	**CAMPING:** None.
HIGHLIGHTS: The largest and highest salt field in the world, glacial lakes.	**FEES:** Entrance to Avaroa Reserve Bs30, with a tour agency US$5. Entrance to Isla de Pescadores (Inkawasi) Bs7.

🔋 PRACTICAL INFORMATION

Tours of the southern lagoons reach heights upward of 5000m, making **altitude sickness** a serious risk—acclimatize before going, and bring lots of water. For **park information,** head to the Avaroa Reserve's **central office,** at Laguna Colorada (p. 290), where you can purchase park entrance tickets (Bs30). The Uyuni **tourist office** (see p. 286) sells **maps** of Salar; tour agencies supply free maps. Tour agencies rent sleeping bags (US$5), but it's best to bring your own. Nights can drop to -25°C, so warm clothes are a necessity; other supplies to bring include snacks, boots, and toilet paper.

🏔 HIKING

DAY I: THE SALAR. Most tours enter the Salar from **Colchani** (pop. 300), 22km north of Uyuni. As the only people allowed to harvest Uyuni salt, villagers here mine, refine, and iodize the mineral for national consumption. Around Colchani, mountains of salt nearly 3m high are scraped together while circular blocks are cut out by hand from a salt field that ranges from a few centimeters to 4m in depth. Near Colchani and scattered through the Salar are **ojos de sal,** the weakest part of the field where salt has worn away to reveal underground water wells. These bubbling, sulfuric holes may look like hot springs, but are actually cold, mineral-rich pits with a pink hue because of the iron that saturates the ground.

After a 10min. drive, two buildings as eerie as their surroundings appear. **Hotel Playa Blanca** and **Hotel Palacio de Sal** were both working hotels up until two years ago. The hotels were amazing: walls, beds, tables, and chairs were constructed of salt blocks and held together with salt and water mortar. The *altiplano* heat warmed the blocks during the day, which insulated the bedrooms at night when outside temperatures dropped. However, you might wonder where the hotels put their sewage on a plain with nothing but salt. So did the government, which shut down both hotels for pollution in 2001. From the outside, the hotels are still an impressive sight, made entirely out of striped salt bricks. Forty minutes farther lies **Isla de Pescadores (Inkawasi),** an earthen oasis amid the sea of salt, covered by an army of ancient, giant **cacti.** It's possible to spend a frigid night here (Bs15), but for most, this otherworldly island serves as a mere lunch stop (entrance Bs7, modern bathrooms Bs5).

The journey continues to **San Juan** (pop. 400), where harsh white land opens to sparsely vegetated, burgundy hills. This small town thrives on tourism, with five different **alojamientos ❶** catering to tour groups. (Singles Bs15, with warm shower Bs20; doubles Bs30, Bs40.) There is little to see in San Juan other than the town's simple **colonial cemetery.** Additional days can be taken to scale **Volcán Tunupa** (5432m), on the northern edge of the Salar.

DAY II: LAGUNAS AND THE EDUARDO AVAROA RESERVE. Day 2 begins with a short drive to **Chiguana,** the military checkpoint. Most jeeps stop an hour or so down the road to admire distant **Volcán Ollague** (5865m), **Bolivia's only active volcano,** located on the Chilean border. In this case, Bolivia got the better half of its deal with Chile—the summit technically belongs to Bolivia, while its geothermal activity resides in Chile. Thirty kilometers later there are a series of **glacial lakes.** Next stop is a series of crystal-clear lakes: **Lagunas Cañapa, Hedionda** (named "smelly lake" for its strong sulfur composition), **Charkota, Honda,** and **Ramaditas.** Despite the freezing temperatures, a smattering of seemingly displaced flamingos inhabit the lake year-round. The Andean, Chilean, and rare James flamingos are best seen farther on at Laguna Colorada. En route to Laguna Colorada, jeeps enter the **Eduardo Avaroa Bird Reserve** (Bs30) and the impressive **Desert of Ciloli** (25 sq. km). A highlight is the **Arbol de Piedra** (Stone Tree), a stoic rock worn away by millennia of harsh winds. The area is also home to *viscachas* (rabbit-like rodents) and over 80 bird species. Pick up a copy of *Aves de la Reserva Nacional de Fauna Andina Eduardo Avaroa* at the Uyuni tourist office.

Finally, the bumpy road leads to **Laguna Colorada** (4121m), a striking pool of water 60 sq. km and only 80m deep that appears to change color throughout the day. Deposits of white borax and other minerals along the shoreline add a glacial element to an already surreal landscape. Creeping close to the sanguine waters lapping the shore may be tempting, but be wary of quicksand. If you purchase your entrance ticket (Bs30) here, don't lose it; you need it to leave the park. Most tours stay in one of the lodgings here, although late-comers may have to drive to a nearby village (2hr.).

DAYS III AND IV: SOL DE MAÑANA AND LAGUNA VERDE. A very early start gets tourists to the geyser region of **Sol de Mañana** (5000m; 29km from Laguna Colorada) by sunrise. **Geysers** (some man-made by a geothermal energy plant) shoot columns of steam 50 to 100m in the air. In a nearby lunar landscape pock-marked with bubbling craters, **hot springs** spew boiling mud and sulfuric gases. **Thermal baths** are a short drive away at **Laguna Chalviri;** many tours stop to thaw in the warm waters. Heading over a mountain pass 65km later, the road opens to the final destination: **Laguna Verde** (4315m), named for the cobalt that colors this lake an incandescent emerald-green. In the background is hulking **Volcán Llicancabur** (5868m), whose summit is included in 5- and 6-day packages. There is a **refuge** at Laguna Blanca, but most tours just drop off Chile-bound travelers here and head back toward Uyuni. However, few manage to get back that same day; most spend a night in either **Villa Alota** or, if heading back on the same route, **San Juan.** More inventive tour companies throw in a trip to blue **Laguna Celeste** (US$100), halfway to Alota, but most are content to head straight back to Uyuni.

PARQUE NACIONAL SAJAMA   ☎08

Inspiring awe in all who stand in its shadow, **Nevado Sajama** (6548m), **Bolivia's highest peak,** challenges mountain climbers the world over. Parque Nacional Sajama's 800 sq. km were set aside in 1946 to conserve Bolivia's fragile *altiplano* wildlife and to shelter the region's intense volcanic activity. West of Sajama, on the Chilean border, volcanoes **Parinacota** ("Lake of the Flamingos" in Aymara; 6132m) and **Pomerape** ("Peak of Pumice;" 6222m), known collectively as **Las Payachatas,** invite more mountain trekking.

AT A GLANCE	
AREA: 800 sq. km.	**GATEWAYS:** Patacamaya (below) and La Paz (p. 329).
CLIMATE: Rainy season Dec.-Mar., mountaineering allowed Apr.-Oct. (best conditions June-Aug.).	**CAMPING:** Permitted and free.
HIGHLIGHTS: Nevado Sajama (Bolivia's highest mountain), the Patacamaya volcanoes, kenua trees, geysers.	**FEES:** Entrance Bs10. Register your name with the ranger.

▐═ TRANSPORTATION

There are two ways to reach Parque Nacional Sajama within Bolivia. From La Paz, take a **bus** bound for **Arica,** Chile; tell the bus company that you are going to Parque Sajama and want to get off at Lagunas, just before the Chilean border. From Lagunas, it's 12km up the main dirt road to Sajama. **Buses** from Arica to **La Paz** can also drop you off at the park (5hr., 10am, Ch$7000). From Patacamaya, **buses** leave for **Sajama** (4hr., 1pm, Bs15). Return buses to **La Paz** leave Lagunas at 10am; buses to **Patacamaya** leave Sajama at 7am. If traveling in a 4x4, arrange a car the day before at the **park information office** (see below).

NORTE GRANDE

■ 🔢 ORIENTATION AND PRACTICAL INFORMATION

The park centers on Nevado Sajama, while Parinacota and Pomerape lie west of Sajama, near the Chilean border. The northern section of the park encompasses valleys and frigid lakes, as well as the best wildlife watching. The park's eastern ridge houses the world's highest forest, while the most geothermically active area lies a few kilometers northwest of Nevado Sajama. Rangers at the **Park Information Office,** the blue building as you enter Sajama, can help you find 4x4s. (☎115 260. Maps are scarce. Open 8am-6pm.) It's best to buy a **map** (Bs40) in **La Paz** (see **Tours,** p. 333). Topographical maps (Bs40) can be purchased in **Oruro** from the **Instituto Geográfico Militar,** in Edificio Prefectura del Departamento on the plaza. (☎254 577. Open M-F 9am-6:30pm.) Get all **supplies** in La Paz as the park does not rent mountaineering equipment. Bring winter gear: warm clothes, tent, sleeping bag, mat, stove, food, and water. Since trails are often unmarked, it's best to go with a **guide.** Only experienced trekkers and campers should go alone. The **Association of Porters and Guides** in Sajama can arrange Spanish-speaking guides (US$15-20 per day). In Oruro, the **IGM** (see above) can help arrange a guide.

🏠 ACCOMMODATIONS AND CAMPING

Although small, the village of Sajama boasts some basic lodging along its main street. **Laka Uta ❶,** just behind the park office, is new and has double walls for extra warmth. (☎02 513 52 60. Bs10.) You can **camp** throughout the park. The only hot bath is in a natural pool 5km north of the village. There are similar accommodations in **Lagunas,** 8km from Sajama on the road to Patacamaya.

👁 🥾 SIGHTS AND HIKING

MOUNTAINEERING. The main reason people visit the park is to ascend Nevado Sajama, one of the most difficult climbs in the Cordillera Occidental, and the **highest mountain in Bolivia.** The summit can be reached in 3-4 days by the south, west, or north side. **Parinacota** is best approached from the southwestern snowfields. When ascending from the Bolivian side, trekkers usually tackle **Pomerape** via its western ridge. Both climbs take about 2 days round-trip. Call the park office a few days ahead of time to arrange a local guide (about US$40), and/or porters and mules (Bs70). A more expensive but reliable alternative is to plan a climb through one of the many agencies in La Paz, like **Andes Expediciones,** Camacho 1377 (☎231 96 55), which also rents climbing equipment (see **Tours,** p. 333).

OTHER SIGHTS. Herds of endangered **vicuña** roam the Patoca valley, 20km north of the park. Other park animals (especially birds) drink from **Laguna Huaa Kkota,** 12km northeast of Sajama. No stranger to superlatives, the eastern side of Nevado Sajama also houses the **world's highest forest,** home to the valuable (and endangered) **kenua trees,** which were previously used as train fuel. At altitudes of up to 5200m, kenuas, with their yellow flowers and red bark, only grow to 3-4m tall. The **yaneta**—hard, green, moss-like growths that secrete a sticky, sweet smell upon contact—have also been used as fire fuel and are now protected. Finally, 8km northeast of Sajama, 30 **geysers** and **pools** spread out over the incredible geothermal terrain, giving this intensely active valley a steamy aura. A popular **day-hike** from Sajama treks west to **geysers** (8km, 3-4hr.), **thermal baths** (3km, 2hr. from geysers), and **forest** (1km from baths) before returning in the late afternoon (3hr.).

CENTRAL NORTE GRANDE

IQUIQUE
☎ 57

A coveted beach town drawing visitors from all over Chile and neighboring countries, Iquique (pop. 150,000) is also a major port with a thriving fishing industry. Iquique was the main shipping outlet for Northern Chile's once-booming nitrate mining industry. Today, this legacy is reflected in the well-preserved historical town center, the opulent Municipal Theater on Plaza Prat, and the rows of stately 19th-century wooden buildings that line Baquedano, the main thoroughfare. Victorian houses, remnants of the mining industry's British capitalist origins, seem incongruous beside the miles of white-sand beaches south of downtown flecked with palm-trees and Florida-style high-rise hotels. North of downtown, Zona Franca, a duty-free import/export zone, is a haven for trade and consumerism. Businessmen and shoppers alike from Chile, Bolivia, and other countries flock here for great deals on everything from automobiles and electronics to clothes and perfumes.

Iquique's mild and dry year-round climate makes its beaches among the best in the Southern Cone of South America, both for swimming and surfing, while steep mountains rising up from town and ideal wind conditions make Iquique the best spot in South America for paragliding. Daytrips to fascinating geoglyphs and petroglyphs, oases offering excellent wines and fruits, thermal baths, and deserted nitrate mining towns all make a stay in Iquique both enjoyable and interesting.

◰ TRANSPORTATION

Iquique, 1843km from Santiago and 300km south of Arica, is well connected by both air and bus routes to domestic and international destinations.

Flights: Aeropuerto Diego Aracena (☎ 407 000), 40km south of town on Ruta 1, is connected to downtown by **Airbus** (☎ 470 181 or 407 045), a minibus service that costs CH$2500 per person. **Radiotaxi Aeropuerto** (☎ 416 388) charges CH$2500 per person from the airport to downtown. Three major airlines serve Iquique:

LanChile, Tarapaca 459 (☎ 427 600), open M-F 9am-1:30pm and 4-7:30pm, Sa 10am-1pm. Flies to: **Arica** (30min., 6 per day 7am-10:30pm, US$25); **La Paz, BOL** (1¾hr.; 10:35am; one-way US$123, round-trip US$170); **Santiago** (3hr.; 5 per day 8:25am-7:55pm; one-way CH$80,000, round-trip if booked a week in advance CH$135,500) via **Antofagasta** (50min.; one-way CH$21,000, round-trip CH$29,000).

Sky Airlines, Ramírez 411 (☎ 428 266). This new airline serving northern Chile offers comparatively cheaper flights to: **Antofagasta** (50min.; 8am and 2pm; one-way CH$16,000, round-trip CH$25,000); **Arica** (35min.; 7, 11am, 1, 10:30pm; one-way CH$12,000, round-trip CH$20,000); **Santiago** (3hr.; 7:30am; CH$118,000, CH$75,000 if booked a week in advance).

TAM, Tarapaca 451 (☎ 390 600; fax 390 604), is a Brazilian airline. Open M-F 9am-6pm, Sa 9am-1pm. Flies to **San Paulo, Brazil** (M, W, F 2:50pm; round-trip US$413) via **Asunción, Paraguay** (one-way US$212, round-trip US$369).

Buses: Most major intercity bus companies have offices at the somewhat decrepit **bus terminal** on Patricio Lynch north of downtown.

Tur Bus (☎ 472 984 or 472 986) goes to: **Arica** (4hr.; 1, 9:30am, 5:30, 6pm; CH$3000); **Calama** (9hr.; 8:30am, 3:45, 4, 5, 11:30pm; CH$4600); **Salta, ARG** (20hr.; Tu, Sa 11:30pm; CH$27,000) via **Calama; Santiago** (24hr.; 10am, 2:30, 4:15, 6pm; *semi cama* CH$15,000, *salon cama* CH$24,000) via **Tocopilla** (3hr., CH$3100), **Antofagasta** (6hr., CH$6000), **Copiapó** (12hr., CH$10,500), **La Serena** (18hr., CH$14,000), and **Valparaíso** (24hr., CH$13,500).

Ramos Cholele (☎ 411 650), goes to **Arica** (4hr., 6 daily 2am-6:15pm, CH$3000) and **Santiago** (20hr., 1:30 and 7:30pm, CH$13,000) via **Tocopilla** (3hr., CH$3000), **Antofagasta** (6hr., CH$5000), **Chañaral/Copiapó** (10-12hr., CH$10,000), and **La Serena** (14hr., CH$12,000).

Iquique

Iquique

🏠 ACCOMMODATIONS

America Hostal, **18**
Freddy Taberna, **11**
Hotel Caiti, **14**
Hotel Carani, **8**
Hotel Carlos Condell, **12**
Hostal Casa Blanca, **7**
Hostal Catedral, **1**
Hotel Dona Genoveva, **9**
Hotel Sunfish, **24**
Hotel Vivar, **23**
Hostal Wilson, **13**
Residencial J.J. Perez, **17**

🍎 FOOD

Barracuda, **16**
La Protectora, **6**
Boulevard, **10**
Cafetería Vizzio, **2**
Casino Español, **5**
Club Croata, **3**
Restaurant-Cafeteria
 Colonial, **4**
Restaurant La Carreta
 de Antonio, **19**
Ta Chang, **15**

🍷 NIGHTLIFE

Anaconda, **20**
La Caldera de Salón, **21**
Pharos, **22**

Zanbrano (☎ 421 135 or 413 215) goes to **Arica** (4hr., 8:30am, CH$3000) and **Valparaíso** (24hr., 4:30pm, CH$13,000) via **Antofagasta** (6hr., CH$7000), **Copiapó** (9hr., CH$8000), **La Serena** (19hr., CH$10,000), **Ovalle** (20hr., CH$10,000), **Viña del Mar** (23hr., CH$13,000).

Pullman Santa Rosa (☎ 431 796) goes to: **Arica** (4hr., 7 per day 1:45am-9:30pm, CH$3000); **Antofagasta** (6hr., 10:30pm, CH$4500); **Calama** (9hr., 10:45pm, CH$4500).

Pullman Bus (☎ 429 852 or 420 139) goes to **Calama** (6hr., 11pm, CH$5000); **Santiago** (4 per day, CH$15,000); **Valparaíso** (3 per day, CH$15,000).

Pullman Santa Angela, Barros Arana 971 (☎ 423 751), on the corner with Zegers, has frequent departures to **Pica** (2hr., 8am-9:30pm, CH$1500) via **Humberstone/Santa Laura** (45min., CH$900), **Pozo Almonte** (1hr, CH$900), **La Tirana** (1¼hr., CH$1200), **Huayca** (1¾hr., CH$1300). Buses leave from company office.

Agencia Barreda, Barros Arana 965 (☎ 411 425), goes to **Pica** (8am-9:30pm, CH$1500) and **Mamiña** (2½hr.; daily 8am, 4pm; CH$2500). Buses leave from company office.

NORTE GRANDE

Mass & Kiss (☎417 106) goes to **Colchane** (5hr.; W, Th, F 10:30pm; CH$4000) via **Chusmiza** (3hr., CH$2500). Buses leave from company office.

Pullman Cuevas, Esmeralda 1000 (☎517 897), on the corner with Juan Martínez, goes to **Oruro, BOL** (14hr., F 10pm, CH$6000) and **La Paz, BOL** (16hr., M-Sa 10pm, CH$8000). Buses leave from company office.

Colectivos and Taxis: *Colectivos* cost CH$320 within Iquique and CH$350 to the outskirts of town. **Radio taxis** cost at most CH$800 anywhere in town during the day, CH$1500 after 10pm—try **Pacífico** (☎451 111) or **Rocar** (☎446 768). **Taxi Tour**, San Andres 783 (☎414 875), and **Turis Cargo**, Barana 295 (☎412 191), go to Arica for CH$7000 per person. Taxis to **Mamiña** (CH$30,000), **Pica** (CH$25,000), **Pozo Almonte** (CH$15,000), and **La Tirana** (CH$20,000) leave from Mercado Centenario.

Car Rental: Hertz, Aníbal Pinto 1303 (☎/fax 510 432, airport ☎410 924; www.hertz.cl). **Budget**, Bolívar 615 (☎416 332, airport ☎407 034; fax 416 095; www.budget.cl). Both charge between CH$29,000 (small sedan) and CH$75,000 (4WD) per day, and offer cheaper weekly rates. Other agencies include **Econorent** (☎600 200 0000; www.econorent.net) and **Aventura Iquique** (☎390 305).

▟ ▐ ORIENTATION AND PRACTICAL INFORMATION

Historical **Plaza Prat,** flanked by a white-washed clock tower, is at the center of town. **Baquedano,** the main thoroughfare, runs north-south from Plaza Prat's southeastern corner down to the beach, providing a pedestrian zone between Thompson and Zegers. The streets between Plaza Prat and **Plaza Condell** are lined with large stores and are always crowded with eager shoppers. Beaches, including **Playa Cavancha** and **Playa Brava,** lie south of downtown along Avenida Balmaceda. Like Arica and the rest of northern Chile's coastal area, Iquique's climate is among the driest in the world (there has been no measurable rainfall for decades). Even during the winter, it is warm enough during the day to sunbathe on the beaches here, although the water may be cold.

TOURIST AND FINANCIAL SERVICES

Tourist Office: Sernatur, Aníbal Pinto 436 (☎312 238), on the corner with Serrano. Offers information and can provide brochures but lacks English-speaking staff. Open M-F 9am-5pm. Try the new, and notably more helpful, private agency **Información Turística,** Serrano 396 (☎517 961; infonorte@entelchile.net), on the corner with P. Lynch. English spoken. Open M-F 8:30am-5:30pm, Sa 10am-5:30pm. English-speaking Darinka Goravica at **Croacia Tours,** 18 de Septiembre (☎422 122 or 099 543 0347; autotek@entelchile.net), between S. Aldea and Latorre, is friendly and well informed.

Tours: The most common offerings in the area are full-day tours to the **thermal baths** in Mamiña, or to the desert oasis towns of **Pica** and **Matilla**. The ghost towns of **Humberstone** and **Santa Laura**, the **Pintados geoglyphs**, and **La Tirana** also tend to be popular destinations. Daytrips to **Gigante de Atacama, Pisagua,** and **Parque Nacional Isluga** via **Colchane** are available as well.

Mane Tour, Baquedano 1067 (☎/fax 473 032 or 099 543 2485; www.iqq.cl/manetour), between Zegers and O'Higgins. Runs full-day tours to **Mamiña** (CH$18,000 per person, 4-person min.). Tours to **Pica, Matilla, Pintados, Humberstone, Santa Laura,** and **La Tirana** available. (CH$13,000 per person, 4-person min.). The **Pisagua daytrip** (stopover at Gigante de Atacama; CH$18,000 per person, 4-person min.) and **Isluga daytrip** (CH$27,000 per person, 5-person min.) are popular choices. Lunch and drinks included in all packages. Open M-F 9am-1:30pm and 4:30-8pm, Sa 9:30am-1pm.

Avitours, Baquedano 997 (☎473 775 or 519 135; www.avitours.cl), on the corner with Zegers. Offers similar daytrips to **Mamiña** (CH$13,500 per person, 4-person min.); **Pica, Matilla, Pintados, La Tirana, Humberstone,** and **Santa Laura** (CH$13,500 per person, 4-person min.); and **Isluga** (CH$30,000 per person, 4-person min.). Open M-F 8am-2pm and 4-8pm, Sa 10am-2pm.

NORTE GRANDE

Turismo Unita, Baquedano 1054 (☎450 422; turismounita@terra.com), runs a 3-day tour of **Parque Nacional Lauca, Parque Nacional Isluga,** and **Salar Surire.**

Turismo Jaws, Latorre 324 (☎418 336; iqq.cl/transjaws), on the corner with Baquedano, offers a daytrip to **Arica** (CH$15,000 per person, 10-person min.).

Consulates: Bolivia, Gorostiaga 215 (☎/fax 421 777). **Peru,** Zegers 570 (☎411 466).

Banks and Currency Exchange: These are widespread, especially on Serrano near Plaza Prat. Most banks have **24hr ATMs. AFEX Money Broker** (☎414 324), on the corner of Serrano and P. Lynch, cashes AmEx traveler's checks. Open M-F 8:30am-5:30pm, Sa 10am-1:30pm. Also try **BankBoston,** Serrano 385 (☎472 181; www.bankboston.cl). Open M-F 9am-2pm and 3-7pm.

LOCAL SERVICES

Supermarkets: Downtown, try **Palmira Supermercados,** on the corner of Vivar and Sargento Aldea. Open daily 9am-10:30pm. Or try **Santa Isabel,** Héroes de la Concepción 2855-1 (☎439 696), near Playa Cavancha, inside the shopping mall. Open daily 9:30am-11:30pm.

Outdoor Equipment: Fallabela (☎394900), on Héroes de la Concepción, in Mall Las Americas. Sells camping, surfing, and other sports and outdoor equipment. Open daily 11am-10pm. **Vertical,** Balmaceda 580 (☎391 077 or 099 450 3298), on the corner with Ramírez on the beach, sells surf boards (new and used), skate boards, and other sports equipment. Also rents surf boards (CH$5000 for 3hr., CH$10,000 per day, discounts for longer rentals). Miguel (miguelcombinaiqq@starmedia.com) offers surfing classes (CH$5000 per 1½hr. class; CH$20,000 for 8 classes). Open 10am-10pm.

Laundromats: Try **Lavandería La Moderna,** 18 de Septiembre 457 (☎232 006), or **Lavandería y Tintorería Olympia,** Lastarria 1235 (☎232 659).

EMERGENCY AND COMMUNICATIONS

Police: ☎133 or 413 110.

Pharmacies: Several are located at Vivar near the corner with Tarapaca. **Salcobrand Farmacias,** Vivar 647 (☎410171). Open daily 9am-midnight.

Hospitals: Hospital Ernesto Torres Galdames, Héroes de la Concepción 502 (☎415 555).

Internet Access: Internet access is readily available all over town. Try **Mundo Clinic Internet,** Latorre 370 (☎517 895), between Lynch and Baquedano (CH$250 for 30min.) Open M-Sa 9am-4am, Su 9am-midnight.

Courier Service: DHL/Western Union, Zona Franca, Puerta 4 (☎414 470 or 429099; www.dhl.com), north of downtown. Open M-F 9am-7pm, Sa 10am-1pm.

Post Office: Bolívar 458 (☎422 148 or 473 539), between P. Lynch and O. Labbe. Also handles **Western Union** service. Open M-F 9am-1:30pm and 3:30-6:30pm, Sa 9:30am-12:30pm.

⚑ ACCOMMODATIONS

Iquique's lodging varies drastically, from humble *residenciales*, to restored colonial mansions on Calle Baquedano, to luxury beachfront hotels. Public camping is permitted on beaches south of Playas **Cavancha** and **Brava** (20km or more away from downtown). However, camping is advisable only in summer, when many people camp on the beaches.

Residencial J.J. Perez, J.J. Perez 650 (☎421 820), between Ramírez and Vivar. Seek out the wooden doorway, not easily visible from the street, that leads into one of the best *residenciales* in Iquique. This newly renovated, multi-story building offers great proximity to the beach, and the staff is charming and friendly. Immaculate rooms with a private baths and TV. Breakfast included. CH$5000 per person. ❷

Hotel Dona Genoveva, Latorre 458 (☎414 058 or 411 578; fax 390 405), between Lynch and Labbe, is among the best medium-priced accommodations in town. The distinctive wood-panel exterior houses comfortable rooms with a private baths, TV, fridges, and phones in a welcoming family atmosphere. Breakfast included. Singles CH$14,000; doubles CH$19,000; triples CH$23,000. AmEx/DC/MC/V. ❸

Hotel Carani, Latorre 426 (☎399 999 or 399 996; fax 399 998), between Lynch and Labbe. A good bet for business travelers and others desiring a comfortable stay in a central location. The pink 5-story cubic building has a quiet backyard garden in which to relax. Rooms equipped with private baths, TV, fridge, and phone. Breakfast included. Singles CH$16,000-19,400; doubles CH$23,700-24,900; triples CH$29,900. AmEx/DC/MC/V. ❹

Hotel Caiti, Gorostiaga 483 (☎/fax 423 038), between Lynch and Labbe. A nice, new hotel in a charming 3-story red building with windows overlooking the street. Rooms with private baths, TV, and fridges enclose a serene inner patio. Breakfast included. Singles CH$13,000; doubles CH$17,000; triples CH$23,000. ❸

Hotel Carlos Condell, Baquedano 964 (☎/fax 313 027), between Zegers and Wilson. Iquique's colonial history comes alive in this newly renovated wooden building hearkening back to the 19th century. The sparkling white, neo-classical facade encloses a meticulous interior decorated with miniature ship models, steering wheels, and mounted period photos. The grandeur of some rooms is accentuated by high ceilings. Breakfast included. Singles CH$14,000; doubles $22,000; triples $30,000. AmEx/DC/MC/V. ❸

Freddy Taberna (formerly Hotel Bellavista), Bellavista 106 (☎099 849 4828), on the corner with Covadonga. The proximity to the beaches increases the value of these adequate lodgings tenfold. Rooms within this red, 5-story buildming contain a private bath, TV, and fridge. Breakfast included. Singles CH$15,000; doubles CH$20,000; triples CH$25,000. ❹

Hostal Catedral, Obispo Labbe 253 (☎391 296), opposite the cathedral. This worn-out building provides clean rooms enclosing a pleasant inner courtyard decorated with hanging plants. Breakfast included. CH$5000 per person for all rooms with shared bath. Singles with private bath CH$9000; doubles CH$12,000; triples CH$18,000. ❷

THE BIG SPLURGE

SUNFISH HOTEL

Amunategui 1990 (☎419 000; fax 419 001; www.sunfish.cl), on the corner with Sur 1, next to Playa Cavancha. Definitely one of the better luxury hotels on the coveted Playa Cavancha, Sunfish Hotel, with its elegant rooms and spacious balconies that afford expansive ocean views, manages to avoid the kitschy Florida-motel feel that some neighboring beachfront hotels evoke. Each large room is tastefully furnished with mahogany furniture, and is equipped with a TV, well-stocked minibar, telephone, hairdryer, and safety box. The hotel's classy bar/restaurant is a great favorite with locals and tourists alike, while businessmen have been known to frequent the bar to escape from the frenzy of Zona Franca. The roof-top swimming pool is one of the best places in Iquique to lounge, savor a fruity cocktail from the terrace bar, and enjoy the beachfront view below. Breakfast included. Sunfish Hotel offers a car rental and room package with Econorent (CH$51,000 per day for either a single or double room and a Toyota compact sedan). Singles CH$53,000; doubles CH$60,000; triples CH$66,000; rates significantly lower during the low season. ❺

THE HIDDEN DEAL

CLUB CROATA

It is establishments like these that make visible Chile's significant Croatian population, and prove that the Croatian community has become an integral part of Chilean society, consequently increasing its cosmopolitan flavor. Club Croata (☎427 412), on the northeastern corner of Plaza Prat., is a sophisticated sampling of southeastern Europe that has been transplanted to Iquique. Coats of arms from different regions of Croatia adorn the walls, creating an authentic atmosphere. The subtle beige walls are complemented by tastefully decorated tables adorned with freshly cut roses. Those seated upstairs are privy to a great view of Plaza Prat. The international menu includes Croatian favorites such as *corvina à la Croata* *cevapcici* (CH$6500) and exquisite seafood (CH$3900-6500). The cafeteria downstairs serves sandwiches CH$1700-2200), salty pancakes CH$1400-2000), and seafood CH$5600-6500). The best deal at Club Croata is the weekday lunch buffet—for CH$2500 you can enjoy a choice of a salad, appetizers, three hot entrees, and dessert including fresh fruit. The Sunday buffet offers all this plus a glass of *pisco sour* or a glass of wine for CH$5000. Open M-Sa 9am-11:30pm, Su noon-4pm. Cafeteria open M-F 9am-8pm. Lunch buffet available M-F noon-3:30pm. Su buffet available noon-4pm. AmEx/DC/MC/V. ❷

Hostal Casa Blanca, Gorostiaga 127 (☎420 007; fax 415 586), close to the corner with Pedro Lagos. Rooms with high ceilings come equipped with a private bath and TV. Kitchen facilities available. Breakfast included. Singles CH$9500; doubles CH$15,000; triples CH$18,000. ❸

Hostal Wilson, Wilson 422 (☎423 789; fax 415 522), between Labbe and Lynch. The slightly shabby street facade gives way to a spacious 3-story interior with a large, comfortable lounge area. Rooms have a private bath, phone, and TV. Breakfast included. Singles CH$9500; doubles CH$15,000; triples CH$19,000. ❸

Hostal Vivar, Vivar 1770 (☎099 971 2919), on the corner with Libertad. This is a run-down establishment that offers no-frills accommodations close to the beach. Rooms have private baths and TV. Laundry service available (CH$2000 per 5kg). Breakfast included. Doubles CH$9000; triples CH$10,000. ❷

America Hostal, Manuel Rodríguez 550 (☎427 524), between Labbe and Ramírez. Like Hostal Vivar, this hostel is located near the beach and provides just the bare essentials. Rooms have shared baths. Singles CH$3000; doubles CH$5000. ❶

🍴 FOOD

Boulevard, Baquedano 790 (☎413 695), between Latorre and Gorostiaga. A colorful taste of France behind a sea-blue street facade with a drawing of the Eiffel Tower. Artsy French posters and photos bedeck the brightly painted walls. Enjoy a perfect *café* while taking advantage of the charming outdoor seating, or order an excellent seafood entree (CH$3800-5800). 3-course lunch specials with a drink CH$2900. Open May-Nov. daily 10:30am-4pm and 7pm-2am; Dec.-Apr. 10:30am-2am. AmEx/DC/MC/V. ❷

Casino Español and Restaurant Carlos Flambeau's (☎423 284), at the northeast corner of Plaza Prat next to Club Croata. Don't let this impressive Moorish building, reminiscent of Spain's Alhambra, intimidate you—it is not that expensive here, the service is exceptional, and the food is notably good. An older clientele regularly enjoys tasty soup (CH$1900-3700), seafood (CH$5800-10,300), steaks (CH$5100-8000), and salads (CH$4900-5000). Beer CH$1000. Open daily 10am-2am. AmEx/DC/MC/V. ❸

Restaurant La Carreta de Antonio, Playa Brava 1858 (☎442 909 or 323 209), across from the Shell Station. One of the better eateries in town, pleasantly located on the beach. Excellent seafood (CH$2500-6000) and meat dishes (CH$4700-6600) are served up impeccably. Open daily 10am-7pm. AmEx/DC/MC/V. ❸

Barracuda, Gorostiaga 601 (☎427 969; www.tabernabarracuda.cl), on the corner with Ramírez. An authentic English-style pub and restaurant complete with an oak wood bar, gas lamps, wooden ceiling fans, and walls plastered with old newspaper cuttings. A mature clientele keeps the place packed on weekends, making this one of the most laid-back places to spend an evening in Iquique. Seafood entrees CH$5900-6400, meat dishes CH$6500-7900, pastas CH$5300-5500, salads $3300-6200. Cocktails CH$2700-3700, beer CH$1300-1500. Open M-Sa 8pm-2am. ❸

Restaurant-Cafeteria Colonial, Baquedano 702 (☎ 312 502), on the southeast corner of Plaza Prat. Pretty stained-glass windows, chandeliers, photos of old Iquique, and charming street seating come together to create a homey atmosphere. The 3-course lunch specials (CH$2000) are a good value. Entrees CH$3000-5500. Open M-Sa noon-4pm and 8pm-midnight. ❷

Cafetería Vizzio, Tarapaca 400 (☎390 271 or 099 543 1293), on the corner with Lynch. A good bet for a satiating cup of coffee (CH$500-950), tea, or light sandwiches (CH$1900-2200). Popular with locals, this cafe/restaurant also serves breakfast (CH$2000) and has competitive lunch specials (CH$2500 for soup, an entree, and coffee). Open daily 8am-midnight. ❷

Ta Chang, Sargento Aldea 765 (☎317 625), between Barros Arana and Vivar. Despite the nondescript interior, the portions at this top-notch *chifa* are huge and tasty. Some authenticity is ensured by the fact that the owners are a couple from Guangdong, China. Chicken CH$1900-2300, beef CH$2000-2400, fish CH$2500-3500, 4-course meals for 2-4 people CH$5000-10,000. Open daily noon-4pm and 8pm-midnight. ❷

La Protectora (☎421923), inside the Sociedad Protectora de Empleados de Tarapaca building on Plaza Prat. The impressive building and self-proclaimed guarantee of good service may disappoint. The service can be lacking and the funky, junk-decorated interior won't jive with everyone's aesthetic. Worth a try for the familiar Sinatra tunes, the occasional band, and good seafood entrees. Soups CH$1400-2200, salads CH$1100-2800, fish CH$3200-5500. Beer CH$800-1200. Open daily 1-4pm and 8pm-midnight. ❸

🔘 SIGHTS

A good place to start a walking tour of historical Iquique is the **Torre del Reloj,** a national monument built in 1877. This imposing, white clock tower—an architectural mélange using both Gothic and Moorish elements—located in the center of Plaza Prat proudly flies a Chilean flag. On the southern side of the plaza lies the **Teatro Municipal,** the cultural center of Iquique since its inauguration in 1890. The neo-classical facade delicately balances a harp on its pinnacle, while an ornate theater resembling an opera-house lingers inside. Until the 1920s, grand European companies that visited the nitrate-mining port during its economic heyday staged performances here. Allowed to deteriorate after the nitrate boom, the theater was restored in 1987 and now stages ballet, classical music, folkloric, theater, and jazz performances (☎411 292. Open daily 10am-1pm and 3-9pm. CH$400). Adjacent to the Teatro Municipal, built 1911-13, is **La Sociedad Protectora de Empleados de Tarapaca,** the former quarters of one of Chile's first labor unions. Today, this opulent mansion with Corinthian friezes and stone balustrades is home to a popular restaurant/bar, **La Protectora** (see p. 299).

Moving south from Plaza Prat, stroll along Baquedano, which is lined with historical Victorian buildings from colonial times. The street is maintained as a pedestrian walkway for tourists—period gas lamps are lit in the evening, ornate fountains trickle, and a trolley track leads down to the intersection with Zegers.

FROM THE ROAD

BOOZE 'N' CRUISE, AND YOU LOSE

All too often, scenes from bad Hollywood films featuring helpless tourists at the mercy of shady and irrational police officers prove true to life in the developing world. Accustomed to presuming that policemen in Latin American countries are synonymous with the mafia, I had planned to keep my distance from Chilean policemen, the pervasive *carabineros*.

But as visible members of the Chilean community and the only source of info in smaller towns, the *carabineros* I encountered were helpful, reliable, and courteous law enforcers with an infallible sense of integrity. Indeed, officers often insist on enforcing the strict letter of the law (no, not to obtain a bribe, but for the sake of law-enforcement itself).

But a warning to all hell-raisers and ne'er-do-wells: while the assurance of scrupulousness among *carabineros* is a comforting thought as you navigate the culture and terrain of Chile, it can be a mixed blessing. Over-zealous officers have been known to detain tourists for driving without several forms of ID along with a driver's license, and they tend to crack down on anyone driving after consuming alcohol (even one drink is one too many in cautious *carabinero*-consciousness).

So don't hesitate when approaching *carabineros* with fumbling, touristy questions in the wilds of northern Chile. But if you get detained for doing something naughty, do not try to bribe a *carabinero*. You'll find yourself in serious trouble as those melodramatic movie scenes will come to life.

—*James Lee*

Make a stop at the **Museo Regional,** Baquedano 951, between Wilson and Zegers. Built in 1892, the museum has informative displays about the region's ethnographic heritage from Chinchorro culture up to the nitrate period. (Open M-F 8:30am-4pm, Sa 10:30am-1pm. Free.) Just a block south of the museum is the two-story **Palacio Astoreca,** O'Higgins 350, on the corner with Baquedano. Built in 1904 by an affluent tycoon of the nitrate industry, this mansion is now a museum featuring rotating exhibits. (Open Tu-F 10am-1pm and 4-7:30pm, Sa 10am-1:30pm, Su 11am-2pm. CH$400.)

If you'd rather head north from Plaza Prat, visit the two-story **Centro Español** on the plaza's northeast corner. A colorful rendition of the Alhambra in Granada, Spain, this mansion was built for the local Spanish community in 1904. Typical blue mosaic tiles and imposing Moorish arches give way to a posh, domed interior. Intricate sabers and knights' armor enhance the charm of wall paintings featuring scenes from *Don Quixote* (painted in 1908 by the Spanish painter Vicente Tordecillas) and Spanish history (painted in 1931 by the Chilean Sixto Rojas). The first floor is a functioning restaurant and club (see p. 298), but you can enter for free to look around. Farther north of Plaza Prat lies the **Museo Naval** (☎ 402 121), at the end of Aníbal Pinto next to the port. Built in 1871 as the office of the Peruvian governor and the customs house, this classical stone building now houses a museum dedicated to testimonies from the Naval Battle of Iquique during the War of the Pacific (1879-1884).

For beach-goers, there are plenty of places to sunbathe on Iquique's beautiful white-sand beaches. Close to downtown, **Playa Cavancha** is the most popular choice with locals and tourists alike. The kitschy boardwalk lined with cacti, palm trees, and fountains leads to a mini llama ranch. Farther south, **Playa Brava** and other beaches along Ruta 1 are good for surfing and sunbathing (*taxi colectivos* from downtown to Playa Brava CH$350). Add some excitement to a lazy day at the beach by taking advantage of Iquique's reputation as the best **paragliding** spot in South America. Join dozens of the sport's enthusiasts as they jump off steep mountains on weekends. However, remember that changing wind directions and the fact that you're jumping off a cliff make this a dangerous sport—trust the small emergency parachute, but follow the rules carefully. **Escuela de Parapente Manutara** is a French-run local paragliding operator. (☎/fax 418 280. CH$25,000 per tandem jump; 2-3hr.; no experience necessary. CH$80,000 for a 3-day course.)

ᴦᴉ SHOPPING

Iquique offers the avid shopper everything from duty-free shopping in Zona Franca (known in the vernacular as Zofri) to quaint hand-made products available at decent *artesanías* (crafts/souvenir shops). The new Mall Las Americas, an American-style shopping mall, and small "Mom and Pop" stores add to the array of shopping options. Established in 1975, **Zona Franca** is a veritable beehive of wholesalers and retailers. This retail mall harbors smaller stores rather than large, nationwide chain stores. (☎515 600 or 515 405; www.zofri.cl. Open M-F 9am-1:30pm and 3-8pm, Sa 9am-1:30pm for wholesalers; M-Sa 11am-9pm for retail shoppers.) Any *colectivo* going north from downtown takes you to Zofri for CH$300 per person. The prices tend to be slightly higher in **Mall Las Americas,** on Héroes de la Concepción, near Playa Cavancha. (Open 11am-10pm.) For **artesanías** selling woolen garments and intriguing souvenirs, stroll around the area near the corner of Thompson and Juan Martínez, northeast of Mercado Centenario. (Open 10am-2pm and 5-10pm.)

ᴗ NIGHTLIFE

Iquique is the nightlife hotspot in northern Chile—most bars and clubs stay rockin' all night long. With a high concentration of gay and lesbian residents, Iquique accordingly offers a happening gay/lesbian nightlife scene. Pleasure-seekers will find sinful sanctuaries all over town, but most dance clubs are located at Playa Brava, south of downtown. A taxi from downtown to the clubs costs CH$1500.

Pharos, Av. Arturo Prat (☎381 682), on Playa Brava south of downtown. When the proprietors decided to a bring frat-boy Greek scene to Iquique, they took their project a little too literally. If the triumphant entrance lined with commanding statues of Zeus, Poseidon, centurions, centaurs, and chariots isn't enough, the 2 large dance floors surrounded by imposing Greco-Roman columns will probably inspire you to new heights of revelry and rambunctiousness. When in Chile, do as the Chileans do and groove with the mostly 20s crowd to house DJ tunes. Beer CH$1000. Cover CH$4000 for men, CH$3000 for women. Open F-Sa midnight-5am.

La Caldera del Salón, Vía 3 km 7 (☎385 066), at Bajo Molle, farther south from Pharos. This glitzy 2-story Salsoteca whips up salsa, salsa, and more salsa. An older, more upscale crowd jives among brightly lit artificial palm trees below the glowing circular ceiling. Cover CH$6000, including a drink. Open F-Sa 11pm-5am.

Anaconda, Playa Brava 1882 (☎447 395), on Playa Brava across from the Shell Station. A real 9m-long anaconda hide hangs creepily over the bar. Although the wall paintings of the Amazon jungle are less than realistic, this lively and intimate bar with a dance floor is a fun place to spend an evening. Beer CH$1500. Open M-Sa 10pm-5am.

ᴗ DAYTRIP FROM IQUIQUE: HUMBERSTONE AND SANTA LAURA

Buses between Iquique and Pozo Almonte stop at Humberstone and Santa Laura (45min. from Iquique; CH$900 to Iquique, CH$300 to Pozo Almonte). Colectivos CH$1000 to Iquique, CH$500 to Pozo Almonte. Free; voluntary donations requested.

Learn about Iquique's thriving nitrate-mining industry of the past through an informative daytrip to these ghost mining towns. Located within a short walk of each other, 45km east of Iquique on Ruta 16, these company towns (originally called *oficinas*) were developed in the 1870s. Humberstone (named after an early British company manager) and Santa Laura housed thousands of miners and factory workers and together composed the economic backbone of the region through colonial times. Economic hardship lead to the closure of the *oficinas* in 1960, but the deteriorating, abandoned facilities were declared historical monuments in 1970. Today, Humberstone is managed by the family of the *oficina*'s last owner, and is bigger and better preserved than Santa Laura. Walk through Humberstone's pleasant Plaza de Armas and visit the town's hospital, 400-seat theater, and large metal swimming pool to get a sense of life in a turn-of-the-century British company town. Santa Laura is managed by the municipality of Pozo Almonte (☎ 751 220, ext. 234) and offers a look at the large industrial plant with a rusted and corroded, yet imposing, smoke stack. Both sites have small museums that are open daily during daylight.

SOUTH OF IQUIQUE

POZO ALMONTE   ☎ 57

South of Iquique, Pozo Almonte (pop. 10,000) is a transportation hub that offers visitors heading to more remote destinations a chance to refuel and avail of several practical services. If dallying here, check out the **Museo Histórico Salitrero** on the **Plaza de Armas. (**☎ 751 477. Open 9am-10pm.)

Frequent **buses** go to **Iquique** (1hr., CH$900) and **Pica/Matilla** (1hr., CH$600) via **La Tirana** (30min., CH$300). **Taxi colectivos** to **Iquique** cost CH$1300. Taxis available at Betty Market in the Plaza de Armas go to **Pica/Matilla** (CH$15,000), **Mamiña** (CH$15,000), **La Tirana** (CH$13,000), and the **geoglyphs** at Pintados (CH$15,000).

The **gas station** has a **24hr. ATM,** while free **Internet access** is available at the **municipal government office. (**☎ 751 477, ext. 234. Open M-Sa 9am-7pm.) A **post office** (open M-F 8:30am-12:30pm and 3-6:30pm, Sa 8:30am-12:30pm), **hospital** (☎ 751 214), and four supermarkets including **Betty Market** (open daily 7am-11pm) are available as well. If you decide to stay overnight in Pozo Almonte, the **Hotel Estancia Inn ❸** offers clean rooms with a TV and private hot water bathrooms. (☎ 752 242. 7-bed dorms CH$6000; singles CH$9500; doubles CH$13,000.) The large dining hall serves **breakfast** (CH$1000; open 6-10am) and **lunch** (CH$1800; open noon-4:30pm), while a few simple restaurants in town offer options for dinner.

RESERVA NACIONAL PAMPA DEL TAMARUGAL

South of Pozo Almonte, the Reserva Nacional Pampa del Tamarugal is sprawled across 100,000 hectares. A wooded area featuring *tamarugo*, the *reserva*, with fauna including mice, lizards, and reptiles, is a less than thrilling stop for most visitors excepting enthusiastic ecologists or biologists. *Tamarugo* is a native tree species that once covered a vast area of Norte Grande but is presently nearly extinct due to waterlogging that occurred during the area's nitrate boom. The *tamarugo* scattered throughout the *reserva* today are a result of Conaf's restoration efforts. **Buses** between Iquique and Antofagasta/Calama stop at the Conaf office at the Reserva Nacional (1½hr. from Iquique, CH$2000). The **Conaf** office, 25km south of Pozo Almonte, just off the Panamericana, offers exhibits about the Reserve's ecology. (☎ 751 055. Open M-F 8am-6:20pm but staffed during the daytime on weekends as well.) Conaf also has three **cabins** with four rooms each, kitchen facilities, a refrigerator, and shared hot-water bath available (CH$5000 per cabin). Camping is also permitted (CH$4000 per site).

Although the campgrounds here are complete with BBQ facilities, picnic tables, sinks, and power outlets, the only reason to stay overnight is to visit the amazing **geoglyphs** at the Salar de Pintados in the Reserva Nacional. The **Cerro de**

Pintados is world famous for the 390 geoglyphs that can be viewed here. Drawn between AD 800 and 1300, these fascinating depictions of human and animal figures and geometric shapes are visible on the slopes of a barren hill. Some geoglyphs were restored by the Universidad de Tarapaca in 1982. Look out for the souvenir shop at the entrance to the geoglyphs. To reach the Pintados geoglyphs, drive south from the Conaf office for a few minutes or walk for an hour. From Pozo Almonte, hire a taxi for CH$15,000. Pay admission fees at the Conaf office (CH$1000).

MATILLA ☎ 57

Matilla, a charming desert oasis, lies 40km east of the Reserva Nacional Pampa del Tamarugal on the Panamericana. Like Pica, Matilla (pop. 700) is famous for its succulent fruits and rich wines. A popular weekend retreat since the 19th century, when captains of the nitrate industry rewarded their efforts with a few too many glasses of wine, Matilla still draws visitors looking for some rest and recreation from all over Chile, especially in the summer. Visit Matilla's interesting **Iglesia de San Antonio,** a national monument with a pink baroque facade and a large bell tower with a cupola. The present building was rebuilt in the 19th century after the original 17th-century church was destroyed. To get inside, ask for the key at the shop next to the church. Just a stone's throw from the church is **Lagar de Matilla,** a small open-air museum enclosed within mud-brick walls that is the site of another national monument, a 17th-century wooden wine press. Ask for the museum key at the same shop that keeps keys to the church.

To get to Matilla, take the hourly **bus** from Iquique to Pica (2hr., CH$1500). Prepare to be greeted by boisterous fruit vendors selling mouth-watering mangos. A **first-aid clinic** and two small **supermarkets** are also available. The hard-to-miss yellow building houses Matilla's **post office.** (☎741 068. Open M-F 8am-3:30pm.) To make the most of your trip here, check into ▧ **El Parabien ❷,** located a few kilometers west of Matilla on the road to Pozo Almonte. Situated on the vast *pampa,* picturesque El Parabien comprises 10 delightful, rustic cabins. Each cabin sleeps five people in two rooms and includes a TV, fridge, kitchen facilities, and a shared bath. Enjoy the rejuvenating scent of citrus that wafts into the cabins from the orchard of lemon, orange, and grape trees located on the premises. Or order a platter of local fruit while lounging about the large swimming pool. (☎741 588 or 440 862. CH$22,000 per cabin.) For simple meals, amble over to the **Restaurant Don Carlos ❶.** (☎741 707. Open 9am-3pm and 7-11pm.)

PICA ☎ 57

Pica's limes are reputed to make the best *pisco sours* in Chile—but don't down so many drinks that you disrupt the serenity of this veritable haven of tranquility. A bigger and better version of Matilla, Pica offers equally luscious fruits and wines in addition to calming rock pools and charming *artesanías.* Pica's picturesque **Plaza de Armas** is home to the **Iglesia de San Andres** (annual feast celebrated on November 30), with its beige classical facade and twin bell towers. The present building dates from 1886 after earlier 17th- and 18th-century buildings were destroyed by earthquakes. A visit to the **municipal museum,** Avenida Balmaceda 178, in an attractive new building, is worth the time and effort. Exhibits presenting the region's paleontology, archeology, and history are on display—look out for the dinosaur footprints found near Chacrialla and a 1500-year-old mummy. (☎741 665 or 741 156; www.pica.cl. Open T-F 9am-1pm and 4-8pm, Sa 9am-1pm. Free.) The **natural rock pool** is run by the municipality, offering showers and changing rooms.

NORTE GRANDE

Frequent **buses** run between Iquique and Pica (2hr., CH$1500) via Pozo Almonte. A **taxi** to Iquique costs CH$40,000. In terms of amenities, Pica's offerings include a **tourist office**, on Balmaceda at the entrance to Cocha Resbaladero. (☎741 310 or 741 340; fax 741 330; www.pica.cl. Open Tu-Sa 11am-1:30pm and 3-7pm.) Other services include a **gas station, supermarkets, Internet access, a car rental agency** (☎741 105) on Resbaladero, and a **courier service** Chile Express at Balmaceda 255 (☎741 378), which also serves as a **Western Union** and a **centro de llamados** (open daily 9am-11pm). Numerous **fruit vendors** and **artesanías** sell handicrafts and souvenirs. (Open 11am-9pm.) The **post office** is located at Balmaceda 371. (Open M-F 9am-12:45pm and 2:30-5pm.)

The best to place to stay in Pica is **Cafe y Hostal Suizo** ❸ at General Ibañez, a short walk from Cocha Resbaladero. The Danish owners have set up a delightful Swiss-style two-story lodge that offers comfy rooms with a hot-water baths. (☎741 551. Doubles CH$14,000-16,000.) **Guayito** ❷, General Ibañez 69, is a tourist complex that has rooms with private baths. (☎741 663 or 741 358; fax 741 270. Doubles CH$10,000; triples CH$15,000.) Used by tour groups from Iquique, this complex also has a swimming pool, a wooded picnic area, a conference room, and a campground. Other lodgings include **Hotel Camino del Inca** ❷, Esmeralda 14, a pink building with a large, open-air dining area which offers rooms with private hot-water baths. (☎/fax 741 008. Breakfast included. Singles CH$4500; doubles CH$12,000.) Another decent budget option is **Hostería O'Higgins** ❷, Balmaceda 6, with spartan rooms with TV and hot-water baths. (☎741 524. Breakfast included. Singles CH$5000.) **Hostal San Andres** ❷, Balmaceda 797, is an old building with worn rooms. (☎741 319. Breakfast included. Singles CH$4000.)

Make sure you sample *alfajores*, a sweet pastry unique to Pica and Matilla sold at several vendors around town. For heartier meals, **Cafe y Hostal Suizo** ❶ serves large breakfasts (CH$3000), pizzas (CH$3000), and sandwiches (CH$1700). **Guayito** ❶ serves soups (CH$1000), meats (CH$1500-2000), fish (CH$2000-3000), and beer (CH$500-1000). **Hostal San Andres** ❷ serves simple four-course meals for CH$3000. **Restaurant La Palmera** ❶, Balmaceda 115, serves simple meals for CH$1800. (☎741 144. Open daily 8am-11pm.) For a hoppin' Saturday night, try the *discoteca* at **El Palmear** at Balmaceda 414. (☎741 026. Open midnight-5am.) Or head to **El Socavon**, Arturo Prat 208. (☎741 576. Open 11am-2am.)

LA TIRANA

La Tirana (pop. 560) occupies an important place in Chilean religious consciousness. During the town's annual religious feast of **Virgen del Carmen** (July 12-18), tens of thousands of pilgrims from all over Chile overflow this tiny village, which is virtually deserted through the rest of the year. The feast revolves around **Sanctuario de la Tirana,** the large town square housing an unusual church at one end. The spectacular dancing in elaborate masks and colorful costumes during the feast distracts from the church, which stands out on other occasions. Constructed in the 1930s on the ruins of an earlier church destroyed by an earthquake, the yellow metal exterior of this church incongruously recalls a Masonic Temple. Opposite the church, the **Museo Regional del Salitre** (☎751 601) is a single-room exhibit containing an odd collection of paraphernalia including radios, stuffed birds, a movie projector, and a piano made in 1840.

While some pilgrims are moved to crawl to La Tirana on their knees all the way from Iquique, a less spiritual means of arrival is available—**buses** connecting Iquique and Pica stop here on a daily basis (1¼hr., CH$1200). There are no accommodations in La Tirana (opt for a holier experience and camp on the outskirts of town like the pilgrims). Small shops that serve basic meals are scattered throughout town.

MAMIÑA
☎ 57

Mamiña (pop. 430) has long been famous for its reviving thermal baths. This is an absolutely delightful village with pre-Hispanic ruins, petroglyphs, and geoglyphs scattered throughout.

📟 TRANSPORTATION AND PRACTICAL INFORMATION. Buses to Iquique leave regularly (2½hr., 8am and 6pm, CH$2500) via **Pozo Almonte** (1½hr., CH$1500). As you enter Mamiña, the paved road dissolves into gravel streets with no names. The north section of town is defined by the **Iglesia de Nuestra Senora del Rosario** (also called the Iglesia San Marcos), a brick building built in the 17th century. The southern section of town houses most accommodations and the limited amenities that are available here. Mamiña has no bank or ATM, gas station, or Internet access; however, a few grocery stores, a paramedic clinic, and a *centro de llamados* (open 9am-1pm and 2-10pm) are available.

🛏 🍴 ACCOMMODATIONS AND FOOD. If you're looking to spoil yourself, **Hotel Los Cardenales ❺**, a colorful chalet overlooking the valley, is the place to hang your hat. Owned by Lithuanians, this magical, 4-star complex boasts a large indoor thermal swimming pool, tastefully decorated rooms that include a jacuzzi and TV, three meals, charming stained-glass windows, and terraces ideal for sunbathing. Guests are invited to luxuriate in the owners' spacious and elegant living room. Make sure to book ahead, or you may just have to settle for lunch and the use of the swimming pool and jacuzzi for a day. (☎099 545 1091; fax 517 000. Singles CH$25,000; lunch option CH$8000). Low on cash? **Hotel Tamarugal ❷** offers a nice view of the valley from four-person cabins with thermal baths. (☎099 660 2910. Breakfast included. CH$5000 per person.) A luxurious, yet affordable, alternative to the Hotel Los Cardenales is the **Hotel Llama Inn ❸**, with comfortable glass-walled rooms, thermal baths, and two-room cabins that sleep four to six people. A large hall with a lounge and bar, satellite TV, and a sizeable outdoor thermal swimming pool make a stay here rather enjoyable. (☎099 540 0295. Singles CH$12,000, including breakfast; CH$20,000 including all meals. Lunch and use of the swimming pool CH$5000.) **Restaurant Cerro Morado ❸** has comfy rooms in a chalet-style wooden building. All cabins have thermal baths. The restaurant serves breakfast (CH$800-1200), and the hearty lunch (CH$2500) is a nice treat. (☎099 244 6093. Singles CH$12,000 including all meals.) For a more spacious setup, visit **Hotel Nina de Mis Ojos ❹**. Twenty-four clean room containing thermal baths flank the dining hall where breakfast (CH$1200) and four-course lunches (CH$2500) are served. (☎519 132. Singles CH$15,000 including all meals.)

📷 SIGHTS. While most hotels have private thermal baths, a dip in public baths is possible at **Baños de Ipla**. Water temperature is maintained at 45 degrees Celsius. (☎751 298. Open daily 8am-2pm and 3-9pm. CH$800 for 20min.) **Baños el Chino**, located near the bottling plant for Mamiña-brand mineral water, is a public mud bath in an outdoor setting named after a Chinese visitor in the 19th century who was miraculously cured of all ailments after a mudbath. (Open daily 9am-3pm. CH$1000 per day; children CH$500.) **Kespikala Centro de Arte y Artesanía Indígena** (☎099 364 4762) is housed in the rustic stone building with a straw-covered ceiling. A space for the promotion, display, and sale of indigenous arts and crafts, the *centro* also functions as the unofficial **tourist office** for the village.

  Pukará del Cerro Inca, a fortress on the southern outskirts of the village, is the most impressive pre-Hispanic ruin. A wonderful 30min. hike from the village is facilitated by the trail marked clearly with green pegs. From Pukará, enjoy a panoramic view of the village, valley, and surrounding desert. Look out for petro-

NORTE GRANDE

glyphs and fragments of Inca ceramics scattered throughout the fortress. A natural thermal pool lies on the way to Pukará from the village, and at the foot of the hill stands a statue of an Inca fertility goddess. Next to Pukará is a peak (3100m) displaying a cross erected to mark the site of pre-Hispanic religious ceremonies, including the Aymara New Year festival (June 21).

NORTH OF IQUIQUE

Northern destinations can be reached from the paved road that branches east of the Panamericana at Huara and continues to Colchane on the Bolivian border and farther to Oruro inside Bolivia. However, this scenic route between Huara and Colchane has little traffic and no regular bus service from Iquique. International buses that run between Iquique and Oruro are not supposed to pick up or drop off passengers along the way. That said, some bus drivers can be quite accommodating if you arrange a pick-up well in advance.

HUARA   ☎57

Huara (pop. 2000) is 80km northeast of Iquique. Unless you've been driving all night and are too tired to continue to Iquique or Pozo Almonte, there is no reason to stop at Huara. Other than a few grocery stores, there are no amenities in town— this is not the place to come looking for gas stations or ATMs. If crashing here overnight, stay at the **Residencial Manuelito ❷**, which houses a *centro de llamados* and offers clean rooms. (☎751 385. Singles CH$5000, with bath CH$10,000).

EL GIGANTE DE ATACAMA

Fourteen kilometers east of Huara, El Gigante de Atacama, standing tall at 85m, is the largest geoglyph of a human figure in the world. The geoglyph is inscribed upon Cerro Unita, a lone barren hill that eerily interrupts the consistent flatness of the terrain. This bizarre figure is comprised of a large, apparently crowned, head and a long-limbed body with outstretched arms. The peculiarity of El Gigante is augmented by his equally bizarre companion, a smaller, unidentifiable creature sporting a long protuberance—a tail, perhaps? Or maybe a...nose? Public transport to the figures is not available, so you'll have to avail of a guided tour from Iquique, hire a taxi, or drive yourself. To see the geoglyphs, walk 1km off the road to reach the side of the hill that displays these geoglyphs. The side of the hill visible from the road flaunts geometric geoglyphs resembling airport landing strips.

TARAPACA   ☎57

If you're wondering why Region I, the northernmost administrative region of Chile is called Region de Tarapaca, find your answer here. Nine kilometers east of Cerro Unita and a further 7km along the road, the town of Tarapaca, a dusty town littered with deteriorating adobe houses, was the capital of the northernmost region of Chile when the area was under Peruvian rule. Sadly, for a town with such an illustrious history, there is little reason to stop here unless a visit to the **Iglesia San Lorenzo** strikes your fancy. A national monument built in 1717, the church holds its annual festival on August 10. The church is undergoing restoration after damage incurred during the 1987 earthquake. (To get in, ask at the shop on the corner of the plaza for the key-keeper.) At the entrance to Tarapaca is a monument dedicated to a battle fought here in 1879 during the War of the Pacific. Tarapaca offers no accommodations and no amenities other than a small grocery store and a *centro de llamados*. Since international buses do not pass by here, arrange a guided tour or hire a taxi to see Tarapaca.

CHUSMIZA

Home of the ubiquitous mineral water brand of the same name, Chusmiza, a town comprising eight families, offers little to the budget traveler. **Buses** between Iquique and Oruro, Bolivia may stop at the turnoff to the village, but the only reason to get off would be some barely visible pre-Hispanic agricultural terraces. If making Chusmiza an overnight stop, try **Hostal Munata Cabanas ❷**, which has clean rooms with hot-water baths. (☎443 216 or 443 612. Singles CH$5000.)

COLCHANE

A diversification of the landscape—deep canyons, interesting cacti at lower elevations, shrubbery at altitudes over 4000m—indicates your arrival at Colchane, on the Bolivian border. The turnoff point for the Parque Nacional Volcán Isluga, this wind-swept, almost deserted town lies 100km north of Chusmiza. The international **bus** to and from Iquique arrives and departs at irregular hours (5hr., CH$4000). When making travel plans, remember that the wet season can render this road impassable. Amenities offered include a police station, a paramedic clinic, small shops, and a *centro de llamados* (open 9am-9pm). Expensive **gas** is available from Andrés García (ask a villager to direct you to Andrés). There are no banks or ATMs here, so get cash before you leave Iquique. Basic accommodations include **Pension Gomez ❶**, with humble rooms, hot water, and breakfast for CH$3000, and **Residencial Choke ❶**, which offers sparse rooms without hot water for CH$3000 and simple meals for CH$1200. The **customs office** for entering Bolivia may not always be staffed. (Open 7:30am-7pm.)

PARQUE NACIONAL VOLCÁN ISLUGA

Six kilometers north of Colchane, the tiny settlement of Isluga marks the southern entrance to Parque Nacional Volcán Isluga. The only way to get here from Colchane is by renting a car, biking, or hiking. Sprawled across 180,000 hectares, the park's expansive *altiplano* wilderness is interrupted only by a beautiful 17th-century church. A recent robbery keeps the church's doors locked, but this quintessential Andean colonial church makes a view of the park picture-perfect. The stunning landscape, unfolding leisurely beneath towering snow-capped peaks, features vast green *bofedal* plains dotted with llamas, alpacas, and vicuñas. Nearby, at the base of the active volcano, Volcán Isluga (5530m), lies another small settlement called Enquelga. The park exit lies north of Enquelga; from there you can continue north to the Salar de Surire and Parque Nacional Lauca. Much of the land in the park belongs to the local Aymara Indian community, therefore there is no admission fee. However, camping within the park is not recommended. In general, when tackling such altitudes of over 3500m, it is wise to spend up to three days acclimatizing—you should not attempt to climb the peaks here until you have successfully adjusted to the altitude and taken precautions against altitude sickness.

Other than a **paramedic clinic** staffed with a nurse in Enquelga, no amenities are available in Parque Nacional Volcán Isluga. Since Volcán Isluga is located very close to the Bolivian border, you need a special **permit** from Direccion de Frontera y Limites in Santiago (also obtainable from Gobernacion Provincial in Putre or Iquique). A **Conaf** *refugio* located within the park is staffed with a ranger who will arrange a local guide for CH$10,000-15,000 per day. The climb takes 6hr. from the Conaf *refugio* to the peak—start early in the morning as you cannot camp on the soft volcanic soil. Hiking boots and ski poles or walking sticks are recommended for this mildly strenuous climb, which should be avoided during wet summer weather. The *refugio* offers basic **accommodations**

NORTE GRANDE

as well—two 4-bed rooms are complemented by a hot shower, kitchen facilities, and a comforting fire place (CH$5500 per person). If you call Conaf in Arica in advance, even if the *refugio* is full, basic rooms can be arranged in houses in Enquelga (CH$3500, including use of the *refugio*'s shower and kitchen). Some **tour operators** in Iquique arrange 3-day trips that end in Arica and visit Parque Nacional Volcán Isluga, Parque Nacional Lauca, and the Salar de Surire.

THE NORTHERN BORDER

ARICA   ☎ 58

An attractive beach resort town with a dry, mild climate year-round, Arica (pop. 190,000) is Chile's northern gateway to Peru and Bolivia. Arica's pre-Columbian archaeological heritage is evident in the nearby Azapa and Lluta Valleys, which are decorated by numerous geoglyphs and petroglyphs. Developed as a port for the inland mining industries under the Spanish settlers, the formerly Peruvian territory of Arica became part of Chile only after the War of the Pacific (1879-1884). Chile's victory is still celebrated annually in Arica during *Semana Ariquena* in early June. The beaches here offer some of the best surfing in the country and draw tourists from all over Chile and Bolivia, while the town itself serves as a base for excursions into the hauntingly beautiful *altiplano* landscape of the Parque Nacional Lauca, Reserva Nacional Las Vicuñas, and Monumento Natural Salar de Surire.

▐ TRANSPORTATION

As a transportation hub for travelers going to and from Peru and Bolivia, Arica has reliable international flights as well as bus connections to Tacna, Peru on the Panamericana highway, and to La Paz, Bolivia on Ruta 11. It is also a starting point for trips along Ruta 11 to *precordillera* and *altiplano* destinations of Chile's far north, including Parque Nacional Lauca.

INTERCITY TRANSPORTATION

Airport: Aeropuerto Internacional Chacalluta (☎211 116) is 20km north of Arica, near the Peruvian border. There is no shuttle bus, so use **Radio Taxi Aeropuerto** (☎254 812), which runs regular service to and from **Arica** (CH$5000; CH$2000 as *colectivo*). **LanChile** (☎231 641, 251 641, or 252 725), on 21 de Mayo between Colón and Baquedano and at the airport. Open M-F 10am-1:30pm and 5-9pm, Sa 10am-1pm. Flies to: **Antofagasta** (2¾ hr., 7:25 and 11:55am, US$44) via **Iquique**; **Santiago** (3½ hr.; 7:25, 11:55am, 2:50, 6:50pm; one-way US$205, round-trip US$344, discount if booked one week in advance) via **Iquique** (30min., US$25); **La Paz, Bolivia** (30min., 11:45am, US$112). **Aero Continente** (☎252 491) has no office in Arica, but tickets can be purchased at **Mar y Tour,** Colón 301. Open M-F 9am-1:30pm and 4-8pm, Sa 10am-2pm. **Aero Continente** runs inexpensive flights to **Santiago** (4¼ hr.; W, F, Su 7pm; one-way US$100, round-trip US$188).

Buses: There are two **bus terminals** in Arica, the **Terminal de Buses** and the **Terminal Internacional.** The names are misleading, as most international buses to **Bolivia** and **Argentina** leave from Terminal de Buses, while Terminal Internacional is used mostly for buses and *colectivos* to **Tacna, Peru.** There is a large proliferation of bus companies, all with their own schedules and fares. Differences in fares can be substantial, so it is worth shopping around—fares in the low season can be significantly lower than in the

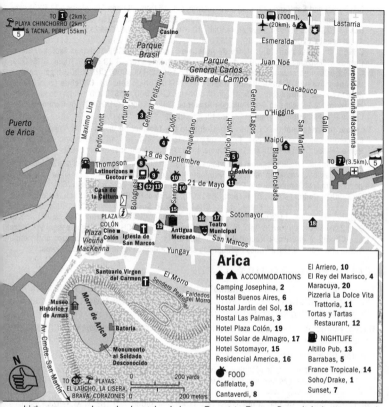

Arica

🏠🏠 ACCOMMODATIONS
Camping Josephina, **2**
Hostal Buenos Aires, **6**
Hostal Jardín del Sol, **10**
Hostal Las Palmas, **3**
Hotel Plaza Colón, **19**
Hotel Solar de Almagro, **17**
Hotel Sotomayor, **15**
Residencial America, **16**

🍽 FOOD
Caffelatte, **9**
Cantaverdi, **8**

El Arriero, **10**
El Rey del Marisco, **4**
Maracuya, **20**
Pizzería La Dolce Vita Trattoria, **11**
Tortas y Tartas Restaurant, **12**

🍸 NIGHTLIFE
Altillo Pub, **13**
Barrabas, **5**
France Tropicale, **14**
Soho/Drake, **1**
Sunset, **7**

high season and can be bargained down. To get to Tacna, Peru, it is better to go by *colectivo*, as it is faster and only slightly more expensive than by bus.

Terminal de Buses, Av. Diego Portales 948 (☎241 390). The **information office** can help you find the best company for your destination. Open 7am-11pm. **Pullman Santa Rosa** (☎241 029) goes to: **Iquique** (4hr.; 7 per day 6:30am-9:30pm; CH$3000, CH$3500 in high season); **Antofagasta** (10hr.; CH$6000, CH$9000 in high season); **Calama** (10hr.; CH$6000, CH$9000 in high season). **Zambrano** (☎241 587 or 226 453) goes to: **Iquique** (4hr., 8 per day 8am-2am, CH$3000); **Valparaíso** (28 hr.; 11:30am; CH$12,000, CH$20,000 for *salon cama*); **Santiago** (28hr.; CH$13,000, CH$20,000 for *salon cama*) via **Antofagasta** (10hr.; CH$6000, CH$9000 in high season). **Pullman Bus,** also known as **Fichtur** (☎800 320 320; www.pullman.cl), goes to: **Santiago** (28-30hr.; 8:30, 9:30, 10:30am, 3, 6, 11:30pm; CH$11000 for *ejecutivo*, CH$13,000 for *semi cama*, CH$25,000 for *salon cama*) via **Copiapó** (15hr., CH$11,000) and **La Serena** (23hr., CH$12,000); **Antofagasta** (10hr.; 8:30 and 11:30pm, CH$6000); **Valparaíso** (28hr., 12:30pm, CH$13,000); **Calama** (10hr., 9:30pm, CH$6000). **Tur Bus** (☎222 217 or 241 059; www.turbus.cl) goes to: **Santiago** (28hr.; 11am, 3:30, 9, 11pm; CH$16,000, CH$23,000 high season) via **Iquique** (4hr., CH$3099), **Maria Elena** (8hr., CH$5000), **Mejillones** (8hr.; CH$5500, CH$6500 high season), **Antofagasta** (10hr.; CH$6000, CH$7500 high season), **Chañaral** (12hr.; CH$10,000, CH$12,000 high season), **Copiapó** (15hr.; CH$12,000, CH$18,000 high season), **Vallenar** (20hr.; CH$12,499, CH$20,000 high season), **Coquimbo/La Serena** (23hr.; CH$14,000, CH$21,000). The same **Tur Bus** departures for Santiago go on to **Mendoza, Argentina** (CH$26,000, CH$30,000 high season) but it is cheaper to buy tickets for Argentina in Santiago. **Pullman Carmelita** (☎241 591) goes to **Iquique** (4hr.; M-Sa 7 per day 6am-10pm; Su 8am;

CH$3000) and **Santiago** (32hr., M-Sa 8am-2pm, CH$15,000). **Ramos Cholele** (☎221 029) goes to: **Iquique** (4hr., 5:45am-8:30pm, CH$3000) and **Santiago** (30hr., 3pm, CH$15000). **Flota Barrios** (☎223 587) goes to: **Santiago** (30hr.; 10:30pm; CH$12,000, CH$21,000 high season) via **Antofagasta** (10hr.; CH$5000; CH$7000 high season); **Calama** (8hr.; 11pm; CH$4500, CH$6500 high season); **San Pedro de Atacama** (10hr., CH$8000). **Turismos Iquique/Buses Cuevas y González** (☎241 090) goes to: **La Paz, Bolivia** (7hr.; 3:30 and 9:30am; CH$6000, CH$12,000 high season); **Viña del Mar** (30hr.; 1pm; CH$13000, CH$26000 high season); **Iquique** (CH$3000); **Antofagasta** (CH$6000, CH$8000 high season). **Chilebus** (☎222 817) goes to **La Paz, Bolivia** (8hr.; 10am, 2pm in summer; CH$6000, CH$10000 in high season). **Geminis** (☎241 647) goes to **San Pedro de Atacama** (13hr., 10pm, CH$7000) via **Calama** (10hr., CH$5000) and **Salta, Argentina** (24hr.; Tu, Sa 10pm; CH$29,000).

Terminal Internacional (☎ 261 092), next door to the Terminal de Buses on Av. Diego Portales. Numerous **colectivos** to **Tacna, Peru** (1hr., CH$1500-2000) are in this terminal, such as **San Remo** (☎260 509; CH$2000). To continue on to Lima, it is cheaper to buy tickets in Tacna.

Other Terminals. Smaller regional companies that run smaller and slower buses depart from their own offices but also keep offices in Terminal Internacional. **La Paloma,** also known as **Transportes Humire,** German Riesco 2071 (☎260 164 or 222 710), goes to: **Belen** (6hr.; Tu, F 7am; CH$2000); **Codpa** (4½hr.; Tu, F 7am; CH$1800); **Parinacota/Chucuyo** in **Lauca National Park** (5hr., 7am, CH$2500) via **Putre** (3½hr., CH$1500) and **Socoroma** (3hr.; CH$1500); **Charana, Bolivia** (7hr.; Tu, F, 11:30am; CH$4500) via **Visviri** (5hr., CH$4000). **Trans Cali** (☎261 068 or 221 220) serves **La Paz** (8-9hr.; Tu, Th, F 8:30am; CH$6000, CH$8000 high season) via **Putre** and **Chungará** in **Parque Nacional Lauca. Bus Lluta,** on the corner of Chacabuco and Vicuña Mackenna, goes to **Lluta Valley** destinations such as **Poconchile;** inquire at **La Paloma.**

LOCAL TRANSPORTATION

Taxis: These are numerous. Try **RadioTaxi Estrellas del Norte** (☎266 000; 24hr.) or **Pucarani RadioTaxis** (☎255 907; 24hr.) Taxis from downtown to town outskirts (beaches, discoteques etc.) CH$1000-1500.

Buses: Public buses run 5:30am-11pm (CH$230) and **taxi colectivos** cost CH$300 per person for anywhere inside the city.

Car and Bike Rentals:

Budget, Av. Comandante San Martín 599 (☎/fax 258 911; www.budget.cl), inside Hotel Arica and at the airport. Charges between CH$29,000 (small compact sedan) and CH$74,000 (4WD) per day. Cheaper weekly rates.

Hertz, Baquedano 999 and at the airport (☎231 487, at airport 219 186; www.hertz.cl), charges similar rates.

Cactus Rent A Car, Baquedano 635 (☎257 430 or 099 541 7067; cactusrent@latinmail.com), at the corner of Maipú, inside the shopping arcade. A more economical alternative (CH$20,000-35,000). Also rents bicycles (CH$2000 per hr., CH$7000 per day). Open 8am-9pm.

✳ 🛈 ORIENTATION AND PRACTICAL INFORMATION

The main thoroughfare, **21 de Mayo,** runs east-west and forms a pedestrian mall between **Baquedano** and **Prat.** El Morro, a rocky mountain located some 100m from the beach on the town's southwestern corner, towers over the rough rectangular grid of downtown Arica and its surrounding coastal desert landscape. The picturesque **Plaza Colón,** with its palm fringed lawns and the **Iglesia San Marcos,** sits close to the waterfront at the foot of El Morro. Beaches lie both to the south (**Playa El Laucho, Playa La Lisera, Playa Brava,** and **Playa Corazones**) and north (**Playa Chinchorroo** and **Playa Las Machas**) of downtown Arica.

TOURIST AND FINANCIAL SERVICES

Tourist Office: Sernatur (☎232 101; fax 254 506), on Prat near the corner with San Marcos, offers **brochures** on the Arica area and the Norte Grande region. Open M-F 8:30am-5:20pm. The municipal-run **Dirección de Turismo,** Sotomayor 415 (☎206

245), between Baquedano and Colón, sometimes has an English-speaking staff member. Open M-F 8:30am-5:30pm. Dirección de Turismo also maintains a **tourist information kiosk** (☎800 201 489), on Plaza Colón across San Marcos from Sernatur, that is sometimes manned by an English speaker. Look for the small beige-painted metal kiosk with a thatched roof. Open 8am-8pm.

Tours: The Belgian-owned **Latinorizons,** Bolognesi 449 (☎250 007; www.latinorizons.com), between Thompson and 21 de Mayo, is one of the better tour operators and has English-speaking staff and guides. Open M-Sa 9:30am-9pm. **Geo Tour,** Bolognesi 421 (☎253 927; fax 251 675; www.geotour.cl), is the biggest operator in town with additional offices in Iquique and San Pedro de Atacama. They have English-speaking guides and offer a half-day tour of archaeological sites in **Azapa** and **Lluta Valleys** (CH$12,000 per person, min. 2 people). Open M-Sa 9am-10pm. **Turismo Lauca,** Prat 430 (☎/fax 252 322 or 220 067), opposite McDonalds, has the best vehicles. Open M-Sa 9am-10pm. **Parinacota Expediciones,** Prat 430 (☎/fax 256 227), inside the shopping arcade on the corner with Thompson, is the oldest operator in town and charges slightly cheaper rates. Open M-Sa 9am-9pm. All of the tours offer 1 or 1½ day trips to **Parque Nacional Lauca** that include stops along the Ruta 11 for Lluta Valley geoglyphs and precordillera villages and attractions such as **Poconchile, Pukará de Copaquilla,** and **Socoroma** (1 day trip CH$12,000 per person, min. 6 people; 1½ day trip CH$40,000 per person, min. 4 people). They also run 2½ or 3-day trips that add **Surire Salt Lake** and **Isluga National Park** to the itinerary (2½ day trip CH$80,000 per person, min. 4 people; 3 day trip CH$130,000 per person, min. 4 people; the 3 day trip can end either in Iquique or back in Arica). Most of them also operate **day trips** through Arica and the nearby Azapa Valley (CH$12,000 per person, min. 2 people). Although 1-day trips are the most popular, some travelers react badly to altitude on the Andean highlands and prefer the 1½ day trip, which allows for acclimatization by spending a night in **Putre** (altitude 3500m). All trips to **Lauca,** including the 1-day trip, come with meals, coca tea (supposed to help with acclimatization), guides (usually only Spanish-speaking), and on-board emergency oxygen.

Travel Agencies: Global Tours, 21 de Mayo 260 (☎232 909), between Colón and Bolognesi, sells airplane tickets and package tours. Open M-F 9am-1:30pm and 4pm-8:30pm, Sa 10am-1pm.

Consulates: Bolivian Consulate, Patricio Lynch 292 (☎231 030). Open M-F 9am-2pm. **German Consulate,** Prat 391 (☎254 663 or 231 655). Open M-F 10am-noon. **Spanish Consulate,** Av. Santa Maria 2660 (☎224 655 or 222 780; fax 221 829). Open M-F 8am-12:30pm. **Peruvian Consulate,** San Martín 235 (☎231 020). Open M-F 8:30am-1pm.

Bank: Atlas Citybank, 21 de Mayo 170 (☎231 720), between Prat and Bolognesi. Open M-F 9am-2pm and 4-6:30pm. All banks have ATMs.

Currency Exchange: Cambios Yanulaque Ltda, 21 de Mayo 175 (☎231 175), between Bolognesi and McDonald's. Open M-F 9:20am-2pm and 4-8pm, Sa 10am-2pm.

Work Opportunity: University of Tarapaca (☎205 300 or 205 100) holds cultural events such as concerts and other performances. Qualified native English speakers may inquire here to find jobs **teaching English**.

LOCAL SERVICES

Supermarkets: Ekono, Diego Portales 2291 (☎248 192 or 248 198). Open 9am-10pm.

Laundry: There are no coin-operated public laundries in Arica—you leave your laundry to be washed at a *lavandería*. Try **Lavandería La Moderna S.A.,** 18 de Septiembre 457

(☎232 006). Open M-Sa 10am-1:30pm and 5-9pm. **Lavandería y Tintorería Olympia,** Lastarria 1235 (☎232 659), keeps similar hours.

National Park Administration: Conaf, Vicuña Mackenna 820 (☎250 207 or 250 570), on the corner with Chacabuco, provides information on weather, camping, hiking, and driving conditions in the national parks and reserves. Also makes bookings for stays in Conaf's *refugios* inside the parks. Register here if you plan on hiking, camping, or driving. Open M-F 8:30am-5:20pm.

Outdoor Gear: Gringo Surf and Skate Shop, Bolognesi 440 (cell ☎ 099 849 5524; gringosurf@hotmail.com), sells surf and skateboard equipment and rents surf boards (US$10 per day). Open 10am-10pm. **Din S.A.,** 21 de Mayo 184 (☎252 719), between Baquedano and Lynch, sells fishing gear and wet suits. **CM Prat,** 21 de Mayo 161 (☎225 067), sells camping equipment.

EMERGENCY AND COMMUNICATIONS

Emergency: ☎131

Police: ☎133, on Lastarria between Gallo and San Martín.

24-hour Pharmacy: There are many in town, especially on 21 de Mayo. Try the 24-hour **Farmacias Redfarma** (☎232 155), at the corner of Colón and 18 de Septiembre.

Hospital: Hospital Dr. Juan Noe, 18 de Septiembre 1000 (☎229 200), east of downtown. Open 24hr.

Internet Access: Internet cafes abound, especially on and around 21 de Mayo. Try **Galera Internet,** 21 de Mayo 211 (☎251 388), inside the shopping arcade next to Entel Internet. CH$100 for 10 min., CH$500 per hr. Open M-Sa 8:30am-12:30am, Su and holidays 10am-10pm.

Post Office: Prat 305 (☎231 316), next to Sernatur. Offers **lista de correos** and **Western Union** services. Open M-F 8:30am-1:30pm and 3-6:30pm, Sa 9am-1pm.

Courier Service: DHL, Colón 351 (☎256 753; fax 256 761; www.dhl.com), between Sotomayor and 21 de Mayo, also functions as a **Western Union.** Open M-F 9am-6:30pm, Sa 10am-1pm.

ACCOMMODATIONS

Arica offers an abundance of **hostels, hotels,** and **residenciales.** Although **camping** is free on beaches north of town, good campgrounds that usually feature swimming pools, BBQ, kitchen, and shower facilities are available in **Villa Frontera** north of town and in the **Azapa Valley** southeast of town. Prices go up during the holiday season (Dec.-Feb., Easter, and mid-Sept.) but can be bargained down during the rest of the year.

Hostal Las Palmas, Velásquez 730 (☎255 753; LasPalmas-LasCondes@tie.cl), between Maipú and O'Higgins. Easily the best hostel in town. A light beige interior and red-brick walls flank spotlessly clean rooms with bath and TV. Relax on the 3rd fl. terrace to enjoy great harbor view. Laundry CH$1000 per kg. Sells day trips to Lauca National Park (by Turismo Lauca; $12,000 per person). Singles CH$6000; doubles CH$12000; triples CH$18000. ❷

Hotel Solar de Almagro, Sotomayor 490 (☎224 444; fax 221 248), on the corner with Patricio Lynch. Friendly staff and large, comfy rooms with bath, balcony, TV, fridge, and phone make up for an earthquake-damaged interior (restoration forthcoming). Breakfast included. Singles CH$16,540; doubles CH$19,700; triples CH$23,810. AmEx/DC/MC/V. ❹

NORTE GRANDE

Hostal Jardin del Sol, Sotomayor 848 (☎232 795; fax 231 462), between San Martín and Arturo Gallo. One of the better hostels in town, set in tranquil surroundings. Features ultra-new laundry machines (CH$4000 per 2kg), a kitchen with microwave, and small but comfortable rooms with bath and ceiling fans. Breakfast included. Singles CH$6500; double and twin CH$10,000; triples CH$18,000. ❷

Hotel Plaza Colón, San Marcos 261 (☎/fax 231 244, 254 424 or 253 640; www.hplaza.cl), on the corner with Bolognesi. This pink 5-story building in 2 wings has comfy rooms with bath, A/C, TV, fridge, and phone. Ask for one of the rooms in the new wing. Restaurant on the top floor has a nice harbor view. Breakfast included. Singles US$24; doubles US$35; triples US$45. Major credit cards accepted. ❹

Hotel Sotomayor (formerly **San Marcos**), Sotomayor 367 (☎232 970 or 232 149; fax 251815; www.hotelsotomayor.cl), between Colón and Baquedano. An old concrete building houses passable rooms with bath, TV, and A/C. Breakfast included. Singles US$17-20; doubles US$21-26; triples US$26-30. ❸

Hostal Buenos Aires, Maipú 740 (☎253 111), between Blanco Encalada and San Martín. Small but adequate rooms with bath and TV enclose an inner courtyard. Singles CH$5000; doubles CH$9000; triples CH$12,000. ❷

Residencial America, Sotomayor 430 (☎254 148; www.resamerica.terra.cl), between Baquedano and Patricio Lynch. A family set-up offers no-frills, clean rooms with a TV. Breakfast included with multi-night stays. Singles CH$4000; doubles with bath CH$8000; triples CH$9000, with bath CH$12,000. ❷

Camping Josephina, Pedro Lagos 14 (☎213 995), in Villa Frontera near the airport. From Arica, go north on Panamericana Norte past the turn-off for Rt. 11 (to La Paz) and exit at **Villa Frontera.** Follow the signs for camping or take a taxi (CH$2000). One of the better camp grounds in the Villa (CH$1500 per person) has a swimming pool, tennis court, BBQ, kitchen, and a hot water shower. 5min. walk to the beach. Reservations recommended in the summer. House with 12-15 beds (triples CH$10,000, entire house CH$30,000). ❶

◘ FOOD

In addition to the typical **chifas** (Chinese restaurants à la Peru), pizzerias, and chain eateries such as **Bavaria,** Arica has a lively gastronomical scene with several fine restaurants offering signature Chilean seafood cuisine.

▧ **Maracuya,** Comandante San Martín 0321 (☎227 600; fax 255 448), on the beach near the pier connecting with **Isla de Alacran.** Offers a refined, tranquil atmosphere, and is frequented by an older clientele. Waiters in formal attire serve up excellent seafood in a romantic seaside setting. Relax on the comfortable sofas in the lounge or admire the beach-inspired decor. Everything on this sophisticated international menu is likely to satisfy the most discerning taste—try the *corvina salsa amazonica* (steak with mango salsa; CH$6600), the *camarones ecuatorianos al ajillo* (shrimp in a garlic cream sauce; CH$13,500), or the *crema de salmon* (salmon with cream and curry; CH$2800). Open-air seating available. Open 12:30pm-2pm and 8pm-1am. ❹

▧ **Cantaverdi,** Bolognesi 453 (☎258 242), between Thompson and 21 de Mayo. Jazzy, mellow space with soft colors and a sunburst motif. Locals and tourists alike flock to this hip bar/restaurant for a light meal. Sandwiches CH$1800-4000, pizzas CH$2200-3800, beer CH$850-900, mixed drinks CH$1500-3500. Open M-Sa 9am-5pm. ❷

Tortas y Tartas Restaurant, 21 de Mayo (☎258 538), between Bolognesi and Colón. Patrons fill this trendy eatery to sample from the chic menu. Try the delicious chicken pancakes in white sauce (CH$3100). Breakfast specialties CH$1200-2500, filets CH$4100, fish CH$3300-4900, salads CH$2600-3800. Open 9:30am-11pm. ❸

Caffelatte, 21 de Mayo 248 (☎231 881), between Colón and Gen. Velásquez. Crowded café/restaurant charmingly decorated with photos of old Arica. Pleasant penthouse seating overlooking the street available. Try the 3-course lunch specials (CH$1800). Sandwiches CH$1300-1900, pizzas CH$2000-2500, milk shake CH$1500. Open M-Sa 8am-midnight, Su 10am-3pm and 6pm-midnight. ❶

El Arriero, 21 de Mayo 385 (☎/fax 232636), between Baquedano and Colón. Wind through the long corridor and step down into the main dining room adorned with paintings, maps, photos, wooden wheels, and musical instruments. The yellow and orange cellar gives off a relaxing vibe. Soups CH$1300-2500, fish CH$4000-5400, chicken CH$2500-3700, fillets CH$4000-5000. Open noon-3:30pm and 7-11pm. Major credit cards accepted. ❸

Altillo Pub, 21 de Mayo 260 (☎231 936), between Bolognesi and Colón. With its candle-lit tables and kitschy Hollywood interior, this pub caters to a yuppie crowd. Try the *mariscos* (CH$2900-4300). Sandwiches CH$1700-2400. Stocks 24 brands of beer (CH$950-2400). Open M-Sa 6pm-3am. AmEx/MC/V. ❷

France Tropicale, 21 de Mayo 384 (☎/fax 257 217), between Colón and Baquedano. Dark jungle decor and candle-lit tables make the upstairs bar/restaurant a mellow after-hours hangout for an older clientele. Large pizzas CH$3800-5000, beer CH$1000-1200. Open Su-Th 6:15pm-2:30am (or until last customer), F-Sa 6:15pm-4am. ❸

El Rey del Marisco (☎229 232), on Colón near the corner with Maipú. A nondescript interior with wooden paneling define this upstairs seafood joint. *Paila marina* (seafood stew; CH$1990), *pescado a la margarita* (fish in margarita sauce; CH$4550), and *carnes* (meats; CH$2200-3500) are popular. Open noon-1am. AmEx/DC/MC/V. ❷

Pizzeria La Dolce Vita Trattoria, 21 de Mayo 501 (☎230 928), on the corner with Patricio Lynch. Rustic 2-story eatery serves decent thin-crusted pizzas (CH$3000-5000 for large, CH$1500-3500 for small) and pasta (CH$2800-4200). Beer CH$600. Happy hour 6-10:30pm (CH$3500 for a pizza and 1 liter of beer). Open noon-2am. ❷

🔘 SIGHTS

A climb to the top of Arica's **El Morro** offers a panoramic vista of the town, ocean, and surrounding desert landscape. This is also the perfect spot to watch a glorious Chilean sunset. To reach the top of El Morro walk up the easy zigzagging footpath starting at the southern end of Colón or take a taxi from downtown Arica (CH$1000). At the top of El Morro you will also find the **Museo Histórico y de Armas** (est. 1974), which is filled with military paraphernalia and miniature model enactments of Chile's victory over Peru in the **War of the Pacific.** (Open 8am-8pm. CH$400, children CH$250)

After a trip to El Morro, descend the footpath and check out **Casa Bolgnesi** on the corner of Colón and Yungay, a 2-story historical mansion with verandas that houses the Peruvian Consulate General. A block northwest on the **Plaza Colón** is the colorful quasi-Gothic **Iglesia San Marcos** (1875), a small, beige, prefabricated building designed by Gustave Eiffel, of the Parisian tower fame. Simple stained glass windows decorate the interior.

Another Eiffel creation is the **Casa de la Cultura,** the ex-customs house dating to 1874, next to Sernatur and across San Marcos from Plaza Colón. The small, elegant brick building has a marble facade and features an interior composed of a wood panel ceiling, corrugated metal columns, and a spiral staircase. Some permanent displays of photos and historical mementos are on display, but most of the space is used for rotating art and cultural exhibitions. (☎206 366. Open M-F 8:30am-8pm, Sa-Su and holidays 9am-9pm. Free.)

◙ BEACHES

From the foot of **El Morro**, it is a 20min. walk to the beaches south of downtown (**El Laucho** is the nearest, followed by **La Lisera** and **Brava; Corazones** is further south). Enclosed by a rock embankment and thus suitable for swimming, La Lisera is the best beach in the area. Clean public toilets with showers, changing rooms, and a children's playground make a day spent here even more pleasant. (Take bus No. 8 or pay CH$1000 for a taxi). The waves at Brava and Corazones are too strong for swimming, but Corazones features the occasional seal as well as coves and rock pools for bathing, making it a delightful hiking, biking, or fishing trip from downtown. No buses go to Corazones but *colectivos* cost CH$2000; walking takes 2 hours. The beaches north of town, **Chinchorro** and the farther away **Las Machas** (locals often lump these together, calling both Chinchorro), stretch all the way to the Peruvian border and are good for surfing, camping, and sometimes swimming. (Take bus No 12 or a *colectivo* for CH$400).

■ SHOPPING

A good bet when shopping for **Andean handicrafts** is **Poblado Artesanal,** Hualles 2825, a mock *altiplano* village of whitewashed stone houses with thatched roofs. During the summer, Poblado Artesanal hosts cultural events and folk music performances on Friday and Saturday evenings. Numerous *colectivos* (numbers 7 and 8; CH$300 per person) and buses (numbers 3, 7 and 9) come here from downtown. (☎ 222 683. Open Tu-Su 9:30am-1:30pm and 3:30-8pm.)

A great place to buy fresh produce from all over Chile and Peru is **Terminales Agropecuarios,** referred to by locals as **Agro** and located 15-20min. northeast of downtown by bus (CH$230). *Colectivos* with "Agro" written on them cost CH$300 per person. Agro also sells many items other than produce, both wholesale and retail, including second-hand clothes, for reasonable prices.

The narrow alley of Bolognesi, between 21 de Mayo and 18 de Septiembre, also has stalls where locals sell arts and crafts. (Open 6am-6pm.)

◪ ◨ ENTERTAINMENT AND NIGHTLIFE

Arica has a hoppin' nightlife, one of the liveliest in northern Chile. A good place to hang out on summer nights is **Isla de Alacran.** Jutting out from the foot of El Morro is the hotspot where local youth park their cars to party and socialize into the wee hours of the morning.

Cine Colón, 7 de Junio 190 (☎231 165), on Plaza Colón. Shows recent flicks from Hollywood and elsewhere. Shows run 2-10pm. M-W CH$1700, Th-Su CH$2600.

Barrabas, 18 de Septiembre 524 (☎230 928), close to corner with Patricio Lynch. 20- to 30-somethings down beers (CH$1000) in the dimly lit casual interior. Occasional band on weekends. Small dance floor. Cover Th-Sa CH$1000. Open 9pm-6am.

Drake, Buenos Aires 209 (☎215 891), near the beaches north of downtown (CH$1000 by taxi from downtown). Wooden statues of Santa María hover over a two-story dance floor packed with a youngish crowd dancing to varied house music. Erotic show on Th. Cover CH$2500 for Chileans, CH$3500 for foreigners (includes a drink). Beer CH$1500. Open Th-Sa midnight-5am.

Soho, Buenos Aires 209 (☎215 891), in the same building as Drake. Young locals and expats alike crowd onto the large two-story dance floor and big concrete bleachers. This steamy meat-market of youngsters is incongruous with the industrial, minimalist structure. Connected to Drake after 2am—roam through both clubs for only one late-night cover. Occasional live music. Beer CH$1500, mixed drinks CH$1500-3000. Cover F CH$500-1000, Sa CH$2000-2500. Open F-Sa 10pm-5am.

Sunset (☎ 223 730), in the Azapa Valley, 3½ km from downtown. A young crowd writhes into the morning hours in front of the two large video screens on the cavernous dance floor. A generic interior with a tacky tropical themed bar. Beer CH$1500. Erotic show on Tu. Cover CH$2500. Open Tu, F-Sa midnight-5am.

🎒 DAYTRIPS FROM ARICA

Arica is situated between two fertile valleys, **Azapa** to the south and **Lluta** to the north, each of which is known for its corn, alfalfa, tomato, and olive cultivation and is home to an abundance of wild plants such as the *cola de caballo* and *totora*. Both valleys, lush strips of green in stark contrast with the surrounding desert terrain, contain scattered archeological sites dating from pre-Inca times and are famous for their numerous geoglyphs and petroglyphs.

■ **MUSEO ARQUEOLÓGICO SAN MIGUEL DE AZAPA.** A visit to this superb regional museum, administered by the **University of Tarapaca**, is a must for an overview of the area's archaeological heritage. The arid climate of this northernmost area of Chile has ideal conditions for the archaeological preservation of relics. The **mummies** from the Chinchorro culture (6000-2000 BC) exhibited in the Museo are thought to be among the oldest ever uncovered. The museum (est. 1967) has exhibits on the lives, dress, and shelter of people from the area from 7000 BC until the 18th century. A **museum shop** and guided tour in English, French, German, and Portuguese are available. Arica's tour operators include a visit to this museum and nearby geoglyphs in 1-day tour itineraries. You can also get there from downtown Arica by *taxi colectivo*. (☎ 205 555; www.uta.cl/masma. *Colectivos depart from corner of Chacabuco and Patricio Lynch 10am-6pm; CH$700 one way; CH$4000 for a private tour including stops along the way at geoglyphs. To return to Arica, walk to the main road and flag down a colectivo. Open Mar.-Dec. 10am-6pm, Feb. 9am-8pm. CH$1000, children CH$300.)*

■ **SOCOROMA.** A charming **Aymara farming village, Socoroma** (altitude 3000m; 120 residents) lies 5km down from Ruta 11. Lined with cobbled streets, Socoroma's picture-perfect mini square is complete with a quintessential Andean bell-tower church, red and white geranium flowers, and a towering snow-capped peak in the background. This is a smaller, more quaint version of neighboring **Putre,** making for a good overnight stay for acclimatization. (*Lodging in Socoroma with basic amenities is offered by Emilia Humire and her family* ❶. ☎ 099 545 2635. *CH$2500 per person. Emilia also serves meals with home-made bread and jam; CH$1000 for soup or salad. Call ahead 2 weeks in advance, as Emilia is sometimes out of town. La Paloma (see Arica Transportation, p. 308) runs buses to and from Arica 2-3 times a week.)*

LLUTA VALLEY AND POCONCHILE. The fascinating **Lluta Valley geoglyphs,** dating from the 12th century A.D. and restored in the 1980s, are included in the trips to Lauca run by Arica's tour operators. **Geo Tour** in Arica covers both Lluta and Azapa Valleys in its archaeological day tour. **Bus Lluta** also services this area on its buses to Molinos (*1hr. to Poconchile; 7 per day from corner of Chacabuco and Vicuña Mackenna in Arica; CH$500 to Poconchile).*

East of the Lluta Valley along Ruta 11 sits the tiny village of **Poconchile** with its 17th century **Iglesia de San Geronimo.** Damaged by an earthquake in 2001, this atypical Andean church has wooden towers that were added in the 19th century. There is a small shop and restaurant across the road from the church (see above for bus schedule to Poconchile). After Poconchile, Ruta 11 climbs steeply eastward on the precordillera and one begins to see the bizarre **cactus candelabros** ("candle-bearer") that dot the landscape and grow 3-4cm a year depending on the amount of moisture they get from the coastal mist known as *camanchaca* (also called *garua*).

Just before you reach **Pukará de Copaquilla,** a circular pre-Inca stone fortress erected to protect trade caravans and restored in 1987, you can stop at **Pueblo de Maillku ❷,** the solar-powered "eco-friendly" abode of a Chilean couple with their small children, for a cup of coca leaf tea and homemade bread *(CH$1500 for tea and bread. maillku@Latinmail.com. The couple offers a plain room for lodging. CH$5000 per person; camping CH$2500 per person. Guided tours that help with acclimatization also provided.)* The lookout point for the Pukará is a good place to let out a shout and hear the valley echo. Next on Ruta 11 is **Tambo de Zapahuira,** a pre-Inca ruin which was most likely a place to collect taxes and store grains in cellars.

NORTH TO PERU

BORDER CROSSING INTO PERU: CHACALLUTA
The road from Arica to Tacna, Peru is well-maintained and heavily traveled. The best way to cross the border is in one of the giant 1970s American sedans that leave, when full, from either the international bus terminal in Arica, or the Tacna bus terminal. Leaving from Arica, the road runs 20km north through Chacalluta before crossing the border and continuing on to Tacna. Customs is open 8am-midnight. The process is fairly simple and involves no more than a brief search of your luggage for contraband and various food products and a passport stamp (see **Essentials: Border Crossings,** p. 65, for info on visas and fees).

MOQUEGUA, PERU   ☎054

Moquegua (pop. 47,208) sits on the border of the Atacama desert, the driest in the world, living up to its Quechua name, "Quiet Place," with cobblestone streets, a small center, and sun that offers respite from the coastal fog. Unfortunately, parts of the town met with destruction in a June 2001 earthquake centered directly off the coast. Undeterred, tourists and archaeology-lovers continue to make the journey to Moquegua's fascinating ruins and museums.

🖃🗃 TRANSPORTATION AND PRACTICAL INFORMATION. The fountain of water-spitting frogs, designed by Gustave Eiffel, in the **Plaza de Armas** marks the center of town. **Ayacucho, Moquegua, Ancash,** and **Tacna** border the plaza. Two blocks to the left of the plaza (facing downhill), **Piura** leads down to the traffic circle where its name changes to **La Paz.** The bus terminal for **Ormeño,** La Paz 524 (☎761 149), is at the traffic circle; the terminals for **Flores** and **Cruz Del Sur** lie 5min. farther down La Paz. Buses go to: **Arequipa** (3½hr., 10 per day 6:45am-11:30pm, s/20); **Lima** (18hr., 6 per day 3:15-6:45pm, s/35); and **Tacna** (2hr., 16 per day 5:30am-8:30pm, s/5-7). The **Oficina de Información Turística,** Ayacucho 1060, distributes **maps** and informative Spanish brochures. (☎762 236. Open M-F 7:30am-3:30pm.) **Banco de Crédito,** Moquegua 861, has the only 24hr. AmEx/MC/V **ATM.** (☎761 325. Open M-F 10am-6pm, Sa 9:30am-12:30pm.) Other services include the **police,** at Ayacucho 808 (☎761 391, emergency 105) and **Es Salud hospital,** on Urbanación Villa Hermosa (☎763 990 or 761 565; open 24hr. for emergencies). **Cafe Internet,** Moquegua 478, is on the corner of the Plaza de Armas. (☎761 245. s/2 per hr.; s/5 for whole night F-Sa. Open 7:30am-11pm.) **Serpost,** Ayacucho 560, is also on the plaza. (☎762 551. Open M-Sa 8am-noon and 3-6:30pm.)

⌐⌐ ACCOMMODATIONS AND FOOD. Moquegua's accommodations come in all shapes and sizes. On the lower end of the spectrum is **Hostal Carrera ❷**, Lima 320, with bare but adequate rooms and hot common baths, but cold private baths. (Singles s/12, with bath s/15; doubles s/24, s/27.) **Hostal Piura ❸**, Piura 255, offers handsome rooms with comfy mattresses, oriental rugs, mirrors, hot baths, and cable TV. (☎ 763 974. Singles s/27; doubles s/37.) Moqueguan restaurants serve the local specialties—*palta* (avocado), wine, and pisco—and a surprising amount of Italian food. **Casa Vieja Pizzeria Bar ❶**, Moquegua 326, serves delicious lasagna (s/6) and vegetarian dishes. (☎761 647. Open M-Th 6-11pm, F-Sa 6pm-1am.)

◨ SIGHTS. The dry desert has perfectly preserved the relics (and sometimes the bodies) of earlier cultures, making Moquegua an area of intense archaeological interest. **Museo Contisuyo,** Tacna 294 (entrance on the plaza), is a great source of regional information. Its interactive exhibit (with English explanations) traces cultural development since the Archaic period, 12,000 years ago. (☎/fax 761 884. Open W-M 9am-1pm and 3-5:30pm, Tu 9am-noon and 4-8pm. s/1.5.) The museum can arrange a visit to the **Paleolithic Caves of Toquepala.** (Guided trips in Spanish s/ 50 per person, with public transportation.) **Cerro Baúl** ("Storage Trunk Hill"), named for its boxy appearance, lies 12km from town, where the pre-Inca Huari constructed a city in AD 600-750. The city's ruins (it burned down mysteriously around AD 950) sit on the summit. The excursion involves an uphill hike (1½hr.), most pleasant in the morning when it's cooler. Frequent **colectivos** from the corner of Balta and Tacna, 2 blocks downhill from the Plaza de Armas, pass **Cerro Baúl** (30min., s/2.) At the Ayacucho corner of the plaza, **Catedral Santa Catalina** holds the remains of 13th-century Italian martyr Santa Fortunata, whose legacy is honored with fireworks every October 14. (Open 6:30am-noon and 3-7:30pm.)

TACNA, PERU   ☎054

<table>
<tr><td rowspan="4">NUEVO SOL</td><td>CH$1 = 0.0055</td><td>1 SOL = CH$182.3</td></tr>
<tr><td>US$1 = 3.742</td><td>1 SOL = US$0.267</td></tr>
<tr><td>UK£1 = 5.744</td><td>1 SOL = UK£0.174</td></tr>
<tr><td>EUR€1 = 3.680</td><td>1 SOL = EUR€0.272</td></tr>
</table>

Tacna (pop. 294,000), Peru's southernmost city and principal crossing point into Chile, lies only 36km from the border. Lost to Chile in the 1879 War of the Pacific, Tacna's citizens voted themselves back into Peru on August 28, 1929, earning the city the nickname "Heroic Tacna." Despite its present nationality, Tacna's well-maintained streets, relatively high prices, and good health care are a testament to the Chilean influence. Regardless of its confused nationality, the city and its periphery offer good shopping, hot springs, and remarkable rock paintings.

⌐ TRANSPORTATION

Flights: Aeropuerto Carlos Ciriani Santa Rosa (☎844 939), 5km south of town. Taxi s/ 10. **AeroContinente,** Apurimac 265 (☎747 300), flies to **Lima** (1½hr.; 12:30 and 7pm, US$72).

Trains: Estación Ferroviaria (☎724 981), at Albarracin and 2 de Mayo. Follow Blondell beyond the cathedral in the Plaza de Armas, turn right onto Dagnino just before the railroad tracks, and continue until it ends. Service between Tacna and Arica, Chile (1½hr., US$2), following repairs on the tracks, is expected to resume October or November 2002. Call for schedules.

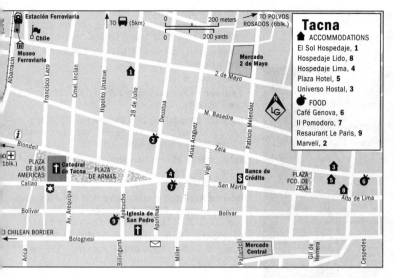

Tacna

🏠 ACCOMMODATIONS
El Sol Hospedaje, **1**
Hospedaje Lido, **8**
Hospedaje Lima, **4**
Plaza Hotel, **5**
Universo Hostal, **3**

🍴 FOOD
Café Genova, **6**
Il Pomodoro, **7**
Resaurant Le Paris, **9**
Marveli, **2**

Buses: Terminal Terrestre, a 20min. walk north of the Plaza de Armas on Hipólito Unanue. Taxi s/2. **Ormeño** (☎723 292) has service to: **Arequipa** (6hr.; 5am, 2:30, 10pm; s/13) via **Moquegua** (2hr., s/5); **Lima** (20hr., 4:30 and 7pm, s/40; *servicio especial* 2pm, s/50). **Flores** (☎726 691) has the most frequent service to **Arequipa** (6hr., 13 per day 5:30am-10:15pm, s/15) via **Moquegua** (2hr., s/8).

International Colectivos: Sedans to **Arica, Chile** (1hr., leave when full 6am-11pm, s/3.5-7) leave from next to the bus terminal.

✈🚌 ORIENTATION AND PRACTICAL INFORMATION

The main street in town, **San Martín,** houses most of Tacna's tourist services. San Martín intersects the **Plaza de Armas,** where it splits at the cathedral into **Callao** to the left and **Blondell** to the right. Another major street, **Bolognesi,** runs parallel to San Martín two blocks to the south. **Hipólito Unanue,** which intersects San Martín at the Plaza de Armas, runs north to the **bus terminal** and the Panamericana.

PERU COUNTRY CODE	☎51

Tourist Office: Blondell 50, 4th fl. (☎/fax 722 784), in the municipal building behind the cathedral, has thorough information and **maps.** Open M-F 7:30am-4pm.

Consulates: Bolivia, Bolognesi 1721 (☎745 121), about 1km east of the Plaza de Armas. Open M-F 9am-noon. **Chile** (☎723 063), on Presbitero Andia at Albarracin, 100m past the train station. Open M-F 8am-1pm.

Banks: Banco de Crédito, San Martín 574 (☎722 541), exchanges AmEx and Visa traveler's checks, gives Visa cash advances, and has an AmEx/MC/V **ATM.** Open M-F 10am-6pm, Sa 9:30am-12:30pm. **Cambios Tacna,** San Martín 612 (☎743 607), exchanges currency. Open M-Sa 8:30am-8pm.

Markets: Shopping opportunities abound in Tacna. The most convenient public market is the **Mercado Central,** on Bolognesi at Paillardelli. Open 6am-8pm. The mother of all Tacna markets is **Polvos Rosados,** on Pinto, just past Industrial, the road that intersects

FROM THE ROAD

the bus station. Taxi s/2. Find everything from athletic shoes to chocolates, liquor to electronic goods, at prices 35-60% lower than in Lima. Open 8am-8pm.

Police: Callao 121 (☎ 714 141), on San Martín, at the Plaza de Armas. Open 24hr.

Emergency: ☎ 105.

24-Hour Pharmacy: Inka Farma, San Martín 537 (☎ 728 080).

Hospital: Hospital Hipólito Unanue (☎ 723 361, emergency 723 872), on Blondell beyond the cathedral. Open 24hr. for emergencies.

Telephones: Office, San Martín 442 (☎ 725 254). Open 7am-11pm. Telefónica del Perú **pay phones** are on the plaza.

Internet Access: The many cafes tend to be full, especially at night. **InfoRed Internet,** San Martín 735 (☎ 727 573), is fast. s/2 per hr. Open 8am-11pm.

Post Office: Serpost, Bolognesi 361 (☎ 724 641). Open M-Sa 8am-8pm. **DHL,** Pasaje Vigil 178 (☎ 725 225). Open M-F 9am-1pm and 3-7pm.

ACCOMMODATIONS

The most notable joy of Tacna's accommodations is that you'd be hard-pressed to find a TV *without* cable. Most mid-range hotels are centered around the Plaza de Armas and up San Martín, while the bare-bones places cluster at the southern end of town, across Bolognesi. It can be difficult to find a free room in mid-December, when Chileans arrive en masse to do their Christmas shopping.

El Sol Hospedaje, 28 de Julio 236 (☎ 727 711). Rooms with baths have balconies or big windows; those without baths are smaller and darker. All are spotless and have cable TV. Singles s/20, with bath s/30; doubles s/30, s/35. ❷

Hospedaje Lido, San Martín 876-A (☎ 741 598). Well-maintained rooms include the basic amenities. Baths are hot, and the price is right. Singles s/20; doubles s/30. ❷

Hospedaje Lima, San Martín 442 (☎ 744 229), presents elegant trappings: a red carpet leads up the stairs, and beds have faux-leather headboards. Don't be fooled by first impressions, though; rooms aren't particularly luxurious. Private baths. Restaurant (breakfast s/5-7). Cable TV s/5. Singles s/28; doubles s/38. ❷

Universo Hostal, Zela 724 (☎ 715 441), at the end of the walkway off San Martín, between Vizquerra and Varela. Clean, carpeted rooms in a quiet building, with an emphasis on safety and solitude. Rooms with baths have phones and cable TVs. Singles with bath s/25; doubles with bath s/40. ❷

Plaza Hotel, San Martín 421 (☎ 722 101), has clean well-maintained rooms—all with private baths and cable TVs. Well-furnished lobby has elevators. Continental breakfast included. Singles s/50, doubles s/68. ❸

🍴 FOOD

Most restaurants cluster on San Martín, just up from the plaza. The regional specialty, *picante a la tacneña*, is a spicy mix of potatoes, beef, and *ají* sauteed in oil. Italian restaurants abound, especially on Libertad, the pedestrian street before the 600th block of San Martín.

Café Genova, San Martín 649 (☎ 744 809). Where sophisticated locals come to mingle at outdoor tables. Elaborate salads s/9-20. Exquisite pasta dishes s/14-27. Open 8am-midnight. ❷

Marveli, Zela 495 (☎ 711 037). This vegetarian restaurant has nutritional charts of each meal and plenty of soy products. *Menú* s/6. Open 7am-8pm. ❶

Restaurant Le Paris, Ayacucho 88-A, half a block off San Martín. The only thing remotely French about this popular place is its name. Boasts an array of Peruvian specialties (*mariscos* s/8-10), Italian dishes (sausage ravioli s/8), and Spanish refreshments (pitcher of sangria s/15) at budget prices. *Menú* s/5. Open 8am-11pm. ❶

Il Pomodoro, San Martín 521 (☎ 726 905). Something of a Tacna staple, this 10-year-old eatery features pizza (personal s/15, large s/30), pasta (s/12-17), and more expensive meat dishes in a spacious dining area. Open 11am-11pm. MC/V. ❷

👁 SIGHTS

PLAZA DE ARMAS. The plaza features a fountain known as the **Pileta Ornamental,** designed in the 19th century by **Gustave Eiffel,** who designed similar fountains for Buenos Aires, Lisbon, Paris, and nearby Moquegua (see p. 317). Facing the plaza, the simple but elegant neo-Renaissance **cathedral** was finished in 1854. A giant chandelier hangs over the altar inside and small, round, stained-glass windows line the nave. *(Open 7am-noon and 4-6:30pm. Mass M-Sa 7:30am and 5:30pm, Su noon.)* On the other side of the plaza, an 18m **commemorative arch** honors Miguel Grau and Francisco Bolognesi, two heroes from the War of the Pacific.

hotspot, so we get more varied flora, fauna, and landscape here than in San Pedro.

LG: What is it like living here? Doesn't it get a bit lonely here sometimes? What do you do for fun, for example?

BK: I like Putre because it is small enough and the people are nice enough that you can leave your door open most of the time, yet you have an essential infrastructure like the bank, the post office, etc. I work in our office with a view of two volcanos all day long and have flowers in my garden all year long, which I couldn't do in Alaska. What do I do for fun? I work on my computer and construct presentations and power-points for flowers, birds, and other aspects of nature. And I have a huge library and read and write about birds and flowers and find different places to go.

LG: Has the September 11 terrorist attack affected the tourism industry here in Putre and Chile in general?

BK: No, at least not with the tours I run. I think this is partly because Chile is a relatively safe country to travel in, especially now in comparison to Argentina, which is having problems. Chile is in a good position for tourism in the future because of the range of attractions it offers from the northern deserts down to Torres del Paine in the south and also because of the range of activities it offers, from mountain climbing to rafting to bird watching in its many national parks and reserves.

OTHER SIGHTS. The **Museo Ferroviario** consists of two exhibit rooms along the tracks at the train station displaying old newspaper clippings, route maps, collections of train stamps from all over the world, and railroad equipment and machinery. Antique locomotives are on display across the tracks and at the end of the station. *(Knock at the green door on 2 de Mayo 412, to the right of the clock.* ☎724 981. *Open M-Sa 7am-5pm. s/1.)* **La Casa de Cultura** (or **Museo Regional Histórico**), above the public library, displays local pre-Inca artifacts and large oil paintings representing the War of the Pacific. *(Apurimac 202, at Bolívar. Open M-Sa 9am-1pm and 1:30-3:30pm. s/3.)* Francisco Antonio de Zela y Arizaga, who shouted the first cry for Peru's independence in 1811, lived and died in the **Casa de Zela,** one of the oldest colonial houses remaining in Tacna. *(Zela 542. Open 8am-noon and 3-7pm. Free.)*

🎵 ENTERTAINMENT

Trendy bars and *discotecas* populated primarily by Tacna's students and their tourist friends lie amidst the flashy casinos of San Martín. **Pub El Tablón,** Libertad 83, halfway down the pedestrian walkway, offers live music and karaoke in a cozy, dimly lit bar room. *(*☎744 444. *Cocktails s/7-12. Th 2-for-1 drink specials. Open M-Sa 7pm-late.)* **Korekenke,** San Martín 841, is a little pub with a friendly atmosphere. Larger and louder is the attached *discoteca.* *(*☎743 758. *Live music F-Sa nights. Cover s/10-15. Open Th-Sa 10:30pm-3am.)*

WEST OF ARICA

PUTRE   ☎58

At 3500m, Putre (pop. 1400), the capital of Parinacota Province, sits at the base of nearly 6000m-high **Nevados de Putre**. A popular overnight acclimatization stop for travelers heading to nearby destinations in the national parks, Putre is similar in feel to Socoroma but a bit bigger and blander. Putre offers a number of lodging and eating options as well as a hip bar that is the center of nightlife. As one might expect from a town at this altitude, it gets very cold at night—warm clothes are a must for visitors. The town comes alive during the February Carnaval and the September-October Ferán (Feria Regional Andino), a three-day fair with animals, fresh produce, crafts, and musicians from Chile, Bolivia, and Peru.

▣ TRANSPORTATION. Departing from **Arica**, **Trans Call** buses (☎261 068 or 221 220) go to **La Paz, Bolivia** (Tu, Th, F 8:30am). **La Paloma** buses depart for **Arica** (2½hr., 1:30pm, CH$1500).To reach **Lauca National Park** from Putre without taking a car or guided tour, go to **Cali Supermarket** to book a reservation on the **Arica-La Paz** international bus (expect to pay full fare to La Paz). To return, you can then stand on Ruta 11 to catch the bus back.

▣▣ ORIENTATION AND PRACTICAL INFORMATION. Putre is a tiny town with no available map, so street names and numbers don't mean much. Services in the town rarely have phone numbers—almost everyone uses the *centro de llamados* to make and receive phone calls. There are also **no ATMs** or facilities for cash advances on credit cards, so it is imperative to stock up on cash and other necessities in Arica or Iquique before going on to Putre.

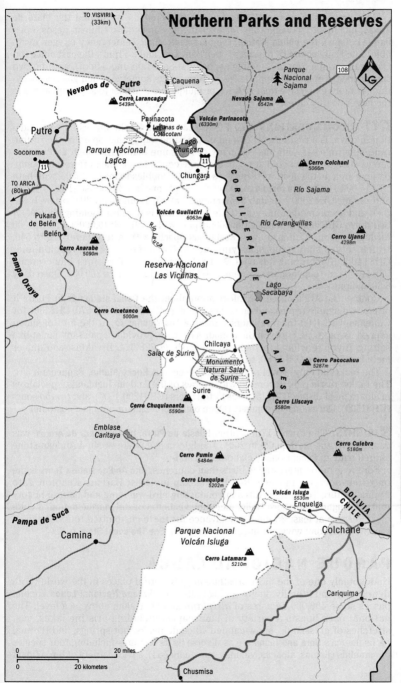

Northern Parks and Reserves

TO VISVIRI
(33km)

Nevados de Putre

Caquena

Cerro Larancagua
5439m

Parque Nacional
Sajama

Nevado Sajama
6542m

Putre

Parinacota

Volcán Parinacota
(6330m)

Socoroma

Lagunas de
Cotacotani

Lago
Chungará

Parque Nacional
Lauca

Cerro Colchani
5066m

TO ARICA
(80km)

Chungará

Río Sajama

Pukará
de Belén

Belén

Cerro Anarabe
5090m

Volcán Guallatiri
6063m

Río Caranguillas

Cerro Ujansi
4298m

Pampa Oxaya

Reserva Nacional
Las Vicuñas

Río Lauca

Lago
Sacabaya

Cerro Orcetunco
5000m

Chilcaya

Salar de Surire

Monumento
Natural Salar
de Surire

Cerro Pacocahua
5287m

Surire

Cerro Chuquiananta
5590m

Cerro Lliscaya
5580m

Emblase
Caritaya

Cerro Culebra
5180m

Cerro Pumin
5484m

Cerro Llanquipa
5202m

Pampa de Suca

Volcán Isluga
5530m

Enquelga

Camina

Parque Nacional
Volcán Isluga

Colchane

Cerro Latamara
5210m

BOLIVIA
CHILE

Cariquima

0   20 miles
0   20 kilometers

Chusmisa

CORDILLERA DE LOS ANDES

108

N

LG

Most services, shops, and lodgings are clustered on or around the **Plaza de Armas,** including the **bank** (only for exchanging currency to Chilean pesos; open 9am-11:30am), the **police station,** the **paramedic clinic** (emergency oxygen available), the Entel **centro de llamados** (open 8am-1pm and 2-11pm), the **post office** (on Carrera between Prat and O'Higgins; open M-Sa 9-1am and 3-9pm), and the two **supermarkets** (open 8am-10pm). The supermarkets sometimes sell gas but everything is more expensive than in Arica or Iquique, so it is best to stock up on gas in the larger nearby cities.

▌▐ ACCOMMODATIONS AND FOOD. La Paloma ❷, the biggest accommodation in town, is a *residencial* owned by the same family that operates the restaurant, supermarket, and bus company of the same name. Although **La Paloma's** rooms sometimes get cold at night, the large concrete complex offers a nice sunbathing area on the upstairs terrace. (☎ 222 710. Doubles/twins CH$3500, with bath CH$15,000.) **La Paloma restaurant ❶** serves simple meals. (Breakfast CH$600; lunch and dinner CH$2000.) **Hostal/Supermarket Cali ❷,** Baquedano 399, offers basic food and accommodations—the triple with a bath is the best rooming choice. (7-bed dorm CH$2500; doubles CH$6000; triples with bath CH$10,000; add CH$1000 for high season.) Cali also owns **Restaurant Apacheta ❶,** Arturo Perez Canto 540, which serves simple but satisfying meals. (Breakfast CH$750, lunch/dinner CH$1400.) **Restaurant Rosamel ❶,** La Torre 400c, offers both basic meals (CH$1500) and super-spartan rooms (CH$3000) for lodging. (☎ 300 051. Open daily 8:30am-9pm.)

Contact the Arica office for information about the **Conaf station ❷** in Putre. It offers two simple triples and one 6-bed dorm. (☎ 250 207 or 250 570. CH$3000 for Chileans, CH$4000 for foreigners.) **Hostería Las Vicuñas ❺,** at the foot of snow-capped Nevados de Putre on the outskirts of town, provides a pleasant chalet-like setting, if you're willing to shell out the cash. (☎ 228 564. Breakfast and dinner included. Doubles US$55-80; triples US$72.)

The real (and only) jewel of the nightlife scene is **Kuchu Marka,** Baquedano 351. The funky, rustic pub, decorated with murals of the Andean highlands, specializes in alpaca meat dishes (CH$1500), assorted beers (CH$1200-1500), and *tumbo* sours (CH$1500). Occasional live music. (Open daily noon-2am or until last customer.)

◪ SIGHTS. The town's 17th century **Iglesia de Putre,** on the **Plaza de Armas,** was damaged by the earthquake in 2001. The Iglesia is a white-washed Andean stone church with an exceptionally elaborate facade.

For those more interested in birds than churches, **Alto Andino Nature Tours** is the only tour operator in town. Run by Alaskan biologist Barbara Knapton, Alto Andino Nature Tours specializes in conducting bird-watching and natural history tours throughout northern Chile, including visits to coastal marine mammal colonies. Reserve at least 2 months in advance for these customized tours. (beknapton@hotmail.com; www.birdingaltoandino.com. See **The Local Story,** p. 320).

PARQUE NACIONAL LAUCA

Undoubtedly one of the most breathtakingly beautiful places in the world (both figuratively and literally due to its high altitude), **Parque Nacional Lauca** encompasses some 400,000 hectares of *altiplano* at 4000-6300m above sea level. The national park boasts a variety of landscapes, including pristine lakes, vast stretches of grasslands, snow-capped volcanic peaks, hot springs, and thermal baths. Lauca's **flora and fauna** are as diverse as its terrain—including four species of camelids (llamas, alpacas, vicuñas, and guanacos), a wide variety of birds (giant

Parque Nacional Lauca

coots, Andean geese, three species of flamingo, and nadus, a type of South American ostrich), and plants found in dense forests (such as quenoa and llareta), just to mention a few. Several peaks in the park offer hikers and alpinists easy access to the otherwise elusive 6000m mark.

AT A GLANCE

AREA: 138,000 hectares.

CLIMATE: Dry climate; average of 280mm. of precipitation annually, some rain in the summer and snow in the winter. Temperature ranges 12°C to 20°C during the day; -3°C to -10°C at night.

GATEWAYS: Main entrance at Las Cuevas.

HIGHLIGHTS: Remarkable variety of wildlife, including llamas, alpacas, vicuñas, and flamingos. Also mountain climbing, hot springs, thermal baths.

FEES: Free entry; open 24 hours.

CAMPING: Conaf's campsite at Chungará; free camping throughout the park possible but risky.

⊟ TRANSPORTATION

Parque Nacional Lauca lies on the border of Bolivia. It is an easy three hour drive from **Arica** on the paved **Ruta 11** to La Paz, Bolivia. A high-clearance **4WD vehicle** is strongly recommended for driving on the gravel roads inside the park, especially during the wet months in summer when roads get flooded or washed away. Although it is possible to navigate the park alone with a good map, a **hired guide** often facilitates the trip and is a necessity for those going on to Reserva Nacional Las Vicuñas and Monumento Natural Salar de Surire.

For information on **public transportation** to the park, see **Transportation and Tours in Arica** (p. 308). Please note that hitchhiking inside the park or from the park to RN Las Vicuñas and MN Salar de Surire is not recommended, as traffic is sparse on the unpaved roads, one can easily get lost without a guide, and the inherent risk involved in hitchhiking remains a valid concern.

NORTE GRANDE

☀ ⓘ ORIENTATION AND PRACTICAL INFORMATION

Lauca National Park is flanked in the south by **Reserva Nacional Las Vicuñas** and **Monumento Natural Salar de Surire,** which were once part of the park but became separate in the 1980s to permit mining.

There are **Conaf** ranger stations, located at **Las Cuevas** (the park's western entrance), **Parinacota,** and **Chungará,** which provide information concerning hiking trails and the latest conditions for climbing nearby peaks. (Open 9am-12:30pm and 1-5:30pm.) Only the Conaf location at Chungará, however, offers a **refugio** and **camping** (see accommodations and food, below). There is a **police station** in Chucuyo village.

It may be possible to enter the park without registering with the Conaf, but it is strongly recommended that you **register** at Conaf's Arica office if you plan to go hiking in the park, in case of an emergency. To climb **Volcán Parinacota, Volcán Guallatire,** or other peaks adjacent to the Bolivian border, you need a special permit from the **Dirección de Frontera y Limites** in Santiago, which can also be obtained at **Gobernación Provincial** in Putre or Iquique (if you go with a guided tour, the guide will take care of this paperwork). Although it is possible for experienced climbers with proper equipment to tackle Volcán Parinacota or Volcán Guallatire on their own, it is strongly recommended that everyone climb with an experienced guide, such as Jorge Barros (☎220 269 or 099 866 2030; info@suritrek.cl; www.suritrek.cl).

It is important to note that you cannot get **fuel, cash,** or **provisions** in the park, so it is necessary to stock up in Arica or Iquique (even Putre and Colchane offer no place to get cash). Driving inside the park after sunset is certainly not recommended, as it is easy to get lost in the frigid darkness, and it is almost impossible for Conaf or the police to find broken-down cars. For those planning on hiking or climbing in the park, remember that high altitude can have devastating consequences for some people, and even a seemingly easy hike can turn into a major exertion at this altitude. Be careful to eat and drink moderately, carry plenty of water, and avoid more physical activity than your body can handle.

▲ ⓕ ACCOMMODATIONS AND FOOD

The Conaf location at Chungará maintains a **refugio,** which is a great place to spend a night on the shores of Lake Chungará. The *refugio's* amenities include a hot shower, kitchen, fire place, and emergency radio communication. Advance reservations at the **Arica Conaf ❷** (see National Park Administration, Arica, p. 312) are recommended, but it is sometimes possible to arrive without a reservation and find a bed. Bring a sleeping bag in case the beds are full. (6 beds; CH$4000 per person for Chileans, CH$5500 for foreigners.) Conaf's Chungará **campsite ❶,** located next to the refugio, is protected by a 1.2m high stone wall. Campers have access to the shower and kitchen facilities at the *refugio.* Those brave enough to camp should bring an insulated sleeping bag and warm clothing, since the nights are frigid at 4500m above sea level. (CH$5500 per tent.) It is feasible to **camp** anywhere inside the park without permission, but this is highly discouraged, as most of the land belongs to Aymara owners who reserve the right to ask campers caught on their land to leave.

Restaurante Copihue de Oro ❶, in **Chucuyo** village, serves simple meals (CH$1500) and maintains a basic 6-bed dorm for lodgers. (No hot water. CH$2000.) Chucuyo has several other restaurants that offer similarly priced meals; most of these cater to truck drivers stopping en route to and from La Paz, Bolivia. **Florentina Alvarrez ❶,** in **Parinacota** village, offers a no-frills, 6-bed room. (No hot water. CH$2000.) There is no place to eat in Parinacota or in any location in the park.

☉ SIGHTS

Beyond the **Las Cuevas** entrance at the western end of PN Lauca, there is nothing except the lonely Conaf station. As you ride on **Ruta 11**, Volcán Parinacota and other peaks are visible from the road. The tiny village of **Chucuyo** is next with its police station and a couple of restaurants.

The tiny village of **Parinacota** (about 20 residents) includes a beautiful **church,** a **small school,** and stalls where the Aymara residents sell their **crafts.** Ask for permission before photographing the Aymara villagers. Enclosed within a walled compound, the 17th-century stone church is a **national monument,** featuring a thatched roof, a bell tower, an otherworldly interior, a fine display of gold and silver from Bolivian mines, and colorful mural paintings. No flash photograhy of the murals is permitted. Ask for caretaker Cipriano Morales Huanca to open the door. Parinacota is a good place to start a **hike** to the top of nearby **Cerro Guane Guane** (5097m), which offers expansive views over the park. There is no **sendero** (marked trail) to the top, but the hike from the Conaf *refugio* takes only a few hours. Although climbing gear is not necessary, some people prefer to travel with a local guide—ask the Conaf ranger to help you find a guide (CH$10,000-15,000 per day).

Continuing past **Laguna Cotacotani,** a shallow lake near Parinacota, you soon reach **Lago Chungará,** the highest lake in the world at 4500m above sea level, flanked by twin volcanos. Formed out of lava from the neighboring (and dormant) **Volcán Parinacota, Volcán Pomerape** (6232m) is rather shallow (deepest point 37m) but is still a wonder of nature. The Conaf *refugio* offers an unbeatable location for spending a night and is also a base for hiking the nearby **Cerro Choquelimpie.** (5228m. No marked trail but a straightforward 4hr. hike to the top; 2 hours down. No climbing gear necessary, but you can ask the Conaf ranger to get you a local guide.) If you are an experienced climber with the necessary gear, you can undertake the multi-day climb to the top of Volcán Parinacota (there is a marked trail from Chungará *refugio* to the base of the volcano but no trail from then on to the top). However, as explained previously, attempting this challenging climb is advisable only with an experienced guide and is discouraged during the wet season. Most visitors end their tour of PN Lauca at the *refugio* at **Chungará,** heading back to Arica.

RESERVA NACIONAL LAS VICUÑAS AND MONUMENTO NATURAL SALAR DE SURIRE

Once part of Parque Nacional Lauca until separated for mining purposes, **Reserva Nacional Las Vicuñas** and **Monumento Natural Salar de Surire,** although less accessible than PN Lauca, remain beautifully undisturbed. The reserve and the monument offer equally stunning landscapes with immense pampas, verdant *cienegas* (swamps), dramatic mountains, an ominously smoking volcano, and eerie bub-

AT A GLANCE

AREA: 209,131 hectares.	**FEATURES:** Salar de Surire, Volcán Guallatire, Río Lauca.
CLIMATE: Temperatures oscillate between 5°C and 15°C during the day, and -5°C and -15°C at night. The annual rainfall average is 260mm.	**HIGHLIGHTS:** Diverse fauna including vicuñas, llamas, and alpacas at Chilcaya; 3 species of flamingo and several hot springs at Polloquere; salt plains of Surire; spectacular views from the peak of the volcano.
CAMPING: No sites available; *refugios* in Surire (CH$5500).	
GATEWAYS: Arica.	

bling pools known as **Salar de Surire** (the salt lake of Surire). Wildlife includes great herds of vicuñas, llamas, and alpacas, as well as three species of pink flamingo. This area offers hikers and alpinists breathtaking opportunities to climb to particularly high altitudes.

▐ TRANSPORTATION. Getting to this sublime territory takes some effort, as the only way to get here is by means of a **guided tour** (see Arica Tours, p. 311) or by driving on your own. Most visitors to this area come down south from PN Lauca on the gravel road (Ruta A 232) that turns into Ruta 235 as it reaches Río Lauca and enters RN Las Vicuñas.

▟▐ ORIENTATION AND PRACTICAL INFORMATION. It is recommended to drive in **RN Las Vicuñas** and **Salar de Surire** with a guide, as even good maps are of little help in areas where there are no road signs and you could end up illegally in Bolivia. (Be careful not to walk off the beaten path near the Bolivian border, as there are **land mines.**) A high-clearance **4WD** is strongly recommended for driving on the gravel roads inside RN Las Vicuñas and Salar de Surire. Upon arrival at **Guallatire**, visitors are required to register at the **police station**, given the close proximity to the Bolivian border.

▐▐ ACCOMMODATIONS AND FOOD. The **Conaf refugio** in **Surire ❷**, located on a hill overlooking MN Salar de Surire, is an absolutely terrific place to spend a night—an oasis of warmth and comfort with a breathtaking view of the surrounding landscape. There is a 4-bed room in the building where the ranger lives that has a hot shower, a fireplace, and a kitchen. Bring a sleeping bag in case the room is full and you have to sleep on the floor. (CH$5500 per person.) Another building next door offers 5 rooms and a kitchen, providing 12 beds total. In this **refugio ❷**, hot water may not always be available. (CH$5500 per person.)

◙ SIGHTS. Located at the foot of **Volcán Guallatire**, Guallatire has a small 17th-century **church**, but its Conaf station is no longer in operation. Climbing Volcán Guallatire, which last erupted in 1961, is not technically challenging but can be hazardous given the emissions of poisonous gas and changing wind directions—climbing with a specialist guide is strongly recommended. (See the previous section on climbing Volcán Parinacota in Parque Nacional Lauca, p. 327).

Beyond Guallatire, cross **Río Lauca** on a bridge, but avoid this during the wet summer months, as the bridge often floods and becomes impassable, even with a high-clearance 4WD. The nearby **police station** in **Chilcaya** affords a magnificent view of Salar de Surire. At sunset, this landscape is particularly beautiful and eerie, with glowing purple mountains, warm hues of the salt and borax sediments, and blue pools. No trees, only scrub vegetation, survive at this altitude (4200m).

After traveling around the Salar for some 15km, you reach the Conaf station/*refugio* in **Surire** on a hill overlooking the salt pan (see food and accommodations, above). After a night in the *refugio*, get ready to hike the nearby peaks (about 5000m high), which have no marked trails but do offer easy climbs lasting a few hours. Ask the ranger to recommend a local guide if you did not come with one already.

A 20km drive around the Salar will take you to **Polloquere**, also called **Aguas Calientes,** which is close to a lookout point for watching colonies of flamingos (don't climb the wooden lookout tower, as it is unstable). Polloquere is a magnificent place with several **thermal pools** and steaming **hot springs.** Bathing in one of the more tepid thermal pools (some pools are almost at boiling temperature) is an exhilarating experience. Camping next to the pools is not recommended, as the sulfur smoke can give you a bad headache at night.

Most tours of Surire end at Polloquere but those who wish to press farther south can continue on towards the Conaf station/*refugio* at **Enquelga** inside **Parque Nacional Volcán Isluga,** another pristine expanse of *altiplano* with an active volcano similar to that in RN Las Vicuñas. Although it can be impassable in the wet season, the gravel road from Polloquere to Enquelga, passing through sweeping pampas and steep mountain passes, ranks as one of the most stunning scenic drives in the world.

CONTINUING TO BOLIVIA

BORDER CROSSING INTO BOLIVIA: CHUNGARÁ

Ruta 11, the road that runs from Putre to Parque Nacional Lauca, continues through the park to Chungará, 7km from the border. This little frontier town is home to the Chilean customs office. Just over the border is Tambo Quemado and the Bolivian customs. The road goes on from there all the way to La Paz.

Although this route is heavily traveled and well-maintained, the pass can be closed in winter due to inclement weather, so it's worth your while to double-check with Conaf or the authorities in Arica before attempting the crossing. The customs office at Chungará is open from 8am-8pm. The process is fairly simple and involves no more than a brief search of your luggage for contraband and various food products and a passport stamp (see **Essentials: Border Crossings,** p. 65, for info on visas and fees).

LA PAZ, BOLIVIA ☎02

BOLIVIANO (BS)		
CH$1 = B$0.0111	B$1 = CH$90.54	
US$1 = B$7.535	B$1 = US$0.133	
UK£1 = B$11.56	B$1 = UK£0.865	
EUR€1 = B$7.410	B$1 = EUR€0.135	

Originally founded in 1548 as *"La Ciudad de Nuestra Señora de La Paz,"* Bolivia's capital was first settled by Spaniards along the road to the ancient capital of Tiahuanuco, now located in Laja. Before long, however, the cold and wind of the harsh *altiplano* surface proved more than they could handle, so they relocated to La Paz (pop. 2.5 million; 3650m). Nestled deeply and densely in the Chuquiago Marka Valley, the city lies enclosed by a wall of mountains that keeps the wind out and life's energy in. It's also a great place for hiking, with a mountainous terrain that brings a variety of climates and breathtaking encounters with nature.

Today, "peacefulness" remains notably absent from La Paz's vocabulary. Micros zoom down the street, within inches of the sidewalk markets (not to mention vendors and shoppers) carrying everything under the sun. On Sagárnaga, tourists clamor for alpaca wool and luck-bringing llama fetuses, while south of Plaza del Estudiante, students and backpackers bridge the cultural gap over *cerveza* and thumping beats. From El Prado's broad boulevard, where jutting skyscrapers compete with the ancient heights of the *cordillera*, to the narrow cobblestone passes of Jaén, where bemused children peer into Museo Casa de Murillo's wishing well, La Paz is a vibrant mix of pop and folk, international and traditional, hustle and tranquility, stirring it up as only Bolivia can.

La Paz
Overview

✈ INTERCITY TRANSPORTATION

Airport: El Alto Aeropuerto (☎810 120 or 810 123), 30min. from the center. Information desk open 5am-8pm. Take an "Aeropuerto" microbus (Bs3.8) headed northwest from the Plaza Isabel la Católica or anywhere along El Prado, 16 de Julio, or Mariscal Santa Cruz. Minibuses run 6am-6pm. Taxi Bs30. Radio-taxi Bs40. Departure tax of Bs120 for visitors who have been in Bolivia over 90 days. Exit tax Bs10; international exit tax US$25.

International Airlines:

AeroContinente, 16 de Julio 1490 (☎310 707). Open M-F 9am-7pm, Sa 9am-noon. All flights are in the afternoon. To **Cusco** (1hr., US$142) and **Lima** (1¾hr., US$262).

LanChile, El Prado 1566 (☎358 377 or 322 370). Open M-F 8:30am-6:30pm, Sa 9:30am-noon. Flies to **Santiago** (5hr., 1 per day, round-trip US$349) via **Arica** (45min., round-trip US$125) and **Iquique** (2¼hr., round-trip US$140).

Varig Airlines, Mariscal Santa Cruz 1392 (☎314 040). Open M-F 9am-6:30pm, Sa-Su 9:30am-noon. To **Río de Janeiro** (8½hr., 2:20pm, US$388) and **São Paulo** (5hr., 2:20pm, US$362).

American Airlines, Edificio Herman on El Prado (☎351 360), flies to **Miami** (7am).

Domestic Airlines:

AeroSur, 16 de Julio 1616 (☎313 233). To: **Cobija** (1hr.; M 8:30am, F 3:35pm; Bs964); **Puerto Suárez** (3hr., M and Th 2:10pm, Bs1169); **Santa Cruz** (1½hr; F-Tu 2 per day, W 3 per day; Bs730); **Sucre** (50min.*).*

Lloyd Aero Boliviano (LAB), Camacho 1466 (☎371 020, reservations 0800 30 01). To: **Cusco** (1hr.; Tu, Th, Sa 9am; US$104); **Lima** (1¾hr., US$184); **Sucre** (1½hr., US$71).

Transporte Aero Militar (TAM) (☎359 288), at Montes and Serrano. Open M-F 8:30am-6pm, Sa 9am-noon. To: **Cobija** (1¾hr., W and F 9am, Bs590); **Cochabamba** (45min., Tu 8:30am, Bs290); **Guayaramerín** (3½hr., Tu 8:30am, Bs640); **Puno** (4½hr., Tu 8:30am, Bs640); **Reyes** (1hr., Th 8:30am, Bs350); **Riberalta** (3½hr.); **Rurrenabaque** (1hr.; M and Sa 9am, W-Th 9:30am; Bs350); **San Ignacio** (4½hr., M 8am, Bs320); **Santa Cruz** (1½hr., Tu and Th 8am, Bs350); **Sucre** (1¾hr., Sa 8am, Bs350); **Tarija** (3hr., Sa 8am, Bs490); **Trinidad** (2½hr., Th 8:30am, Bs360).

Buses: La Paz has 3 long-distance bus terminals.

International Bus Terminal, Caseta 40 (☎02 280 551). Taxi Bs6. **Expreso Cruz del Sur** (☎282 077) goes to: **Bogotá** (5 days, 8am, US$250) via **Puno** (6½hr., Bs50); **Guayaquil** (3½ days, 8am, US$130); **Lima** (2 days, 8am, US$50); **Quito** (4 days, 8am, US$135). **Ramos Cholele** (☎284 439) goes to: **Iquique** (12hr.; Tu, Th, Su 6am; Bs90); and **Santiago** (36hr.; Su, Tu, Th 6am; Bs320) via **Arica** (8hr., Bs80). **Cooperativo de Servicios Turísticos** (☎281 686) goes to: **Arequipa** (18hr., Bs130); **Copacabana** (4hr., 8am, Bs20); **Cusco** (15hr., Bs120); **Lima** (2 days, 8:30am and 3pm, US$50) via **Chacaltaya** (2hr., Bs50); **Tiahuanuco** (2½hr., 8:30am and 3pm, Bs50). **El Dorado** (☎281 672) goes to: **Cochabamba** (7hr., 15 per day 7am-10:30pm, Bs20-30); **Potosí** (10hr., 8pm, Bs50); **Santa Cruz** (7hr., 5:30 and 7:30pm, Bs120). **Expreso Tupiza** (☎282 153) goes to **Tupiza** (7:30pm, Bs60) via **Potosí** (10hr., Bs30). **Expreso San Roque** (☎281 959) goes to: **Bermejo** (36hr., 5pm, Bs110); **Buenos Aires** (3 days, 5pm, US$70) via **Camargo** (4hr., Bs70); **Tarija** (24hr., 5pm, Bs80); **Yacuiba** (36hr., 5pm, Bs100). **Jumbo Bus Bolívar** (☎281 963) goes to: **Cochabamba** (7hr., 8 per day, Bs25); **Santa Cruz** (18hr., 7pm, Bs80); **Valle Grande** (26hr., F 8 and 9:30am, Bs70). **Transporte 6 de Junio** (☎280 892) goes to **Cusco** (24hr., 8 per day, 8am-6pm) via **Copacabana** (4hr., Bs20) and **Puno** (6½hr., Bs40). MC/V.

Villa Fatima Terminal, at the far northeast tip of the city, sends buses to: **Chulumani** (3hr., 4 per day, Bs25); **Coroico** (3hr., 8 per day, Bs20); **Guyaramerín** (2 days, 2 per day, Bs180); **Rurrenabaque** (18hr., 3 per day, Bs85). Taxis (Bs6) and micros (Bs2) depart frequently 7-11am. Companies include: **TransBolivia** (☎210 469); **Trans 10 de Febrero** (☎210 146); **Tourbus Total** (☎212 526); and **Flota Yungueña** (☎213 527).

El Cementerio Terminal, on Baptista, above the Mercado de Brujas in the western part of town, serves: **Copacabana** (4hr., 15 per day, Bs20) via **Huatajata** (1½hr., Bs15); **Desaguadero** (2½hr., 2 per day, Bs25); **Sorata** (4hr., 10 per day, Bs20); **Tiahuanuco** (1hr., 10 per day, Bs15). Most buses leave before 2pm.

✸ ORIENTATION

One of the biggest benefits to a city in the heart of a valley is that it is almost impossible to get lost: to re-orient yourself, just walk downhill. The most activity lies along **El Prado,** the long main street that changes its name several times; in central La Paz, going east, it's **Mariscal Santa Cruz, 16 de Julio,** or **El Prado;** to the west, it becomes **Montes.** At its opposite end, it converts into **Villazón** briefly before splitting into **Arce** and **6 de Agosto. Sagárnaga** ascends from El Prado by the **Iglesia de San Francisco,** leading to many shops, hostels, and tourists. Nightlife picks up south of **Plaza del Estudiante** around **20 de Octubre.**

⊏ LOCAL TRANSPORTATION

Buses: Both **micro-buses** (large) and **minibuses** (small) run fixed routes all day throughout the city but can be hailed at any point. "Fixed routes" should be taken in the loosest sense. Destinations are displayed on the windshields. Pay upon boarding (Bs1 within the city, up to Bs3 outside). To get off yell *"bajo aquí."*

Taxis: Within the city Bs4-10, outside Bs30. **Radio-taxis** (☎222 525 or 242 525).

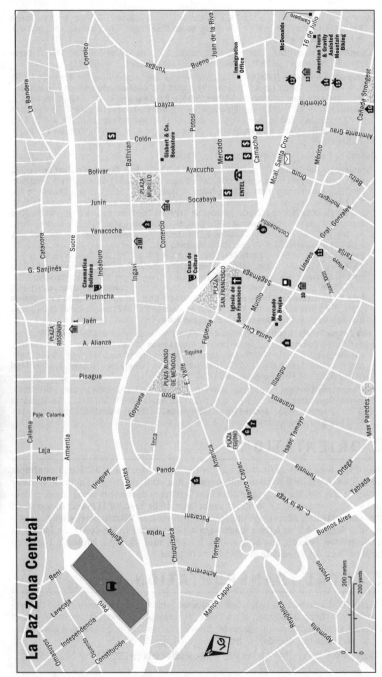

La Paz Zona Central

NORTE GRANDE

Car Rental: American Rent-A-Car, Camacho 1574 (☎202 933). The selection is small (mostly 4-wheel-drive), but the safety standards are higher than most other places in town. Ford Explorer US$89, Nissan US$69 per day. US$290-590 per week. Open M-F 8:30am-7pm. AmEx/MC/V.

◪ PRACTICAL INFORMATION

BOLIVIA COUNTRY CODE	☎591

TOURIST AND FINANCIAL SERVICES

Tourist Office: (☎371 044), at El Prado and Mexico. Sells **maps** of La Paz, Bolivia, and Lake Titicaca (Bs15-17), but has little else. Open M-F 8am-noon and 2:30-7pm. **Angelo Colonial Tourist Services,** Linares 922-24 (☎360 199), has a tour guide library, bulletin board, Internet access (Bs7 per hr.), and book exchange. Open M-F 2:30-10pm.

Tours: There are numerous tour agencies on Sagárnaga, but don't just go for the lowest price—they're often low for a reason. **Andean Summits** (☎422 106; www.andeansummits.com) offers reliable guides and trekking advice. **Bolivian Journeys,** Sagárnaga 363 (☎357 848; bolivianjourneys.org) has equipment rental, maps, and experienced guides. Open M-F 9am-noon and 2:30-7pm, Sa 9am-noon and 2:30-6pm. **America Tours SRL,** 16 de Julio 1490 office 9 (☎310 023 or 374 204). Open 9am-5:30pm. Home to **Gravity Assisted Mountain Biking** (☎313 849; fax 310 023; gravity@unete.com), for extreme sports freaks and confused travelers alike. Incredibly knowledgeable owners run bike trips down the **"World's Most Dangerous Road"** (the road to Coroico, US$49) and help oxygen-deprived new arrivals gather their thoughts and their breath. Multi-day tours for experienced cyclists. Those interested in the Coroico ride should email at least a week in advance. Open M-F 9am-6pm, most Sa 10am-2pm.

Embassies: Australia, Arce 2081, Edificio Montevideo Mezzanine (☎440 458 or 442 946; fax 400 801; chf@wara.bolnet.bo). **Canada,** 20 de Octubre 2475 (☎431 215; fax 432 330; lapaz@dfait.maeci.gc.ca), on Plaza Avaroa. **Ireland,** Sánchez Lema 2326 (☎411 873; fax 421 408; amtrac@ceibo.entelnet.bo). **Peru,** 6 de Agosto, Edificio Allianza (☎441 250). **UK,** Arce 2732-2754, Casilla 425 (357 424; fax 391 063; ppa@mail.rds.org.bo). **US,** Arce 2780, Casilla 425 (☎430 251 or 430 120; fax 433 900; www.megalink.com/usembalapaz).

Immigration Office, Camacho 1433 (☎203 028, naturalization office 08 003 007). Visa extensions. Open M-F 8:30am-4pm.

Currency Exchange: *Casas de cambio* are the only places to change traveler's checks. **Casa de Cambios América,** Camacho 1233 (☎204 369). Open M-F 9am-12:15pm and 2:15-6:15pm, Sa 9am-noon. **Casa de Cambios,** Colón 330 (☎374 866 or 343 226). Bs1 commission. Open M-F 9am-6:30pm.

ATMs: Can be found in most tourist districts, especially in El Prado, along 16 de Julio.

La Paz Zona Central

♠ ACCOMMODATIONS
Arcabucero Inn, 11
Estrella Andina, 7
Hostal Señorial, 3
Hostal Sucre, 16
Hotel Majestic, 8
Hotel Pando, 5
Hotel Rosario, 6
La Paz City Hotel Anexo, 14

♦ FOOD
Dumbo, 12
La Llave, 15
Rest. Discoteca Jackie Chan, 9

🏛 MUSEUMS
Museo de Arte Contemperáneo, 13
Museo de Coca, 10
Museo Etnografía, 2
Museo Nacional de Arte, 4
Museos Municipales de la Paz, 1

NORTE GRANDE

American Express: Capitan Ravelo 2101 (☎442 727; fax 443 060; magri_emete@megalink.com). Open M-F 9am-noon and 2-6:30pm, Sa 9am-noon.

LOCAL SERVICES

English-Language Bookstores: Los Amigos del Libro, Mercado 1315 (☎320 742). Open M-F 9:30am-12:30pm and 2:45-7:30pm. **Libros del Amigo** (☎328 164), on 16 de Julio. Small selection of best-selling paperbacks. Open M-F 9:30am-8:30pm, Sa 9:30am-2pm.

Library: Biblioteca Central *(☎378 477)*, at México and Stronguest. Open M-F 9am-9:30pm, Sa 9am-1pm.

Cultural Centers: The following are great sources of information on cultural events. **Alliance Française,** Guachalla 399 (☎325 022). Open M and F 9am-1pm and 3-9pm, Tu-Th 7:30am-1pm and 3-9pm, Sa 9am-1pm. **Goethe Instituto,** 6 de Agosto 2118 (☎442 453). Open M-F 9am-1pm and 3-7pm.

Language Schools: La Casa de San Antonio, N. Cordozo and Murillo 29, 2nd fl. (☎461 329; escuespa@ceibo.entelnet.bo). Spanish lessons US$7 per hr. **Homestay option.** Open M-F 8:30am-1pm and 3-8pm. **Centro Boliviano Americano** (☎441 508), Edificio El Estudiante, on Batallón Colorados. $150 for 50hr. of lessons.

Laundromat: Nueva Polar, Mayor Lopera 444 (☎212 068). Open M-Sa 8-11am and 1-9pm. Many accommodations also offer laundry services. Average price Bs6 per kg.

EMERGENCY AND COMMUNICATIONS

Emergency: ☎110.

Police: Edificio Olimpia 1314 (☎225 016), on the Plaza Tejada Sorazano.

24-Hour Pharmacy: Farmacia Gloria, Arce 2670 (☎434 344). Bang on the doors if they're locked and the owners will let you in.

Hospital: AMID Clinic, Claudio Sanjinés 1558 (☎221 949 or 226 767). Ambulance services available. Open 24hr. MC/V.

Telephones: Entel, Ayacucho 267 (☎313 030). Can connect to La Paz cell phone numbers (commonly beginning 01). Open 9am-12:30pm and 3-6:30pm.

Internet Access: Every couple of blocks. **International Call Center Internet,** Sagárnaga 227, has fast computers and cheap international calls. Bs4 per hr. Open M-Su 9am-11pm. **Café Internet Pla@net,** Sagárnaga 213 (☎111 261). Bs4 per hr., students Bs3.5 per hr., includes free coffee. Open 7am-10pm.

Post Office: Mariscal Santa Cruz 1278 (☎374 143 or 374 144). Open M-F 8:30am-8pm, Sa 9am-6pm, Su 9am-noon. **DHL/Western Union** (☎785 522), at Mariscal Santa Cruz and Loayza. Open M-F 8:30am-7pm, Sa 9am-noon. **FedEx,** Capitán Ravelo 2401 (☎443 537). Open M-Sa 8am-8pm.

⛰ ACCOMMODATIONS

La Paz has no shortage of places to spend the night. Generally, you'll have to pay a little more for a serviceable room, bath, and alarm clock.

▨ **Estrella Andina,** Illampu 716 (☎456 421; jupame2000@hotmail.com). Excellent value. Murals of Bolivian landscapes decorate every room—enough to make staring at the wall worthwhile. Top floor patio and restaurant offer great views. All rooms with private bath and cable TV. Breakfast buffet included. May-Sept. Singles US$20; doubles US$30. Oct.-Apr. US$16; US$26. MC/V. ❹

Arcabucero Inn, Viluyo 307 (☎313 473; ar_hostal@hotmail.com). Two blocks from Sagárnaga, by a park where children practice celebratory soccer dances. This well-kept, homey inn has a central 4-story solarium with terraces, vines, oil paintings, and food service. June-Sept. singles Bs80; doubles Bs120. Oct.-May Bs60-70; Bs100. ❸

Hostal Sucre, Colombia 340. Gives bang for your buck, with lots of amenities including cable TV. Enviable location on Plaza San Pedro. Singles Bs50, with bath Bs70; doubles Bs70, Bs110; triples Bs105, Bs165. ❷

Hotel Majestic, Santa Cruz 359 (☎451 628). Conveniently located near Sagárnaga with unbelievable views of the city. Bath (with scalding hot showers) and breakfast included. Cable TV Bs15. Singles Bs70; doubles Bs90; triples Bs130. MC/V. ❷

Hotel Pando, Pando 248 (☎454 922). Great perks for the price in a location convenient for quick stays. Internet cafe and tourist agency downstairs. Cable TV, phone, and well-scrubbed bath in each room. Breakfast included. Singles Bs70; doubles Bs120; triples Bs150; quads Bs170. Bs10 discount per night for stays over 3 nights. ❷

Hotel Rosario, Illampu 704 (☎451 658; fax 451 991; reservas@hotelrosario.com; www.hotelrosario.com). Three-star establishment with information center, charming cafe with free Internet, and safe box. All rooms have private bath, cable TV, heater, and panelled windows to keep out noise and cold. Breakfast buffet included. Singles US$28; doubles US$37. MC/V and traveler's checks. ❹

La Paz City Hostal Anexo, México 1539 (☎368 380). Basic but charming, with sunny rooms, common area, and bag deposit. Dorms Bs26; singles Bs30. ❶

Hostal Señorial, Yanacocha 540 (☎406 042). Extra comfy rooms have high ceilings, and some have windows. Communal atmosphere, since guests wine and dine together in the kitchen every evening. Bustling common rooms. Well-scrubbed common bathrooms. Bs40 per person. ❷

◖ FOOD

From the early morning until long after dark, **street vendors** in La Paz dispense fresh fruit, hot bread, and grilled sausages. Before noon, the **salteña** (a small pouch-like pastry filled with spicy beef, chicken, or eggs and potatoes and onions) sells best. In small, family-owned joints (distinguished by the Coca-Cola advertisements above their doors), lunch is cheap (Bs6-10) and quick. Restaurants line both **El Prado** and the side streets that stem from it. South of **Plaza del Estudiante,** pricier options serve up great cuisine of nearly every variety. As a rule of thumb, prices increase the farther south you go. For packaged goods, try supermarket **Hipermercado Ketal S.A.,** at Arce and Pinilla. (☎335 433. Open 7am-10:30pm.)

🍴 **La Bodeguita Cubana,** on Federico Zuazo. Zesty, caribbean flavors inspire customers to write poems of praise on the walls. Don't leave without sampling the delectable passion fruit mousse (Bs7). Entrees Bs26-30. Open M-F noon-3pm and 6pm-midnight, Sa 6:30pm-midnight, Su noon-4pm. ❶

Restaurante Discoteca Jackie Chan, Cochabamba 160 (☎339 231). Lives up to its name with Chinese food that kicks butt. Enormous menu. Fast, friendly service. Lunch Bs10. Entrees Bs15-25. Appetizers Bs8-25. Open noon-11:30pm. ❷

La Quebecoise, 20 de Octubre 2387 (☎121 682). Romantic restaurant feels like an old world inn and serves some of the best food in town. Entrees Bs45-54. Open M-F noon-3pm and 7-11pm, Sa 7-11pm. AmEx/MC/V. ❺

Pronto, Jáuregui 2248 (☎441 369), in the basement. Excellent Italian cuisine served in a cozy room with a checkered floor. Bring a date or an empty stomach for hefty portions. Pasta Bs18-30. Entrees Bs28-40. Open M-Sa 6:30-10:30pm. ❸

Wagamomma's, Arce 2557 (☎434 911). Indulgent Japanese fare with a simple, inviting decor. Reserve a table in advance. Sushi Bs30-61. Open Tu-Sa noon-2:30pm and 7-10pm, Su noon-2:30pm. MC/V. ❹

Vienna, Federico Zuazo 1905 (☎441 660). Live classical piano accompanies some of the best food in town. Excellent filet mignon Bs39. Chocolate mousse is secretly coveted by most of the capital city (Bs15). ❹

Tamboro Colonial, inside Hotel Rosario. Legendary breakfast buffet. Live *peña* music provides a backdrop for exquisitely prepared dinners (entrees Bs29-39). Breakfast 7-9:30am, dinner 7-10:30pm. ❸

Dumbo, 16 de Julio 1543 (☎313 331). An ice cream lover's paradise, Dumbo also serves hearty main courses, although you'll be hard pressed to resist jumping straight for the sweet stuff. Play pen for kids. Entrees Bs10-30. Ice cream Bs4-18. Open 8am-11:30pm. ❷

La Llave, México 1522 (☎350 499). A local favorite. Keys speckle the wallpaper near posters of Elvis, Lennon, and Marilyn Monroe. Native tunes performed live at lunch on weekends. Entrees Bs10-30. Open noon-midnight. MC/V. ❷

◎ SIGHTS

PLAZAS AND PARKS. With their nearly 3hr. siesta every afternoon, the people of La Paz need somewhere to rest their feet and enjoy the sun—plazas scattered throughout the city never fail to oblige. **Plaza Avaroa,** on 20 de Octubre in Sopocachi, is a haven for the young at heart—children test-drive electric cars, dogs romp, and brilliant balloons fill the sky. **Las Velas,** on Bolívar on the way to the stadium, has a similarly youthful atmosphere, with go-carts, flying chairs, and loud Latin pop music. **Mirador Laikakota,** on El Ejército, is worth the walk for anyone who wants to see the bustle of La Paz laid out below them (Bs50). **Plaza Murillo,** on Comercio, was founded as and still serves as the center of town. A refined **cathedral** resides on its southern side; the presidential palace (also know as the **Palacio Quemado,** or Burnt Palace, because of the fires that have gutted it twice) sits next door. At 6pm the crisply-uniformed guards take down the flags. **Plaza San Francisco,** impossible to miss from the top of Mariscal Santa Cruz, has become an activity center of its own—nearly every mode of transportation passes by it. Minor hippie circuses perform on the central strip that divides **16 de Julio.**

▨**SAN PEDRO PRISON.** This prison takes the concept of a guided tour to its most absurd limits. An English-speaking inmate leads packs of gringos through a free trade zone where the man with the most bolivianos rules. In wealthier areas, inmates have hot water, cable TV, access to a sauna, and permission for their families to move in with them. Learn about the Coca-Cola sponsored *fútbol* team, torture methods (like putting red hot chilli peppers where the sun don't shine), and tons of anecdotes that should never be put in print. *(Entrance fee Bs73, but bring extra for a Bs3 "tax" and other possible charges. No cameras. Tours Th-Su every hr. 9am-5pm.)*

IGLESIA DE SAN FRANCISCO. Elegantly decaying in the center of town, San Francisco (constructed in 1549) imposes its presence on all who enter La Paz. Its enormous dome is visible from the highest points in town and its open plaza hosts all sorts of festivities. Religious ceremonies take up most of the interior's activity. *(Off Mariscal Santa Cruz. Open 7am-11pm. Free.)*

VALLE DE LA LUNA. Appropriately named "Valley of the Moon," Valle de la Luna is covered with bizarre land forms due to decades of erosion. Tall stone peaks are divided by deep gullies, each with its own unique perspective of La Paz. There are a number of slippery dirt paths that allow you to navigate across, around, and between the incredible formations, seemingly miles away from the big city bustle

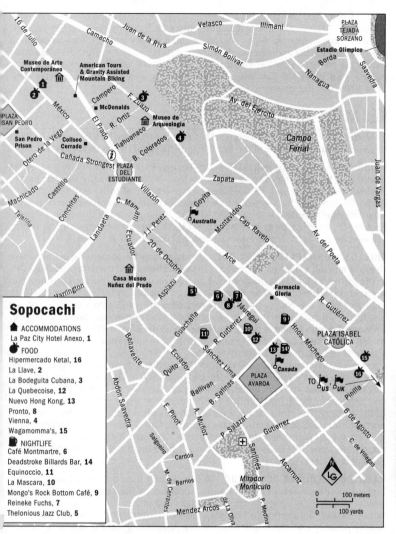

Sopocachi

▲ ACCOMMODATIONS
La Paz City Hotel Anexo, **1**

🍴 FOOD
Hipermercado Ketal, **16**
La Llave, **2**
La Bodeguita Cubana, **3**
La Quebecoise, **12**
Nuevo Hong Kong, **13**
Pronto, **8**
Vienna, **4**
Wagamomma's, **15**

🍸 NIGHTLIFE
Café Montmartre, **6**
Deadstroke Billards Bar, **14**
Equinoccio, **11**
La Mascara, **10**
Mongo's Rock Bottom Café, **9**
Reineke Fuchs, **7**
Thelonious Jazz Club, **5**

NORTE GRANDE

and any earth-bound civilization. Guided tours to Chacaltaya include a brief stop at Valle de la Luna, but those looking for time to indulge childhood fantasies of space travel should go it alone. *(Take Mallasa-bound micro 11 or minibus 231 or 237 from the Plaza del Estudiante near México (30min., Bs1.80). Get off at Valle de la Luna, right before Mallasa. Micros and minis return to La Paz until 6pm.)*

JARDÍN BOTÁNICO. La Paz's botanical garden provides a soothing midday respite from the downtown bustle. The park is filled with a small, well-maintained network of paths lined with trees, flowers, and most importantly, benches. *(In Miraaflores. ☎ 225 274. Open M-F 8am-6:30pm, Sa 9-5pm.)*

ZOOLÓGICO. The zoo contains a diverse collection of animals, but the inhumane condition of the cages makes it a bit harder to fully enjoy the site. See jaguars, monkeys, giant vultures, ducks, and more. Such variety makes it easy to overlook the ordinary llamas and alpacas that also call this zoo home. *(Take a Mallasa-bound micro 11 or minibus 231 or 237 from the Plaza del Estudiante, off México, to the zoo (35min., Bs1.80). It's a 15min. walk from Valle de la Luna. Return buses leave from the zoo until closing. Open 10am-6pm. Bs3, children Bs1.)*

🏛 MUSEUMS

Though not as strong a pull as some other activities offered by the capital, La Paz's museums illuminate some of the more unique facets of the city's life and history.

MUSEO DE COCA. Part cultural history lesson, part modern public-awareness campaign, this museum examines the coca leaf—first, as a healthy, historic part of Andean culture; second, as the integral component of today's deadly cocaine trade. Visitors are challenged with the central question of contemporary debate: how can one combat the drug trade without waging war on Andean traditions? *(Linares 906, behind Iglesia de San Francisco. ☎ 333 032; www.coca-museum.magicplace.com. Info available in Spanish, English, French, Hebrew, and German. Bs7.)*

MUSEOS MUNICIPALES DE LA PAZ. Also known as the Museos de la Calle Jaén, these four small museums warrant a short visit. **Museo Costumbrista** provides a thematic history of La Paz through small but colorful dioramas, masks, figurines, pictures, and scattered paintings. **Museo Litoral,** established in 1979 to honor the 100th anniversary of the War of the Pacific, recreates one of Bolivia's military defeats and has a fantastic collection of maps and historical documents. **Museo de Metales Preciosos Precolombianos** is unofficially known as the *Museo del Oro*, and it's easy to see why. The *Sala de Oro* (Room of Gold) is a subterranean vault where the ancients' gold glows as brightly as ever. The *Salas de Plata* and *Cerámica* (Rooms of Silver and Ceramics) recount the religious, decorative, and ceremonial uses of two more elements that were important in the Tiahuanuco and Inca cultures. **Museo Casa de Pedro Domingo Murillo** pays tribute to a hero of independence and indigenous medicine. Murillo's old home is now a shrine to a political history of the country. The stern expressions of Bolivia's presidents adorn the president's portrait room. An additional small room presents local handicrafts, from masks to dolls to dog-shaped shoes. *(Museo Costumbrista is on Sucre. The other 3 lie around the corner, on Jaén. Open Tu-Su 9:30am-12:30pm and 3-7pm, Sa-Su 10am-1pm. Admission to all Bs4. Ticket office in Museo Costumbrista.)*

CASA MUSEO NUÑEZ DEL PRADO. Once a family mansion, this building now houses hundreds of stone and wood sculptures by the late Marina Nuñez del Prado. A contemporary and friend of Picasso and Neruda, and Bolivia's most famous artist, del Prado died in 1995. Also on display are student works from nearby primary and secondary schools. The sculpture garden is one of the greenest nooks around. *(Ecuador 2034, 2 blocks up Pérez from Villazón. Open Tu-F 9:30am-1pm and 3-7pm, Sa-M 9:30am-1pm. Bs5, students Bs2, under 10 and over 65 free.)*

MUSEO NACIONAL DE ARTE. Previously a palace, the national art museum was built in 1775, making it the oldest building in La Paz. An eclectic collection of 20th-century Bolivian art and contemporary paintings from other parts of Latin America adorns the top floor. The main floor displays colonial paintings that revisit the theme of the crucifixion inexhaustibly, while the ground floor holds a collection of local artwork. The entire museum centers around a peaceful courtyard where visitors can rest and let the full power of the canvas take effect. *(At Comercio on Plaza Murillo. Open Tu-F 9am-12:30pm and 3-7pm, Sa-Su 10am-1pm. Bs5, under 18 free.)*

MUSEO DE ARTE CONTEMPORÁNEO. Housed in a decadent club building, the newest museum in La Paz displays the immense talent of today's Bolivian artists as well as works by international artists of rising repute. Renovation plans include a cafe, library, and map room. *(El Prado 1698. ☎335 905. Open M-F 9am-6pm.)*

MUSEO ETNOGRAFÍA. Although you can't miss the Aymara influence in La Paz, you might need to go to the city's ethnographic museum to understand it. The museum presents a comprehensive and insightful look into indigenous Bolivian life, from clothing to agriculture, festivals, food, and history. *(Two blocks from the Plaza Murillo on Ingavi. Open Tu-F 9am-12:30pm and 3-7pm, Sa-Su 9am-1pm. Free.)*

MUSEO DE ARQUEOLOGÍA. Discover the relics of an ancient empire in this castle-like building. Treasures date back to the first known life in the Andes—the Tiahuanuco culture. The collection holds mummies, stone jugs, metalwork, and figurines. *(Tiahuanuco 93, 1½ blocks from El Prado. ☎311 621. Open M-F 9am-12:30pm and 3-7pm, Sa 10am-12:30pm and 3-6:30pm, Su 10am-1pm. Bs5.)*

MUSEO TAMBO QUIRQUINCHO. This museum documents La Paz's growth and development, using "then and now" photographs to trace the city's evolution. Its varied displays cover every aspect of life in La Paz, including an investigation of the *chola* persona (a stereotyped image of Bolivian women as hardworking, builders of the nation). The exhibits also include contemporary paintings and sculptures. *(Evaristo Valle 176. ☎390 969. Open Tu-F 9:30am-1pm and 3-7pm, Sa-Su 10am-12:30pm. Bs1.)*

🔊 ENTERTAINMENT

ARTS
The **Teatro Municipal,** at Sanjinés and Indaburo, puts on the most consistent and popular theatrical performances. There are several **movie theaters** in town; most show major pop culture imports with Spanish subtitles. One is on El Prado, another on 16 de Julio just north of Plaza del Estudiante; there are also a couple near Plaza Murillo. **Cinemática Boliviana** (☎406 444), at Pichincha and Indaburo, shows international art house films, many with Spanish subtitles. The **Casa de Cultura,** on Mariscal Santa Cruz, across from Iglesia de San Francisco, has an information center for cultural events around town. A small theater upstairs sometimes hosts performances. (☎374 668. Open M-F 8:30am-noon and 2-7pm.) The weekly **Bolivian Times** (Bs6) offers sparse cultural advice.

FESTIVALS
If there's a street named after it, there's probably a parade or party on that date (and the day before, and the day after) as annual celebrations shake up the city on a fairly regular basis. Throughout the last week of December and the first week of January, vendors pack every street and plaza, and the entire city center becomes an open-air market. In celebration of Christmas and New Year's Eve, the **Feria de Alasitas** (Jan. 24) is a time to make wishes. The most familiar face during this holiday is Ekeko ("dwarf" in Aymara), a chubby, jolly little man not unlike St. Nicholas. Every family hangs miniature versions of the things they most desire (cars, houses, food, etc.) around his neck. **Carnaval de Oruro,** the largest regional festival, takes place on the third Saturday in February and is a gathering of towns in the La Paz region. Later in the year, a preponderance of La Paz flags, banners, and decorations marks the **anniversary** of the La Paz district (July 16). Dance troupes take over during the evening, and the sidewalks fill to capac-

NORTE GRANDE

ity with stands selling hot sausages, candied apples, and *ponche*, a hot drink made of milk and liquor. Along El Prado, the festivities last long into the night, and bands burst into song for days afterward. Later in July, the festival of **El Gran Poder** rolls into town. For most, it's a spectator event, but those who desire a more interactive experience should check out the **Entrado Folklórico Universitario.** The university students' version of El Gran Poder incorporates all the traditional dances; they also provide free lessons in the afternoon and evening on the plaza in front of the university. Finally, on August 6, Bolivia's **Independence Day** is celebrated loudly and proudly. Festivities start on August 5, with Plaza Murillo in the spotlight. August 6 and 7 are both considered *feriados* (holidays), so don't expect to find much open.

SPORTS

If you haven't been hit by a stray soccer ball or assisted in spotting an acrobatic celebratory goal formation, then you haven't had the authentic Bolivian experience. **Fútbol** is everywhere and dominates the sports section in almost every newspaper, which always has information on the next big game. Alternatively, head to the stadium, and ask at the ticket window. Tickets for big matches (Bs50) often sell out, but it's usually possible to show up the day of the match and purchase them from hawkers, albeit at a slight mark-up. Historically, Bolivia's team hasn't fared as well as South America's other powerhouses, but it usually does well at home, when thousands of screaming fans are rooting for them and the high altitude fazes opponents quickly. **Coliseo Cerrado** on México, by the Plaza del Estudiante, holds **wrestling** matches and cultural **festivals.**

['] SHOPPING

In La Paz's markets, anything and everything is for sale—from fossils and toilets to llama fetuses and skiing equipment. More than just a tourist indulgence, a day at the markets is a true experience of life in the capital city. The largest market, **Mercado Rodríguez,** convenes on weekends at Calle Rodríguez and offers everything from oranges to underwear. **Mercado de Brujas,** along Santa Cruz and Sagárnaga, behind Iglesia de San Francisco, is for the superstitious. Indigenous women sell coca tea and dried llama fetuses to cure ailments and scare away bad luck. Meanwhile, hundreds of other merchants sell the staples most tourists just can't leave without: alpaca sweaters, reed pipes, silver and gold trinkets, and brightly colored bags. **Mercado Camacho,** at the end of Camacho, is a never-ending farmer's market. **Mercado Negro,** along Max Paredes, is five department stores and a chain of pharmacies that spill onto the street. Everything you could ever want is balanced pyramid-style on tables. Take the **Bus Ceja,** 16 de Julio, to **El Alto** for massive, anything-goes markets on Thursdays and Sundays that close around 3pm.

⌨ NIGHTLIFE

Friday nights bring live music to clubs and restaurants and a *paceña cerveza* (local beer) into almost every hand. Bars have a monopoly on the early action, filling around 9pm; clubs take over around midnight and go well into the morning.

BARS

Mongo's Rock Bottom Café, Hermanos Manchego 2444 (☎ 440 714). Where most gringos go to hit rock bottom. Serves up great American-style burgers, sandwiches, and attitude. Packed by 10pm with chatting people. Entrees Bs20-30. Beer Bs13, mixed drinks Bs15. Open M-F noon-1:30am, Sa 6pm-2:30am.

Reineke Fuchs, Jáuregui 2241 (☎08 124 874; reineke@mail.megalink.com; www.reinekefuchs.com). Means "red fox" in German, as its sign depicts. Astonishing selection of imported beers from German to Czech (Bs12-18). A good, quiet place to start the night, though beer aficionados usually end up spending the night after starting it. Open M-Sa 6pm-1am.

La Máscara, 20 de Octubre. Here, a slightly older crowd sheds the many masks of adolescent life. Live rock, samba, and Brazilian music on Th and F. Open Th-Sa 7pm-2am.

Deadstroke Billiard's Bar, 6 de Agosto (☎434 784). Run by an ex-marine. A mix of gringos and locals come here to wield cues and match skills. Beer Bs12. Billiards Bs10 per hr. Open M-F 5pm-late, Sa 7pm-late.

Diesel Nacional, 20 de Octubre 2228 (☎310 434). An upscale, trendy bar. Train tracks lead to a diesel engine motif. Beer Bs12, mixed drinks Bs18-30. Open M-Sa 8pm-3am.

Café Montmartre, Guachalla 363, off 20 de Octubre. Catch the big soccer game or nibble a dainty pastry. The Alliance Française (the official French Cultural Center) is right next door. Open M-F noon-3pm and 4pm-2am, Sa 8pm-2am.

Beer's Pub, Sanjinés 2688 (☎411 668). Breathes life into La Paz's Th nights. Often hosts new bands. Well-dressed crowd. Cover Bs25. Open Th-Sa 9:30pm-2:30am.

CLUBS

Thelonius Jazz Club, 20 de Octubre 2172 (☎337 806). Cozy atmosphere and fantastic jazz, both traditional and Latin. A local crowd gives you the chance to escape the gringo-dripping joints. Cover Bs20. Open W-Sa 9pm-3am.

Underground Club, Medinacelli 2234 (☎312 365). Follow the signs from 20 de Octubre. Loud beats and flashing lights satisfy the raver in everyone. Diverse international crowd. For a mid-week rush, try the W night Rave Party, when this place is the only one drawing a crowd. On the weekend, don't come before midnight unless you want to dance alone. Cover Bs15. Open W-Sa 10pm-3am.

Equinoccio, Sánchez Lima 2191 (☎01 245 667), between Aspiazu and Guachalla. A bar and dance club, Equinoccio brings live music to an active crowd. On weekends, live music doesn't start until midnight, about the same time that the crowds do. The stage is big, the dance floor bigger. Cover Bs10-25. Open W-Sa 9pm-3am.

Forum (☎413 669), on Sanjinés. You have to walk through a 20 ft. high gate and twin spotlights before you can bump with the local crowd. While people gather in front 30min. before it opens, the real action isn't until later. Cover Bs25. Open W and F-Sa 11pm-4am.

⚑ DAYTRIPS FROM LA PAZ

▨ CHACALTAYA

There is no public transportation to Chacaltaya, but tour agencies run minibuses during the week (US$10, min. 5 people). Club Andino Boliviano, México 1638 (☎324 682), sends a bus most weekends (US$10). Vehicles stop in the resort parking lot, about a 1hr. uphill walk from the top. Weather may hinder transportation in rainy season (Nov.-Mar.).

The "world's highest ski resort" puts more emphasis on "highest" than "resort." Perched on a windy cliff at 5300m, the lodge overlooks the Cordillera Real's snowy peaks unraveling in every direction. Skiing is possible when weather permits, but equipment rental and tow-rope to the top are only available Jan.-Mar.

MUELA DEL DIABLO

Take minibus #288 (40min., Bs30) from Plaza del Estudiante to the end of the line. From the parking lot, continue up the dirt road to the right. At the small cemetery, continue up and to the right (2hr.). Buses back to La Paz leave until 4pm.

Rocky hills that change color every few meters frame the path to the top of Muela del Diablo (molar of the devil), named for the way it juts out of the mountainside like an aching wisdom tooth. The colors provide an interesting contrast to the characterless architecture that lies at the trailhead below, in the village of Ovejuyo. Those traveling alone may want to take a taxi from the *zona sur*, as bandits are known to frequent the area.

VALLE DE LAS ÁNIMAS

Take minibus or micro Ñ from Plaza del Estudiante to Ovejuyo (40min., Bs2.30); ask the driver to tell you when to get off. From there, follow the rocky uphill path (1hr.). Minis and micros head back to La Paz until late afternoon.

On a hillside populated by enormous stone peaks, narrow paths lead up to where the views appear to belong on another planet. From the base, the path (1hr.) is not very well-defined; it becomes more difficult to discern as the walls of rock close in. It's also easy to slip on the loose ground; as the track meanders its way around the needles of stone, a good handhold may be the only means of continuing upward. From the perch at the very top, the crumbling dirt is easy to forget as the world looks tiny, nestled in the valley below. Beware of crevices too narrow for broad shoulders or backpacks—step gingerly but plant your feet securely, and you'll be duly rewarded at the top. Those traveling alone should also be cautious, as robberies are said to occur.

TIAHUANUCO

Take a Guaqui-bound bus (1½hr., every 30min., Bs6) from the corner of José María Azin and Eyzagu to Tiahuanuco. Head right from the fork and look for the flat, orange museum on the right, just off the railroad tracks. To get back to La Paz, catch a minibus in the plaza or along the main road. Almost all the tour agencies on Sagárnaga offer daytrips to Tiahuanuco (8am-3pm, US$8-10). Though more expensive, they can fill in a lot of blanks, turning the dusty and dull into the mysterious and ancient. Open 7am-5pm. Bs15.

The ruins of Tiahuanuco provide an extensive history lesson about the barren *altiplano* and fodder for archaeological, historical, pseudo-historical, occult, science fiction, and conspiracy theories of every kind. The Tiahuanuco Empire (2500 BC to AD 1172) stretched through what are now Bolivia, Peru, Chile, and Argentina before mysteriously disappearing. Present-day *campesinos* living near the ruins are trying to emulate the Tiahuanuco agricultural system that once fed eight million people, equal to today's Bolivian population. The **Museo Regional de Tiahuanuco** displays relics of the great empire, including elongated skulls (probably a status symbol) and a mummy in the fetal position. The ruins themselves represent three levels of the Tiahuanuco religious framework: **Pirámide de Akapana** was probably a religious temple that honored the mighty surrounding mountains. Scientists estimate that it stood 18m tall, but today it is almost completely buried. Distinctive stone heads emerge from the walls of the **Templete Semisubterraneo,** a large quadrangular temple, while a stone map of the Tiahuanuco region hides in **Kantat Hallita,** a semi-underground temple. Different theories attempt to explain the jutting heads—one claims that they represent the heads of defeated enemies, while another asserts that they are heads of all the nations of the world, with whom the empire had contact when crossing the ocean in reed boats. **Kalasaya,** an enormous open-air temple, houses detailed structures that suggest it served as an agricultural calendar. Three stone statues—**monolito Ponce, monolito Fraile,** and **Puerta del Sol**—probably played important roles in measuring time. **Putuni,** also known as the Palacio de Los Sarcáfagos (Palace of the Sarcophagi), is still under excavation, but already alluring with hundreds of religious designs decorating the polished stone floor. Finally, the wondrous massive stones of **Pumapunku,** some weighing up to 130 tons, cover the site. Where they came from and how anyone moved them remains a mystery.

HIKING NEAR LA PAZ.

EL CHORO

This mainly-downhill **hike from Cumbre to Coroico,** the most popular trek in the La Paz area, promises spectacular views and a stunning variety of climates. Travelers who brave the road, on foot or bike, start in fleece and finish in shorts. Most of the trek follows a pre-Hispanic road.

AT A GLANCE

LENGTH: 4800m.	**TIME:** 3-4 days.
CLIMATE: Heavy rains in Dec.-Feb. make the trek extremely difficult. Apr.-Oct. is ideal, but there is snow year-round.	**ALTITUDE:** 2000-5000m. **DIFFICULTY:** Medium.
FEATURES: Spectacular views, rivers, wildlife, various climates.	**FEES:** The town of Choro charges Bs10 to pass.

⌐? TRANSPORTATION AND PRACTICAL INFORMATION

The hike starts in Cumbre, a 1½hr. car ride from La Paz. Towns along the route may provide food, water, batteries, and occasionally lodging, but don't count on it. **Buses** leave all day from Villa Fátima to **Cumbre** (8am, Bs20). At the end of the hike, *colectivos* leave Chairo for nearby **Coroico** (Bs25), where it's possible to catch a bus back to La Paz.

Maps of the park are available at the **Instituto Geográfico de Bolivia,** on Linares (Bs20). Bring clothing for all climates, extensive camping supplies, and three days' worth of food. Weather can be unpredictable; it's best to hike with a group.

Most hikers spend the first night at the ranger camp in **Chucura,** a 5hr. hike from Cumbre. Stop in **Sandillani** the second night, about 8-9hr. from Chucura. There are a number of campsites and locals sometimes house hikers. If you choose to stay in **Chairo** the third night, there a number of free campsites.

⚑ OUTDOOR ACTIVITIES

HIKING. Day 1 starts in **Cumbre** (30min. drive from La Paz) and winds along an ancient road carved into a hillside. The trail is entirely uphill, and you reach the hike's highest altitude (5000m) in the mountain town of **Chuchura.** On **Day 2,** the downhill trek to **Choro** (3000m) brings poorer road conditions but more breathtak-

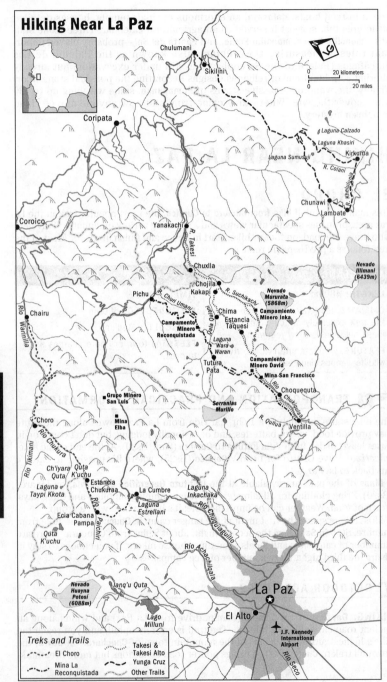

Hiking Near La Paz

Chulumani
Sikilihi
Coripata
Kirkuma
Laguna Calzado
Laguna Khasiri
Laguna Sumusiji
R. Colani
R. khellchuca
Coroico
Chunawi
Lambate
Yanakachi
R. Takesi
Nevado Illimani (6439m)
Chuxlla
Chojila
Kakapi
R. Suchikach
Nevado Mururata (5868m)
Pichu
R. Churi Umani
Chima
Campamento Minero Inka
Chairu
Río Warnilla
Campamento Minero Reconquistada
Estancia Taquesi
Laguna Wara Waran
Tutura, Pata
Campamento Minero David
Mina San Francisco
Grupo Minero San Luis
Río Chuquaqita
Río Chuquiguara
Choro
Mina Elba
Serranías Murillo
R. Quilua
Ventilla
Río Tikimani
Ch'iyara Quta Quta
Quta K'uchu
Estancia Chukuraa
La Cumbre
Laguna Inkachaka
Río Chuquiaguillo
Laguna Taypi Kkota
Río Chukura
Laguna Estrellani
Ecia Cabana Pampa
Río Paichiri
Quta K'uchu
Río Achachilaia
Nevado Huayna Potosí (6088m)
Janq'u Quta
La Paz
El Alto
Lago Milluni
J.F. Kennedy International Airport
Río Seco

Treks and Trails
- El Choro
- Mina La Reconquistada
- Takesi & Takesi Alto
- Yunga Cruz
- Other Trails

NORTE GRANDE

ing vistas—rivers and waterfalls abound. **Day 3** is a lengthy 6hr. descent to **Sandillani** but rewards travelers with bountiful wildlife, including hummingbirds endemic to Bolivia, spider monkeys, small tigers, and porcupines. On **Day 4,** the hike ends with a 5hr. trek down to the town of **Chairo.**

MOUNTAIN BIKING. Catch a glimpse of snowy mountains and Yungas jungle as you zip down the **"World's Most Dangerous Road"** from Cumbre to Coroico. Biking is the safest means of descending this road, and tours provide guides leading and following the biking group (usually 10-12 people) along with a van to bring up the rear and carry spare helmets, gloves, and vests (equipment checks every 30min.). Tours leave from La Paz at 9am and end in Coroico around 4pm, then return to La Paz (3hr.). Dozens of agencies offer biking tours (to other locations as well), but only two offer quality bikes. ▨**Explore Bolivia,** Sagarnaga 339, offers 1-day tours (US$39-49). Rafting and kayaking packages are also available (US$100-120) and include resort-like accommodations and excellent meals. (☎391 810; madness@caoba.entelnet.bo. Open 8am-7pm.) **Gravity Assisted Mountain Biking,** 16 de Julio 1490 (☎374 204), in America Tours SRL, Edificio Avenida. Service isn't great, but the bikes are, and lots of customized 1- to 3-day riding options are available (from US$49).

YUNGA CRUZ

This adventurous hike, stretching from Andean mountaintops to thick jungle lowlands, is a favorite among tour guides because it traverses a range of climates, offers stunning views, and is less crowded than other treks. It is also one of the most difficult hikes done regularly.

AT A GLANCE	
DISTANCE: 31km from Chuñavi, 40km from Lambate.	**TIME:** 3-4 days.
	ALTITUDE: 1700-4200m.
CLIMATE: May-Sept. (especially June-Aug.) is the best time to go.	**DIFFICULTY:** Medium-Difficult.
	FEES: None.
FEATURES: Khala Ciudad and Yunga Cruz mountains, Río Kheluluni, forests.	

NORTE GRANDE

⊟🛈 TRANSPORTATION AND PRACTICAL INFORMATION

Three-day hikes begin in the town of **Chuñavi;** four-day treks start from **Lambate.** After **Cerro Khala Ciudad,** the two trails converge. **Buses** to Chuñavi (6hr., 9am, Bs20) leave from Luís Lara in La Paz. Return buses depart at the trail's endpoint, in Chulumani (6hr., Bs25). **Private transport** is necessary to reach the 4-day hike trailhead at Lambate. Tour agencies in La Paz supply maps (see **Tours,** p. 333). Color **maps** of the Yungas cost Bs60. Water is scarce along the trail. Temperature changes drastically, so bring clothes for different climates. Tour agencies in La Paz rent equipment. **Elma Tours,** Naupanasi 888 (☎456 823), rents **tents** (US$4 per day). Since the trail is hard to follow, it's best to go with a guide. Tours run about US$25 per day, but transportation is additional US$40. (see **Tours,** p. 333). Trips from Lambate spend the 1st night in the town of Kirkuma and the 2nd below Cerro Khala Ciudad (where trips starting in Chuñavi camp their first night). After the two trails converge after Cerro Khala Ciudad, groups camp atop Cerro Yunga Cruz the final night.

HIKES

4-DAY HIKE. If starting in Lambate, **Day 1** first heads downhill to **Río Kheluluni** (2hr.), then follows the river (5km, 4hr.) up to **Kirkuma,** a small village where groups camp for the night. **Day 2** heads steeply uphill (9km, 5½hr.) toward the **Cerro Khala Ciudad** campsite, which offers stunning views of **Laguna Khasiri,** the town of **Illimani,** and **Nevado Illimani.** On **Day 3,** leave the lake and head to the pass around Khala Ciudad (2km, 2hr.), where the trails converge after a kilometer. As the trail continues to a spectacular campsite atop **Cerro Yunga Cruz** (3-4hr.), the scenery transforms from cool Andean landscape to wild vegetation. Thick greenery covers **Day 4**'s hike into **dense forest** (3-4hr.) and eventually a fork in the road appears; bear right. When you reach a clearing by **Cerro Duraznuni,** follow the path to the left, and continue about 2hr. to the top of a **ridge** where you can camp or keep moving; the path continues to the towns of Sikilini (1hr.) and ultimately Chulumani (2hr.). Do not follow the road to Chulumani; it takes longer than the trail. On M and Th, **buses** run from Sikilini to **Chulumani** (10am and noon, Bs5-10).

3-DAY HIKE. This 3-day hike starts in Chuñavi and goes directly uphill to spend the first night at **Cerro Khala Ciudad.** From there, the trail is identical to that of the 4-day hike above.

MINA LA RECONQUISTADA

For a history lesson much more entertaining than that of any textbook, La Reconquistada offers encounters with old Bolivian mines set against an awe-inspiring backdrop. The trail traverses the diverse landscape of the Yungas, offering mountainous ascents and a tunneling descent into thick lowlands.

AT A GLANCE

DISTANCE: 25km from Mina San Francisco, 34km from Ventanilla.

CLIMATE: It's best to go during dry season (May-Sept.), especially June-Aug.

FEATURES: Reconquistada mine, the Yungas, 200m tunnel, rivers, small lakes.

TIME: 2-3 days.

ALTITUDE: 1950m-4000m.

DIFFICULTY: Medium.

FEES: None.

TRANSPORTATION AND PRACTICAL INFORMATION

Buses to **Ventanilla** via **Mina San Francisco** leave every morning from Luís Lara in La Paz. From Ventanilla, it's 7km to the trailhead. Obtain **maps** of the park before leaving at tour agencies in La Paz (see **Tours,** p. 333). While the tour is easily done alone, going with an organized group makes transportation easier.

3-DAY HIKE

Those who start in Ventanilla must follow the uphill road to **Mina San Francisco** (8.5km), via the town of Choquelchota along the way (1½hr.). From the trailhead at the mine, the path is a strenuous uphill trudge with great Andean vistas. After 1hr., a small lake appears; from there, it's another hour (5.5km) to the pass between **Cerro Zorra Quillo** and **Cerro Huanakuni.** After the pass, the trail is mostly downhill until you reach the **campsite** in a flat, grassy plain. Along the way, you'll pass the village of **Tutura Pata,** which lies along the **Río Zorra. Day 2** takes you from the campsite down to **Río Qala Qalami** (45min.), where the path splits. Follow the route that goes up out of the river to **Mina La Reconquistada** (2½hr.). From the mine, it's a 20min. walk to a dark, descending **tunnel** 200m long. Go slowly, bring a flashlight, and be careful to stay on the proper trail while inside. After the tunnel, the path goes uphill (1½hr.) before reaching a **pass.** From the pass, hike 40min. downhill to a **campsite** by a stream. **Day 3** is an easy downhill hike (4hr.) through the **Yungas.** Because the final stretch is easy, many hikers opt to finish the trail in two days, but finding a return bus to La Paz in the late afternoon can be difficult.

THE LAKES DISTRICT

Imagine standing in a rolling field, looking over a clear, blue lake at a towering volcano covered in a deep green forest that spreads for miles around. You are imagining a typical scene in Chile's Región Los Lagos, the Lakes District. Home to an incredible diversity of natural attractions from roaring waterfalls to smoldering volcanoes, from bubbling hot springs to vast, pristine lakes, this region has become increasingly more popular among Chileans and foreigners alike. This diversity, however, is not limited to natural wonders. From a more civilized perspective (or at least one more focused on civilization), Los Lagos is home to major industrial cities, unmapped rural farm towns, and even wild beach resorts.

The cultural heritage of the region has also made it extremely fascinating for many visitors. This is the region where the fierce Mapuche stood their ground, confounding would-be Spanish colonizers for over 300 years. Despite their eventual defeat in the mid-1800s, their culture and traditions have had a major impact on the local way of life and in many places has been faithfully carried on by their descendants. Germanic influences spice up the cultural flavor of the region as well. German migration here during the 19th-century sparked a major agricultural and small industries boom—the region is now famous for its dairy farms, its breweries, and its stalwart German food. No rural, frontier land, however, would ever be complete without its cowboys. The Chilean *huasos* are, like most lone riders of the world, an oft-mythologized but rapidly dying breed. You can still see some of the remnants of their lifestyle in the ever popular rodeos and *cueca* dances.

The Lakes District begins just south of **Los Angeles** and runs all the way to the industrial port of **Puerto Montt.** The myriad small towns and cities provide such a variety of experience as to satisfy any type of traveler. The wild and free can bask on the Pacific coast in little towns like **Niebla** just south of **Valdivia,** or around some of the pristine lakes in beach resorts like **Pucón, Puerto Varas,** and **Frutillar.** The more reserved and cultured can encounter Mapuche, present and past, in **Temuco,** or discern the German influence in **Osorno.** If you seek natural beauty, stick to the foothills of the Andes, where nearly a dozen national parks provide access to challenging mountain ascents and beautiful forest hikes. Finally, if overwhelmed by this onslaught of natural and cultural beauty, escape to some of the quieter, undiscovered towns of **Coñaripe, Calbuco,** and **Lago Ranco Village.**

HIGHLIGHTS OF THE LAKES DISTRICT

CLIMB up to the fiery crater of Volcán Villarrica in **Parque Nacional Villarrica** (p. 372).

STOP and smell the roses in **Panguipulli,** which won't be hard since thousands of them line the streets of this little town (p. 379).

DISCOVER the intricacies of traditional Mapuche jewelry at the **Museo Regional de la Araucanía** in **Temuco** (p. 358).

EASE into the soothing Aguas Calientes of the **Parque Nacional Puyehue** (p. 392).

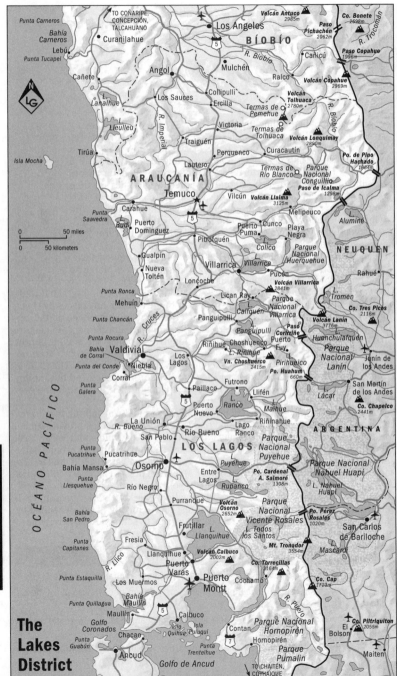

The Lakes District

SOUTH TO TEMUCO

PARQUE NACIONAL TOLHUACA ☎ 43

Tolhuaca means "Front of the Cow" in Mapuche—the name might seem rather bizarre, until you make the 50km drive from the Panamericana to the park's secluded entrance. The sometimes rock-strewn, sometimes muddy, and always treacherous path will lead you past several curious bovine observers, just about your only company for the one and a half hours of automobile rattle-and-hum. More than 6000 hectares of forestland sprawl over hills and along the banks of the **Río Malleco,** featuring a terrific diversity of fauna from the Andean condors to the Pudú, the smallest deer in the world. The flora isn't too shabby either—*araucaria* line the hills while *coïhue* and oak trees thrive at lower elevations. The center of the park lies around its serene **Laguna Malleco,** whose western edge unravels into a 49m high waterfall, the **Salto Malleco.** Seven well-marked trails, ranging from 1.5km to 8.6km in length, wind their way around the park from the base camp at the lagoon; some trace a course within view of **Volcán Tolhuaca** (2806m), or along the flight path of the Andean condors.

AT A GLANCE

AREA: 6000 hectares.

CLIMATE: Cool and rainy.

GATEWAYS: Temuco, Los Angeles.

HIGHLIGHTS: Hiking around Volcán Tolhuaca; Andean condors; *pudús; coïhue* and *araucaria* trees.

FEATURES: The beautiful trio of Río Malleco, Laguna Malleco, and Salto Malleco; Volcán Tolhuaca.

FEES: CH$1700, children CH$600.

CAMPING: Sites at Laguna Malleco CH$7200.

Getting to the Parque Nacional Tolhuaca is tricky even for those with 4WD, and is almost impossible using public transportation. One way to drive there is to follow the Panamericana to the exit marked "Inspector Fernandez" and "Parque Nacional Tolhuaca," 98km south of Los Angeles and 4km north of Victoria (make sure to exit at the blue sign that says "Salida"—not the service road before it). Once you exit the highway, the bumpy dirt-and-sharp-rock road begins, and will take you over wooden bridges and muddy hills for 50km—it's especially dangerous at night, when there's absolutely no lighting. An alternate route follows the paved road from Victoria east to the town of Curacautín. Drive 39km north on that dirt road to the Termas de Tolhuaca, and continue 9km west to the park entrance. Remember to drive slowly and watch out for the cows.

Entrance to the park costs CH$1700 for adults, CH$600 for children. Visitors can enter at any time for information on the park. At Laguna Malleco is a small **campground** among moss-covered trees. (CH$7200 per site with showers and toilets.) If you follow the dirt road 9km further down from the park entrance, you'll reach the **Termas de Tolhuaca,** a hot springs resort with luxury hotel accommodations.

TEMUCO ☎ 45

After three centuries of bloody fighting against gold-hungry Spanish conquistadores and then land-hungry Chilean settlers, the defeated Mapuche laid down their arms and signed a treaty in 1881 on the top of Cerro Ñielol, ceding their land in exchange for peace. The once-proud Mapuche were soon shunted off to small scraps of land far away from that hill, while in its shadow a new city emerged in the very south of the young republic of Chile: Temuco.

In spite of the machinations of early Chilean settlers, the city of Temuco never shook loose its Mapuche roots. Even today, the city maintains the feel of a bustling frontier town, a gateway to Chile's more savage South. First and foremost, Temuco (pop. 280,000) is a transportation and commerce hub that draws people and goods from around Chile—including significant numbers of Mapuche, who live in communities either in the city or in the long stretches of countryside beyond its borders. The city is a good place to learn about the ancient indigenous cultures, both in the above-average Museo Regional de la Araucanía and in the Mapuche craft shops littered throughout the city's lively marketplaces. The presence of several universities and other research institutions has also helped to raise awareness of the city's rich, hybrid cultural heritage.

Despite its ethnic history, the hustle and bustle of Temuco's thriving commercial life has favored convenience over aesthetics. As a result, downtown lacks the charm of older, less frenzied city centers elsewhere in the south. Nevertheless, Temuco provides an indoctrination to Mapuche traditions that can be observed more intimately as you flee south from the old lands of colonial conquest. The city is also an excellent jumping-off point for a range of nearby parks, including the lush forestland of the Monumento Natural Cerro Ñeilol, just a few blocks north of the city center. Fortifying the cultural foundation of the city is its connections to Chile's two literary masters, poets Pablo Neruda and Gabriela Mistral, (Neruda was born nearby in Parral, and Mistral taught school here), although you're unlikely to notice this detail unless you stay at the city's century-old landmark, Hotel Continental, where the two used to lodge.

▌ TRANSPORTATION

Flights: Aeropuerto Maquehue, 7km southwest of Temuco. **Taxi** CH$3000-4000. Alternatively, try one of the several transfer services. **Transfer & Turismo de la Araucanía** (☎/fax 339 900; www.transtouraraucania.cl; info@transtouraraucania.cl) will get you to the airport in 15-20min. for CH$1000-3000. **Tours Plus Transfer** (☎386 000) offers a comparable service.

  LanChile, Bulnes 687 (☎272 312), next to Plaza Aníbal Pinto, on the corner of Varas and Bulnes. Open M-F 9am-1:30pm and 3-7pm, Su 10am-1:30pm. Flies to: **Concepción** (40min., 8:35pm, CH$23,746); **Punta Arenas** (5hr., 6:15pm, CH$113,864) via **Puerto Montt** (45min., CH$14,932); **Santiago** (1¼hr.; 10:25am, 1:20, 7:25, 8:10, 8:35pm; CH$93,932).

Trains: Estación Temuco, Barros Arana 191 (☎233 416), at the very eastern end of Lautaro. There is also a **ticket office** at Bulnes 582 (☎233 522), next to the Sernatur office. Open M-F 9am-7pm, Sa 9am-2pm. Goes to: **Chillán** (7½hr.; 8:30pm; economy CH$2300, tourist CH$2800, *salon* CH$3400); **Santiago** (13hr.; 8:30pm; economy CH$5400, tourist CH$6800, *salon* CH$84,000); **Talca** (9½hr.; 8:30pm; economy CH$3400, tourist CH$4600, *salon* CH$5000).

Buses: Terminal Rodoviario de la Araucaría, Vicente Pérez Rosales 01609 (☎225 005 or 404 040), a 10-15min. drive north of the city center, off the Panamericana. **Colectivos** #11P, 9, and 7 run from the terminal to the city center for CH$250. **Taxis** run between the terminal and Plaza Aníbal Pinto (CH$2000-3000).

  Tur-Bus (☎258 338) goes to: **Angol** (2hr., 2:35 and 7:20pm, CH$1400); **Osorno** (4hr., every hr. 1am-6pm, CH$3100); **Pucón** (2hr., 8 per day 6:35am-7:50pm, CH$2200); **Santiago** (9hr., every 30min. 7am-1pm and 8pm-12:15am, CH$5000); **Villarrica** (1½hr., 8 per day 6:35am-7:50pm, CH$1900).

  Inter Sur (☎258 338) goes to: **Chillán** (4hr., 9 per day 8:45am-10:45pm, CH$3900); **Los Angeles** (2½hr., 8 per day 8:45am-10:45pm, CH$2800); **Osorno** (4hr., 4pm, CH$3100); **Pucón** (2½hr., 5:35pm, CH$2100); **Puerto Montt** (6hr., 4pm, CH$4100); **Santiago** (9hr.; 8:45, 10:30am, noon, 1:20pm; CH$11,000; overnight buses 9:40, 10, 10:30, 10:45pm; CH$13,300).

  Igi Llaima (☎257 074) goes to **Santiago** (9hr.; 9:30, 10, 11:30pm; CH$5000).

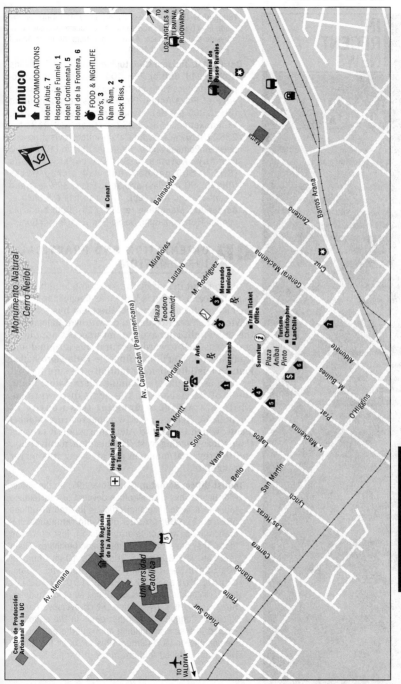

Temuco

▲ ACCOMMODATIONS
Hotel Aitué, **7**
Hospedaje Fumiel, **1**
Hotel Continental, **5**
Hotel de la Frontera, **6**

● FOOD & NIGHTLIFE
Dino's, **3**
Ñam Ñam, **2**
Quick Biss, **4**

Monumento Natural
Cerro Ñeilol

■ Conaf

Balmaceda

Miraflores

Lautaro

M. Rodríguez

Plaza
Teodoro
Schmidt

■ Mercando
Municipal

Av. Caupolicán (Panamericana)

Portales

■ Avis

CTC

■ Turacamb

Sernatur ⓘ

Plaza
Aníbal
Pinto

■ Train Ticket
Office

Turismo
■ Christopher
■ LanChile

M. Montt

Marva

Solar

Varas

Bello

San Martín

Las Heras

Carrera

Blanco

Freire

Prieto Sur

✈ TO
VALDIVIA

Hospital Regional
de Temuco

Museo Regional
de la Araucanía

Centro de Producción
Artesanal de la UC

Universidad
Católica

Av. Alemana

General Mackenna

Zenteno

Barros Arana

Cruz

Aldunate

M. Bulnes

Prat

V. Mackenna

Lagos

O'Higgins

Lynch

$

Terminal de
Buses Rurales

Maria

TO
LOS ÁNGELES &
TERMINAL
RODOVARNO

LAKES DISTRICT

IN RECENT NEWS

[L]EISURELY STROLLS WITH AUGUSTO

Augusto Pinochet, the retired dicta[t]or of Chile, is now a spry eighty-six [y]ears of age, and continues to make a [s]plash on the nation's front pages [f]rom time to time. Politicians in the [l]eft-of-center coalition that ousted him [f]rom power keep trying to figure out if [t]hey really want to see him punished, [o]r if they just want him shoved into a [v]ery dark closet and forgotten.

In 2002, Pinochet made the news [a]s his political opponents demanded [h]is resignation from his post as sena[t]or-for-life, citing his medical diagno[s]is of dementia. The public pressure [w]orked, and Pinochet dropped the [s]inecure and seemed to fade once [a]gain into oblivion. A few weeks later, [h]owever, Pinochet was once again in [t]he news. He was living in Iquique, in [t]he north of Chile, and had taken up [t]he habit of daily walks—with his thug[g]ish armed entourage—through the [c]ity.

One day in July, that armed entou[r]age came upon a car with three men [i]nside with rifles stashed in the back [s]eat. Needless to say, these hired [g]uns were instantly subdued and [a]rrested before a single shot could be [f]ired at the venerable former head of [s]tate.

As it turned out, the deadly rifles [w]ere air rifles, and the "men"—aged [1]6, 17, and 23—had not intended to [p]op the ex-commander-in-chief of the [C]hilean army, but rather, a few liz[a]rds, seagulls, and crabs.

Terminal de Buses Rurales, Pinto 032 (☎210 494), on the corner of Balmaceda and Pinto, serves locations in the countryside around Temuco. A taxi to and from the Plaza Aníbal Pinto costs CH$3000-4000.

Car Rental: Turismo Christopher, Bulnes 667, Oficina 202 (☎211 680 or 218 400; www.turismochristopher.cl; temuco@turismochristopher.cl), on the eastern edge of Plaza Aníbal Pinto. Rents cars starting at CH$25,000 per day. Manual transmission only. **Avis,** V. Mackenna 448 (☎237 575 or 238 013; fax 238013; www.avischile.cl; temuco@avischile.cl), between Portales and Montt. Rates start at CH$24,800 per day, Automatic Subaru Legacy sedans (CH$70,500 per day) and 4x4 pickup trucks (CH$70,500 per day) available. Prices 30% less during off-season. Apr.-Sept. Avis also has a branch at **Aeropeurto Maquehue** (☎337 715). Both branches open M-F 8:30am-8pm, Sa-Su 9am-1pm and 3-8pm.

✈ 🛈 ORIENTATION AND PRACTICAL INFORMATION

Temuco is cut in half by the sweeping length of the Panamericana, which is known as **Caupolicán** within the city center and connects the main bus terminal at Vicente Pérez Rosales to downtown. **Balmaceda,** the other split-lane avenue, intersects Caupolicán and heads east toward the rural bus terminal and train station. You'll also find the **Feria Libre Aníbal Pinto,** a bustling open-air market—be sure to visit by day, as it's unsafe at night. **Plaza Aníbal Pinto,** south of Balmaceda, is the heart of downtown, while **Plaza Teduro Schmidt** lies nearby at Caupolicán. Between the two squares runs **Manuel Montt,** which turns into Alemania when it crosses Caupolicán heading west. The hospital, a university, and the regional musuem are all along this major thoroughfare.

Tourist Office: Sernatur, Claro Solar 897, on the corner with Bulnes, has a small office devoted just to Temuco tourism. A larger, regional office is located at Bulnes 586 (☎211 969; fax 215 509; info.sernatur@chilearaucania.cl; www.chile-araucania.cl), just down the block. They have maps of Temuco and brochures. Open Jan.-Feb. M-F 8:30am-8:30pm, Sa 10am-6pm, Su 10am-2pm; Mar.-Dec. M-F 9am-1:30pm and 3-5pm. **Conaf,** Bilbao 391 (☎298 100, 298210; temuco@conaf.cl; www.conaf.cl), has an office complex. However, the forestry division, which oversees Parque Nacional Conguillío and other parks in the region, is located in a smaller building opposite the entrance to the complex, in its D Corridor (Pasillo D), on the 2nd fl. They offer detailed fold-out maps of Parque Nacional

Conguillío for sale and have a helpful, knowledgeable staff. Open M-F 8:30am-1:30pm and 2-5:30pm.

Tours: Turismo Christopher, Bulnes 667, Oficina 202 (☎211 680; temuco@turismochristopher.cl; www.turismochristopher.cl), on the eastern edge of Plaza Aníbal Pinto. Offers tours of Parque Nacional Conguillío (CH$35,000), Parque Nacional Huerquehue (CH$35,000), Villarrica, Pucón, other scenic areas around Lago Villarrica (CH$35,000), and the Siete Lagos (CH$45,000). Indigenous-area tours to Chol-Chol, Isla Huapi, and Lago Budi (CH$35,000). Open M-F 9am-7:30pm, Sa 10am-5pm.

Bank/ATM: Banco de Chile, Varas 818 (☎207 911), at corner of Varas and Prat. Cashes traveler's checks and US dollars. **24hr. Redbanc ATM.** Open M-F 9am-2pm.

Currency Exchange: Turismo Christopher (see **Tours,** above) changes traveler's checks and various foreign currencies. **Turacamb,** Claro Solar 733 (☎237 829), between V. Mackenna and Prat, changes foreign currency and cashes traveler's checks. Open M-Sa 9am-2pm and 4-8pm.

Laundromat: Marva, Montt 415 (☎952 201), near Caupolicán. Wash and dry single load CH$3000 per load. Open M-F 9am-8:30pm, Sa 9am-7pm.

Police: The *carabineros* (☎211 604) have headquarters at Claro Solar, on the corner with Barros Arana. Another small office (☎211 029) is on a traffic island in the middle of the intersection of Balmaceda and Pinto, across from the Feria Libre.

Late-Night Pharmacies: Farmacias Ahumada, Bulnes 413 (☎237 066 or 211 119), on the corner with Portales. Open 8am-11pm. **Salcobrand,** Montt 701-703 (☎237 321), on the corner of V. Mackenna and Montt. Open M-Sa 9am-10pm.

Hospital: Hospital Regional de Temuco, Montt 115 (☎296 100), between Blanco and Prieto Norte.

Telephones/Fax: Turacamb (see **Currency Exchange,** above) has telephone service through Telefónica CTC. International faxes CH$1200 per page, domestic CH$300. Open M-Sa 9am-2pm and 4-8pm. **CTC,** Montt 629 (☎239 472; fax 239 473), between Lagos and V. Mackenna. International faxes CH$1000 per page, domestic CH$250. Open M-Sa 8am-10pm.

Internet Access: There are a number of Internet cafés on Montt, near Caupolicán, including **Ciber Temuco,** Montt 404 (☎275 817), at the corner with Las Heras. CH$600 per hr., students with ID CH$400. Open 8:30am-4pm. **CTC** (see **Telephone/Fax,** above) also has Internet access. CH$400 per hr.

Post Office: Portales 801 (☎295 100), on the corner with Prat. Open M-F 9am-7pm, Sa 9am-1pm.

After news of the arrests reached the media, government officials immediately urged the ex-dictator to keep a lower profile, and to stop taking his walks in broad daylight. In response, Pinochet's irate aides tartly replied that their boss was not about to "hide" anymore. Besides, a man of eighty-six needs exercise to stay trim.

As for the three would-be assassins, they were questioned and released later that same day. "I would have had to have been crazier than he is to shoot him with a rifle," said Felipe Muñoz, 23, after leaving the police station.

ACCOMMODATIONS

Although one of Chile's more important travel hubs, Temuco is surprisingly short on comfortable lodgings that are worth the price.

Hotel Aitué, Varas 1048 (☎212 512 or 329 191; fax 212 608; reservas@hotelaitue.cl; www.hotelaitue.cl), 2 blocks east of the Plaza de Armas. This small hotel offers comfortably modern rooms with spotless bathrooms. Attentive staff. Cable TV, private parking, laundry service, minibar, security safes, and central heating (radiators) are available. Internet access CH$2500 per hr. Breakfast included. English spoken. Reservations recommended 1 week in advance. Singles CH$28,000; doubles CH$33,000; triples CH$40,900. IVA discount available to foreigners paying cash. AmEx/MC/V. ❺

Hotel Continental, Varas 708 (☎238 973; fax 233 830; hcontine@ctcinternet.cl), across from Quick Biss restaurant. As the former residence of Chilean poet Pablo Neruda, fellow Nobel laureate Gabriela Mistral, and ex-President Salvador Allende, this hotel has had its share of famous guests. And although this 113-year-old hotel may be a bit past its prime, if you don't mind dark hallways and old-fashioned accommodations, the rooms are actually quite charming, with their plaid bed spreads and hardwood floors. Radiator heating, private parking, and laundry service available. Breakfast included. Reservations recommended up to 4 days in advance Jan.-Feb. Singles with shared bath in hallway CH$9000, with shared bath between adjoining rooms CH$15,000, with private bath CH$17,000; doubles CH$16,000/CH$20,000/CH$25,000; triples CH$21,000/CH$25,000/CH$30,000; quads with private bath CH$35,000. AmEx/MC/V. ❸

Hotel de la Frontera, Bulnes 726 (☎200 400; fax 200 401; r726@hotelfrontera.cl), just south of Plaza Aníbal Pinto. This luxury hotel has pleasant, well-heated rooms with an indulgent amount of hot shower water—though the beds themselves are rather limp. Private parking, laundry service, central heating, cable TV, minibar. Free Internet access. Breakfast included. Reservations recommended in advance. Singles or doubles CH$31,900; triples CH$39,500; suites CH$54,000. AmEx/MC. ❺

Hospedaje Furniel, Claro Solar 625 (☎313 327), between Lagos and V. Mackenna. This is one of the cheapest places you'll find in Temuco—and it shows, with drab, musty rooms, sagging mattresses, and forlorn bathrooms. Parking CH$2000 per night. Gas-burning space heaters. Rooms with shared bath CH$3500 per person. ❶

FOOD

Temuco doesn't have any culinary specialties of its own, but it attracts quite a few national chains while providing Chilean staples at reasonable prices. For cheap eats, the **Mercado Municipal** is the best place, with its innumerable food stands serving all types of Chilean dishes. (Entrances on Rodríguez, Portales, and Aldunate. Open in the summer, M-Sa 8am-8pm, Su 8:30am-4pm; rest of year M-Sa 8am-7pm, Su 8:30am-4pm.)

Dino's, Bulnes 360 (☎403 301), between Rodríguez and Portales. Don't be deterred by the beaming green dinosaur waving a fork on the restaurant's sign—inside the dining is quite classy, and quite pricey. Entrees include a wide range of pastas, fish, and meats (CH$3450-6900). If beef is your thing, try the *Escalopa "Dino's,"* a slab of steak draped in ham and cheese (CH$5500). Downstairs cafe open M-Sa 8:30am-midnight, Su 11am-7pm. Restaurant open M-Sa noon-4pm and 7:30pm-midnight, Su noon-4pm. AmEx/MC/V. ❸

Hotel Continental, Varas 708 (☎238 9731; fax 233 830), restaurant is inside hotel, straight through the doors to the right of the reception desk. This French-style dining hall within the venerable hotel boasts old-world charm, with high ceilings, marked hardwood floors, and polished bronze chandeliers casting a moody light on the white tablecloths. Entrees CH$2900-5400, pasta CH$3300-4100, tortillas CH$2900-3500, salads CH$1200-3500. Open 12:30-3:30pm and 8-10:30pm. AmEx/MC/V. ❸

Quick Biss, Varas 755 (☎211 219 or 237 504), between V. Mackenna and Prat. This branch of the nationwide chain allows for fast dining, with a lunchtime self-service center where you pick and choose among individually-priced entrees and appetizers (noon-4pm only). Quick Biss also has offerings suitable for more leisurely dinners, such as the steak (CH$2100) and the lemon-seasoned boneless chicken breast (CH$1700). Hamburgers CH$1150-1750, hot dogs CH$550-650, sandwiches CH$1100-1550, pizzas CH$1320-1820. A smattering of vegetarian options are available. Open M-Sa 8:30am-10pm, Su 9am-4pm. AmEx/MC/V. ❶

Ñam Ñam, Portales 802 (☎316 282), on the corner of Portales and Prat. Sit in the old-fashioned leather-lined booths in this bustling sandwich shop and you'll find yourself wreathed in cigarette smoke within minutes. Still, it's a good place to go for *churrascos* (CH$1250-2350), hamburgers (CH$750-1550), and other sandwiches (CH$630-2850). Lunch specials CH$1290-1590. Open 9am-midnight. AmEx/ MC/V. ❶

■ SHOPPING

Temuco is a modern metropolis ringed by countryside, situated advantageously close to significant Mapuche settlements and other communities where traditional ways of life have not yet died. What's more, Temuco is the main transport hub in the Chilean South—all of which makes the city an excellent place to pick up fine Chilean pottery, wood carvings, and wool items. The **Mercado Municipal** is a good place to start: an entire city block chock-full of small handicraft shops and food stands, it is one of the largest liveliest municipal markets in all of Chile. (See intro to **Food,** p. 356). If you're looking for fine indigenous craftsmanship, head to the **Casa de la Mujer Mapuche,** Prat 283, on the eastern edge of Plaza Teodoro Schmidt. It is a collective run by Mapuche women from communities throughout the region who work in clay, wool, and cloth in traditional styles. (☎233 886. Open M-F 9:30am-1pm and 3-6pm. In summer, also open Sa 10am-6pm.) The **Centro de Producción Artesanal de La Universidad Católica,** Alemania 0442 (☎212 081 or 205 306), on the corner of 18 de Septiembre and Alemania, a few blocks west of the Museo Regional, is another excellent place to look for Mapuche workmanship, especially for silver and ceramic works. (Open M and W 9am-1pm and 3-6pm; T, Th, F 9am-1pm and 3-7pm; longer hours in the summer.)

For a wilder shopping experience, keep a firm hand on your pocketbook and head out to the **Feria Libre Aníbal Pinto,** located along Pinto near the train station. Among the swirling crowds you'll find rows upon row of stands selling fruits, vegetables, meats, dairy products, and crafts—about 700 in total. Locals describe this area as *superpeligroso* (very dangerous), especially at night, so watch where you go and keep an eye on your belongings at all times. (☎210 968. Open M-Sa 8am-6pm, Su 8am-4pm.)

◎ SIGHTS

Temuco is unexpectedly low on tourist attractions, and those that exist tend to be somewhat of a long walk from the central plaza (fortunately, *colectivos*, taxis, and buses are not in short supply). A convenient place to start a tour of the city is at the **Plaza Aníbal Pinto,** located between Bulnes and Prat and Claro Solar and Varas. In the center of the plaza, ringed by palm trees, is the **Monumento a la Araucanía,** which pays homage to the many threads of culture that have been woven into modern Temuco, from defiant Mapuche warriors to Chilean soldiers.

MUSEO REGIONAL DE LA ARAUCANÍA. The Museo Regional is housed in a pleasant white adobe house with green roof tiles, dating back to 1924. Surrounded by towering trees—palms and even a California sequoia—the museum is worth a visit, even if just for its peaceful setting. On the first floor you'll find a sizable collection of Mapuche pottery, wooden masks, and weavings. The second floor is devoted to history, including displays from Spanish armor and rifles dating to the Spanish conquest in the 16th century, to old photographs of Mapuche forced into reservations *(reducciones)* in the 19th century. Unlike many other museums in Chile, the Museo Regional de la Araucanía has stylish, professional-looking interpretive signage in Spanish, with *mapudungun* (the Mapuche tongue) translation for the exhibits on the first floor. *(Alemania 084. Walk west on Montt from the central plaza. Montt turns into Alemania once it crosses Caupolicán. The musuem is just past the hospital and the Universidad Católica. Colectivos and buses head in that direction on Montt. ☎ 730 062. Open M-F 9am-5pm, Sa 11am-5pm, Su 11am-2pm. CH$600, children CH$300. Free Su.)*

MONUMENTO NATURAL CERRO ÑIELOL. The 89 hectares of tree-studded hilltop, at 200m above sea level, that comprise the Monumento Natural Cerro Ñielol, provide splendid views of the city and the surrounding countryside. In fact, the view is so good that there is an observatory at the very top—the Observatorio Volcanológico de los Andes del Sur (SERNAGEOMIN)—the only one of its kind in Chile. The park houses a native forest of lingüe, laurel, raulí, coigüe, and oak trees, and among them you might be able to spot the Copihue, Chile's national flower. Considering how close the park is to downtown Temuco, there is an amazingly wide assortment of wildlife hiding in the woods—buff-necked ibises, foxes, and even the *monito del monte*, the smallest marsupial in the world. On its grounds you'll find walking trails, picnic sites, and even a restaurant nestled amid the forest grounds and small lakes. Conaf administers the park. *(Observatory ☎ 270 700, not normally open to the public. For information about the park, contact Conaf's Temuco office at Bilbao 391. See **Tourist Office,** p. 354. The park entrance is located at the northern end of Prat, several blocks north of the city center. ☎ 298 222. Open Oct.-Mar. 8:30am-10pm, rest of the year 8:30am-8pm; those visiting on foot should leave before sundown. The park's Environmental Information Center, the Centro de Información Ambiental, is open from 8:30am-6pm, Oct.-Mar. until 7pm. CH$700, children 12 and under CH$200.)*

PARQUE NACIONAL CONGUILLÍO ☎ 43

The ⚑**Parque Nacional Conguillío's** two most prominent features are a smoldering volcano and a serene lake. Throughout 60,832 hectares of unspoiled wilderness, the park embodies vivid contrasts: on its northern stretches lie dense thickets of *araucaria*, a vast forest that has lingered there for millennia; while toward **Volcán Llaima** (3125m) in the south sprawls a wasteland of hardened lava, evidence of the still active volcano's periodic outbursts (its last major eruption was in 1957). The diversity of landscape translates into an impressive range of hiking options, from

AT A GLANCE	
AREA: 60,832 hectares.	**HIGHLIGHTS:** Hiking Sendero las Vertintes and Sendero Travesía a Malalcahuello.
CLIMATE: Temperate; Nov.-Mar. average 15°C; June-July average 6°C; annual rainfall 2000mm.	
	GATEWAYS: Temuco via Vilcún, Curacautín, or Melipueco.
FEATURES: Volcán Llaima and Lago Conguillío.	
FEES: CH$2800, children CH$800.	**CAMPING:** Plentiful sites at Lago Conguillío (CH$12,000) and Laguna Captrén (CH$8000).

Parque Nacional Conguillío

Curacautín
R. Cautín
Termas de Manzanar
Manzanar
Malalcahuelto
Lonquimay
Salto de la Princessa
Estero Valgara
Tunel las Raices
CORDILLERA DE LAS RAICE
R. Captren
Termas Río Blanco
R. Lonquimay
Reserva Nacional Lago Gualletue
Laguna Quepe
Guardaparque
Lago Conguillío
Administracion Centro de Visitantes
Volcán Llaima 3125m
Quinquen
Laguna Gualletue
R. Quetrojeutun
TO VOLCÁN TEMUCO
Centro de Esqui las Araucarias
Salto de Truful
R. Trufquennahue
Guardaparque
R. Rilpe
Cerro Allillonco 1314m
Reserva Nacional China Muerta
Reduccion Laguna de Iclama
Icalma
Melipeuco
R. Allipen
0   4 miles
0   4 kilometers

simple 800m walks past lush vegetation on **Sendero las Vertintes,** near the southern guard post, to daunting multiple-day expert hikes over ice and snow. To hike the **Sendero Travesía a Malalcahuello,** an estimated 48hr. excursion, regulations require you to bring climbing equipment and report your route to the park authorities before embarking. Visitors are also allowed to hike their way to the volcano's center, provided they show credentials verifying their climbing experience and bring the necessary gear; it's an 8hr. trek, if all goes well, but park staff say that the view of the surrounding landscape from the volcano's 3125m summit will blow you away (if the high altitude winds don't).

There are three approaches to the park: one through the turns of Vilcún and Cherquenco from the west (50km from Temuco to **Vilcún,** and then 30km over a dirt road from Vilcún to **Sector Los Paraguas** within the park). Another route goes through **Curacautín** from the north (35km over dirt roads). A third approach is from **Melipueco** from the south (22km over dirt roads). All these towns can be reached from Temuco by bus (see Temuco **Transportation,** p. 352). A taxi from Curacautín to the park is CH$8000.

The park is open year-round, but during the winter, heavy snowfalls block off many of the trails and permit access only from the west and south. (Open Nov.-Apr. 8:30am-6pm. CH$2800, children CH$800.) A small ski center is located on the western end of the park, in Sector Los Paraguas. **Centro de Esquí Las Araucarias** is open June September, snow permitting.

The park has **campgrounds** at the southern edge of **Lago Conguillío** (90 sites) and a smaller 11-site camping area at **Laguna Captrén** to the west. (Sites have hot showers, toilets, and sinks. Lago Conguillío sites Jan.-Apr. CH$12,000; Nov.-Dec. CH$9000. The sites at Laguna Captrén are comparable but cost CH$8000.) *Cabañas* with kitchens, private baths, and hot water are also available at Lago Conguillío, between Nov.-Apr. for CH$35,000 (for up to 8 people) or CH$50,000 (for up to 12). For reservations, call **Conaf** in Temuco (☎ 45 298 213).

More information about Parque Nacional Conguillío can be obtained at Conaf's Temuco office, Bilbao 391, just north of Caupolicán, at the center of Bulnes. The division of Conaf that handles national parks can be found in the smaller building opposite the entrance, in Pasillo, on the second floor. (☎ 45 298 100 or 45 298 210; www.conaf.cl or www.parquenacionalconguillio.cl; temuco@conaf.cl. Open M-F 8:30am-1:30pm and 2-5:30pm).

LAGO VILLARRICA

VILLARRICA   ☎ 45

Villarrica (also spelled "Villa-Rica") has long sat in the shadow of its perfectly picturesque sister, Pucón—even locals here admit that their neighbor across the lake is a little more aesthetically pleasing. Nevertheless, Villarrica is worth the trouble for those looking for more than (pricey) thrills: not only is it easier on the wallet than Pucón, but it is also quieter, with smaller mobs of carousing tourists in the summertime, and a magnificent view of Lago Villarrica, in all its varied shades of blue. The area around Villarrica also has a significant Mapuche population, who are proud and up front about their heritage. As a result, Villarrica is an excellent place to learn about the indigenous culture, and also pick up some authentic handicrafts. Beware the months outside of December-February, though—it is decidedly wet, and when it rains in Villarrica, it rains for weeks.

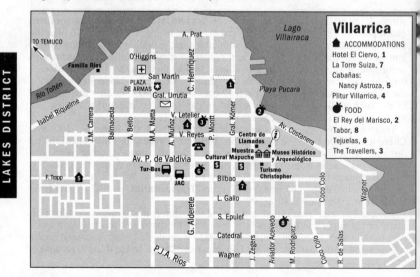

Villarrica

🏠 ACCOMMODATIONS
Hotel El Ciervo, **1**
La Torre Suiza, **7**
Cabañas:
  Nancy Astroza, **5**
  Plitur Villarrica, **4**

🍴 FOOD
El Rey del Marisco, **2**
Tabor, **8**
Tejuelas, **6**
The Travellers, **3**

LAKES DISTRICT

⊏ TRANSPORTATION

Buses: The two major bus lines are **Tur Bus** and **Jac,** which have terminals facing each other across Anfión Muñoz, a block south of Pedro de Valdivia.

Tur Bus, Anfión Muñoz 657 (☎413 652), goes to **Pucón** (25min.; every hr. 8am-9:15pm; Dec.-Mar. CH$400, Apr.-Nov. CH$300) and **Temuco** (1¼hr.; every hr. 7:20am-12:50pm, every 2hr. 12:50-9:25pm; Dec.-Mar. CH$2100, Apr.-Nov. CH$1900).

Jac, Bilbao 610 (☎411 447), to: **Lican Ray** (30min.; every 15min. 7am-9:15pm; Dec.-Feb. CH$400, Apr.-Nov. CH$300); **Pucón** (30min.; every 15min. 7am-9:15am; CH$300, Dec.-Feb. CH$400); **Temuco** (1½hr., every 30min. 6:25am-9:20pm, CH$2000); **Valdivia** (2¼hr.; 7, 9, 11:15am, 4:30, 7pm; CH$1900).

Lago Villarrica/Seven Lakes

Taxis/Colectivos: Taxis cost CH$800 for anywhere in the city and can be found near the bus stations along Anfión Muñoz (CH$1000 after midnight). *Colectivos* (CH$200) and buses (CH$150) run a circuit through the city center (Camilo Henríquez and Pedro de Valdivia), along Pedro de Valdivia, and around the circle inscribed by Carrera, San Martín, and Anfión Muñoz. *Colectivos* only run from 7am-10pm.

Car Rental: Turismo Christopher, Pedro de Valdivia 1033 (☎414 230), across from the museum and tourist office. Rates start at CH$30,000 per day. Manual transmission vehicles only.

Bike Rental: The hostel **La Torre Suiza** (see **Accommodations,** p. 363) rents out bikes for CH$5000 per day.

◼ ▮ ORIENTATION AND PRACTICAL INFORMATION

Villarrica is located 85km south of Temuco, on the western edge of Lago Villarrica, 25km east of Pucón. It is easily walkable, a few blocks of short storefronts and houses stretching out from the lip of Lago Villarrica. The main thoroughfare, **Av. Pedro de Valdivia,** cuts across the town center from west to east; **Camilo Henríquez** bisects it from the north, and becomes Alderete heading further south. Most of the banks and shops are clustered around that main intersection. The **Plaza de Armas** lies three blocks north and two blocks west of that intersection, where you'll find the hospital, post office, and police.

Tourist Office: The municipality has its **Oficina de Turismo** at Pedro de Valdivia 1070 (☎206 619 or 206 618; fax 206 641; turis@entelchile.net; www.villarrica.co.cl), next to the museum and public library. They offer maps of Villarrica and the Lago Villarrica area. Pick up *Datos Araucanía* for a schedule of events here and in Pucón. In summer open M-F 8:30am-9pm, in winter 9am-6pm.

Tours: Familia Ríos, San Martín 256 (☎412 408), at the very western end of San Martín, offers fishing tours in rowboats on Lago Villarrica (CH$5000 per hr.) and at selected spots along the length of Río Toltén. There are also river trips to the Prado Chico fishing site (3hr. CH$25,000, 8hr. CH$50,000). The fishing season begins the second week of Nov. and lasts until the first week of May. Tour rates are for 2 people accompanied by one guide. Open 8am-9pm. **Politur Villarrica,** Camilo Henríquez 475 (☎/fax 414 547; foresta007@hotmail.com; politurvillarrica.enynter.net or www.politur.com), between Valentín Letelier and Vicente Reyes, usually with a placard in the sidewalk outside advertising tours. Open M-Sa 9am-1:30pm and 3-9pm; Su 9am-1:30pm and 7-9pm. Tours include the following:

Ascents of Volcán Villarrica: The company will supply you with slides to transport you down the volcano slopes in style (4-5hr. up, 50min. down; 6:30am, returns 6pm; min. 2-people; CH$22,000 per person, includes all necessary equipment). From July-Nov., they also offer *ski randonee* ascents of the volcano. Skiers wear special skis that permit uphill hiking and then skiing down. Snowboarders have the option of lugging their boards up the mountain and grinding on down (intermediate and expert skiers only; CH$29,000). English-speaking guides available.

White-water rafting: There are packages on the upper and lower rapids of nearby Río Trancura, which include transport, equipment, and an English-speaking guide accompanying the raft in a kayak. The gruelling up-river excursion amounts to 2hr. of Class IV or V rapids suitable only for experienced rafters. Rapids are roughest during the winter. (4hr.; Nov.-Mar. CH$12,000 per person, Apr.-Oct. CH$15,000 per person, groups of 6-7 CH$12,000 per person). There are also outings to the slightly tamer lower stretches of Río Trancura. The hour of Class III rapids isn't smooth sailing but the tour company claims it's suitable even for kids (3hr.; Nov.-Mar. CH$5000 per person, Apr.-Oct. CH$8000 per person, groups CH$5000 per person).

Other packages: Trips available to the ritzy **Termas Huife hot springs resort,** 33km east of Pucón, or to the more rustic **Termas Los Pozones** a little farther down the road, where you'll bathe among the rocks outdoors. (10:20am; Nov.-Mar. returns 8pm, Apr.-Oct. 6pm. Huife CH$15,000 per person, Pozones CH$14,000 per person). Guided tours of the frozen lakes and snow-buried trails of **Parque Nacional Huerqueque** (snow trekking gear included; CH$15,000 per person). Round-trip transport to the **ski center** on Volcán Villarrica (ski equipment rental CH$5000; 9am, returns 6pm; CH$5000 per person).

Currency Exchange: Turismo Christopher, Pedro de Valdivia 1033 (☎414 230), across from the museum and tourist office. Changes traveler's checks, US dollars, and Argentine pesos. Open Dec.-Mar. M-F 9:30am-2pm and 4-10pm, Su 9:30am-2pm and 4-8pm; Apr.-Nov. M-F 9:30am-2pm and 5:30-10pm, Sa 9:30am-1:30pm.

Bank/ATM: Banco de Chile, Pedro de Valdivia 799 (☎411 668), on the corner with Montt. Has a **24hr. Redbanc ATM.** Open M-F 9am-2pm. **Banco Estado,** Pedro de Valdivia 957 (☎411 085), across from the Municipalidad. Open M-F 9am-2pm.

Work Opportunity: Politur Villarrica (see **Tours,** p. 362) looks for up to two guides or office workers to help out Dec.-Feb. and possibly at other times of the year. Contact Erna Avello Aedo. For details, see **Alternatives to Tourism,** p. 84.)

Library: Biblioteca Pública Dictino Niño de la Horra, Pedro de Valdivia 1050 (☎412 445), on the corner with Julio Zegers. Open M-F 9am-1pm and 3-7pm.

Market: There are traditional craft stores scattered all throughout the downtown area. One of the better ones is **Feria Artesenal Huimpay,** Julio Zegers 570 (☎410 003), next to the Mapuche *ruca* on the corner with Pedro de Valdivia. This market sells all sorts of objects fashioned by local artisans—from polished wooden toys to wool scarves and leather purses. Open Jan.-Feb. 9am-midnight, Mar.-Dec. 10am-6pm.

Emergency: ☎133.

Police: The *carabineros* have their headquarters at M.A. Matta 230 (☎411 433), on the eastern end of the Plaza de Armas.

Hospital: Hospital Villarrica, San Martín 460 (☎411 169), on the northern end of the Plaza de Armas.

Telephones/Fax: Centro de Llamados, Camilo Henríquez 590 (☎410 965 or 410 961), just north of Pedro de Valdivia. Offers telephone service through CTC. International faxes CH$1500 per page, domestic CH$300. Open Dec.-Mar. 8:30am-midnight, Apr.-Nov. 8:30am-10pm.

Internet Access: Centro de Llamados (See **Telephones/Fax,** above) will connect you. CH$1000 per hr.

Post Office: Anfión Muñoz 315 (☎412 860), near the Plaza de Armas. Open M-F 9am-1pm and 2:30-6pm, Sa 9am-1pm.

ACCOMMODATIONS

As the less fashionable sister of the two towns along the lake, Villarrica has had to find a different tactic to woo travelers. Rather than bombarding them with sensory pleasures, Villarrica recognizes the true way to a tourist's heart—through her pocketbook. On almost every block of the town, and especially near the lake, you'll find cheerfully painted signs advertising *cabañas* and *hospedajes*, and the prices tend to be well below what you'll find just across Lago Villarrica.

La Torre Suiza, Francisco Bilbao 969 (☎/fax 411 213; info@torresuiza.com; www.torresuiza.com), between General Körner and Julio Zegers. It sounds like a *Let's Go* backpackers' dream adventure: Beat and Claudia Zbinden quit their jobs in Switzerland and began a 2½-year journey on bike through Asia, Australia, New Zealand, and South

America, landing in Villarrica and setting up a little hostel geared to other wayfarers far from home. The 3-story building does "tower" over its vertically challenged neighbor, but inside, the 9 new rooms and their bathrooms are low-ceilinged and cozy. The Zbindens are a great source of information on local adventure touring. English spoken. Book exchange, wood-burning stove, laundry (CH$3000), parking. Internet access CH$1000 per hr. Breakfast included. Reservations during summer recommended. Dorms Sept.-May CH$5000 per person, June-Aug. CH$4000; doubles CH$12,000/CH$10,000, with private bath CH$15,000/CH$12,000. ❷

Hotel El Ciervo, General Körner 241 (☎411 215; fax 410 925; reserva@elciervo.cl; www.elciervo.cl), north of General Urrutia, to the left of a pedestrian walkway. Don't be scared off by the antlered *ciervo* (stag) skulls near the hotel entrance—this four-decade-old converted German mansion offers some of the finest lodging to be had in Villarrica, at fairly reasonable prices. The colorful floral-print bedspreads, plaid chairs and stools, and aroma of potpourri give the rooms a homey feel. Gleaming white bathrooms and views of the smoldering Volcán Villarrica add to the experience. Outdoor pool, central heating, private parking, laundry facilities. Internet access CH$500 per hr. Breakfast included. English spoken. Reservations recommended 1 week in advance. Singles in main building Dec.-Feb. CH$35,000, Mar.-Nov. CH$24,000, in annex CH$30,000/CH$20,500; doubles CH$47,000/CH$32,000, in annex CH$40,000/CH$27,500; suites CH$57,000/CH$38,000; additional beds CH$14,000/CH$10,000. ❺

Plitur Villarrica, Camilo Henríquea 475 (☎414 547; foresta007@hotmail.com; politurvillarrica.enynter.net), north of Pedro de Valdivia. Like many establishments in Villarrica and Pucón, this travel agency doubles as a *hospedaje*, offering 4 serviceable if unexciting rooms on the top floor, with hardwood floors and shared bathrooms. Reception M-Sa 9am-1:30pm and 3-9pm, Su 9am-1:30pm and 7-9pm. Laundry facilities. Internet access CH$800 per hr. English spoken. Reservations recommended. Pickup from bus terminal available. Doubles Nov.-Mar. CH$5000, Apr.-Oct. CH$3500. ❷

Cabañas: If you don't mind being a bit outside the town center, call up **Nancy Astroza,** Federico Trapp 157 (☎419 558), to reserve the comfy *cabaña* just behind her house. Señora Astroza is a kind-hearted woman who is very familiar with all of the private *cabañas* in the area and runs her own with her bubbly daughters and granddaughters. The 2-story *cabaña* can house up to 5 people in its 2 bedrooms and full kitchen and bath. Jan.-Feb. CH$15,000, Mar.-Dec. CH$12,000. ❹

🍴 FOOD

Seafood is an obvious specialty for a lakeside town like Villarrica, but locals also pride themselves on their savory *cazuelas*—rich beef stews laden with sweet potatoes and a creamy mush of rice.

🍴 **The Travellers,** Velentín Letelier 753 (☎/fax 412 830; intertravellers@mixmail.com; www.surf.to/travellers), between Camilo Henríquez and Montt. Just off Villarrica's broadway, you'll find what might be Chile's most cosmopolitan restaurant south of Santiago—a delightful mix of cultures, exuberantly displayed in the wide range of food on the menu (Asian, European, and Panamerican), the prints on the wall, and the grooving music. Try the curry fried rice, with sliced beef, prawns, and veggies (CH$3950) or just kick back at one of the bare, wooden tables with a mug of Schop (CH$1000) and amuse yourself with the decks of cards and other games they have available. Wide variety of Chinese noodle and rice dishes CH$2300-3750, dinner entrees CH$3250-4950. Open Dec.-Mar. 9am-3am, Apr.-Nov. 10:30am-1am. AmEx/MC/V. ❸

El Rey del Marisco, Valentín Letelier 1030 (☎412 093), on the shorefront near Julio Zegers. The fabulous seafood at El Rey is prepared by local chef extraordinary Daniel Leighton. His cozy restaurant at the eastern end of town has a view of the striking blue backdrop of Lago Villarrica. Even a simple dish like *crema de espárragos* (CH$1200) is heavenly from his kitchen. Try the *parrillada marisco* (CH$5200), an exuberant medley of grilled clams, mussels, calamari, baby shrimp, and salmon. Various fish dishes CH$3100-5300. Open M-Sa 11am-4pm and 7-11pm, Su 11am-4pm. AmEx/MC/V. ❸

Tabor, Saturnino Epulef 1187 (☎411 901), between Acevedo and Rodríguez, 3 blocks south of Pedro de Valdivia. Seashell chandeliers hang from the ceiling and fat wooden fish decorate the walls at this fine seafood restaurant. The adventurous should try the *erIzos al matico* (CH$4900), sliced-up sea urchins doused in lemon juice, diced onions and cilantro, though those with weaker stomachs will be better off with the *congrío paraíso*, sea bass lovingly drenched in a cream sauce of crab meat and baby shrimp (CH$4700). Fish entrees CH$3800-5200. Open 11:30am-midnight. AmEx/MC/V. ❸

Tejuelas, Gerónimo de Alderete 632 (☎410 619), near the intersection with Pedro de Valdivia. Here they serve up sandwiches (CH$1600-2200) and pizzas (CH$2900-4500), but this is really a place to get a good, stiff drink. Try that bizarre mix of orange Fanta and beer, the *fanschop* (CH$800). Open Nov.-Mar. 9am-midnight, Apr.-Oct. M-Sa 9am-midnight, Su 7pm-midnight. ❷

🔆 SIGHTS

Villarrica's most breathtaking scenic attractions are, of course, Lago Villarrica and Volcán Villarrica—the latter, though some 30km away, is visible in all its fuming glory throughout the town. To enjoy the lake, head out to **Playa Pucara,** at the intersection of General Urrutia and Julio Zegers. Once a volcanic black sand beach, it's now more of a muddy grass field than a beach. Nevertheless, it's still a great place to admire the huge expanse of softly undulating water. Head farther north along the lake's edge and you'll eventually reach the **Embarcadero Municipal,** a wide, concrete dock where locals tie up their boats. Take a stroll down that narrow pier and you'll be close enough to touch the water. Here, you can fully appreciate the mist-shrouded mountains in the distance and the incredible array of blues that paint the horizon.

Villarrica also has an active indigenous community and, during the summer, the town draws Mapuche from all over the area, who congregate at the **Muestra Cultural Mapuche** at the corner of Pedro de Valdivia and Julia Zegers. There, Mapuche artisans sell handmade crafts and clothing and also have demonstrations of their centuries-old traditions of weaving, jewelry, and craft making. Year-round, you'll find on the grounds a straw **ruca,** the traditional dwelling of Mapuche families, which was erected in 1998 after four days of work by six Mapuche masters. The straw roof has been treated with smoke to make it impenetrable to water, and animal skins cover the earth floor. (Muestra Cultural Mapuche open from first Monday of Jan. until Feb. 25 daily 9am-11pm. Free.)

Just down the road from the *ruca,* on the top floor of the public library, you'll find the small but enthusiastically run **Museo Histórico y Arqueológico Municipal de Villa-Rica,** Pedro de Valdivia 1050. On display is a wide assortment of Mapuche paraphernalia, including grinding stones made from volcanic rock, ceremonial wood and leather drums (the *kultrún*) and other musical instruments, pouches made of animal scrotums and bladders and a fascinating selection of silver stirrups. The helpful museum staff is glad to show you the collection and even tell you the complex meaning behind the *kultrún* drum. (☎413 445. Open Jan.-Mar. 15 M-Sa 9:30am-1pm and 6-10pm, Su 6-10pm; off-season M-F 9:30am-1pm and 3:30-7pm. CH$100.)

LAKES DISTRICT

PUCÓN   ☎45

The charming town of Pucón looks like it was made to be on a postcard—oh-so-quaint wooden cabins line leafy streets at the ashen lip of a vast still lake in the shadow of mist-ringed mountains. Towering over everything is the picturesque Volcán Villarrica, the most active volcano in South America, a smoldering core of pent-up geological angst, just minutes away from downtown. Unlike Villarrica, Pucón has learned to exploit its natural bounty to the hilt—numerous guides hawk tours of the volcano and the river rapids to the hordes of tourists that inundate the town in the summer. Once you've sampled some of Pucón's fine international cuisine, enjoyed a few glittering sunsets on its lakeside beach, and lost several week's wages at Hotel del Lago's gleaming casino, you'll want to leap into one or many of the nearby national attractions, such as climbing onto the crater's edge at Volcán Villarrica, whitewater rafting on the famous Río Trancura, horseback riding in the vast parkland, or unwinding in the pungent warmth of the numerous nearby hotsprings resorts.

⌐ TRANSPORTATION

Flights: Aeroport Necluman (☎878 8914 for the administrator), 6km east of Pucón. A **taxi** there will cost you CH$2000. This very small airport operates only during summer and for special holiday flights. **LanChile** has 2 flights per week to **Santiago** in summer.

Buses: JAC, Uruguay 505 (☎443 693), 2 blocks south of O'Higgins along Palguin, goes to: **Lican Ray** (30min.; M-Sa every 10min. 7am-9:30pm, Su every 10min. 8am-9:30; Nov.-Mar. CH$400, Apr.-Oct. CH$300); **Temuco** (2hr.; M-Sa every 30min. 6am-8:30pm, Su every hr. 7am-8:30pm; CH$2300); **Valdivia** (3hr.; M-Sa 6:15, 8:15, 10:30am, 3:45, 6:15pm; Su 8:15, 10:30am, 3:45, 6:15pm; CH$2100); **Villarrica** (30min.; M-Sa every 10min. 7am-9:30pm, Su every 10min. 8am-9:30pm; Nov.-Mar. CH$400, Apr.-Oct. CH$300). Additional buses during the summertime. **Tur Bus,** O'Higgins 910 (☎443 328), a 10min. walk east on O'Higgins out of town, goes to: **Temuco** (30min.; M-Sa 8 per day 6:45am-7:45pm, Su 7 per day 7:50am-7:45pm, CH$400); **Valdivia** (3hr., Su 10:30am, CH$2200); **Villarrica** (30min.; M-Sa 8 per day 6:45am-7:45pm, Su 7 per day 7:50am-7:45pm; CH$400).

Taxis/Colectivos: Taxis can easily be found on O'Higgins and the Plaza de Armas. CH$1000 anywhere in town. *Colectivos* run along O'Higgins and elsewhere throughout town (8am-9pm CH$250, 9pm-midnight CH$350).

Car Rental: Sierra Nevada Rent a Car has two branches in Pucón: one at O'Higgins 524 (☎444 210; fax 444 214; sierranevada@entelchile.net; www.sierranevadaitgo.com), on the northeast corner with Palguin; another at O'Higgins 211 (☎099 585 0249), on the corner with Lincoyán. Offers manual transmission 4X4 trucks (CH$30,000-33,000 per day, off-season CH$28,000-30,000), as well as cars, some of them automatics (CH$25,000-28,000 per day, off-season CH$20,000-25,000). Insurance (with CH$400,000 deductible) included. Reserve at least 1 day before in summertime. Open Dec.-Mar. 8:30am-9pm, Apr.-Nov. 9am-7pm. AmEx/MC/V. **Turismo Christopher** (see **Currency Exchange,** p. 369) rents cars starting at CH$20,000 per day. Offers jeeps and trucks, but no automatic transmission vehicles.

Bike Rental: Turismo M@yra (see **Tours,** p. 368). Rents mountain bikes for CH$5000 per day. Will provide maps and information on self-guided half- or full-day bike tours to Lago Caburgua and the Ojos de Caburgua, a series of subterranean pools of water.

Ski Rental: Sol y Nieve (see **Tours,** p. 368) rents ski equipment (boots, poles, and skis) for CH$7000 per day. Rents snowboard equipment (boots and board) for CH$11,000

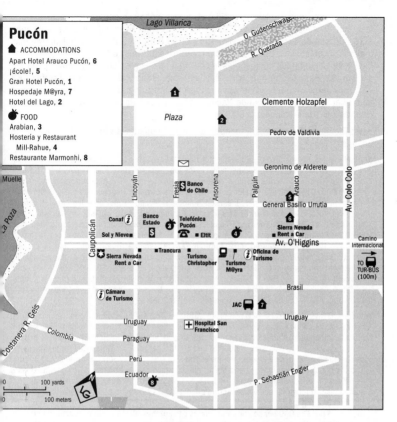

Pucón

🏠 ACCOMMODATIONS
Apart Hotel Arauco Pucón, 6
¡école!, 5
Gran Hotel Pucón, 1
Hospedaje M@yra, 7
Hotel del Lago, 2

🍎 FOOD
Arabian, 3
Hostería y Restaurant
  Mill-Rahue, 4
Restaurante Marmonhi, 8

LAKES DISTRICT

per day. Available June-Aug. only. **Turismo M@yra** (see **Tours,** p. 368) rents skis (CH$5000 per day), ski *randunee* equipment (CH$12,000 per day), and snowboards (CH$10,000 per day).

✳ 🔢 ORIENTATION AND PRACTICAL INFORMATION

Seven-block-wide Pucón lies on the eastern edge of Lago Villarica, 25km down the road from the town of Villarrica. The east-west span of **O'Higgins** is the town's main thoroughfare, which during busier months looks like a catwalk for all the 4WD pick-ups and SUVs to strut their stuff. Along this strip you will find a horde of adventure tour outfits, alongside upper-end retail stores (even United Colors of Benetton and the Nike Store have made an appearance). Three blocks north of O'Higgins is the **Plaza de Armas,** flanked by the ritziest hotels in town; just around the Gran Hotel Pucón you'll find Pucón's **beach.** Heading south of O'Higgins, the roads are named after other South American countries (Brasil, Uruguay, etc.), and here you'll find some of the cheaper lodging.

Tourist Office: The signs that say "*Oficina de Turismo,*" right off the highway actually lead you to the privately run **Cámara de Turismo,** Brasil 115 (☎/fax 441 671; info@puconturismo.cl), at the corner with Caupolicán. The English-speaking staff offers maps and will direct you toward (affiliated) hotels, *cabañas,* and travel agencies. Open Dec.-Mar. 10am-9pm, Apr.-Nov. 10am-2pm and 3-7pm. More helpful is the Municipalidad's **Oficina de Turismo,** O'Higgins 486 (☎293 003; fax 293 001; ofturismo@municipalidadpucon.cl; www.puconturismo.cl), on the southwest corner with Palguin. They have a long counter full of brochures, including maps. English-speaking staff. Open Dec. 15-Feb. 28 8am-10pm, Mar.-Nov. 8:30am-7pm. **Conaf,** Lincoyán 336 (☎/fax 443 781; pnvillarrica@conaf.cl), between O'Higgins and General Urrutia. They have maps and other information on Parque Nacional Villarrica and Parque Nacional Huerquehue. Open M-F 8:30am-1pm and 2:30- 6pm.

Tours: There are several major tour operators in town offering a wide variety of adventure outings.

Sol y Nieve (☎/fax 441 070; solnieve@entelchile.net; www.chilesolnieve.com), on the corner of O'Higgins and Lincoyán, with another office in the lobby of Gran Hotel Pucón (☎444 761). Leads hikes up Volcán Villarrica (min. 4 people; Dec.-Mar. CH$25,000 per person, Apr.-Nov. CH$30,000). Their whitewater rafting excursions to the lower Río Trancura (Class III rapids) entail 1 hour in the water, with guides, lifejacket, windbreaker, and helmet provided (min. 4 people; Dec.-Mar. CH$6000, Apr.-Nov. CH$10,000). Taking it up an notch, you can try their whitewater rafting tours of the upper Trancura (Class IV rapids), a 3hr. excursion (min. 5 people; Dec.-Mar. CH$12,000, Apr.-Nov. CH$15,000). Also offers: hikes on horseback through local forests (min. 2 people; CH$15,000); guided tours through Parque Nacional Huerquehue (min. 4 people; CH$18,000); full- or half-day fishing excursions on the Liucura or Trancura rivers, with guide, equipment and transport (half-day CH$45,000 per person, full-day CH$65,000 per person; 20% discount for groups of 2+ for half-day excursions); trips to nearby hot springs (min. 4 people; CH$9000 per person); various tours of Pucón and the surrounding region (min. 4 people; CH$3000-9000). Open 9:30am-1:30pm and 3:30-8:30pm.

Trancura, O'Higgins 211C (☎441 189 or 441 959; fax 441 189; turismo.trancura@entelchile.net; www.trancura.com). Guides speak limited English. Offers guided tours up Volcán Villarrica that include transport, equipment, and entrance into park. (7:30am, returns 6pm; min. 3 people, max. 9 people, off-season max. 5 people; CH$20,000 per person). Whitewater rafting packages also available, including 1 hour in the lower Trancura (CH$5000-7000 per person) and another 4 in the Maichin River's Class IV and higher rapids, which can be attempted Nov.-Mar. and is for experienced rafters only (8hr., min. 4 people, CH$35,000 per person). Other tours include: guided hikes through Parque Nacional Huerquehue (CH$12,000 per person); horseback riding in the forests along the Trancura and Liucara rivers (3hr., CH$12,000 per person); trips to the Termas Huife (CH$15,000 per person) and Termas Los Pozones (CH$13,000 per person); and other surrounding sights. Open 9am-midnight, off-season 9am-8pm.

¡ecole!, General Urrutia 592 (☎441 675; ecole@entelchile.net; www.ecole.cl), on the corner with Arauco, offers guided tours of Cañi, a private nature reserve 20km from Pucón, run by a foundation of ecological organizations. The 140-hectare sanctuary is an excellent place for bird-watching, and contains a number of lagóons and streams and a 9km trail for which you'll need snowshoes to follow in the wintertime (snowshoe rental CH$1500; includes transport, guide, and entrance to the reserve; 9am, returns 6pm; CH$9000 per person). They also arranges tours of Termas Los Pozones (3hr. at resort, min. 4 people, CH$8000 per person); tours of Termas Huife or Termas Panqui (CH$10,000 per person); horseback riding in the countryside near Termas Los Pozones (half-day CH$15,000, full-day CH$30,000) or in Antilco (half-day CH$14,000, full-day CH$30,000).

Turismo M@yra, O'Higgins 447 (☎444 514; myhostel@hotmail.com), between Ansorena and Palquín. Tours include: guided ascents of Volcán Villarrica (includes transport, insurance, equipment, entrance fee, and English-speaking guide; 7am, returns 5pm; min. 2 people; CH$22,000 per person); horseback riding in the countryside (3hr., CH$12,000 per person); whitewater rafting in lower Trancura (3hr. in water, CH$5000 per person) and upper Trancura (3hr. in water, CH$12,000 per person); and trips to Termas los Pozones and Termas Huife (3-4hr. at springs, CH$8000 per person).

Bank/ATM: Banco de Chile, Fresia 223 (☎442 718), between Alderete and General Urrutia, has a **24hr. Redbanc ATM.** Open M-F 9am-2pm. **Banco Estado,** O'Higgins 240 (☎441 100), between Lincoyán and Fresia, has **24hr. ATM.** Open M-F 9am-2pm.

Currency Exchange: Turismo Christopher, O'Higgins 335 (☎/fax 449 013), between Fresia and Ansorena. Cashes traveler's checks and changes US dollars, Euros, and other foreign currency. Open Jan.-Feb. 9:30am-3am, Mar.-Dec. 9:30am-7:30pm. **Telephonica Pucón** (see **Telephone/Fax,** p. 369) changes US dollars.

Work Opportunity: Hostería y Restaurant Mill-Rahue (see **Food,** p. 371), hires 3 or more waiters and 3 or 4 cooks for summertime work Jan.-Mar. **Turismo M@yra** (see **Tours,** p. 368), hires secretaries and salespeople to work in their office Dec.-Feb. For detailed info on both positions see **Alternatives to Tourism,** p. 83.

Language Lessons: ¡école! (see **Tours,** p. 368) offers Spanish classes starting at CH\$9000 for a 2hr. class. One-on-one instruction also available. For details see **Alternatives to Tourism,** p. 80.

Supermarket: Eltit, O'Higgins 336 (☎441 103 or 441 342), between Fresia and Ansorena. Open Jan.-Feb. 9am-11pm, Mar.-Dec. 9am-9:30pm.

Police: The *carabineros* have an office at O'Higgins 135 (☎ 441 196), at the corner with Caupolicán.

Hospital: Hospital San Francisco, Uruguay 325 (☎441 177), on the block between Fresia and Ansorena.

Telephones/Fax: Telefonica Pucón, O'Higgins 312 (☎442 052 or 442 054), between Fresia and Ansorena. Offers telephone service through Entel. International faxes CH\$500 per page, domestic CH\$350. Open M-Sa 10am-2pm and 4-8pm.

Internet Access: Unid@d G, O'Higgins 415, local 2 (☎444 918; unidadg@hotmail.com), between Ansorena and Palguín. CH\$800 per hr. Open 10am-11pm. **Telefonica Pucón** (see **Telephone/Fax,** above) offers Internet access for CH\$500 for 30min.

Post Office: Fresia 183 (☎441 164), on the corner with Alderete. Open M-F 9am-1pm and 3-6pm, Sa 9am-12:30pm.

ACCOMMODATIONS

As a premier destination for tourists around the globe, Pucón has some of the most luxurious—and most expensive—hotels in all of Chile. These are mostly located near the Playa Grande, along the Plaza de Armas. Luckily, many *hospedajes* cater to the needs of the young backpacking crowd, so the rates can be quite reasonable, especially outside the peak months of December to February. You'll find that almost any Pucón resident with four walls and a roof will be willing to rent out a room to you, given the right price. Lots of *hospedaje* owners and workers are also tapped into the adventure tour business, so they can be a great source of advice.

¡école!, General Urrutia 592 (☎441 675; www.ecole.cl; ecole@entelchile.net), on the corner with Arauco. One of Chile's most enjoyable—and educational places to stay, ¡école! was started in 1994 as a joint Chilean and North American venture, a base for sending out ecologists and other workers to the private nature reserve Cañi. It offers a wealth of information on the region's natural wonders, besides being just a really good place to lay your backpack for a few nights. The cheerful, colorful rooms are named after trees (*araucaria, cipres, alerce*), while the gleaming new, shared bathrooms bear the names of birds (*loica, chucao*). In the summertime, the best place to chill out is on the outside patio, under grapevines trellis, where you can sit at a table with a cup of herbal tea or just snooze in one of their hammocks. Laundry, radiator heating. English-speaking staff. Reservations recommend in summer. Dorms CH$3500, with sheets Dec.-Mar. CH$7500, Apr.-Nov. CH$6500; singles Dec.-Mar. CH$12,000, Apr.-Nov. CH$9000, with private bath CH$17,000/CH$15,000; doubles with private bath CH$17,000/CH$15,000; triples with private bath CH$23,000/CH$21,000. IVA discounted for foreigners. 10% HI discount on dorms. AmEx/MC/V. ❷

Gran Hotel Pucón, Hozapfel 190 (☎441 001, www.granhotelpucon.cl), occupying the entire northern end of the Plaza de Armas. Gran Hotel Pucón is the town's 2nd oldest hotel, built in 1934, and it has obviously snagged the best spot in town, with lakeside vistas stretching across almost the entire length of the volcanic gray beach. There are different options for accommodations here: rooms in the old building or single or multi-bedroom condominiums in the two towers on either side of the hotel. You'll probably want to spend most of your time in the hotel's huge backyard plaza, with neatly trimmed lawns and the best views of Pucón's awe-inspiring sunsets. Guests can borrow bikes for free and make use of the hotel's sizeable sports facilities, including squash courts, a multi-purpose auditorium, and indoor and outdoor pools. For those less anxious to burn calories, there are massage services, jacuzzis, and an Italian restaurant with a separate buffet area. Cable TV, laundry, radiator heating, A/C 3rd and 4th floor. Internet access. Breakfast included. English-speaking managers. Reservations recommended 2 weeks in advance. Singles US$152; doubles US$228. AmEx/MC/V. ❺

Hotel del Lago, Ansorena 23 (☎291 000; fax 291 200; www.hoteldlelago.cl), on the eastern end of the Plaza de Armas. If you're looking for the finest in modern comfort (and are willing to pay for it), forget about that old hotel on the beach and head to Hotel del Lago, the place where Pucón's high rollers go to live it up. Hotel del Lago features Pucón's one and only casino, and its huge entry hall, equipped with the requisite glass elevator, is indubitably one of Pucón's modern wonders. The luxury complex features a gourmet restaurant, 3 bars, a health club and spa, outdoor and indoor pools, a cinema, and, lest we forget, its very own bingo hall. As for the rooms, even the least expensive ones have bathrooms sporting fine Italian marble. A/C, private parking, cable TV, minibar, laundry. Internet access 30min. free, then CH$3000 per hr. Breakfast included. Reservations recommended 1 month in advance during summer. Doubles Dec.-Mar. US$180-240, Apr.-Nov. US$130-180; suites US$270-1100/US$210-1100. AmEx/MC/V. ❺

Hospedaje M@yra, Palguín 695 (☎442 745; myhostel@hotmail.com), just south of the JAC bus terminal, with another similar branch at Colo-Colo 485. Decent rooms in a pine-wood house, decorated with pictures of skiers zooming down fluffy mountains and the occasional deerskin. Caters to groups of backpackers, with an 8-person dorm with bunkbeds at the top floor of an annex. Full kitchen, private parking, space heaters. Internet 15min. free, CH$1000 per hr. Staff speaks some English. Check-out 10:30 am. Rooms with shared bath Nov.-Feb. CH$5000 per person, Mar.-Oct. CH$4000, with private bath CH$7000/CH$5000. Guests receive 10% discount on tours with Turismo M@yra. AmEx/MC/V. ❷

Apart Hotel Arauco Pucón, Arauco 440 (☎/fax 441 711; araucopucon@hotmail.com; www.araucopucon.itgo.com), between O'Higgins and Brasil. This establishment offers *cabaña*-like lodging off a pleasant, brightly lit walkway. The owners are adamant about keeping the place quiet after 10:30pm and between 2:30-5:00pm for the afternoon *siesta*. TV, private parking, gas heaters. Laundry CH$2000 per load (wash and dry). Reception 7am-1am (guests have keys to gate). 2-person apartments Dec.-Mar. CH$25,000, Apr.-Nov. CH$15,000; 4-person apartments CH$35,000/CH$20,000. IVA discounted for foreigners. AmEx/MC/V. ❹

FOOD

As a tourist town *par excellence*, Pucón has a rather cosmopolitan culinary scene, Attention vegetarians: Pucón is your town—locals don't try to pass off ham as an ingredient in veggie dishes.

Arabian, Presia 354B (☎443 469), between General Urrutia and O'Higgins. A tiny restaurant owned by Chileans of Arab descent who cook up fantastic Middle-Eastern dishes with a large number of vegetarian options. Try the vegetarian sandwiches (CH$2900-3300) named after various Arab countries–the "Qatar" is stuffed with falafel, hummus, and tabbule (CH$3300), and the "Jordania" has cheese, tomato, avocado, and mayo (CH$2900). For those more carnivorously inclined, there are shish-kababs (CH$4200) and other interesting delicacies, such as vegetables stuffed with spicy meat and rice (CH$4100-4700). It's worth stopping by just for the piping hot pita bread accompanied by mashed garbanzo beans that they serve for free. Wrap up the meal with an Arabian coffee, *Kahue* (CH$900). Open 9am-2am, off-season 10:30am-3:30pm and 7-10:30pm. ❸

¡école! (see **Accommodations,** p. 369) serves up entirely meatless dishes in a chill atmosphere, amid leafy plants and peacefully soporific tunes. A young palm tree even grows right up through the center of one of the tables. There is a wide range of meal-sized salads (CH$2500) and omelettes (CH$2500-4400) to choose from. Try the *tabruli* (CH$1000), made from Andean Quinoa, tomatoes, parsley, mint, and herbs or one of the quiches (CH$3500-4800). "Vegetarian" here also seems to apply to salmon and trout fillets (CH$4400), doused in butter, white wine, and cream. Open 8am-midnight, off-season 8am-10pm. AmEx/MC/V. ❸

Hostería y Restaurant Milla-Rahue, O'Higgins 460 (☎441 610), between Ansorena and Panguín. A pleasant restaurant shod in pine wood, offering hearty dinner entrees. Wide array of soups, from *creme de la tomate* (CH$1800) to *paila marina* (CH$4200); a decent selection of fish, from Mexican trout (stuffed with spicy bits of chicken; CH$4800) to Sicilian salmon (with mushrooms; CH$4800) and juicy steaks, including *filet estragon* (with taragon sauce; CH$4900) and *lomo pabre* (steak laden with onions and fried eggs; CH$4700). Vegetarian options are sparse, but you might try their *past cesara* (CH$3500). Open Jan.-Mar. 8am-1am, Apr.-Dec. 10am-11pm. AmEx/MC/V. ❸

Restaurante Marmonhi, Ecuador 175 (☎/fax 441 972), between Caupolicán and Lincoyán. The prime decorations are the jigsaw puzzles of colorful landscapes hung up on the walls. Locals congregate here for their inexpensive, filling lunches and pricier dinners. English menus. *Menú* with soup, entree, and dessert CH$3880. Soups CH$1000-2900, fish CH$3900-4980, other meat dishes CH$2500-4980. Open Jan.-Feb. 10am-midnight, Mar.-Dec. M-Sa 10am-10pm, Su 10am-6pm. Accepts US dollars. ❸

SIGHTS

The main attraction in Pucón is, of course, its beach. **Playa Grande** lies on the northern end of town, behind the Gran Hotel Pucón. The "beach" is really a dark gray, gravelly collection of crushed volcanic rock—not very suitable for building sandcastles. Still, the view of the lake, flanked by snow-capped mountains, is impressive. The mountains are often shrouded in clouds and their rugged, lava-built sides can sometimes be pelted with rain for 15 days straight, especially during the winter. The waters of Lago Villarrica, however, are wondrously still, shimmering softly in the light breezes of the valley. You can rent **boats** or **jetskis** here if you want to make some waves of your own. Whatever you do, though, don't miss the breathtaking sunsets, when the blues of the lakewaters drain away into fiery red. Playa Grande ends at a rocky outcropping to the west, where the hilly peninsula sticks a long thumb into the lake. At the other end is Pucón's other lake shore, **La Poza.** There are not even gray rocks here—just a marshy stretch of grass along the lip of the lake—but you'll find the wooden wharf where many of the lake's sailboats are moored.

Pucón's **Plaza de Armas,** just south of the Playa Grande, is not very inspiring, with its dirt paths amid trees and a graffitied antique train engine. Nevertheless, it is surrounded by the town's most insanely expensive hotels, the distinctive turquoise-painted facade of Gran Hotel Pucón to the north, and the modern, gleaming Hotel de Lagos to the east. In the latter you'll find a **casino** where you can shake hands with the one-armed bandits on the first floor for free but be ready to shell out CH$2000 to access the card games on the second floor. (Casino open Jan.-Feb. 24hr., Mar.-Dec. 11am-4am, card tables 8pm-4am).

PARQUE NACIONAL VILLARRICA

The most active volcano in South America, Volcán Villarrica (2847m) dominates the skyline for miles around with its distinctive smoldering crown, visible on clear days from across the lake in Villarrica. The volcano has spewed lava more than 30 times since its first recorded eruption in 1558. Its last major outburst was in 1971, when a violent explosion triggered avalanches and unleashed a blizzard of ash upon Lago Villarrica and Lago Calafquén. However, since its last minor eruption in 1984, which produced a spectacular but harmless river of fire, the mountain has been fairly quiet. Still, scores of tourists make the ascent hoping to see a pit of liquid, hot magma, although they are often disappointed by thick sulfur clouds that blanket the crater. Nevertheless, Volcán Villarrica is quite accessible for a snow-capped mountain—physically grueling but not technically difficult—and it's worth the five hours of hiking to gamble on seeing the impressive lava bowl.

Though the celebrity status of Volcán Villarrica tends to eclipse all else, the 63,000 hectare park offers much more in the way of breathtaking beauty. Formed around a spur jutting from the spine of the Andes, Parque Nacional Villarrica is home to three other major volcanoes—Volcán Quetrupillán (2360m), Volcán Quinquilil (2002m), and the mammoth Volcán Lanín (3747m). Along the southern slopes of the four sibling volcanoes, from Villarrica in the west to Lanín in the east, stretches a thick forest of Monkey Puzzle (*araucaria*) trees, some that have seen as many as three millennia. Oddly enough, the lava-spewing craters of the park's volcanoes are also surrounded by huge natural reservoirs of water, the result of perpetual alpine snowfalls.

LAKES DISTRICT

AT A GLANCE	
AREA: 63,000 hectares.	**GATEWAYS:** Villarrica, Pucón.
CLIMATE: Average 2,500-3,500mm of rain Mar.-Aug. Average high temp. Jan.-Mar. 23°C; average low temp May-Aug. 4°C.	**HIGHLIGHTS:** Volcanes Villarrica, Quetrupillán, and Lanín; Monkey Puzzle trees.
CAMPING: Near entrance to Quetrupillán.	**FEES:** Entrance fee CH$3000.

ORIENTATION

Conaf has three offices located in the park—one at the entrance of **Sector Rucapillán** (at the western end, where ascents to Volcán Villarrica begin and the ski center is located), one at the entrance of **Sector Quetrupillán** (in the center, wedged between Volcán Villarrica and Volcán Quetrupillán), and the third along the route through the mountains to Argentina, at **Sector Puesco** (between Volcán Quinquilil and Volcán Lanín). (Conaf administration open Jan.-Mar. 8:30am-9pm; Apr.-Dec. 8:30am-6pm. Entrance fee CH$3000.)

HIKES

SECTOR RUCAPILLÁN (VOLCÁN VILLARRICA). The park's most frequented sector (thanks to its hot-headed volcano), sector Rucapillán has two principal **trails**— one up the **volcano** (5km, 6hr.) and one around its **southern edge** (23km, 12hr.). The trip up the volcano begins at the Conaf administration office at the park entrance, where those brave enough to make the ascent without a guide must show proof that they have sufficient climbing experience (alpine club ID or the like) and the proper equipment. All climbers will want to bring a gas mask with them (provided by tour agencies) to fend off the poisonous sulfur fumes that spill from the perpetually burning crater. You'll also want a good pair of shades. Children 12 and younger need a parent accompanying them. (5hr. up, 2hr. down. Ascents must begin between 7 and 10am.)

The trek up the volcano starts on the road to the ski center covering the slopes of Villarrica. There is a **ski lift** that cuts 1-1½ hr. off the hike; however, it is expensive (CH$3500) and only runs from 8am-9am outside of the ski season. After getting beyond the ski center, it's another three to four hours of slogging up the snow-blanketed slopes until you reach the lip of the crater, where—volcano spirits willing—you'll see some lava bubbling below you.

Getting down the volcano slopes can be a refreshing change of pace. Walking will take you two hours, but many tour agencies will lend you **slides** so you can shimmy down a bit more playfully than you came up. Some tour agencies will also let you climb the slope **ski randonee,** wearing skis specially modified so that you can walk uphill and ski back down (must be intermediate skier). **Snowboards** are also allowed but you have to haul it to the top yourself.

The trail around the volcano, **Sendero Challupen Chinay,** offers stunning views of a landscape of dramatic contrasts, from the volcano wrapped in ice to the two lakes, Calafquén and Villarrica, glinting in the sunlight, with broad expanses of *araucaria* coating the ridges and valleys in between. It's a 12hr. hike in total (23km), which brings you to the Conaf administration office at Sector Quentrupillán. Visitors who forego the ascent for this less vertical hike pay only CH$2000 for a seven day pass at the entrance. *(The entrance to Sector Rucapillán is 9km from Pucón and tour buses frequently make the trip. No public transportation available. Taxis from Pucón CH$8000-10,000.)*

SECTOR QUETRUPILLÁN. About 37km from Pucón, down the dirt road that passes by the **Termas de Palquín** hot springs resort, you'll find the entrance to Parque Nacional Villarrica's Sector Quetrupillán. This is an often overlooked, but abundantly rewarding swath of pristine forestland stuck between two volcanoes. The prime attraction here is the horseback riding provided by a number of businesses along the road to the park (half-day CH$10,000).

LAKES DISTRICT

The shortest trail in Sector Quetrupillán is **Sendero Pichillancahue,** a low-difficulty jaunt through a forest of stout Monkey Puzzle trees, with views of Volcán Choshuenco to the south and Volcán Quetrupillán to the north. It also gives you the opportunity to observe the glacial movement of ice on Volcán Villarrica (3.3km, 1¼hr.). Longer trails stretch around Volcán Villarrica's far end to the west, and to Volcán Quetrupillán to the east—eventually ending up, some 32km of hiking later, at Sector Puesco, on the other side of the volcano. *(Access to the trails CH$3000 instead of the usual CH$2000. 4WDs allowed on the 9km stretch of muddy dirt road, accesible only in summer. The park's only bonafide camping facilities are located near the entrance to the sector and are only open during the summer. Max. 6 people; CH$5000 per site).*

SECTOR PUESCO. Right before the highway cuts through the Andes at Paso Mamuil Malal, the gateway to Argentina, it passes through the most secluded segment of Parque Nacional Villarrica, Sector Puesco. A customs post stands guard at the entrance here, where you'll have to show identification (i.e. your passport) and also the registration of your vehicle. Those who want to visit the park will have to hand over their passports, which they'll give back when you leave the park.

The trails in Sector Puesco lie in the shadow of the massive Volcán Lanín. At 3747m, it's a few heads taller than its more famous brother to the west and sits only partially in Chile. There are numerous shorter trails—**Sendero Lagos Andinos** makes a lazy circuit around several small Andean lagoons replete with wildlife (12km, 6hr.), while another extended trail heads west toward Sector Quetrupillán, alongside the southern slopes of the volcano. *(The entrance to Sector Puesco is 69km from Pucón, with another 18km of road leading to the mountain pass and international border. To get there, take a bus headed from Pucón to Argentina and get off at the customs post. Visitors enter free at this end of the park, though charges apply for other areas of the park.)*

⛷ SKIING

Situated on the slopes of Volcán Villarrica inside Sector Rucapillán is the ski center, **Ski Pucón Chile,** run by Gran Hotel Pucón. It boasts 20 trails serviced by nine ski lifts and a wide range of difficulty levels. Lava flows have carved out channels into the mountain face, creating natural half-pipes that will challenge expert skiers and snowboarders. Most trails sit at 1200m above sea level with a few lifts taking you up to 1800m. (☎ 197 2872, in Pucón 441 901; www.granhotelpucon.cl. Open July 7-Sept. 22 9am-5pm. Priciest seasons July 7-28 and Sept. 15-22.)

LAGO CALAFQUÉN AND PANGUIPULLI

LICAN RAY   ☎ 45

For Chilean youths, Lican Ray is the ultimate vacation getaway. Summers at this beach resort just 30km from Villarrica are an endless party—by day the beach is covered with Chilean students trying to get that perfect tan and by night the clubs are hopping those bronzed and beautiful bodies. The hedonism is being tamed, however, by the increasing presence of families who have caught on to this great holiday destination.

CHILE'S ECONOMIC MIRACLE
The Inside Story on the Chilean Peso

Amongst political economists, Chile is often regarded as Latin America's developmental miracle. And with the collapse of the Argentine economy, the one-time Latin darling of free-market economists, Chile stands alone as the only sound South American economy. Its balance of free-market liberalism with selective state intervention is unique within a region prone to extremity. Furthermore, its successful economic and social policies have added to greater ideological debates about how to define and quantify poverty and inequality, and how to reduce their severity.

Economic turmoil in Latin America prompted the United Nations Economic Commission for Latin America (ECLA) to call the period 1997-2002 the "lost half-decade" in evocation of the "lost decade" of the 1980s, when Latin economies collapsed under the debt crisis. But while Brazil, Uruguay, and Argentina were reeling during the summer of 2002, the Chilean economy, while not immune to the regional meltdown, remained remarkably stable.

Chile's below-3 percent growth rate (GDP) projected for 2002 paled in comparison with its 7 percent growth rate during the 1990s, but that compared favorably with the projected stagnation in Latin America overall and Argentina's 13.5 percent projected contraction (International Monetary Fund 2002). The Financial Times predicted that only Chile and Mexico would escape the regional fallout. Mexico, they said, would stay afloat due to its close ties with the United States, while Chile would survive as a result of nearly 20 years of fiscal prudence fortifying the state with a low foreign debt and a relatively strong social safety net.

Economic stability has allowed Chile to remain politically calm amidst regional turmoil. In Argentina and Brazil during the summer of 2002, left-wing political figures appealed to popular despair, piquing anti-free-market, and naturally anti-US, sentiment.

The most heated political debate in Latin America today centers around an ideology known as neo-liberalism. (Utter the term "neoliberalismo" to spark debate on any Latin street from Tierra del Fuego to Tijuana.) The fundamental idea underlying neo-liberalism is the reduction of the state's role in the economy. This means drastic reductions in trade tariffs and opening businesses to international competition while encouraging foreign investment, activities that should lead to more and better jobs, a reduction in poverty, and increased prosperity across economic and social spectra.

Unfortunately, although many Latin American nations have experienced periods of marked growth after free-market reform, inequality has often worsened and poverty reduction has fallen short of aspirations. More people now support the idea that good governance is necessary for prudent market integration; chronically corrupt or inefficient governments cannot simply be circumvented.

Credibility for this assertion comes not only from myriad failures, but also from the success—indeed, the sole regional triumph—of Chile. Over the past 20 years the Chilean government has opened its markets selectively and/or gradually while, relative to other free-market transition countries, heavily regulating the banking (i.e., lending) industry. Experts say that state intervention has led to the successful development of high-risk (fruit) and long-term (forestry) export industries that might not otherwise attract investments from private institutions (Marcus Kurtz 2001). Chile's rapid growth from 1987-98 led to a reduction in poverty from 40 percent to 17 percent, while extreme poverty fell to 4 percent (World Bank 1998).

Chile's mix of state regulation with economic liberalism could be the result of historical lessons learned. A failed experiment with socialism in the 1970s led to Pinochet's 17-year dictatorship. Pinochet's radical neo-liberalism and the banking collapse of 1982 put Chile in hard times. Mark Mulligan of the Financial Times asserts that culture and national character evolved in step with political and economic transformations: "Most agree it was those two shocks that helped shape the Chilean economic model of free trade and fiscal prudence, and created a nation of austere, risk-averse, largely law-abiding people" (Aug. 5, 2002).

Like other newly internationalized economies, however, inequality continues to be an issue in Chile. From 1994-98, the income of the lowest income decile increased by 15 percent while the top decile's income increased by 31 percent (World Bank 1998). One obstacle to higher equity has been information flow: small businesses and poor households do not always know what services are available to them (Kurtz 2001, World Bank 1998).

Once we look beyond income per se and evaluate inequality as a function of social, political, and economic empowerment, however, Chile's inequality situation improves tremendously; indeed, it truly excels in comparison with its neighbors. Chile's standard testing system used to determine household eligibility for social services such as family allowances, water and housing subsidies, education, and health care has in effect transferred income from the rich to the poor via public services. (World Bank 1998).

Chile's current president, Ricardo Lagos, exemplifies Chile's unique blend of free trade and social spending. A socialist, Lagos has tried to remain investment-friendly while strengthening Chile's democracy through social investment. At the outset of his term Lagos said: "I imagine a country where there will be further advances in infrastructure, where there will be more social justice and more equality" (Financial Times, April 3, 2001).

Lagos has claimed victories on both the free trade and social reform fronts, although his popularity has suffered from the effects of the regional meltdown. Labor reforms aimed at improving pension and unemployment programs, encouraging worker organization, and fortifying other rights are meant to empower the non-rich. Lagos maintains that his measures are necessary to prevent class friction. At the same time, Lagos was busy finalizing a free-trade agreement with the European Union that left Washington scurrying to complete their own deal with Chile.

The future is still uncertain for Chile due to the instability of its neighbors and to questions regarding its ability to integrate small businesses, rural laborers, indigenous workers, and other groups, but Chile remains the paragon for economic development in Latin America south of Mexico. Its example should also quell the highly contentious global ideological debate pitting the neo-liberalists against all those to the left, for in Chile, a little from the left and a little from right has so far proven to be the proper balance.

Derek Glanz was the Editor of Let's Go: Spain, Portugal, and Morocco *1998. He is now a freelance journalist who recently began pursuing postgraduate studies in international relations. He has been published in* The Associate Press *and* The Miami Herald, *and served as a guest TV analyst on Colombia's* TeleCartagena.

TRANSPORTATION. **Buses** pull into and out of the east side of the plaza at Urrutia. **Buses** and **vans** leave frequently for **Coñaripe** (every 15min., CH$1000) and **Panguipulli** (M-F 7 per day 7:50am-5:15pm; Sa 8, 8:30am, noon, 1, 5:30pm; CH$2000). Buses also go to **Liquiñe** via **Coñaripe** and the **Termas de Coñaripe** (M-Sa noon and 6pm, CH$1500). **Transtur,** Urrutia 319, goes to the Termas (round-trip CH$3000-6000). Tours of Valdivia are available (CH$10,000). They also offer transport to the **airport** in **Pucón** (CH$20,000) and to **Temuco** (CH$50,000).

ORIENTATION AND PRACTICAL INFORMATION. The main road in town is **General Urrutia,** which runs east toward **Lago Calafquén** past the **Plaza de Armas** and heads west to the main road running between Villarrica and Coñaripe. The **Oficina de Turismo** is located in the plaza at Urutia 310. (☎431 201. Open 9am-9pm; off-season M-F 9am-5pm.) Continuing east on Urrutia, you'll arrive at **Playa Chica** on the lakefront. This beach is extremely popular with locals as it boasts lower prices than the more touristy **Playa Grande.** Grande, Lican Ray's answer to the French Riviera, manages to attract hordes of tourists. **Cacique Punulef,** runs parallel to Urrutia two blocks south, along Playa Grande. Walking south almost anywhere from Urrutia takes you to the beach in about 2min. Like many of its rural, lakeside neighbors, Lican Ray is lacking in ATMs, banks, express mail services, and car rental agencies. The **Posta de Salud** is a small clinic which is always open for emergencies, but has shorter hours for visits to the doctor. **Internet access** is available at two terminals in the tourist office (CH$400 per hr.) and also across the street (CH$600 per hr.). The **post office** is also located in the tourist office kiosk on the plaza, and is only open five hours per day.

ACCOMMODATIONS. **Hotel Refugio Inaltulafquén ❸,** Punulef 510, is a great, fun place to stay. Right on the beach, it has an attached restaurant and bar with pleasant outdoor patio seating in warm weather. The bright rooms, some of which have charming lake views, are filled with books that are part of the hotel's growing collection. The amiable English-speaking owners take pride in their cosmopolitanism—they have accommodated guests from all corners of the world. (☎412 543. Singles CH$10,000, with bath CH$15,000.) If you can't get a room at the sought-after Refugio, consider the expensive **Hotel Becker ❹,** Manquel 105, which although nice, is not worth splurging on. (☎431 553. Doubles CH$35,000; quads CH$50,000.) Alternatively, the solid budget option, **Hospedaje Victor's Playa ❷,** on Punulef, has been a popular choice over the last few summers—the lakefront bar complements the low prices. (☎099 596 3616. Singles CH$5000; doubles CH$8000.) **Residencial Temuco ❷,** Mistral 515, is another cheap stay farther from the water. If all other options are booked, this is as solid a back-up plan as any. The rooms are basic but comfortable, and the staff is friendly and caring. The shared baths are kept spotless. (☎431 130. CH$5000 per person; suites CH$15,000.) Quality **cabañas** abound in Lican Ray. Hit the tourist office for an updated list of what's open and to make a price comparison—the list is too long and variable to put down here. Try **Cabañas Limay ❶,** Urutia 901, for the cheap sixperson *cabaña*—a great place to crash after a night of partying (CH$12,000 per night). **Camping** is not allowed on either Playa Chico or Playa Grande, but just off the road, toward Coñaripe, there are sites on the lake front such as **Camping Vista Hermosa ❷,** 4.5km away.

FOOD. The **Ñaños ❷,** Urrutia 105 (☎431 021), is the most popular dining spot in town with locals and tourists alike—some diners travel from other towns just for its food. The huge clay oven outside can cook up to 50 *empanadas* and soft bread rolls at a time. Meanwhile, **Nietos ❷** is renowned for its seafood, particularly their *trucha* (fresh trout; CH$2800). Most seafood dishes are quite a bargain (CH$4000 and under). **Restaurant El Coyote ❷**, Urrutia 370, has cheap, yet delicious, set meals all day—warning: not to be confused with the Coyote butcher shop around the corner. (☎431 596. Open 11:30am-10pm.) A popular **pizza place** at Urrutia 201 is open all summer long, but changes names each year.

🟦 🔳 **SIGHTS AND ENTERTAINMENT.** Between **Playa Grande** and **Playa Chica** lies a peninsula which is grassy and forested—stroll through this welcoming splash of green that provides respite from the sunny beaches. In addition to its fine beaches, Lican Ray has several unique churches that are worth checking out. Stop by at the Victorian-inspired blue and white **Parroquia San Francisco of Cariman,** lying just before crossing the small bridge from town out to the road to Coñaripe. The **Semana de Lican Ray** typically takes place on the 2nd week of February, and the festivities promise to be great—in past years, the town has consistently broken records for world's largest barbecue. And while this grilling en masse is dwindling, the week is still full of not-to-be-missed beach events—for more details, check with the tourist office after November. **Boat rentals** are a fun way to explore the lake, and are generally cheaper on Playa Chica (CH$3000 per hr.). **Expediciones Trancura** runs **hydrofoil rides** in the summer (CH$11,000) and organizes hiking trips up Volcán Villarrica (CH$20,000).

This tiny town has some serious nightlife during its peak months. **Jaranero Pub,** on Heununman, next to the Coyote butcher shop displaying a Wily Coyote, is a trendy Lican Ray hotspot during the summer. **Desibelius,** a hip disco, lies a short 3km drive out of town on the road towards Villarrica. Jam-packed with grooving youths in the summer, the *discoteca* only runs on weekends during the rest of the year. Before hitting these clubs, start the evening at the nearby bar, **Donde el Flaco.**

COÑARIPE
☎ 63

Nestled along the banks of Lago Calafquén, the tiny town of Coñaripe offers pristine, undisturbed views of the lake and Volcán Villarrica. Until recently, Coñaripe was overlooked by Chilean students in favor of the more flamboyant party town of Lican Ray. But quiet Coñaripe has begun to steal away some of those tourists, and the spectacular views, serenity, and particularly, the development of the Termas de Liquiñe are making Coñaripe and the less-frequented Lago Calafquén a mustsee for those who visit the Villarrica region.

🔳 🔳 **TRANSPORTATION AND PRACTICAL INFORMATION. Buses** leave for **Lican Ray** and **Panguipulli** every 15min. From either of these towns, board other buses to Valdivia and Osorno. Upon arriving in town, the road from Lican Ray turns into **Guido Beck de Ramberga,** the main thoroughfare in Coñaripe. The road passes along the **plaza** on the right, and the **bus station** lies 200m farther along on the left, just before the road forks right towards Panguipulli. The curvy and scenic road continues left towards the refreshing **Termas de Coñaripe** and further down to the **spa** at Liquiñe. The **Oficina de Turismo** is located in a kiosk on the plaza. (☎317 403. Open in summer 9am-9pm; in winter Sa-Su 9am-5pm.) The nearest banks are in Panguipulli or Villarrica, so make sure you have enough cash with you before arriving here. **Currency exchange** is possible in Coñaripe, but at poor rates. The **health clinic** is across from Chumay and is always open for emergencies.

🔳 🔳 **ACCOMMODATIONS AND FOOD. Hotel Entre Montañas ❹**, Beck 496, is a bright hotel with a popular restaurant and bar. The rooms are equipped with clean private baths. (☎317 298. Singles CH$15,000, off-season CH$11,000; doubles CH$25,000/CH$15,000). **Hostal Chumay ❷**, Los Pellines 11, on the other side of the plaza, is a good budget option with a boisterous, fun owner named Leo who speaks some English and leads tours for guests during the summer. Some rooms have private baths or clear volcano views; ask for a room where you get the best of both worlds. (☎317 287. Breakfast included. CH$6000 per person, off-season CH$3000.) **Cabañas ❷** are located just past Chumay, away from the plaza, right next to a **campground.** Depending on the location of a campsite or *cabaña,* the amenities included, and the length of stay, camping or renting a *cabaña* averages between CH$4000-8000 per night. The facilities here are much more affordable than similar offerings in Lican Ray. Try **Camping Cordillera ❷** (☎240 522). There is one **bar/restaurant** on the waterfront, but otherwise, Coñaripe's beach is not very commercial. A quaint **cafe/bakery** suffuses the main road with the warm smell of freshly baked goods, near where the road forks toward Liquiñe and Panguipulli. Good, affordable *empanadas* and *postres* can be consumed here in the charming upstairs seating area that enjoys views of the lake and surrounding mountains.

NEAR COÑARIPE: LAS TERMAS DE COÑARIPE Y LIQUIÑE

The **Termas de Coñaripe** are 15km from the town of Coñaripe along a slow, uphill gravel road. Budget travelers who have been passing up the opportunity to take a dip in more expensive, soothing baths in other parts of Chile will be glad to finally pamper themselves without breaking the bank. Entrance to the thermal baths is CH$6000 for adults (CH$3000 for children under 10). Unfortunately, it's pricey to stay overnight at the **hotel ❹**, so plan on returning to Coñaripe before nightfall. (CH$20,000-45,000 per person depending on the meal plan and other services chosen.) If you don't splurge for a room, spend the money to indulge yourself instead—the spa here is elaborate and well-equipped, offering a variety of rejuvenating and healing therapies ranging from mud baths and massages to herbal treatments and aromatherapy (CH$10,000). To really earn your massage, spend the day horseback riding (CH$4000 per hr.).

The more remote **Termas de Liquiñe** are even kinder to budget travelers; prices are cheaper and the emphasis on a purely natural experience is heartening. However, the ride up can be harrowing, especially after bad weather. The open-air pools here are completely isolated and facilitate an almost ethereal exchange with nature (CH$3000, children CH$2000). Pricey **rooms ❹** with meals are available as well. (CH$22,500 per night, children CH$13,500.)

PANGUIPULLI ☎63

Panguipulli (pop. 8000) is the main town on one of the larger lakes in the area, its namesake Lago Panguipulli. Known as the romantic town of a thousand roses, its streets are lined with literally thousands of these bushes. The downtown is vibrant, not to mention beautifully scented, and is situated a 10min. walk away from the lakefront.

TRANSPORTATION. Buses leave frequently for **Coñaripe** (1hr., every 30min., CH$2000); **Lican Ray** (2hr., every hr.); **Valdivia** (2hr., every 30min., CH$2500); **Villarrica** (3hr., every hr.). Long distance buses on a somewhat varying schedule go to **Termas, Temuco,** and **Santiago.**

ORIENTATION AND PRACTICAL INFORMATION. The road to Panguipulli from the Panamericana passes under a large welcome banner and then weaves into downtown via O'Higgins, up to the **Plaza de Armas.** The post office and the tourist office both lie near the northeast corner of the plaza. O'Higgins is on the left of the plaza while the next street over to the south, Martínez de Rozas, is a commercial strip that then leads eastward towards the lakefront five blocks away.

LAKES DISTRICT

Recently, tourism has really started to pick up in Panguipulli. Although the town is larger and more complicated than any other settlement on Lago Ranco or Lago Calafquén, the **tourist office** (☎311 311 or 311 312; turmpanpui@telsur.cl; www.panguipulli.cl), at the intersection of O'Higgins and the plaza, is excellent; the office is occasionally staffed with English-speakers, and clear maps are readily available.

An organization called **Tourisme Panguipulli** is a conglomeration of all the tourist industry proprietors in town and works to provide efficient tourism services. The current manager of Tourisme Panguipulli is **Carlos Tejo**, a.k.a Tío Carlos (☎311 215). An amiable, beloved older gentleman who speaks some English and is revered throughout town. He runs popular rafting trips and expeditions to various nearby attractions, including ecological parks and *termas*.

There is one **ATM** in town at the combination Esso **Tiger Mart** and **gas station** on Martínez de Rozas 367 (☎311 313). The other *cajero* in town is only for local bank account holders. The town **hospital** is on Cruz Coke, off O'Higgins on the way to the Panamericana. **Internet access** is at several points along Martínez de Rozas.

⌨️ ACCOMMODATIONS AND FOOD. Hotel España ❹, O'Higgins 790, boasts an enviable central location and makes for a charming night's stay. Proprietress Señora Gabriela España keeps the small rooms very tidy and well-decorated. The downstairs cafe has pleasant outdoor seating and is the perfect place to loll away a warm summer evening. (☎311 166. Breakfast included. Singles CH$18,000; doubles CH$25,000.) If you're willing to splurge a bit, try **Cabañas Tío Carlos ❸**, at Ethegaray 375, a set of attractive *cabañas* lying just beyond downtown. Run by the renowned Tío Carlos, you can bet that the rooms are as charming as he is. (☎311 215. CH$20,000.) Alternatively, **Hospedaje Monserat ❷**, O'Higgins 112, is a cheap stay in a standard hostel-style room. The *hospedaje* is popular with industrious Chilean backpackers, although there are only two bathrooms for the eight rooms. (☎311 443. CH$6000-9000 per person depending on the season.) When feeling famished, mosey on over to **Gardylafquen ❶**, at Rozas 722 (☎311 887), where great salmon dishes go for under CH$3000. The upstairs dining room has quite an ambiance with nice views of town. **Café Central ❷**, Rozas 880, serves up mediocre meals (CH$2000-4000) in a pretty enclosed courtyard. You'll leave happy if you order coffee after dinner—their brews for CH$500-800 are memorable. To really make an evening of it, stop by the bar on your way out and have a "special coffee" (spiked with a variety of alcohol; CH$2500).

WEST COAST

VALDIVIA   ☎63

Surrounded by the rich, fertile hills of the Lakes District, Valdivia (pop. 124,000) is often labeled as one of the most attractive cities in Chile, and with its annual rainfall of 2300mm, it is definitely the wettest. The urban dwelling itself is an appealingly curious city—neither coastal nor inland, neither beautiful nor ugly, and neither bustling nor quiet, it has everything a tourist needs and most of what one wants. Once touted for its pervasive and rich German heritage, the manifestations of these roots have been reduced to a few restaurants and street names since the catastrophic earthquake of 1960 leveled the city. Nevertheless, a visit to southern Chile would be incomplete without seeing what this pearl has to offer.

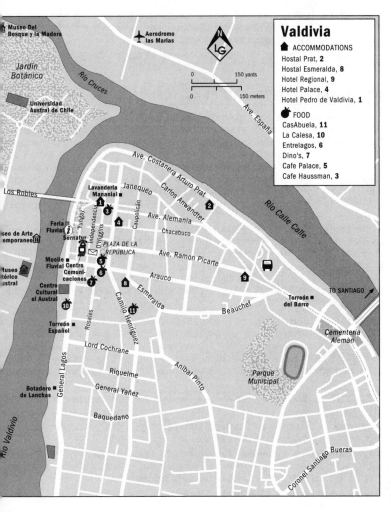

Valdivia

ACCOMMODATIONS
Hostal Prat, **2**
Hostal Esmeralda, **8**
Hotel Regional, **9**
Hotel Palace, **4**
Hotel Pedro de Valdivia, **1**

FOOD
CasAbuela, **11**
La Calesa, **10**
Entrelagos, **6**
Dino's, **7**
Cafe Palace, **5**
Cafe Haussman, **3**

TRANSPORTATION

Buses: Long-distance buses run from the **Terminal de Buses,** Anfión Muñoz 360 (☎212 212). **Cruz del Sur** (☎213 840), **Buses Norte** (☎212 800), **Tur Bus** (☎226 010), and **Buses JAC** (☎212 925) all have departures every 30min. to: **Osorno** (2hr., CH$1500); **Puerto Montt** (4hr., CH$3500); **Temuco** (3hr., CH$2000); **Villarrica** (3hr., CH$2000). **Cruz del Sur** and **Andimar** (☎224 665) make the international trip to **Bariloche, ARG** (2 per day, CH$10,000). Regional buses also run from this terminal. **Linea Verde** and **Buses Pierhueco** (☎218 609) run to **Panguipulli** several times per day (2hr., CH$1500). **Buses Futrono** (☎202 225) goes to **Valdivia** via **Paillaco** (2hr., every hr., CH$1500) and **Futrono** (several per day, CH$1000).

Local Buses: Local buses to Niebla can be caught along Prat, especially near the Sernatur offices (30min., CH$500). Inexpensive city buses also pass through the plaza area frequently and go by the bus station as well.

Colectivos: *Colectivos* are much cheaper than regular buses, although they aren't quite as accessible.

◀▮ ▮ ORIENTATION AND PRACTICAL INFORMATION

Three rivers meet at Valdivia. **Río Calle Calle** runs northwest along the eastern border of the city until it meets **Río Cruces** coming south and turns into **Río Valdivia**. Valdivia heads southwest to the Pacific Ocean, separating mainland Valdivia from the section on Isla Teja to the west. From the bus station on the eastern side of the city, **Prat** (known as the Costanera) runs a block from the water along Río Calle Calle. When it reaches the northern tip of the city at the confluence of Calle Calle and Cruces, Costanera turns south and ducks under the **Puente Pedro de Valdivia**, the bridge to Isla Teja, and ends on the edge of the downtown in the western part of the city.

Two blocks to the east, the **Plaza de República** is the center of activity. Bordered by **Henríquez** to the east, **O'Higgins** to the west, **Maipú** to the south, and **Libertad** to the north, the plaza stretches two blocks. **Picarte** heads east from the center of the plaza and is the most commercially developed street in town, with many budget hotels along the way to the bus station. In the opposite direction, at the entrance to the bridge to **Isla Teja,** is a smaller plaza with the Municipal building and the grand Hotel Pedro de Valdivia.

Tourist Office: Sernatur, Prat 555 (☎213 596), at the Feria Fluvial, has tour boats and tours waiting just outside its doors. Organized and efficient. English-speakers are always available in the summer. Open M-F 8:30am-7pm, Sa 10am-4pm, Su 10am-2pm; off-season 8:30am-1pm and 2:30-6:30pm, Sa 10am-4pm, Su 10am-2pm. The **Municipal tourism office** has a **kiosk** in the bus terminal and in the Mercado Fluvial, just across the street from Sernatur.

Banks: Many **banks** are in the plaza area and **24hr. ATMs** are scattered all across the *centro.*

Currency Exchange: There is a **currency exchange** on Alemania, between Henríquez and Caupolicán and many more along Picarte.

Language Schools: Universidad Austral de Chile, Casilla 567 (☎213 911). Students interested in learning Spanish can enroll directly in the university, or arrange private lessons. For more information see **Alternatives to Tourism,** p. 80.

Laundromat: Lavanderia Mananial, on the corner of Henríquez and Alemania, has efficient laundry service.

Telephones: There are several *centros de llamados* around the plaza.

Internet Access: Centro Comunicaciones, on Libertad between Yungay and Independencia, is a great Internet cafe with phones, faxes, printers, and a scanner. CH$1000 per hr. Open 10am-11pm. There are slightly cheaper cyber joints on Esmeralda, Henríquez south of Arauco, and Chacabuco east of Henríquez.

Post Office: O'Higgins 575, facing the plaza.

▮ ACCOMMODATIONS

The lodging in town isn't the cheapest in Chile but with a little hunting you can find a good place that won't break the bank.

Hostal Prat, Prat 595 (☎222 020), comes highly recommended by locals. Sitting right on the waterfront, the living room, dining room, and several of the guest quarters look out over Río Calle Calle. Simple but clean rooms all have private baths. Breakfast included. Singles CH$12,000-15,000; doubles CH$18,000-CH$20,000. ❸

Hostal Esmeralda, Esmeralda 651 (☎215 659), is also a good value. It is a big, old mansion that is somewhat run down, but rooms are nice and neat. Located on a pleasant and fairly quiet side street, the location is quite central, with several restaurants and services nearby. ❸

Hotel Regional, Picarte 1005 (☎216 027), opposite the bus terminal. Rooms are fairly clean, although they can feel a little cramped. Your aesthetic sense may be irked by the lack of decor. Singles CH$5000; doubles with private baths CH$10,000-14,000. ❷

Hotel Palace, Chacabuco 308 (☎213 319), at the corner with Henríquez, is bigger than it looks from the crowded street below, though its lobby and breakfast room are a bit crowded. Rooms here are bright and pleasant, and some have street views. Singles CH$20,000-22,000; doubles CH$24,000-26,000; triples CH$31,000. ❹

Hotel Pedro de Valdivia, Carampangue 190 (☎212 931), is the most distinctive landmark in town. The interior is palacial and the beautiful rear courtyard adds to the luxury. The rooms are fairly simple for such a grandiose establishment, although the lack of ornamentation doesn't translate directly into a lack of quality. Good restaurant on the hotel premises. Breakfast included. Rooms CH$50,000-125,000. ❺

◻ FOOD

Valdivia's culinary choices are where its mixed heritage really comes out.

CasAbuela, Henríquez 540 (☎218 807), specializes in homestyle regional Chilean cuisine. You can get good set meals with soup and drink (CH$3000-4000) and delicious homemade desserts. Meat dishes CH$3000-4000. ❸

La Calesa, Yungay 735 (☎213 712), is a fine dining experience featuring Peruvian cuisine. The pretty garden, river views, and an attentive staff are enough of a reason to eat here—and that's even before sampling the food. Try any of the seafood entrees on the menu—marine munchies are their specialty (CH$4000-6000). ❸

Entrelagos, Rosales 630 (☎218 333), is perfect for travel-weary tourists. The menus are in English, and familiar dishes including sandwiches (CH$2000-4000), salads (CH$2000), and fajitas for two (CH$5000), are served up in a friendly fashion. Don't leave without trying the specialities here—fine chocolates and aromatic coffee. One side of the restaurant is the tempting *chocolatería* and the other is the tea house. Valdivianos love to make their own Entrelagos hot chocolate by melting fine bars of chocolate into steaming milk (*submarinos* CH$1500). ❷

Cafe Haussman, O'Higgins 394 (☎213 878), one block north from the plaza, is a local tradition serving hundreds of *crudos* daily. These are slices of bread slathered with uncooked beef, onions, a herbal dressing, and fresh lemon juice—an unlikely combo which actually works quite well (CH$800). If you can handle the meat, give one of these Germanic edibles a try. ❶

Dino's, Maipú 191 (☎213 061), at the corner with O'Higgins. The chain restaurant actually has a high quality buffet room downstairs (CH$4500) and is one of the few places that, in keeping with the revered tradition of Starbucks-style coffee chains, will provide coffee to go in cups with lids. ❸

Cafe Palace, Rosales 580 (☎213 539) is a Chilean diner which is very popular with Valdivian students but has older regulars as well. The set menu is always a good deal (CH$3000) and the desserts are also notable. Sandwiches CH$2000-3000, Entrees CH$3000-4500. ❷

👁 SIGHTS

EL CENTRO
Most of Valdivia's main attractions lie across the river on Isla Teja. The mainland, however, does have some exciting areas. The most popular is the **Costanera,** where locals like to jog, walk or just lounge and relax. You can follow the paved running path along the river all the way from the bus terminal to the **Feria Fluvial.**

FERIA FLUVIAL. Lying on the western edge of town, along Río Valdivia, the Feria Fluvial is one of the city's most exciting areas. The **Mercado Central,** at the north-end, is a great place to shop around or catch a cheap seafood meal while the port area often plays host to families of seals who come in search of food scraps or just a little sun. This area is also the central place to catch a boat tour. With almost a dozen companies hawking various tours, you are sure to find something that suits your fancy. If you're feeling aggressive, you can definitely bargain with boat owners and tour guides, but be sure to find out if the package you choose includes a meal and any actual landings. Many of the tours head to nearby nature preserves around Isla Negra, and out to the ocean (near Niebla) and back.

OTHER SIGHTS. There are also a couple interesting places in town. Several blocks south of the Feria at the corner of General Lagos and Yerbas Buenas is one of the two **Torreones de Valdivia**—an old Spanish watchtower. The second stands next to the bus station. They are not very noteworthy but are still local objects of pride. A block north is the **Centro Cultural el Austral,** Yungay 733 (☎213 658), a lovely building with free entry to view its art galleries. Painting lessons are offered by the artists in residence and a calendar of cultural events is available as well.

ISLA TEJA
Thousands of people walk across the Pedro de Valdivia bridge to Isla Teja every day, although most of them are students heading to the Universidad Austral de Chile, which sits at the center of the island. There are, however, a few nice attractions on Teja for the inquisitive traveler.

MUSEO HISTÓRICO Y ARQUEOLÓGICO. The museum is an interesting stop—if only for the view. The old mansion has nice views of Valdivia, the river, and the university crew teams that row along it. The contents and displays in the museum itself are somewhat interesting, but all labels are in Spanish. Of most interest are the Mapuche Indian exhibits displaying the traditional skills and lifestyles of these indigenous people. (*Cross the bridge and take the first left, follow the signs.* ☎212 872. *Open 9:30am-1pm and 2:30-6pm. CH$800.*)

MUSEO DE ARTE CONTEMPORANEO. This is not quite as nice as the Centro Cultural on the mainland, but is a good place to check out new exhibits by local and university artists. (*Next to the History Museum. Open Tu-Su 10am-1pm and 3-7pm. CH$500.*)

PARKS. Behind the University are the **Botanical Gardens** and the **Parque Saval.** Both make for a lovely walk in nice weather with thousands of species of plants and flowers, many of them well-labeled. (*Closes at dusk. Free.*)

NEAR VALDIVIA: NIEBLA   ☎ 63
Lying at the mouth of Río Valdivia, Niebla serves primarily as a summer haven for Valdivianos wanting to escape the city for a while to languish in a *cabaña* by the beach and soak up some sun. The rest of the year, the only attraction here is the nearly 400-year-old **fort** built by Spanish colonizers to guard the mouth of Río Valdivia from seafaring invaders. The fort itself is not the most exciting sight in the

region, boasting simply an ammunition storage area and a battery of guns. However, if you have the time for a tour, haggle a fair price with a guide (CH$1500), and learn the interesting history of Valdivia and the surrounding area. (Open Tu-Su Nov.-Mar. 9am-8pm, Apr.-Oct. 10am-5:30pm.) If forts are not your cup of tea, stroll over to the picturesque cliffs offering breathtaking views over the crashing waves far below. All **buses** going to or from Niebla stop by the fort before returning to Valdivia (30min. from the Sernatur office, CH$300).

The town of Niebla itself features a short, yet pleasant, waterside walkway. Speckled with a few seafood restaurants and budget *hospedajes*, the otherwise-quiet town gets lively and brims with energy in the summer. Splurge and enjoy the biggest Niebla draw, a spacious and comfortable **cabaña ❷** suitable for families or a group of friends. (CH$25,000-50,000 per night.)

LAGO RANCO

FUTRONO   ☎ 63

Futrono is the largest town that lies on the banks of the Lago Ranco, a still, gorgeous lake that is yet to be taken over by tourism. Besides a beautiful view of this vast body of water, the town has little to offer, even though it boasts two main streets rather than the standard one of other lake towns.

⬛ TRANSPORTATION. Almost all **buses** to Futrono originate in Valdivia or Paillaco. **Buses Futrono** (☎ 481 279) and **Buses en Directo** (☎ 481 413) go to **Lago Ranco Village** via the dirt road circling the lake (1½hr., every 30min., CH$500). **Tur Bus** (☎ 481 402) goes to **Villarrica** (2hr., CH$1500). From **Valdivia**, buses going farther south can be boarded. **Minibuses** leave every 30min. for **Valdivia** (CH$1000) and **Paillaco** (CH$500).

⬛⬛ ORIENTATION AND PRACTICAL INFORMATION. Balmaceda is the main strip with a quarter-mile stretch of stores, restaurants, and bars. The helpful **tourist office** is located at the intersection of the two main streets, on the western end of town. (☎ 481 389 or 482 636; turiftrn@telsur.cl. Open M-F 9am-9pm, off-season 9am-5pm.) The police linger nearby on the way in from the Panamericana Carretera (1hr. drive from the highway). The nearest **banks** are in Valdivia, so make sure to withdraw cash there before heading to Futrono. **Currency exchange** is possible, but at poor rates. **Internet access** is available inside the sundry **store** at the intersection of LeoDegario and Balmaceda.

⬛ ACCOMMODATIONS. Hostería Rincon Arabe ❷, on Gaston Guarda Paredes, lies just down the road from the discoteque, near the *carabineros*. The airy *cabañas* are a 5min. walk from Lago Ranco. Señora Jemila is from Egypt and serves up delectable Arab cuisine in the restaurant adjoining the *hostería*. Get some food and then relax on the porches outside the *cabañas* to enjoy views of the lake. (☎ 481 406. CH$10,000-20,000 per night.) **Camping ❷** by the lake is popular with budget travelers. (CH$5000-10,000 per site.) Or splurge at the new and luxurious **Caja Compensación Los Andes ❹,** a hotel complex at Acharan Arche, including both rooms and individual *cabañas*, behind the municipality. Possibly the nicest place to stay in Futrono, the complex has rooms that overlook the lake as well as the lush Parque Futronhue. After a day of splashing around in the lake, you can rejuvenate yourself with an evening dip in the complex's indoor pool and a stop in the sauna, which is free for guests. (☎ 481 208. Singles CH$15,000; doubles CH$30,000; surcharge for non-members.)

◨◧ FOOD AND ENTERTAINMENT. The **restaurant** at Caja Compensación Los Andes is mediocre at best, but a much better option is available at LeoDegario 15, at a new place called **Las Terrazas ❸**. The pleasure of big-city-style fine dining is enhanced by gorgeous views from the restaurant's patio. (Most entrees CH$4000-6000.) A cheaper homestyle meal can be enjoyed at **Hostería De Floro ❷**, at Balmaceda 114 (☎481 271). The hearty soups (CH$1500) are always tasty and wholesome. The nearby **Restaurant Donde Chamullo ❷** at Balmaceda 565 (☎481 343), specializes in shellfish and other seafood delicacies. They fry almost everything on the menu, but if you're feeling adventurous enough, sample from their diverse raw bar; split open the porcupine-like shellfish and swallow its yellow innards whole. Otherwise, stick to the tried and true fish entrees (CH$2400-4500), *paila mariscos* (CH$2000), or *empanadas de mariscos* (CH$2500). The set lunch at **Rincon Arabe ❸** is a little pricey, but well worth the cost for an assortment of Middle Eastern delicacies (CH$5000). On weekends, the **discoteca** on Gaston Guarda opens its doors to townies and tourists alike, and stays thumping till the wee hours of the morning.

▨ OUTDOOR ACTIVITIES. Several parks and beaches can be accessed from Futrono via the 121km dirt road around Lago Ranco. The road is not always passable, and sometimes the only option for cars other than 4WD vehicles is to return to the Carretera (the Panamericana), and get at the lake from a different point. Nearby **Parque Futronhue** is a neatly manicured reserve with clearly labeled signs describing the flora to be found here. Fauna, including wild pigs, roams freely, but is largely harmless and quickly scampers away from curious tourists and children. **Fishing, horseback riding, trekking, boating, rafting trips,** and other ecological excursions can be booked between November and April, but the schedules and offerings vary frequently so consult with the tourist office to plan a trip to the park (see **Practical Information**, p. 385). Also ask about trips to **Isla Huapi,** a small island in Lago Ranco populated by native inhabitants.

Coique, just west of Futrono, is a lakefront resort with various housing complexes on the water. The best known is **Bahía Coique,** an expensive all-amenities-inclusive resort for wealthy Chileans. Coique's **beach** is the best on Lago Ranco and is consequently crowded during summer months.

Nearby **Llifén** is a natural and peaceful beach. Massive **Cerro Huequecura** (1584m) looms over the beach, making it a picturesque place to spend an afternoon swimming, picnicking, and fishing. Adjacent **Hostería Huequecura** is a nice, but somewhat expensive, place to stay on the waterfront. *Hostals* with reasonable rates lie in adjoining areas and **camping** is plentiful and always cheap.

LAGO RANCO VILLAGE ☎ 63

Although a one-road town, there is much more to Lago Ranco Village than the dusty highway running through it. Travelers will enjoy the rustic attractiveness of the town and its back country setting. The addition of a few good budget lodgings make it a good place to just relax and enjoy all that Lago Ranco has to offer. Nevertheless, the village has a long way to go before it can identify itself as a bonafide tourist hotspot—there is a palpable dearth of amenities.

To travel to and from Lago Ranco Village, use Inter Sur, Tur Bus, Buses Pirehueico, or Expreso Panguipulli which connect Lago Ranco to **Osorno** and **Valdivia** several times daily. Tur Bus also goes to **Santiago** in the summer (17hr., 1 per day). If driving, turn off the highway that circuits Lago Ranco at the Rio Bueno exit.

The road into town winds downhill past the pretty **municipal building** to the left, passing Calles Temuco and ending at Calle Viña del Mar on the lakefront. Coming east through town on the main road, the "highway" from Río Bueno, veer left at the sign for the **tourist office,** a helpful shackfull of info. (Open Dec.-Mar.) There is nowhere to change money in town, so get cash while in Valdivia or Osorno.

At Viña del Mar 145 lies the homey **Casona Italiana ❷,** a collection of six nice *cabañas* overlooking the water. The amiable owners permit barbecuing on their property, making for some festive summer nights. (☎491 225. Breakfast included. *Cabañas* CH$15,000-25,000.) Next door, **Hostería Phoenix ❷,** at Viña del Mar 141, has no-frills single and double rooms that are very plain but inexpensive. The pleasant restaurant and bar on the first floor spices up the atmosphere. (☎491 226. Breakfast included. Doubles CH$8000; triples CH$12,000.) The lively dockside restaurant **Ruca Ranco ❶** cooks up good set meals for a pittance. But if you really want to hold on to your cash, try barbecuing at the park along the beach, 50 yards away from Casona Italiana.

OSORNO   ☎64

Osorno (pop. 105,000) has retained the vestiges of its Germanic heritage more than any other city in Chile. The Spanish founded the city in 1558, but were forced south to Chiloé by Mapuche rebellions in 1599. Though they regained the city at the end of the 18th century, their hold on Osorno was always tenuous at best. It wasn't until German immigration in the mid-1800s that the city really began to thrive, soon becoming one of the country's dairy capitals. The German influence, so prevalent today, extends beyond the many farms and *chocolaterias* that cover the area—the values, nomenclature, and lifestyles of the people of Osorno are a unique blend of Germanic and Chilean cultures.

▐ TRANSPORTATION

Flights: Aeropuerto Carlos Hott Siebert, 7km outside of town. **Taxi** from downtown CH$2500. **LanChile,** Matta 862 (☎236 688), has flights to **Santiago** and **Temuco.**

Buses: Long-distance buses leave from the **main terminal,** Errázuriz 1400 (☎234 149). Several companies run buses, including **Cruz del Sur** (☎232 777 or 232 778), **Norte Transporte Turismo** (☎233 319), and **Pullman Sur** (☎232 777). They run to: **Bariloche, ARG** (8hr., 10:30am and 12:45pm, CH$8000); **Puerto Montt** (2hr., every 30min. 7am-10pm, CH$1200); **Santiago** (16hr.; departures in the morning and night; CH$7000, sleeper CH$18,000); **Temuco** (4hr., every 30min. 7am-7:30pm, CH$3000); **Valdivia** (2hr., every 30min. 7am-10:15pm, CH$1500). Local buses leave from the **Terminal Buses Rurales** at the Mercado Municipal, on the corner of Prat and Errázuriz. **Expreso Lagos Puyehue** (☎243 919) and **Buses Puyehue** (☎236 541) run to: **Aguas Calientes** (2hr., CH$1000); **Anticura** (min. 2 passengers; 8 per day 8am-7:15pm, CH$2000); **Entre Lagos** (1hr., CH$500). **Mauricio minibus transport service,** on Freire between Ramírez and Mackenna, will drive as far as Bariloche, ARG. Often goes to **Parque Puyehue** (CH$28,000) for a whole day, or to other regional destinations

Car Rental: A&S Sur Automoviles, Matta 889 (☎310 694), between Rodríguez and Bilbao, rents cars for CH$15,000-30,000 per day including minimal insurance and taxes.

▐▐ ORIENTATION AND PRACTICAL INFORMATION

The **Plaza de Armas** is in the center of town, bordered by **Ramírez** to the north, **Matta** to the east (where Osorno's most distinctive building, a tall, latticed cathedral, faces the plaza), **Mackenna** to the south, and **O'Higgins** to the west. Banks surround the plaza, and several money exchanges operate just off the plaza on Ramírez. The long distance Bus Terminal exits onto Errázuriz; the Plaza de Armas (less than 500m away), by turning right (to the south) out of the terminal and passing the municipal market and Plazuela Yungay (at Avenida Prat), a busy little plaza with benches and foosball tables.

LAKES DISTRICT

Tourist Office: Sernatur, O'Higgins 667 (☎234 104), offers some printed material and will readily answer your questions. English speaker in summer. Open Dec.-Mar. 8:30am-8:30pm; Apr.-Nov. 8:30am-1pm and 2:30-5:30pm. **Summer Kiosk** on the Plaza de Armas. There is a second office at the **main terminal,** 2nd fl. (☎234 149). Open 8am-8pm. **Conaf,** Martínez de Rozas 430 (☎234 393), has some good, detailed information on Parque Nacional Puyehue.

Tours: Club Andino, O'Higgins 1073 (☎232 297), can help arrange transportation to and within Parque Nacional Puyehue.

Banks: Banks surround the Plaza de Armas. **Banco de Chile** is on the corner of Mackenna and Matta, **Banco Santiago** is on the corner of Mackenna and O'Higgins, and there is also a **Banco BHIF.** All open M-F 8am-2pm, Sa 8am-noon.

Currency Exchange: Cambiotur, Mackenna 1004 (☎234 846) is a good, reputable money exchange. Helpful staff also provides travel services. Other money changers are on Ramírez, off the plaza.

Bookstores: Librería Inglés is a small shop in the Patio Freire outdoor mall. Limited collection of English books. **Multilibros,** on Cochrane between Freire and Mackenna, is much bigger, but almost all books are in Spanish.

Laundromat: Lavandería Limpec, Prat 678, just south of Plazuela Yungay. CH$3000 per kg for wash and dry. 5hr. service. Open M-Sa 8am-7pm.

Hospital: Hospital Base (☎235 572) is 10 blocks south of the plaza on Buhler, in the southern part of the *centro.*

Telephones: Many *centros de llamados* are around the plaza and on Ramírez.

Internet Access: Internet Cafe, Ramírez 959 (☎252 841), underground, is cheap but slow. CH$350 per hr. Open 10am-1pm and 3pm-midnight. **GEA.com,** Mackenna 1140 (☎249 671). Quality connection but a bit pricey. CH$750 per hr. **El Patio.com,** Freire 542 (☎269 788), has fast connections. CH$500 per hr. Open 11am-10pm.

Post Office: O'Higgins 645, next to Sernatur, just west of the plaza.

⛺ ACCOMMODATIONS

Osorno can be bitter cold at night, so heated rooms during the winter are almost a must. However, summers are often mild, making air conditioning unnecessary.

Hotel Niltaihuen, Los Carrera 951 (☎232 356 or 234 960), between Cochrane and Matta, is one of the best values in town. A cozy building with heating, it has nice, clean rooms. Breakfast (CH$1500) can be served to your room. There is also a travel and car rental agency below it which are equally helpful, but no English speakers are available. Singles CH$15,000, off-season CH$10,000; doubles CH$20,000/CH$12,000. ❹

Hostal Rucaitue, Freire 546 (☎239 922), has nice rooms with TVs and hot baths. A pleasant cafe serves up sandwiches (CH$1000), and a small bar behind the cafe has draft beers (CH$550). Free parking. Breakfast included. Singles CH$15,000; doubles CH$17,000. ❹

Hotel Interlagos, Cochrane 515 (☎232 581 or 234 695; www.hotelinterlagos.cl), between Los Carrera and Ramírez. The Interlagos is a real stretch for a tight budget, but is worth the splurge. Convenient central location, but situated on a quiet side street away from the noise and bustle of downtown. Large rooms are modern, and elegant. Breakfast included. Check-out 10am. Singles CH$25,400; doubles CH$33,200. ❺

Residencial Schultz, on Freire, between Los Carrera and Ramírez, has hot water and heaters in the small, clean rooms, but service is not very welcoming. The *residencial* also lies on a busy, noisy street. Breakfast included. Singles CH$8000; doubles CH$10,000. ❸

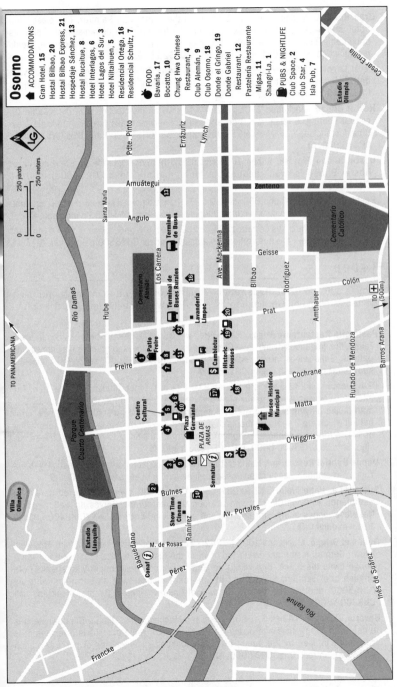

Osorno

▲ ACCOMMODATIONS
Gran Hotel, **15**
Hostal Bilbao, **20**
Hostal Bilbao Express, **21**
Hospedaje Sánchez, **13**
Hostal Rucaitue, **8**
Hotel Interlagos, **6**
Hotel Lagos del Sur, **3**
Hotel Niltaihuen, **5**
Residencial Ortega, **16**
Residencial Schultz, **7**

◆ FOOD
Bavaria, **17**
Bocatto, **10**
Chung Hwa Chinese
    Restaurant, **4**
Club Alemán, **9**
Club Osorno, **18**
Donde el Gringo, **19**
Donde Gabriel
    Restaurant, **12**
Pastelería Restaurante
    Migas, **11**
Shangri-La, **1**

🎵 PUBS & NIGHTLIFE
Club Space, **2**
Club Star, **4**
Isla Pub, **7**

LAKES DISTRICT

Gran Hotel, O'Higgins 615 (☎232 171), on the corner with Ramírez. This classy, old hotel is in need of a little renovation, but still has some of its old-school charm. Its unbeatable location on the northeast corner of the plaza may be worth the price. Breakfast included. Singles CH$18,500; doubles CH$26,500. ❹

Hotel Lagos del Sur, O'Higgins 564 (☎243 244). This upscale venue offers private baths, cable TV, 24hr. room service, central heating, and laundry service. Singles CH$21,400; doubles CH$27,000. ❺

Hostal Bilbao, Mackenna 1205 (☎264 444), at the intersection with Prat. Cable TV, central heating, a restaurant/bar, and laundry service make for a comfortable stay. Breakfast included. Singles CH$17,000, off-season CH$12,000; doubles CH$20,000/ CH$15,000. ❹

Hostal Bilbao Express, Bilbao 1019 (☎262 200), near Cochrane. The new cousin of Hostal Bilbao is even cheaper but more spartan. Dorms CH$4500; doubles CH$10,000. ❷

Residencial Ortega, Colón 602 (☎232 592), just a block away from the bus terminal. Rooms are cheap and come with a continental breakfast. CH$6000 per person. ❷

Hospedaje Sánchez, Los Carrera 1595 (☎232 560), is a good place to stay if you want a cheap room near the bus station. Breakfast included. CH$5500 per person. ❷

FOOD

Osorno's cultural diversity is reflected in its cosmopolitan culinary options—expected Chilean and German fare is spiced up with Chinese and Nepalese offerings.

Pastelería Restaurante Migas, Freire 584 (☎ 235 541), has the best pastries in town. Jaime, the gregarious owner, is of German descent and loves to practice his English with patrons. Sandwiches, pizzas, baked *empanadas* CH$600-3000. *Tarteleta* of coconut, strawberries, and fresh cream CH$750. ❶

Club Alemán (☎232 514) is a palpable vestige of German influence in the area. The interior is covered with gorgeous old-world German decor and has cheery, romantic German music playing softly in the background. Patrons are greeted by a homey lobby behind which are 3 separate rooms that house the restaurant, cafe, and bar (also know as Fogón Bar on a separate entrance). Meals are a fusion of German and Chilean cuisine. Entrees CH$3000-6000. Beer CH$800-1200. ❸

Donde Gabriel Restaurant, Ramírez 1170 (☎232 763), on northwest corner of Plazuela Yungay. A standard lunch of *pollo asado,* fries, and a beer costs CH$2200. ❷

Shangri-La, Patio Freire 542 (☎257 755). The amiable owner Jay moved here from Kathmandu with his Chilean wife to open this restaurant. Serves up well-prepared Nepalese dishes along with fine Chilean specialties. Entrees CH$2000-4000. Open 11am-midnight. ❷

Donde el Gringo, Mackenna 1027 (☎242 797), between Cochrane and Freire. This well-known German restaurant lies in the heart of the Historic District. Locals will tell you a *gringo* owns the place—that would be Gert, a German descendent who speaks both English and German. Specializes in fine meat dishes such as succulent wild pig (CH$5000) and has the largest selection of Chilean wines in Osorno. Steak and fish CH$3000-5000. ❸

Bavaria, O'Higgins 743 (☎231 303), between Mackenna and Bilbao. The downstairs is a cafe with sandwiches and pizzas (CH$1000-3000), while upstairs is a restaurant is constantly infused by the aroma of a slow roasting succulent leg of pork. Set lunch CH$3000, entrees CH$3000-5000. ❸

Chung Hwa Chinese Restaurant, Matta 517 (☎243 445). No self-respecting Chilean city would be caught *chifa*-less, and Osorno's offering is among the finest, offering good 2-person meals for CH$5500. Entrees CH$2000-5000. Open 11am-4:30pm and 6:30pm–midnight. ❷

Bocatto, Ramírez 938 (☎238 000), between Cochrane and Matta, has sandwiches and pizzas (CH$1000-2000). Open 10am-10pm. ❶

Club Osorno, Cochrane 759 (☎234 098), has a laid-back, sports bar type atmosphere. A great place to unwind with a beer and watch a soccer game or Marcelo Ríos tennis match with locals. Entrees and sandwiches CH$3000-5000. Open 9am-11pm. ❸

🔘 SIGHTS

Osorno is not a city for major attractions. That said, the pervasive Germanic influence is still very present in many of the city's buildings and makes for a decent walking tour. The heart of the city's **Historic District** is along Mackenna. Walking west along the avenue will bring you past some of the oldest establishments in town, most built in 19th-century Victorian style. The section between Cochrane and Freire has been well-preserved, and is filled with quaint boutique stores and restaurants including the renown Italian pizza place, **Bell Italia,** an exquisite **hand-icraft store,** Alta Artesania, and the best **wine store** in the city, La Casa del Vino.

The other major attraction in Osorno is the **Museo Municipal,** Matta 896, on the corner of Bilbao. Although the collection is a little eclectic, it has some interesting pieces. Keep an eye out for the classic Wurlitzer jukebox from Germany and a gorgeous old pipe organ. The history of Osorno is also retold through an interesting display using old photos and weapons, but the exhibit is not well-organized. (☎238 615. Open M-Th 9:30am-5:30pm, F 9:30am-4:30pm, Sa 2:30-6pm. Free.)

🎵 🎦 ENTERTAINMENT AND NIGHTLIFE

Like in most major Chilean cities, the main event is always the goings-on of the local soccer team (on or off the field). Although most locals are bitterly disappointed by their team's descent to Chile's second division in 2001, you can still catch a lively game at the Estadio Olímpico (☎233 211). There's also a **Show Time Cinema,** Ramírez 650, that plays subtitled and dubbed English films and the occasional Spanish one as well (CH$2000). To get your **shopping** fix, head to the **Plaza Germania,** on the northern end of the Plaza de Armas. As Osorno's only indoor shopping mall, you can get all the chain-store goodies and food-court snacks you've been missing. The outdoor **Patio Freire,** on Los Carrera and Freire, offers similar features, situated around a pretty, manicured, central garden. Nightlife options are few and far between, but worthy of a night on the town.

Isla Pub, on the corner of Cochrane and Mackenna, has a log cabin exterior and a fun, lively atmosphere inside. The well-stocked bar tends to draw a fairly professional crowd.

Club Space, on Los Carrera, near the corner with Bulnes. The rowdy downstairs attracts mostly university students, while upstairs is a chill bar scene with good drink specials that draw in a corporate clientele. Weekend cover CH$2000.

Club Star, on Bulnes, 2 blocks south from Los Carrera, has an even younger crowd than Space, but a much larger dance floor with several balconies and bars. With a cheaper cover, Thursdays tend to draw an older crowd, but weekends bring more outrageous, crowded partying. Weekend cover CH$3000.

LAKES DISTRICT

PARQUE NACIONAL PUYEHUE

Sitting in the foothills of the Andes at the border with Argentina, Parque Nacional Puyehue is one of the most popular parks in Chile. Ironically, however, this is not because of the vast mountain forests it protects, but rather because the famed hot springs at Aguas Calientes attract visitors from far and wide. Covering 106,000 hectares of rugged *cordillera*, the park is a good bet whether you're looking to rough it on campgrounds or live it up in luxury in ski resorts. Regardless of why you're there, it's hard *not* to enjoy the thick forests, populated with pumas, screaming foxes, coipos, güiñas, vizcachas, and pudús. Look among the diverse flora for attractive birdlife including cóndors, choroys, bandurrias, and hualas.

AT A GLANCE

AREA: 106,000 hectares.

CLIMATE: Temperate with a cool annual average temperature of 8°C.

GATEWAYS: Osorno; Bariloche, ARG.

FEATURES: Sector Anticura, Sector Antillanca, and Aguas Calientes.

HIGHLIGHTS: Hiking Sendero de Excursión al Volcán Puyehue and Volcán Casablanca. Hot springs of Aguas Calientes.

CAMPING: Camping and picnicking grounds are scattered throughout the park. Several *refugios* and *cabañas* are available along the trails.

ORIENTATION

The park is divided into three sectors—Sector Anticura, Aguas Calientes, and Sector Antillanca. **Sector Anticura,** traversed by the Río Gol, Gol is best suited to hiking, with trails extending from the entrance to **Volcán Puyehue** (10km), **Los Baños** (20km), **Pampa Frutilla** (20km), and **Lago Constancia** (28km). **Aguas Calientes** offers hikes to **Lago Rupanco,** but the main attraction here is the renown hotsprings (see **Practical Information,** below). **Sector Antillanca** is home to **Volcán Casablanca,** fabulous ski resorts, and some of the best skiing in the area. The park's **ski center** sits at the base of Volcán Casablanca and the resort boasts facilities for both downhill and cross-country skiers.

TRANSPORTATION

The park lies on Ruta 215, which runs from Osorno over the border to Bariloche, Argentina. At km 76, the road turns north through Sector Anticura and crosses the border at Paso Pajaritos. U-485 splits off at km 76 and heads south past the main *guardaparque* in Sector Aguas Calientes and the hot springs resort before ending at the ski resort in Sector Antillanca. Club Andino or Conaf in Osorno (see **Practical Information,** p. 388) can help arrange transportation within the park. A van and driver from Aguas to Anticura and back costs about CH$18,000; from Aguas to Antillanca and back is CH$15,000. The most economical travel option is to take both trips with the same driver—the fare can be negotiated to CH$25,000. Conaf park guard Luis Santibanez and his son Gerardo (☎ 099 253 9150) also offer trips and tours of the park in their minibus.

PRACTICAL INFORMATION

The main **Conaf office** for the park lies in Sector Aguas Calientes, although Sector Anticura and Sector Antillanca also have central Conaf outposts. **Information centers** are located in Aguas Calientes and Anticura. A small **store** resides in the

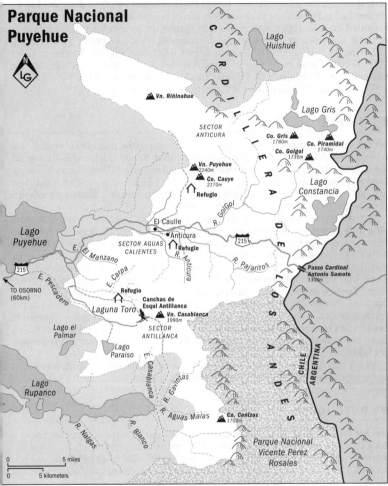

Parque Nacional Puyehue

Lago Huishué

CORDILLERA

Vn. Riñinahue

SECTOR ANTICURA

Lago Gris

Co. Gris
1780m

Co. Piramidal
1740m

Co. Golgol
1730m

Vn. Puyehue
2240m

Co. Cauye
2170m

Refugio

Lago Constancia

R. Golgol

El Caulle
•Anticura

215

SECTOR AGUAS CALIENTES

Refugio

E. El Manzano

R. Anticura

R. Pajaritos

Passo Cardinal
Antonio Samote
1308m

Lago Puyehue

E. Carpa

215

E. Pescadero

TO OSORNO
(60km)

Refugio

Laguna Toro

Canchas de
Esqui Antillanca

Vn. Casablanca
1990m

SECTOR
ANTILLANCA

Lago el Palmar

Lago Paraiso

E. Casablanca

DE LOS ANDES

CHILE
ARGENTINA

Lago Rupanco

R. Gaviotas

R. Aguas Malas

Co. Cenizos
1700m

R. Nalgas

R. Blanco

Parque Nacional
Vicente Perez
Rosales

0   5 miles

0   5 kilometers

Hostería de Aguas Calientes. The **ski resort** (☎235 114; antillanca@telsur.cl) in Antillanca can be reached year-round, although winter is obviously the busiest season. For those looking for value package deals to the park's snowy slopes, check out **Club Andino** in Osorno (see **Tours**, p. 388).

ACCOMMODATIONS AND FOOD

Most of the established lodging in the park resides in Sector Aguas Calientes. There are a variety of *cabañas*, some of which can be rented through **Cabañas Nilque ❺**. These are run by the Nilque family who also own the Hotel Niltaihuen in Osorno (see **Accommodations**, p. 388). Reservations can be made at their travel agency below the hotel. (*cabañas* US$40-65.) Also look into the **hostería** and the **Aguas Calientes resort** (see **Outdoors**, below). In Sector Anticura, there are several

campsites near the *guardparque*. **Termas Puyehue Resort with Gran Hotel and Spa ❺**, resides just outside of the park and is in direct competition with Aguas Calientes. Founded in 1957, this gorgeous hotel is connected to a beautiful, modern spa, which is slightly more expensive than its competitor but also better quality. (☎232 157. Singles CH$32,000-180,000; doubles CH$47,000-200,000; 4-person suites CH$100,000.) There aren't very many options for food outside the resorts but the *hostería* does have a **cafe ❸**. (*Menú* CH$4500, sandwiches and entrees CH$2000-4000.) There are two picnicking sites in the park as well.

📷 HIKING

Sector Aguas Calientes is the smallest, but is home to the main **Conaf** station and several short hikes. The longest of these is **Sendero Berlín** which winds its way all the way to Lago Berlín and terminates at a small *refugio* (11km, 5hr. round-trip). **Sendero Pionero** climbs its way up to the tallest hill in the sector with a great view of Lago Puyehue and Río Chanleufú (1.8km, 1¼hr. round-trip); **Sendero Recodo** is a short jaunt to the picnic grounds (380m, 15min.).

Sector Anticura has the most extensive trail system. For those wanting to start off a little easier, there are several **miradors** that can be easily accessed from the *guardaparque* in this sector. Across from the Conaf office are trails to **Salto del Indio** (900m) and **Salto de La Princesa** (1.2km); each takes at most 15min. each way. Indio is taller with a wider vista, but Princesa is not to be snubbed. For those who want to take on some serious trekking, there are several good excursions. **Sendero de Excursión al Volcán Puyehue** is a two- to three-day hike (16km) that runs past Volcán Puyehue, the Azufreras, and the baths. On the slopes of the volcano rests a *refugio* that can fit up to 12 people. The other major venture is **Sendero de Excursión a la Pampa de Frutilla.** Following an ancient road, this two- to three-day hike starts from the Último Puesto area and winds up at a *refugio* in a dry lakebed.

Sector Antillanca in the south of the park does not have much hiking, other than an excursion between Volcán Casablanca and Lago Rupanco.

🥾 OUTDOORS

The **hot springs** of Aguas Calientes are one of the park's main attractions. Visitors flock to the **resort** for luxurious treatments ranging from a simple dip in one of the thermal pools to massages and aromatherapy. (☎ 197 4529 or 197 4531. Indoor hot pool CH$4500; outdoor hot pool CH$1200; hot tub treatments CH$5000; massage

BORDER CROSSING INTO ARGENTINA: PASO PAJARITOS
Ruta 215, the road that leads from Osorno through Entre Lagos into the Parque Nacional Puyehue, continues on to Bariloche in Argentina. Within the park itself, the road runs through Sector Anticura before arriving at **Chilean customs,** 22km from the border. From there, the road continues just north of the majestic Cerro Frutilla before winding up eventually in **Bariloche,** Argentina.

The pass can be closed in winter due to inclement weather, so it's worth your while to double-check with authorities in Osorno before attempting the crossing. The customs office at Pajaritos station is open from 8am-7pm. The process is fairly simple and involves no more than a brief search of your luggage for contraband and various food products and a passport stamp (see **Essentials: Border Crossings,** p. 65, for info on visas and fees).

CH$12,000; mudbath CH$10,000; aromatherapy CH$7000.) The resort also has four-person **cabañas** ❺ that it rents out to guests with a little advance notice. (CH$62,000 per cabin, off-season CH$35,000.) The Osorno office, O'Higgins 784 (☎232 881) runs **daytrips.** If booking through them, opt for the package deal including lunch and pool fees to get the best value (with open air pool CH$8000, indoor pool CH$10,000).

LAGO LLANQUIQUÉ

PUERTO OCTAY   ☎ 64

While Frutillar's German colonial architecture is well-preserved and cultivated as a quaint tourist attraction, the colonial architecture that graces the southern stretches of Puerto Octay is authentic, but many of the town's colonial structures are in some stage of disrepair and ruin. Off the main tourist route but still (barely) on Llanquihué's transportation network, this northern lake port is a quieter, less convenient alternative to towns like Frutillar and Puerto Varas. Architecture and history buffs will enjoy a stroll through town and a look at the museum, but it might not be worth a long trip out of your way.

▐ TRANSPORTATION. Buses depart from the station on top of the hill, at Balmaceda and Esperanza, for **Osorno** (5 bus companies; every 15-30min., M-F 6:30am-8pm, Sa-Su 8am-8pm; CH$500) and **Puerto Montt** (5 per day, CH$1200) via **Puerto Varas** (CH$1000) and **Frutillar** (CH$600).

▰▱ ORIENTATION AND PRACTICAL INFORMATION. The tourist information kiosk, next to the municipal offices on Esperanza to the east of Plaza de Armas, has a map posted year-round to help travelers find important municipal services. (☎391 750. Open Dec.-Mar.) To change money, try **Banco Estado,** Pedro Montt 345, north of Independencia. (☎391 332. Open M-F 9am-2pm.) Conveniently below the Hospedaje Teuber (see **Accommodations and Food,** below), **Supermercado Teuber** offers the best selection of groceries in town. (Open in summer 8:30am-midnight, in winter 8:30am-9:30pm.)

For emergency services, the **police station,** Pedro Montt 507 (☎391 615), can be found on the road to Osorno across from the Shell station. The **hospital,** Pedro Montt 601, is across the diagonal street northeast of the Plaza de Armas. (☎259 265 or emergency ☎259 260. Primary care M, F 5-7pm and T-Th 5-6pm. Emergency room open 24hr.) The **call center,** Pedro Montt 387, is north of the bank. (☎391 554. Open 9am-10pm.) For **Internet,** the Municipal library, at Esperanza and Independencia, gives people 30min. free. (☎391 523. Open M-F 8:30am-12:30pm and 1:45-6:30pm.) Find the **post office,** Esperanza 555, in the municipal building. (M-F 9am-12:30pm and 2:30-5:30pm, Sa 9am-12:30pm.)

▐▛ ACCOMMODATIONS AND FOOD. Probably the best reason to stay in Puerto Octay is ▨**Zapato Amarillo Backpacker** ❷, 2.5km north of town on the road to Osorno. Frequent buses run this way and will know where to stop if you ask. Look for the yellow boot, follow the driveway past the first cluster of houses, and go right at the gate and along the hedgerow. The multilingual family is a great travel resource, offering all sorts of perks from their warm, cozy "grass roof chalet." (☎391 575; ledgemaster@zapatoamarillo.8k.com. Call from town for pickup, but reserve ahead. Bicycles, canoes, laser sailboats, and mountaineering equipment for rent. Tours and transport around the lake offered. Internet CH$1000 per hr. Laundry. Kitchen access. Breakfast included, other meals offered. Dorms CH$6000; doubles CH$14,000.) A cheaper, plainer, in-town option is **Hospedaje Teuber ❶**, German Wulf 712, above the grocery store. The rooms are nothing to scream about, but they do come with breakfast. (☎391 348. Kitchen access. Shared baths. Doubles CH$7000.)

For some good eats, **Baviera ❶**, German Wulf 582, is a jack-of-all-trades joint with a restaurant, bar, and the best *almuerzo* deal (CH$2000) in town. (☎391 460. Open daily 10am-11pm.)

◙ SIGHTS. The Puerto Octay's main (and perhaps only) attraction is its German ancestry. For some historical background, peruse the **Museo el Colono,** Independencia 591, at Esperanza, which has devoted its second floor to preserving the spirit and some specific articles of the colonial period. During the off-season, only one room is open, but the museum is still well worth a visit. (☎391 523. Open Dec.-Mar. Tu-Su 10am-1pm and 3-7pm, Apr.-Nov. M-F 8:30am-12:30pm and 1:45-6:30pm. CH$600; Apr.-Nov. free.) A more informative walking tour of the town's history is in the brochure **Histórico Paseo de Puerto Octay,** which will direct you to the town's oldest and occasionally most decrepit buildings. Find copies of the brochure at the museum or in Zapato Amarillo (see **Accommodations and Food,** above).

FRUTILLAR   ☎ 65

Hugging a crescent-shaped shoreline, **Frutillar Bajo** is a resort town that exists for for only two blocks and about four months per year. From December through March, the town hops with Chilean and foreign visitors—almost every residence puts out a *"hospedaje"* sign, and festivities peak with the **Semana de Musical Frutillar** (in late January or early February), a celebration of classical and jazz music. For the rest of the year, however, the town is not known for rocking 'n' rolling—even sports and picnics are prohibited on the inviting shoreside park. Peaceful and quiet perhaps to a fault, this historic German settlement offers rest and relaxation to those who seek its sheltered shores.

Frutillar Alto is only 3km west of Frutillar Bajo, which is indisputably the more rowdy and practical of the towns, offering **supermarkets, laundromats, bars,** a **police station,** a **medical center,** and **buses** to the outside world.

▐ TRANSPORTATION. Frequent **buses** (CH$200) and **colectivos** (CH$300) connect Frutillar Bajo with Alto. From there, *micros* run to **Puerto Montt** (every 5min., CH$900) via **Puerto Varas** (CH$600) and **Puerto Octay** (every 2hr., CH$600).

▐ ORIENTATION AND PRACTICAL INFORMATION. The two towns are separated by **Av. Carlos Richter.** In Frutillar Bajo, the main drag along the shoreline is **Av. Philippi,** with **Av. Vicente Peréz Rosales** one block back from the lake.

The **visitor information** kiosk (☎420 198), in the middle of town on the Plaza de Armas, operates seasonally from December through March. **Banco Santander,** Phillipi 555, at the north end of town, has a **24hr. ATM.** (☎421 228. Open M-F 9am-2pm.) The **police station** (☎422 435) stands on Carlos Richter, the road between the two towns. **Internet access** is only to be found in Frutillar Alto's call centers. Mail leaves town from the **Correos de Chile,** at the corner of San Martín and Vicente Peréz Rosales. (Open M-F 9am-1:30pm and 3-6pm, Sa 9am-12:30pm.)

ᚠᚢ ACCOMMODATIONS AND FOOD. In summer, it pays to reserve accommodations well in advance, especially around the music festival. *Hospedajes* in town charge a premium for the scenery and small-town ambience. **Turismo el Arroyo ❸,** Philippi 989, operates a spacious, year-round *hospedaje* that offers one of the best values in town. (☎421 560. Breakfast included. Rooms with shared bath CH$8000 per person, CH$5000 off-season; with private bath CH$12,000/ CH$6000.) **Hotel Am See ❺,** Philippi 539, north of town center, is the warmest and most personal of the town's accommodations, with grand views. It is worth the splurge, especially in the off-season. (☎421 539; fax 421 858; ciberg@123mail.cl. Breakfast included. Cable TV. Private baths. Singles CH$30,000, off-season CH$14,000; doubles CH$40,000/CH$20,000.) For the HI faithful, **Hostería Winkler ❹,** Philippi 1155, at the south end of town, is a German colonial mansion with central heating, crowded rooms, and droopy beds. (☎421 388. Dec.-Mar. CH$15,000-20,000 per person, Apr.-Nov. CH$8000-12,000; HI members CH$13,000/CH$7000.)

Shaded tent sites are available about 1.5km south of town at **Camping Los Ciruelillos ❶,** visible from town with its long, cookie-cutter hotel building and pre-fab *cabañas*. (☎420 163 or 339 123. Showers and kitchen. 2-person sites CH$5000; 6-person CH$10,000; *cabañas* for 6 CH$40,000.)

Tourist prices are also applicable to Frutillar's restaurants. A notable exception is **Trayen Salon de Té ❶,** Philippi 963, which offers affordable *kuchen* (a German fruit tart) and *churrasco con palta y tomate* (grilled meat with avocado and tomato; CH$1900). The coffee and tea may be a bit overpriced, but the view of lake and the volcano make it all worthwhile. (☎421 346. Open in summer daily 8am-10pm, sometimes later on weekends.)

◙ SIGHTS. The **Museo Colonial Alemán,** on Rosales at the north end of town near Richter, provides some insight into the German colonial exodus to the Llanquihué area following the Democratic Revolution of 1848 in Germany. The building with the waterwheel houses a textual record of the history of Germans in Chile, while the two outlying houses replicate the abodes of both wealthy and modest German settlers. (☎421 142. Open Tu-Su 10am-1:30pm and 3-6pm. CH$1600; children CH$500.) The **Bosque Nativo Chile,** at the Centro Experimental Forestal Edmundo Winkler, is a sort of woodlands observatory. With a short nature trail illustrating different local arborial species, this 33-hectare park satisfies the contemplative outdoors enthusiast. (☎421 291. Open daily 8am-6pm. CH$1000, children CH$500.)

PUERTO VARAS   ☎65

Twenty kilometers inland from its seaport neighbor of Puerto Montt, the lakefront town of Puerto Varas (pop. 28,000) is a little less industrial. In fact, it has only one pier, which supports a visitor information staff rather than a fleet of fishing boats. Puerto Varas may be a bit too touristy for some—tour agencies line nearly every downtown avenue, hawking treks, rafting trips, and tours to various parts of the southern Lakes District. Nevertheless, with plentiful *hospedajes* and all of the conveniences of home, this German colonial town makes a great jumping-off point for exploration of the surrounding region, including many picturesque destinations around Lago Llanquihué. On sunny days, views are breathtaking—waves lap against Costanera Drive, offering a brilliant contrast to the thundering volcanoes and toothy peaks that mark the border with Argentina.

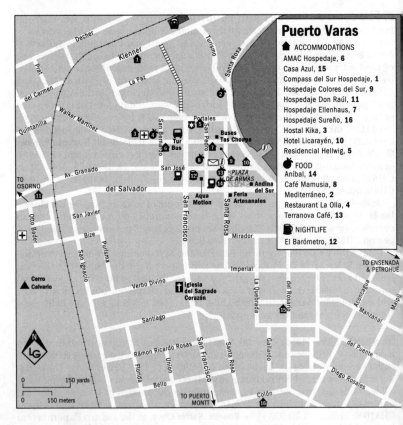

Puerto Varas

🏠 ACCOMMODATIONS
AMAC Hospedaje, **6**
Casa Azul, **15**
Compass del Sur Hospedaje, **1**
Hospedaje Colores del Sur, **9**
Hospedaje Don Raúl, **11**
Hospedaje Ellenhaus, **7**
Hospedaje Sureño, **16**
Hostal Kika, **3**
Hotel Licarayén, **10**
Residencial Hellwig, **5**

🍴 FOOD
Aníbal, **14**
Café Mamusia, **8**
Mediterráneo, **2**
Restaurant La Olla, **4**
Terranova Café, **13**

🌙 NIGHTLIFE
El Barómetro, **12**

📷 TRANSPORTATION

Flights: The **airport** is 45km away, beyond Puerto Montt, but **LanChile**, Granado 560
(☎234 799), operates an office in town. Open M-F 9:30am-1:30pm and 3:30-8pm, Sa
10am-2pm. To get to the airport, take a *micro* to Puerto Montt (see below; CH$600)
and then board a big, blue Pullman airport bus (CH$900). A taxi to the airport costs
CH$11,000-12,000.

Buses: The buses in town do not leave from a single terminal, but there are 4 different
consolidated offices in town. **Tur Bus,** W. Martínez 227A (☎233 787), runs to **Santiago** (6, 8, 9:30pm, CH$15,900; *cama* 6:45 and 8:50pm, CH$31,000) and **Temuco**
(5-6 per day, CH$3700) via **Osorno** (CH$1100). **Andes Mar** and **Buses Lit,** W. Martínez 227B (☎237 255), go to **Bariloche, ARG** (W, F, Su 8:50am; CH$9000) and
Santiago (8:30am, 7:20, 9:20pm; CH$10,000). **Tas Choapa,** W. Martínez 230
(☎233 831), goes to: **Bariloche, ARG** (10:30am, CH$9000); **Osorno** (CH$1000);
Santiago (6:15 and 8:15pm, CH$8000; *cama* 8:30pm, CH$20,000). **Pullman Sur**
and **Cruz del Sur,** San Pedro 210 (☎231 925), go to: **Bariloche, ARG** (daily 8:50am,
additional trip Th, Su 11:15am; CH$8000); **Castro** (5 per day, CH$3500) via **Ancud**

(CH$2500); **Santiago** (5 per day, CH$11,000-24,000); **Temuco** (5-10 per day, CH$4000) via **Valdivia** (CH$2500) and **Osorno** (CH$1200). **Cruz del Sur** buses depart from a terminal southeast of town, on San Francisco. **Andina del Sud,** Del Salvador 72 (☎232 811; www.crucedelagos.cl), is the only operator that runs the expensive hybrid bus/boat trip to **Bariloche, ARG,** including 3 bus jaunts and 2 lake crossings (in summer 1-2 days, 8:30am, US$130 not including lodging and food; in winter 2 days, night in Peulla, M-F). Office open M-F 8:30am-1pm and 3-7pm, Sa 8:30am-1pm.

Micros: All *micros* heading east leave from the front of La Olla Restaurant (see p. 401); those going to the north also stop in front of El Mesón de Nueva Branau, on San José, just northwest of San Bernardo. **Expressos** (☎232 253) run to **Llanquihué** (every 5-10min., CH$300) and **Puerto Montt** (every 5-10min., CH$600). **Thaebus** goes to **Frutillar** (every 10-15min., CH$600) via **Llanquihué** and **Puerto Octay** (every 2½hr.; CH$1000). **Interlagos** (☎257 015) goes to **Ensenada** (every 30min., CH$1000) and **Petrohué** (every hr., CH$1200). **Buses Fierro** (☎253 022) goes to **Ensenada. Suyai** also runs buses to **Puerto Chico** and **Puerto Montt.** Fares are fixed. Look for the destination on the windshield and flag the bus down.

Taxis: Can be found at the taxi stand across from the Vyhmeister supermarket (see **Orientation and Practical Information,** p. 400) and at the intersection of Santa Rosa and El Salvador. If you need pick-up at an accommodation, call **Radio Taxi** (☎234 200). *Colectivos* run to **Puerto Chico** and other neighborhoods.

ORIENTATION AND PRACTICAL INFORMATION

It is fairly easy to get oriented downtown—look for the main lakeside quadrant, the **Plaza de Armas.** The major northwest-southeast thoroughfare is **San Francisco,** which continues south to access **Ruta 5 Sur** to Puerto Montt. Running northeast-southwest, **San José** and **Del Salvador** extend beyond town to **Ruta 5 Norte** towards Osorno. **Costanera,** along the shoreline, heads east through Puerto Chico along the south side of the lake to Ensenada and Petrohué. **San José** becomes **Granado** beyond San Bernardo, but the changeover is unmarked and somewhat confusing.

Tourist Office: Informatur (☎338 542), at the corner of San José and Santa Rosa. Its status as a subscription-based tourist promotion agency undermines its quantity and quality of information. Open 8am-11pm, off-season 10:30am-12:30pm and 3-7:30pm. **Información Turística** (☎237 956), on the pier, has less biased info and better maps. Open 9am-11pm; off-season M-F 9am-1:30pm and 3-7pm, Sa-Su 10am-1:30pm and 3-7pm.

Tours: There are a handful of adventure tour operators in town, but two of them do most of the walk-in, independent traveler business. **Al Sur Expeditions,** Del Salvador 100 (☎232 300; www.alsurexpeditions.com), on the lake side of Plaza de Armas, offers rafting on the Petrohué (5hr., CH$18,000-20,000), horseback riding (1 day; CH$30,000), and an ascent of Osorno (12hr., US$108 including equipment and insurance). **Aqua Motion Expediciones,** San Pedro 422 (☎232 747; www.aquamotion.cl), has similar packages for rafting (CH$18,000) and climbing Osorno (from US$80). **Ko' Kayak,** San José 320 (☎346 433; www.paddlechile.com), offers lake and river kayaking as well as trips on Estuaria Reloncavi.

Currency Exchange: Exchange Ltda., Del Salvador 257, local #11 (☎232 019), cashes traveler's checks and changes cash. Open M-F 9am-2pm and 3-7pm. **AFEX,** another exchange, is right across the hall.

Banks: There are a host of banks in the downtown area, most with **ATMs.** Try **Banco Estado,** Santa Rosa 414 (☎232 296), and **Banco de Santiago,** San José 291 (☎235 670), between Santa Rosa and San Francisco.

Bookstore: El Libro del Capitán, 418 W. Martínez (☎234 501), boasts a stack of books in English and German for exchange and purchase. Open M-Sa 10:30am-7:30pm.

Supermarkets: Vyhmeister, Granado 565 (☎232 831), just past San Bernardo. Open M-Sa 8:30am-10pm, Su 9am-9:30pm. Also **Las Brisas,** Del Salvador 451 (☎346 400), across from the Esso station. Open 8:30am-10pm.

Laundromat: Lavandería Alba, 511 W. Martínez (☎232 908), offers wash and dry services for CH$1400 per kg. **La Garza Azul Lavandería,** San Pedro 563 (☎099 458 3677), washes and dries for CH$1500 per kg.

Emergency: ☎133.

Police: 24hr. operator (☎237 449 or 237 455), at the northern end of San Francisco, past W. Martínez on the right.

Pharmacy: Salcobrand (☎234 544), at the corner of Del Salvador and San Francisco. Open M-Sa 9am-10pm.

Medical Services: Clínica Alemana, Otto Bader 810 (☎232 336), has a good reputation. Another option is **Centro Médico,** W. Martínez 576 (☎232 792).

Telephones: For the longest hours among the call centers in town, try **Crell Centro de Llamados,** San Francisco 430 (☎234 530). Open M-Sa 9am-10pm, Su 2-9pm. Also, **Entel** (☎234 905), near San José and San Francisco. Open M-Sa 9am-8:30pm.

Internet Access: Cyber Service, Del Salvador 264 (☎237 911), charges CH$15 per min. Open M-Sa 10:30am-1pm and 3-9pm. **Crell Centro de Llamados** (see **Telephones,** p. 400), is a cheaper option, offering CH$400 for 30min., CH$700 per hr.

Post Office: San José 242 (☎232 304), at the corner of San José and San Pedro. Open M-F 9am-1:30pm and 3-6:30pm, Sa 9am-1:30pm.

▐ ACCOMMODATIONS

Puerto Varas has some of the best variety and most consistent quality of accommodations in the southern Lakes District. Consequently, many travelers sleep here and take daytrips to the smaller, more expensive outlying communities along the lake. In summer, **reservations** are advised, and prices rise with the tourist tide. So while Puerto Varas is more attractive than Puerto Montt, be prepared to pay a small premium if you stay here.

▨ **Compass del Sur Hospedaje,** Klenner 467 (☎232 044; mauro98@telsur.cl). Mauricio, the friendly English- and German-speaking owner, will help you get your bearings in this old German colonial house perched over the west side of town. Comfortable beds, a spacious kitchen, and a multilingual crowd make stays a pleasure. Owner will arrange rental cars. Laundry, bike rental (CH$5000 per day), Internet. Free pick-up from town, airport shuttle CH$9000. Breakfast CH$2000. Dorms CH$5000; singles CH$9000; doubles CH$14,000; prices lower in off-season. ❷

Casa Azul, Manzanall 66 (☎232 904; www.casaazul.net), at the intersection with Del Rosario. A new location for an old standby, "New Blue" is scheduled to open for business in Oct. of 2002. Contact owner Andreas ahead of time to make sure everything is up and running. Kitchen, book exchange, central heating. Dorms, singles, and doubles from CH$6000 per person. ❷

Hotel Licarayén, San José 114 (☎232 305). If you are going to splurge for accommodation in Puerto Varas, this is your place. All rooms are bright and well-decorated with cable TV, patios, and beautiful lake views. Breakfast included. Singles US$50-62, off-season US$39-47; doubles US$65-80/US$48-59. ❺

Ellenhaus, W. Martínez 239 (☎233 577; ellenhaus@yahoo.com). Very convenient location near the water and 3 of the 4 bus terminals. Free pick-up at the Cruz del Sur terminal. The living room TV and a chess board in the cozy attic are distraction enough in winter, but during the summer, venture out of the house on one of Ellen's tours through the Lakes District and Chiloé (8 people min.). No cooking, kettle only. Breakfast CH$1500. Singles CH$6000; doubles CH$9000-10,000; triples CH$12,000. Rooms are about CH$1000 cheaper in the off-season. ❷

Hospedaje Colores del Sur, Santa Rosa 318 (☎231 850). With its vibrant, colorful exterior and friendly green, blue, and red interior, this warm 2nd floor apartment is worthy of the name "*Colores*". Homey and bright, but with a cramped kitchen. Dorms CH$5000; singles CH$6000; doubles CH$12,000. ❷

Hostal Kika, W. Martínez 584 (☎234 703). A good value for Puerto Varas, Kika has 5 rooms upstairs with basic private baths. Reservations necessary in summer and shoulder seasons. Restaurant open 11am-midnight. Singles CH$18,000, off-season CH$12,000; doubles CH$25,000/18,000; triples CH$32,000/22,000. ❹

Hospedaje Sureño, Colón 179 (☎232 648). Tucked away to the south of the city, near the Cruz del Sur bus terminal, Sureño offers squeaky-clean facilities. Kitchen and parking available. Breakfast included. Singles and doubles with shared bath CH$6000 per person, off-season CH$4000; with private bath CH$7000/CH$5000; 5-person *cabañas* from CH$25,000. ❷

Hospedaje Don Raúl, Del Salvador 928 (☎234 174), west of town center. The cheapest accommodation in town, Don Raúl is first-come, first-served. Simple rooms house full-time renters in winter, tourists in summer. Kitchen. Singles and doubles CH$4000 per person; camping CH$2000. ❶

Residencial Hellwig, San Pedro 210 (☎232 472), above the Tur Bus office. Although Hellwig has been a fixture in Punto Varas for over a decade, its saggy beds prove that longevity does not guarantee comfort. Nevertheless, the social atmosphere, central location, and airy environs make it a worthwhile consideration. Parking and kitchen available. Singles and doubles CH$5000 per person, off-season CH$4000. ❷

AMAC Hospedaje, San Bernardo 313, 2nd fl. #2 (☎234 216), above Supermercado O'Higgins. With a friendly owner, central location, cable TV, and laundry available, the simple accommodations are not a bad deal. Low ceilings. Singles CH$6000, off-season CH$5000; doubles CH$12,000/CH$10,000. ❷

⌂ FOOD

Because of its proximity to Puerto Montt's salt waters, Puerto Varas features seafood in the majority of its eateries. For inexpensive *comida típica*, there is a row of hole-in-the-wall joints south on San Francisco, near the church.

Restaurant La Olla, San Bernardo 240 (☎234 605). The best combination of quality and value among the local seafood restaurants. The checkered tablecloths are festive, and the *congrio margarita* (fish in a white sauce of wine, lemon, and shellfish; CH$4500) intrigues the taste buds. Excellent *ceviche* CH$3000. Open 11am-midnight; sometimes later in summer. ❸

Mediterráneo, Santa Rosa 068 (☎237 268). The seafood is sure to please at this patioed waterfront restaurant. Large *tapas* menu includes a delicious *ceviche mixto* (CH$3500). As a main course, try one of the pasta dishes (CH$5000) or the salmon with broccoli and potatoes (CH$7500). Vegetarian-friendly. Open Oct.-May 10am-1am; June-Sept. 7pm-midnight. ❸

Café Mamusia, San José 316 (☎233 343). The chocolates displayed out front (CH$800-1000) are just part of the allure here. The lunchtime feast ($3300), which includes a scrumptious dessert and an espresso, will keep you going all day. Tackle the *Volcán Osorno* (cheeseburger with onions and pickles) for CH$3900. Open M-Th 9am-11pm, F 9am-midnight, Sa 10am-midnight, Su 10am-11pm. ❸

Terranova Café, Santa Rosa 580 (☎310 822). Somewhat less exciting than other culinary options, this cafe/bar is nonetheless a good deal. Simple fixed-price *almuerzo* CH$2000, crepes CH$1200-1500, cappuccino CH$900. Live jazz music on F. Open M-F 9:30am-2am, Sa-Su 11:30am-2am. ❶

Aníbal (☎235 222), on the corner of Santa Rosa and Del Salvador, next to Plaza de Armas. A cheap dinner spot for pizza and quality *comida típica*, with a few veggie dishes. Medium (read: very big for one person) vegetarian pizza CH$3600, *churrasco palta* CH$2400. Open 10am-11pm. ❷

👁 📷 SIGHTS AND NIGHTLIFE

Puerto Varas is surprisingly short on sights and attractions for a city so steeped in regional history. Most people simply use the attractive city as a base for day **excursions** to points along and near Lago Llanquihué. A few downtown locales do, however, merit attention. The **Plaza de Armas** spans some impressive lakeside real estate in the center of town, good for lingering on a nice day. The individual boutiques at the **Feria Artesenal,** just south of the plaza on Del Salvador, peddle a range of ceramics, *lapis lazuli*, wood carvings, wool items, and postcards. Prices and quality are consistently higher than at Puerto Montt's craft market. (Open 10:30am-1pm and 4:30-7pm.)

A notable landmark in town is the **Iglesia Parroquial del Sagrado Corazón de Jesús,** built by Jesuits in the early 20th century. A prominent but drab reminder of the German colonial influence in town, the church's yellow-and-brown exterior is surprisingly made of corrugated metal, not wood.

For a night out on the town, try **El Barómetro,** San Pedro 418 (☎346 100). Well-known for its summertime *fiestas*, this bar rises to the occasion, pumping jammin' music, Latin and otherwise, into the early morning hours. Special event notices are posted all over town. (Open 4pm-very late, off-season M-Sa 7pm-late.)

🏃 EXCURSIONS

The extensive list of outdoor activities available in the Lago Llanquihué vicinity could overwhelm even the most active traveler. Puerto Varas is the headquarters for many local adventure travel outfitters. Among the most popular summer excursions are **rafting** the Petrohué River, **horseback riding, trekking,** and **climbing** the nearby volcanoes. Both **Al Sur** and **Aqua Motion** (see tours, p. 399) employ guides for these activities and others, including **canyoning** and **fly fishing.** Consult the companies individually to "choose your own adventure." Keep in mind that independent-minded, budget-conscious travelers can eschew these sort of packaged tours and find their own way to the eastern side of the lake, using Puerto Varas as a stopping point for supplies, inspiration, and advice. Just about any point along the lake (save for sections of the east side) can be a day-trip from town.

A more expensive but nonetheless relaxing and popular way of experiencing the lakes is the **Andina del Sud** (see **Transportation,** p. 398) ferry/bus combination across lakes and passes to **Bariloche, ARG.** A bus runs from town to Petrohué, where a boat crosses to **Peulla,** on the other side of **Lago Todos los Santos.** After two more boat trips and two more bus legs, the trip pulls into Bariloche late in the evening (during summer). For those intent on going to Bariloche, daily buses from Puerto Varas also reach the city for about 8-10% of the cost of Andina del Sud. If you'd rather **cruise** only the beautiful Lago Todos los Santos, buying only the leg from Petrohué to Peulla and back is much cheaper (from CH$20,000) and can be arranged from the small office in Petrohué (see **Petrohué,** p. 405).

WEST OF LLANQUIQUE

ENSENADA ☎ 65

Proximity to several natural wonders and panoramic views of Lago Llanquihué make peaceful Ensenada an enjoyable stop-over for those en route to Petrohué. A smattering of descent accommodations and services have sprung up to oblige travelers passing through the town. Activities here revolve around the Lago Llanquihué and Parque Nacional Vicente Peréz Rosales. Activities nearest to Ensenada include hiking the **Laguna Verde Trail** and climbing or skiing **Osorno's slopes** (see p. 407).

Ensenada is serviced by a fleet of **Interlagos micros,** which run to **Petrohué** (every 2hr. 7am-4pm, CH$550) and **Puerto Varas** (every hr. 7am-8pm, CH$700). **Buses Fierro** goes to **Cochamó** (3 per day, CH$1200). **Southern Chile Expeditions,** in the south of town at km 42, is the main tour operator in town, providing packages for horseback riding, climbing, fly fishing, and trekking right from Ensenada. (☎212 027 or 212 052; www.southernchilexp.com.) **Supermarket Yessely,** on the south end of town, is the best-stocked market, but nevertheless has only the very basics. (☎212 009. Open daily 9am-9pm, later during the summer.) Other services include a **police station,** at the highway intersection on the east side of town (☎212 057; open 24hr.), and a **post office,** next to the Copec station (☎212 038; open Sa 9am-1pm).

The best indoor accommodation for your money is **Hospedaje Yessely ❷,** the northern of two "Yessely" locations in town, at km 43. Small singles, doubles, and quads come with access to a nice kitchen; one room has a private bath. (☎212 009; yessely@entelchile.net. Lake access. Reservations recommended in summer. Breakfast CH$1500. Rooms CH$6000 per person.) More comfortable self-contained lakeside *cabañas* and rooms can be procured at **Brisas del Lago ❺,** Casilla 24, next to green-lit Supermarket Bellavista. (☎212 012; briensen@telsur.cl. *Cabañas* for 2 people Jan.-Feb. US$47-54, Mar.-Dec. US$30; singles with breakfast US$46/$34; doubles with breakfast US$41-48/38.) In-town camping options include the nearby, somewhat littered **Camping Trauco ❶,** with an outdoor toilet and small cooking shelter. (☎212 033 or 212 006. Sites vary CH$1000-4000 depending on view and proximity to road.) Another more remote campsite lies 2.5km from town at **Puerto Oscuro** in Parque Nacional Vicente Peréz Rosales (see p. 405).

Culinary choices are less plentiful—only four restaurants, including the lakefront **Canta Rana** (☎212 010), km 43, populate the town. Most are open for lunch and dinner in summer, but only for the midday meal in the winter.

COCHAMÓ ☎ 65

It's not Bermuda or the Bahamas, Key Largo, or Montego, but you'll want to get here fast and then take it slow. This torpid little fishing village resembles a barn-

FROM THE ROAD

MARLBORO MAN

It's five kilometers from the town of Cochamó to the mouth of the Cochamó River. I'm trying to hitch with virtually zero traffic. Next bus out is in three hours. I think I'll walk. With dust on my shoes and grit in my eyes, I look up and notice him. A ways ahead of me but keeping my pace is a menacing figure moseying along on a stalwart horse. This *caballero's* at home in the wasteland—my fleece jacket and notebook say I don't belong. I'm crunching gravel as I walk, he halfturns at the sound of my footsteps. There's a rifle laying diagonally across his lap. No big deal, I think. This *guaso* doesn't have Old-West vigilanism in him. Besides, I'm from Texas. But I slow down. It's not high noon, but it's the next best thing—2:25pm. Sun glints off his shooter. He brings his horse to a dead stop. I'm a goner. But I keep walking. The maverick looks me up and down. Dirt's in my eyes, I can't make him out. He slowly lights a cigarette and takes a long drag. Bet it's a Marlboro. I could use one right about now—there's sweat in my eyes, cotton in my mouth, and a good-fer-nothin' buckaroo packin' a firearm sizing me up. It's time for a showdown. I say "*Buenas tardes.*" He coolly brings his hand to his hat and nods slightly. Sun moves across the sky and out of my eyes. The *caballero's* got a baby-face. His well-worn boots are covered in camouflage pants. The wide-brim camouflage hat is more grunge than Wild West. The bright red Limp Bizkit hooded sweatshirt shakes the yellow belly out of me. This pardner's more of a rocker. Guess that's why they keep 'em in silhouette in the Marlboro commercials.
—Tom Mercer

yard petting zoo, with frenzied animals spilling into the pot-holed streets. Looking around, you wonder which is more miraculous: the stunning view of the adjacent peaks or the fact that the town's ravenous huskies don't devour the clucking fowl all around them. But in Cochamó, everybody just seems to get along. Maybe it has something to do with the placid waters of the estuary or the vigilant eye of Volcán Yates, which surveys town goings-on from the southern end of the fjord.

There is very little to do in town. Going down to visit the harbor is a colorful experience, if only because of the puttering, pastel-painted fishing boats, many of which are keeled-over on the beach. Much of Cochamó's excitement and activity takes place 5km south of the town's center. **Campo Aventura ❶**, at the mouth of the Cochamó River, has its entrance on the south side of the bridge; the lodge lies about 200m up the driveway. The indoor accommodations and trips offered at Aventura may be a little pricey, but are well worth the splurge—and the budget traveler can still opt to camp for reasonable prices. The base camp at the mouth of the river offers sites with access to shower facilities (CH$3000 per person) or lodge accommodations with vegetarian breakfast and dinner included (CH$25,000 per person). A 17km hike or horseback ride separates the base camp from the La Junta lodge facility, which offers comparable services at similar prices in a spectacular glacier-carved, granite-dome-studded valley. Most people come for the extended horseback riding trips (3½-10 days) or various packages including kayaking, canyoning, hiking, fishing, and farm visits, all of which can get quite costly. (☎232 910; www.campo-aventura.com. Owners speak fluent English, French, German, and Spanish. Reserve ahead. Bike and fly fishing rentals available. Free access to library and beach. Sauna and laundry facilities available for a fee.)

Independent **hikers** can ask Campo Aventura for access to the valley and will most likely be obliged, but at some times of the year, hiking these trails solo can be a very muddy undertaking. Check conditions before planning or attempting any trips in this wet area.

Cochamó lies 20km south of **Ralún** and is currently only accessible from the north, along what will eventually become the northern stretch of the Camino Austral. Beyond Ralún, the road is unpaved and occasionally narrow. The only bus company that runs this route is **Buses Fierro,** which comes from Puerto Montt (3hr., 7:45 and 11:45am, CH$2000) and Puerto Varas (2hr., 9am and 1pm, CH$1800), and returns in the afternoon (2 and 6pm). Services in town are minimal. On the main street, Av. Cochamó, **visitor information** can be gleaned from the municipal offices (☎216 150). Also on Av. Cochamó are well-marked **public telephones** and the **police station** (☎216 233).

Down by the water along Catedral, there are a couple of seasonal **seafood restaurants** that keep flexible hours. **Hospedaje Edicar ❷,** on Arturo Prat, is the best year-round accommodation in town. (☎216 156 or 099 785 5537. 19 beds in 8 rooms. Breakfast included. CH$4500-5000.)

PETROHUÉ
☎65

On the opposite side of Ensenada, on the western edge of Lago Todos Los Santos, Petrohué is a town almost completely bereft of services. Although the town nearly shuts down in the winter, during the mild summer months, it fills with travelers seeking out great views and excursions to nearby natural wonders. The few buildings in "town" are constructed in log-cabin style, and a flotilla of small motorboats is a fixture in high season, ready to shuttle hikers and sightseers to and from trailheads and picnic spots around the pristine lake. Although there are a good number of guides and locals to offer information and assistance from December through March, there is little in the way of formal community services and infrastructure.

Buses are run by **Interlagos** from Puerto Varas and Ensenada (5-6 per day, more in peak season; CH$1500). A small fleet of independent **water taxis** shuttle to trailheads all over the lake and take fishermen out to catch salmon and trout (CH$10,000-15,000).

A large cruise boat operated by **Andina del Sud** runs to Peulla, on the east side of Lago Todos los Santos. Another boat takes 30min. tours of the west side of the lake and longer trips to the picnic-friendly Isla Margarita. (☎232 811. Peulla trip 2hr.; 11am, returning at 3pm; CH$17,000 per person. Isla Margarita trip departs 12:30 and 3pm, CH$4000 per person. Frequent lake tours CH$6000.)

From a small outpost next to the Petrohué Hotel (see below), **Expediciones Vicente Peréz Rosales** operates canyoning (US$60 per half-day), mountaineering (US$120 per person), and fly fishing trips. (☎312 524; fax 258 042; www.petrohue.com. Mountain bike rentals US$20 per day; fly fishing equipment rentals also available.) **Conaf** has its park administration office in town. (☎212 036; vperezrosales@123mail.cl. Open Dec.-Mar. 8am-11pm, Apr.-Nov. 8am-6pm.) Other services include: a **very small store,** selling expensive film and snacks (☎258 042; open 10am-7pm, off-season 10am-noon and 1:30-5:30pm); a **post office** (open M-Sa 10:30-11am); and a **public telephone,** in front of the Conaf office.

The cheapest indoor accommodation in town is **Hotel Küschel ❷,** just a rowboat ride across the mouth of the lake. Rooms are first come, first served, and go quickly in summer. (CH$6000 with breakfast; other meals offered for CH$4000.) **Hotel Petrohué ❺** has more luxurious meals and rooms. (☎258 042. Breakfast included. Singles US$65, off-season US$44; doubles US$90/67.) Camping is available at the Conaf location.

PARQUE NACIONAL VICENTE PERÉZ ROSALES

Established in 1926, this sprawling national park is Chile's most visited and one of its most breathtaking. An intricate sequence of relatively recent geological events have sculpted the area, guiding the path of **Río Petrohué** away from **Lago Llanquihué** and placing **Volcán Osorno** and **Volcán Puntiagudo** prominently on the topographical map. Glacial scouring and melting has also left its mark on the sheer walls and hanging valleys around **Lago Todos los Santos.**

LAKES DISTRICT

In the summer, swarms of Chileans and foreigners descend on this section of the Lakes District to raft, hike, cruise, and climb in and around Volcán Osorno and Lago Todos los Santos. In the center of all of this is the spectacular Lago Llanquihué. Like a great symphony, majestic and expansive Llanquihué suggests themes and variations, developments and denouements along its ample banks. Crumbling Calbuco and stately Osorno dominate views from all parts of the lake, while dramatic Puntiagudo graces only the northern shore with its pinnacle-like volcanic plug. This southernmost and largest of the lakes is one of the most visited, acting as a hydro-highway, ushering a steady stream of cars, buses, and boats along its banks, up to the toothy corridor of the Andes and beyond. Despite the warm-weather influx of visitors, crowds are not much of a problem—those with a little advice from Conaf and an adventurous spirit can easily blaze their own trail into the mountains.

AT A GLANCE

AREA: 251,000 hectares.

CLIMATE: Humid temperate. Average annual rainfall of 2500-4000mm. Temperature ranges from about 16°C in summer to 6.5°C in winter. Snow at the highest points.

CAMPING: 2 Conaf locations: Playa Petrohué and Puerto Oscuro.

GATEWAYS: Ensenada, Puerto Frías.

HIGHLIGHTS: Natural wonders such as Volcán Osorno, Lago Todos Los Santos, the Petrohué waterfalls, and Río Negro; more than 100 species of birds and 30 species of mammals.

FEES: Free, except for Saltos del Río Petrohué (CH$1200).

ORIENTATION AND PRACTICAL INFORMATION

For patient, simple-Spanish information about the park, trails, and services, contact **Conaf,** either at its park **headquarters** in Petrohué (see p. 405) or at its one-man **branch office,** just outside Ensenada on the road to Las Cascadas. (Open M-F 8:30am-1pm and 2-6:30pm, Sa-Su 9am-1pm and 2-6pm.) There are also more specialized offices at **Centro de Esquí Burbuja** and **Saltos del Río Petrohué.** In an **emergency,** try the Conaf cell (☎ 099 375 8388) or dial ☎ 138 for "air rescue." The only part of the park that requires an **admission fee** is Saltos del Río Petrohué (CH$1200).

CAMPING

Conaf offers two camping areas in the park. The biggest and most popular is the expanded **Playa Petrohué ❶,** with great views across the lake. (24 sites. Toilets, water, cooking shelter, and parking available. Up to 3 people CH$6000; 4-8 people CH$12,000; day use CH$3000.) Just 2.5km north of Ensenada on Lago Llanquihué, near the turn-off for the Osorno Refugio and ski area is the more rustic **Puerto Oscuro ❶.** (10 sites. Toilets, shelter, trash disposal. Up to 4 people CH$3000.)

HIKING

Hikers should be well-prepared for cold, wet weather at all times of year and rapid weather changes, as storms coming off of the Pacific slam right into these mountains without much advance warning. Although there is no formal system of accounting for hikers, it is recommended to consult Conaf about your inten-

Parque Nacional Vicente Perez Rosales

Parque Nacional Puyehue

Lago Rupanco

Co. Sarnoso 1630m

TO OSORNO (70km)

Puerto Rico

Co. Patojo 2024m

CORDILLIERA

CHILE

ARGENTINA

R. Negro

Vn. Puntiagudo 2493m

R. Escape

R. Sin Nombre

SIERRA EL RINCON

Co. Techado 1890m

R. Peulla

Peulla

Paso de Pérez 1022m

Refugio la Picada

Las Cascadas

Vn. Osorno 2652m

Lago Todos los Santos

Isla Margarita

CORDILLIERA DE LOS ANDES

Co. Tronador 3491m

Centro de Esquí Burbuja

Salto del Petrohue

Lago Llanquihue

Ensenada

R. Blanco

Cayutué

225

TO PUERTO VARAS (20km)

R. Petrohué

Lago Cayutué

Vn. Calbuco 2003m

Co. Jullet 1240m

Ralún

5 miles

5 kilometers

tions before you leave on a longer excursion. Many of the trails from remote Lago Todos los Santos are very isolated; carry plenty of extra supplies and be sure to arrange a water taxi back. The best readily-available topographical **map** of the area is the red JLM trekking map (#15), available in Puerto Montt and Puerto Varas bookstores.

HIKES AROUND PETROHUÉ AND ENSENADA. For a short, accessible jaunt, try the **Laguna Verde Trail** (200m; 20min.). Beautiful at sunset, the trail leads from the Ensenada Conaf outpost to a bright green, algae-colored pool, which is separated by a thin neck from the main body of Lago Llanquihué. The most scenic beginner hike on Volcán Osorno is the **Paso Desolación Trail** (12km; 5-6hr. round-trip; only one water source en route), extending from Petrohué up to the pass, where Refugio La Picada is located. Along the way, views open in the direction of the lake and Mt. Tronador, as well as toward the peak of Osorno. A pleasant alternative to the bus, the **El Solitario Trail** (6km; 2hr. one-way; no water) goes from the Las Cascadas road near Puerto Oscuro to the Petrohué road 1km south of Saltos del Río Petrohué. Finally, the **Rincón del Osorno Trail** (10km; 4hr. round-trip) winds from Petrohué along the lake, offering variations on the lake-and-peaks theme.

HIKES AROUND LAGO TODOS LOS SANTOS AND PEULLA. Hikes from the remote shores of the lake and Peulla generally require a bit more effort, time, preparation, and gear. Most of these trails should be done as multi-day trips and some don't follow established trails. From Peulla, the well-established **Laguna Margarita Trail** (16km; 8hr. round-trip) ends at a nice pond in a grove of native trees. Along the lake, the most popular backcountry route in the park, **Termas de Callao** (2-3 days), can be done as either a round-trip or one-way hike, leading up Río Sin Nombre and coming out the other side on Lago Rupanco at Las Gaviotas, a remote farming and agro-tourism community. There is a simple cabin at the springs, though it may be full in the summer (use of the springs and cabin CH$4000). Note that a bus from Osorno gives access near to Las Gaviotas for cheaper than the negotiated water-taxi price to the Río Sin Nombre trailhead.

A worthwhile trail also leads up **Río León** (5-7hr.) to a grove of Alerce trees, a popular destination for canyoning operators. A more remote and undeveloped **river-valley route** (2-5 days) loops from Cayutúe to Río Blanco, passing Lago Cayutúe on the south side, heading up Río Conchas, then Río Quitacalzones to the valley containing the natural Baños de Bariloche (overseen by local caretakers), where the trail heads down the Río Blanco back to the lake. Check conditions with Conaf before leaving, as the route can be quite messy after heavy rains.

From the Cayutúe trailhead, a relatively easy trail leads south from Lago Cayutúe over beautiful **Paso Cabeza de Vaca** (6-7hr. one-way) to a gravel road just north of Ralún. For experienced, well-prepared backpackers, the difficult route up to **Paso Bariloche** (2-3 days to pass one-way) follows the length of the Río Blanco until it peters out near the pass on the southern slopes of Tronador. Route-finding skills are required on this hike. Crossing the pass is a complicated proposition, as Argentine park authorities are leery of unguided hikers and climbers. Passports must be stamped by customs officials before crossing, and hikers must check in with Argentine officials as soon as they arrive in civilization on the other side. Consult Conaf or Extranjería officials for details. *Let's Go does not recommend crossing the border here or angering Argentine park authorities in any way.*

⚠ OUTDOORS

Most other outdoor activities must be undertaken through guides or outfitters, because equipment and/or experience may be necessary. **Rafting** trips on the Río Petrohué are popular in the summer—most operators are located in Puerto Varas. **Fly fishing** is another opportunity; those interested should contact **Gray Fly Fishing,** San José 192 (☎232 136 or 310 734; http://grayfly.com), near the Plaza de Armas.

In addition to the Lago Todos los Santos area, much of the park's outdoor activities take place on the slopes of **Volcán Osorno.** Companies based in Puerto Varas, Ensenada, and Petrohué offer guided trips to the peak, which is a technically challenging ascent. If you have experience and want to do the trip solo, contact Conaf by phone or in person at the **Centro de Esquí La Burbuja** (☎252 571), which has the concession for the mountain. After the climbing season, powder buries the peak, and ski season runs from June to September. The ski center has one T-bar lift and one surface lift in operation. Call for details about schedule, tickets, and rentals.

SOUTH OF LLANQUIQUE

PUERTO MONTT
☎ 65

The transportation hub and gateway to the south for both travelers and 18-wheelers, Puerto Montt has an industrial feel that it just can't shake. Visitors on their way to the fjords, surrounding wilderness, or the Camino Austral tend not to linger here. However, the vibrant streets and bustling port boast a charm of their own. With more restaurants, shops, hostels, markets, and amenities available than in other cities and towns in the area, Puerto Montt is the place to take advantage of the services and facilities of city life before heading into the beauty and tranquility that lie ahead.

▆ TRANSPORTATION

Flights: Aeropuerto El Tepual, about 20min. north of town, accessible by bus from the bus station. **LanChile,** O'Higgins 167 (☎ 253 315, in the airport 283 020), flies to: **Balmaceda** (3 per day, CH$52,200); **Concepción** (1 per day, CH$42,200); **Punta Arenas** (3 per day, CH$90,000); **Santiago** (7 per day, CH$78,700); **Temuco** (1 per day, CH$21,700). **AeroContinente,** Gallardo 67 (☎ 347 777 or 316 983), flies to: **Balmaceda** (M, W, F, Su 10am; CH$33,400, round-trip CH$48,700); **Punta Arenas** (M, W, F, Su 10am; CH$41,000); **Santiago** (M, W, F, Su 5:20pm; CH$45,000). Prices rise if tickets are reserved less than 4 days in advance, or if flight is almost full. It is usually cheaper to buy round-trip tickets.

Buses: A state of orderly confusion persists here—although hordes of people rush about searching for the right bus at the right price, crowded buses roll in and out punctually. Buses leave from the **bus station,** but buses to **Fruitillar, Nanguihue,** and **Puerto Varas** can be waved down on **Portales;** just look for the signs in the windshield. Off-season brings cheaper prices to **Santiago**—walk around and look for large posters with times and lowered prices.

Tur Bus (☎ 253 329) goes to: **Concepción** (10hr.; 9:15, 10:30am, 7:45, 9:30pm; CH$6100. *Executivo* 9pm, CH$11,500. *Salón cama* 10hr., 8:45pm, CH$14,600) and **Santiago** (14hr., 8 per day 8am-10pm, CH$6900. Direct *executivo* 12hr.; 7 and 10:35pm; CH$14,800. Direct *salón cama* 12hr., 6:15 and 8:20pm, CH$20,500).

ETM (☎ 256 253) goes to: the **airport** (2hr. before every flight out, CH$900) and **Maullin** (M-Sa every 45min. 7:30am-9pm, Su every 1½hr.; CH$800).

Trans Chile goes to: **Ancud** (3 and 4:45pm, CH$2500); **Castro** (every 1½hr. 7:45am-8:15pm, CH$2500); **Quellón** (7:45am and 3:15pm, CH$3500).

Cruz Sur (☎ 254 731) goes to: **Loncoche** (4hr., CH$3300); **Osorno** (2hr., CH$1200); **Temuco** (7hr., every hr. 7am-7pm, CH$4000); **Valdivia** (3½hr., CH$2500).

Turibus goes to: **Punta Arenas** (32hr.; Tu, Th, Sa 11am; CH$25,000) and **Bariloche, ARG** (6hr., 8:30am, CH$8000).

Inter Sur (☎ 259 320) heads to **Santiago** (14hr.; 3:45, 5:15, 7:15, 8:15pm; CH$7500).

Fierro goes to: **Hornopirén** (4½ hr.; 8am, 1:30, 3pm; CH$2800); **Osorno** (1¾hr., M-Sa 20 per day 6:30am-10:30pm, CH$1200); **Santiago** (13hr., 7:15 and 8pm, CH$8000).

Tas Choapa (☎ 254 828) goes to **Bariloche, ARG** (7hr., M-Sa 10am, CH$8000).

Buses Bohle (☎ 254 526) goes to: **Ancud** (8:30am, CH$7000); **Petrohué** (11am and 7:30pm, CH$4000); **Puyehue** (9am, CH$6500).

Minibuses leave regularly 7:30am-9:30pm for: **Frutillar** (1hr., every 10min., CH$900); **Nanguihue** (45min., every 30min., CH$700); **Puerto Varas** (35min., every 10min., CH$600).

Boats: The **port** lies west of town, and all company offices are directly inside the gate. **Transmarchilay** (☎270 430) goes to: **Chaitén** (12hr.; M noon, Tu 8pm, Th 6pm, F 7pm; CH$16,000). **Navimag** (☎432 300) goes to **Chaitén** (10hr., F 10pm, CH$15,000). **Catamarans** go to **Castro** (2hr.; Tu, Th 6pm; CH$12,000) and **Chaitén** (4hr.; M, W, F 9am; CH$21,500). See p. 415 for information on longer ferry excursions to Puerto Natales and Puerto Chacabuco.

✈ 🛈 ORIENTATION AND PRACTICAL INFORMATION

Look for water to the south and the towering hill to the north to orient yourself. The bustling **port** lies to the west of town, with the vibrant **Angelmo market** just beyond it. Students, businessmen, tourists, and truckers congregate in the **Plaza de Armas,** while the noisy **bus station** sits on the waterfront almost halfway between the port and the plaza. **Antonio Varas** is a lively strip of shops and services along the southern edge of the plaza. There is no need to hail a cab in Puerto Montt, as the 25min. walk from the port to the plaza is well-lit at night. When wandering away from the water, beyond the port, use a taxi—the area may be run-down.

Tourist office: Conaf, Amunategui 500 (☎290 711), at Doctor Martín, is the regional office for the southern lakes, with a wealth of Conaf material for perusal or copying. Open M-Th 9am-1pm and 2:30-5:30pm, F 9am-1pm and 2:30-4:30pm. Basic information can also be found at the office in the bus station, but the **tourist office** (☎254 580), on Varas across from the plaza, is more helpful with useful brochures and a decent town map. Open M-Sa 9am-4pm.

Tours: Travelers and Tours, Angelmo 2186 (☎295 997), gears its business toward budget travelers. 6-day trips along the **Camino Austral** begin at CH$150,000. 2-day trips to **Hornopirén** (CH$45,000); 1-day trips to **Chiloé** (CH$10,000), **Frutillar** (CH$5000), and **Termas Puyehue** (CH$10,000) also available. **Boat trips** from Chiloé to visit **penguins** offered (CH$40,000). To **climb Volcán Osorno** (CH$120,000), **explore canyons** (CH$30,000), or **fly fish** (CH$120,000), book a trip departing from Puerto Varas. The slightly upmarket **Eureka,** Varas 449 (☎250 412), offers similar trips at similar prices, as well as less strenuous tours to nearby lakes and towns.

Currency Exchange: Trans Afex, Portales 516, changes traveler's checks with a small commission. Or try **La Monedo de Oro,** in the bus terminal.

ATM: Santander, on the corner of Varas and Gallardo, accepts Cirrus/MC/Plus/V. **Banks** are located on the same block.

Bookstore: Sotavento Libros, Diego Portales 580 (☎256 650), boasts the town's best collection of Spanish-language regional information and a select but well-chosen collection of English-language literature, both Chilean and international. Open M-F 10am-1:30pm and 3:30-8pm, Sa 10am-2pm and 5:30-8pm.

Supermarket: Las Brisas, on the corner of Lota and Portales, across the street from the bus station, stocks every imaginable item. Open daily 8:30am-midnight.

Laundromat: Lavadario Narly, San Martín 165 (☎311 528), charges CH$1000 per kg. Open M-F 9am-1pm and 3-7:30pm. Also **Altamar,** Angelmo 1564 (☎257 113), near the port, charges the same rate and even cleans sleeping bags. Open M-F 9am-7pm, Sa 10am-4pm.

Emergency: ☎133

Police: Gallardo 519 (☎431 355).

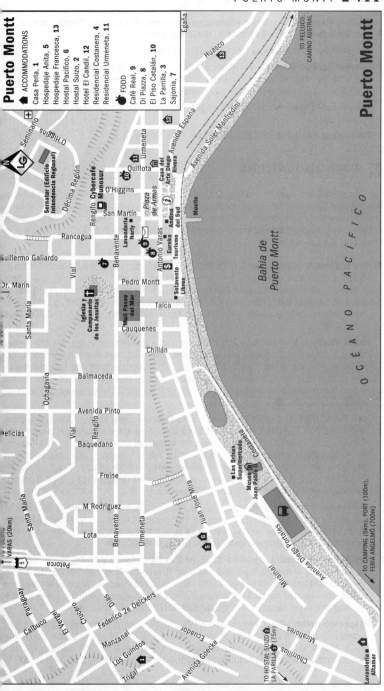

Puerto Montt

♦ ACCOMMODATIONS
Casa Perla, 1
Hospedaje Anita, 5
Hospedaje Francesca, 13
Hostal Pacífico, 6
Hostal Suizo, 2
Hotel El Candil, 12
Residencial Costanera, 4
Residencial Urmeneta, 11

♦ FOOD
Café Real, 9
Di Piazza, 8
El Piso Catalán, 10
La Parilla, 3
Sajonia, 7

Sernatur (Edificio Intendencia Regional)

Iglesia y Campanario de los Jesuitas

Bahía de Puerto Montt

OCÉANO PACÍFICO

Puerto Montt

LAKES DISTRICT

24-Hour Pharmacy: A rotating pharmacy system prevails here—**Cruz Verde,** Varas 952, and **Salcobrand,** Varas 549, display the latest schedule.

Hospital: Hospital Regional (☎261 134), on Seminario.

Internet Access: Internet, in the strip mall connected to the Supermarket Las Brisas, near the bus station. Fast and reliable service CH$1200 per hr. **Cybercafe Munosur,** San Martín 232, connects for the same price. Open M-Sa 9am-11pm, Su 3-11pm.

Telephone: Telecom, Varas 527. Open M-F 9am-9pm, Sa 9:30am-9pm, Su 11am-2pm and 4-9pm.

Post office: Rancagua 126. Open M-F 9am-7pm, Sa 9am-1pm.

ACCOMMODATIONS

Accommodations tend to cluster in three areas of the city: the cheapest choices are located between the bus station and the port. Alternatively, expensive options with immaculate service dot the downtown area near the plaza. East of the town center, moderate options abound—however, if you arrive in town late, hail a cab because its a bit of a walk.

Hostal Suizo, Independencia 231 (☎252 640). Easily the most creative hostel in town, Suizo is decorated exclusively with the owner's art (which is all for sale). The bright rooms are sure to delight, while vivacious guests make an evening spent lolling about the porch a great treat. Dorms CH$5500; doubles with private bath CH$20,000. Large cabin without beds but with a kitchen and space for 10 sleeping bags CH$3000 per person. ❶

Hostal Pacifico, Mira 1088 (☎256 229). More of a business hotel than anything else, this is a great pick for those who want some privacy and are homesick for cable TV. Room service, car rental, tourist information, and laundry services will rejuvenate visitors so they may return to the grueling world of budget travel. 18% discount for guests with a foreign passport. Singles CH$15,000; doubles CH$26,000; triples CH$28,000; quads CH$30,000. ❹

Casa Perla, Trigal 312 (☎262 104; casaperla@hotmail.com), south of the intersection with Crucero, a 10-15min. walk from the bus station. From the bus station, catch the 5, 50, 55, or 57 *colectivo.* The dorm rooms are somewhat cramped, but in this pleasant, warm, and clean house, no one's complaining. Kitchen, laundry, and Internet access available. Breakfast included. Sea-kayaking trips available. 6-day, 7-night package includes a room, 18hr. of Spanish lessons, 1hr. Internet per day (US$165 per person). Singles, doubles, triples, quads CH$5000 per person. ❷

Residencial Urmeneta, Urmeneta 290 (☎253 262). Although this quaint hostel is in the middle of town, it doesn't charge the high prices of other central hotels. Skylights flood most second-floor rooms with warm sunlight. Welcoming owners make guests comfortable in the high-ceilinged kitchen. Dorms CH$6000. ❷

Residencial Costanera, Angelmo 1528 (☎255 244). The large living room with soft couches and a chess set looks over the busy street and offers a glimpse of the water. The second-story rooms filter most of the noise, but light sleepers should avoid the front rooms. The crowded rooms flush visitors out into the living room, which is consequently bustling and lively. Doubles with shared bath CH$6000 per person. ❷

Hospedaje Anita, Mira 1094 (☎315 479). The massive stairway leads up to small rooms with bunk-beds and drab, shared bathrooms. Cable TV and hot water make this basic accommodation near the bus station a solid option for late arrivals. Kitchen access and breakfast included. Dorms CH$3000; doubles CH$4000 per person. ❶

Hospedaje Francesca, Huasco 96 (☎432 955), in the eastern part of town. This small hostel fills up with Chilean students and visitors who come to enjoy a view of the water from the *hospedaje*'s vantage point above town. Its central location makes this hostel an excellent starting point to explore the city. Simple breakfast CH$500. Triples and quads CH$4000. Closed in the off-season. ❷

Hotel El Candil, Varas 177 (☎253 080). The high ceilings and faded curtains of this hulking central building hint at its former glory, but the Candil has gone downhill over recent years. Still, the location is great and the rooms are surprisingly large. Doubles and triples CH$8000 per person. ❸

⬛ FOOD

Be sure to hit the Angelmo market for an obligatory *curanto* plate: a flamboyant combination of mussels, clams, sausage, pork ribs, and chicken. Nicer restaurants that line the market tend to be pricier, but stroll through anyway, as it's fun to get the competing restaurants to woo you to their table. Andrés Bello, several blocks in front of the bus station, has many small eateries serving up daily lunch specials for CH$1500.

Sajonia, Gallardo 231. This fine restaurant caters to Puerto Montt's corporate clientele with a selection of crepes (CH$1800-4000) and house specialties (CH$3900-5900). The caesar salad (CH$1800) is a far cry from anything found in Italy, but is a creamy treat in its own right. The set lunch with soup and an entree is a good deal at CH$2000. Open 10am-midnight. ❷

El Piso Catalán, Quillota 185, 2nd fl. (☎313 900). A variety of fresh vegetables and vegetarian options on the *almuerzo* menu (CH$2500-2900) are served up promptly with finesse. Although the portions are not huge, the quality and prices more than compensate. Open 11am-5pm and 7-11pm; open until 1am on summer weekends. ❷

La Parrilla, Independencia 165. The open grill and wood-paneled dining room create a pleasant atmosphere in which you can enjoy fresh meat grilled to perfection. The basic *lomo* comes with a side-dish of your choice (CH$3000), while zesty sauces like the *pimienta* can spice up your meal for a little more (CH$3500). If you can't decide, be bold and order the complete *asado*: a mélange of chicken, sausage, pork, and beef on a hot mini-grill (CH$8500). Open 11am-midnight. ❸

Café Real, Rancagua 137. Central location, attentive service, and hearty dishes make locals and visitors gravitate to this bright and open cafe. Start with a salad (CH$700-1400) or a heaping bowl of *cazuela* (CH$1900) before attacking a thick *lomo* (CH$3900) or *paella* (CH$4500). Downstairs often rocks with live music on F and Sa after 10pm—check the sign on the door to see who is playing. Open 8am-1am. ❸

Di Piazza, Gallardo 119. Great pizzas and pasta draw crowds to the small top floor of this pizza joint. Thin-crust pizzas and a variety of toppings make for an interesting meal; a large easily serves two people (CH$2000-4200). Open 11am-11pm.

⬛ SIGHTS

ANGELMO MARKET. Just west of the port, this artisan market brings the street to life. The market stretches from the port to the cul de sac, where a busy fish market and a cluster of restaurants attract locals and tourists alike. Fine woolen and leather goods crafted by regional artisans include *huaso*-style hats and antique boot spurs. The fish market is always bustling as the latest catch is cleaned and prepared in front of hungry customers. As you peruse the line of restaurants, enjoy

LAKES DISTRICT

playful banter with white-aproned women who will wink, smile, and gesture coyly to cajole you to their restaurant. Although Angelmo's hustle and bustle is all part of the fun, larger restaurants set apart from the market serve the same items at similar prices. *(Local westbound buses service the area; look for "Angelmo" signs on windshields. CH$200.)*

MUSEUMS. The **Museo Juan Pablo II** is the only real don't-miss museum in Puerto Montt. Although the exhibits for the Pope's visit to town are a little dull, other features make for a fascinating afternoon. A convincing replica of a *chilote*-style cabin, broad explanations of German colonial history, and sensational pictures from the destruction of Puerto Montt in the 1960 earthquake, the largest ever measured, are a few highlights from this eclectic collection. *(Diego Portales 991, just east of the bus terminal. ☎ 261 822. Open Dec.-Mar. M-F 9am-7pm, Sa-Su 10am-6pm; Apr.-Nov. M-F 10am-6pm, Sa 9am-1pm. CH$250, children CH$100.)* Downtown, the **Casa del Arte Diego Rivera** hosts rotating exhibits of local and national exhibits, which are usually worth a look. *(At Quillote and Antonio Varas. ☎ 261 817. Open M-F 10am-1:30pm and 3-7pm. Free.)*

🔹 DAYTRIPS FROM PUERTO MONTT

CALBUCO
Buses Fierro and Buses Bohle run frequent service from the main bus terminal (1hr., every 10-15min. 7am-10pm, CH$700).

If you don't appreciate marine life, don't bother with this jaunt Southeast of Puerto Montt. Calbuco appeared as a colonial settlement when the Mapuche destroyed Osorno in 1602, sending lots of European folk looking for a new home. The hilltop location and peaceful surrounding channels (the connecting causeway is a recent development) must have extended some piece of mind to its rattled founders. A stroll along the present-day shoreline reveals the workings of this coastal town. Colorful boats sputter around the harbor, checking up on shellfish farms and shuttling around customers. In summer, **Turismo Real Calbuco** (☎ 461 210 or 461 300) does some people-moving of its own, showing visitors the surrounding islands, including **Islas Tabon, Puluque,** and **Quenu.** Activities on these trips include picnics, homestays, and cultural interface. Closer to home, **Turismo Chaullin** (☎ 254 0028; turismochaullin@yahoo.com) runs tours and events on **Isla Chaullin Helvetia,** which houses a hostel and a botanical garden. For more info on these and other excursions, visit the information stand on the main coast road, or try the **Office of Tourist Information** (☎ 461 807), on Los Héroes. The fruits of the sea are best prepared at **Costa Azul,** Vicuña Mackenna 202 (☎ 461 516 or 462 411), which offers a succulent *curanto* (CH$2800). Rooms are available at the adjacent *hospedaje*. If you have time to kill before skipping town, see if the wood-work shop opposite the tourist office is open. The proprietor keeps irregular hours, but his unique wood-carved ships are worth a look.

MAULLÍN AND CARELMAPU
From Puerto Montt, ETM buses leave fairly frequently to Maullín (1½hr.; every 45min. 7am-9pm; CH$800) and Carelmapu (2hr.; CH$1000).

Even more isolated than Calbuco, these two communities stand in stark contrast with each other: Carelmapu is exposed to the wind and waves from the Pacific through the **Bahía de Ancud,** while Maullín is located on a sheltered river mouth, carrying fishermen on its gentle lapping currents. Like a flower that blooms only briefly once a year, Carelmapu hosts an annual **Fiesta de la Vírgen de la Candelaria** (February 2), providing an excuse for fishermen and boaters from all over the coast and Chiloé to crowd the town harbor for a huge food festival.

PARQUE NACIONAL ALERCE ANDINO

Buses Fierro goes from Puerto Montt to Hornopirén via Río Chaica, Correntso, and Lago Chapo (M-Sa 12:30pm; CH$1000). Park offices are available on the Río Chaica and in Correntso. If driving: 40km southeast of Puerto Montt on Camino Austral towards Hornopirén, the road intersects the Río Chaica. From here, a dirt road (passable by 4WD vehicles) leads 7km to the park visitor's kiosk. Laguna Chaiquenes is 5.5km farther up. The main office for park is in Puerto Montt. Basic camping (CH$1000) available at Correntso, Río Chaica, and Lago Chaiquenes.

Southeast of Puerto Montt and bordering on Estuario Reloncaví, Alerce Andino preserves a host of *alerce* stands and scores of rugged, bush-covered peaks. Infrequent public transportation makes access virtually impossible without a car. However, diligent backpackers will quench their thirst for wilderness on satisfying trails through these unique, virgin forests.

The most popular and worthwhile trail is **Laguna Fría** that commences at Lago Sargazo and passes through millennia-old stands of alerce to arrive at a rustic *refugio* on Laguna Fría (8km, 4hr.). Also well-established is the trail to **Lago Triangulo** from Laguna Chaiquenes on the southern side of the park (7km). On a map, you'll see a trail between the Laguna Fría and Lago Triangulo trails; in reality, this route has long been overgrown.

NEAR PUERTO MONTT

SAIL THE SOUTH

The Puerto Eden and the Magellanes are similar boats that traverse the glacial south. Dec.-Mar. 4-day trips run for US$200-550, 2-day trips are US$80-250. All prices are for triple or quadruple rooms. Off-season prices drop about 10% (Sept.-Nov.) or 20% (Apr.-Aug.). 10% discount for students with ID or an ISIC card. For more information or to purchase tickets, contact a Navimag office: Coyhaique, Presidente Ibáñez 347 (☎ 233 306); Puerto Montt, Angelmo 2187 (☎ 432 300), in the shipyard; Puerto Natales, Pedro Montt 262 (☎ 414 300); Punta Arenas, Magallanes 990 (☎ 200 200); Santiago, El Bosque Norte 0440, Piso 11 (☎ 442 3120).

In the last decade, Puerto Montt has emerged as a gateway to the desolate beauty of ice-encrusted passages, nameless glaciers, and frosty waterfalls of the far south of Chile. Even in the summer, the nearest hills in the region appear to be trapped in an endless winter as snow creeps down as low as 400m above sea level. Enterprising companies have recently refurbished ships to carry foreign and domestic travelers into the icy tundra. Despite the consistency of the views and close quarters on board, the boats allow travelers to enjoy an almost meditative journey through a frozen world. Large public decks are a respite from the cabins and provide opportunities to socialize with boatmates.

Most travelers begin in Puerto Montt and take the four-day trip to **Puerto Natales.** After passing Chacabuco's sea lions and lone albatrosses, the ships enter exposed waters. The massive cargo ship remains unfazed by increased waves until the **Gulfo de Penas** (appropriately the Gulf of Struggle), where the force of the Pacific swells and upsurges. As the passage narrows, magnificent glacial vistas and unchartered land passes by you in a never-ending reel of ice.

Advance bookings are required for trips taken in **January** or **Feburary,** since the cruise has become increasingly popular among Chileans who plan their trips for the summer. Last-minute purchases may be possible during the off-season, so if acting on impulse, don't hesitate to give it a shot. **Meals** on board are basic—chicken, seafood, or beef with pasta and soup are standard fare. Vegetarians receive little special attention, and are often served the same meal without meat. If you plan to end your evenings on deck with a glass of port with fellow passengers, stock up on wine or spirits before setting sail—alcohol is available at the bar, but it is expensive.

The accommodations are better than most basic hostels, but the cramped living quarters can get stifling. Some bunks on lower decks get hot, and the floors may collect water. Comfortable beds come only with a fitted sheet, so a **sleeping bag** or blanket is necessary. **Security** is very good—all passengers have personal locked cupboards, although some bins don't have enough space to hold an entire backpack.

A popular alternative to this journey south is a visit to **Laguna San Rafael,** which leaves from Puerto Montt or Puerto Chacabuco and avoids the Gulfo de Penas, spending only two days in the ice canals.

CHILOÉ

South of the Lakes District, the rough mountainous terrain plunges into the Pacific Ocean, creating an archipelago of rocky, hilly islands collectively known as Chiloé. Visitors to the islands will quickly become immersed in the flavorful tapestry of rural Chilote life as they sample mouth-watering seafood, explore ancient cultures, and grow to understand the stubbornly independent marine lifestyle that continues to survive. The annual holiday influx does bring a heightened energy to virtually all island communities, where seasonal tourist businesses thrive and lively festivals initiate the unaware into unique Chilote traditions. While a trip to the archipelago will probably be devoid of adrenaline rushes, no other destination in Chile can boast the same storied past and layered culture, which is preserved not only in museums, but in the day-to-day routines of Chilote farmers and fishermen.

The rugged isolation that wears lines on the faces of Chiloé's laborers has also been the principal factor in the development of the island's customs and cultural icons. The pre-existing Huilliche and Chonos societies met the arrival of the Spanish in 1567, and later, the Jesuits in 1608. While the Spanish developed and fortified the cities of Ancud and Castro, the Jesuits began to convert the native population and erect wood churches on practically every street corner. The marriage of Catholic theology and persistent elements of Huilliche and Chonos superstition probably resulted in Chiloé's present-day secular mythology. Other ambient conditions, including the growth of the fishing industry, produced unique craftsmanship, individual boat-building styles, and the rise of the tidal-flat homes known as *palafitos*.

Touched by seismic activity and glaciation, the 40-island-strong archipelago lacks the dramatic volcanic and alpine landforms of the adjacent regions of Los Lagos and northern Patagonia. Instead, Chiloé boasts rolling hills, farmlands, forests, and rocky beaches, which are very, very slowly being pulled down into the sea by the grinding action of the Pacific plate crashing into the South American continent along its western margin.

Despite its moderate topography, any suggestion that Chiloé is a more "gentle" place than the mainland can be dismissed instantly. Most Chilotes survive on their willful perseverance, barely managing to eke out a living. With a wet climate and poor soil, the only crops that grow well on the island are potatoes, garlic, and other root vegetables, and, historically, most locals have had to supplement their diet with either livestock or fish. In the end, subsistence farming continues to this day even as the island's salmon fisheries and mollusk farms have become a sustainable industry.

HIGHLIGHTS OF CHILOÉ

GET AMOROUS in **Achao** by gorging on aphrodisiacal oysters (p. 433).

SCALE the dramatic trail to Río Anay in **Parque Nacional Chiloé** (p. 436)

PUTTER around the archipelago in a pastel-colored launch in quirky **Quemchi** (p. 426).

WRANGLE witches and debate mutants at the Annual Meeting on Folklore in **Ancud** (p. 419).

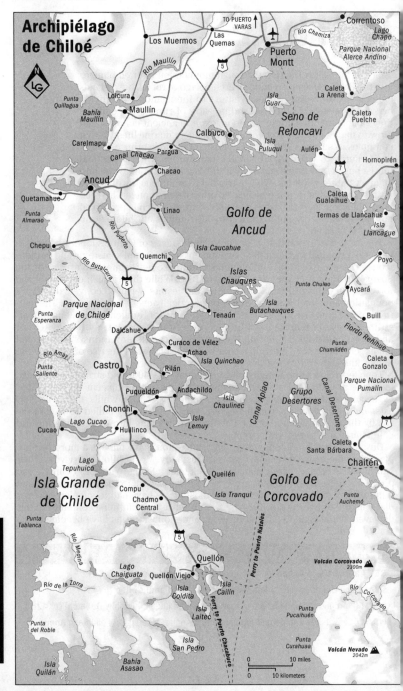

Archipiélago de Chiloé

Correntoso
Lago Chapo
Parque Nacional Alerce Andino
Río Chamiza
TO PUERTO VARAS
Las Quemas
Los Muermos
Puerto Montt
Río Maullín
Caleta La Arena
Isla Guar
Caleta Puelche
Loicura
Punta Quillagua
Bahía Maullín
Maullín
Seno de Reloncavi
Calbuco
Isla Puluqui
Aulén
Carelmapu
Canal Chacao
Pargua
Hornopirén
Chacao
Ancud
Quetamahue
Linao
Golfo de Ancud
Caleta Gualaihue
Termas de Llancahue
Punta Almarao
Chepu
Río Pudeto
Isla Llancague
Río Butalcura
Quemchi
Isla Caucahue
Poyo
Aycará
Islas Chauques
Punta Chulao
Parque Nacional de Chiloé
Punta Esperanza
Isla Butachauques
Buill
Dalcahue
Tenaún
Fiordo Reñihue
Río Amay
Curaco de Vélez
Achao
Punta Chumildén
Punta Saliente
Castro
Rilán
Isla Quinchao
Caleta Gonzalo
Puqueldón
Andachildo
Parque Nacional Pumalín
Chonchi
Isla Chaulinec
Grupo Desertores
Lago Cucao
Isla Lemuy
Cucao
Huillinco
Canal Apiao
Canal Desertores
Caleta Santa Bárbara
Lago Tepuhuico
Queilén
Chaitén
Compu
Isla Grande de Chiloé
Chadmo Central
Isla Tranqui
Golfo de Corcovado
Punta Auchemó
Punta Tablanca
Río Medina
Quellón
Río de la Zorra
Lago Chaiguata
Quellón Viejo
Volcán Corcovado 2300m
Isla Coldita
Isla Caillín
Río Corcovado
Isla Laitec
Punta Pucaihuén
Punta del Roble
Isla San Pedro
Punta Curahuaa
Volcán Nevado 2042m
Isla Quilán
Bahía Asasao
Ferry to Puerto Chacabuco
Ferry to Puerto Natales

0   10 miles
0   10 kilometers

ANCUD
☎ 65

Perhaps Ancud's relatively large size is counter to Chiloé's small-town mentality. Or maybe tourists lament the absence of a traditional Chilote church. Regardless of the reason, it's a fact that many hurried travelers bypass Chiloé's largest town of Ancud (pop. 23,148), heading straight for the island's better-known attractions to the south. That leaves plenty of room for the Chilean families and students who fill the town in January and February seeking rest and recreation, both of which are plentiful here. The fun only just begins with daytrips to Peninsula Lacuy, the small town of Caulín, and the penguined Pacific coast. Puttering around the Costanera, soaking up rays on a crowded beach, or slurping down slippery shellfish are also great ways to fill long, lazy summer days.

▣ TRANSPORTATION

Flights: The nearest **airport** is in Puerto Montt, but **Turismo Proa,** Bellavista 493 (☎ 623 090), sells tickets.

Buses: Buses rurales (short-range buses) in northern Chiloé leave from designated areas within the city. **Regional** and **national buses** depart from a central terminal, a 15-20min. walk east of town at the intersection of Aníbal Pinto and Marcus Vera.

Rural Buses: Bus del Río, on Arturo Prat, across from the Esso station, between Guardia Goycoleta and Pedro Montt, follows the *costanera* interior route east and then heads south to **Quemchi** (10am, noon, 4pm; CH$1500). From the same departure spot on Arturo Prat, **Bus Caulín** heads east to **Caulín** (7am, noon, 4pm; CH$700) and **Bus Chepu** runs south and west to **Chepu** (6:30am and 4pm, CH$1000). From Aníbal Pinto, between Goycoleta and Pedro Montt, **Bus Mar Brava** stops at destinations along the **Lacuy Peninsula,** ending in **Fuerte Ahui** (6:45am, noon, 4pm; CH$1000). This is a list of year-round, daily departures—there are more buses during weekends and over the summer.

National and Regional Buses: Buses Cruz del Sur (☎ 622 265) goes to: **Puerto Montt** (2hr., 18 per day 7:15am-9:45pm, CH$2200); **Quellón** (2½hr., 8 per day 7am-4:30pm, CH$2800) via **Chonchi** (2hr., CH$1800) and **Castro** (1½hr., 20 per day, CH$1000); **Santiago** (6:40pm, CH$16,500; *cama* 5:10pm, CH$33,000); **Temuco** (8 per day 8:45am-6:45pm, CH$6500) via **Osorno** (CH$3500) and **Valdivia** (CH$5000). **Buses Trans Chiloé** (☎ 622 876) goes to **Puerto Montt** (10 per day, CH$1500) and **Quellón** (4 per day 7:15am-6:30pm, CH$2000) via **Chonchi** (CH$1300). **Quellén Bus** (☎ 621 140) heads to: **Castro** (6-8 per day 11am-9pm, CH$1000); **Puerto Montt** (6-8 per day 8:05am-5pm, CH$1500); **Santiago** (5pm, CH$9000).

Taxis: Pudeto 210, east of the Plaza de Armas. Or call **Radio Taxi Ancud** (☎ 622 064).

Car Rental: There is no car rental agency in town—to procure a car for daytrips, head south to **Castro** (see p. 427).

Bike Rental: Hospedaje San Jose, Pudeto 619 (☎ 622 467). CH$500 per hr., CH$300 per day. Bikes are also available through **Turismo Campesina,** Admirante Latorre 58 (☎ 626 753).

▣ ▣ ORIENTATION AND PRACTICAL INFORMATION

Many of downtown Ancud's amenities are a block or so away from the shore. Running east-west, **Arturo Prat** is the main thoroughfare leading out to the bus station. The main city offices, the museum, and the **Plaza de Armas** are located atop a hill, south of Prat, a block east of the water and the primarily residential **Av. Costanera.** East of the Plaza de Armas, **Pudeto** is lined with many of the town's shops, restaurants, and bars.

Tourist Office: Sernatur, Libertad 665 (☎622 800; fax 622 665; sernaturchiloe@hot-mail.com), offers a wide range of information and serves as Sernatur's regional head-quarters for Chiloé. Open M-Th 8:30am-5:30pm, F 8:30am-4:30pm.

Banks: Banco de Chile, Libertad 621, also has a **24hr. ATM.** Open M-F 9am-2pm. Or try **Banco Estado,** Eleuterio Ramírez 229 (☎624 102). There are no *cambios* in Ancud.

Work Opportunities: Fundación Con Todos, Eleutario Ramírez 207, 2nd fl. (☎622 604; contodos@entelchile.net), works with a network of farmers in Chiloé making individual farms available for accommodations under the premise that visitors will participate in farm activities. For details, see **Alternatives to Tourism** (p. 83).

Markets: Mercado Municipal, between Dieciocho and Arturo Prat, to the east of Liber-tad. Buckets of crabs, fish, and shellfish lie out for the taking, along with bundles of seaweed and wood-carved crafts. Stands open 9am-8pm.

Supermarkets: For basic ingredients, try **Supermercado Becker,** Arturo Prat 271 (☎627 100; open daily 9am-10pm), or **Supermercado Correa P&P,** at Dieciocho and Blanco Encalada (☎622 946; open daily 9am-10pm). **Fruits** and **veggies** are best purchased from one of the shops on Pedro Montt, between Prat and Dieciocho (open 9am-8pm).

Laundromat: Lavandería Clean Center, Pudeto 45 (☎623 838), charges CH$1100 per kilo. Open M-Sa 9:30am-1pm and 3-7:30pm.

Police: Plaza Centenario (☎622 333), at the intersection of Banco Encalada and O'Hig-gins. **Guardia** open 24hr.

Pharmacy: Farmacia Buseyne, Libertad 566 (☎622 281), has the longest hours in town. Open M-Sa 9:30am-1pm and 2:30-8pm.

Hospital: Admirante Latorre 301 (☎622 355), at the intersection with Pedro Montt.

Telephones: *Centros de llamados* are available at several locations, including Aníbal Pinto 301 (open 9am-10pm) and Pedro Montt (☎627 992; open 1am-9pm). **Telefónica del Sur** available in the Mercado.

Internet access: Several slow connections available. **ZonaNet,** Pudeto 276 local 2 (☎623 647). CH$1000 per hr., 10am-3pm CH$700 per hr. Open 10am-midnight. Sim-ilar rates at the office at Pudeto 219 local 4 (☎623 068). Open daily 10am-midnight.

Post Office: Pudeto 201 (☎624 843). Open M-F 9am-1:30pm and 3-6:30pm, Sa 9am-1pm.

⛏ ACCOMMODATIONS AND CAMPING

For those equipped with tents, the scenic avenue **Costanera Norte** offers several cliff-top properties on which summer camping is permitted. If you are camping alone, try to negotiate a one-person, backpacker rate. Otherwise, the town's countless *hospedajes* manage to accommodate the summer influx of Chilean students and their foreign counterparts. Ancud specializes in bargain-basement accommodations, so this is not the place to hang your hat if you want to pamper yourself with room service at a luxurious hotel. Most accommodations are open year-round.

Hostal Lluhay, Lord Cochrane 458 (☎622 656). Although the view from the dining area is the clincher, over-the-top hospitality, a "limitless" breakfast, private baths, and taste-ful antique furnishings don't hurt this spotless hostel either. Kitchen facilities available. Internet access CH$1000 per hr. 3-4 person rooms CH$5000 per person; singles from CH$7000; doubles from CH$6000 per person. ❷

Hospedaje Ancud, Los Carrera 821 (☎622 296), just south of the intersection with Errá-zuriz. The amiable, retired teacher who runs this small *hospedaje* will sit you down for

Ancud

🏠 ACCOMMODATIONS
Alojamiento O'Higgins 6, **2**
Complejo Turístico Chiloé, **1**
Hostal Lluhay, **3**
Hostal Madryn, **5**
Hospedaje General
 Baquedario 469, **6**
Hospedaje Vist del Mar, **14**
Hospedaje Ancud, **13**
Hospedaje San Jose, **15**
Hostal Belén, **9**

🍴 FOOD & NIGHTLIFE
Chilote Mena El Unico, **12**
La Pincoya, **7**
Pietro Pub, **11**
Kurantón, **4**
Restaurant Balai, **10**
El Sacho/Mi Casa, **8**

an informative lesson on the region. Internet access, a cozy kitchen, and nice bathrooms make a stay here pleasant and convenient. Breakfast included. Singles, doubles, and triples CH\$4500 per person; off-season CH\$4000. ❷

Hotel Madryn, Bellavista 491 (☎622 128), at the intersection with Prat. A good choice for privacy-seekers and wood-paneling aficionados. Staircases and the low doorframes evoke a ship's interior. Spacious rooms come with cable TV, space heaters, and private baths. Breakfast included. Singles CH\$8000, Apr.-Oct. CH\$6000; doubles CH\$14,000/CH\$12,000; triples CH\$18,000/CH\$14,000. ❸

Hostal Belén, Arturo Prat 269 (☎622 343; hostalbelen@entelchile.net), above Supermercado Becker. In a central and seemingly noisy location, Hostal Belén is amazingly tranquil, with pink and red tones enhancing the plush wood interior. Rooms are not spa-

IN RECENT NEWS

BRIDGE TO NOWHERE?

The ferry from Chacao, east of Ancud, to Pargua, on the mainland, is literally a rite of passage for those entering Chiloé. Spanning over 10km and taking 30min. to complete, the often-times beautiful voyage puts its passengers on Chilote time. By the time they disembark the ferry, people are calmer and less anxious, ready to absorb the wonders of the grand isle. However, for businessmen and some residents who frequently make this trip, the romantic voyage loses its luster and becomes a serious inconvenience, especially in winter, when there are spells of weather so bad that the ferry cannot run.

Which is why the Chilean government had taken bids from investors for the rights to build a 2.3km bridge across the 120m deep channel, shaving 27-28min. off the crossing time. The company that eventually won the contract claims that, "the geographic isolation of Chiloé erects serious impediments to the economic and social development of the population." They believe the bridge will grease the wheels of development via greater commercial and tourist exposure.

Unfortunately, everyone is not so enthusiastic. Various polls have shown that most residents of the island are actually either indifferent or opposed to the bridge. Opponents claim that a bridge is very low on the island's priority list, well below various social and economic concerns that the bridge won't solve.

cious, but some have private baths. Kitchen facilities and 2 parking spaces available. Dorms and doubles CH$5000 per person. ❷

Alojamiento O'Higgins 6, O'Higgins 6 (☎622 266), at the intersection with Lord Cochrane. Take friendly and accommodating hosts, add a stately old house with reasonable rates, and stir briskly. No doubt, this is a recipe for happy travelers. A quirky abundance of avant-garde paintings makes the place quite colorful. Pleasant upstairs dining area, but potentially saggy beds. Breakfast included. Doubles, triples, and quads CH$5000 per person; off-season CH$4000. ❷

Hospedaje Vista del Mar (HI), Costanera 918 (☎622 617; vistaalmar@entelchile.net), just south of Los Cavada. You can't miss these 2 prodigious brown-and-white buildings with multicolor flags out front. An HI affiliate for discount-seekers; a spacious seaside accommodation for others. Great views don't fully compensate for the slightly over-priced rooms with worn carpets and the very small kitchen. CH$5500 per person for members, CH$6000 for non-members; doubles with bath CH$13,500/CH$15,000. *Cabañas* also available. ❷

Hospedaje General Baquedano 469, General Baquedano 469 (☎625 650), with a big blue sign out front. The rooms are basic, the hall illuminated by only one bare bulb, but the mattresses are comfortable and the owner is friendly. Filled with Chilean students in Jan. and Feb. this becomes one of the cheapest deals in town during the off-season. Kitchen facilities available. Breakfast CH$800-1000. Doubles or triples CH$4000 per person; off-season CH$3000. ❷

Hospedaje San José, Pudeto 619 (☎622 467; rocarmu@telsur.cl). Stop by to satiate your inner pilgrim—Biblical images, Jesus posters, and scriptures are imposing fixtures in all rooms. Internet access and laundry service available. 30 new beds will be a welcome part of forthcoming expansion and renovation efforts. CH$4000 per person; 2-person *cabaña* CH$10,000-12,000. ❷

Complejo Turístico Chiloé, Costanera Norte 285 (☎622 961). Just one of several **camping** establishments on this street; if you don't like it, keep walking and shop around for yourself. A popular choice among backpackers, the site is a fun and lively place to hang your hat in the summer. Cooking shelters, Internet access, and phone service available. Sites for up to 5 people CH$7500; spacious *cabañas* for up to 5 people CH$35,000, CH$20,000 in the off-season. ❷

🔒 FOOD AND NIGHTLIFE

There are a multitude of well-stocked stores and cheap market stands for those who are cooking for themselves (see **Supermarkets, p.** 420). **Fish and shellfish** are available in the **Mercado Municipal** (see p. 420).

La Pincoya, Arturo Prat 61 (☎622 613 or 622 511), near the port. Diners enjoy appealing views, good service, and delectable cuisine in 2 stories of semi-elegant dining. The *curanto* (CH$2800) is an obvious favorite, but the *salmon papillon* (CH$3500), salads (CH$1200), and the *pastel de choclo* (CH$3300) complete the balanced menu. Open 10am-midnight; off-season M-F 10am-11pm, Sa-Su 7-11pm. ❷

El Sacho and **Mi Casa** (☎622 260), both located in the central courtyard of the Mercado. Always busy and bustling, these are great, laid-back places to satisfy that fish craving you've had for days. Most tasty options, including *corvina*, salmon, and *congrío* (CH$2000-3000), are a la carte with heady sauces (CH$2000). Fixed lunch menu CH$1500-2000. Open daily 9am-1am. ❸

Kurantón, Arturo Prat 94 (☎622 216), across the street from the central COPEC station. A wide variety of seafood is served in this intimate, boutique-like restaurant. Although Kuranton is famed for its *curanto* (from CH$2500), the *ceviche* is an equally succulent choice. Open M, Th-Sa 10am-11pm; Tu, W, Su 2:30-11pm; liable to close early if customers don't linger. ❷

Chilote Mena El Único, Pudeto 318 (☎625 835 or 626 944). *Comida típica* with good ambience all day, every day. Reliable stand-bys like *churrascos con palta* (CH$1200) and *italiano* (CH$1300) served up daily. Good seafood dishes are prepared occasionally. The pastry display case is sure to tempt even the most health-conscious of eaters. Open 24hr. ❶

Restaurant Balai, Pudeto 199 (☎625 070), adjacent to the plaza. If you're getting sea-sick from all the seafood you've been sampling, stop by for a wider selection, including 4-topping pizzas (CH$3300), *lomo* and *filete* options (CH$3000-4000), and assorted salads (CH$2000). Large lunch specials CH$2600. Open daily 10:30am-1am. ❷

Pietro Pub, Maipú 615 (☎626 410), between Pudeto and Ramírez. A great place to chill and down a beer, or two, or three (CH$800-1300). Don't let the straight-backed chairs fool you: this is no place for the straight-laced. In the summer, 70s and 80s music gives way to sporadic live jazz and rock acts. Happy Hour M-F 7:30-9pm. Open M-F 11am-3am, Sa 8pm-4am. ❶

Moreover, Chiloé's road network that the bridge would link to the mainland is very rough—so much so that many claim road improvement should be a higher priority or even a prerequisite to bridge erection.

Finally, some object entirely to the whole idea of the economic "exploitation" of the island, claiming (in a banner hanging from a window in Castro) that the bridge represents, "the second colonization of Chiloé." Whatever you believe, the US$350 million needed for construction has been raised, and the company is in the process of getting environmental approval for the project.

The government has been hesitant to recognize objections to the plan, partially because it doesn't cost the government a thing. Instead, the builders will recoup their investment from fares levied on passengers that will be quite similar to the fares currently charged ferry-riders. Once the financial wheels are turning, it's quite hard to stop investment on this scale, and residents fear that this might be the crucial step of the homogenization process, a development that may cause rural Chiloé to lose its rural mystique, unique culture, and throwback lifestyle.

🔍 SIGHTS

The best way to see Ancud is to pick a sunny day, start in town, and work your way outwards. Start at the **Museo Regional de Ancud,** Libertad 370, a few buildings south of Sernatur, easily visible with its striking blue base and turreted courtyard. The second-floor displays offer an insightful and comprehensive look at the history, culture, and geography of the Grand Isle. Particularly fascinating are the ceramic, basket-weaving, and textile exhibitions, pictures of the 1960 earthquake's impact on Ancud, and the large 3-D terrain map of Chiloé. Outside, a *fogón* (Chilote cooking hut) and various intriguing marine flotsam adorn the courtyard. (☎ 622 413. Open Jan.-Feb. M-F 10:30am-7:30pm, Sa-Su 10am-7:30pm; Mar.-Dec. M-F 9:30am-5:30pm, Sa-Su 10am-2pm. CH$500.) While the museum's factual displays on Spanish colonialism will bring out the historian in you, a stop at **Fuerte San Antonio** will exercise your imaginative faculties. On the site where Spanish colonial troops were defeated and expelled from Chile in 1828, the open-air grounds of the fort house a collection of seven cannons in the battlements. From the fort, walk east a block, then one block north on Baquedano, and continue east on Antonio Burr following the path to the top of **Cerro Huaihuén,** for the best view of town. In bright, sunny weather, expect panoramic views of the mainland with its peaks and volcanoes. Once the sightseeing is over, amble over to the **Mercado Municipal** (see p. 420) for dinner or souvenir shopping.

In January and February, Ancud comes alive with a variety of gastronomic, cultural, and commemorative events. These include the **Musical Days of Chiloé,** a loose confederation of classical music concerts in the second week of January, and the **23rd Annual Meeting on Folklore,** in the third week of January, when respected scholars gather on the beach to discuss witches and mutants.

🏔 OUTDOOR ACTIVITIES

It's very possible that the best way to spend time in Ancud is to get out of Ancud. North of town, the **Lacuy Peninsula** juts out in the shape of a fishing hook, curving east and clearly visible opposite the town center. In the summertime, this peninsula is awash with industrious campers, eager horseback-riders, and frolicking beach-goers. At **Piedra Run,** 24km from Ancud on the peninsula, intricate volcanic rock formations stand on a pleasant beach with undulating sand dunes. On the far north side of the peninsula, **Faro Corona** will please lone rangers and lighthouse enthusiasts with its remote location 45km by road along the Canal de Chacao. **Fuerte Ahui,** at the eastern tip of the peninsula 40km from Ancud, is the area's biggest attraction. Dating from 1779, its ruined battlements are much more intricate than those of its San Antonio counterpart, and it boasts 14 impressive cannons. The **Amadeus** makes daily trips out to the fort in January and February (3hr., CH$5000 per person), providing visitors a great opportunity to get out on the water.

The most interesting faunal attraction outside Ancud is **Pingüinera Puñihuil,** an island preserve off Chiloé's western coast that hosts a significant population of Humbolt and Magallan penguins. A boat trip (CH$3000) takes visitors to the island, while all-inclusive minibus tours (CH$5000; late Nov.-Feb.) leave from the Plaza de Armas. **Buses Mar Brava** offers basic transportation as well; see **Sernatur** (p. 420) for details on schedules and fares.

A bit farther afield, the **Río Chepu Sector** of Parque Nacional Chiloé has some beautiful coastal trails, but trips here require some logistical planning (see

THE STUFF OF LEGENDS Before immersing yourself in Chilote culture and its throwback farming and fishing lifestyle, it pays to acquaint yourself with Chiloé's pantheon of deformed and debauched mythological figures and icons. You might not be able to cull any pick-up lines from their fetid ranks, but knowing a bit about the creatures will help you explain aberrant pregnancies and deaths of all sorts. It will also help explain the odd names of restaurants and other services all over the island.

Trauco: Probably the most invoked of the mythological figures, this hideous elfen beast lives in the thick, tangled forests of Chiloé. He is best known for his promiscuity, as young women who wander into his lair find themselves transfixed by his gaze and are unable to resist his advances. His lovemaking is reportedly expert, and those impregnated by him find themselves unsatisfied by mere mortals thereafter.

Pincoya: This marine goddess is known as a harbinger of fickle sea harvests. Her sensual dance followed by a glance towards the sea brings fish teeming into shore to be caught by Chilote fisherman. On the other hand, a glance towards land after the dance foretells a poor catch. Her fabled role could evolve with the current phenomenon of *marea roja* (red tide).

Invunche: With a third leg sprouting from his spine, this crazy character guards a witches' cave near Quicavi, where he eats anyone who approaches. His taste for human flesh was acquired during his wayward childhood, when he fed on rotting corpses from Chiloé's graveyards.

Basilisco: With the head of a rooster and the body of a snake, this funny-looking serpent slithers methodically towards his goal, physically and mentally weakening his already-ill victims before sucking their lungs dry.

Caleuche: This ghost galleon manned by specters patrols Chiloé's seas and metes out justice when the fog descends and renders navigation impossible. The ship ushers well-intentioned sailors back to port, but allows others to perish in the mist.

Parque Nacional Chiloé, p. 436). **Caulín,** 26km east of Ancud, not far from the ferry dock at Chacao, is a small town known for its oysters and handicrafts. A bike ride from Ancud to Caulín along the coast can be immensely rewarding, but watch out for the high tide—the water rushes over the coastal road, making it almost impassable.

If you're feeling adventurous and a trip to the Lacuy Peninsula isn't hardcore enough, six- and seven-day kayaking trips to waters in the Pumalín fjords and eastern Chiloé islands are offered by **Austral Adventures.** Pricey daytrips to Puñihuel and the west coast are also available. Ask for Brett at Hostal Llahuy. (☎625 977; www.australadventures.com. Daytrips CH$75 per person, min. 2 people.) For a whole slew of outdoor recreational possibilities, try **Turismo Campesino** (☎623 075; campesino@telsur.cl), which rents bikes, horses, and kayaks for trips on Río Chepu and organizes trekking trips.

SOUTH TO CASTRO

To the southwest, the picturesque east coast of Isla Grande is unified by a road that runs south through Quemchi, west to Tenaún, and south again through Dalcahue before arriving in Castro. This route is worth exploring by car, bike, or bus if necessary. These quaint little towns along the coast are a great way to get to know the slow-paced lifestyle of Chiloé's denizens.

CHILOÉ

QUEMCHI   ☎ 65

This small, sandy bay with pastel-patterned boats is framed by the stunning view across the Gulf of Ancud to the volcanoes of the Hornopirén area, which rise up beyond the island of Caucahué. On the coastal road between Dalcahue and the northeast, Quemchi is representative of all the region's attractions: a laid-back laissez-faire lifestyle and a developing agro-tourism network.

The **information kiosk** is on the waterfront in a plaza in front of the town's **church**, one of its main features. In the summer, along the water, there are **boats for hire**, with which you can explore Chaucahué and see a nearby seal colony (one hour round-trip). Only four kilometers south of Quemchi, **Isla de Aucar** lies 500 yards off the coast; during low tide, it is possible to walk out to the island and visit the pretty botanical garden. You can also hire boats to take you to the island if picnicking there strikes your fancy—time it well and you may be able to walk back. The ▨coastal road from Dalcahue through San Juan, Tenaún, via a detour at Quicavi, and on to Quemchi, is one of the most beautiful rural roads in Chiloé. Renting a car is wise, because regular Castro bus service only runs to Tenaún or via the inland route to Quemchi. Renting a bike from one of the *hospedajes* in Castro is a cheaper option, but plan for a couple of days of travel each way. The views are infinitely better if you're traveling northeast, but make sure to check the forecast; you wouldn't want it to rain on your parade. About three kilometers north of town, **Agroturismo Dougnac-Cordero** (☎691 305) has built a reputation as one of the best agrotourism locations, allowing guests to watch and participate in farmwork. Call ahead for reservations or contact the main Agroturismo office (see **Alternatives to Tourism**, p. 83).

Minibuses service the route to **Ancud** (1½hr., 6-9 per day, CH$1000) both along the northern Costanera road and via the Panamericana. **Buses Quemchi** heads to **Castro** (1½hr., 6-9 per day, CH$1000). All buses leave from the **bus terminal** at the far north of town on the **Costanera**, also known as Centerario in its southern stretches and Yungay on the north end. For a reasonable room in town, **Hospedaje Yungay 71 ❷**, across from the bus terminal, has adequate rooms with low ceilings. (☎691 285. Breakfast included. CH$4000 per person.) A slightly nicer option is the **Hospedaje Costanera ❷**, Diego Bahamonde 141, further south along the coast, which has nice views from some of the rooms. (☎691 230. Singles and doubles CH$6000 per person, off-season CH$4000; with breakfast CH$7500/CH$5000. 6-person *cabañas* CH$16,000.) Good eating is best done at **El Chejo Restaurant ❶**, on the Costanera between the Hospedaje Costanera and the bus terminal, unmistakable with its purple-and-white paint job. A hearty *almuerzo* (CH$2000) includes fish and sometimes salmon.

DALCAHUE   ☎ 65

Famous among visitors for its lively Sunday market, Dalcahue (pop. 3000) serves as a fishing and shellfish farming center, a port for traditional boats, and the departure point for ferries to Isla Quinchao. Life here is a mesh of commercial and rural, with fish-canning factories marking the road to Castro while islanders troll the waters in their old fishing boats. Dalcahue's unique culinary flair should be declared an official tourist attraction—the *curanto* prepared in buckets at the market is out of this world, while *ostras* (local oysters) served up in restaurants are fit for the gods.

🖪🔁 **TRANSPORTATION AND PRACTICAL INFORMATION.** Regular **ferry** service is offered at the dock (10min.; every 20min. 7am-11pm; passengers free, CH$1500 per car). Regular **buses** run to **Castro** (35min.; M-F every 15min. 7am-

9pm, Sa-Su every 30min. 8am-9pm; CH$400) and **Achao** (every 45min., CH$700). **Colectivos** to Castro (CH$600) leave from in front of the **post office** and tend to stop running around 6-7:30pm. Laid lengthwise along the **Dalcahue channel,** the main street **Ramón Freire** runs parallel to the water and **Ana Wagner,** while **Pedro Montt** runs along the coast. The main town amenities are in a little square at the town center, near the intersection of Freire with Mocopulli, which connects with the Panamericana. The market, municipal building, restaurants, cathedral, and *hospedajes* lie to the south and east of this service block. A small **information kiosk** (open only in summer) lies in front of the **consultorio** (☎641 295), near the **post office,** Freire 302 (open M-F 9am-1:30pm and 3-6pm, Sa 9am-12:30pm), and the **police,** Mocopulli 102 (☎641 748). Further west, **Banco Estado,** Freire 645, has a **24hr. ATM.**

⌂ ACCOMMODATIONS AND FOOD. Although value accommodations do not abound in Dalcahue, **Residencial La Fiera ❷,** M. Rodríguez 017, two blocks west of the *iglesia,* is a good bet. A range of rooms is offered on the second and third floors while the restaurant downstairs serves as the only main common area. (☎641 293. Kitchen access in the winter. Singles or dorms CH$5000; doubles CH$10,000, with bath CH$14,000; off-season CH$4000/CH$8000/CH$12,000.) Since the *curanto* here can't be missed, head down the street to **Restaurant Playa ❷,** M. Rodríguez 09, where notably delicious food is served up with a particular Chilote charm. *Curanto* (CH$3500) and *ostras* (CH$2000) are supplemented with a small plate of *erizos* (sea urchin roe; CH$2500), a delectable Dalcahuan delicacy. (☎641 397. Open 10am-11pm.) Cheaper **Palafito Las Brisas ❶,** behind the *mercado,* offers a variety of fish including *ceviche* and *comida típica.* (Open 9:30am-midnight.) The market vends a great selection of food and fresh produce in the summer.

◪ SIGHTS AND OUTDOOR ACTIVITIES. The famous **Sunday market** livens up the waterfront in the winter, but only lasts until mid-afternoon. In the summer, people pour in from Castro, Ancud, and other outlying areas to keep the market bustling and the town sparkling late into the evening. The lesser-known Thursday market is nice, but no match for Sunday's spectacular affair. The **Iglesia de Nuestra Señora de Los Dolores,** north of the open plaza on the east side of town, built in 1858, mimics the style of earlier cathedrals on a more grandiose scale. Inside, a small, unmanned "museum" offers documents, scriptures, vestments, and hymnals from the history of the church. The **docks** are worth a walk any day of the week—watch fishermen pull in bags of shellfish and piles of fish and transport them to the market or to nearby canning factories, and be glad you're on vacation.

North of town, **Altué Expeditions** guides upscale **sea kayaking** trips in the fjords across the gulf and to the outer islands of the Chiloé archipelago. Guests spend a night in the spotless, communal bunkroom before leaving for distant waters. Archipelago trips paddle through the Mechuque and Chauque Islands; guests stay in family houses for a full cultural and culinary experience. Trips are scheduled months ahead of time, but call last-minute for available spots. (☎641 110, in Santiago 2 232 1103; www.seakayakchile.com. Sept.-Apr. 4-day all-inclusive Chiloé trip US$590.)

CASTRO ☎65

Born as a Spanish outpost in 1567, Castro is one of the oldest cities in Chile, yet much of it looks suspiciously like it was built in the 1960s. Well, that's because it was. Like much of southern Chile, Castro was devastated by the 1960 earthquake. Unlike its neighbors, however, it was the only major town in Chiloé not to abandon the *palafito* (a house built on stilts over tidal flats) in its rebuilding effort. Precarious *palafitos* persist in rows, wooing tourists down to the city's waterfront where restaurants and the famous town market are situated. In the summer, daytrip tours run from here all over the archipelago, illustrating an important point: Castro is not an attraction in and of itself but serves as an effective hub for travelers. If you have only a couple of days in Chiloé, Castro will give you a flavor of the island, but for longer visits, stop here, get your bearings, and move on to the real Chiloé, which is locked up in the countryside and not on Castro's busy streets.

▐ TRANSPORTATION

Flights: There is no airport on the island, though **LanChile**, Blanco 299 (☎635 254), on the southeast corner of the Plaza, books flights out of Puerto Montt. Open M-F 9am-1:30pm and 3-6:30pm, Sa 10am-1pm.

Buses: There are two terminals in town. **Buses rurales** to destinations in central Chiloé leave from the **Terminal Municipal,** San Martín 681, just north of the intersection with Sergeant Aldea and set back from the street through a *paseo.* **Buses interprovinciales** leave from the **Terminal Cruz del Sur,** San Martín 486, at the corner of Sotomayor, less than a block north of the church. **Luggage storage** available (CH$700 per day).

Terminal Cruz del Sur: TransChiloé (☎635 152) and **Cruz del Sur** (☎632 389 or 635 158) go to: **Ancud** (1½hr., 26 per day, CH$1300); **Puerto Montt** (3½hr.; 26 per day 6:40am-8:30pm; CH$3200, CH$2500 with TransChiloé); **Punta Arenas** (36hr.; Tu, Th, Sa 7:20am; CH$40,000); **Quellón** (2hr., 17 per day, CH$1000) via **Chonchi** (CH$500); **Santiago** (17hr.; 3:45 and 5:15pm; CH$17,000, *cama* CH$29,000); **Valdivia** (7 per day 7:20am-3:40pm, CH$6000) via **Osorno** (CH$4800).

Terminal Municipal: Buses Arriagada goes to **Achao** (1½hr.; M-F 9 per day, Sa 7 per day, Su 4 per day; CH$1000) via **Dalcahue** (CH$400). **Queilén Bus** runs to **Puerto Montt** (3½hr., 6 per day, CH$2500) via **Ancud** (CH$1200) and **Queilén** (1½hr., 7 per day, CH$1200). **Buses Gallardo** heads to **Pequeldon** on Isla Lemuy (M-Sa 7:30, 9:50am, 6:30pm, Su 2:30 and 6:30pm; CH$1200). **Buses Ojeda** goes to **Cucao** (1½hr.; M-F 12:30 and 4pm, Sa 12:30pm, Su 10am and 6:30pm; CH$1200) via **Chonchi** (CH$500). **Quemchi Bus** goes to **Quemchi** (1½hr.; M-Sa 6 per day, Su 12:20 and 6pm; CH$1000). **Expresos** goes to: **Achao** (2hr., 11-15 per day, CH$1000); **Dalcahue** (35min.; M-F every 15min. 7:15am-9pm, Sa-Su every 30min. 8am-9pm; CH$400); **Quellon** (2hr.; M-F 19 per day 6:30am-9pm, Sa 12 per day 7am-9pm, Su 8 per day 8am-9pm; CH$1000).

Ferries: TransMarChilay, Thompson 273 (☎635 691), does not offer ferry service from Castro, but has information and bookings here for those headed to Puerto Montt and Quellón. **Catamaranes del Sur,** Blanco 299 (☎800 650 015 or 632 361; www.catamaranesdelsur.cl), offers fast transportation from Castro to Chaitén between Dec. and Feb. (3hr., Tu and Th 9am, passengers only).

Taxis and Colectivos: Taxis and *colectivos* running city routes cluster along San Martín. *Colectivos* to Dalcahue (CH$600) are located just east of San Martín, a block north of the Terminal Municipal. *Colectivos* to Chonchi (CH$600) are south of the Terminal Municipal east of San Martín on Ramírez. **Radio Taxis Chiloé** (☎632 828) and **Radio Taxis Milenium** (☎636 565) offer call-based service.

Car Rental: Rent-A-Car, Esmeralda 266 (☎637 900), inside the Esmeralda Hotel, charges CH$30,000 per day. Or try **Ads Rent-A-Car,** Blanco 244 (☎637 777).

Bike Rental: Available for guests at **Hospedaje El Mirador** (see **Accommodations,** p. 431).

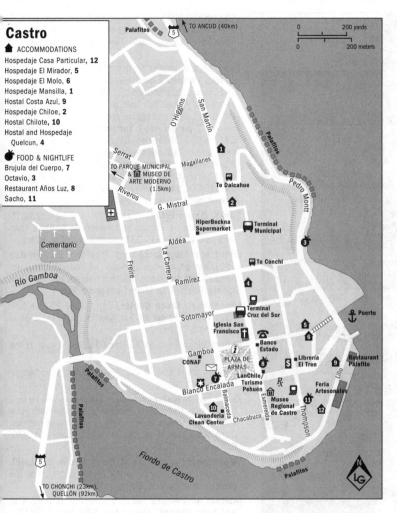

Castro

ACCOMMODATIONS
Hospedaje Casa Particular, **12**
Hospedaje El Mirador, **5**
Hospedaje El Molo, **6**
Hospedaje Mansilla, **1**
Hostal Costa Azul, **9**
Hospedaje Chiloe, **2**
Hostal Chilote, **10**
Hostal and Hospedaje
  Quelcun, **4**

FOOD & NIGHTLIFE
Brujula del Cuerpo, **7**
Octavio, **3**
Restaurant Años Luz, **8**
Sacho, **11**

TO ANCUD (40km)

0   200 yards
0   200 meters

Palafitos

Cementario

Río Gamboa

TO PARQUE MUNICIPAL
& MUSEO DE
ARTE MODERNO
(1.5km)

Serrat
Riveros
O'Higgins
San Martín
Magallanes
To Dalcahue
G. Mistral
Aldea
Freire
La Carrera
Ramírez
Sotomayor
Gamboa
CONAF
Blanco Encalada
Balmaceda
Chacabuco
Esmeralda
Thompson
Lillo

HiperBeckna
Supermarket
Terminal
Municipal
To Conchi
Terminal
Cruz del Sur
Iglesia San
Fransisco
Banco
Estado
Librería
El Tren
Restaurant
Palafito
Feria
Artesonales
Museo
Regional
de Castro
LanChile
Turismo
Pehuén
Lavandería
Clean Center

PLAZA DE
ARMAS

Pedro Montt
Palafitos
Puerto

Fiordo de Castro

Palafitos

TO CHONCHI (23km),
QUELLÓN (92km)

ORIENTATION AND PRACTICAL INFORMATION

Castro is fairly small and easy to navigate. The downtown area follows the typical Chilean grid pattern and is bounded by **Costanera Pedro Montt** to the south and east, by **Freire** to the west, and **Magallanes** to the north. The **Panamericana** splits into the southbound **O'Higgins** and the northbound **San Martín** as it enters town. These two streets form the **Plaza de Armas** when they intersect with **Gamboa** and **Blanco Encalada.** A block to the west, **Serrano** runs from the Terminal de Buses Rurales in the northwestern part of town.

Tourist Office: The **information kiosk** is in the Plaza de Armas. Open Dec.-Mar. 10am-8pm, Apr.-Nov. 11am-3pm. For info on **Parque Nacional de Chiloé,** try **Conaf,** Gamboa

IN RECENT NEWS

MOLLUSK MATTERS

Chiloé's readily available and wonderfully fresh seafood may have you shoveling in every clam, mussel, abalone, or sea urchin that comes your way. And who can blame you? However, issues of freshness and health are especially important with mollusks, which can cause illness or death. Keep an eye out for *marea roja* (red tide) that's progressing north into portions of Chiloé. This ambient organic toxin fluctuates in concentration over the course of a year. When levels are low, eating shellfish is safe and dandy. When levels are high, the high levels of toxin, when consumed, can paralyze the central nervous system and shut down the cardio-respiratory system, causing rapid death. Fortunately, the Chilean government is well aware of the problem. As a result, all shellfish caught and shipped off to market or to restaurants are tested for the *marea roja* toxin. Consequently, exposure risk is very low. However, if you go catch your own dinner or buy shellfish right off the dock, there is a slim chance that you could be putting yourself at risk. No amount of cooking will destroy the toxin, so it's vital to avoid buying shellfish from risky sources. That said, *marea roja* is not the only way to be ill after consuming shellfish. More innocuous but nonetheless unpleasant food poisoning can result from the improper handling of mollusks that aren't fresh. So, when sitting down to an appetizer of *almejas a la parmesana*, look around, and if you see cockroaches crawling up the wall, you might want to think twice about those clams.

424 (☎532 501), just west of the Plaza, although they aren't very accommodating or well-equipped to help travelers with their needs. Open M-F 9am-1pm and 2-5:45pm.

Tours: Trips to locales all over the island originate from Castro. **Pehuén Expediciones,** Blanco 299 (☎632 361; www.pehuentour.com), offers 8hr. daytrips to Dalcahue and Achao, Isla Lemuy, Parque Nacional Chiloé, and a visit to the penguins and seals (CH$18,500 per person, 2 person min.). **Turismo Quelcun,** San Martín 581 (☎632 396), operating out of Hostal Quelcun, has more budget-oriented full daytrips (10am-9pm; 2-3 person min.) Offerings include trips to Parque Nacional Chiloé (CH$10,000), *pingüineras* of Puñihuil (CH$15,000), Isla Lemuy (CH$12,500), and boat trips around Isla Mechuque (CH$15,000).

Banks: Banco Estado, San Martín 397 (☎632 251), on the Plaza de Armas, and **Banco de Chile,** Blanco Encalada 201 (☎635 331), both have **24hr. ATMs.**

Bookstore: Librería El Tren, Thompson 229 (☎633 396), has an eclectic selection of Spanish books for perusal, and the warm hearth creates a homey atmosphere. Open M-Sa 10am-2pm and 4-9pm.

Laundromat: Clean Center, Balmaceda 230 (☎633 132). CH$1100 per kg. 2hr. service. Open M-Sa 9am-1pm and 3-7:30pm.

Police: Diego Portales 457 (☎631 855), west of the plaza.

Hospital: Freire 852 (☎632 444), north of the intersection with Mistral.

Pharmacy: Salcobrand, Blanco Encalada 228 (☎632 010), posts the rotation system 24hr. pharmacy rotation system schedule with address and phone number. Open M-Sa 9am-10pm, Su 9:30am-1:30pm and 3:30-8:30pm.

Telephones: Easy to find all along San Martín. **Entel,** Gamboa 267, is close to the plaza, just east of the church. Open 9am-10:30pm.

Internet Access: The fastest connection in town is at **Bakania Planet,** Thompson 256 (☎532 810). CH$400 for 30min. Open M-F 10am-11pm, Sa 11am-10:30pm, Su 11:30am-9:30pm. The cheapest connection is at **Gyganet,** 279 Sotomayor (☎530 237). CH$700 per hr. Open M-Sa 10am-11pm, Su 4-11pm.

Post Office: Bernardo O'Higgins 333. Open M-F 9am-1:30pm and 3-6:30pm, Sa 9am-1pm.

■ ACCOMMODATIONS

For a tourist hub, Castro's accommodations are relatively lackluster. The mid- to upper-range accommodations are severely wanting, and only a few *hospedajes* stand out as good values. The highest density of *hospedajes* is on **Barros Arana,** the pedestrian-only stairway extension of Sotomayor, a block and a half east of the Cruz del Sur Terminal. Many accommodations are engaged in an amusing advertising campaign, adopting names that proclaim the comparative superiority of the view from their location. Barros Arana *hospedajes* not listed here are generally cheaper, but with fewer amenities and little space in which to accommodate peak-season crowds.

■ **Hospedaje El Mirador,** Barros Arana 127 (☎633 795; maboly@yahoo.com). This towering 3-story mansion has fjord views from some of the rooms. The lovely family makes the spotless, well-maintained rooms and pleasant common facilities homey. Ample breakfast included. Bike rental and Internet access available. Dorms and doubles CH$5000, with private bath CH$6000; off-season CH$4500/CH$5000. ❷

■ **Hospedaje Mansilla,** San Martín 879 (☎635 613). The kind woman here must be the most motherly *hospedaje* owner in town—with a stern demeanor barely masking her warm hospitality, she is sure to charm all guests. Wooden floors, clean bathrooms, and a large dose of TLC make a stay here particularly enjoyable. Hearty breakfast included. Singles and doubles CH$4000 per person; off-season CH$3000. ❷

Hostal Costa Azul, Lillo 67 (☎632 440; costazul@chiloeweb.com), stands inconspicuously among waterfront *hospedajes* near the *feria.* The open staircase and skylight brighten the mood in this practically flawless hotel, the best mid-range accommodation in town. Good for couples. Cable TV, phone, private baths, and breakfast included. Twins and doubles CH$20,000, Apr.-Nov. CH$14,000. ❸

Hospedaje El Molo, Barros Arana 140 (☎625 026). Right across from El Mirador, the space here is more communal, with a bigger kitchen and a larger dining room for summertime meals. Front rooms with clean wooden floors may well have the best views on Barros Arana. Breakfast included. Internet access available. Singles, doubles, and twins CH$5000 per person; Apr.-Nov. CH$4000. ❷

Hospedaje Chiloé, Monjitas 739 (☎635 136; patitejer@hotmail.com), just off San Martín. Economical and hospitable. A spacious downstairs bathroom is kept clean. Breakfast included. Internet access available. Singles CH$4500; off-season CH$3500.

Hostal Chilote, Aldunate 456 (☎635 021). A two-in-one in a quiet neighborhood, hotel-type rooms are upstairs in the main house, while hostel-style rooms are out back in a separate building. Private baths and cable TV make up for the slightly funky odor in the full units. In-house rooms have endearing old-school flowery bedspreads and more light. Homestyle breakfast included. *Hospedaje* singles and doubles CH$5000 per person; hotel singles and doubles CH$8000. ❷

Hostal and Hospedaje Quelcun, San Martín 581 (☎632 396; quelcun@telsur.cl). A full-scale operation with both budget and mid-range options. The oddly tropical-themed *hostal* courtyard lies adjacent to the upstairs dorm-style rooms. Quiet *hostal* rooms are complete with private baths and TV, but feel a little cramped. The *hospedaje* rooms are the better bet. Breakfast included with *hostal* rooms; *hospedaje* breakfast CH$500. For details on excursions offered see **Tours** (p. 430). Singles CH$30,000; doubles CH$35,000; twins CH$36,000; Apr.-Oct. CH$14,000/CH$15,000/CH$18,000. *Hospedaje* beds CH$4500; Apr.-Oct. CH$4000. ❷

Hospedaje Casa Particular, Lillo 159 (☎637 431). With only an unassuming *hospedaje* sign out front, it's a challenge finding this house. Although a good budget option with newly painted rooms, the seasonal rate flexibility may facilitate over-pricing for unsuspecting foreigners. Kitchen access only in the winter. Breakfast included. Beds CH$3000-4000 per person. ❶

◘ FOOD

As in the rest of Chiloé, seafood is the victual of choice, although much of it is brought in from other ports. The tourist dining hot spot is down at the **palafitos restaurants,** behind the *feria.* All establishments offer cheap lunches featuring seafood (CH$1800) and keep similar hours. (Sept.-Mar. 9am-midnight, Apr.-Aug. 9am-6pm.) For groceries, visit the massive, two-story **HiperBekna** at O'Higgins 711. (☎637 100. Open M-Sa 9am-9:30pm, Su 10am-9pm.) A wider selection of **fruit and vegetable** stores can be found down Aldea toward San Martín.

Octavio, Pedro Montt 261 (☎632 855), a block north along the coast from the eastern end of Barros Arana. The decoration is a pleasant mélange including yellow-and-orange tablecloths, Chilote neo-primitivist paintings, and nets draped dramatically on support poles. The family kitchen's food is equally remarkable. The savory *salmon Octavio* is a highly recommended grilled fillet dressed with a fiery red sauce of peppers, onions, capers, and sausage, topped with fried potato slices (CH$3400). Open 10am-midnight. ❷

Sacho, Thompson 213 (☎632 079), a steep walk up Thompson from the southern end of Lillo and the waterfront. In the rarified air of the hill over the waterfront, the prices rise, but so does the complexity of the cuisine. The creamy crab-based *carpacho* (CH$1900) and *almejas Sacho* (clams; CH$3000) make a visit worthwhile. Enjoy the view from the upstairs seating area while dining. Open noon-4pm and 8pm-midnight. ❸

Brújula del Cuerpo, O'Higgins 308 (☎633 229), on the southwest corner of the Plaza de Armas. Service here is perfunctory, but that element is overshadowed by the reasonably priced food. Moreover, the salads (CH$2500) may be one of the best options for vegetarians in a town that blatantly lacks non-seafood options. In mid-morning and mid-afternoon, *onces* (CH$2000) are served with *kuchen.* Profits benefit the volunteer fire squad. Open 9:30am-midnight. ❷

Restaurant Años Luz, San Martín 309 (☎532 700), on the east side of the Plaza de Armas. This restaurant and bar serves fixed-price lunches (CH$1800-2500), but really fills up on the weekends, when its creative cocktail menu draws honky cats from all over Castro. The sprightly *pisco sour* (CH$1300) and hefty *marea baja* (kahlua, *licor de oro,* and cream; CH$1500) are the perfect dichotomy. Open M-W 11am-11pm, Th-Sa 11am-1am, Su 11am-5pm; may stay open until 2am or later in the summer. ❷

◉ SIGHTS

Activities in Castro are limited to the market and museums, as most of the area's cultural goings-on and nature exploration occurs in adjacent areas of the archipelago. Take a stroll along the fjord's shoreline before hitting up the museums in town. Along the southern end of the city, visible from south of the market, and farther along the shoreline north of the port, Castro's much-photographed **palafitos** are anachronistic icons hearkening to a past when poor subsistence fishermen tied their boats to the supporting wooden piers of their modest houses. Although the abodes have long outlived their practicality, they do lend a traditional air to the town. South of the port, the **feria artesanales** easily eclipses the island's other craft markets, save for Dalcahue's renowned Sunday market. Among the items available are woolen Chilote weavings and samples of famous regional wood carvings in the form of bowls, utensils, and other knickknacks. Further north, a primitive **locomotive** from Chiloé's defunct railroad is displayed, appearing as feeble as lore suggests: passengers apparently had to get out and help push the train up any sort

UP, UP, AND AWAY In Chiloé, an unwritten code says that any-
time you move your house to a different locale, you should, if at all possible, use the
same material for construction of the new home. Not only does this save *pesos* and
timber, but it's supposed to be lucky as well. Thus, people have been known to dis-
mantle their homes piece-by-piece (or even to uproot the foundation), harness a few
horses to it, and crack the whip. Although the practice is not as visible these days, the
destruction following the 1960 earthquake spurred quite a boom in the house-moving
tradition, with many folks moving back from the water to avoid future exposure to tidal
waves and the slow, seismic sinking of the island.

of moderate knoll. Castro's large, neo-gothic **iglesia,** constructed in 1912, is hardly
consistent with the style of Chiloé's traditional churches, but it does have an
imposingly plush wood interior.

For an enjoyable and suitably passive intake of Chilote history, culture, and
architecture, stop by the **Museo Regional de Castro,** Esmeralda 255. A maze of oddly
partitioned space has displays on Catholic vestments, boat building, and the
unique Chilote tradition of uprooting houses and hauling them to new locations
(see **Up, Up, and Away,** below). (☎635 967. Open M-Sa 9:30am-1pm and 3-6:30pm, Su
10:30am-1pm; in the summer M-Sa until 8pm. Free; donations requested.) The
Museo de Arte Moderno is located three kilometers north of town on Galvarino Riveros, which departs town from the west end of Gabriel Mistral. In a done-up *fogón,*
it houses an important collection, fusing traditional themes with a modern aesthetic. Look for a bus or *colectivo* that includes Parque Municipal on its route; the
museum is just beyond the park on the right. (☎635 454. Open Jan.-Feb. 10am-
6pm; Nov., Dec., Mar. 11am-2pm. Free.)

Castro's well-known festivals are consistently the best on the island. The **Festival
Costumbrista Chilote** in the second week of February is the largest bash celebrating
all things Chilote with traditional food, culture, and myth on display. Various other
eclectic festivals are peppered throughout the months of January and February,
when the party never ends down in Chiloé.

NEAR CASTRO

The smaller islands of the archipelago lie across narrow, gentle channels, near the
fjord that shelters Castro, decreasing in size as they taper off east toward the mainland. Although there isn't all that much to "do" or "see" on these small offshore
islands, a visitor is forced to slow down to Chiloé's pace and can immerse him or
herself in the culture in order to truly appreciate the people and way of life in
these out-of-the-way locales.

ACHAO   ☎65

Although regional minibuses patrol the streets of this, one of Isla Quinchao's biggest towns, the trip from Dalcahue to Achao seems like a step back in time.
Embedded in a valley along a black gravel beach, alerce-shingled houses and the
oldest church on the island contribute to the old-world charm.

The **Iglesia Santa Maria,** on the east side of town, is the town's biggest attraction because its 1767 birthdate makes it the oldest church on the island and a
must-see for cathedral enthusiasts and architecture buffs. When walking
through town, see how many shapes of **alerce shingle** you can spot on the houses
in town. Varying shapes can inform shingle-experts (yes, there is such a thing) of
the origin of the shingles and the date of the house's construction. When you run
out of houses, rolling sheep pastures on the outskirts of town can provide as

CHILOÉ

much, if not more, enjoyment. Though *Let's Go* does not recommend it, **hitchhiking** in this area is reportedly easy in January and February, although you will be less likely to snag a ride to the tiny hamlet of Quinchao than Curaco de Velez. If you have an insatiable appetite for increasingly rural destinations, you can find a **boat** to take you to the offshore islands of Llingua, Quenac, and Caguache. Tours are informally organized through the information kiosk. If passing through town during the first week of February, check out the annual **Encuentro Folclórico del Archipiélago** that brings impressive musical lineups, traditional food, and handicrafts to town.

Regular bus service makes the town an easy daytrip from Castro or Dalcahue. **Expresos** buses to **Castro** (every 45min., CH$1000) via **Dalcahue** (CH$700) leave from the center of town. Across the way, the **visitor information kiosk** houses an old woman who knits, plies local wares, and answers questions. (Open year-round; hours vary.) For accommodations and food, try the seaside **Hostería La Nave ❷**, at the corner of Prat and Aldea, which offers a *hospedaje* with hotel-type rooms, as well as a tasty seafood menu boasting excellent oysters (CH$2500), both raw and on the half-shell. (☎661 219. Singles CH$6000; doubles CH$10,000, with bath and TV CH$17,000; off-season CH$4000/CH$6000/CH$8000.) **Hospedaje Sol y Lluvias ❸**, the green-and-yellow house on the way into town, and other *hospedajes* near the church also offer rooms.

CHONCHI
☎ 65

It is hard to imagine the gods venting their anger on this unassuming *pueblito*, but 2002 has brought Chonchi more than its share of small-scale natural disasters. First, a huge patch of the northern waterfront burned down in a massive early-morning fire. Then, a freak gust of autumn wind toppled the town's church steeple, leaving an unsightly wooden gash in its place. Reconstruction is well underway, however, and town life ambles on: salmon boats pack the main pier to unload their profitable cargo, and area farmers herd their livestock among passing buses in the town center. One of the handful of authentic Chilote towns that surround the more commercial and sterile town of Castro, Chonchi is also central, making it a convenient base for visitors making daytrips around the island.

⧉ TRANSPORTATION. From their office on the plaza, **Cruz del Sur** and **Trans Chiloé** (☎671 218) go to **Castro** (30min., every 45min. 8am-9:30pm, CH$500) and **Quellón** (1½hr., every 45min. 7:30am-9pm, CH$900). From the rural **terminal** just a few doors down the street, **Queilén Bus** heads to **Queilén** (1½hr., 6 per day, CH$1000). From the same terminal, **Buses Arroyo and Ojeda** goes to **Cucao** (1hr., 2-4 per day, CH$1000). **Minibuses** go to **Huillinco** (3 per day, CH$400) and **Lemuy** (4-6 per day; price varies). From Centenario, next to the church, minibuses (CH$500) and **colectivos** (CH$600) head to **Castro**.

🖼🛈 ORIENTATION AND PRACTICAL INFORMATION. Municipal services cluster around the **Plaza de Armas**, overlooking Costanera and the port. **Centenario** heads south from the center, becoming Ruta 5 to Quellón, while **Sargento Candelaria** goes from just west of the town center north toward Castro. A small, sheltered **tourist information kiosk** is located at the corner of Centenario and Candelaria. (Open Nov.-Mar. 9am-7pm.) Other services include: a **24hr. ATM** at **Banco Estado**, Centenario 28 (☎671 226); **police**, Cerda 224 (☎671 845); **24hr. medical consultorio**, at Candelaria and Andrade (☎671 240 or 671 643); and **Internet access**, at the *centro de llamados* on Andrade near the cross-street leading to the *mercado* (CH$1000 per hr.). The **post office** is at Centenario 421. (☎671 558. Open M-F 9am-1:30pm and 3-6pm, Sa 9am-1pm.)

ACCOMMODATIONS AND FOOD. Without a doubt, the best lodging in Chonchi for independent travelers is **Esmeralda by the Sea ❷**, only 100m southeast of the *mercado* and the terminus of the Irarrázaval Costanera road. After seven years here, the Canadian-born Carlos is a true "Chonchino" and proves to be a great source of info regarding Chilote culture. A variety of excursions are made available for guests upon request. (☎671 328; grady@telsur.cl. Laundry services, kitchen facilities, and the occasional salmon dinner are available. Breakfast included. Internet access. Free use of rowboat permitted. Bicycle, camping equipment, and fishing gear rentals available. Dorms CH$4500; doubles with private bath CH$10,000.) Coming in a distant, although commendable, second place, is **Hospedaje El Mirador ❷**, Ciriaco Alvarez 198, down the street beyond the fire station, on the southeast side of town. A kind and hospitable owner, nice rooms, and free use of the kitchen prove to be big perks. (☎671 351. Breakfast CH$700. CH$4000 per person; off-season CH$3500.)

A variety of food options await the hungry visitor. The ever-accommodating family-run restaurant **El Trébol ❸**, Irarrázaval 187, just a few buildings down from the *mercado*, serves the best fish in town at reasonable prices. Try the *Trébol del Mar* (CH$3600), a decadent fish and shellfish sampler. (☎671 203. Open noon-midnight; times vary off-season.) Further inland, the **Restaurant Alerce ❷**, Candelaria 308, on the second floor, focuses its fare on fowl and beef. The menu depends on what the kitchen has in stock, and prices are determined by the chef's mood, but a tasty *churrasco* with a side order and a drink averages at about CH$2000-3000. (☎671 346. Open noon-11pm, later on weekends.) For a taste of a different sort of *chonchina*, head to the **bakery**, a couple of doors down from Cruz del Sur on the Plaza de Armas, where you can buy the half-pretzel, half-cracker, ring-shaped toasted goodies en masse. Wash them down with a shot of *licor de oro*, Chonchi's most famous creamy aperitif, distilled from milk and distinctly flavored and sweetened.

SIGHTS. Although Chonchi is a beautiful town, walking around can be taxing. Known as the "city of three levels," steep roads between the Plaza de Armas and the Costanera lead further uptown. Fortunately, along Centenario, on the way to the town center, the **Museo de Las Tradiciones Chonchinas** provides a good stop halfway up the hill. Opposite the intersection with Cerda, this is no ordinary small-town museum. The colonial mansion is decorated in period style and is artfully cluttered with old knick-knacks and colorful artifacts. The attic harbors a collection of local tools and photographs, canvassing a wide array of Chonchi activities and experiences. (Open 9am-7pm; off-season M-F 10am-1pm. Free; donation recommended.) Any trip to Chonchi should include a visit to the **Iglesia San Carlos**, which, although temporarily maimed, has quite a beautiful wood interior and adds an imposing presence to the west side of the Plaza de Armas. Since the meaning of "chonchi" is "slippery earth," you may want to investigate the almost annual phenomenon along the northwest end of the Costanera, where a small **landslide** occurs, threatening the same building near the pier—try to find the spot, which may be quite "freshly slid" in the autumn and winter. Or if you're passing through town in the second week of February, eat, drink, and be merry at the **Fiesta Criolla de Chonchi,** one long party flaunting music, crafts, and *curanto* feasts.

DAYTRIPS. Other than excursions that Carlos runs from Esmeralda by the Sea (see **Accommodations and Food,** p. 435), take the **ferry** to one of the most popular independent daytrips in the area, **Isla Lemuy**, 3km south of Chonchi at Huicha (15min.; every 30-45min. 8am-9pm; passengers free, CH$3000 per car).

CHILOÉ

Boats from the Chonchi waterfront may also be available for transport to the other side of the channel. Many of Lemuy's residents have never left the island or gone beyond Chonchi, consequently perpetuating a strong Chilote culture. Carlos can recommend a walking or biking tour, depending on your interests and time constraints.

For those who have time, another interesting daytrip from this area is the forgotten quiet town of **Queilén,** 44km of dirt road from Chonchi, where rocky shores give way to sandy beaches with a great view across the bay to mainland Chile. Buses depart several times per day (see **Transportation,** p. 434).

PARQUE NACIONAL CHILOÉ ☎65

The Parque Nacional Chiloé may explain the lack of roads and settlements in western Chiloé, whose relative isolation contrasts sharply with the harbor towns and rolling farmland that speckle eastern Chiloé. The dense, tangled underbrush of the park's coastal rainforests, the boggy mess of its swamps, and its sandblasted, wave-battered coastline would deter even the hardiest inhabitant. Only Conaf's constant machete maintenance can keep the creeping vegetation from enveloping established trails, and roaring coastal storms frequently cause flooding, landslides, road washouts, and general misery among stubborn hikers who think trekking trails here are just another "walk in the park."

Most visitors spend several days here, hiking up from Cucao to the campsites and *refugios* at Cole-Cole or Anay. Despite the intimidating and seemingly impenetrable terrain, the experience of conquering the Chilote wilds is worth the trouble. On clear, summer days, the views along the weathered coastline are awe-inspiring. At night, the untamed wilderness will inspire talk of Chiloé's mystical creatures, who fit nicely amongst the knotted trunks and hidden recesses of these woods. Even Charles Darwin could not resist the temptation to tackle this back country. Traversing the trans-island route in 1834, he stopped in the small Huilliche settlement of Cucao and wrote a famous account of his impressions of the landscape. Unfortunately, Darwin's little town of native villagers has long been replaced by a sprightly town that opens its doors to tourists in the busy months of January and February.

AT A GLANCE

AREA: 34,000 hectares.

CLIMATE: Warm and humid with frequent and sudden storms.

FEATURES: Hilly terrain covered in rainforests and groves of *alerce* marked by cliffs and sandy beaches.

GATEWAYS: Cucao and Puerto Anguay.

HIGHLIGHTS: Lago Cucao, the coastal bluffs, sea lion colonies on Metalqui, horseback riding on the sparkling beaches.

CAMPING: Chanquín, Cole-Cole, and various other *refugios*.

FEES: Nov.-Mar. CH$1000.

✈ ORIENTATION

The 430 sq. km national park is divided into two main sectors open to visitors. The northern **Sector Chepu** is accessible from the settlement of **Puerto Anguay** only by boat across the Río Chepo. From the river, follow the trail south along the coast to the park's borders. **Sector Cucao,** also known as Sector Anay or Chanquin, is more easily available to the general public. The town of **Cucao** offers access from the south along coastal trails. The smaller, restricted sectors of Metalqui, an island haven for marine wildlife, and Abtao, a northern adjunct to the Cucao area, are so remote that access is naturally restricted. The road to Cucao from the east (constructed in 1983) runs alongside two lakes—**Lago Huillinco** and **Lago Cucao.** The lakes are connected by broad river channels and the water level is often affected by storms. Lying behind the coastal dunes, most of the town of Cucao is on the southern side of the bridge straddling Lake Cucao's outlet stream. However, several campgrounds, *hospedajes*, and restaurants are located on the northern side of the bridge, where the road continues on into the park.

▐➋ TRANSPORTATION AND PRACTICAL INFORMATION

Bus service to the park is available from **Ancud** to Chepu (see **Ancud: Transportation,** p. 419) and from **Castro** (see **Castro: Transportation,** p. 428) via **Chonchi** to Cucao on a daily basis. **Buses Ojeda** is infamous for canceling service if the bus isn't full. **Boats** for the trip across the Río Chepu (CH$8000) can be hired at the dock at the end of the road. A **taxi** from Chonchi to Cucao can be hired (CH$12,000, round-trip CH$26,000); fares should be negotiated before departure. Although the main **park administration** is in Castro (☎532 502; see p. 429), there are **Conaf outposts** near the northern border of the Chepu sector at **Río Lar.** The **visitor's center** in the south, one kilometer past the Cucao bridge on the right, houses a second Conaf outpost and has modest displays about the flora, fauna, culture, and agriculture of the area. (Open Nov.-Mar. 9am-1pm and 2-8pm; Apr.-Oct. 9am-1pm and 2-6pm. Entry fee Nov.-Mar. CH$1000). For safety reasons, it is recommended that visitors register their trip with Conaf officers.

▐▌ ACCOMMODATIONS, CAMPING, AND FOOD

Outside park boundaries in Cucao, there is a proliferation of small *hospedajes*, ranging from clean and friendly to basic and squalid. You should always see your living and sleeping space before committing for the night. On the town side of the bridge, along the main road, the bright pink **Hospedaje El Paraíso ❷** boasts cleaner rooms than most places in town, and the price reflects it. (☎09 296 5465. Breakfast included; other meals available for extra. Dec.-Mar. CH$5000; off-season CH$4000.) A popular alternative near the bridge on the right side of the road heading north is **Cocineria and Hospedaje Las Luminarias ❶,** which is renowned for its cheap rooms and good food. Get lunch early before all the food is lapped up. (*Empanadas* CH$150; hearty fixed-menu lunch CH$2500. Restaurant open when there's food. Singles CH$3500; off-season CH$3000.) Even if you aren't hiking or camping, it pays to **bring your own food supplies** because the selection available in town is severely wanting.

Although campgrounds in town abound, there's no good reason not to camp on the scenic sites that lie across the river instead. Just pick a site, find out who owns the land, and offer to pay CH$1000-1500 for a night there. Or look for houses with "camping" signs out front. The official **Conaf concession ❶** at Chanquín is more luxurious than some *hospedajes* in town, with access to toilets and showers. More expensive *cabañas* are also available. (☎09 919 1314. Cooking shelter. Sites CH$3000 per person. 6-person *cabañas* CH$30,000.) Primitive camping at **Cole-Cole ❶** includes pit toilets and a basic shelter (CH$1000 per person). A range of **refugios ❶,** usually equipped with a cooking shelter or stove, can be found at Río Anay, Cole-Cole, and at Río Refugio, in the northern Sector Chepu. (CH$1000 per person.)

🔲 HIKING

The network of trails in the park is not very extensive, but the trails that do exist are well-maintained and provide wonderful opportunities to see coastal rainforest in all its glory. Depending on the weather, bridges may wash out, trails may become overgrown, and campsites may flood—all in a matter of hours. Check with Conaf for trail conditions before you leave, but be prepared for anything. Big storms can turn a weekend getaway into an exercise in survival. Don't brave the weather if there's a bad forecast or if it looks ominous. For those who venture into the park, especially important are a sturdy pair of waterproof boots, good raingear, and warm clothes. Hiking off-trail in Parque Nacional Chiloé is not just inadvisable, it's suicidal, and would probably require a chainsaw.

SECTOR CUCAO. This sector, also known as Sector Anay or Chanquín, can be reached from the visitor's center along a number of trails of varying lengths and difficulty levels. The **Sendero Interpretivo El Tepual** (1km, 45min.) leads through bog and forest, with eye-catching flora along the way. It's a good way to get acquainted with the forest when you're under time restraints. Another easy walk is the **Sendero Dunas de Cucao** (1.7km, 45min.), which showcases the area cleared of vegetation by the tidal wave in 1960. **Lake Cucao** is said to be layered with saltwater on the bottom and fresh water on the top because of that tidal influx. Fishermen report that both saltwater and freshwater specimens can be caught in the lake. The stark beach between the lake and ocean is daunting on a gray, windy day, and stunning on a clear one. Access to the beach is also available from the small Huilliche town three kilometers further north, west of the bridge over the outlet river from Lago Huelde. There are trails around **Lago Huelde,** but it's more practical to hire a boat that runs to trails on the other side of the water. From here, a trail (12km, 4hr. one-way) leads northeast to the **Rancho Grande,** an *alerce* forest at a 600m high point in the park (ask at the visitor's center if the trail is open). Further north, car access becomes difficult and the hardcore walking trail really begins. The path goes north to **Río and Playa Cole-Cole** (20km, 6hr. one-way) and continues to **Río Anay** (5km, 1½hr. one-way). In bad weather, you should allow more time for the obligatory wading and splashing around. Some water crossings may be necessary regardless, depending on the maintenance of the trail. Follow the trail until it terminates on the beach, then follow the beach until it ends at the cliffs. At this point, the trail enters the forest and heads up and over **Punta Chaiquil** and down to Cole-Cole. From here the hike to Anay is straightforward. This is the most popular trail in the park and sees heavy traffic in January and February.

OTHER SECTORS. South from Cucao, a trail (2-3 days round-trip) leads through private land to a popular sea lion hangout called **Punta Pirulil.** Locals or Conaf officials will be able to tell you about the condition of the trail and nearby campgrounds. In the northern Sector Chepu of the park, the esteemed **Chepu-Lar-Refugio Trail** leads from the southern banks of the Río Chepu to the Conaf ranger station at **Río Lar** (14km, 4hr. one-way) and further on to the mouth of the **Río Refugio** (6km, 1½hr. one-way). The trail is less frequented than Cole-Cole and lends itself well to a tranquil day in the great outdoors. Plus, the beaches along the way are stunning. There is also a trail along a "dirt road" between Dalcahue and Castro to the **Abtao Sector** (18km, 8hr. one-way) where a *refugio* is open and maintained. However, ask a ranger before attempting it, as the trail is often overgrown and impassable.

⚠ OUTDOORS

If hiking isn't your forte, other outdoor activities are available. The Chanquín campsite rents **kayaks** (CH$3000) for use on Lake Huelde. In Cucao, on the other side of the bridge, a **horseback riding** guide charges an arm and a leg for a day of horseback riding in the park (US$100 per day). Alternatively, those with riding experience can rent horses in town at their own risk (CH$2000 per hr.).

QUELLÓN   ☎ 65

On an island of port towns, Quellón is the port town that tops them all. Regular ferry service in the summer, the largest fishing fleet on Chiloé, a naval installation, and a more rough-'n'-tumble sailor feel win this town the nautical trump card. Quellón's harbor represents a variety of moods from misty and romantic to clear and bustling, but the town itself is a little less colorful—born in the early 20th century, Quellón lacks the indigenous cultural depth possessed by much of Chiloé. The lack of nearby attractions makes this little more than a stopover for people riding the ferry east or south.

🖃 TRANSPORTATION. From the **bus terminal,** Cerda 052 (☎681 284), **Cruz del Sur** heads to **Ancud** (7 per day, CH$2800) via **Chonchi** (CH$900), **Castro** (CH$1000), and **Santiago** (1 and 2:30pm, CH$15,000). **Trans Chiloé** goes to **Puerto Montt** (6:40, 8am, 12:15, 2, 5pm; CH$3500) via **Chonchi** (CH$900), **Castro** (CH$1000), and **Ancud** (CH$2000). **Regional Sur** goes to **Castro** (4 per day, CH$800-1000). **Ferry** times can change drastically and often times won't go in the winter due to low demand. **Navimag** (☎680 511), on Costanera just east of Gómez García, sends ships to **Chaitén** (15hr.; Oct.-Mar. Th 8am and midnight; CH$10,000, cars CH$55,000) and **Chacabuco** (Oct.-Mar. Su 8pm, Apr.-Sept. Sa 6pm; CH$7500, cars CH$41,000). **Transmarchilay** (☎681 331; www.tmc.cl), located on the first floor of the Romeo Alfa Hotel building at the corner of Cerda and Costanera, offers trips at similar prices.

🔳🔳 ORIENTATION AND PRACTICAL INFORMATION. Av. Pedro Montt (known to locals as **Costanera**) follows the coast in an east-west direction. Most of the town's attractions and services lie within three blocks of the coast between the north-south streets of **Pedro Aguirre Cerda** and **Ramón Freire.** When Ruta 5 Sur comes within city limits, it becomes the east-west **Av. Juan Ladrilleros,** the main commercial stretch in town. Accessing Costanera is difficult because three of the north-south streets don't reach the coast east of **Av. A. Gómez García,** although there is a stairway down to Costanera near the end of **Av. 22 de Mayo.**

The small **information kiosk** on the Plaza de Armas, at the corner of Santos Vargas and Gómez García, can be helpful. (Open Dec.-Mar. 9am-9pm.) **Banco Estado,** 22 de Mayo 399, at the corner of Ladrilleros, has a **24hr. ATM,** but exchanges and cashes checks for a premium. (☎681 266. Open M-F 9am-2pm.) Other amenities include the **police** (☎682 865), on Ladrilleros west of Gómez García; a **hospital,** Eduardo Ahues 305 (☎681 243), two blocks north of Ladrilleros and a block east of La Paz; and **Internet access** at Cyber@Quellón, across from the bottom end of the Feria Artesanal on Gómez García, just south of Ladrilleros. (☎682 301. CH$1000 per hr. Open noon-midnight.) A **post office,** on 22 de Mayo, next to the municipal building, also offers **Western Union** services. (☎681 862. Open M-F 9am-1pm and 3-6pm, Sa 9am-12:30pm.)

🔳🔳 ACCOMMODATIONS AND FOOD. In a bind, there is a plethora of accommodations along Costanera, but the best bets for value are further inland. On the warm, friendly side, **Hotel La Pincoya ❸,** La Paz 64, just north of Ladrilleros, offers

CHILOÉ

slightly overpriced, spartan rooms that are somewhat compensated for by the warm hearth downstairs and the huge, clean kitchen available for guest use. (☎681 285. Singles CH$7000; doubles CH$11,800.) **Residencial Esteban ❷**, Pedro Aguirre Cerda 355, sports a pleasant common space upstairs and basic, small rooms in one of the best budget accommodations in town. (☎681 438. Breakfast included. CH$5000; off-season CH$4000.) **Los Suizos Hotel ❹**, Ladrilleros 399, at the southeast corner with La Paz, offers a significant step up in both quality and price. (☎681 787; lossuizos@entelchile.net. Private baths and cable TV. Breakfast included. Excursions available. Singles CH$14,000; doubles CH$18,000.) **Camping** can be found south and west of the city. **Restaurant El Chico Leo ❷**, Pedro Montt 325, is hailed by locals as the best lunch in town. The famous fixed lunch special (CH$2000) includes a fish entree. The *curanto* (CH$3500) might strike the fancy of more culinary ambitious folk. (☎681 567. Open 7am-midnight.) **Entre Islas ❷**, 1½ blocks north of Ladrilleros on Freire, offers a parting drink with snacks or a meal for ferry-catchers. (Steak medallions CH$3300. Pisco sour CH$1100. Open M-Sa 12:30pm-1am.)

🟦 **SIGHTS.** Quellón does not offer enough activities to distract visitors from the inconsistent ferry schedule. However, the two museums in town are worth a look. The more inspired of the two, **Museo Nuestro Posado**, Ladrilleros 225, east of the center, includes a striking sculpture and arboreal garden. The real draws are reconstructions of the ubiquitous *fogón*, a *companaría*, and a primitive mill. (☎681 213. Open Dec.-Mar. during daylight. CH$600.) **Museo Municipal,** on the Plaza de Armas, is cluttered with a miscellaneous collection of regional artifacts. (Open in summer 9am-7pm; in winter M-F 9am-1pm.) The **feria artesanales,** on Gómez García, features carved and knitted wares, but doesn't compare with its counterparts in Castro and in Dalcahue.

AISÉN & THE CAMINO AUSTRAL

The Aisén—over 1000km of wild, rugged, mountainous terrain—is Chile's least developed region. Indeed, with less than 100,000 people inhabiting this untamed land, it is almost entirely *un*developed. In colonial days, Spanish and British sailors making the journey through the Straits of Magellan reported that this was an inhospitable land lacking any trace of human civilization. Even after subduing the fierce Mapuche in the 19th century, few Chileans ventured south of Puerto Montt. The reason is not hard to fathom. Just beyond Puerto Montt, the lush valley running through Middle Chile and the Lakes District plunges into the Pacific Ocean, creating a maze-like coastline of inlets, fjords, and archipelagos, while the interior is dominated by snow-capped mountains, thick forests, and raging rivers.

Nevertheless, the government has not been completely oblivious to this underutilized region. In the 1960s, government subsidies and incentives started a minor migration south. However, the only lasting result was the uncontrolled clearing of many forests for lumber and farmland. In 1976, General Pinochet, worried about a possible attack from Chile's archrival, Argentina, through this totally undefended region, initiated a project to improve communication and development in the south, which entailed the construction of the grand Camino Austral. Despite its smooth beginnings in Puerto Montt, this roadtripper's dream-come-true quickly turns into a rough, partially built road that disappears entirely in some places. Although this mega-highway failed in its goal to encourage growth in the Aisén, it has opened up previously inaccessible areas of the south to adventurous travelers.

The best place to begin an exploration of the area is in **Chaitén,** just south of Puerto Montt. Its proximity to some incredible national parks and the still passable Camino Austral slowly introduces travelers to the ruggedness of the region. Those ready for a little more can continue south to **Futaleufú.** This up-and-coming hot spot is the center of adventure tourism in the Aisén, offering everything from horseback riding to whitewater rafting. If you're not quite so excited about being tossed against rapids, but don't mind braving more conquerable waves, boats from Puerto Montt and Chiloé often stop in **Puerto Chacabuco** before winding their way south through the impressive fjords. The easiest way to drop into the middle of it all (literally) is to fly into **Coyhaique.** With the only major airport in the area and buses departing to most towns in the area, the city has become Aisén's transportation center.

HIGHLIGHTS OF AISÉN & THE FAR SOUTH

BATTLE the raging rapids of the mighty **Río Futaleufú** in a fragile kayak (p. 449).

GAPE at the incredible hanging glacier, suspended over the placid waters of a blue-green lake in **Parque Nacional Queulat** (p. 452).

WHILE away the hours, fly-fishing in the rolling rivers of **Reserva Nacional Río Simpson** (p. 457) outside of **Coyhaique** (p. 453).

MEANDER through the largest private park in the world, **Parque Natural Pumalín** (p. 445), created by business mogul Douglas Tompkin, founder of Esprit clothing company.

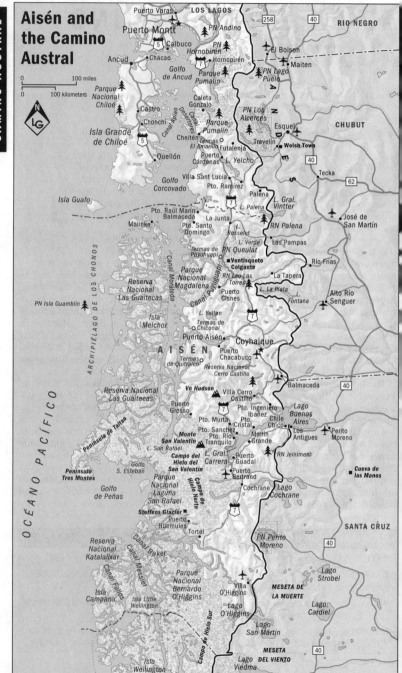

Aisén and the Camino Austral

CHAITÉN ☎ 69

This rugged town serves as a bustling port, receiving local flights and crowded ferries from Chiloé and Puerto Montt. The popular and well-serviced Parque Natural Pumalín lies just to the north, providing visitors with a fine opportunity to explore the region's wilderness. The striking Volcán Michinmáhuida stands to the northeast and the subtler Volcán Corcovado sits to the southwest, but this flat town has little more to offer passing visitors.

TRANSPORTATION

Flights: The local airport is located 6km south of town. **Aeromet,** Todesco 42 (☎ 731 844), flies to **Puerto Montt** (M-Sa noon, CH$35,000). **Aeropuelche,** Corcovado 212 (☎ 731 800), flies to **Puerto Montt** (M-Sa 12:30pm, CH$38,000). Same-day tickets may be available for lower rates. Companies include transport from their offices to the airport in the cost of the flight.

Buses: The **bus station** is located on O'Higgins. **Chaitur,** in the bus terminal, manages most local departures to: **Caleta Gonzalo** (M, W, F 8am); **Coyhaique** (Tu, Th, F, Su 9:30am, CH$15,000); **Futaleufú** (M-Sa 3:30pm, CH$6000); **Puyuhuapi** (M-Sa 3pm, CH$8000).

Chaitén

🏠 ACCOMMODATIONS
Hostal Puma Verde, **5**
Residencial Astoria, **7**
Hostal Los Chicos, **8**
Cabañas Brisas del Mar, **3**
Hospedaje Sebastián, **1**
Hosteria-Cabañas
Corvocado, **6**

🍴 FOOD
Flamengo, **2**
Quijote, **4**

Ferries: Transmarchile, Corcovado 266 (☎731 272), goes to: **Puerto Montt** (12hr.; M, W midnight, F 7am, Su 7pm; CH$16,000) and **Quellón** (5hr.; W, Sa 9am, Su 7am; CH$13,000). After the summer season (Dec.-Feb.), ferries are less frequent—call to confirm the next departure. **Navimag,** Ignacio Carrera Pinto 188 (☎731 570), heads to: **Puerto Montt** (10hr.; Tu, Th, Sa 8am; CH$16,000) and **Quellón** (5hr.; M, W, F 9am; CH$14,000). The high-speed **catamaran** run by **Catamaránes de Sur,** Ignacio Carrera Pinto 188 (☎731 199), zips to **Puerto Montt** (4hr.; M, W, F 1pm; CH$21,500).

◼◼ ⚡ ❷ ORIENTATION AND PRACTICAL INFORMATION

Two blocks east of the bay, the **Plaza de Armas** is surrounded by some of the town's basic services. The main street running from the water to town is **O'Higgins,** while simple accommodations line **Av. Ignacio Carrera Pinto.** The road along the coast goes by two names: officially **Av. Corcovado,** locals mostly refer to it as **Costanera.** Chaitén's tourism industry has set up shop between the park and the waterfront.

Tourist office: In a small glass booth on Corcovado, near Padre Juan Todesco. Offers basic brochures and a helpful staff member to answer questions. However, Nicolás at **Chaitur** is the best source of information.

Tours: Chaitur, O'Higgins 70 (☎731 429), in the bus station. Nicolás, with his easy charm and eye for detail, has become the most sought-after tour operator and source of info. He accommodatingly arranges all types of tours in Parque Natural Pumalín or in the northern region of the Camino Austral, where tourists can visit lesser-known volcanoes and glaciers.

Bank and ATM: Banco del Estado, on the corner of O'Higgins and Libertad, on the plaza, has decent rates for US dollars, but takes time to complete the transaction. Changes traveler's checks with a US$10 commission. Open M-F 9am-2pm. **ATM** only accepts cards with both MC and Cirrus affiliation.

Laundromat: Lavadaria Masol, Todesco 272. Washes a load for CH$4000. Open M-Sa 10am-1pm and 3-6pm.

Supermarket: Michinmáhuida, Corcovado 203. A good place to stock up before long trips, offering a wide selection and a decent deli. Open M-Sa 9:30am-1pm and 3-8pm.

Police and Emergency telephone: ☎133

Hospital: Jimenes Romero, Ignacio Carrera Pinto 160 (☎731 244).

Telephone and Internet Access: Entel, on the corner of Libertad and Cerda. Offers speedy Internet access. CH$1000 per hr. Open daily 9am-1pm and 3:30-10:30pm.

Post Office: O'Higgins 253, in the municipal building on the park. Open M-F 9am-1pm and 3-5:30pm, Sa 9am-1pm.

⌂ ACCOMMODATIONS

O'Higgins, one block from the bay, offers some of the cheapest options in town, but check the rooms before you commit, as they can be run-down. The strip of hotels and hostels on the waterfront charge a little more, but in the off-season most establishments are willing to give guests a small discount.

Hostal Puma Verde, O'Higgins 54 (☎731 184, in Puerto Montt 65 250 079). A total steal, these new, pristine, apartment-style rooms hold big beds covered in soft duvets and overlook a serene garden. You can access the charming kitchen with its hanging copper pots anytime, or just stop by to enjoy the hearty continental breakfast. Single beds in the triple, CH$10,000; 5-person cabins CH$45,000. ❸

Residencial Astoria, Corcovado 442 (☎731 263). The spacious plant-filled living room on the second floor makes up for the cramped bedrooms. With a view of the bay, a small restaurant, and basic breakfast, Astoria is an easy place to pass a day or two. Doubles and triples CH$5000 per person. ❷

Hostal Los Chicos, Portales 441 (☎731 547). Spread throughout the one-story house, big bright rooms welcome visitors looking for quiet afternoons and good service. Clean common baths. The open-front living room is a nice touch, since Chaitén is low on outdoor space to relax in. Breakfast CH$500. Doubles and triples CH$4500. ❷

Cabañas Brisas del Mar, Corcovado 278 (☎731 284). The string of small connected cabins each holds four guests in cozy quarters with TVs and small galley kitchens. CH$35,000 per cabin. ❸

Hospedaje Sebastián, Almirante Riveros 163 (☎731 225), has a restaurant, homey rooms, transportation service, and arranges excursions. Spacious doubles and triples fill up with both Chilean and foreign guests looking to enjoy nearby adventures every summer. Lunch or dinner served for CH$3000 with advance notice. Breakfast included. CH$4500 per person. ❷

Hostería-Cabañas Corcovado, Corcovado 408 (☎731 221). Tight rooms with large beds overlook the bay. The small restaurant downstairs only serves a few dishes each day, but they can whip up anything with a little warning. Doubles CH$5000 per person, with private bath CH$7000. ❷

☐ FOOD

With so many restaurants in hostels, the dining options in town are pretty limited. If you plan to eat at your *residencial*, be sure to notify the manager and maybe even pre-order so that they can shop and prepare your meal later.

Flamengo, Corcovado 218, serves up a variety of fish and other seafood with sauces ranging from creamy to dreamy (CH$3500-5000). The chicken dishes are less glamorous, but the juicy steak *al pobre* served with a heap of french fries and two fried eggs will conquer any beastly appetite (CH$4500). Open 11am-9pm. ❸

Quijote, O'Higgins 42. The small and simple dining area of Quijote foreshadows the simple menu that offers only a handful of items. The hamburger barely counts as a meal (CH$2000), but the salmon can fill a hungry stomach. Open 11am-9:30pm. ❶

☐ EXCURSIONS

The dearth of formal tours in the region gives industrious visitors a chance to leisurely craft their own plan of action. The impressive **Alerce** forest is a common destination for visitors. The simplest way to enjoy the beautiful landscape is a daytrip or extended visit to **Parque Natural Pumalín.** Buses head to the park regularly in the summer months. Park office in town, O'Higgins 62 (☎731 341), offers basic information and some excellent photography of the park. The nearby **Volcán Michinmáhuida** is accessible as well, but time, some foresight, and a dash of persistence is necessary to arrange these trips—call or stop by **Chaitur** (see **Orientation and Practical Information,** p. 444) to customize a trip.

CALETA GONZALO AND PARQUE NATURAL PUMALÍN

The largest private park in the world, Parque Natural Pumalín is made up of 300,000 hectares of virgin wilderness between the Argentine border and the area just south of Puerto Montt in Chile. The land was gradually acquired during the 1990s by wealthy American environmentalist Douglas Tompkin, who later

FU FIGHTERS

The majestic power of the Futaleufú river has attracted more than just the new group of rafting and kayaking junkies. Over the last five years, a large Canadian metals company, Noranda, has been politically positioning itself to harness the valley's substantial waterflow to power a proposed aluminum smelting plant. The constant high levels of water would power three separate facilities and require six dams. The hydro plants alone would bring about US$2.75 billion to the region and constitute the single largest capital investment in Chilean history, but many activists warn against the known and unknown dangers of the project. Beyond the 8000 hectares of farmland that will be lost, little is known about potential water and soil contamination and the effects on local flora and fauna.

One of the largest questions is why Noranda has chosen this region, since the raw material, bauxite, would need to be imported from Brazil, Jamaica, or Australia. The region's dammable rivers have been cited as one major factor, but some suggest that lax environmental laws and low population density are the major draw for Noranda.

Despite some very overpowering environmental risks, the government has been seriously considering opening the area to development because of the immediate economic benefits. The influx of capital spending would bolster the economy while providing many new jobs to workers with limited options in the area.

donated the land to the Fundación Pumalín to ensure its preservation in the future. Despite ongoing controversy stemming from political pressure to keep the precious territory open to eco-tourists and the general public, much of the park remains inaccessible due to the owners' restrictions and a lack of trails.

Four well-traveled day-hikes, however, facilitate an exploration of the park. A perfect picnic spot is along the **Sendero Cascada,** just south of **Caleta Gonzalo,** the small port town 56km north of Chaitén. The path carves through rainforest before reaching the impressive waterfall (3hr. round-trip). Twelve kilometers south of town, the **Laguna Tronador** trail winds uphill to a lake with gently trickling streams near a welcoming campground (3hr. round-trip). Another kilometer further south, the short **Sendero Alerce** makes possible a personal visit to some of the most admired trees in the region. The **Hidden Falls Trail,** 14km south of Caleta Gonzalo, passes three spectacular waterfalls along a wet, idyllic path (1½hr. round-trip).

Plan to spend the night in Chaitén, as accommodations in Caleta Gonzalo are expensive. The **Cabañas Caleta Gonzalo ❺,** offer excellent service in small rooms. (☎ 1812 960 4151. Doubles US$55.) Three-hundred meters south of town, **Camping Río Gonzalo ❶** has good facilities and plenty of sites (CH$1000 a night). At the trailhead of the **Hidden Falls** path, a covered **campground ❷** permits visitors to car-camp or rest in a massive shelter (CH$4000 per person). Food is only available in the small cafe in town, so pack what you'll need and take it along with you.

FUTALEUFÚ ☎ 65

Branching off the main Camino Austral, the road to Futaleufú runs along the green ribbon of the Río Espolón before catching up with the mighty Futaleufú river. The powerful waters of the "Fu" carve through the lush landscape, creating some of the best whitewater in the world. The Futaleufú is revered among guides from around the world—it will give any rafting or kayaking enthusiast an adrenaline rush to last a lifetime. Although group rafting trips are a relatively new venture, expert guides drawn by the Futaleufú's exciting and challenging waters are readily available. However, despite an upsurge in outdoor-adventure services, Futaleufú remains a quiet town because the tourist season is short (Nov.-Apr.) and access to the region is seasonally limited.

⌨ TRANSPORTATION

Buses: Cordillera Buses, Prat 239 (☎ 721 249), goes to **Chaitén** (4hr., M-Th 7am, CH$6000) and the **Argentine border** (20min.; M, F 8am, 5:30pm; CH$1500), where buses going on to **Esquel** and **Trevelín** are available. **Transportation Sebastián,** Balcameda 511 (☎ 721 288), also heads to **Chaitén** (4hr., M-Sa 6:30am, CH$5500). In the summer, buses leave for **Puerto Montt** on Tuesdays if there is enough demand. Departure time for the 33hr. ride through Argentina is irregular, so call for more information (☎ 721 280). **Bus Norte C. Austral** leaves for **Coyhaique** from Hospedaje Carahue (Su 8am, CH$15,000).

◤✱ ⓘ ORIENTATION AND PRACTICAL INFORMATION

Futaleufú sits on a plateau on which streets are laid out in an organized grid system. Buses enter town from the south. Two blocks east of the bus station, the central square serves as the town's hub. However, many restaurants and services are sprinkled throughout the town's orderly dirt roads.

Tourist office: O'Higgins 536, on the southern edge of the square. Offers little more than a regional map.

Tours: Expediciones Chile, O'Higgins 397 (☎ 721 320), run out of the Hostería Río Grande, is the only rafting and kayaking operation that has a full-time office in town. 4-day and 1-week all-inclusive packages available for US$1300 and US$2500 respectively. Kayaking lessons begin at US$200 per day per person; price reduces with more people. When manned boats are available, and if there is enough demand, they will organize trips for travelers to various destinations along the river. Half-day boat trips are US$70. More experienced groups can hit the powerful class V parts for US$90. Min. 5 people; lunch included. This operation is highly regarded because of its focus on safety. There are other operations that have offices along the river, which are most easily contacted by stopping at **Sur Andes,** Pedro Aguirre Cerda 308 (☎ 099 824 3180). The helpful owner also runs a variety of combination trips in the area, including a 4-night horseback riding tour of a valley that stops at secluded villages in the wilderness (US$330 per person). One-day horseback riding trips are CH$12,000 per horse plus an obligatory CH$15,000 guide. Fishing tours without equipment run CH$30,000 per person.

A group of North American and European observers have organized themselves to publicize these events in an attempt to stop the project, which would effectively close the river to tourism and other benign forms of economic development. Many believe that tourism is the most feasible and sustainable option that can facilitate an eco-friendly use of the area's resources. The tourism industry has only just sown its seeds in the region, but the initial response has been very positive. Some of the new river adventure companies have made small but significant investments in increasing opportunities in the region while maintaining a strong focus on local involvement. Through free kayaking classes and other training for locals, tour owners hope to build a crop of regional guides and expand the number of tourists that spend money to enjoy the river. Tourism may never bestow the colossal economic benefits of the proposed smelting plan, but the long-term health of the region may be better managed through its less intrusive use of the land.

Further information about alternatives to damming the Futaleufú and ways for individuals to support this effort are available through Futa Friends at www.futafriends.org.

Bank: Banco Estado, on the park at the corner of Rodríguez and O'Higgins. Changes US dollars and traveler's checks at fair rates with a US$11 commission. Open M-F 9am-2pm. There presently are **no ATMs** in Futaleufú.

Police and Emergency: ☎ 131

Hospital: A large regional hospital, Balcameda 382, offers basic services, but lacks English-speaking staff.

Telephone: Telephone office, Balcameda 419. Open M-Sa 9am-1pm and 2:30-9pm, Su 4-9pm.

Post office: On the corner of Rodríguez and O'Higgins in the municipal office, opposite the bank. Open M-F 9am-12:30pm and 2:30-6pm, Sa 9am-12:30pm.

ACCOMMODATIONS

During the summer season, several *hospedajes* north and east of the plaza offer cheap accommodations with kitchen facilities. The following is a list of establishments that remain open throughout the year.

Hostería Río Grande, O'Higgins 397 (☎ 721 320). With its central location and pleasant, professional staff, Río Grande sets the standard for hotels in town. The small restaurant serves select dishes and wonderful grilled meats. All rooms have private baths and simple, rustic decor. Singles CH$25,000; doubles CH$40,000; triples CH$45,000. ❺

Hospedaje Adolfo, O'Higgins 302 (☎ 258 633). Soft beds, a warm fire, and a filling breakfast awaits all guests at Adolfo. The floral couches in the living room welcome you to laze away a rainy day, but the cabins in the backyard may be better for small groups looking to relax with a little more privacy. Singles CH$5000, 4-bed cabins CH$45,000. ❷

Hospedaje Carahue, O'Higgins 332 (☎ 721 221). If you can get beyond the run-down rooms with a slight draft, you can enjoy a respite in the lively family room with satellite TV. Breakfast leaves a little to be desired, but cheap, basic meals are available with some advance notice for about CH$2000. Kitchen facilities available. Doubles and triples CH$4000 per person. ❷

Hospedaje el Campesino, Prat 107 (☎ 721 275). The basic rooms and worn beds in this small house have a cozy feel, which is enhanced by the working fireplace. Kitchen facilities and a clean eating area compensate for the limited common space. Doubles and triples CH$3500 per person. ❶

FOOD

Restaurants open seasonally—if passing through town during the off-season, ask around town to find out what is open.

Escorpio, Gabriela Mistral 255. In the high-season, ravenous rafters crowd Escorpio to enjoy the popular *curanto*, a combination of mussels, sausage, and chicken. A range of seafood dishes, grilled chicken, and a well-stocked bar are available as well. Open 11am-10pm. ❷

Futaleufú, on the corner of Pedro Aguirra Cerda and Sargento Aldea. The salmon, beef, and chicken dinners (CH$3500) are simple yet filling meals, served up in a large, welcoming space. The egg and toast breakfast is delicious (CH$4500). Open 8am-10pm, varying off-season hours.

⚡ EXCURSIONS

The area's magnificent waters make **rafting** and **kayaking** the most popular activities. However, one-day excursions (starting at US$65) are run only during the summer, as tourism is a new venture along the Futaleufú. Don't underestimate the river's potential to get vicious—although it is possible to find cheaper trips through less reputable companies, unless you're sure that the guides and equipment you choose can ensure your safety, stick to the big names. **Kayaking lessons** are also available, but preparation is recommended. (For complete information, see **Tours**, p. 447.)

For those not wanting to be flung around by the Futaleufú, other opportunities to explore the area exist. There are many small operations along the drive up the valley into town that offer riverside **camping** and **horseback riding.** The best way to take advantage of these is to start in town and leisurely trek downhill from one operation to another in order to enjoy their sites along the majestic river. Companies in town offer horseback riding trips that go further up the valley and visit some of the small communities embedded in the wilderness. **Fly fishing** is also growing in popularity, but most operations do not have extensive equipment for the novice angler.

Day hikes from town are a simple way to enjoy the woodlands and impressive rivers. A pleasant trail starts at the town center; go west down Balmaceda down the slope to the bridge. The road curves out of town and continues up the hill that looms over Futaleufú. The hike to the large flag visible from town lasts one and a half hours. Weather can change rapidly, so bring rain gear and drinking water.

SOUTH TO COYHAIQUE

PUERTO PUYUHUAPI

The original German settlers left their mark on this small town, which hugs the northern edge of **Parque Nacional Queulat.** Most Camino Austral travelers who stop at Puyuhuapi are looking to enjoy the nearby hot springs, located 11km and a boat ride away from town. Three large European-style houses that dominate the landscape, and an interesting rug factory, **Fábrica de Alfombras,** (on Aisén, in the west end of town, recently converted into a museum and shop), are legacies of German settlers in the region. Thirty-minute weekday tours of the factory are conducted between 10:30am and 5pm. Stop by **Café Rosdbach** if the museum staff is not immediately available. Any minibus headed north or south can easily drop travelers off at Puyuhuapi, since the Camino Austral runs through the heart of town. Most buses stop at Ventisquero, where useful info is available. **Transportes Emanuel,** in the Supermercado Carretera Austral, next to the police station, runs buses north to Chaitén (☎325 119; M-Sa 7:30am, CH$8000).

Choices for accommodations are limited in Puyuhuapi, but there are a few good options. **Casa Ludwig ❷,** on the eastern side of town, offers quaint and clean rooms. The real treat is the massive sun-filled living room with soft wooden paneling. (Breakfast included. Singles CH$20,000; doubles CH$25,000; attic rooms CH$6000.) **Residencial Marly ❷,** on the Camino Austral in the middle of town, offers comfortable beds in slightly crowded rooms (CH$6000). Local fish and the lunch of the day are available for CH$3000. **Café Rossbach ❷,** on Aisén, is run by

A USER'S GUIDE TO CHILEAN FLORA:
Or, How to Impress Friends While Hiking Through *Parques Nacionales*

Chile's *parques nacionales*, from Torres del Paine to Vicente Perés Rosales and Alerce Andino to Volcán Isluga, are the highlights of any trip to Chile. A five-hour hike through any of these spectacular nature reserves can be enriched by an appreciation for Chile's diverse flora resulting from the country's unique topography. Stretching from the teen latitudes all the way to 56° south, Chile is subject to the influence of a cold current running up the side of the continent that causes unusual rain patterns along the coast. Furthermore, the range of altitude provided by the Andes gives rise to many distinct plant communities. Any attempt to summarize or characterize the consequently varied flora of the country as a whole is futile. Instead, an introduction to the more conspicuous and interesting native plants, which are found in different habitats ranging from the northern deserts to far south temperate rainforests, will bring out the amateur botanist in any traveler, making him or her an instantly interesting hiking companion.

The deserts of Northern Chile are some of the driest in the world, experiencing rainfall only once every decade or so. Consequently, they are largely devoid of vegetation except near streams or areas of frequent fog. Nonetheless, many different plants (including a relative of the potato) are specially adapted for life in these deserts, and over 20 species of cactus in the genus *Copiapoa* are found in the Atacama desert. One species (or, to be precise, one variety, *Copiapoa columna-alba*) comprises what is surely one of the strangest natural sights in Chile. This *Copiapoa* is often the dominant plant in the landscape where it occurs, and all individuals of the variety lean markedly northward, giving rise to the optical illusion that the entire landscape is tilted. This behavior has been explained as a tactic by which the cactus minimizes the surface area exposed to the direct rays of the sun. In this environment where light is not limited but water is, plants actually avoid excess exposure to the sun. Thus, the sun hits the top of the leaning cactus at a 90° angle, and the long trunk of the cactus receives only indirect light.

Further south, these eerily tilted cacti give way to more verdant, yet similarly unusual, species of flora. Central Chile was once home to luxuriant forests of the Chilean wine palm, *Jubaea chilensis*, but it is now found only in isolated and generally inaccessible populations in the wild. The beautiful palm tree grows to six feet in diameter and has a gray trunk that is smooth in appearance but bears diamond-shaped leaf scars. It is known locally as the *coquito* because its fruits (nuts) are edible and resemble small coconuts, both in appearance and in taste. The harvesting of the fruits does the tree little harm, but it has suffered extensive decline due to the harvest of its sweet sap. The sap is harvested by cutting the crown of leaves causing the sap to rise. A single full-grown tree can house up to 90 gallons of harvestable sap, which is released over the course of a few months. The sap serves as the tree's nourishment; thus, individuals cannot survive many such harvests. Once harvested, the sap is either fermented to make wine, or boiled to make a sweet syrup called *miel de palma*, or palm honey. Much of the commercially available palm honey comes from wine palms grown on plantations.

Perhaps the most recognizable native Chilean tree is the so-called Monkey Puzzle tree, *Araucaria araucana*, which grows in southern Chile at mid-elevations. These conifers are popular garden and arboretum specimens the world over, and once you have seen one, you are unlikely to forget it. The juveniles are covered all over with hard, triangular, spiky "leaves"—even on the trunk! It was this zealous anti-herbivore protection that caused a gentleman from Cornwall in the 19th century to remark that it would puzzle a monkey to climb it. (Nevermind the lack of monkeys in Chile.) In the wild, adult Monkey Puzzles can reach extraordinary heights exceeding 180 feet. The trunk is very straight and typically devoid of branches for three quarters or more of its length. The branches are long and straight, covered with a cylinder of spiky leaves, and slightly pendant. The Monkey Puzzle often occurs in dense forests in which it is the dominant canopy tree. Where it shares the forest with other tree species,it vastly overshadows all other species in height,so that the canopy looks likean even layer punctuated by strange toothpicks topped in a pyramid of green.

Monkey Puzzle trees are known locally by the native name of *pehuén*. The trees served as a major food source for many of the indigenous peoples, particularly the Pehuenche. The seeds of the monkey puzzle (*piñones*) are delicious and abundant wherever the trees are found. The female cones are in fact so massive, and the trees so tall, that many places prohibit the planting of female trees for fear of falling cones braining passersby. The seeds are starchy and can be eaten raw, but are typically dried and roasted and eaten either whole or ground into flour (keep this in mind in case you get stranded at the peak of Volcán Osorno). An early German visitor to Chile, remarking on the plentiful nuts and their widespread consumption by locals, suggested that it would take 18 araucaria trees to provide all the food necessary for a person for a year.

Fossil evidence has shown that Monkey puzzle trees are part of an ancient conifer family dating back over 200 million years. In addition, araucarias participate in what is probably the oldest known insect-plant interaction. Cones of the genus Araucaria that date to the Jurassic Age have been found in Argentina with damage that closely resembles the damage inflicted on present-day Argentine araucarias by beetles. One of the best places to see large populations of Monkey Puzzle trees is in Santuario Cañi, a privately owned reserve that is dedicated to promoting local guide training and sustainable interactions with the remaining forests. There are no roads, so be prepared to hike it. If you're willing to hike to the high mirador, you will be afforded a simultaneous view of four spectacular volcanoes and an equally spectacular old growth araucaria-nothofagus forest.

European visitors to Chile made several unsuccessful attempts at growing the first Monkey Puzzle trees in England until Sir Joseph Banks finally got it right. This fascination with the Monkey Puzzle tree cannot, however, prevent its declining numbers. The straight trunk and enormous size make the tree a valuable lumber product and, despite being nominally protected, illegal logging continues at a prodigious rate.

Venturing still further South from Monkey Puzzle land, you may be lucky enough to see the majestic alerce, which resembles the giant redwoods, but is actually related to the cypress. While not as tall as the sequoias (only reaching heights of 150 feet), it can live over 3500 years and grow to four meters in diameter. The wood contains protective resins that made it a popular timber for exterior structures like shingles and decks. Only 15% of the area originally forested by alerce remains, but the recent establishment of Parque Pumalín, funded largely by the philanthropist Douglas Tompkins, founder of North Face and Esprit, will hopefully go a long way towards ensuring the long-term survival of this unique species.

Amity Wilczek is a graduate student in evolutionary biology at Harvard University.

the daughter of one of the founding settlers. The cafe mixes standard salmon and potato fare with a few German dishes for about CH$6000 a meal. The rundown **Ventisquero ❶**, on O'Higgins, around the corner from the central police station, offers only one simple dish a night (CH$3500) and whichever soap opera that's on TV.

NEAR PUYUHUAPI

TERMAS DE PUYUHUAPI

Once an inauspicious getaway where locals could soak away worries, the thermal baths are now owned and run by a five-star resort, with five-star prices. **Hotel Termas de Puyuhuapi ❺** (☎325 103), charges US$120 for a single bed—if that sounds excessive, a day visit is CH$15,000 (extra for seaweed baths and lunch). Since the springs are south of town and across the bay, find transportation to the docks 11km south of town and catch a boat heading to the resort (9:30am, noon, 7pm; returns immediately after; US$5).

PARQUE NACIONAL QUEULAT

The thick, temperate rainforest of Queulat limits visitors to the two major marked trails, one of which leads to one of the world's rare "hanging" glaciers. As the astounding ice mass hangs over the tranquil lake, waterfalls speckled with bits of ice rush down all around it. To reach the hanging glacier, enter the park through the southern entrance, 22km south of Puerto Puyuhuapi. Follow the valley path of **Río Guillermo** for 1½hr. before reaching the stone walls shaped by the retreating glacier. No public transportation heads directly to the park, but any north- or south-bound transportation on the Camino Austral will be happy to drop you off at the park entrance—just be attentive, as drivers can easily pass it without a second thought. **Camping** is permitted, but there are no facilities or shops for food. (Camping free. Entrance to park CH$4000.)

PUERTO CISNES

The small town was one of the first in the region to serve as an outpost to the surrounding unchartered territory, but has developed slowly since. The dolphins in the bay are one of the most delightful points of interest, but the tranquil, easy way of life may seduce some visitors. **Bus Hernandez**, 12 Octubre 337 (☎254 600), rolls into town from Coyhaique (M-F 4pm, returns 6:30am; CH$5000), but no regular service heads to town from the north. To continue north on the Camino, ask around town for a ride back to the road and wave down a scheduled bus headed north. It is best to call ahead to a company with regular northern service and confirm the time a bus will pass—then arrive with plenty of time and patience. In town, **Hospedaje Bellavista ❷**, Septimo de Linea 112, will put you up in simple rooms with nice company for CH$6000. **Guairao ❷**, Piloto Pardo 58, cooks up the widest range of seafood and chicken dishes around.

PUERTO CHACABUCO

This small port town is the last stop for freight boats headed south through the famous Chilean fjords. Although most passengers on these trips travel the whole distance between Puerto Montt and Puerto Natales, Puerto Chacabuco can be a good place to begin or end a fjords trip for those that want to take on the difficult but rewarding task of traversing the Camino Austral. To get to Chacabuco, take one of the many buses to **Puerto Aisén** and then wait on the main street, Sgto. Aldea, for one of the many buses with a sign for "Puerto Chacabuco" (CH$350). Chacabuco offers little to visitors other than a place to dock, but if you're stuck in town, **Hotel Moraleda ❷** (☎315 155), about five minutes from the port on the only paved road, has basic rooms (CH$6000) and even more basic food.

COYHAIQUE   ☎ 67

The busy streets and heaving diesel buses of Coyhaique, the only substantial city in this region, may be jarring for visitors traversing the tranquil Camino Austral. But along with the bustling energy of the city come bountiful shops, a range of dining options, and a wider selection of accommodations. In addition to being a useful place to stop and refuel, Coyhaique offers a plethora of natural attractions, including rivers and parks heralded by fly fishers and hikers in the know.

⌐ TRANSPORTATION

Flights: There is no airport in Coyhaique, but local flights use the municipal airport in **Balcameda,** 30min. away and accessible by regular minibuses. **Aero Continente,** Prat 470 (☎240 144), flies to: **Puerto Montt** (1hr., 3:50pm, US$24); **Punta Arenas** (2½ hr.; M, W, F, Sa 12:40pm; CH$25,000); **Santiago** (3hr., US$120). **LanChile** (☎231 300), on the corner of Parra and Moralada, heads to **Santiago** (CH$100,000) via **Punta Arenas** (CH$31,000) and **Puerto Montt** (CH$50,000). **Transportes Don Carlos,** Subteniente Cruz 63 (☎231 981, call for all departure times), heads to: **Chile Chico** (M-W, F; CH$19,300); **Cochrane** (M-Th, CH$36,000); **Tortel** (W, CH$18,000); **Villa O'Higgins** (M-Th, CH$56,200).

Buses: These tend to be minibuses that can better navigate the Camino Austral. Choose your seat carefully, as the ride is almost always longer than expected and very bumpy. It is recommended to book ahead. Schedules change seasonally, but the tourist office keeps an up-to-date listing of buses for the entire region. Some minibuses leave from the **bus station** at the corner of Magallanes and Lautaro.

Bus Norte C. Austral, Parra 337 (☎232 167), goes to **Chaitén** (Tu, Th, Sa 8:30am; CH$15,000) and **Futaleufú** (Sa 8am, CH$15,000).

Nadis (☎258 203), in the bus station, goes to **Cochrane** (8hr.; Tu, Th, F, Su 10am; CH$8000) and **Puyuhuapi** (5hr.; Tu, W, F, Sa 1pm; CH$7,000).

Bus Sur (☎211 460), in the bus station, goes to: **Puerto Natales** (25hr., CH$27,000) and **Punta Arenas** (22hr., Tu 4pm, CH$25,000).

Sr. Reinaldo Cea, Simpson 829 (☎231 555), offers summer service only to **Chaitén** (9hr., M-Th 9am, CH$15,000).

Bus Hernandez, 12 Octubre 337 (☎254 600), goes to **Puerto Cisnes** (M-F 4pm, CH$5000).

Acuario 13 (☎522 143), in the bus station, goes to **Cochrane** (10hr.; M, F, Su 10am; Sa 1pm; CH$9500).

Buses Pilchero (☎239 218), in the bus station, goes to **La Junta** (6½hr., W-Sa 9am, CH$8000).

Buses Don Carlos, Subteniente Cruz 63 (☎232 981), goes to **Puerto Aisén** (every 30min. 7:45am-9:30pm, CH$1200).

Other Buses: Dario Figueroa Castro (☎233 286), **Tour Aisén** (☎253 232), **Minibus Don Tito** (☎250 280), and **Yamil J. Ali. M.** (☎250 346) each depart daily for **Puerto Ibáñez** to catch the 9am ferry to **Chile Chico.** Call for departure schedule.

FROM THE ROAD

ON THE ROAD AGAIN

It's appropriate that as Herman, a local trucker, cruises home to Coyhaique, he croons "take me home...country roads..." Like John Denver and Willie Nelson (the grooving driver's top picks for sing-alongs), Herman appreciates the value of a good road. As a southerner in Chile, Herman is intimately acquainted with and personally invested in the difficult history of the highway he moves along—the infamous Camino Austral.

Over a jovial chicken dinner set to rocking 60s tunes, Herman explains that although the flourishing lumber industry and the not-so-sparse-anymore population of the far south should ensure that a city like Coyhaique is fully connected to the rest of the nation, this fluidity of transportation is not something he takes for granted.

The Camino Austral was Pinochet's major project, integral to his vision of a homogenous and united Chile. The first to admit that the rough-cut road is an incomplete venture (two ferries are still necessary to traverse the breaks in the road), Herman is well-aware that his persistent allegiance to the ruthless dictator is a tense issue. However, Herman's explication of the road's real benefits for the people of the Aisén region—electricity, water, schools, hospitals, effective police services, a standard of life on par with the rest of Chile—makes the citizens' loyalty to the deposed tyrant seem a little less absurd. What a long strange trip it's been for southern Chile.

—Alex Leary

ORIENTATION AND PRACTICAL INFORMATION

It seems that Coyhaique's founders were fed up with the grid system that characterizes most Chilean towns—instead, they formed a pentagonal **central plaza**. Only a couple of blocks out from the plaza, however, the city returns to the conventional format with perpendicular streets. From the manicured plaza, **Av. Horn** meets **Arturo Prat** to form a lively strip of restaurants and shops, while in the opposite direction from the center, **Condell** harbors many banks and travel services.

Tourist Office: Bulnes 35 (☎231 752). Extensive written materials and maps, and a small but helpful staff. Up-to-date listings of the variable and decentralized transportation available. Open in summer 8:30am-8:30pm, may be closed for lunch.

Tours: Gran Patagonia, General Parra 97 (☎214 770; info@granpatagonia.cl). This American-run operation specializes in **kayaking** (US$100), **fly fishing, horseback riding** (CH$15,000-25,000), **rock climbing** (full-day US$100), and **hiking. Bike rentals** CH$8000 per day. Longer combination trips can be arranged, starting at US$100 per day per person. **Boulder Outdoor Adventure** (☎099 565 1022) has its office in the town square during the summer. Catering to students and backpackers, they offer **horseback riding, trekking, rock climbing,** and **rafting.**

Currency Exchange: Turismo Prado, 21 de Mayo 417, exchanges traveler's checks at slightly poorer rates than cash. Open M-F 9am-1:30pm and 3:30-7pm, Sa 9am-1:30pm and 5-7pm. Also try **Emperador Exchange,** Bilboa 222 (☎232 727). Open 10am-1pm and 3-8:30pm.

ATM: Beginning at the park, **Condell** has many large banks with ATM access, including **Banco Santiago,** 141 Condell. Cirrus/MC/Plus/V.

Supermarket: Hiper Multimas, Lauturo 331, stocks every food imaginable. Open 9am-10pm.

Market: Just west of the central plaza, a small collection of booths sell regional wool crafts and leather goods at negotiable prices.

Laundromat: Natti, Simpson 417 (☎231 047), can turn around a load of laundry in a day for CH$4000.

Emergency: ☎ 131, **ambulance** ☎ 133.

24-hour Pharmacy: Rotation system; check the central **Salcobrand,** 326 Bilbao (☎ 210 465), on the corner with Horn.

Hospital: Aisén Regional Hospital, on the corner of Ibar and Carrera.

Telephone/Internet: Entel, Prat 326, is usually very busy, but is run efficiently, offers several phones and fast Internet access for CH$1000 per hr. Open M-F 8:30am-10:30pm, Sa 10am-10:30pm, Su 11am-7pm. **Cyber Pat@gonia,** Prat 360 2nd. fl., or on the corner of Condell and 21 de Mayo. Fast connections CH$960 per hr. Open 9am-11pm in the summer, 9am-2pm and 3-9pm in the winter.

Post Office: Cochrane 226, near the plaza. Open M-F 9am-12:30pm and 2:30-6pm, Sa 9am-12:30pm.

ACCOMMODATIONS

Hospedaje Chiloé, Baquedano 274 (☎ 251 381), is a solid choice for groups who want to cook—triple-occupancy apartments include a small kitchen. Singles and doubles CH$4000-5000 per person; apartments CH$15,000. ❷

Hospedaje Luis Roco, 21 de Mayo 668 (☎ 231 285). Common spaces and a clean kitchen are adorned with bright paintings and matching bedspreads. Breakfast included for campers. Singles, doubles, and triples CH$7500 per person. Camping CH$3000 per tent. ❸

Hostal Bon, Serrano 91 (☎ 231 189). The fly-fisherman owner cooks and services this quiet and clean establishment. Both the hotel-style rooms in the main building and smaller rooms for traveling students have TVs and big, soft beds. Guided overnight fly fishing trips US$120 per person per day. Lunch and dinner available if you ask ahead of time (CH$3500). Breakfast included. Singles CH$16,500; doubles CH$24,000; triples CH$31,000; student rooms (up to five with a separate kitchen) CH$8000 per person. ❸

Hostal Belisario Jara, Bilbao 662 (☎ 234 150), boasts a pristine decor, marvelous views, an apple tree garden, and excellent service. Guests enjoy a glimpse of rustic patagonian living with a touch of luxury. The lookout spire and charming bedrooms with private baths complete the aesthetic experience. Breakfast included. Singles CH$40,000; doubles CH$53,000; triples CH$69,000. MC/V. ❺

Señora Pochi, Freire 342 (☎ 234 547). This centrally located lodging welcomes visitors to mingle with the many generations of the Pochi family that drop by the family-oriented common space. Just like home, Señora Pochi shoos you out of the kitchen. The doubles and triples are cramped and worn, but with private baths are a deal at CH$6000. ❷

Hospedaje Lautaro, Lautaro 269 (☎ 238 116), set back from the busy corner. Blankets are generously provided to counter the draft in these sparse and often cold bedrooms. The large living room is much warmer and always bustling with other guests. Kitchen access available to the very tidy. Doubles, triples, and quads CH$5000 per person. ❷

Hospedaje Nathy, Simpson 417 (☎ 231 047). Down a dirt driveway, the small but warm rooms provide respite from the city just outside the doorway. The odd collection of singles, doubles, and triples all share clean but cold bathrooms. CH$3500 per person. ❶

Coyhaique

▲ ACCOMMODATIONS
Hospedaje Chiloé, **1**
Hospedaje Lautaro, **12**
Hospedaje Luis Roco, **3**
Hospedaje Nathy, **13**
Hostal Belisario Jara, **7**
Hostal Bon, **4**
Señora Pochi, **8**

● FOOD
Café El Torreno, **9**
Cafetería Alemana, **2**
El Comedor, **11**
Histórico, **6**
La Olla, **5**
El Tunnel, **10**

◘ FOOD

Look out for CH$2500 lunch specials in the restaurants that line Prat.

▨ **La Olla,** Prat 176. For a little more than the set lunch price at other restaurants, La Olla tantalizes the tastebuds with delicately prepared, sumptuous dishes. The gracious owner will tempt you with the day's offerings, such as lamb chop, beef ribs, or crab that come with a hearty soup or a generous *ceviche* (CH$3000). Soothe your eyes as you contemplate the intricate woodcarvings while waiting for your order. Menu items like *paella* (CH$3000) and steak (CH$4500) are also prepared with great care. Dinner is a bit more expensive, but worth every peso. Open 11am-9pm. ❷

Cafe El Torreno, Prat 470. The boisterous local crowd enjoys *fútbol* (soccer) games while chowing on some of the best lunch *menú* options on the street. Specials served through dinner (if they last) for CH$2500. The tasty chicken dishes (CH$3200) and soups (CH$1200) are also good choices if the special runs out. Grab a half-liter beer with your meal for only CH$1000. Open 10:30am-11pm. ❷

Histórico, Horn 48. Often filled with Europeans and Americans, Histórico offers the local specialty dish *pastel de choclo* (CH$4500) and other creative vegetarian options (CH$3500). Great presentation spices up the chicken dishes (CH$3200) and pizzas (CH$3000). The wood fire and rustic furniture allure guests to linger over their fresh coffee in the evenings. Open 8am-11:30pm. ❸

Cafetería Alemana, Condell 119. The German-influenced menu is mainly dominated by local dishes, including *bife el pobre* (CH$3800) and pizzas (CH$2000-2800). The extensive sandwich offerings (CH$1800-3000) deliver enticing combos of meats and vegetables on fresh bread, including hot turkey with guacamole. Breakfast available. Open 9am-11pm. ❷

El Tunnel, Prat 497. Although *lomo* (CH$3900) and personal *parillas* with a variety of grilled meats are the specialty, the large portions of *congrío* (conger eel) and salmon (CH$3500) are also hot choices. Many guests also linger over beers (CH$950) while enjoying the big-screen TV and the dark decor. Open 9am-1am. ❸

El Comedor, 12 de Octubre 317. With one of the cheapest menus in town, Comedor attracts frugal travelers with the rotisserie chicken in the window and a set lunch for only CH$2000. More plentiful options are worth a look, too—sample the cream soups (CH$600) or the *congrío Cecilia* (CH$3200). Open 10am-10pm. ❷

◪ DAYTRIPS FROM COYHAIQUE

RESERVA NACIONAL COYHAIQUE. This small national reserve offers visitors good views of the bustling town and a few simple walks along two small lakes. Proximity has made this wooded area popular among locals looking to relax, but it remains relatively secluded. Since the park is within the city limits, it can be reached by an hour and a half walk north along Baquedano. Once you cross the bridge over the Río Coyhaique, the Reserva will be on your left. *(Conaf collects a CH$2000 fee at the entrance and offers basic information for Laguna Verde and Laguna Venus. Camping sites are available around both lakes for CH$10,000 a night for up to 6 people; basic bathrooms and fresh water are available but you will need to bring all food and other provisions.)*

RESERVA NACIONAL RÍO SIMPSON. Often attracting fly-fishers, the reserve's namesake river and its tributaries hold many trout. The evergreen forest veils a majestic waterfall, **Cascada La Vírgen,** where the river meets Río Correntoso. Thirty-seven kilometers from Coyhaique toward Puerto Chacabuco, a **visitor center**

BORDER CROSSING INTO ARGENTINA: CHILE CHICO
Sitting just three kilometers from the border, Chile Chico provides easy access to Argentina from where you can start your trek southward to the glacier parks and Tierra del Fuego. A rough road runs across the Chile-Argentina border to **Los Antiguos** five kilometers on the other side, where it becomes Ruta 43. Sixty kilometers later it runs through the town of Perito Moreno, where it meets Ruta 40, the main road to El Calafate.
   The pass remains open unless Chile Chico itself is buried in snow. The customs office at the border is open from 8am-9pm. The process is fairly simple and involves no more than a brief search of your luggage for contraband and various food products and a passport stamp (see **Essentials: Border Crossings**, p. 65, for info on visas and fees).

has a small museum and botanical garden. *(Take any bus from Coyhaique to Puerto Chacabuco and ask to be let off at the park entrance (see **Transportation**, p. 453). Camping CH$10,000 per site.)*

PARQUE NACIONAL LAGUNA SAN RAFAEL. Located in the northern region of the frozen, desolate Chilean fjords, the national park harbors many animals, mostly birds and marine life. Hanging fog and ominous peaks set the backdrop for the impressive **San Rafael glacier,** which lures many of this park's visitors. Most visitors access the park for a short one- to two-hour tour of the glacier and lake by plane from Coyhaique. Other visitors take one of the cruise ships from Puerto Chacabuco that navigate the narrow opening connecting the lake to the ocean. *(Contact any of the travel agents in Coyhaique to arrange transportation. Min. 4 passengers to take off. US$150 per person.)*

CHILE CHICO   ☎ 67

Chile Chico's cedar trees barely hinder the powerful winds that blow over from the adjacent Patagonian plains. This quiet town remains a pleasant getaway, with its dramatic blue water and nearby secluded parks, paying little attention to the stream of tourists on their way to Argentina. Chile Chico's greatest claim to adventure fame is the west-bound road to Cochrane that mountain bikers hail as the most inspiring in the region, despite the difficult climb and tight curves.

TRANSPORTATION. Minibus Padilla, O'Higgins 420 (☎411 904), rolls to **Los Antiguos, ARG** (1½hr.; M-Sa 9am and 1:30pm, returns 10am and 2:30pm; CH$4000). **Condor,** O'Higgins 420 (☎411 904), goes to **Puerto Río Traquilo** (4¼hr.; M, Tu, Th 5pm; CH$7000) via **Puerto Guadal** (2½hr., F 5pm, CH$5000). **ALE,** Rosa 880 (☎411 739), near the stadium, goes to **Cochrane** (5-6hr.; W 10am, returns Th; CH$10,000). ALE offers additional service on Saturdays during the summer.
   Ferries go to **Puerto Ibáñez,** leaving from beneath the cliff in the northwest corner of town (2¼hr.; M-F 4pm, Su 2pm; CH$1800). "Combination" minibuses leave directly from the port upon arrival of the ferry, heading to **Coyhaique** (2½hr., CH$3000).

ORIENTATION AND PRACTICAL INFORMATION. Most basic services can be found on the main street, **Avenida O'Higgins.** The **tourist office** (☎411 123), on the corner of O'Higgins and Lautauro, lists local events and has a simple regional museum. **ALE tours** (☎411 739) arranges transportation and basic fishing and horseback riding trips to nearby parks including **Lago Jeinimeni,** but is best for groups of six to ten people. **Banco del Estado,** Gonzalez 112, changes US dollars at poor rates. (Open M-F 10am-1pm.) The local **Entel** office can be found at O'Higgins 420. The **post office** is at Manuel Rodríguez 121.

ⓇⒸ ACCOMMODATIONS AND FOOD. The name of the game in Chile Chico is simple but friendly. **Eben-Ezer ❸,** 302 Rodríguez, has doubles and triples with low ceilings but good company and a living room. (☎411 535. CH$5000 per person, including breakfast.) Although known predominantly for transportation and tours, **ALE ❷** continues to expand its services, offering cozy beds and a new outdoor grill for guest use. (Breakfast included. Singles CH$5000.) **Don Luis Hospedaje ❷,** Balmaceda 175, is the cheapest in town, but a last-resort choice because of its small, misshapen rooms and worn bedding. (☎411 384. CH$3500 per person.) The hearty plates of grub served at **Elizabeth y Loly ❷,** Pedro Antonio Gonzalez 25, are satisfying for lunch or dinner. The lunch specials at **Cafe Refer ❷,** O'Higgins 440, featuring only local meats and fish, are a great pick for only CH$3500.

TIERRA DEL FUEGO & THE FAR SOUTH

Picking his way slowly along the rock path, the hiker emerged from the lush evergreen forest into a grassy alpine field. Looking up at the craggy, twisted towers of rock that dominated the landscape, he smiled and wished he could stay there forever. Shaking his head, he zipped up his jacket as the eternally blowing wind sent a chill through his body. After one last look at the soaring mountains, he set off quickly towards the shimmering turquoise lake ahead of him. The glaciers awaited him.

Most travelers who spend time in the South of Chile and Argentina say that you have to experience it to understand it. A rugged region of looming mountains, pristine lakes, and barren plains marked by little pockets of civilization, the region has become one of the most popular in South America. Despite the bitter tension between Chileans and Argentines, most will admit that you can't visit this part of one country without visiting the other. **Campo del Hielo Sur,** the vast ice fields of the Andes, covers the mountains on both sides of the border and the islands of **Tierra del Fuego** are split almost down the middle. This is definitely just one big playground for those in love with adventure hiking and boat touring through incredible terrain, quaint sheepherding villages, and frontier cities.

Most travelers visiting from Chile, start their journey in **Punta Arenas** and head north to **Puerto Natales** from where most of the biggest draws on the Chilean side can be explored. Be sure to leave yourself plenty of time to explore the enormous **Parque Nacional Torres del Paine,** which is one of the most well-known parks in the world. The Argentine cities of **Calafate** and **Chaltén** sit just on the opposite side of the Andes at the edge of the vast, barren Patagonia. To the west of Punta Arenas lies the Isla Grande of Tierra del Fuego. The northern part of this area around **Río Grande** is dominated by the windswept steppes of Patagonia. This slowly gives way to the mountainous, forest regions surrounding **Ushuaia** and **Parque Nacional Tierra del Fuego.** Just to the south and back in Chile is the rustic **Puerto Williams,** lying a few hundred kilometers from Antarctica.

HIGHLIGHTS OF TIERRA DEL FUEGO & THE FAR SOUTH

FROLIC with "jackass" penguins, otherwise known as Magellanic Penguins, in the **Monumento Nacional Los Pingüinos** (p. 467) outside **Punta Arenas.** (p. 461).

SLIP across fields of ice as you hike the Andean glaciers of **Parque Nacional Los Glaciers** (p. 483) above Chaltén (p. 480).

INDULGE in decadent King Crabs and sophisticated Argentine wine at the "End of the World," as the Ushuaians label their town (p. 488).

MARVEL at the green-blue glacial lakes, the lush forests, and the twisted towers that sit atop the Paine massif in **Parque Nacional Torres del Paine** (p. 472).

FLOAT through the Beagle Channel on a local fishing boat (p. 494).

PUNTA ARENAS ☎ 61

This self-proclaimed "capital of Patagonia" is often just a stopping point for outdoor adventurers on their way to the region's world-famous attractions. While the local sites are of some interest—especially the renowned **Las Pingüineras** (Penguin Colony)—Punta Arenas's main draw is its position as a transportation hub and supply center for those venturing to more remote parts of Patagonia. Still, the town retains the same charm it had when it was founded in 1848 as a trading post, and, if nothing else, is a pleasant place to spend a day or two.

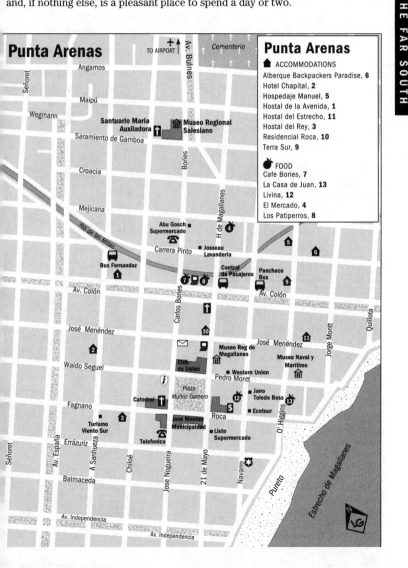

Punta Arenas

🏠 ACCOMMODATIONS
Alberque Backpackers Paradise, **6**
Hotel Chapital, **2**
Hospedaje Manuel, **5**
Hostal de la Avenida, **1**
Hostal del Estrecho, **11**
Hostal del Rey, **3**
Residencial Roca, **10**
Terra Sur, **9**

🍴 FOOD
Cafe Bories, **7**
La Casa de Juan, **13**
Livina, **12**
El Mercado, **4**
Los Patiperros, **8**

TIERRA DEL FUEGO & THE FAR SOUTH

TIERRA DEL FUEGO
& THE FAR SOUTH

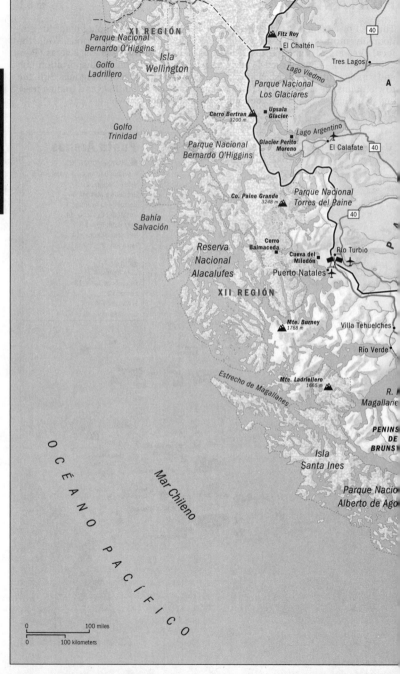

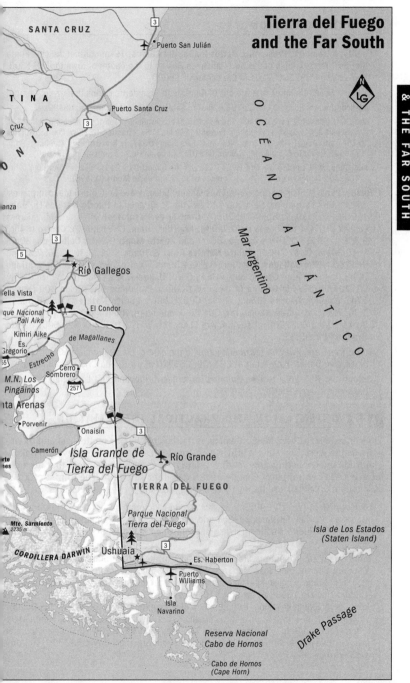

Tierra del Fuego and the Far South

SANTA CRUZ

Puerto San Julián

TINA

Cruz

Puerto Santa Cruz

anza

5

Río Gallegos

ella Vista

El Condor

que Nacional
Pali Aike

Kimiri Aike
Es.
Gregorio

Estrecho

de Magallanes

M.N. Los
Pingüinos

Cerro
Sombrero

257

ta Arenas

Porvenir

Onaisin

3

Camerón

Isla Grande de
Tierra del Fuego

Río Grande

rte
nes

TIERRA DEL FUEGO

Mte. Sarmiento
2235 m

Parque Nacional
Tierra del Fuego

CORDILLERA DARWIN

Ushuaia

3

Es. Haberton

Puerto
Williams

Isla
Navarino

Reserva Nacional
Cabo de Hornos

Cabo de Hornos
(Cape Horn)

OCÉANO ATLÁNTICO

Mar Argentino

Isla de Los Estados
(Staten Island)

Drake Passage

TIERRA DEL FUEGO
& THE FAR SOUTH

⊫ TRANSPORTATION

Flights: Aeropuerto Presidente Carlos Ibáñez del Campo, 19km north of the city. Punta Arenas-Puerto Natales buses and Pancheco Bus go to the center of town for CH$1500. Van service CH$2500. Taxis to the center CH$6000.

Airlines: Several airlines operate out of Aeropuerto Presidente Carlos Ibáñez del Campo:

Aerocontinente, Roca 924 (☎220 960), flies to **Santiago** (4hr.; M, Tu, Th, Sa; US$90).

DAP, O'Higgins 891 (☎223 240). There's often space available even if the flights are "full," so keep asking. Sends small planes to: **Porvenir** (20min., M-Sa 2 per day, US$23); **Puerto Williams** (1hr.; Apr.-Aug. T, Th, Sa 1pm; Nov.-Mar. T-Sa 3pm; US$71); **Río Grande** (45min., F 9am; US$90); **Ushuaia** (45min.; M, W 9am; US$100); **Cabo de Hornos** (infrequent, US$300).

Lan Chile, 999 Lantaro Navarro (☎241 232, at the airport 213 211), flies to: **Santiago** (4hr., US$230); **Concepción** (US$123); **Temuco** (US$105); **Puerto Montt** (US$98).

Buses: Punta Arenas has no central bus station; buses leave from individual companies' offices. **Bus Fernandez,** Samueza 745 (☎242 313), goes to **Puerto Natales** (8, 9am, 1, 2:30, 5, 6:30, 7, 8pm; CH$2500). **Central de Pasajeros,** Colón and Magallanes (☎220 967), sends buses to: **Calafate, Arg** (6hr., 9am, CH$13,000); **Castro** (34hr., 9:30am, CH$28,000) via **Osorno** (30hr.) and **Puerto Montt** (32hr.); **Coihaique** (30hr., M 10:30am, CH$25,000); **Puerto Natales** (3hr.; 8:30am, 1:30, 3:30, 4:30, 7:30pm; CH$2500); **Río Gallegos, Arg** (6hr.; daily 11:30am, Th also 3pm; CH$7000); **Santiago** (40hr., transfer from Osorno bus, CH$41,000); **Ushuaia, Arg** (14hr.; M, W, Th, F, Su; CH$20,500) via **Río Grande** (10hr., CH$13,000). **Pancheco Bus,** Colón 900 (☎242 174), goes to: **Osorno** (35hr., W, Sa, CH$28,000); **Puerto Natales** (3hr.; 8:30am, 1:30, 7:30pm; CH$2500 one-way, CH$4500 round-trip); **Río Gallegos, Arg** (4hr; Tu, F, Su 11:30am; CH$7000); **Ushuaia, Arg** (14hr.; M, W, F 7:15am; CH$20,500) via **Río Grande** (9hr., CH$13,000).

Taxis: There are always a few waiting around the central plaza or cruising Colón, Magallanes, and Bories. Fares start at CH$200, CH$220 at night, and CH$250 Sundays.

Colectivos: #15 goes to **Tres Puentes** for ferries to Porvenir and Los Pingüinos. Most destinations are CH$200.

✳ ⁊ ORIENTATION AND PRACTICAL INFORMATION

The central plaza, **Plaza Muñoz Gamero,** is flanked by the bay on the east and mountains on the west. The simple grid system and logical numbering of every block by hundreds makes estimating distances fairly easy. Only the streets that actually intersect the central plaza change names on either side of it. The tourist office is efficient and officials are happy to give out maps and locate destinations.

Tourist office: (☎220 990; infopuq@chile.com) Victorian-style kiosk in Plaza Muñoz Gamero. Has helpful transportation and accommodations information for both Punta Arenas and Puerto Natales. English spoken. Open M-F 8am-8pm, Sa 9am-7pm, Su 9am-3pm.

Tours: Many tour operators are scattered east of the central plaza on Lautar Navarro between Errázuriz and José Menandez. The tourist office has a list of other tour operators in the area. English-speaking staff available at all tour offices. **Jano Toledo Boss,** Lautaro Navarro 1013 (☎/fax 224 510; www.inhospitapatagonia.cl), has a wide range of tours including kayaking, fishing, mountaineering, and tours to the Penguin Colony. Prices are somewhat higher than competitors, but there is more flexibility. Open M-Sa 10am-1pm and 3-8pm. **Turismo Viento Sur,** Faguano 585 (☎225 930). Offers tours at competitive rates. Mountain bike rentals available (half-day CH$7000, full-day CH$9000).

Consulates: The tourist office has a more complete list of consulates. Consulates in the area include **Argentina** (☎261 912), **Brazil** (☎241 093), and **Great Britain** (☎211 535). There is no consulate for the US.

Currency Exchange: Central de Pasajes, Colón and Magallanes (☎220 967). Changes cash and travelers checks at good rates. Open daily 9am-9pm.

ATM: Many large banks with 24hr. ATMs circle the central plaza. **Banco de Chile,** Roca 864, accepts Cirrus/MC/Plus/V without a service charge. Open 24hr.

Western Union: Pedro Montt 840 (☎228 462). **DHL** express mail service available. Open M-F 8:30am-7:30pm, Sa 9:30am-2pm.

Laundromat: Josseau, Ignacio Pinto 766 (☎228 413). Same-day service if dropped off before 10am. Open M-F 8:30am-7:30pm, Sa 8:30am-2pm. AmEx/MC/V. CH$1000 per kilo.

Supermarket: Listo, 21 de Mayo 1133, near the central plaza. Open M-Sa 10am-1pm and 3-8pm. DC/MC/V. Or try **Abu Gosch,** Bories 647. Open M-Sa 9am-10pm, Su 10am-9pm. DC/MC/V.

Emergency: ☎133

Fire: ☎132

24-hour Pharmacy: There is a rotating system between local pharmacies which is posted on the front door of each one.

Hospital: Hospital Regional, Angamos 180 (☎205 000).

Telephones: Telefonica, Bories 674. Also has **Internet** access (CH$900 per hr.). Open M-Th 9:30am-1:30pm and 3-9:30pm, F 9:30am-1:30pm and 3-10:30pm, Sa 10:30am-11pm, Su 4-9:30pm. **Telefonica (CTC),** Noguiera 1100, on the southeast corner of the central plaza, connects to the US for CH$476 per min. and CH$10 per min. locally. Open M-Sa 8:30am-10pm, Su 9am-10pm.

Internet: Calafate Internet, Magallanes 922 (☎241 281). Central location, fast connections. CH$1200 per hr. **Ciber Cafe,** Colón 780, 2nd fl. A bit slower than Calafate, but cheaper. CH$1000 per hr.

Post Office: Bories 911 (☎222 796).

ACCOMMODATIONS

As the gateway for trekkers to Parque Nacional Torres del Paine, Punta Arenas has a range of accommodations, although reservations are recommended in the summer. The tourist office also has listings for lodging within 15min. of the plaza. The accommodations listed below are generally within 6 blocks of the central plaza:

Hostal de la Avenida, Avenida Colón 534 (☎/fax 247 532). Quiet, private rooms with private bath, a small garden, and central location seem to keep this hostel booked. Breakfast included. Reservations recommended. Singles CH$25,000; doubles CH$30,000; triples CH$35,000; quads CH$40,000. ❺

Terra Sur, O'Higgins 730 (☎225 618; hostalterrasur@entelchile.net). Spacious dorm-style rooms decorated with posters of American movies and Victorian images create a homey atmosphere. Sheets not included. Kitchen access available. 4-bed dorms with private bathrooms and shared shower CH$4000. ❷

Hospedaje Manuel, O'Higgins 648 (☎242 411), 4 blocks north and 2 blocks east of the *plaza central.* The most central of the ultra-cheap. Communal bathrooms are clean and hot water is readily available, although there can be lines when the hostel is filled to capacity. Free kitchen access. Dorms CH$3000. ❶

Hostal del Estrecho, José Menendez 1045 (☎/fax 421 011), one block north and 3 blocks south of the central plaza. The friendly owner takes good care of the bright and clean rooms. Common and private baths are worn, but well maintained. Singles CH$10,000, with bath CH$19,000; doubles CH$16,000/CH$24,000; triples CH$21,000/CH$27,000; quads with bath CH$32,000. ❸

Residencial Roca, Magallanes 888 (☎/fax 243 903). Despite squeaky floors, loud traffic, thin walls, and oddly shaped rooms, Roca has a great central location. Pleasant and helpful owners make up for the chaotic decor. Continental breakfast included. CH$6000 per person. ❷

Hostal del Rey, Fagnano 589 (☎223 924; www.chileaustral.com/hdelrey), two blocks west of the central plaza. Family-run and group-oriented. Rooms are small and eclectic, but like the communal bathrooms, are clean and well-kept. Living room with cable TV. Reservations recommended. Doubles CH$10,000; apartment for 2-3 guests CH$15,000. ❷

Hotel Chapital, A. Sanchues 974 (☎223 163), one block west and half a block north of the plaza. The bland, gray exterior houses sparsely decorated, hotel-style rooms near the center of town. Doubles with private bath and TV CH$15,000. ❸

Albergue Backpackers Paradise, Pinto 1022 (☎222 554). Always lively, Paradise fills up almost every night because of its kitchen, small living room, and free Internet. A great place to meet other travelers if you can handle the tight and noisy dorms. CH$3000 per person. ❶

⬛ FOOD

Los Patiperros, Colón 782 (☎245 298). Friendly staff serves up a sumptuous and warming chicken *cazuela* (hearty stew) full of sweet potatoes, corn, rice, and carrots. Other options include fish (CH$3800) and beef (CH$4500). Open daily 11am-1am. AmEx/DC/MC/V. ❸

El Mercado, Mejicana 617, 2nd fl., at the intersection of Chiloé, 4 blocks north and one block west of Pl. Muñoz Gamero. A relaxed atmosphere (diner-style) and helpful wait-staff makes this local favorite appealing to visitors as well. Hearty portions of beef or local seafood CH$4000-6000. Open 24hr. AmEx/MC/V. ❸

Livina, Lantaro Navarro 1048. Tantalizing sweets and delightful fresh bread compliment a wide variety of eat-in or take-out meals in this clean, orderly, and popular restaurant/bakery. A great place for take-out sandwiches (cold CH$990, hot CH$1300-2300). Chicken and rice or potatoes eat-in special CH$1300. Sinful desserts CH$310-2000. Open M-F 10am-8pm, Sa 10am-2:30pm. AmEx/DC/MC/V. ❶

Cafe Bories, on the corner of Bories and Colón. Grills up the usual collection of hamburgers, *lomos* (chops), and pizzas (CH$800-2000). Try the cozy basement seating area to get away from kitchen noise. Combination plates CH$1000-1500. Set lunch of soup, pasta, dessert, and beverage CH$1490. Open daily 11am-7pm. ❶

La Casa de Juan, O'Higgins 1021 (☎229 910). Locals flock here for the especially good salmon (CH$3400), plentiful salads (CH$2800), and good wines (CH$2000-3500). With some advance notice, they are eager to arrange a complete barbecue in other locations for six or more people. Open 11am-midnight. ❷

⬛ SIGHTS

CLUB DE LA UNION. Built in 1895 by Sara Braun, the widowed wife of local leader José Noguiera, this ornate building is one of Punta Arenas's architectural wonders. For many years after Sara's death, the palace was maintained by local socialites for private use. Although an exclusive group of local citizens still meets in the marble-floored salons and wood-paneled music room, the club—named a national monument in 1982—is open to the public. If it is particularly quiet, the guard may allow access to the terrace and dining rooms now used by the new five-star hotel that shares the building. *(Pl. Muñoz Gamero 716. ☎241 489; clunion@entelchile.net. Open Tu-Th and Su 11am-1pm and 6:30-8:30pm, F and Sa 11am-1pm and 8-10pm. CH$1000.)*

MUSEO REGIONAL DE MAGALLANES. Also known as the Casa Braun-Menéndez, this decadent mansion has been restored to reveal the prosperous lifestyle of late 19th century Punta Arenas. Although some rooms can only be viewed from the threshold, visitors are permitted into a few of the restored rooms decorated with their original furnishing. Native artifacts and an interactive station detailing the lives and customs of the three distinct Chilean cultures are wonderful additions. *(Magallanes 900 block, north of the central plaza. ☎244 216. Open M-Sa 10:30am-5pm, Su and holidays 10:30am-2pm. CH$800, children CH$400. Extra charge for cameras.)*

CEMETARIO MUNICIPAL. An easy 15min. walk from the center of town, the immaculately maintained cemetery is a pleasant display of both the wealthy and common elements that characterize old Punta Arenas society. The central and ornate tombs of leading figures like José Menéndez and Sara Braun give way to manicured avenues to the many family mausoleums. *(Bulnes 949, 10 blocks north of the central plaza. Open dawn to dusk. Free.)*

■ DAYTRIPS FROM PUNTA ARENAS

MONUMENTO NACIONAL LOS PINGÜINOS. In 1892, Marta and Magdalena Islands were finally established as a national monument park that now attracts hundreds of vacationing Chileans and tourists alike. The park is home for more than 50,000 pairs of Magellanic Penguins, sometimes known as "jackass" penguins because of their distinctive bray-like call. After the 2hr. trip to the island, visitors are given about an hour to watch the flightless birds struggle overland and roam about the shore. Those who brave the 30min. walk to the lighthouse can enjoy excellent views of the entire island and obtain further information. The real treat, however, is back on the boat where the elevated position allows for splendid views of these adorable aquatic animals as they return from the sea. *(For information, contact the República de Chile Minesterio de Agricultura Corporación Nacional Forestal, José Menéndez 1147. ☎223 420. Purchase tickets at any tour office. Boats leave daily from Tres Puentes Port, easily accessible by colectivo 15 that passes Magallanes every few minutes. Tours CH$21,000, children CH$10,500.)*

SENO OTWAY. One hour north of town, Seno Otway allows for good viewing of the "jackass" penguin, but it is noticeably smaller and less personal than the more popular Monumento Nacional Los Pingüinos. Despite the smaller penguin population here, it may be better for those short of money or time. *(Most tour offices sell morning and afternoon transport to Seno Otway for about CH$7000. Entrance fee CH$6000.)*

FUERTE BULNES. Founded in 1843, Fuerte Bulnes was the first Chilean settlement along the Magellan Strait. As Pedro Sarmiento de Gamboa's outpost, Fuerte Bulnes only lasted a few years before citizens moved 55km north to Punta Arenas for better soil and protection. The present-day reconstruction of the settlement includes a chapel, horse stalls, a jail, and an ominous fence of sharpened stakes. However, the real gem is the coastal walk and expansive view across the Magellan Strait. The trip takes about three hours, with an hour at the site itself. The cafe has reasonably priced food and is a great place to enjoy a picnic. *(Tickets can be purchased from any tour office in town for CH$7000 per person. Some hostels will also arrange trips, although prices can vary greatly. Taxis will make the round-trip journey for CH$25,000.)*

RESERVA FORESTAL MAGALLANES. Just west of town and overlooking the bay, the reserve is an easy escape from Punta Arenas's gusty winds. Local families often come up to enjoy a barbecue or a pleasant walk in the picturesque forest, but this is no spectacular highlight for most travelers seeking Patagonia's natural wonders. The mountain, given over to cheap, although comparatively unexceptional, skiing in the winter, doubles as a hiking site during the summer. A 1hr. circuit trail and a 45min. hiking trail to the peak provide a great view of town. *(Turismo Viento Sur offers trips to the reserve's ski club at 10am and 1pm that return at 1:30 and 5pm, CH$1500 each way. Lift tickets and rental equipment CH$20,000. In the summer, Viento Sur rents bikes with helmets; half-day CH$7000, full-day CH$9000. To bike back to town, follow the coast back to the plaza.)*

PUERTO NATALES ☎ 61

Founded in 1911 as a sheep-herding settlement, Puerto Natales now attracts flocks of tourists and trekkers. Its proximity to Parque Nacional Torres del Paine and Cerro Balmaceda makes this an ideal place to stock up on camping equipment and supplies for heading out into the wilderness. However, the port's scenic coastline on the Seno Última Esperanza and its variety of nature outings will tempt you to stay put. You can easily keep yourself busy with the incredible camping, fishing, and sights, including the fascinating Cueva del Milodón. With its variety of ser-

Puerto Natales

🏠 ACCOMMODATIONS
Casa Cecilia, **1**
Casa Lili, **2**
Danicar, **11**
Nancy Hospedaje, **8**
Magallania, **9**

🍴 FOOD
Concepto Indigo, **3**
El Maritimo, **6**
el Living, **5**
Restaurante Cristal, **10**
Restaurant Última Esperanza, **4**
El Rincón de "Don Chico" 2, **7**

vices, good food, and accommodations, Puerto Natales satisfies both the casual nature lover and the hardcore hiker.

▐ TRANSPORTATION

Flights: 6km west of town. This small local airport is usually very quiet, with almost no major airlines. **DAP** has the only regular service to **El Calafate, ARG** (45min., M-Sa 9am, US$50). Taxis to the airport cost about CH$5000.

Buses: Bus Sur, Baquedano 558 (☎411 325), goes to: **Coyhaique** (10hr., M 8:30am, CH$27,500); **El Calafate, ARG** (5hr., M-Sa 9am, CH$13,000); **Osorno** (34hr., W and Sa 7am, CH$30,500) via **Puerto Montt** (32hr., CH$30,500); **Punta Arenas** (3hr.; M-Sa 7, 8:30am, 12:45, 3, 7pm; Su 8am, 3, 7pm; CH$2500); **Río Gallegos, ARG** (6hr., Tu and Th 6:30am, CH$8000); **Río Turbio, ARG** (1hr.; M-F 10am and 6pm, Su 9am; CH$2000). Most buses leave from the office, but confirm ahead of time, as some early ones leave from the plaza. **Cootra,** Baquedano 266, also heads to **El Calafate, ARG** (5hr., 6:30am, CH$13,000). **Pancheco,** Baquedano 244 (☎412 783), goes to **Río Turbio, ARG** (1hr.; 6:30am, 6:15, 9:15pm; CH$2000). **Buses Fernández,** Eberhard 566, runs regular buses to **Punta Arenas** (3hr.; 8, 9am, 1, 3:30, 5, 6:30, 7, 8pm; CH$3000). From Puerto Natales, many bus companies run their own circuit to 3 destinations in **Parque Nacional Torres del Paine: Laguna Armaga** (2½hr.), **Lago Pehoé** (3½hr.), and the **Conaf office** (4½hr.). Buses that make the park loop include: **Buses JB,** Prat 258 (☎412 824; 7, 8am, 2:30pm; CH$3000); **Pancheco** (7am and 2:15pm, CH$3500); **Bus Sur** (7am, CH$3500).

Taxis: Although they are generally unnecessary, taxis can be found around the plaza. Fares start at CH$700.

Boats: Navimag, Costanera Pedro Mont 380, runs well-known 2- and 4-day boats to **Puerto Montt** and **Puerto Chacabuco.**

✳ ▐ ORIENTATION AND PRACTICAL INFORMATION

Around the manicured Plaza de Armas, Puerto Natales' streets extend in a standard grid system. Most of the town's services line **Av. Bulnes,** which runs from the waterfront to the outskirts of town, one block from the plaza. North of the square, the intersection of **Blanco Encalado** and Bulnes is also a center of activity.

Tourist Office: Costanera Pedro Montt 19 (☎412 195). The out-of-the-way office is probably less helpful than your friendly hostel owner.

Tour offices: Most offices offer similar packages. **Path@gone,** Eberhard 595 (☎/fax 413 291; www.chileaustral.com/pathgone), is centrally located and extremely helpful, offering ice hiking, sailing, trekking, and combination packages. Open 9am-10pm. **Big Foot,** Bories 206 (☎414 611; www.bigfootpatagonia.com), runs a top-notch adventure tour operation with guided tours of the national park, sea kayaking, glacier trekking, and almost anything else if you ask ahead of time. Also try **Onas,** Eberhard and Blanco Encalada (☎412 707; open 9am-10pm) and **Comapa,** Costanera Pedro Montt 380 (☎414 300).

Currency Exchange: Mily Travel Agencies, Blanco Encalada 277 (☎411 262), exchanges US dollars and traveler's checks. Open M-Sa 10am-1pm and 3:30-7pm.

ATM: Banco Santiago, on the corner of Bulnes and Blanco Encalada, accepts AmEx/MC/V.

Ticket Agencies: Lan Chile, Tomás Rogers 78 (☎411 236), flies out of Punta Arenas, but the local office is helpful for questions. **DAP** has no official office, but tickets to El Calafate, ARG can be purchased from **Turismo Natales,** on Bulnes and Ladrilleros.

Laundromat: Catch, Bories 218 (☎ 411 520), takes about 2-3hr. CH$1000 per kg; CH$3500 for a full load. Open 9am-10pm.

Supermarket: Super, on the corner of Esmeralda and Blanco Encalada, has more options and better prices than other markets in town. Open 9am-10pm.

Equipment Rental: Many hostels offer reasonable equipment at fair prices. Check out the yellow Internet office, @, Bulnes 368, for tents, sleeping bags, stoves, and mats.

Emergency: ☎ 131

Police: ☎ 133 or ☎ 411 133

Information: ☎ 139

24-Hour Pharmacy: Puerto Natales runs on a rotating system for all-night pharmacies, so check the schedule at any one. **Farmacia Puerto Natales,** Esmeralda 701 (☎ 411 306), is central. Open 9:30am-1pm and 3-10:30pm.

Internet Access: Although many offices offer Internet access, finding a reliable and inexpensive service can be a challenge. **ForTaleza,** Blanco Encalada 170, is popular and has usually fast connections. CH$1000 per hr. Open 10am-11pm. **Patagoni@ Net,** Blanco Encalada 330, is comparable, with printing and scanning services as well. Internet CH$1000 per hr. Open 10am-10pm.

Telephones: Telefónica, Blanco Encalada 298, is great for phone calls, but charges a hefty CH$1500 per hr. for Internet access. Open M-F 9am-11:45pm, Sa and Su 10am-11pm. **Entel,** Baquedario 244, just one block north, is generally quieter and cleaner. Open M-Sa 9am-10pm.

Post Office: Correos de Chile, Iberhard 429, on the plaza. Open M-F 8:30am-12:30pm and 2:30-6pm, Sa 9am-12:30pm.

⌂ ACCOMMODATIONS

▓ **Casa Cecilia,** Tomás Rogers 60 (☎/fax 411 797; redcecilia@entelchile.net). Cecilia and her husband have tailored their quaint, clean home to their guests' every need. The new mattresses, open kitchen, welcoming lounge areas, clean bathrooms, and useful information keep visitors coming back for more. Breakfast included. Laundry CH$4000. Camping equipment for rent. Will reserve *refugios* and buses. English, German, and Spanish spoken. Reservations recommended. Dorms CH$6000; matrimonials with private bath CH$30,000. ❷

▓ **Nancy Hospedaje,** Bulnes 343 (☎411 186; www.patagoniadiscovery.cl). Follow the rainbow sign to Nancy's relaxed lodging, with comfortable beds and cozy common spaces. Despite the slightly run-down decor, it remains clean, bright, and friendly, with an airy kitchen, Internet access, and free storage. Breakfast included. 2-4 bed dorms CH$4000 per person. ❷

Magallania, Tomás Rogers 255 (☎414 950). Magallania makes up for its tight bedrooms with a fun common space reminiscent of a college dorm room, featuring eclectic groupings of couches and poster-covered walls. Kitchen facilities and camping available. Dorms CH$3000. Camping CH$2000. ❶

Casa Lili, Bories 153 (☎414 063), by the coast, offers large, well-lit rooms. Although the decor is a little worn, the helpful managers provide information and equipment rental for those heading on to PN Torres del Paine. Luggage storage, laundry, and Internet access available. Breakfast included. Singles and doubles CH$3500 per person. ❶

Danicar, O'Higgins 707 (☎412 170). This centrally located hostel is managed by an entire family. Friendly owners have loads of helpful information on the town and surrounding area. Breakfast included. Doubles and matrimonials CH$3500 per person. ❶

◪ FOOD

▨ el Living, Arturo Prat 156 (☎ 411 140), on the plaza. For a healthy alternative to heavier local cuisine, indulge in the creative vegetarian dishes at el Living. Delicious salads (without mayo; CH$1200-1900) and unique sandwiches (CH$1900-2300) are complemented by the full coffee bar. Daily specials are always fresh, and the lasagna will satisfy any appetite. A leisurely pace and plenty of international magazines make it difficult to leave. Open 11am-10:30pm. ❶

Restaurante Cristal, Bulnes 439 (☎ 411 850). Local families crowd around the long tables at cozy Cristal for a hearty lunch. The basic menu has enough surprises to appeal to adventurous palates, and the substantial half-liter beers (CH$1000) are great for a big thirst. Memorable pork chops (CH$2000) and pan-grilled chicken (CH$2200) come with a salad or potatoes. *Tostados* CH$800. Soups CH$800. Open 11am-midnight. ❷

El Rincón de "Don Chicho" 2, Eberhard 169. Generous, delicious meals make up for the ambience—or lack thereof—supplied by the fake fire and rustic bar-hut. Salads (CH$700) and cream soups (CH$800) are great for a snack, but heaping portions of grilled pork, chicken, beef, and sausage in the *Tenedor Libre* (CH$5000) are the true highlight. Decent pizzas CH$1800-3600. Open 11am-4pm and 7pm-midnight. ❸

Restaurant Última Esperanza, Eberhard 354 (☎ 413 626 or 411 630). Esperanza serves good portions of some of the best seafood in town in a slightly upscale ambience. The chicken *cazuela* (CH$2400) or the *bife de lomo* (CH$3500) are good options for meat lovers, but the real treats are the salmon and the *centolla* (crab; CH$4500). Open 11am-midnight. ❷

El Marítimo, Pedro Montt 214 (☎/fax 410 819). Specializing in seafood but also offering beef and chicken dishes, Marítimo is often recommended by locals. The bay views and helpful waitstaff add to the lively atmosphere, but tables can be hard to come by. *Centolla* CH$5000, *lomo* CH$4000. Open noon to midnight. ❸

Concepto Indigo, Ladrilleros 105 (☎ 413 609; www.conceptoindigo.com), at the port. The large windows overlooking the bay make this a picturesque spot for an afternoon coffee (CH$800). Although the pies, cakes, and cookies are tasty, indulge in one of Indigo's famous brownies. The rest of the menu is pricey, but delicious and creatively presented. Outdoor climbing wall. Open 11am-11pm. ❸

◉ SIGHTS AND TOURS

The sights around Puerto Natales are rather limited, but one particularly fascinating attraction is the **Cueva del Milodón,** a cave containing the skeleton of an enormous pre-historic ground sloth, discovered by Hermann Eberhard in 1890. Today, a reconstructed Milodón towers over visitors to the cave. The **Museo de Sitio** offers further information about the harmless beast and the era it lived in. Some tour companies offer trips to the cave, but taxis are more flexible. (Open 8am-8pm. CH$5000 entrance fee to the cave, CH$10,000 for up to 4 people.)

A wide variety of **guided tours** are available in Puerto Natales. A relaxed full-day bus tour of **PN Torres del Paine** gives an excellent taste of the park without the work of trekking. (Tours 7:30am-7:30pm. CH$18,000 plus CH$6500 park admission.) A boat trip and short hike around Serrano or Balmacera has spectacular views of nearby fjords and the glacier. (Tours daily 8am-5pm. CH$35,000.) A tour to **Perito Moreno** glacier and **El Calafate, Argentina** is a 12-hour trip—a 10-hour round-trip boat ride with 2 hours to observe one of the most magnificent glaciers in the world. (Tours 7am-10pm. CH$30,000 plus ARG$5 park entrance fee.) The two trips offered to the **Estancia Rosario,** just across the bay, give a good taste of life on a Patagonian ranch. The lunch trip includes a full *asado*. (Tours 12:30-4:30pm. CH$12,500.) Some trips only have a snack, but leave more time for exploring the ranch. (Tours 2-6pm.)

Most of these tours are offered by all of the agencies, but **Path@gone** (see **Practical Information,** p. 469) comes highly recommended. For more high-paced tours, **Big Foot** (see **Practical Information,** p. 469) has a three-day sea kayaking tour to or from the national park (US$380), but requires two days lead time to prepare. Big Foot also offers guided and plush tours of the park with food, camp, guides, and equipment for seven or more days, starting at US$690 per person for larger groups. **Onas** (see **Practical Information,** p. 469) also has kayak tours of Serrano River, starting at US$150 per person for two days. The most thrilling adventure may be the zodiac tour that includes the Serrano Glacier, the Serrano River, and some sea lions. (Tours 8am-8pm. US$85.)

PARQUE NACIONAL TORRES DEL PAINE

As the southernmost park in Chile, Parque Nacional Torres del Paine is the longtime mecca of South American outdoor adventure. The park's main focal point is its eerie landscape, with the enormous granite towers that give it its name. The grand circuit that was once the only option for visitors has now become more manageable for less serious hikers because of frequent organized tours, which include magnificent shorter hikes and excursions. The famous "W" hike, boat trips, horseback riding, glacier trekking, and even one-hour walks permit a wide variety of travelers to be enchanted by the dramatic landscape.

◪ TRANSPORTATION

From Torres to **Puerto Natales, Buses JB** leaves from: the **Conaf administration office** (1:45 and 6:30pm, CH$3000); **Lago Pehoé** (2:30 and 7pm, CH$3000); and **Laguna Armaga** (3:30 and 7:30pm, CH$3000). **Pancheco** and **Bus Sur** leave from: the **Conaf administration office** (2:45pm); **Lago Pehoé** (1:30pm); **Laguna Amarga** (12:30pm). There are also shuttles that meet arriving and departing buses at **Laguna Armaga** to transport visitors to **Hostería and Camping Las Torres** (CH$3500 round-trip).

By **boat,** the **Hielos Patagónicos** crosses Lago Pehoé three times per day in the summer, less frequently off-season. Leaving from **Refugio Pudeto,** the boat offers amazing views (30min.; 9:30am, noon, 6pm; returns 10am, 12:30, 6:30pm; CH$9000). From the **Hostería Lago Grey** (see below), a three-hour tour of Lago Grey goes to the glacier and back (CH$30,000).

Horses are available for rent at the Conaf (CH$15,000 and up per hour).

AT A GLANCE	
AREA: 181,000 hectares.	**GATEWAYS:** Puerto Natales, Punto Arenas.
CLIMATE: Strong winds throughout the year. Mean summer temperature is 11°C. Average rainfall 700mm per year. Altitude from 50m to 3000m above sea level.	**HIGHLIGHTS:** Wildlife including guanacos, ñandús, condors, mountain lions, foxes, and a variety of birds. Glaciers, lakes, lagoons, rivers, and the famous granite towers.
CAMPING: Various privately owned campsites throughout the park. Some free camping possible.	**FEATURES:** Paine Massif, Paine Grande, "Cuernos del Paine", Salto Grande, Salto Chico.
FEES: Park entrance CH$6500.	

✦ ORIENTATION

A good dirt road follows much of the southern portion of the park and reaches a number of nice hotels and other service points of the park. Of the two entrances, **Laguna Armaga** is a more common starting point, as it is near the major trailhead, but the **Conaf administration office** is a good entrance for visitors who are not traveling the circuit. **Lago Pehoé** is also an important point, with its regular ferry that visitors use at the beginning of the "W" trek.

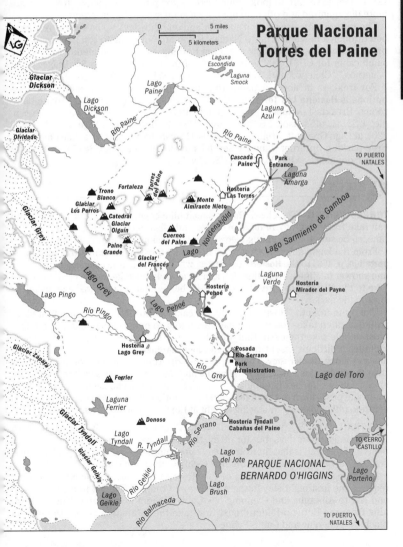

Parque Nacional
Torres del Paine

0   5 miles
0   5 kilometers

Glaciar Dickson

Laguna Escondida

Lago Paine

Laguna Smock

Lago Dickson

Laguna Azul

Glaciar Olvidado

Río Paine

Río Paine

Cascada Paine

Park Entrance

TO PUERTO NATALES

Laguna Amarga

Fortaleza

Torres del Paine

Trono Blanco

Hostería Las Torres

Glaciar Los Perros

Monte Almirante Nieto

Catedral

Glaciar Olguín

Lago Sarmiento de Gamboa

Glaciar Grey

Cuernos del Paine

Paine Grande

Glaciar del Francés

Lago Nordenskjöld

Laguna Verde

Hostería Mirador del Payne

Lago Pingo

Hostería Pehoé

Río Pingo

Lago Grey

Lago Pehoé

Glaciar Zapata

Hostería Lago Grey

Posada Río Serrano

Park Administration

Lago del Toro

Ferrier

Río Grey

Laguna Ferrier

Glaciar Tyndall

Donoso

Hostería Tyndall Cabañas del Paine

TO CERRO CASTILLO

Lago Tyndall

R. Tyndall

Río Serrano

Lago del Jote

PARQUE NACIONAL BERNARDO O'HIGGINS

Lago Porteño

Glaciar Geikie

Río Geikie

Lago Brush

Lago Geikie

Río Balmaceda

TO PUERTO NATALES

ACCOMMODATIONS

Within the park there are many lodging options, ranging from free campsites to luxury hotels starting at US$500 per night. Campsites at **Camping Las Torres ❶**, located at Hostería Las Torres (see below), are free. **Camping Lago Pehoé ❶**, at the east end of its namesake lake, is another central site. **Camping Pass ❶**, **Las Carreteras ❶**, and **Camping Los Guardes ❶**, on the Torres Circuit (see p. 474) are free; others on this loop, including **Camping Seron ❶**, **Camping Dickson ❶**, and **Los Perros ❶**, cost CH$2250 per person and have small shops that charge steep prices for extra food. Take care to look around before you pitch your tent, as free sites are more disorganized and often do not have a good system for bathrooms.

The *refugios* are crowded in summer and on rainy days, so be sure to reserve a bed through a hostel in Puerto Natales if you are not going to bring a tent. These privately run, rustic lodgings are often nothing more than a mediocre bed in a small cabin for CH$15,000. A bed at one of the three **Fantástico Sur Lodges ❸**, at "Cuernos," "Chileno," and "Las Torres," costs US$17 per night.

For trekkers in need of pampering after the tough trails, a more luxurious options is **Hostería Las Torres ❺**, Ruta 9 norte km 387. (☎226 054. Private bathrooms. Breakfast included. Free parking. Internet, laundry services available. Singles US$131, off-season US$79; doubles US$149/89.) **Hostería Lago Grey ❺** (☎410 220), at Lago Grey, offers similar services. (Private bathrooms. Breakfast included. Free parking. Internet, laundry services available. Singles US$173, off-season US$82; doubles US$199/95; triples US$228/109.)

HIKES

TORRES CIRCUIT. The classic **Torres circuit** hike begins at the **Laguna Armaga** and can take from seven to 10 days. Weather and blisters can easily add unexpected time, so be sure to have enough leeway and provisions to enjoy the hike.

From the Laguna Armaga, many visitors take the 30-minute minibus (see **transportation**, p. 469) to the **Hostería Las Torres,** where there is free **camping**, bathrooms, and shower facilities. From this site, almost all trekkers take the seven-hour return hike to the **Mirador Las Torres** (see "W" trek, below), one of the most awe-inspiring sites in the park.

The route from the Hostería Las Torres campsite to Glacier Grey is a four-stage path that often takes four to five days, with four to nine hours of hiking each day. Most people take the extra time to split up the final nine-hour stage, because it includes a difficult assent through the **John Gardner Pass** and the equally trying descent along **Glacier Grey**. The simple side trip from Camp Dickson that reaches **Lago Quemodo** adds a day. From **Albergue** and **Camping Glacier Grey,** the rest of the circuit follows the newly popular "W" trail. Some hikers choose not to follow this route and push down to **Lago Pehoé** and then another five hours to the Conaf administration office, passing or staying a night at the free campsite at **Las Carretas.**

"W" TRAIL. The "W" trail can be hiked in either direction. It is possible to rush through in just four days, but for many, the trek is better enjoyed in five. A major benefit of this trail is that there are many opportunities to leave a full pack at camp and use only a day pack to see the real focal points of the park.

Beginning from **Laguna Armaga** or the Hostería Los Torres is simple, but often requires the first night stay in the Albergue or Camping Chileno to make the second day to Albergue and Camping Los Cuervos more manageable. Those beginning from the Refugio Pudeto must first take the catamaran across the lake to reach the Albergue and Camp Pehoé.

The first stage runs along **Lago Grey** to the Albergue and Camping Grey. From the campsite, the rocky points that face the enormous glacier are only 15 minutes farther and other spectacular views from above the glacier are only another hour. If you are trying to do the "W" in four days, you will need to take the noon boat and return to Lago Pehoé with little time at the glacier in order to avoid walking after sunset.

From Lago Grey, return to Lago Pehoé and continue east to **Campamento Italiano** or push on up the **Valle de Frances** to the **Campamento Británico** if your legs aren't sore. If you stay at Italiano, the next day is a six-hour return hike up the valley with magestic views of the horns and backs of the towers, but it is best to press on for two hours more to the **Albergue** and **Camping Los Cuervos.**

The next stage can take you to **Albergue and Camping Chileno** in six hours or the free **Campamento Torres,** only one hour further. The second option will permit a short but cumbersome morning climb to the base of the ring of towers for what will easily be the highlight of any trek. This *mirador* can get crowded and even noisy during the day, but these distractions hardly detract from the three powerful batholith peaks.

TORRES DEL PAINE MIRADOR TRAIL. This trail is essentially the final leg of the "W" trail, but begins and ends near the manicured Hostería Las Torres, winding up the **Río Asencio** before turning up a steep and time-consuming boulder field. The first two hours are on a moderate uphill trail followed by a much calmer wooded and exposed trail. The final hour up the neck-wrenching crest should be taken with care, as there is no single path and some boulders are not completely secure. It is a spectacular place to rest and think, so a box lunch is almost obligatory.

SENDERO MIRADOR CUERNOS AND OTHERS. This very short hike is extremely rewarding, since it places visitors in the beaming glow of the Central Horn after only a one-hour walk. The hike begins just above the **Refugio Pudeto** after a short walk along a dirt road. The **Salto Grande** waterfall, only 15 minutes from the Refugio, marks the beginning of the walk and is a nice bonus walk for those waiting for the catamaran. Many day trips to the park are sure to include this easy walk. Other hikes in the park include the three-day trip to **Lago Pingo,** west of Lago Grey, and the short trip to **Laguna Verde.**

BORDER CROSSING INTO ARGENTINA: CANCHA CARRERA
Heading north from Puerto Natales to Parque Nacional Torres del Paine, the road branches off of at Km 65 to Villa Cerro Castillo. The frontier road continues on from there to Ruta 40, the main road north to El Calafate. The customs office at Cerro Castillo is open from 7am-11pm. The process is fairly simple and involves no more than a brief search of your luggage for contraband and various food products and a passport stamp (see **Essentials: Border Crossings,** p. 65, for info on visas and fees).

EL CALAFATE, ARGENTINA ☎ 02902

Sitting between the rough Patagonian plains and the craggy edges of the Andean range, El Calafate provides a minor break from the relentless elements. Tucked just south of Lago Argentino, El Calafate has relatively calm breezes and good views. Its position near the astonishing Perito Moreno glacier and the Fitz Roy range has built up a relatively organized tourism trade, but there are plenty of reasonable options left for the informal adventure seeker.

FROM THE ROAD

PATAGONIAN PEACE

After a six-hour bus ride, I arrived in El Calafate with a friend I had met in Puerto Natales. Hours staring across the lonely Patagonian plains on the rocky road had put me in a daze. I sat down for a coffee while my friend went to check email. While I waited, I watched the lazy clouds tumble and unfold under the merciless winds.

"This is a great place to be alone," the waiter broke in, as he placed my cup on the table. Although I explained that I was with someone, he continued, "No, you haven't been here long enough—you'll see."

Looking back on my couple of weeks in Tierra del Fuego and Torres del Paine, I can begin to understand what he meant. Although buses and hostels were full of other adventure-seekers, the landscape of the far reaches of South America had impressed upon me a peaceful solitude—the unrelenting winds and glacial rivers seemed to have swept everything else away.

I now understand why European pioneers who came to this region are often depicted as weathered, weary, and almost always alone. I began to think that their distant stare was an attempt to reconcile the massive expanse around them and accept the personal endurance required to survive within it.

Today, this region remains a powerful collection of nature's mighty forces that inevitably affect every person who traverses the region. The opportunity to single-handedly brave the intensity of the Patagonia brings out the fortitude and integrity in anyone—surrender to this transforming experience.

—Alex Leary

⌐ TRANSPORTATION

Flights: El Calafate's new **airport** is about 15min. from town. **Remises** will shuttle up to 4 people to or from the airport (ARG$14). **Aerobus** (☎492 492) also shuttles passengers for ARG$5 and waits for incoming flights. Tickets for **Aerolineas Argentinas** can be purchased at **Rumbo Sur** (see **Ticket Agencies** in Practical Information, p. 477) for trips to: **Bariloche, ARG** (W and Sa 8:30pm, ARG$131); **Buenos Aires, ARG** (7:15pm, ARG$108); **Trelew, ARG** (M, Tu, Sa 7:15pm; ARG$140); **Ushuaia, ARG** (3:15pm, ARG$78). **LAPA,** San Martín 1015 (☎491 171), flies to: **Buenos Aires, ARG** (3:15 and 3:45pm, ARG$108); **Puerto Madryn, ARG** (Su 1:15pm, ARG$140); **Ushuaia, ARG** (M-Sa 3:15pm, ARG$85). The only international flight is with **DAP** to **Puerto Natales** (M-F 10am in summer, US$60). There is a ARG$20 **departure tax** for international flights and a ARG$7 one for domestic flights, paid at the airport.

Buses: Buses arrive and depart from the orderly **bus station** on Julio Roca, up the stairs from Av. San Martín. All bus companies have desks in the terminal; many have offices in town as well. Many companies serving El Chaltén give a ARG$5 discount if you purchase an open return with them, but be sure they have the return time you want. **Cootra** (☎491 444) goes to **Puerto Natales** (5½hr., 6am, ARG$25). **Interlagos** (☎491 179) heads to **El Chaltén, ARG** (8am and 6pm, ARG$25) and **Río Gallegos, ARG** (2½hr., 8am and 3pm, ARG$20). Ask for the 10% student discount. **Tasqua** (☎491 843) goes to **El Calafate, ARG** (7:30am and 2pm, ARG$25) and **Río Gallegos, ARG** (2½hr.; 3, 8am, 2:45pm; ARG$25). **Chaltén Travel** (☎491 833) sends buses to **El Chaltén, ARG** (8am and 6pm, returns at 7am and 6pm; ARG$25) and along **Route 40** to **Perito Moreno, ARG** and **Los Antigos, ARG** (15hr.; northbound on odd number days, southbound on even days at 8am; ARG$88). **Los Glacieres** (☎492 212) goes to **El Chaltén** (7:30am and 5:30pm, returns 5:30pm and 3:30am).

⬥ 🛈 ORIENTATION AND PRACTICAL INFORMATION

The main avenue, **Av. del Libertador General José de San Martín,** is locally known simply as Libertador or San Martín. A majority of the town's services line this street, and nearly everything else worth seeing is within easy walking distance. The **bus station** sits atop this hill with convenient access to town.

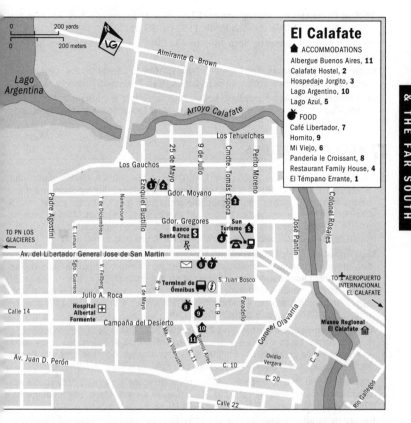

Tourist Office: Roca 1004 (☎491 090), in the bus terminal. Has helpful pamphlets and books of hostels and restaurants to peruse. Open 9am-9pm.

Tours: Many hostels and bus companies will sell tickets for trips to **Glacier Perito Moreno** and other excursions. **Sur Turismo,** 25 de Mayo 23 (☎491 266; www.surturismo.com.ar), has a wide range of options, mostly formal excursions to lakes and *estancias* in the area. Although glacier "minitrekking" seems available everywhere, **Hielo y Aventura,** San Martín 935 (☎492 205), runs hikes on Perito Moreno.

Currency Exchange: Many large shops on San Martín offer poor to moderate rates for US dollars and traveler's checks. Try **Thayler,** San Martín 1309. Open M-Sa 10am-noon and 5-8pm.

ATM: Banco Santa Cruz, 24 de Mayo 22, takes MC/V.

Ticket Agencies: Rumbo Sur, San Martín 960 (☎492 155), sells Aerolineas Argentinas and DAP tickets.

Laundromat: Lavadería, 25 de Mayo 43, in back of the shopping area, cleans a load in about 2hr. for ARG$7. Open M-Sa 8:30am-12:30pm and 3-8:30pm, Su 4-8:30pm.

Supermarket: ALAS, 9 de Julio 71, has the widest selection in town and many goodies for the trail.

Emergency: ☎ 101.

24-Hour Pharmacy: The rotating system of 24hr. pharmacies prevails here, so check the list at **Farmacia El Calafate,** San Martín 1192 (☎493 311).

Hospital: Albertal Formente, Roca 1487 (☎491 001), is just down the street from the bus terminal.

Internet and Telephones: The large and busy **Telefónica Locutorio,** San Martín 996, has 8 admittedly slow machines. ARG$3 per hr. Open 7:30am-12:30pm.

Post Office: Correo Argentina, San Martín 1102, at the foot of the stairs to the bus terminal. Open M-F 9am-4pm and Sa 9am-1pm. Most tourist shops that sell postcards also sell stamps.

ACCOMMODATIONS

Calafate Hostel, Moyano 1226 (☎492 450). Often filled with Argentine youths and weary Europeans, the long halls and sunny common space of this log-cabin hostel are always clean and buzzing. With reasonable promotions for trips to the glacier and El Chaltén, the friendly front desk staff doubles as a budget travel agent. Kitchen, Internet access, free shuttle from local bus station. Reservations recommended in Jan. and Feb. 4-bed dorms ARG$12, with private bath ARG$15. HI discount available. ❶

Lago Argentina, Campaña del Desierto 1050 (☎491 423), near the bus station. Argentina provides basic accommodations with tight rooms and concrete bathrooms. The small common area stocks plenty of information, but some of it is outdated. The larger private singles, doubles, and triples are worth the extra cash. Lockable personal storage, laundry, room service. 4-bed dorms ARG$6; singles with bath ARG$30; doubles with bath ARG$40; triples with bath ARG$50. ❶

Albergue Buenos Aires, Buenos Aires 296 (☎491 147). The large and quiet accommodations are run by an informative, friendly owner. The dark wood and low lights make the hostel a little dreary, but add to the relaxed atmosphere. Common area with TV and kitchen access. 4-bed dorms ARG$12; doubles with private bath ARG$40. ❶

Lago Azul, Perito Moreno 83 (☎491 419). This small house run by an elderly couple has a laid-back, homey feel, with pictures of relatives all around. Clean, bright bathrooms. Quiet but central location. 2-bed dorms ARG$10. ❶

Hospedaje Jorgito, Moyano 943 (☎491 323). This family-run *hospedaje* has a variety of small but bright rooms and good garden camping with a covered kitchen. Visitors are often invited to share a cup of tea or relax in the living room. 2- and 3-bed dorms ARG$12; doubles with private bath ARG$30. Camping ARG$6. ❶

FOOD

Café Libertador, San Martín 1101. The simple, family atmosphere at this central cafe compliments the cheap and varied dishes. Jovial service all day and into the night. Omelettes ARG$6, salmon with fries ARG$8, garlic and parsley chicken ARG$7. Open 7am-1am. ❶

El Témpano Errante, Mayano 1226, in the Calafate Hostel. The relaxed atmosphere, enthusiastic service, and home-cooking with a twist make this one of the best restaurants in town. The excellent "chop suey" incorporates stir-fried peppers, zucchini, and carrots with chicken, pork, or beef and plenty of soy sauce (ARG$8). The *bife de chorizo* is also a hearty choice (ARG$10). Open 8am-11:30pm. ❶

Restaurante Family House, Comadante Espora 18 (☎492 156). Although the inexpensive chicken and salad (ARG$6.50) may attract your eye, local *platos* such as the *bife de chorizo* (ARG$8) have a much better chance of filling your tummy. The seafood is a bit pricier (ARG$9), but a nice alternative to classic Argentine beef dishes. Open noon-midnight. ❶

Mi Viejo, San Martín 1111. Inside the bright yellow building, the simple *tenedor libre* heaps grilled chicken, lamb, pork, and beef on your plate (ARG$11) until you are stuffed. Fresh veggies fill the salad bar, but the focus is on the typical Argentine *asado*. Be sure to tell the waiter your preferences. Pasta and other limited options available. Open noon-1am. ❶

Hornito, Buenos Aires 155, near the bus terminal. This pizza restaurant offers a slight variation on the normally greasy Argentine pies. Simple cheese crepes (ARG$6-7) are a good snack, but the pastas are more satisfying (ARG$6-9). The set *menú* (ARG$7) has a simple pizza and basic dessert. Pizzas ARG$7-15. Open 10am-1am.

Panadería le Croissant, on the corner of Buenos Aires and Roca, right next to the bus terminal. The friendly bakery has many sweet treats to begin your day or to pack for a long bus ride. The prepared sandwiches, made fresh daily, are more appetizing than the hot take-out food. Open 7am-11pm.

🎯 SIGHTS

RESERVA LAGUNA NIMEZ. The new **Reserva Laguna Nimez,** a short walk north of town, protects an enormous collection of local birds. The powerful breezes off of Lago Argentino and the open vistas of the distant mountains make visitors feel like they are back in the patagonian climate. The entire circuit around the *reserva* takes about 45 minutes to complete and passes through the feeding grounds for a whole range of local birds. (*Head away from town on Ezequiel Bustillo for three blocks, go left for half a block, and cross the only bridge. Continue north another five minutes, take a right and a quick left, then continue for another block. ARG$1. Unnecessary auto guide ARG$1.*)

PERITO MORENO. As one of the world's few advancing glaciers, **Perito Moreno** is clearly the number one sight for visitors in El Calafate. Located one and a half hours west of town, the glacier attracts endless buses packed with national and international visitors. With only a short boat "safari" to the face of the southern wall (purchase at the park; ARG$20), the full-day excursion is usually spent walking the well-maintained decks waiting for the inevitable cracking and breaking-off of chunks of ice. On sunny days, this is an especially relaxing daytrip to watch an exquisite force of nature at work. Glacier trekking is available (see **Tours,** p. 477.) Almost every tour office, bus office, and hostel sells transport to the glacier for ARG$25—ask for student discounts. Simple food is available at the cafeteria, but a packed lunch is best enjoyed watching the glacier. (*ARG$5.*)

GUIDED TOURS. 4x4 tours for three hours (ARG$10) or seven hours (ARG$100 with lunch) ride along the tough terrain, but usually don't pass by much flora or fauna. Tours on the great Lago Argentina go for ARG$171, while a trip to Lago Roca is only ARG$40. To see a well-polished ranch, visit **Estancia Alice** for ARG$40 or pretend to be a gaucho on full-day horse rides around **Cerro Frias** for ARG$55. A short and perhaps unnecessary **city tour** is also available (two and a half hours, ARG$25).

"**Minitrekking**" is probably the most intense guided tour available, as it takes you across the southern Brazo Rico lake and up on the Perito Moreno glacier, a five-hour tour of the rivers, lakes, and paths that run throughout the glacier. (*Daily at 8:30 and 10am. ARG$90 plus ARG$5 park admission.*) On the "**Safari Nautico,**" a 130-person boat cruises along the southern arm of the glacier for astonishing vistas of the glacial ice towers. (*One-hour tour, 11am and 4pm. Tickets ARG$20, available at the dock.*)

EL CHALTÉN, ARGENTINA ☎02962

At the foot of the striking Monte Fitz Roy, El Chaltén is a charming mountain village perfect for hiking and relaxing. Although it has only 300 permanent residents, El Chaltén has actually been declared the trekking capital of Argentina. Lying almost on the trailhead itself, it is an excellent hub from which to explore the pristine paths of Parque Nacional Los Glacieres.

▐ TRANSPORTATION

Most buses head to and from El Calafate, so most visitors book return trips before leaving for El Chaltén (see p. 476). If you have an open return ticket, be sure to notify the company you are traveling with when you plan to leave to be sure they will have a seat for you at that time.

The following companies go to **El Calafate: Chaltén Travel,** from Rancho Grande Hostel (7am and 6pm, ARG$25); **Interlagos,** from the Fitz Roy Inn (8am and 6pm, ARG$25); and **Tasqua,** from Pangea (7:30am, ARG$25). Chaltén Travel also goes north to **Perito Moreno** and **Lagos Antiguos** (15 hours, leaving on odd number days and returning on even days 8am, ARG$68). It is easy to cross over to Chile Chico in the southern region of the Aisén region of Chile.

▐▐ ORIENTATION AND PRACTICAL INFORMATION

Güemes, a main street running through the heart of town, is perpedicular to **Lago del Desierto.** A block to the right is the beginning of the other main stretch, **San Martín.** Many points of interest lay around Lago del Desierto, but San Martín also has a number of hostels and services. Most buildings are *sin numero* (without a number), but everyone knows where to find most shops and offices.

Tourist Office: First building on the left on Güemes. Has most basic information. **Rancho Grande** also serves as a good information source.

Tours: MRZ, San Martín 493 (☎493 098). Very helpful, with a wide range of tours. Open M-Sa 8:30am-12:30pm and 5-9:30pm. Also try **Fitz Roy Expeditions** (☎493 017), on Güemes, and **Camino Abierto Expedition** (☎493 043), on Cronnel Terray.

Currency Exchange: There is **no ATM, bank,** or **currency exchange** in El Chaltén. **Ranch Grande** does exchange traveler's checks, but at poor rates.

Laundry: Lavandería Isabel, on San Martín, will do a load for ARG$8 in half a day.

Supermarket: El Gringuito, on San Martín before Rancho Grande, has a decent selection, with fresh fruit and veggies. Also try **Supermercado,** at the corner of Lago del Desierto and Güemes.

Equipment Rental: Vicento Oeste (☎493 021), at the far end of Av. San Martín, rents sleeping bags (ARG$4 per night), stoves (ARG$2), tents (ARG$10-12), and other camping equipment.

Emergency: ☎101

Pharmacy: Farmacia del Cerro, Halvor Halvorsen (☎493 911), has limited selection. Open M-Sa 10am-1pm and 3-9pm.

Hospital: El Chaltén Hospital, between Adalas and De Agostini.

Internet Access: Although the town doesn't have a public site, go to **Zafarrancho Bar** to send an email from their account (ARG$1).

Telephones: Try **Telefónica,** on Güemes, but expect to wait almost a minute to make the initial connection.

Post Office: The tourist office also sells stamps and will send out packages, but anywhere that sells postcards can also sell stamps and send your message on its way.

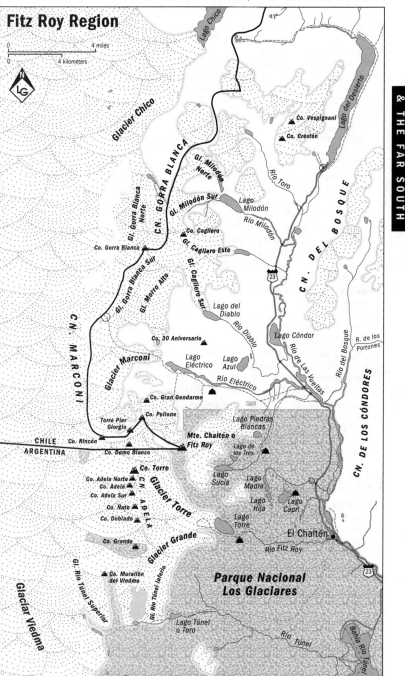

Fitz Roy Region

ACCOMMODATIONS

Rancho Grande (☎ 493 005), on San Martín. The massive common space doubles as an informal cafe and living room. The large 4-bunk dorm rooms and the bathrooms are kept sparkling clean, and the friendly staff knows the answer to almost any travel question. Reservations recommended in Jan. and Feb. Dorms ARG$10; doubles with bath ARG$45; triples ARG$70; quads ARG$80. ❶

Albergue Patagonia (☎ 493 019), on San Martín, at the crest of the hill. The small house packs a lot of beds into its tiny but adequate rooms. A comfy common space, kitchen, and library are added perks. Owner is a great source of information. The restaurant next door also gives guests a 10% discount. 4-6 person dorms ARG$12; HI members ARG$10. ❶

Familio Trajo (☎ 493 046), on San Martín, just past Rancho Grande. Beyond the drab concrete exterior, quaint rooms are attended by a warm family. This new hostel may not be as flashy as its neighbor, but is a great spot for a good night's sleep before hitting the park. Dorms ARG$10; doubles with private bath ARG$30. ❶

Condor de los Andes (☎ 493 101), at the corner of Río de las Vuelatas and Halvorsen. Often filled with Argentine students, the Condor welcomes all visitors. To escape the tight 6-person dorms, you will want to spend most of your time in the spacious front room with a fireplace and open kitchen. Some simple meals available. Dorms ARG$12; HI members ARG$10. ❶

Hostería Lo Nires (☎ 493 009), on Lago del Desierto. Most of the basic but cozy rooms with private bathrooms have views of the Fitz Roy peaks. The starker dorm rooms have kitchen access and more limited views of the range. Dorms ARG$12, HI members ARG$11, without sheets ARG$10; matrimonials ARG$60; doubles with private bath ARG$60; triples ARG$70. ❶

Albergue Del Lago (☎ 493 010). In lieu of a common area, most visitors spend time hanging out in the open kitchen. Rooms are small and there are occasionally lines for the bathrooms, but the jovial manager keeps all guests happy with smiles and advice. 4-5-bed dorms ARG$10, with sheets ARG$12. ❶

La Base (☎ 493 031), on Lago del Desierto. The cabin-like accommodations are great for groups because of the private bathrooms and common kitchen. Enjoy views of Fitz Roy during the day and peruse the enormous collection of videos in the main building after the sun goes down. Off-season discounts available. Doubles ARG$50; triples ARG$60; quads ARG$72. ❷

FOOD

Zafarrancho, on Leone II Terray, behind Rancho Grande. The "music bar" doesn't actually have live tunes, but the eclectic selection of music goes well with the creative dishes. Sample the carrot and pumpkin soup (ARG$4) or savory lamb stew (ARG$12). The chef adds an international flair with Mexican specialties like cheese quesadillas (ARG$5) and heaping nachos (ARG$7) and the Italian basics of pizza (ARG$9-13) and pasta (ARG$10). Once a week, two movies are projected in the great open space, beginning at midnight. Open 12:30pm-late. ❶

Patagonicu's, at Güemes and Madsen. Behind the massive wood door, a welcoming staff serves good pizzas (large ARG$9-16) and pastas (ARG$8). The *bife de chorizo* (ARG$7) goes well with their range of wines (ARG$1.50-35). Open noon-1am. ❶

Pangea, at Lago del Desierto and San Martín. Although pizzas (ARG$4-14) and chicken (ARG$6) are rather unexciting, the massive and juicy *bife de chorizo* (ARG$7) will challenge any hearty appetite. Salads ARG$4. Open noon-midnight. ❶

Casita, mid-way down San Martín. This little restaurant offers the classic *asado* and other basic options. The long menu has few surprises, with chicken (ARG$8) and lamb (ARG$10) as the major options. Basic continental breakfast ARG$5. Open 8:30am-midnight. ❶

⊙ SIGHTS

PARQUE NACIONAL LOS GLACIERES. Dominated by the massive Upsula glacier, this national park is largely inaccessible for extensive hiking. The Perito Moreno glacier is in the southern sector, but it is only from El Chaltén that managed trails carve into the park. In the north, the two major sights of **Fitz Roy** and **Cerro Torre** attract visitors. Although most trails are return hikes to and from El Chaltén, the terrain and views vary so much that it is necessary to see every trail twice to fully appreciate it. All the water in the park is currently potable; visitors are asked to stay 100m away from water to use the bathroom in order to keep it that way.

CERRO TORRE MIRADOR (LAGO TORRE). Easily handled in a daytrip, this relaxing trail follows the Río Fitz Roy to reach Lago Torre and the needle-shaped Cerro Torre. Up San Martín, a massive sign directs you left to the trail. The first hour is a slow climb through rough grass, briefly dipping down before rising again to catch a glimpse of the beautiful vista ahead. Across a peaceful but muddy plain, the cut-off to Fitz Roy is past the Tres Lagunas. The path then moves toward the river, skirting another hill before opening to a massive rock field. To the left among the trees is **Camp D'Agostini,** an excellent but sometimes busy campsite, where glacial rivers sing guests to sleep. Another 15 minutes will bring you to Laguna Torre. There is no formal *mirador*, but many follow the ridge on the right side of the lake to get a closer look. Cerro Torre usually hides behind white cloud wisps even when the rest of the park is sunny. A night at D'Agostini gives you a better chance to see the peak.

FITZ ROY LOOKOUT. This return hike is a long, full-day walk, but almost obligatory for anyone able to do it. Similar to the Torres Mirador hike, the final section is a difficult scramble up boulders, but it delivers you to an astonishing peak-encircled bowl. Beginning at the far end of San Martín in town, the first hour carves up green wooded paths before setting into a more moderate climb up along a small stream. Signs will direct you left toward **Camp Capri,** but continue on through the pastures and occasionally wooded stretches. At the end of a thick forest of tall trees, **Camp Poincenot** offers sheltered campsites with easy access to Río Blanco for water. Over the river and through the woods, **Camp Río Blanco** waits for mountaineers attempting to summit some of the park's major peaks; casual hikers should not camp here. Once you emerge from this final thicket, an imposing stack of boulders greet you to the final one and a half hours of work before the vista. Take this section slowly, as the stones are not always stable and there is no single path. From the crest, the centerpiece of the park boasts in all its glory with a number of other famous peaks by its side. If you plan to rest for some time, it is best to seek some break from the relentless winds down in the bowl.

OTHER HIKES IN FITZ ROY. Some visitors travel to both Fitz Roy and Cerro Torre in one multi-day trip without returning to El Chaltén by using the Laguna de los Tres path, which is about an hour-long walk with excellent views of the lush area around the ponds. It is also possible to push down the boulder-covered river bed of Río Blanco from camp Poincenot before cutting up to Río Electrico

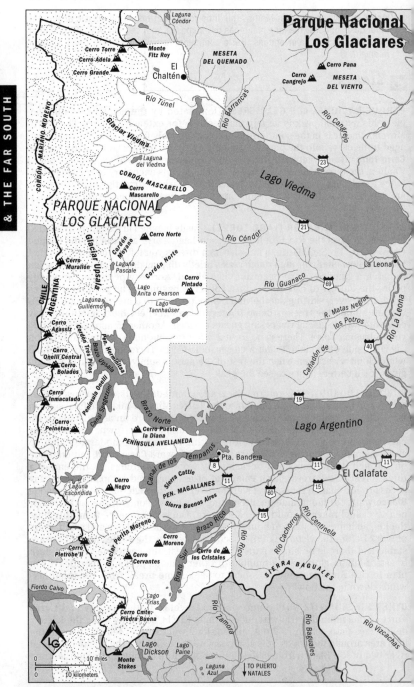

Parque Nacional Los Glaciares

and making a half-circle around Fitz Roy. The final portion of this three- to four-day trip is on private property, but you are welcome use to the path with a one-night stay at **Piedra del Fraile.** This trek can also begin after a ride up to the meeting of Río de las Vueltas and Río Electrico and then down to camp Poincenot before returning to town. Finally, there is a path south of town to **Lago Toro** and its less impressive glacier. The six hours each way requires an overnight stay, but the simple beauty of the entire walk and the relative solitude is just right for some visitors.

■ GUIDED TOURS

The most exciting and popular excursion in town is the ice trekking and climbing under Cerro Torre. The pros at **Fitz Roy Expeditions** begin the full-day adventure by traversing a glacial river, later setting out for ice-walking climbing. Begin in El Chaltén at 7:30am or camp below Laguna Torre at Camp D'Agostini in the Fitz Roy mega-tent for free. (Tours ARG$65, lunch not included.) **Camino Abierto Expediciones** offers the same adventure as well as one- to five-day rock climbing courses for as little as ARG$20 per day.

Excursions from **MRZ** include buses to **Lago del Desierto** to see the beautiful lake (9am, ARG$20 round-trip). Horse rides to Río Blanco take the work out of seeing the park (ARG$45). If you want to get even closer to a glacier, take the boat on Lago Viedma to visit the glacial ice caves and enjoy the cosmic blue light from within the glacier. (Tour 8am-3:30pm, ARG$70). **Albergue Patagonia** also rents mountain bikes that are great to bring to Lago del Desierto (ARG$20 per day).

All companies are listed under **Tours,** see p. 480.

WEST TO TIERRA DEL FUEGO

PORVENIR ☎ 61

Usually only a stopover for travelers en route to Ushuaia, Argentina, Porvenir has a peaceful feel that makes for an enjoyable night's stay. The services and attractions of this tiny fishing and sheep-herding town remain quite limited, but the beautiful Plaza de Armas and the waterfront park are worth a look. Beyond that, Porvenir is a tranquil jumping-off point for wilder adventures and excursions into Argentina's southernmost national park, Parque Nacional Tierra de Fuego.

◰ **TRANSPORTATION. DAP,** Manuel Señoret 705, flies to **Punta Arenas** (M-Sa 8am and 9pm, US$23). The **ferry** to **Punta Arenas** usually leaves Tu-Sa at 1 or 2pm and Su at 5pm. To get to the port, take a taxi from town (CH$1500), but plan on leaving early to avoid departure traffic. **Bus Pacheco** heads to **Río Grande** twice a week— stop by the office in the Club Croata, Manuel Señoret 542, to check dates and times. **Local buses** also head to **Cameron** (Tu and F, CH$1000) and **Cerro Sombrero** (M, Tu, F; times vary; CH$2000). Check local bus schedules posted at most hostels.

◰ **PRACTICAL INFORMATION.** The **tourist office,** at the corner of Schythe and Zavattaro, has only limited information, but the staff is very helpful. (☎ 580 098. Open M-F 9am-5pm, Sa-Su 11am-5pm.) **Cordillera Darwin Tours,** Croacia 653 (☎ 580 450), sells: excursions to the Cordillera Darwin (5-day min., US$90 per person per day); fishing and camping trips along the western coast of Tierra del Fuego (3-day

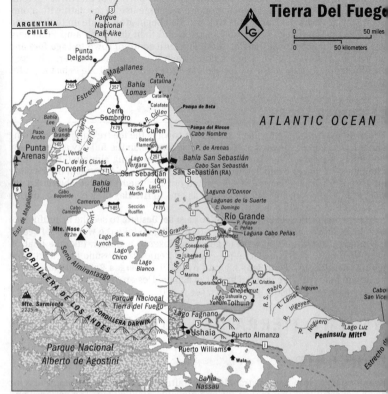

Tierra Del Fuego

min., US$65 per person per day, min. 2-4 people); and horseback excursions to see highlights of the region's gold rush (1 day, US$25). All trips include guides and equipment. **Banco del Estado de Chile,** Phillipi 241, has an **ATM** that accepts Cirrus and MC cards. **Telephones** are available at **Entel,** Phillipi 279. Open 9:30am-11pm. There is no public Internet access in town.

⌂⌂ ACCOMMODATIONS AND FOOD. Most hotels and hostels serve hearty meals at reasonable prices. **Residencial Colón ❷,** Damián Riobó 198, is perpetually full and fun. (☎581 157. Breakfast included. Lunch CH$2000. Dorms CH$4000.) **Hotel España ❷,** Croacia 698, has a greater variety of rooms and friendly management, but slightly uncomfortable beds. (☎580 160. Lunch CH$2300, dinner CH$2800. Dorms CH$5000; doubles with private bath CH$15,000.) All the rooms at **Hotel Rosas ❹,** Phillipi 296, have TVs and private baths in small but decorative rooms. (☎/fax 580 088. Breakfast included. Singles CH$13,750; doubles CH$19,620; triples CH$25,200.) The dining options in town are limited, but the casual atmosphere at the **Club Croata ❸** compliments the tasty seafood and beef fare. (☎580 053. Dinner CH$4000-6000. Open daily for lunch and dinner with flexible hours.)

◎ SIGHTS. Porvenir's rich history as a gold-mining community is reflected in its tourist attractions. Curious travelers can visit its historical **gold rush sites** on horseback—but these trips are better for their beautiful vistas than their historical information. In the tourist office building, at the corner of Schythe and Zavattaro, the **Museo Provincial Fernando Cordero Rusque** has an interesting display of local artifacts and photos. The most amazing exhibit is certainly the Selk nam mummies, left by a group of aborigines on the Isla Grande of Tierra del Fuego. Other eclectic features of considerable interest include displays on the gold rush of 1881, Chilean cinematography, and local natural history. *(Free.)*

RÍO GRANDE, ARGENTINA

Often just an inadvertent stop on the way to Ushuaia, Río Grande has very little to offer most visitors. Committed fly fishers will find this to be a resourceful and accommodating base for the lesser-known but still abundant fishing holes in Tierra del Fuego. Recent efforts to increase the appeal of the town are visible, but Río Grande remains a simple petroleum town, rather than a tourist hot spots.

 TRANSPORTATION. Aerolineas Argentinas flies almost daily to **Buenos Aires** (ARG$98) and **Ushuaia** (ARG$28), but the schedule varies, so stop by the office at the corner of Belgrano and San Martín for up-to-date schedules. **Taxis** are the only way to the airport (ARG$3-4). **Buses** leave from the station at Belgrano 58, next to the YPF station on the shore. **Lider** (☎420 003) and **Montiel** (☎420 997) buses both head to **Ushuaia** (3hr.; 8 per day, last at 9:30pm; ARG$12-15). **Bus Pancheco** (☎423 382) goes to **Ushuaia** via **Puerto Espora** (Tu, Th, Sa 11:30am; ARG$28) and **Porvenir** (M and F 11:30am, ARG$20); continues to **Punta Arenas** via **ferry**.

 ORIENTATION AND PRACTICAL INFORMATION. The principle streets of interest are Belgrano, running north-south, and San Martín and Periot, running east-west. The **tourist office,** Belgrano 319, has maps and friendly advice. (☎422 887. Open M-F 10am-6pm.) Stock up on groceries at **La Anonima Supermarket,** San Martín 536. (Open daily 9am-9pm.) The 100-200 block of San Martín is dotted with **ATMs—Bansud,** Rosales 241, accepts most cards. The **Telecom** office, Belgrano 678, also has **Internet access** for ARG$2 per hour. Check out what's playing at Río Grande's ultra-modern **movie theater,** Perito Moreno 211. (☎422 463. ARG$5.) A great source of information and equipment for **fly fishing** is **Anglers Aventuras,** Rosales 644, which also arranges week-long excursions with advance notice. (☎/fax 423 341. www.anglerstdf.com.)

 ACCOMMODATIONS AND FOOD. There are few budget accommodations and even fewer good ones in Río Grande. **Hospedaje Noal ❶,** Obligado 557, is a good pick. (☎422 857. ARG$15 per bed with shared bath; doubles with private bath ARG$35.) **Hotel Rawson ❷,** Estrada 750, isn't an especially good deal, but clean rooms, private baths, and TVs make it a better option than other places in town. (☎430 352. Singles ARG$22; doubles ARG$33; triples ARG$40; quads ARG$50; quints ARG$58.) Most restaurants have the basic pizza and *lomo* fare.

BORDER CROSSING INTO ARGENTINA: SAN SEBASTIÁN
Over 140km east of Porvenir, on the road to Río Grande in Argentine, lie the twin cities of San Sebastián, one on each side of the border. Separated by 14km, they hold the respective customs offices of Chile and Argentina. The customs process is fairly simple and involves no more than a brief search of your luggage for contraband and various food products and a passport stamp (see **Essentials: Border Crossings,** p. 65, for info on visas and fees).

Some decent options are **La Fuente Azul ❶**, Perito Moreno 638, where a simple chicken and fries platter (ARG$4) is among the more popular choices, or the easy-going **Cafe Americano ❶**, (medium pizza and two drinks ARG$5.50), situated right next door.

USHUAIA, ARGENTINA ☎ 2901

Welcome to the "end of the world." This fast growing Argentine city, once a backward fishing town, has remade itself as the center of tourism in the Austral region. Fed by the swarms of affluent tourists brought by international cruise ships, many excursions have become pricey. However, with a little investigating, the budget traveler can still fully experience the trekking and fishing that draw travelers from all corners of the world to Ushuaia.

▐▀ TRANSPORTATION

Flights: Aeropuerto Internacional Malvinas Argentinas is one of the country's newest airports, boasting airstrips long enough for the three Concord arrivals it has every year. The only transportation to or from the airport is by taxi (ARG$4-5 to town). **Aerolineas Argentinas** (☎ 421 218; www.aerolineas.com.ar) flies to **Buenos Aires** (3½hr.; 2-4 per day) and **El Calafate** (1¼-2hr., 2-4 per week). **AIRG** flies to **Buenos Aires** (1 per day, ARG$160-220) and **El Calafate** (Su 11:50am, more in summer; ARG$82-128).

Buses: Techni Austral goes to **Punta Arenas** (12hr.; Apr.-Sept. M, W, F 6:30am, more frequent Oct.-Mar.; ARG$52, includes ferry). **Tolkeyen** also goes to **Punta Arenas** (12 hr.; Apr.-Sept. M, Tu, Th, Sa 8am; more frequent Oct.-Mar.; ARG$60, includes ferry).

▞▞ ▊ ORIENTATION AND PRACTICAL INFORMATION

Framed by white-capped mountains and looking down upon the picturesque Beagle Cannel, Ushuaia is simple to navigate. The five-by-fifteen block area of most interest to visitors lies upon a hill with logically laid out north/south streets. Most businesses are on, or just off, San Martín, located one block up from the gusty Maipú, which is situated directly on the port. Be particularly cautious of traffic going up or down the hill, as stop signs are rare and traffic has the right of way.

Tourist Office: San Martín 674 (☎ 424 550). Plentiful information on the city and region. Also books daytrips and longer excursions. Be sure to get your official certificate proving you have been to the most southern city in the world. English spoken.

Tours: Most offices sell identical packages. **All Patagonia,** Juana Fadul 60 (☎ 433 622), is central and helpful. **Rumbo Sur,** San Martín 350 (☎/fax 430 699), is also a good agency. Excursions include: half- and full-day boat trips in the Beagle Channel to see sea lions, penguins, and other wildlife (ARG$35-65); canoeing and trekking in the national park (ARG$50); horseback riding (2hr., ARG$30); glacier trekking (2hr., ARG$60); plane trips over town (½hr., ARG$35); and 4x4 daytrips around Lago Fagnano (ARG$80). Most longer trips begin at 9am, include lunch, but will only go if 2 or more people sign up. All Patagonia also has boat excursions to Antarctica for 10 days to one month (ARG$3000-6000). **Wind Fly,** San Martín 54 (☎/fax 431 713), organizes fly-fishing excursions to the area's excellent fishing holes. Prices start at ARG$180 for a one-day trip. Equipment included.

Consulates: Chile, Jainen 50 (☎ 430 909). There are only a few European consulates and none for the US. Contact the tourist office for more info.

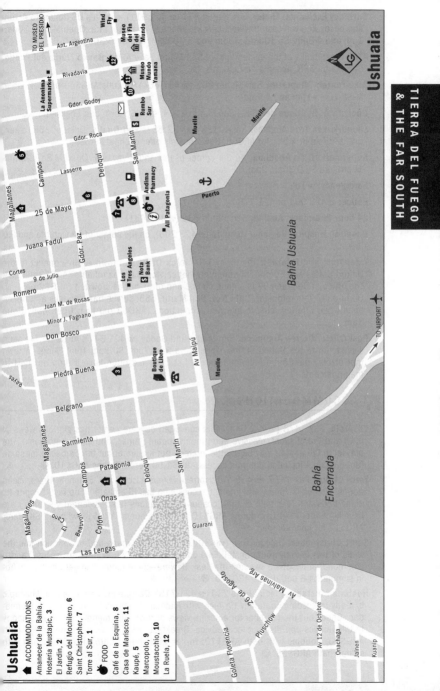

TIERRA DEL FUEGO
& THE FAR SOUTH

Currency Exchange: Thaler, San Martín 877 (☎ 421 911), changes US dollars to Argentine pesos and will cash travelers checks, although at a poor rate. Open M-F 10:30am-1pm and 4-8pm, Sa 10am-1:30pm and 5:30-8pm, and Su 5:30-8pm.

ATM: Most banks at the eastern end of San Martín have ATMs. **Banco Tierra del Fuego,** San Martín 388, accepts AmEx/Cirrus/MC/Plus/V.

Bike rental: 7Deportes, San Martín 802 (☎ 437 604). Rentals ARG$20 per day. Open M-Sa 10am-1pm and 4-9pm.

Bookstore: Boutique de Libro, San Martín 1129, sells Spanish and English books.

Laundry: Los Tres Angeles, Rosas 139 (☎ 422 687) and **Qualis,** Deloqui 368, clean, dry, and fold in 4-5hr. for ARG$8. Some hostels offer cheaper services.

Supermarket: La Anonima, on the corner of Paz and Rivadavia. Open M-Sa 9:30am-10pm and Su 9:30am-2pm.

Emergency: ☎ 101

Police: ☎ 422 001 or 421 773

24-hour Pharmacy: Andina, San Martín 638 (☎ 423 431).

Hospital: Hospital Regional Ushuaia (☎ 423 200), on the corner of 12 Octubre and Fitz Roy.

Telephone and Internet: The many **Telefónica Offices** in town easily connect to the United States and Europe, but their internet service is not as reliable (ARG$3 per hr.). The office at Belgrano 97 is a good choice and often not as crowded (ARG$2 per hr.). Open daily 9am-midnight. **Cafe Net,** San Martín 565, serves basic snacks and beverages while offering reliable Internet connections (ARG$3 per hr.). Open daily 8am-3am.

Post Office: Correo Argentino, San Martín and Godoy (☎ 421 347). ARG$1.75 to send a postcard to the United States. Open M-Sa 9am-7pm, Su 9am-1pm. Shops in town that display the Correo Argentino sign sell stamps and often have a drop box next to their postcards.

▐ ACCOMMODATIONS

▨ **El Jardin,** Paz 1478 (☎ 422 044). This converted daycare center has glorious views of town and the channel, massive dorm rooms, board games, and clean bathrooms. The playset in the garden may be of little interest, but inquire about the barbecue for some fun. Breakfast included. Internet access ARG$1.50 per hr. Dorms ARG$10. ❶

Torre al Sur, Paz 1437 (☎ 430 745; torresur@impsat1.com.ar). Stunning views, clean dorms, kitchen facilities, and Internet access help this HI affiliate fill up fast. Despite its many beds and less than central location, reservations (also accepted via email) are usually needed. 2-4 bed dorms ARG$10 for HI members, ARG$11 with an ISIC card, ARG$12 for non-members. ❶

Saint Christopher, Deloqui 636 (☎ 430 062). Trekking maps and information line the walls of this friendly youth hostel. Free coffee or tea, cable TV, Internet access, and a communal atmosphere sweeten the deal. Beware—some rooms can get blisteringly hot in summer. 4-6 bed dorms ARG$10. ❶

Hostería Mustapic, Piedrabuena 230 (☎ 421 718). Despite the hotel-like feel, Mustapic is ready to accommodate any traveler, with kitchen access and tons of tourist information. Check out the top floor for amazing views of town. The friendly manager is happy to talk politics and dish out local advice. Breakfast included. Singles with private bath ARG$50; doubles with bath ARG$70; triples with shared bath ARG$50; quads with shared bath ARG$55. ❸

El Refugio del Mochilero, 25 de Mayo 241 (☎436 129). Laid back and accommodating, Mochilero is another budget hot spot because of its kitchen facilities, plenty of hot water, and tons of adventure tourism information. Constant music and free beverages maintain a steady flow of chatter and fun, but it can easily become distracting in the wee hours of the morning. Laundry available. 6 bed dorms ARG$10. ❶

Amanecer de la Bahía, Magallanes 594 (☎424 405), at the top of 25 de Mayo. Join the family and break from the normal travel circle in this relaxed and clean hostel. The friendly owners are a good source of information. Thin walls and heavy traffic may keep some guests awake. Kitchen access. Breakfast included. 4-6 bed dorms ARG$10. ❶

🍴 FOOD

La Casa de Mariscos, San Martín 232. The small and rustic surroundings go nicely with the spectrum of seafood dinners. The region's king crab specialty (ARG$15) is prepared a number of ways, while the hearty *cazuela de mariscos* (seafood stew; ARG$12) tosses together all the local seafood offerings. Some non-seafood dishes also available (half-chicken ARG$9). Open daily 11:30am-3pm and 6pm-midnight. ❷

Moustacchio, San Martín 298 (☎423 308). With its extensive menu, relaxed atmosphere, and great quality food, this *tenedor libre* is a good place to fill up on Argentine meats. Open daily 11:30am-4pm and 7pm-1am. ❶

La Ruela, San Martín 193 (☎436 540). Pack it in at La Ruela's *tenedor libre* for only ARG$9, but you will have to purchase a beverage (ARG$1-2.50). Take your time enjoying the extensive salad bar and full range of grilled meats, but beware—there's a ARG$2 surcharge for wasting food. Fish and other entrees also available. Open daily 11:30am-4pm and 7:30pm-1am. ❶

Marcopolo, San Martín 672. If the same old cafes get you down, Marcopolo will renew your taste buds with its extensive menu and excellent service. The almost regal atmosphere attracts a local clientele. The set lunch (ARG$9, dessert not included) or stuffed chicken (ARG$11) are a nice break from *lomo* and pasta. Unlimited breakfast of coffee and pastries ARG$4.50. Open daily 7:30am-1am. AmEx/MC/V. ❶

Café de la Esquina, San Martín 601. This Argentine cafe serves a basic menu of *milanesa* (thinly sliced, breaded meat; ARG$7) and sandwiches (ARG$4.50-6) and is often bustling with locals and visitors all day long. The ever-changing set lunch (ARG$7-8) is usually served within minutes. Open M-Th 7:30am-3:30am, Sa 9am-3:30am, Su 4pm-1:30am. AmEx/ MC/V. ❶

THE BIG SPLURGE

KAUPÉ

Roca 470 (☎422 704). Although locals in every city often claim to have the best food in the world, Ushuaia actually means it in regard to its small, intimate restaurant, Kaupé, which serves up unmatched delicacies. "Kaupé" is an indigenous word meaning "to be at home," and the welcoming, entirely family-run establishment lives up to its name, with father-chef Ernesto Vivian preparing the meals while his wife and daughter wait tables. Sample the savory Chilean sea bass, baked in paper and served with a light, creamy sauce (ARG$15), or the steamed king crab (ARG$15), which is so delicately prepared you will be sure to enjoy every bite. The selection of fine Argentine wines also satisfies any palate. A good deal for a big appetite is the set menu of "tastings," offering a choice of two appetizers, an entree of tenderloin or fish, dessert, coffee, and a half-bottle of wine (ARG$50). The restaurant's location high above the city makes for incredible views of the Beagle Channel. Scrub off some of that travel dirt and go all out—Kaupé is the place for your big splurge. Open daily 7:30pm-close. AmEx/MC/V. ❸

◎ SIGHTS

MUSEO DEL PRESIDIO AND MUSEO MARITIMO DE USHUAIA. Like another place down under, Ushuaia got its beginnings as a penal colony when 14 convicts arrived here in January 1896. It quickly became the sight of a national prison as the convicts built their own cells and performed other services for the rest of the town. The impressive structure of over 380 cells, at one time holding more than 800 prisoners, was finally shut down in 1947. Within the walls of the now defunct building are two museums and other frequent expositions. The smaller but very detailed **Museo Marítimo** houses numerous models and descriptive maps that thoroughly highlight the exploration and defense of Argentina's extensive coastline from as early as 1520. The **prison museum** begins in one of the five outstretched arms of the prison complex, with many separate displays set up in the rows of cells. Although the detail may be excessive, the many artifacts and displays are quite engaging. Be sure to visit the middle arm of the prison, which remains largely unchanged and gives visitors a more chilling impression of the dreary existence of Argentina's worst convicts. (*Within the naval base, access museum from the Paz and Yuganes entrance.* ☎/fax 437 481. www.ushuaia.org. Open daily 10am-8pm. ARG$9.)

MUSEO DEL FIN DEL MUNDO. This meticulously organized museum displays the entirety of Ushuaia's history. Beginning with the region's role in the age of exploration with notable artifacts from initial encounters with indigenous peoples, the museum also displays photos and items from Ushuaia's days as a penal colony. The general store and an impressive collection of stuffed animals from the region complete what is a detailed but small exhibition. (*Maipú 175.* ☎ 421 863; fax 431 201. www.tierradelfuego.org.ar/museo. Open daily 10am-1pm and 3-7:30pm. ARG$5, students ARG$2.)

MUSEO MUNDO YAMANA. This museum details the indigenous population's origins and customs through artifacts and models. Although the first rooms speak generally about the movement of Asians to the Americas, the final rooms present astonishing miniatures depicting how the Yamana lived, hunted, and traveled. All displays have descriptions in both English and Spanish. (*Rivadavia 56.* ☎ 422 874. mundoyamana@infovia.com.ar. Open daily 10am-8pm. ARG$3.50, students ARG$2.50.)

▨ OUTDOORS

GUIDED TOURS. Don't get confused if it seems as if the tourist industry in Ushuaia is managed by one company—extensive collaboration between tour companies ensures that one office provides all the services offered. All Patagonia, Rumbo Sur, and Wind Fly (see tours, p. 488) are particularly reputable companies that run most of the tours they sell. The **city tour** is a half-day jaunt through town in either a van or a double-decker bus. Coffee and tea are served between frequent stops at easily accessible sights and local museums. (1½hr., ARG$10-12.) **Boat excursions** are either half or full-day tours that reach combinations of destinations within the bay, including the sea lion colony, bird sanctuary, lighthouse, Magellan Penguins, and the historic Harberton Estancia. (Full-day trips depart at 9:30am and return at 3pm. Lunch included. ARG$36-65.) **Tourist flights** over the Beagle Channel in 8-person planes last only a half-hour, but afford majestic views. (ARG$35.)

WILDERNESS TOURS. Few guided tours through Parque Nacional Tierra del Fuego are available because much of the park is easily navigable without help. The **bus tour** is informative, although slightly removed from the natural surroundings. (ARG$20). A full-day trek to and canoe trip back from a **beaver habitat** is available (ARG$65), but you can opt to spend only 3 hours with the beavers as well (ARG$35). The **Train to the End of the World** is a small-track locomotive that recreates the route along which lumber was transported out of the park. It is, however, a slow journey that can easily be skipped. (Estación del Fin del Mundo, Ruta 3. ☎431 600. www.trendelfindelmundo.com.ar. English spoken. ARG$26.) Check out the variety of outdoor activities available beyond the confines of the park, including **glacier trekking** (ARG$60-65), **4-wheel drive excursions** to Lago Faghano (ARG$80), and visits to local **ranches** (ARG$60). Well-organized **fly fishing** trips including all equipment, transport, and food are also available (starting at ARG$180 per day).

WINTER ACTIVITIES IN USHUAIA. The winter season in Ushuaia is not as happening as the summer, but the tourism board is developing several attractions in an attempt to maintain interest despite the short, bleak days and meager snowfall. The **festival of the "Longest Night"** at the end of June kicks off the winter season and is soon followed by the **"End of the World Car Rally"** in July. August ushers in the **"Snow Sculptors Meeting"** and the cross-country **"White March"** competition to keep up spirits in Ushuaia. Otherwise, mediocre downhill skiing and cross-country skiing will keep visitors busy at **Cerro Castor** (27km from town, hourly shuttle ARG$10, rentals and lift ticket ARG$50).

NEAR USHUAIA: GLACIER MARIAL

This scenic 3-hour hike 7km from town rewards industrious visitors with excellent views of Ushuaia and ultimately leads to the glacier. The chairlift runs until 6:45pm, and saves an hour's walk, but is not necessary (ARG$5). To get to the base of the hike, take a van with Bella Vista from 25 de Mayo that leaves every hour on the half-hour 4:30am-6:30pm, and returns on the hour (ARG$5). Or take a taxi (ARG$5 for up to 4 people).

PARQUE NACIONAL TIERRA DEL FUEGO

This southernmost part of the Andean-Patagonian forest is well-maintained and easily accessible to the budget traveler thanks to the interest and dedication of the Argentine tourist board. Inside the park, enjoy walks through soft, fragrant underwood consisting of moss and fern around glacial lakes, or cut up to a craggy peak for expansive views of other summits that rise over the Beagle Channel.

AT A GLANCE	
AREA: 33,000 hectares.	**GATEWAYS:** Ushuaia.
CLIMATE: Humid.	**WILDLIFE:** Diverse wildlife including white *cauquenes* (mackerel), black eyebrowed albatross, diving petrel, *chungungo* (a rare otter), and a particular variety of Tierra del Fuego red fox.
HIGHLIGHTS: Black Lagoon, viewing the grand panorama from Lookout Point, meeting the beavers 400m upstream Los Castores.	
FEES: Park admission ARG$5. Round-trip shuttle services ARG$8-14.	**CAMPING:** Foreigners permitted to camp in designated areas; free campsites available (campsites with services ARG$2-4).

Most trails commence at either **Lago Roca, Bahía Enseñada,** or **Bahía Lapataia,** the drop-off sites for most tour companies. Although all the marked trails take only half a day to complete, there are a handful of rustic campsites for hikers who would like to spend a night at the park. There's always more to explore at **Black Lagoon** (400m. from Route 3), named for its dark color caused by the presence of peat; the **Island** (800m of coast along the Lapataia and Ovando rivers); **Lookout Point** (through the lengas wood at Bahía Lapataia); and the **beaver habitat** at Los Castores stream. Although Parque Nacional Tierra del Fuego may not attract swarms of hardcore hikers like other national parks in the region, its quality sights, friendly service, and easy access make for memorable and relaxing outdoor adventures.

To access the park, use the **shuttle service** provided by most tour companies in Ushuaia. From 25 de Mayo and Maipú, Bella Vista buses leave on the hour and Eban Ezer service is on the half-hour (ARG$8-14 round-trip, not required to return the same day if you pay for tickets at the van). The tourist office has adequate information on the park, but stop by the **main park office** for more information. (San Martín 1395. ☎421 315. Open M-F 9am-4pm.) Pay park admission (ARG$5) at the park entrance, where free maps are available as well. **Camping** is available at **Lago Roca** near a friendly but pricey *confitería* with showers and bathrooms. Free camping can be found at the beaver site on the island and at the beginning of the **Costerna Trail,** but neither of these free sites have any services. Some trails to check out include:

Cerro Guanaco Trail (5km; 4hr. to top, 2½ to return; difficult). This, the only summit trek in the park, begins at Lago Roca and heads straight up to the top. The arduous ascent is interrupted by 2km of mountain pasture that is often soggy, but remains manageable. The peak of the summit is almost totally exposed, so wear layers to stay warm. Despite the challenge, you'll be rewarded with a view of the city and surrounding land.

Hito XXIV Trail (5km, 3hr. round-trip, medium). Also starting from Lago Roca, this path follows the northern shore of the lake, skirting in between surrounding trees. The pleasant breeze over the lake and the variety of small birds and rabbits make this a relaxing and enjoyable hike.

BORDER CROSSING INTO ARGENTINA: PUERTO WILLIAMS

Finding a way to cross the Beagle Channel between Puerto Williams and Ushuaia may seem difficult at first, as boats heading west to Punta Arenas or Puerto Natales cannot stop by Ushuaia on their journey because of geopolitics and border worries on both sides. Inform the naval office of your dilemma—since boats coming into town must check in at their office, they might provide information or arrange a border crossing. Some lucky visitors have caught a lift with the Chilean Navy, but these are informal and irregular opportunities. Most opportunities await at the far end of the port at the Club Naval Yates Micalvi.

In Ushuaia, begin by asking guests and managers at hostels about finding private transport, as many local boats often make the trip and take passengers for about US$65. The Asociación de Actividades Navales is a fruitful place to make inquiries as most smaller boats dock and depart from here.

Boats entering or leaving both ports need to contact the border control office which provides the necessary stamps and paperwork. It is a good idea to contact them a few hours before you depart to ensure that everything goes smoothly (see **Essentials: Border Crossings,** p. 65, for info on visas and fees).

Costera Trail (6½km, 3hr. round-trip, medium). Largely following the channel, this course winds through two types of forest and affords great viewing of flora and fauna.

Pampa Alta Trail (4.9km, 1hr. one-way, medium). An optional longer route lies along the Pilato stream, but this lazy trail eventually reaches an open plane with a panoramic view of the Beagle Channel.

ISLA NAVARINO

PUERTO WILLIAMS

Although difficult to reach and unspectacular by itself, Puerto Williams sits on the doorstep of some excellent wilderness, allowing a glimpse of the so called "end of the world." Puerto Williams, the world's southernmost town, is dominated by the Chilean naval base. Nevertheless, friendly locals and the natural beauty make it a great stopping point before heading into the lush surrounding landscape.

■ TRANSPORTATION. Planes from Punta Arenas arrive at **Aerodromo Guardi-marina Zañartu.** Taxis wait for new arrivals and are the only way to town. **DAP,** next to Turismo Sin Limita, is the only commercial airline servicing Puerto Williams, and flights departing at varying times go only to Punta Arenas (M-Sa, US$71). Some private **boats** take passengers to Ushuaia and Punta Arenas (see **border crossings** p. 494). **Austral Broom,** east of town before the river, has a weekly **ferry** between Punta Arenas and Puerto Williams, but it is rather uncomfortable and long. Contact Sr. Godoy to arrange ferry trips. (in Puerto Williams ☎621 015, in Punta Arenas 218 100. 36hr.; departs W returning F or Sa; US$120, US$150 for a bed.)

⊡ PRACTICAL INFORMATION. For **tourist information,** head to **Turismo Sin Límite** (☎621 150), one block north of the Plaza de Armas. Information about the town and plane ticket bookings are readily available. With advance notice, they can arrange sailboat trips to Cabo de Hornos (7 days) and Antarctica (29 days). There are two **telephone offices** in the central plaza, and the **Telefonica** office offers **Internet access** for CH$1800 per hr. **Banco de Chile,** one block north of the plaza on Yelcho, changes a minimum of US$100 to Chilean pesos. (Open M-F 9am-2pm.)

▟⊡ ACCOMMODATIONS AND FOOD. ▧**Refugio Coiron ❸,** Ricardo Maragañ 168 is a popular lodging, providing great information about the area to boot. (☎621 227. Dorms CH$8000.) **Onashaya Residencia ❸,** on the Plaza de Armas, has rustic accommodations and serves a hearty dinner upon request. (Dorms CH$8000. Dinner CH$2800.) **Posaky Hostel ❸,** two blocks east of the Plaza de Armas, has friendly service and dinner is available on request. (☎621 116. Dorms CH$7500. Breakfast included.) Or just stop by **Cabo de Hornos ❷,** on the Plaza de Armas, which serves hearty meals, but maintains irregular hours.

AROUND PUERTO WILLIAMS

Most visitors to Puerto Williams come for the four-day hike through **Los Dientes** that weaves through the jagged mountains visible from town. The less adventurous can begin the circuit and reach the Cerro Bandera (Flag Point) in just a couple of hours, or push ahead to the first campsite, the Laguna El Salto, and return in a day. The best attraction of the hike is the excellent view across Isla Navarino to Cape Horn, as well as the diverse wildlife. No formal maps are available in town, but the tourist office and some hostels have copies of what serves as a trail map. The best source of extra information is Christian at the popular Refugio Coiron (see accommodations above). The path begins south of town at the "Gruta," the image of Virgin Mary well known to locals. No guides or equipment are readily available in Puerto Williams, so only knowledgeable and prepared hikers are advised to make the loop. Before leaving, be sure to check in with the Chilean Navy, who will collect your passport number and contact information in the event of an emergency.

APPENDIX

SPANISH QUICK REFERENCE

PRONUNCIATION

Each vowel has only one pronunciation: A ("ah" in father); E ("eh" in pet); I ("ee" in eat); O ("oh" in oat); U ("oo" in boot); Y, by itself, is pronounced the same as Spanish I ("ee"). Most consonants are pronounced the same as in English. Important exceptions are: J, pronounced like the English "h" in "hello"; LL, pronounced like the English "y" in "yes"; Ñ, pronounced like the "gn" in "cognac." R at the beginning of a word or RR anywhere in a word is trilled. H is always silent. G before E or I is pronounced like the "h" in "hen"; elsewhere it is pronounced like the "g" in "gate." X has a bewildering variety of pronunciations: depending on dialect and word position, it can sound like English "h," "s," "sh," or "x." Spanish words receive stress on the syllable marked with an accent (´). In the absence of an accent mark, words that end in vowels, "n," or "s" receive stress on the second to last syllable. For words ending in all other consonants, stress falls on the last syllable. The Spanish language has masculine and feminine nouns, and gives a gender to all adjectives. Masculine words generally end with an "o": él es un tonto (he is a fool). Feminine words generally end with an "a": ella es bella (she is beautiful). Pay close attention-slight changes in word ending can have drastic changes in meaning. For instance, when receiving directions, mind the distinction between derecho (straight) and derecha (right).

SPANISH PHRASEBOOK

ESSENTIAL PHRASES

ENGLISH	SPANISH	PRONUNCIATION
Hello	Hola	OH-la
Goodbye	Adiós	ah-dee-OHS
Yes/No	Sí/No	SEE/NO
Please	Por Favor	POOR fa-VOHR
Thank you.	Gracias.	GRA-see-ahs
You're welcome.	De nada.	DAY NAH-dah
Do you speak English?	¿Habla inglés?	AH-blah EEN-glace
I don't speak Spanish.	No hablo español.	NO AH-bloh EHS-pahn-yohl
Excuse me.	Perdón.	pehr-DOHN
I don't know.	No sé.	NO SAY
Can you repeat that?	¿Puede repetirlo?	PWAY-day reh-peh-TEER-lo

SURVIVAL SPANISH

ENGLISH	SPANISH	ENGLISH	SPANISH
Again, please.	Otra vez, por favor.	I'm sick/fine.	Estoy enfermo(a)/bien.
What?	¿Cómo?/¿Qué?	Could you speak more slowly?	¿Podría hablar más despacio?

ENGLISH	SPANISH	ENGLISH	SPANISH
I don't understand.	No entiendo.	How are you?	¿Qué tal?/¿Comó está?
What is your name?	¿Cómo se llama?	Where are (the elephants)?	Dónde están (los elefantes)?
How do you say (jackass) in Spanish?	¿Cómo se dice (burro) en español?	Where is (the center of town)?	¿Dónde está (el centro)?
Good day/night	Buenas días/noches	Good morning	Buenos días
How much does it cost?	¿Cuánto cuesta?	I am hot/cold.	Tengo calor/frío.
Why (are you staring at me?)	¿Por qué (está mirándome)?	I want/would like...	Quiero/Me gustaría...
That is cheap/expensive	Es muy caro/barato.	Let's go!	¡Vámanos!
What's up?	¿Qué pasa?	Stop/ that's enough.	Basta.
Who?	¿Quién?	What?	¿Qué?
When?	¿Cuándo?	Where?	¿Dónde?
Why?	¿Por qué?	Because	Porque

YOUR ARRIVAL

ENGLISH	SPANISH	ENGLISH	SPANISH
I am from the US/Europe.	Soy de los Estados Unidos/Europa.	What's the problem, sir/madam?	¿Cuál es el problema, señor/señora?
Here is my passport.	Aquí está mi passporte.	I lost my passport.	Perdí mi passporte.
I will be here for less than six months.	Estaré aquí por menos de seis meses.	I have nothing to declare.	No tengo nada para declarar.
I don't know where the drugs came from.	No sé de donde vinieron las drogas.	Please do not detain me.	Por favor no me detenga.

GETTING AROUND

ENGLISH	SPANISH	ENGLISH	SPANISH
How do you get to (the bus station)?	¿Cómo se va a (la terminal de autobúses)?	Is there anything cheaper?	¿Hay algo más barato/económico?
Does this bus go to (Tierra del Fuego)?	¿Este autobús va a (Tierra del Fuego)?	On foot.	A pie.
How do I get to...?	¿Cómo voy a...?	How far is...?	¿Qué tan lejos está?
Where is... street?	¿Dónde está la calle...?	What bus line goes to..?	¿Qué línea de buses tiene servicio a...?
When does the bus leave?	¿Cuándo sale el autobús?	Where does the bus leave from?	¿De dónde sale el autobús?
I'm getting off at...	Bajo en...	I have to go now.	Tengo que ir ahora.
Can I buy a ticket?	¿Podría comprar un boleto?	¿How can you get there?	¿Cómo se puede llegar?
How long does the trip take?	¿Cuántas horas dura el viaje?	Is it near/far from here?	¿Está cerca/lejos de aquí?
I am going to the airport.	Voy al aeropuerto.	The flight is delayed/cancelled.	El vuelo está retrasado/cancelado.
Turn right/left.	Doble a la derecha/izquierda.	Is it safe to hitchhike?	¿Es seguro pedir aventón?
I lost my baggage.	Perdí mi equipaje.	Stay straight.	Siga derecho.
I would like to rent (a car).	Quisiera alquilar un coche.	Please let me off at the zoo.	Por favor, déjeme en el zoológico.
How much does it cost per day/week?	¿Cuánto cuesta por día/semana?	Does it have heating/air-conditioning?	¿Tiene calentadora/aire acondicionado?
Where can I buy a cellphone?	¿Dónde puedo comprar un teléfono celular?	Where can I check email?	¿Dónde se puede chequear el email?

ENGLISH	SPANISH	ENGLISH	SPANISH
Could you tell me?	¿Podría decirme?	Are there student discounts available?	¿Hay descuentos para estudiantes?

DIRECTIONS

ENGLISH	SPANISH	ENGLISH	SPANISH
(to the) right	a la derecha	(to the) left	a la izquierda
next to	al lado de	across from	en frente de
straight ahead	todo derecho	to turn	doblar
near	cerca	far	lejos
above	arriba	below	abajo
traffic light	semáforo	corner	esquina
street	calle/avenida	block	cuadra

ACCOMMODATIONS

ENGLISH	SPANISH	ENGLISH	SPANISH
Is there a cheap hotel around here?	¿Hay un hotel económico por aquí?	Are there rooms with windows?	¿Hay habitaciones con ventanas?
Do you have rooms available?	¿Tiene habitaciones libres?	I am going to stay for (four) days.	Me voy a quedar (cuatro) días.
I would like to reserve a room.	Quisiera reservar una habitación.	Are there cheaper rooms?	¿Hay habitaciones más baratas?
Can I see a room?	¿Podría ver una habitación?	Do they come with private baths?	¿Vienen con baño privado?
Do you have any singles/doubles?	¿Tiene habitaciones sencillas/dobles?	Can I borrow a plunger?	¿Me prestas una bomba?
I need another key/towel/pillow.	Necesito otra llave/toalla/almohada	My bedsheets are dirty.	Mis sabanas están sucias.
The bathroom is broken.	El baño está roto.	I'll take it.	Lo tomo.
There are cockroaches in my room.	Hay cucarachas en mi habitación.	They are biting me.	Me están mordiendo.

EMERGENCY

ENGLISH	SPANISH	ENGLISH	SPANISH
Help!	¡Ayúdame!/¡Socorro!	Call the police!	Llame a la policía/los carabineros!
I am hurt.	Estoy herido(a).	Leave me alone!	¡Déjame en paz!
It's an emergency!	¡Es una emergencia!	I have been robbed!	¡Me han robado!
Fire!	¡Fuego!/¡Incendio!	They went that a-way!	¡Fueron en esa dirección!
Call a clinic/ambulance/doctor/priest!	¡Llame a una clínica/una ambulancia/un médico/un padre!	I will only speak in the presence of a lawyer.	Sólo hablaré en presencia de un abogado(a).
I need to contact my embassy.	Necesito contactar mi embajada.	Don't touch me there!	¡No me toque allí!

MEDICAL

ENGLISH	SPANISH	ENGLISH	SPANISH
I feel bad/better/worse.	Me siento mal/mejor/peor.	I have a stomach ache.	Tengo dolor de estómago.
I have a headache.	Tengo dolor de cabeza.	It hurts here.	Me duele aquí.
I'm sick/ill.	Estoy enfermo(a).	Here is my prescription.	Aquí está la recta médica.

APPENDIX

ENGLISH	SPANISH	ENGLISH	SPANISH
I'm allergic to (Monkey Puzzle Trees).	Soy alérgico(a) a (las araucanias).	I think I'm going to vomit.	Pienso que voy a vomitar.
What is this medicine for?	¿Para qué es esta medicina?	I haven't been able to go to the bathroom in (four) days.	No he podido ir al baño en (cuatro) días.
Where is the nearest hospital/doctor.	¿Dónde está el hospital/doctor más cercano?	I have a cold/a fever/diarrhea/nausea.	Tengo gripa/una calentura/diarrea/náusea.

(INFORMAL) PERSONAL RELATIONSHIPS

ENGLISH	SPANISH	ENGLISH	SPANISH
What is your name?	¿Cómo se llama?	Pleased to meet you.	Encantado(a)/Mucho gusto.
Where are you from?	¿De dónde es?	I'm (twenty) years old.	Tengo (viente) años.
This is my first time in Chile.	Este es mi primera vez en Chile.	I have a boyfriend/girl-friend.	Tengo novio/novia.
Do you come here often?	¿Viene aquí a menudo?	I'm a communist.	Soy comunista.
Do you have a light?	¿Tiene fuego?	It's true. Politicians can never be trusted.	De véras. No se puede confiar en los políticos.
Did I dance on the table last night?	¿Bailé en la mesa anoche?	No thanks, I have many diseases.	No gracias, tengo muchas enfermedades.
Please stop kissing me.	No me beses más, por favor.	I love you.	Te quiero.
Do you want to have sex with me?.	¿Quieres tener sexo conmigo?	What a shame: you bought Lonely Planet!	¡Qué lástima: compraste Lonely Planet!

NUMBERS, DAYS, AND MONTHS

ENGLISH	SPANISH	ENGLISH	SPANISH
0	cero	1000	un mil
1	uno	1 million	un millón
2	dos	Sunday	Domingo
3	tres	Monday	Lunes
4	cuatro	Tuesday	Martes
5	cinco	Wednesday	Miércoles
6	seis	Thursday	Jueves
7	siete	Friday	Viernes
8	ocho	Saturday	Sábado
9	nueve	today	hoy
10	diez	tomorrow	mañana
11	once	day after tomorrow	pasado mañana
12	doce	yesterday	ayer
13	trece	day before yesterday	antes de ayer/anteayer
14	catorce	weekend	fin de semana
15	quince	January	enero
16	dieciseis	February	febrero
17	diecisiete	March	marzo
18	dieciocho	April	abril
19	diecinueve	May	mayo
20	veinte	June	junio
21	veintiuno	July	julio

ENGLISH	SPANISH	ENGLISH	SPANISH
22	veintidos	August	agosto
30	treinta	September	septiembre
40	cuarenta	October	octubre
50	cincuenta	November	noviembre
100	cien	December	diciembre

EATING OUT

ENGLISH	SPANISH	ENGLISH	SPANISH
breakfast	desayuno	lunch	almuerzo
dinner	comida	mid-day snack/teatime	las onces/el té
dessert	postre	drink	bebida
fork	tenedor	Bon Apétit	Buen provecho
napkin	servilleta	knife	cuchillo
spoon	cuchara	cup	copa/taza
I am hungry/thirsty	Tengo hambre/sed.	Do you have hot sauce?	¿Tiene salsa picante?
Where is a good restaurant?	¿Dónde hay un restaurante bueno?	Table for (one), please.	Mesa para (uno), por favor.
Can I see the menu?	¿Podría ver la carta/el menú?	Do you take credit cards?	¿Aceptan tarjetas de crédito?
This is too spicy.	Pica demasiado.	Disgusting!	¡Guácala!/¡Que asco!
I would like to order the eel.	Quisiera el congrio.	Delicious!	¡Qué rico!
Do you have anything vegetarian/without meat?	¿Hay algún plato vegetariano/sin carne?	You can't have your pudding if you don't eat your meat.	No puede tener su budín, si no coma su carne.
Where is the bathroom?	¿Dónde está el baño?	Check, please.	¡La cuenta, por favor!

MENU READER

SPANISH	ENGLISH	SPANISH	ENGLISH
a la plancha	grilled	kuchen	pastry with fruit
al vapor	steamed	leche	milk
aceite	oil	legumbres	vegetables/legumes
aceituna	olive	lima	lime
agua (purificada)	water (purified)	limón	lemon
ajo	garlic	limonada	lemonade
almeja	clam	locos	abalone (white fish)
arroz	rice	lomo	steak or chop
arroz con leche	rice pudding	macedonia	syrupy dessert
ave-palta	sandwich with chicken and avocado	maíz	corn
Barros Luco	sandwich with beef and cheese	mariscos	seafood
Barros Jarpa	sandwich with ham	miel	honey
bisteca	beefsteak	naranja	orange
bundín de centolla	crab with onions, eggs, cheese	nata	cream
café	coffee	paila marina	soup of various shellfish
caldillo de congrio	eel and vegetable soup	pan	bread
caliente	hot	pan amasado	a common, heavy bread
camarones	shrimp	papas	potatoes

SPANISH	ENGLISH	SPANISH	ENGLISH
carne	meat	papas fritas	french fries
cazuela	clear broth with rice, corn, and chicken or beef	parrillas	various grilled meats
cebolla	onion	pasteles	desserts/pies
cerveza	beer	pastel de choclo	corn cassarole with beef, chicken, raisins, onions, olives
chacarero	sandwich with beef, tomato, chili, green beans	pebre	mild or spicy salsa eaten with many foods
chupe de marisco/locos	sea scallops/abalone with white wine, butter, cream, cheese	pernil de chanco a la chilena	braised fresh ham with chili sauce
churrasco	steak sandwich	pescado	fish
chorizo	spicy sausage	picoroco	dish using barnacle meat
coco	coconut	pimienta	pepper
congrio	eel	pisco	liquor made with grapes and egg whites
cordero	lamb	plato	plate
curanto	hearty stew of fish, chicken, pork, lamb, beef, potato	pollo	chicken
dulces	sweets	porotos granados	cranberry beans with squash and corn
dulce de leche	caramelized milk	puerco	pork
empanada	dumpling filled with meat, cheese, or potatoes	queso	cheese
ensalada	salad	sal	salt
entrada	appetizer	tragos	mixed drinks/liquor
gaseosa	soda	vino tinto/blanco	red wine/white

SPANISH GLOSSARY

aduana: customs
agencia de viaje: travel agency
aguardiente: strong liquor
aguas termales: hot springs
ahora: now
ahorita: "now in just a little bit," which can mean anything from 5 minutes to 5 hours
aire acondicionado: air-conditioned (A/C)
a la plancha: grilled
al gusto: as you wish
alemán: German
almacén: (grocery) store
almuerzo: lunch, midday meal
alpaca: a shaggy-haired, long-necked animal in the cameloid family
altiplano: highland
amigo/a: friend
andén: platform
anexo: neighborhood
araucaria: Monkey Puzzle Trees
arroz: rice

arroz chaufa: Chinese-style fried rice
artesanía: arts and crafts
avenida: avenue
bahía: bay
bandido: bandit
baño: bathroom or natural spa
barato/a: cheap
barranca: canyon
barro: mud
barrio: neighborhood
biblioteca: library
bistec/bistek: beefsteak
bocaditos: appetizers, at a bar
bodega: convenience store or winery
boletería: ticket counter
bolivianos: Bolivian currency
bonito/a: pretty/beautiful
borracho/a: drunk
bosque: forest
botica: drugstore
bueno/a: good

buena suerte: good luck
buen provecho: bon appetit
burro: donkey
bus cama: buses with sleeping facilities
caballero: gentleman
caballo: horse
cabañas: cabins
cajeros: cashiers
cajeros automáticos: ATM
caldera: coffee or tea pot
caldo: soup, broth, or stew
calle: street
cama: bed
camarones: shrimp
cambio: change
caminata: n: hike
camino: path, track, road
camión: truck
camioneta: small, pickup-sized truck
campamento: campground
campesino/a: person from a rural area, peasant
campo: countryside
canotaje: rafting
cantina: drinking establishment, usually male dominated
carne asada: roast meat
capilla: chapel
caro/a: expensive
carretera: highway
carro: car, or sometimes a train car
casa: house
casa de cambio: currency exchange establishment
casado/a: married
cascadas: waterfalls
casona: mansion
castellano: Castilian or Spanish language
catedral: cathedral
centro: city center
cerca: near/nearby
cerro: hill
cerveza: beer
ceviche: raw fish marinated in lemon juice, herbs, veggies
cevichería: ceviche restaurant
chica/o: girl/boy, little
chicharrón: bite-sized pieces of fried meat, usually pork
chifa: Chinese restaurant
chuleta de chancho: pork chop
churrasco: steak
cigarillo: cigarette
cine: cinema
club: stripclub
ciudad: city
ciudadela: neighborhood in a large city
coche: car
colectivo: shared taxi
coliseo: coliseum/stadium
comedor: dining room
comida criolla: regional, Spanish-influenced dishes
comida típica: typical/traditional dishes
con: with
consulado: consulate
correo: post office
cordillera: mountain range
corvina: sea bass

criollos: people of European descent born in the New World
croata: Croatian
crucero: crossroads
cruz roja: Red Cross
cuadra: street block
cuarto: a room
cuenta: bill/check
cuento: story/account
Cueca: Chilean national dance
cueva: cave
curandero: healer
damas: ladies
desayuno: breakfast
descompuesto: broken, out of order; spoiled/rotten food
desierto: desert
despacio: slow
de turno: a 24hr. rotating schedule for pharmacies
dinero: money
discoteca: dance club
dueña: owner, proprietress
dulces: sweets
edificio: building
email: email
embajada: embassy
embarcadero: dock
emergencia: emergency
encomiendas: estates granted to Spanish settlers in Latin America
entrada: entrance
estadio: stadium
este: east
estrella: star
extranjero: foreign/foreigner
farmacia: pharmacy
farmacia en turno: 24hr. pharmacy
feliz: happy
ferrocarril: railroad
fiesta: party, holiday
finca: a plantation-like agricultural enterprise or a ranch
friajes: sudden cold winds
frijoles: beans
frontera: border
fumar: to smoke
fumaroles: hole in a volcanic region which emits hot vapors
fundo: large estate, or tract of land
fútbol: soccer
ganga: bargain
gobierno: government
gordo/a: fat
gorra: cap
gratis: free
gringo: North American
guanaco: animal in the camelid family
habitación: a room
hacer una caminata: v: hike
hacienda: ranch
helado: ice cream
hervido/a: boiled
hielo: ice
hombre: man
huaso: Chilean cowboy
iglesia: church
impuestos: taxes

APPENDIX

impuesto valor añadido (IVA): value added tax (VAT)
indígena: indigenous, refers to the native population
Internet: Internet
isla: island
jarra: 1-liter pitcher of beer
jirón: street
jugo: juice
ladrón: thief
lago/laguna: lake
lancha: launch, small boat
langosta: lobster
langostino: jumbo shrimp
larga distancia: long distance
lavandería: laundromat
lejos: far
lente(mente): slow(ly)
librería: bookstore
lista de correos: mail holding system in Latin America
loma: hill
lomo: chop, steak
mal: bad
malecón: pier or seaside thoroughfare
maletas: luggage, suitcases
máneje despacio: drive slowly
manjar blanco: a whole milk spread
Mapudungun: the Mapuche language
mar: sea
mariscos: seafood
matas: shrubs, jungle brush
matrimonial: double bed
menestras: lentils/beans
menú del día/menú: fixed daily meal often offered for a bargain price
mercado: market
merienda: snack
mestizaje: crossing of races
mestizo/a: a person of mixed European and indigenous descent
microbus: small, local bus
mirador: an observatory or look-out point
muelle: wharf
muerte: death
museo: museum
música folklórica: folk music
nada: nothing
niño(a): child
norte: north
obra: work of art/play
obraje: primitive textile workshop
oeste: west
oficina de turismo: tourist office
Pakistán: Pakistan
pampa: a treeless grassland area
pan: bread
panadería: bakery
panga: motorboat
parada: a stop (on a bus or train)
parilla: various cuts of meat, grilled
paro: labor strike
parque: park
parroquia: parish
paseo turístico: tour covering a series of sites
payaso: clown
pelea de gallos: cockfighting
peligroso/a: dangerous
peninsulares: Spanish-born colonists

peña: folkloric music club
pescado: fish
picante: spicy
pisa de uves: grape-stomping
pisco: a traditional Chilean liquor made from grapes
pisco sour: a drink made from pisco, lemon juice, sugarcane syrup, and egg white
plátano: plantain
playa: beach
poblacion: population, settlement
policía: police
pollo a la brasa: roasted chicken
pudú: a Chilean wild goat
pueblito: small town
pueblo: town
puente: bridge
puerta: door
puerto: port
queso: cheese
rana: frog
recreo: place of amusement, restaurant/bar on the outskirts of a city
refrescos: refreshments, soft drinks
reloj: watch, clock
río: river
rodeo: rodeo
ropa: clothes
sabanas: bedsheets
sabor: flavor
sala: living room
salchipapa: french fries with fried pieces of sausage
salida: exit
salto: waterfall
salsa: sauce (can be of many varieties)
seguro/a: n: lock, insurance; adj: safe
semáforo: traffic light
semana: week
Semana Santa: Holy Week
sexo: sex
shaman/chaman: spiritual healer
SIDA: the Spanish acronym for AIDS
siesta: mid-afternoon nap, businesses often close at this time
sillar: flexible, white, volcanic rock used in construction
sol: sun/Peruvian currency
solo carril: one-lane road or bridge
soltero/a: single (unmarried)
supermercado: supermarket
sur: south
tarifa: fee
tapas: bite-size appetizers served in bars
telenovela: soap opera
termas: hot mineral springs
terminal terrestre: bus station
tienda: store
tipo de cambio: exchange rate
trago: mixed drink/shot of alcohol
trekking: trekking
triste: sad
trucha: trout
turismo: tourism
turista: tourist
valle: valley
vicuña: a llama-like animal
volcán: volcano
zona: zone

INDEX

INDEX

INDEX ■ **509**

WHO WE ARE

A NEW LET'S GO

With a sleeker look and innovative new content, we have revamped the entire series to reflect more than ever the needs and interests of the independent traveler. Here are just some of the improvements you will notice when traveling with the new *Let's Go*.

MORE PRICE OPTIONS

Still the best resource for budget travelers, *Let's Go* recognizes that everyone needs the occassional indulgence. Our "Big Splurges" indicate establishments that are actually worth those extra pennies (pulas, pesos, or pounds), and price-level symbols (❶ ❷ ❸ ❹ ❺) allow you to quickly determine whether an accommodation or restaurant will break the bank. We may have diversified, but we'll never lose our budget focus—"Hidden Deals" reveal the best-kept travel secrets.

BEYOND THE TOURIST EXPERIENCE

Our Alternatives to Tourism chapter offers ideas on immersing yourself in a new community through study, work, or volunteering.

AN INSIDER'S PERSPECTIVE

As always, every item is written and researched by our on-site writers. This year we have highlighted more viewpoints to help you gain an even more thorough understanding of the places you are visiting.

IN RECENT NEWS. *Let's Go* correspondents around the globe report back on current regional issues that may affect you as a traveler.

CONTRIBUTING WRITERS. Respected scholars and former *Let's Go* writers discuss topics on society and culture, going into greater depth than the usual guidebook summary.

THE LOCAL STORY. From the Parisian monk toting a cell phone to the Russian *babushka* confronting capitalism, *Let's Go* shares its revealing conversations with local personalities—a unique glimpse of what matters to real people.

FROM THE ROAD. Always helpful and sometimes downright hilarious, our researchers share useful insights on the typical (and atypical) travel experience.

SLIMMER SIZE

Don't be fooled by our new, smaller size. *Let's Go* is still packed with invaluable travel advice, but now it's easier to carry with a more compact design.

FORTY-THREE YEARS OF WISDOM

For over four decades *Let's Go* has provided the most up-to-date information on the hippest cafes, the most pristine beaches, and the best routes from border to border. It all started in 1960 when a few well-traveled students at Harvard University handed out a 20-page mimeographed pamphlet of their tips on budget travel to passengers on student charter flights to Europe. From humble beginnings, *Let's Go* has grown to cover six continents and *Let's Go: Europe* still reigns as the world's best-selling travel guide. This year we've beefed up our coverage of Latin America with *Let's Go: Costa Rica* and *Let's Go: Chile;* on the other side of the globe, we've added *Let's Go: Thailand* and *Let's Go: Hawaii.* Our new guides bring the total number of titles to 61, each infused with the spirit of adventure that travelers around the world have come to count on.

MAP INDEX

MAP LEGEND

⊞ Hospital	✈ Airport	🏛 Museum
⬛ Police	🚌 Bus Station	● Hotel/Hostel
✉ Post Office	🚋 Train Station	▲ Camping
ⓘ Tourist Office	M METRO STATION	🍴 Food & Drink
$ Bank	⚓ Ferry Landing	● Shopping
Embassy/Consulate	✝ Church	℞ Pharmacy
■ Site or Point of Interest	✡ Synagogue	● Nightlife
☎ Telephone Office	☪ Mosque	☕ Cafe
Theater	♜ Castle	💻 Internet Café
Library	🚕 Taxi/Collectivos	Pedestrian Zone

The Let's Go compass always points NORTH.